Levels 3–5

Level Up Maths

Series editor: Keith Pledger

Author team: Amanda Bearne, Sharon Bolger, Ian Boote, Greg Byrd, Meryl Carter, Gareth Cole, Crawford Craig, Jackie Fairchild, Anna Grayson, June Hall, Mark Haslam, Fiona Mapp, Phil Marshall, Avnee Morjaria, Keith Pledger, Robert Ward-Penny, Angela Wheeler

Heinemann

Heinemann is an imprint of Pearson Education Limited, a company incorporated in England and Wales, having its registered office at Edinburgh Gate, Harlow, Essex, CM20 2JE. Registered company number: 872828

www.heinemann.co.uk

Heinemann is a registered trademark of Pearson Education Limited

First published 2008

12 11 10 09
10 9 8 7 6 5 4

British Library Cataloguing in Publication Data is available from the British Library on request.

ISBN 978 0 435537 30 2

Edited by Jim Newall, Jane Glendening, Gwen Burns, Nicola Morgan and Harry Smith
Designed by Debbie Oatley (room9 design), Nikki Kenwood (hakoona matata designs) and Tom Cole (Seamonster design)
Typeset by Techset, Gateshead
Original illustrations © Pearson Education Limited, 2008, apart from Origami Cube (page 301) © Paul Jackson
Illustrated by Beehive
Cover design by Tom Cole (Seamonster design)
Cover photo/illustration © Pearson Education Limited
Printed in China (CTPS/04)

Acknowledgements

We would like to thank all of those schools who provided invaluable help in the development and trialling of this course.

The author and publisher would like to thank the following individuals and organisations for permission to reproduce photographs: Shutterstock/David W Kelly p2, Corbis/Corbis Sygma, O. Prevsto p4; Alamy/Jim Batty p6; Getty Images/PhotoDisc pp**8**, **36** (sunglasses, pen & alarm clock), **42**, **44**, **58**, **70**, **86**, **88**, **96**, **100**, **132** top, **142**, **170**, **178**, **190**, **192**, **195** bottom, **196**, **202**, **214**, **216**, **225**, **230**, **238**, **248** top, **248** bottom, **254**, **260**, **274**, **284**, **296**, **306**; Pearson Education Ltd/Arnos Design pp**10**, **186**, **258**; Alamy/MedioImages p**14**; Pearson Education Ltd/Steve Shott p**16**; Pearson Education Ltd/Tudor Photography pp**18**, **54**, **94**, **144**; Corbis/Annie Belt p**20**; Corbis pp**22**, **30**, **46**, **64**, **98**, **108**, **174**, **176** top, **176** bottom, **184**,**188**, **218**, **228**, **232**, **234**, **236**, **240**, **268**, **308**; Pearson Education Ltd/Martin Sookias pp**24**, **102**, **290**; Alamy/View Stock China p**26**; Digital Vision pp**28**, **122**, **132** bottom, **140**, **224**; iStockPhoto/Ismet Salahor p**31**; Dreamstime/Matty Symons p**32**; Pearson Education Ltd/Jules Selmes pp**34**, **82**, **154**, **204**, **246**, **266**, **278**; Corbis/Graham Tim p**35**; Superstock p**36** (ice cream); Pearson Education Ltd/MM Studios p**36** (car & vase); Alamy/Jon Arnold p**38**; Science Photo Library/Chris Bjornberg p**40**; Still Pictures/Shehzad Noorani p**48**; Corbis/Richard T Nowitz p**50**; Alamy/Bananastock p**52**; Alamy/Stock Image p**56**; Brave PR p**62**; Jupiter Images/Photos.com pp**66**, **124**, **128**, **138** bottom, **222**, **226**, **286**; Getty Images/Photonica p**68**; Alamy/Steven May p**76**; Dreamstime/Pablo Eder p**77**; PA Photos/Michael Regan/Empics Sport p**78**; Alamy/Popperfoto p**84**; Illustrated London News p**85**; iStockPhoto p**90**, **146**; Pearson Education Ltd/Phil Bratt p**104**; Corbis/Kevin Fleming p**106** (water ski); Corbis/Kay Niefeld, epa p**106** (javelin); PA Photos/AP/Thomas Kienzle p**106** (long jump); Corbis/David Madison p**106** (sports field); Dreamstime/Lane Erickson p**110**; iStockPhoto/Willi Schmitz p**114**; Alamy/SDBPhoto Travel p**116**; Pearson Education Ltd/Trevor Clifford p**118**; Corbis/Bob Krist p**130** (background); Alamy/Nishan M p**130** (small coins); Brand X Pictures p**134**; Shutterstock/Joel Blit p**136**; iStockPhoto/Jose Fuente p**138** top; Alamy/Linda Richards p**148**; Pearson Education Ltd/Malcolm Harris pp**150** (background), **208**, **304**; Pearson Education Ltd/Devon Olugbena Shaw pp**150** (5 petals), **252**; iStockPhoto/Nikita Tiunov p**150** (8 petals); Alamy/Bill Brooks p**151** (13 petals); iStockPhoto/Mary Gascho p**151** (3 petals) Pearson Education Ltd/Debbie Rowe pp**152**, **195** top, **294**; iStockPhoto Jarno Gonzalez Zarraonandia p**156** (chess); Alamy/Jennie Hart p**156**; Tristain Leverett p**157** (snooker); iStockPhoto/DSG PRO p**157**; Alamy/Michael Jenner p**158**; Alamy p**164**; Richard Smith p**162**; Alamy/TNT Magazine p**166**; iStockPhoto/Willem Dijkstra p**168**; Getty Images/AFP/Indranil Mukherjee p**172**; Rex Features p**182**; Corbis/Bettmann p**194** (man); Corbis/Alan Schein Photography p**194** (background); Corbis/Blue Syndicate p**198**; iStockPhoto/Alexander Hafemann p**200**; Pearson Education Ltd/Peter Morris p**206**; V and A Museum p**212**; Shutterstock/mumbojumbo p**213**; Illinois Bureau of Tourism p**244**, Corbis/The Gallery Collection p**250**; Shutterstock/Mikael Damkier p**256**, iStockPhoto/Dean Walker p**262**; Corbis/Jason Hawkes p**264**; Corbis/Loop Images/Phil O'Connor p**270**; Pearson Education Ltd/Chrissie Martin p**272**; Pearson Education/Gareth Boden p**276**; Alamy/Brand X Pictures p**281**; The Moviestore Collection pp**282** top, **282** bottom; Dreamstime/Shariff Che'lah p**288**; Shutterstock/Pichugin Dmitry p**292**; Australia Reed International/Lindsey Edwards Photography p**298**; Pearson Education Ltd/Liz Alexander p**300** (swans); Corbis/M Angelo p**300** (background); Alamy/Oleksiy Maksymenko p**301**; Pearson Education Ltd/Jill Brischbach p**306**

Every effort has been made to contact copyright holders of material reproduced in this book. Any omissions will be rectified in subsequent printings if notice is given to the publishers.

Contents

Expanded contents

Unit 17 Algebra rules – Algebra 5

Unit 18 Getting into shape – Geometry and measures 5

Welcome to Level Up Maths!

Level Up Maths is an inspirational new course for today's classroom. With stunning textbooks and amazing software, Key Stage 3 Maths has simply never looked this good!

This textbook is divided into 18 units. Here are the main features.

Why learn this?

'One third more free texts when you swap packages.' Are you getting the best deal?

Why are you learning this? For each topic there's a reason why it is useful.

Unit introduction

Each unit begins with an introduction. These include a striking background image to set the scene and short activities to check what you know.

Here's a quick quiz to see how much you already know. The arrows tell you where to look for help.

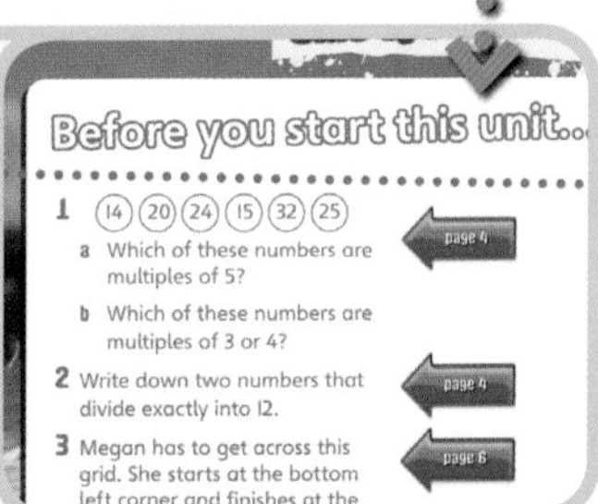
Before you start this unit...

1 (14) (20) (24) (15) (32) (25)
  a Which of these numbers are multiples of 5? — page 4
  b Which of these numbers are multiples of 3 or 4?

2 Write down two numbers that divide exactly into 12. — page 4

3 Megan has to get across this grid. She starts at the bottom left corner and finishes at the — page 6

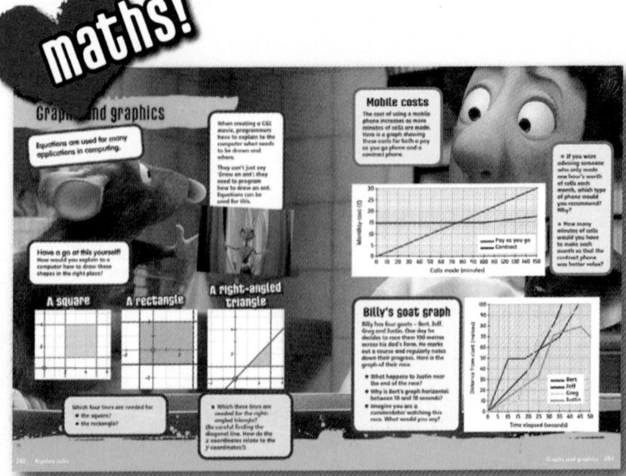

Twelve sets of special activities highlight some intriguing **applications and implications of maths**. Where in history and culture does today's maths come from? How does it affect our lives? Why is it so important to get it right?

Main content

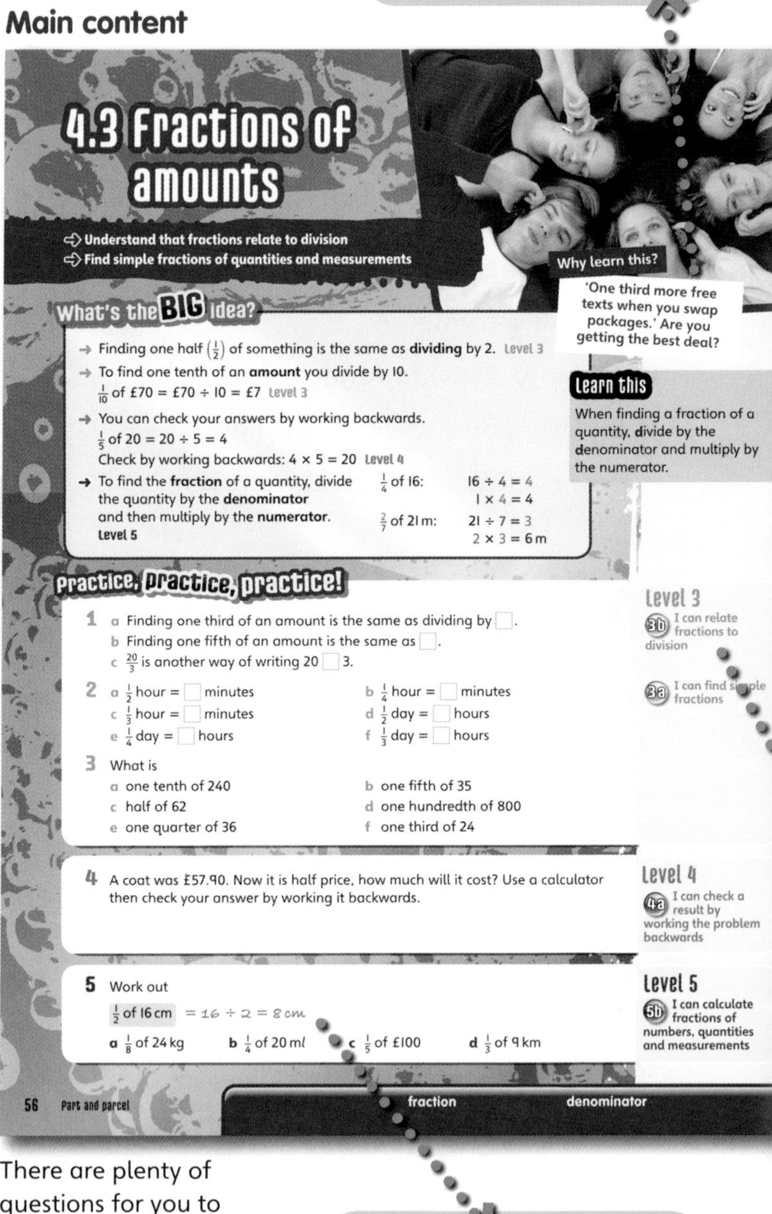
4.3 Fractions of amounts

- Understand that fractions relate to division
- Find simple fractions of quantities and measurements

Why learn this? 'One third more free texts when you swap packages.' Are you getting the best deal?

What's the BIG idea?

- Finding one half $(\frac{1}{2})$ of something is the same as **dividing** by 2. Level 3
- To find one tenth of an **amount** you divide by 10. $\frac{1}{10}$ of £70 = £70 ÷ 10 = £7 Level 3
- You can check your answers by working backwards. $\frac{1}{5}$ of 20 = 20 ÷ 5 = 4. Check by working backwards: 4 × 5 = 20 Level 4
- To find the **fraction** of a quantity, divide the quantity by the **denominator** and then multiply by the **numerator**. Level 5 — $\frac{1}{4}$ of 16: 16 ÷ 4 = 4, 1 × 4 = 4; $\frac{2}{7}$ of 21 m: 21 ÷ 7 = 3, 2 × 3 = 6 m

Learn this When finding a fraction of a quantity, **divide** by the denominator and multiply by the numerator.

Practice, practice, practice!

1 a Finding one third of an amount is the same as dividing by ☐.
  b Finding one fifth of an amount is the same as ☐.
  c $\frac{20}{3}$ is another way of writing 20 ☐ 3.

2 a $\frac{1}{2}$ hour = ☐ minutes b $\frac{1}{4}$ hour = ☐ minutes
  c $\frac{1}{3}$ hour = ☐ minutes d $\frac{1}{2}$ day = ☐ hours
  e $\frac{1}{4}$ day = ☐ hours f $\frac{1}{3}$ day = ☐ hours

3 What is
  a one tenth of 240 b one fifth of 35
  c half of 62 d one hundredth of 800
  e one quarter of 36 f one third of 24

Level 3 — 3b I can relate fractions to division; 3a I can find simple fractions

4 A coat was £57.90. Now it is half price, how much will it cost? Use a calculator then check your answer by working it backwards.

Level 4 — 4a I can check a result by working the problem backwards

5 Work out
  $\frac{1}{2}$ of 16 cm = 16 ÷ 2 = 8 cm
  a $\frac{1}{8}$ of 24 kg b $\frac{1}{4}$ of 20 ml c $\frac{1}{5}$ of £100 d $\frac{1}{3}$ of 9 km

Level 5 — 5b I can calculate fractions of numbers, quantities and measurements

56 Part and parcel — fraction — denominator

There are plenty of questions for you to practise on. All the questions have been **levelled** and **sublevelled**, so you can see how well you are doing. The '**I can** …' statements confirm what you can do.

of 16 cm = 16 ÷ 2 = 8 cm

Highlighted sample questions show you how to set out your working.

Now try this!

A Fraction investigation

You need some 4 by 3 rectangles for this

Two '**Now try this!**' activities give you the chance to **solve problems** and explore the maths further, sometimes with a partner. Activity B is generally more challenging than Activity A.

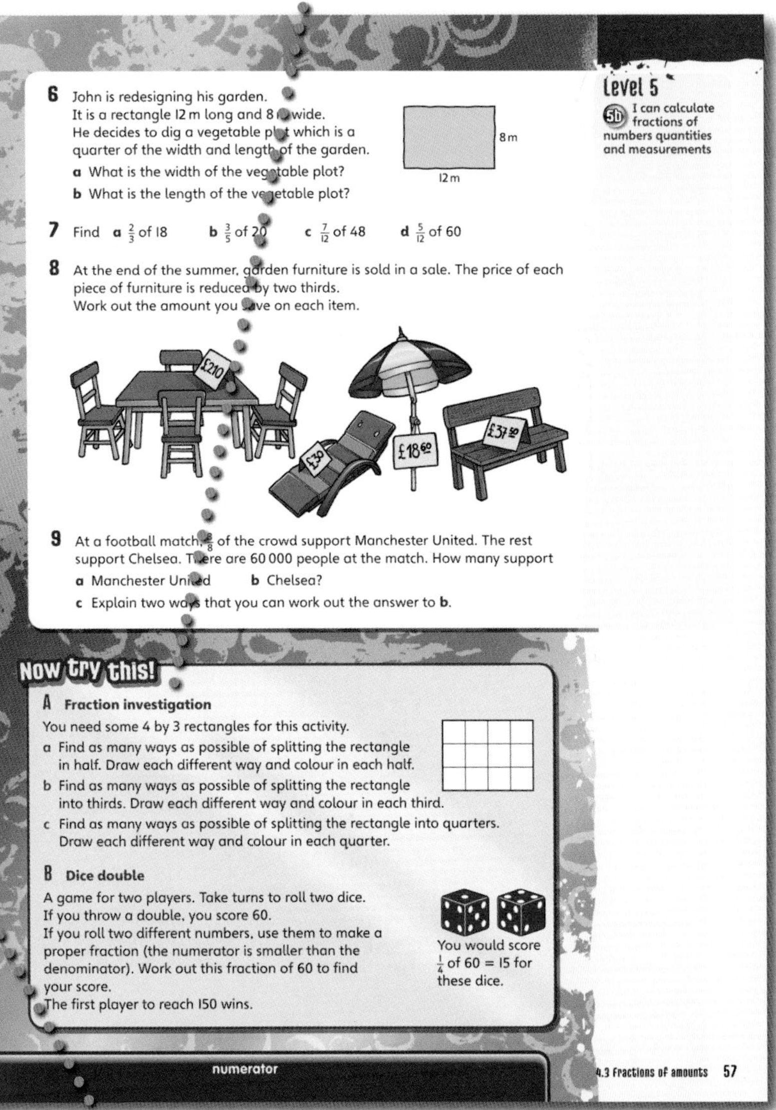

6 John is redesigning his garden. It is a rectangle 12 m long and 8 m wide. He decides to dig a vegetable plot which is a quarter of the width and length of the garden.

a What is the width of the vegetable plot?

b What is the length of the vegetable plot?

Level 5

5b I can calculate fractions of numbers quantities and measurements

7 Find **a** $\frac{2}{3}$ of 18 **b** $\frac{3}{5}$ of 20 **c** $\frac{7}{12}$ of 48 **d** $\frac{5}{12}$ of 60

8 At the end of the summer, garden furniture is sold in a sale. The price of each piece of furniture is reduced by two thirds. Work out the amount you save on each item.

9 At a football match, [illegible]/8 of the crowd support Manchester United. The rest support Chelsea. There are 60 000 people at the match. How many support

a Manchester United b Chelsea?

c Explain two ways that you can work out the answer to **b**.

Now try this!

A Fraction investigation

You need some 4 by 3 rectangles for this activity.

a Find as many ways as possible of splitting the rectangle in half. Draw each different way and colour in each half.

b Find as many ways as possible of splitting the rectangle into thirds. Draw each different way and colour in each third.

c Find as many ways as possible of splitting the rectangle into quarters. Draw each different way and colour in each quarter.

B Dice double

A game for two players. Take turns to roll two dice.
If you throw a double, you score 60.
If you roll two different numbers, use them to make a proper fraction (the numerator is smaller than the denominator). Work out this fraction of 60 to find your score.
The first player to reach 150 wins.

You would score $\frac{1}{4}$ of 60 = 15 for these dice.

numerator

4.3 Fractions of amounts 57

This shows that the questions are at Level 3.

- 'c' questions are easiest.
- 'b' questions are of medium difficulty.
- 'a' questions are hardest.

Level 3

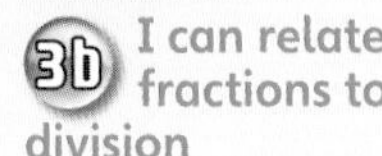

3b I can relate fractions to division

3a I can find simpl fractions

We've scoured the planet to find examples of the World's greatest maths for you to try. You may find yourself helping to build a colony on Mars, saving the wildlife on an endangered island, breaking out of a deadly dungeon or designing a trap to catch a monster!

Unit plenary

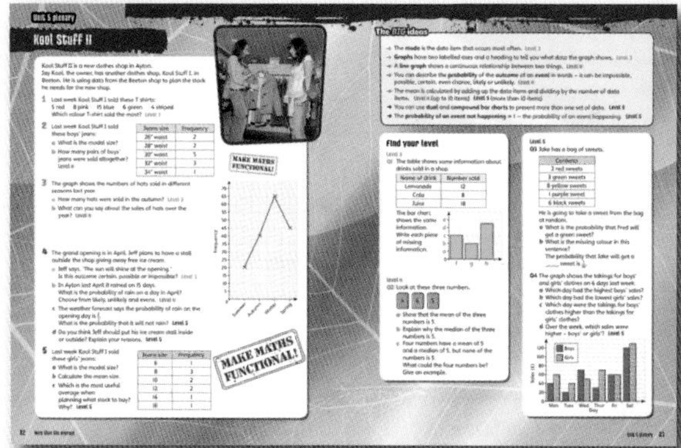

Each unit ends with an extended, levelled activity to help you practise **functional maths** and demonstrate your understanding. There are also Find your level questions to help with assessment.

Revision activities

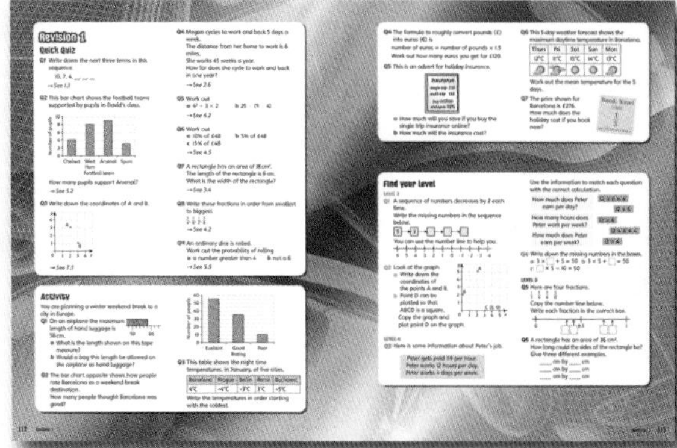

Three revision sections (one for each term) give you the chance to double-check your understanding of previous units. Each consists of a quick quiz, an extended activity and Find your level questions.

LiveText software

The LiveText software gives you a wide range of additional materials – interactive explanations, games, activities and extra questions.

Simply turn the pages of the electronic book to the page you need, and explore!

Interactive explanations

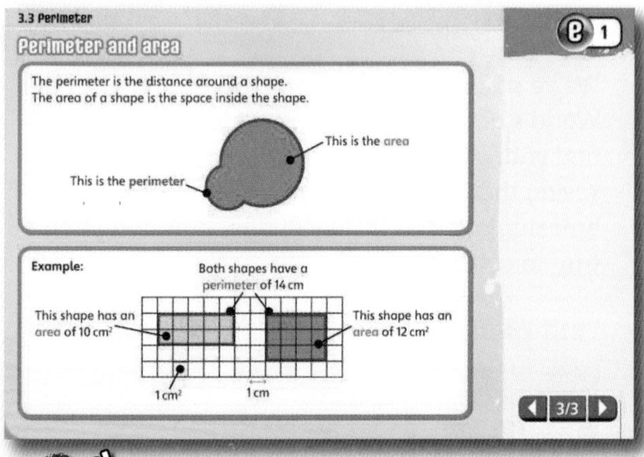

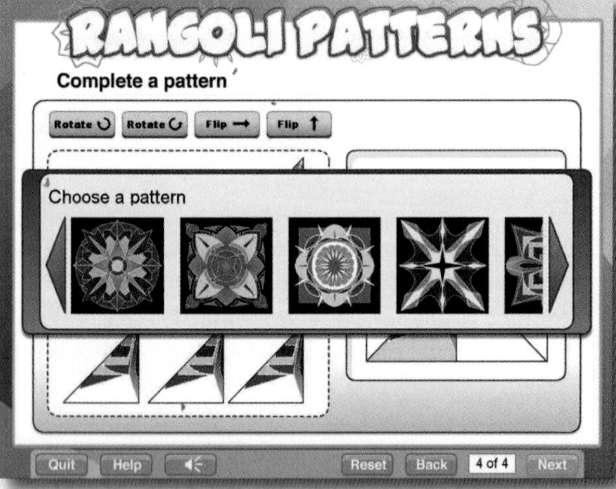

Competitive maths games

- Measure lines to within one millimetre
- Draw lines to within one millimetre
- Calculate the perimeter of a rectangle
- Find the perimeter of other shapes
- Solve problems involving perimeter

Zoom in on any part of the page with a single click.

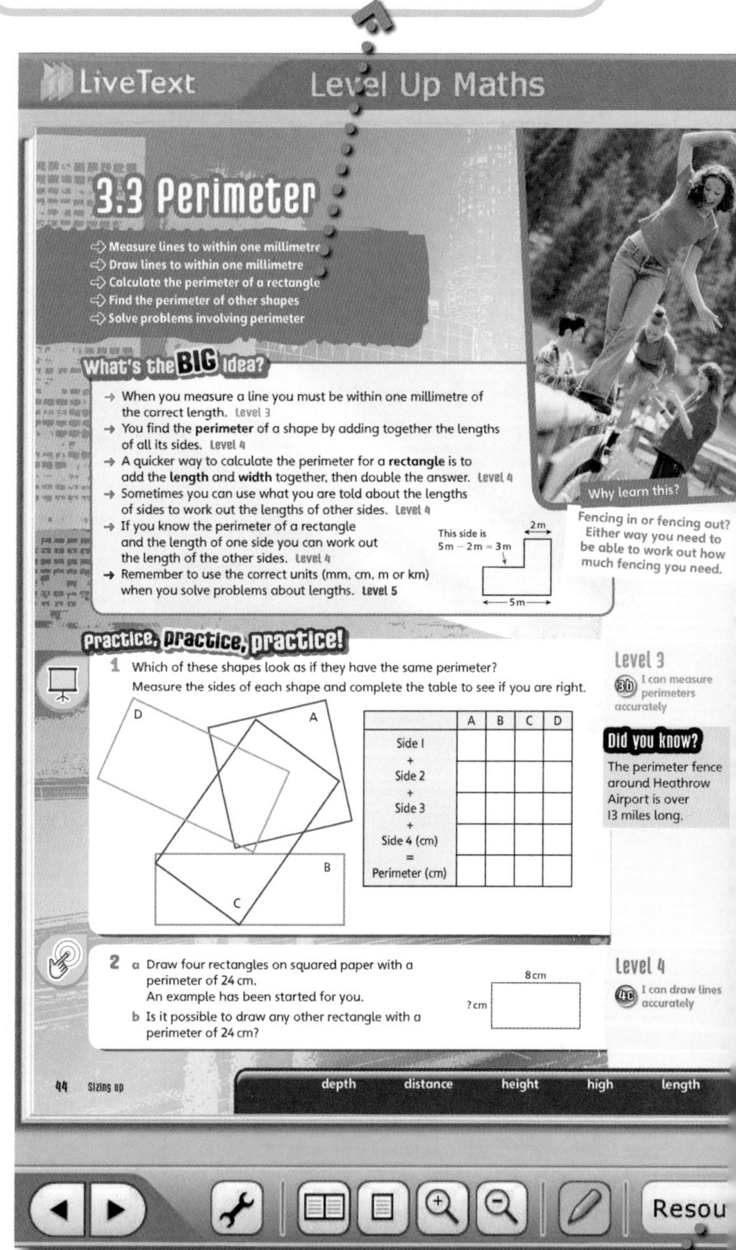

Resources – a comprehensive list of all relevant resources plus lesson plans. It includes a glossary with definitions of key terms. Play audio to hear translations in Bengali, Gujarati, Punjabi, Turkish and Urdu.

Click on the icons to access the extra resources.

- Explanations
- Booster questions
- maths! Interactive
- Extra questions
- Resource sheets
- Worked solutions

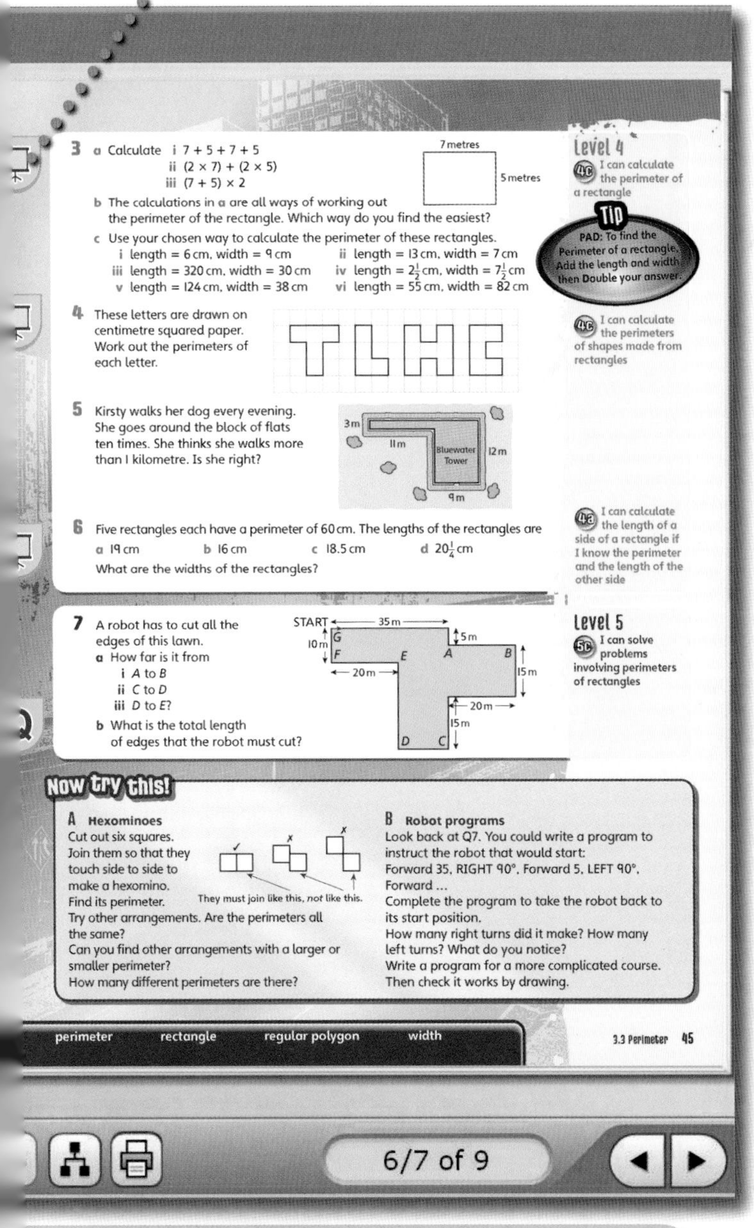

3 a Calculate i 7 + 5 + 7 + 5
ii (2 × 7) + (2 × 5)
iii (7 + 5) × 2

7 metres

5 metres

b The calculations in a are all ways of working out the perimeter of the rectangle. Which way do you find the easiest?

c Use your chosen way to calculate the perimeter of these rectangles.

i	length = 6 cm, width = 9 cm	ii	length = 13 cm, width = 7 cm
iii	length = 320 cm, width = 30 cm	iv	length = $2\frac{1}{2}$ cm, width = $7\frac{1}{2}$ cm
v	length = 124 cm, width = 38 cm	vi	length = 55 cm, width = 82 cm

Level 4

4c I can calculate the perimeter of a rectangle

Tip

PAD: To find the Perimeter of a rectangle, Add the length and width then Double your answer.

4 These letters are drawn on centimetre squared paper. Work out the perimeters of each letter.

4c I can calculate the perimeters of shapes made from rectangles

5 Kirsty walks her dog every evening. She goes around the block of flats ten times. She thinks she walks more than 1 kilometre. Is she right?

3 m 11 m Bluewater Tower 12 m 9 m

6 Five rectangles each have a perimeter of 60 cm. The lengths of the rectangles are
a 19 cm b 16 cm c 18.5 cm d $20\frac{1}{4}$ cm
What are the widths of the rectangles?

4a I can calculate the length of a side of a rectangle if I know the perimeter and the length of the other side

7 A robot has to cut all the edges of this lawn.
a How far is it from
i A to B
ii C to D
iii D to E?
b What is the total length of edges that the robot must cut?

START 35 m 5 m 10 m G F E A B 20 m 15 m 20 m 15 m D C

Level 5

5c I can solve problems involving perimeters of rectangles

Now try this!

A Hexominoes
Cut out six squares.
Join them so that they touch side to side to make a hexomino.
Find its perimeter.
Try other arrangements. Are the perimeters all the same?
Can you find other arrangements with a larger or smaller perimeter?
How many different perimeters are there?

They must join like this, not like this.

B Robot programs
Look back at Q7. You could write a program to instruct the robot that would start:
Forward 35, RIGHT 90°, Forward 5, LEFT 90°, Forward …
Complete the program to take the robot back to its start position.
How many right turns did it make? How many left turns? What do you notice?
Write a program for a more complicated course.
Then check it works by drawing.

perimeter rectangle regular polygon width

3.3 Perimeter 45

6/7 of 9

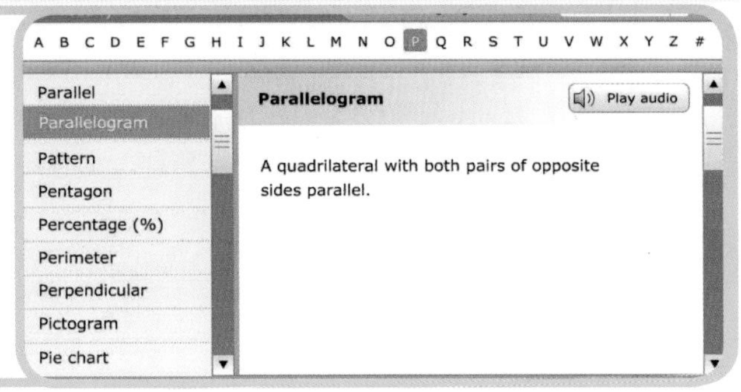

A B C D E F G H I J K L M N O P Q R S T U V W X Y Z #

Parallel
Parallelogram
Pattern
Pentagon
Percentage (%)
Perimeter
Perpendicular
Pictogram
Pie chart

Parallelogram Play audio

A quadrilateral with both pairs of opposite sides parallel.

Interactive

Boosters

Extra practice questions

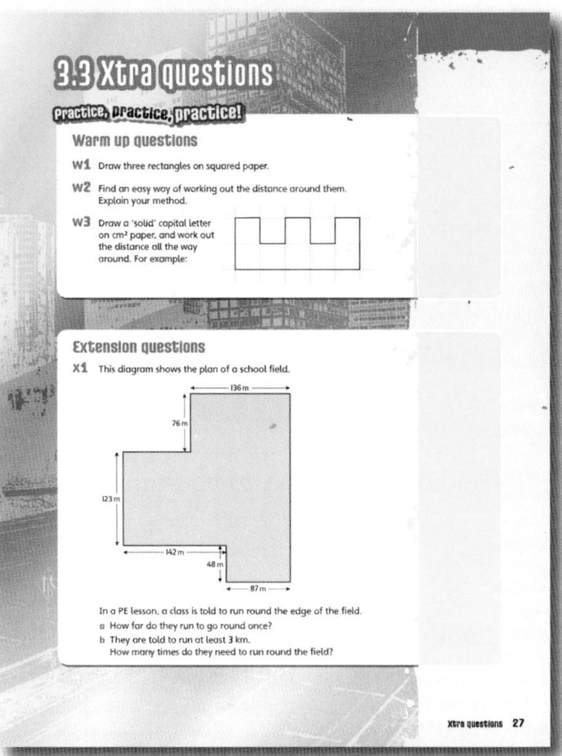

3.3 Xtra questions

Practice, practice, practice!

Warm up questions

W1 Draw three rectangles on squared paper.

W2 Find an easy way of working out the distance around them. Explain your method.

W3 Draw a 'solid' capital letter on cm² paper, and work out the distance all the way around. For example:

Extension questions

X1 This diagram shows the plan of a school field.

136 m 76 m 123 m 142 m 48 m 87 m

In a PE lesson, a class is told to run round the edge of the field.
a How far do they run to go round once?
b They are told to run at least 3 km.
How many times do they need to run round the field?

Xtra questions 27

1 All in order

This unit is all about number patterns and how we can use letters to represent numbers.

The dates of many regular events follow a sequence. When you know the rule of the sequence, you can use it to predict in what years the event will take place.

The football World Cup happens every four years. England won it in 1966. When will the next football World Cup take place?

One year is 365 days. The Earth takes $365\frac{1}{4}$ days to orbit the Sun. Every four years we have a leap year to catch up. We add the four $\frac{1}{4}$ days to make an extra day. Which is the next leap year? How can you tell from the date if a year is a leap year?

Activities

A Find as many ways as you can to make this equation true.

$\square + \square = 12$

B Look at a calendar to find out when the last full moon was. Work out when the next three full moons will be.

Before you start this unit..

1 What is missing from each of these patterns?

Level Up Maths 1-2 page 3

a B, C, D, …, F, G, H

b S, R, Q, …, O, N, M

c 5, 10, 15, …, 25, 30, 35

d 12, 10, 8, …, 4, 2, 0

Describe how you know in your own words.

2 Copy and continue these patterns.

Level Up Maths 1-2 page 3

a ■□■□■□■

b X + X + X +

c   

Describe how you worked out the answers in your own words.

3 Which of these numbers are even?

Level Up Maths 1-2 page 3

(7) (10) (25) (32) (56) (87)

You can use a number pattern to predict when there will be a full moon. On average there is a full moon every 29.531 days. There was no full moon in February in 1866, 1885, 1915, 1934, 1961 or 1999. Why do you think this was?

1.1 Multiples, square and triangle numbers

- Recognise multiples up to 10 × 10
- Continue and describe simple sequences
- Know and recognise square numbers

What's the BIG idea?

- 3, 6, 9 and 12 are all multiples of 3.
  10, 20, 30 and 40 are all multiples of 10. Level 3
- A number multiplied by itself is a **square number**. Level 4
- Square numbers make a square pattern of dots. Level 4
- **Triangle numbers** make a triangular pattern of dots. Level 4

Why learn this?

The Olympics are held in years that are multiples of 4. London will host the Olympics in 2012. You can use multiples to work out when the next Olympics after London will be.

Practice, practice, practice!

Level 3

3b I know multiples of 2, 5 and 10

1 a Copy the table and tick the numbers that are multiples of 2, 5 or 10.

	15	4	20	55	30	7	6	8	40	10	100
Multiple of 2		✓									
Multiple of 5	✓										
Multiple of 10											

b Which numbers in the table are multiples of 2, 5 *and* 10?

c Think of another number which is a multiple of 2, 5 and 10.

d Copy and complete these sentences.

i Multiples of 2 end in… . ii Multiples of 5 end in… .

iii Multiples of 10 end in… .

Did you know?

Leap years occur every 4 years. But years ending in 00 are only leap years if they are multiples of 400. So 2000 was a leap year, but 2100 won't be.

3a I know multiples of 2, 3, 4 and 5

2 The numbers in the boxes are multiples of 2 because they are in the 2 times table.

[6] [12] [8] 15 25 [30] [16] 27 [24]

a Which of the numbers in the list are multiples of 4?

b Which of the numbers in the list are multiples of both

i 2 and 4 ii 3 and 5?

Level 4

4b I know square numbers up to 5 × 5 and 10 × 10

3 These patterns of dots show the first four square numbers.

1	4	9	16
1 × 1	2 × 2	3 × 3	4 × 4

Draw the dot pattern for the fifth square number.

difference even multiple

4 Triangle numbers can be arranged into a triangular pattern of dots.

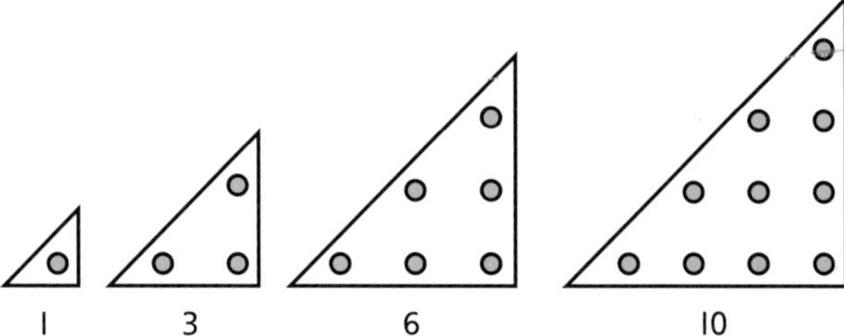

a Continue the pattern to work out the next three triangle numbers.
b Find the pattern in the sequence of numbers. Describe it in your own words.

5 36 is a square number because 6 × 6 = 36.
Write down two other square numbers between 37 and 100.

Level 4

4b I can recognise square and triangle numbers

4a I know square numbers from 6 × 6 to 9 × 9

6 Sanjiv said

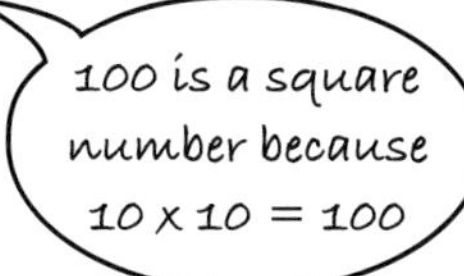

Which of these numbers are also square numbers?

143 121 231 169 123 144 245

7 From the numbers in the cloud, write down:

a the square numbers
b the multiples of 2
c the multiples of 5
d the multiples of 4.
e Which number haven't you used?

Level 5

5c I know square numbers beyond 10 × 10

Now try this!

A Multiple line

A game for two players. You will need counters, a dice and a copy of this grid.

7	2	35	9	4
16	25	40	24	18
3	11	10	6	13
8	15	12	20	15
1	5	17	14	36

Take turns to roll the dice. Choose a multiple of the number you threw from the grid and put one of your counters on it.

If you cannot put a counter on the grid you miss a turn.

The winner is the first to get four in a line (horizontal, vertical or diagonal).

B Square magic

Some square numbers make another square number when added together.
For example 9 + 25 = 36.

Find other square numbers that make another square number when added.

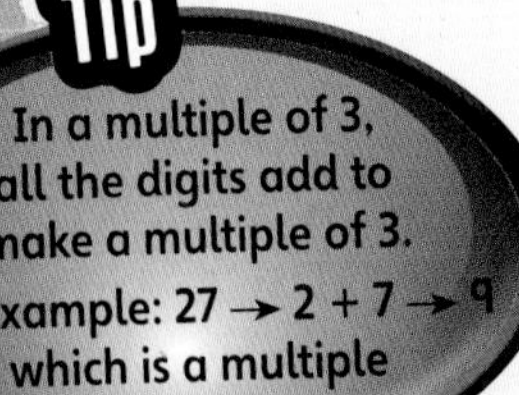

Learn this

You need to learn the square numbers between 1 and 100.

odd square number triangle number

1.2 Number patterns

- Continue simple number sequences by counting on and back in constant steps
- Describe a sequence by using a rule

Why learn this?

If you spot patterns you can make predictions – for example, where to find number 30.

What's the BIG idea?

- A **sequence** of numbers can be made by **counting on** or **counting back** by the same amount each time. Level 3 & Level 4
- Each number in a sequence is called a **term**. Level 3
- You can find the missing terms of a sequence by working out the **difference** between the terms. Level 3
- A sequence can be described using the **first term** and the **term-to-term rule**. Level 4

Super fact!

In Japan, the sequence in which buildings are numbered is often the order they were built in.

Practice, practice, practice!

Level 3

3c I can work out number sequences by counting on

1 These number chains follow a pattern.
Copy the number chains and find the next three numbers in the chain.

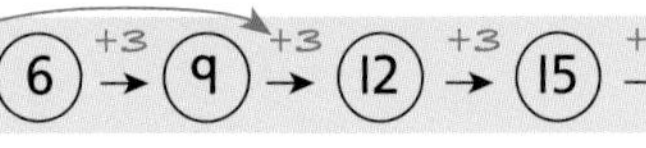
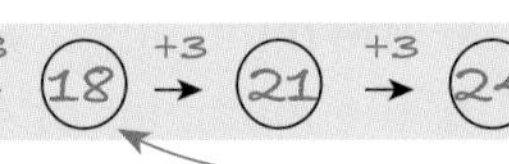
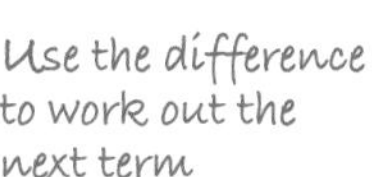

a 5 → 10 → 15 → 20 → 25 → ☐ → ☐ → ☐

b 8 → 18 → 28 → 38 → ☐ → ☐ → ☐

c 3 → 7 → 11 → 15 → ☐ → ☐ → ☐

Tip

A sequence is a pattern of numbers or shapes which follow a rule.

3b I can work out sequences by counting back

2 Copy these sequences and find the next three terms.

a 34, 32, 30, 28, …

b 80, 70, 60, 50, …

c 100, 95, 90, 85, …

d 47, 42, 37, 32, …

3a I can find missing terms in a simple sequence

3 Copy these sequences and find the missing numbers that should go in the boxes.

a 14, 19, ☐, ☐, 34, ☐, ☐

b 25, 21, ☐, ☐, ☐, 5

c 26, ☐, 20, 17, ☐, ☐, ☐

d ☐, 5, ☐, 11, 14, ☐

Level 4

4c I can count on and back in decimal jumps

4 a Copy this number line and fill in the missing numbers in the boxes.

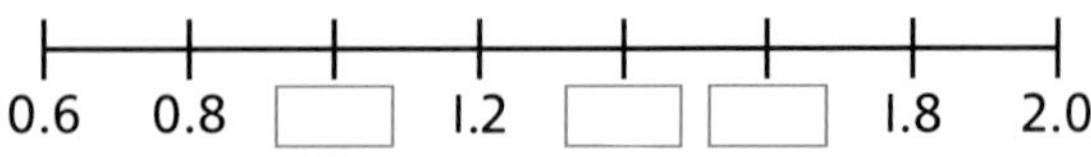

b Continue the number line.
What would the tenth number be?

c Sarah started at 4.5 and counted back in steps of 0.25. She said

> If I count back by 0.25 five times I will get the number 4

Is she correct? Use a number line to help you.

counting back counting on difference first term

Level 4

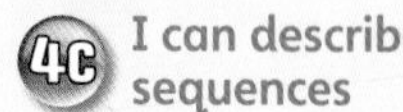

4c I can describe sequences

5 Look at this sequence: 4, 8, 12, 16, 20, … Saima said: *This sequence contains even numbers*

a Write a sentence describing this sequence. Use the word 'multiple'.
b Think of another way of describing this sequence.
c Will the number 81 be in this sequence? Explain your answer.

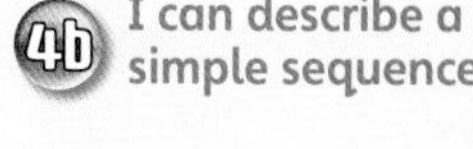

4b I can describe a simple sequence

6 **a** Match each description with one of these sequences.

	Descriptions	Sequences
i	The sequence starts at 1 and increases in steps of 3	12, 10, 8, 6, 4, …
ii	The sequence starts at 12 and decreases in steps of 2	15, 18, 21, 24, 27, …
iii	The sequence starts at 15 and decreases in steps of 3	5, 9, 13, 17, 21, …
iv	The sequence starts at 15 and increases in steps of 3	1, 4, 7, 10, 14, …
		15, 12, 9, 6, 3, …

b One of the sequences doesn't have a description.
Write a description for this sequence.

4a I can describe a sequence using the first term and the term-to-term rule

7

+6 +6 +6 +6 +6

5, 11, 17, 23, 29, …

first term = 5 *term to term rule: +6*

Describe these sequences, the first term and the term-to-term rule.

a 7, 17, 27, 37, 47, …
b 4, 16, 28, 40, 52, …
c 6.5, 5.5, 4.5, 3.5, 2.5, …
d 3.7, 3.9, 4.1, 4.3, 4.5, …

Level 5

5c I can find a term of a sequence

8 Four people can comfortably sit around one table. Tables are added as shown.

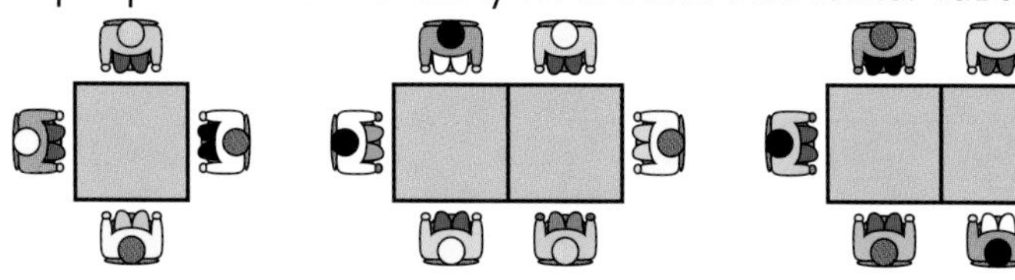

a Copy the table and complete it to show the numbers of people that can sit around the tables.

Number of tables	1	2	3	4	5
Number of people	4				

b How many people can sit around 10 tables? Explain how you worked it out.
c How many tables would you need to seat 30 people?

Now try this!

A Crack the code!

Look at the number lines at the top of Resource sheet 1.2.
Complete each one to help crack the code.
Now decipher the hidden message at the bottom of the Resource sheet.
Make up a hidden message for a partner using this code.

B Make up a sequence

Write a number sequence for a partner. Ask them to find the next three terms.
Can they find the tenth term without continuing the pattern?
Can they describe the rule? Is it the same rule as you used to make the sequence?

pattern sequence term term-to-term rule

1.3 Terms of a sequence

- Extend sequences including into negative values
- Generate a sequence using a term-to-term rule
- Generate a sequence in a practical context
- Generate a sequence using a position-to-term rule

Why learn this?

You can use a sequence to work out which note is which on the neck of a guitar.

What's the BIG idea?

→ You can **generate** a sequence if you know the **first term** and the **term-to-term rule**. Level 4

→ You can find a term in a sequence if you know its position, the first term and the **position-to-term rule**. Level 5

Tip

The term-to-term rule takes you from one term to the next.

Practice, practice, practice!

Level 3

3a I can recognise and extend number sequences below zero

1 Write down the next three terms in these sequences.

−2 −2 −2 −2 −2 −2 *Work out the difference between terms*

6, 4, 2, 0, *−2, −4, −6* *Use the difference to work out the next term*

a 4, 3, 2, 1, __, __, __

b 8, 5, 2, −1, __, __, __

c 40, 30, 20, 10, __, __, __

d 3, −1, −5, −9, __, __, __

e 8, 0, −8, __, __, __

f 4, −1, −6, __, __, __

Level 4

4b I can generate a simple sequence

2 Write down the next five terms of these sequences.

	Rule	First term	Next terms
	add 3	6	
a	subtract 4	35	
b	subtract 10	30	
c	multiply by 2	2	
d	divide by 2	128	

6 + 3 = 9
9 + 3 = 12
12 + 3 = 15
15 + 3 = 18
18 + 3 = 21

4b I can generate terms of a simple sequence

3 Paul decided to create a path across his garden. His path was to be made out of black and green paving slabs.

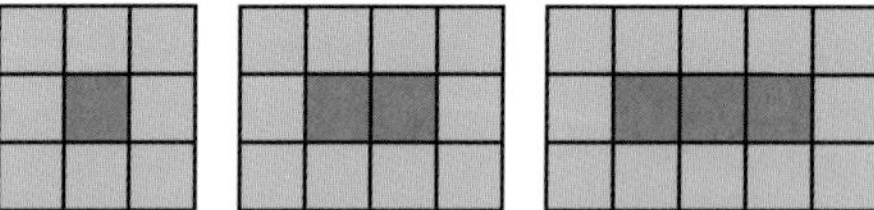

Copy and complete the table to show how many green slabs he will need.

Black slabs	1	2	3	4	5	6
Green slabs						

4a I can generate terms from a more complex pattern

4 Count how many matchsticks are in each shape. Copy and complete the table below to show these numbers of matchsticks.

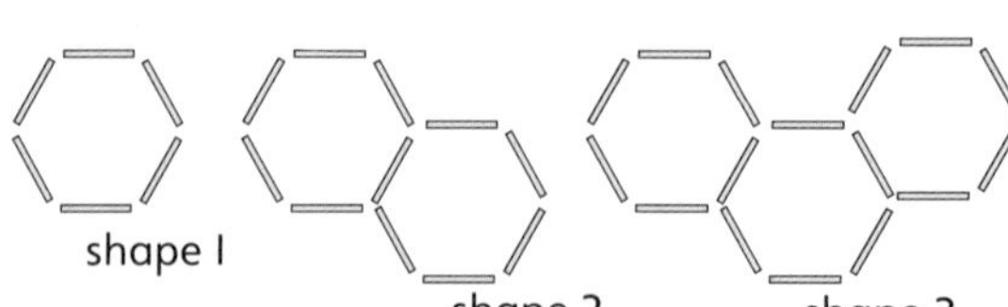

Draw the next three diagrams and complete the table.

Shape number	1	2	3	4	5	6
Number of matchsticks	6					

generate position position-to-term rule

5 Write two different ways to continue these number sequences.
Write down the term-to-term rule you have used and the next three numbers.

1, 4, … Rule: add 3. Next three numbers: 7, 10, 13
Rule: multiply by 2 and add 2. Next three numbers: 10, 22, 46

a 1, 3, … **b** 1, 5, … **c** 3, 5, … **d** 0, 4, …

Level 4

4a I can generate a more complex sequence

6 Write down the next five terms of these sequences.

	Term-to-term rule	First term	Next terms
a	add 3	0	
b	subtract 4	2	
c	+5	−2	
d	−6	1	

7 **a** The position-to-term rule of this sequence is 'multiply by 6'.
Copy and complete the table using this position-to-term rule.

Position	1	2	3	4	5
Term		12			

b The position-to-term rule of this sequence is 'multiply by 3 then add 2'.
Copy and complete the table using this position-to-term rule.

Position	1	2	3	4	5	6
Term	5					

c The position-to-term rule of this sequence is 'multiply by 5 then subtract 1'.
Copy and complete the table using this position-to-term rule.

Position	1	2	3	4	5	6
Term						

Level 5

5b I can generate terms of a linear sequence

5a I can generate terms using a position-to-term rule

Watch out!

Remember that the position-to-term rule is different from the term-to-term rule. Don't get them mixed up.

Now try this!

A Spreadsheet sequences 1

The term-to-term rule for finding the sequence of multiples of 5 is 'add 5'.
You can use a spreadsheet to find the terms of this sequence.

	A	B	C	D	E
1	Term	1	= B1 + 1	= C1 + 1	= D1 + 1
2	Sequence	5	= B2 + 5	= C2 + 5	= D2 + 5

a Use a spreadsheet to find the first 15 multiples of
i 7 **ii** 9 **iii** 18 **iv** 24

b Use a spreadsheet to find the first 15 terms of these sequences.
i 3, 8, 13, 18, … **ii** 102, 98, 94, 90, …

B Spreadsheet sequences 2

The position-to-term rule for finding the sequence of the multiples of 6 is 'multiply by 6'.
You can use a spreadsheet to find the terms of this sequence.

	A	B	C	D	E
1	Term	1	= B1 + 1	= C1 + 1	= D1 + 1
2	Sequence	= B1 * 6	= C1 * 6	= D1 * 6	= E1 * 6

Repeat parts **a** and **b** of Activity A using this method.

sequence term term-to-term rule

1.4 Functions and mappings

- Solve problems involving multiplication and division
- Find the inputs and outputs of functions using a function machine
- Write mappings to express functions

Why learn this?

Function machines can be used to convert one measure into another, for example money into cups of drinks.

What's the BIG idea?

- → Multiplication is the **inverse** or opposite of division. Level 3
- → You can find the **output** of a **function machine** if you know the **input**. Level 4
- → You can find the input of a function machine by using the inverse operation. Level 5
- → You can find the rules of a function machine if you know the inputs and outputs. Level 5
- → You can represent function machines using **mappings** and **equations**. Level 5

Practice, practice, practice!

Level 3

3b I can solve whole number problems

3a I can use inverse operations

1 Use the digits 3, 4 and 5 once in each calculation to make it correct.

a ☐☐ × ☐ = 170 b ☐☐ ÷ ☐ = 15

2 a Use the fact that 40 × 6 = 240 to complete the diagram.

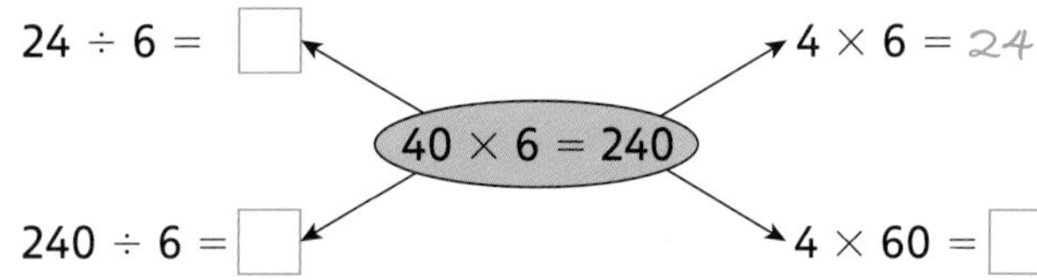

b What other calculations can you work out using this fact?

Level 4

4a I can find outputs of simple functions

3 Copy these function machines and find the missing outputs.

a 3, 5, 7 → +2 → 5, ☐, ☐

b 7, 9, 10 → ×6 → ☐, ☐, ☐

c 14, 18, 20 → −8 → ☐, ☐, ☐

d 20, 30, 24 → ÷2 → ☐, ☐, ☐

equation function machine input

5c I can find inputs and outputs of more complex functions

Tip: To find the input of a function machine remember to do the 'inverse' operation.

4 Copy these function machines and find the missing inputs and outputs.

a

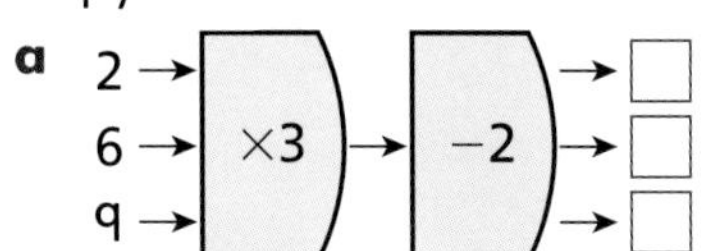

b 6, 18, 20 → ÷2 → +4 → □, □, □

c

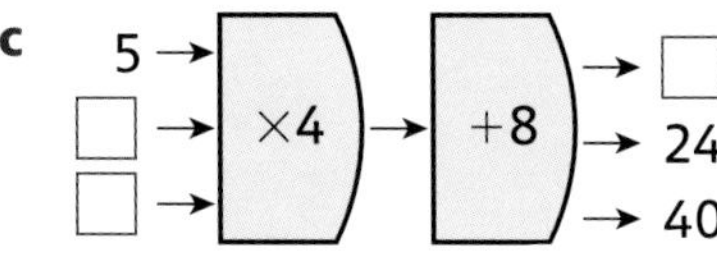

d 10, □, □ → ÷2 → −3 → 2, 5, 7

5b I can construct functions to describe mappings

5 Find the rule to complete these function machines.

a 2, 6, 8 → □ → 4, 12, 16

b 3, 5, 7 → □ → □ → 7, 11, 15

5a I can represent mappings using positive integers

6 Write these function machines as a mapping, $x \rightarrow \ldots$ and an equation $y = \ldots$.

$x \rightarrow$ ×4 → −1 → y $\quad x \rightarrow 4x - 1 \quad y = 4x - 1$

a $x \rightarrow$ ×5 → +4 → y

b $x \rightarrow$ −3 → ×4 → y

5a I can represent mappings using negative integers

7 Ben said: "My function machine subtracts 3 from a number then multiplies the result by 2"

a Which one of these mappings represents Ben's function machine?

A $x \rightarrow 3x - 2$ B $x \rightarrow 2x - 3$ C $x \rightarrow 2(x - 3)$ D $x \rightarrow x - 3 \times 2$

b Copy and complete this table using Ben's mapping.

x	1	2	3	4	5
y					

Watch out! The mapping $x \rightarrow 2(x - 1)$ means subtract 1 first before multiplying by 2

Now try this!

A Single function guessing game

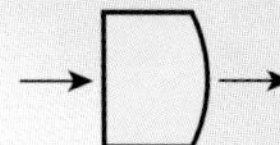

A game for four people. Draw a blank single function machine. Choose one person to be the leader. The leader thinks of a rule to go in the function machine and writes it down secretly. The other players take turns to write an input number for the function machine.

The leader writes the output number using his/her rule.
The first player to guess the correct rule is the new leader.

B Double function guessing game

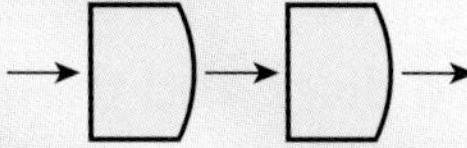

A game for four people. Draw a blank double function machine. Choose one person to be the leader. The leader thinks of a rule to go in the function machine and writes it down secretly. The other players take turns to write an input number for the function machine.

The leader writes the output number using his/her rule.
The first player to guess the correct rule is the new leader.

inverse **mapping** **output**

maths!

Functions and sequences

Functions and sequences lead to lots of puzzles. Some of them are hundreds of years old!

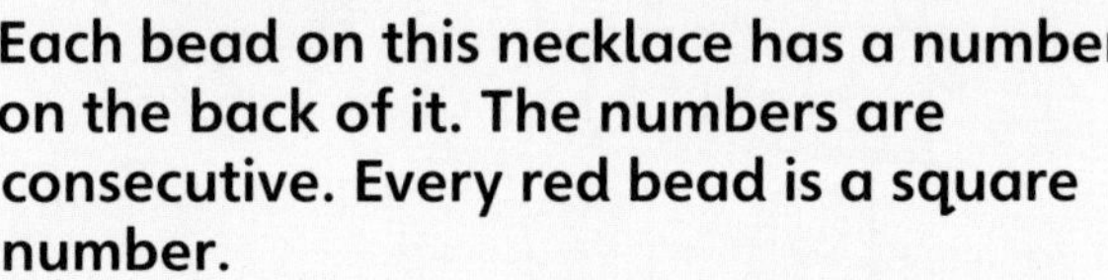

Each bead on this necklace has a number on the back of it. The numbers are consecutive. Every red bead is a square number.

- If the bead with the # is the first bead, what number is it?
- What happens to the number of blue beads between each pair of red beads?

The Tower of Hanoi

The Tower of Hanoi is a game that comes from an old story.
To win you need to move the tower of discs from one peg to another. However, you can only move one disc at a time, and you must not put a larger disc on top of a smaller one.

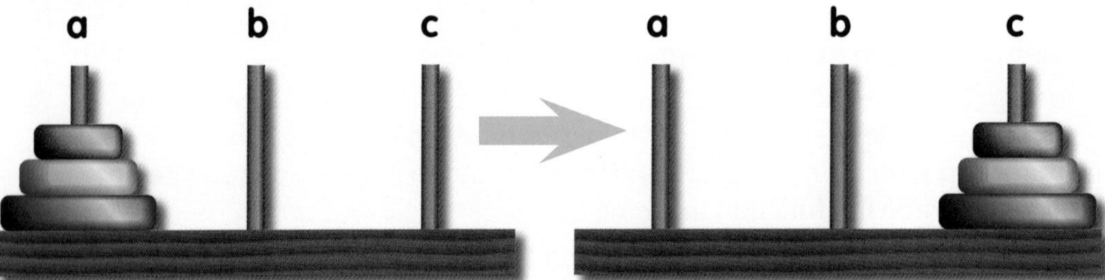

You can play the game with different numbers of discs.

- Try playing with three discs and then four discs to start completing the table below.

Discs	1	2	3	4	5
Fewest moves	1	3			

- Can you find a function that would tell you the least number of moves five discs would take?
- What about six discs?

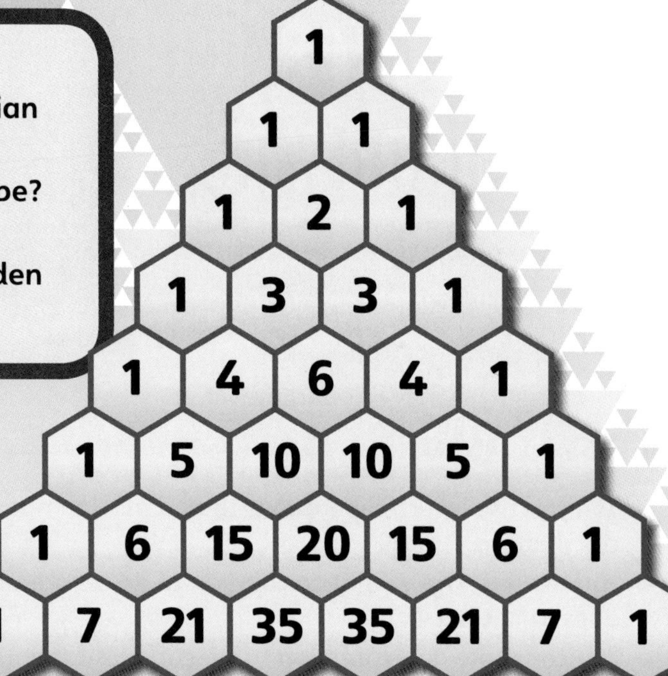

Pascal's triangle is named after the seventeenth-century French mathematician Blaise Pascal.

- What will the next row of the triangle be? How did you work it out?
- How many sequences can you find hidden in Pascal's triangle?

What comes next?

- 1220, 1255, 130, 205, 240, ...
- 31, 28, 31, 30, 31, 30, 31, ...

The Sierpinski triangle is a shape that was first described in 1915. It is made by repeating a simple instruction as many times as possible. Start with one large, black, equilateral triangle. At each next stage, remove a triangle from the middle of each black triangle.

- Try drawing the Sierpinski triangle. How many times can you follow the instruction?
- How many black triangles are there at each stage? Describe this sequence.
- Use Resource sheet A1: Pascal's triangle. Colour all the odd numbers black. What do you notice?

Sequence cross-number

- Solve this sequence cross-number. The rule is always to add or subtract the same amount each time.
- Does the bottom row count as a sequence?
- See if you can create your own sequence cross-number.

1.5 Letters and unknowns

- Construct expressions from worded descriptions
- Identify the unknowns in an equation
- Find the rule for the nth term of a sequence

What's the BIG idea?

- You can use inverse operations to find missing numbers in calculations. **Level 3**
- You need to know what calculation to do before answering a question. **Level 4**
- You can write an **expression** to describe a situation. **Level 5**
- You can write a **position-to-term rule** as an expression. **Level 5**

Why learn this?

You can use letters as a shorthand. If Alex's age is x and Sam is three years older than him, Sam's age will always be $x + 3$

Practice, practice, practice!

Level 3

3a I can use inverse operations

1 Find the missing number in each of these calculations.

$3 + \boxed{12} = 15$

a $14 - \square = 9$ **b** $7 + \square = 13$ **c** $\square \times 4 = 32$

d $\square \div 2 = 6$ **e** $8 + \square = 10$ **f** $15 \div \square = 5$

Level 4

4c I can use appropriate calculations to solve problems

2 Write down the calculation you would do to solve these problems.
Do *not* work out the answer.

There are 25 rows of chairs. There are 28 chairs in each row.
How many chairs are there altogether?

Total number of chairs = number of chairs in a row × number of rows
= 25 × 28

a A school has 420 pupils to divide equally between 20 classes.
How would you work out how many pupils should be in each class?

b Pete wants to make 24 kites. He needs 17 staples to make each kite.
How would you work out how many staples he needs?

Level 5

5c I can construct simple expressions

3 **a** Sunil had b books in his bag when he arrived at school. Write an expression for the number of books he had at the end of the day if he had
i two more **ii** six fewer **iii** five more **iv** four fewer.

b John brought £x to school.
Write an expression for how much money he had later if he
i spent £1 **ii** was given £3.

expression nth term position-to-term rule

4 Bill is b years old. Asma is a years old.
Write expressions for the ages of their teachers:
a Mrs Bright is twice as old as Bill.
b Mr Smith is the sum of Bill's and Asma's ages.
c Mrs Old is three times as old as Asma.
d Mr Stevens is four times Bill's age minus six years.
e Miss Young is three times Bill's age.

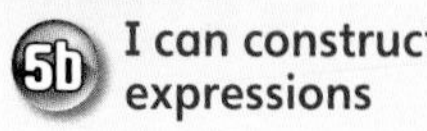

5b I can construct expressions

5 x is a mystery number.
Match the descriptions in words to the expressions.

5a I can construct more complex expressions

	Descriptions	Expressions
a	The mystery number multiplied by six and added to two	$x + 3$
b	Two divided by the mystery number	$50 \div x$
c	Three more than the mystery number	$6x + 2$
d	The mystery number add two then multiplied by six	$x \times x$
e	The mystery number divided by two	$x \div 50$
f	The mystery number divided by fifty	$2 \div x$
g	Fifty divided by the mystery number	$x \div 2$
h	The mystery number multiplied by itself	$6(x + 2)$

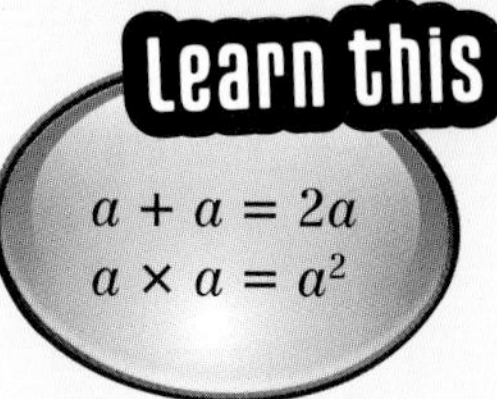

$a + a = 2a$
$a \times a = a^2$

6 $x + y = 15$
What numbers could x and y be?

5a I can identify the unknowns in an equation

7 Look at this table. Copy the sentences and fill in the gaps.

5a I can write linear expressions

a

Position (n)	1	2	3	4	5	…	n
Term	6	12	18	24	30		

i The position-to-term rule is: multiply the position by ____.
ii Using algebra, the position-to-term rule is:
$n \rightarrow$ ____ $\times\, n$ (This is called the rule for the nth term.)

b

Position (n)	1	2	3	4	5	…	n
Term	2	5	8	11	14		

i The position-to-term rule is: multiply the position number by ____ and subtract ____
ii Using algebra, the position-to-term rule is:
$n \rightarrow$ ____ $\times\, n -$ ____

Now try this!

A 'Expression noughts and crosses'
A game for two players. One of you is 'noughts' and the other is 'crosses'. Take turns to choose a statement from Resource sheet 1.5. If you can match a statement to one of the expressions correctly, circle or cross the expression. The first person to get three in a row (horizontally, vertically or diagonally) wins the game.

B Mystery ages
Use the letter x to represent your age. Write expressions for the ages of 4 people you know.
For example: Mum $3x$ Pete $2x + 7$
Give your partner your expressions to work out the ages.

rule variable

1.6 Patterns and sequences

- Investigate sequences
- Find patterns and rules in sequences
- Test whether the rule works

Why learn this?

When you play a computer game you get better at it as you play more. This is because you remember the sequences and patterns you met before in the game.

What's the BIG idea?

- To find terms of a sequence of shapes you need to draw some more shapes. **Level 4**
- You can find the **term-to-term rule** by finding the difference between the terms. **Level 4**
- To check your rule works, use your rule to find the next term in the sequence and then check it by drawing the next shape. **Level 5**

Practice, practice, practice!

Matchsticks investigation Q1–6

These shapes are made from matchsticks.

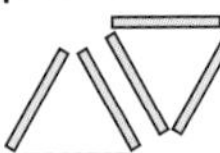
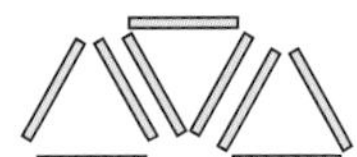

1 There are six matchsticks in the second shape.

a How many matchsticks are in the third shape?

b Draw the next three shapes.

c How many matchsticks are there in the fifth shape?

2 Would any of the shapes have exactly 13 matchsticks in it? Explain your answer.

Level 3

3b I can continue a simple pattern

3 Copy and complete the table. Use the pictures above as a starting point.

Shape number					
Number of matchsticks					

4 Describe the term-to-term rule.

Level 4

4b I can generate a simple sequence

4b I can describe the term-to-term rule

5 Write the position-to-term rule of the pattern above in words.

6 **a** Use your rule to predict how many matches there are in the tenth shape.

b Test whether your rule works by drawing the tenth shape.

Watch out!

Don't forget – the position-to-term rule is different from the term-to-term rule.

Level 5

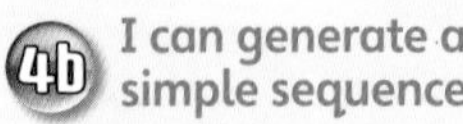
5c I can describe the position-to-term rule

5b I can generate terms of a sequence

investigate pattern predict

Counters investigation

A number sequence is made from counters.

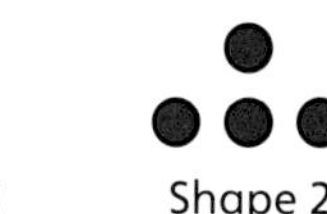

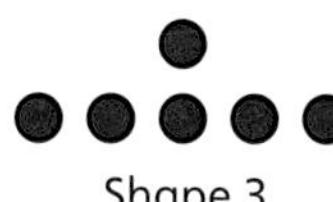

Shape 1 1 counter | Shape 2 4 counters | Shape 3 7 counters

7 a Draw the next three shapes in the pattern.

b How many counters are there in the sixth shape?

8 Would any of the shapes have exactly 11 counters in it? Explain your answer

Level 3

3b I can continue a simple pattern

9 Create a table showing the shape number and the number of counters in each shape.

10 Descrbe the term-to-term rule.

Level 4

4b I can generate a simple sequence

4b I can describe the term-to-term rule

11 Write the position-to-term rule of the pattern in words.

12 **a** Use your rule to predict how many counters there are in the eighth shape.

b Test whether your rule works by drawing the eighth shape.

Level 5

5c I can describe the position-to-term rule

5b I can generate terms of a sequence

Squares investigation

John makes the first letter of his name with squares.

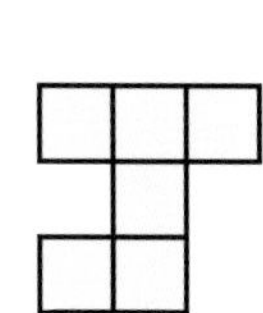

Shape 1 6 squares

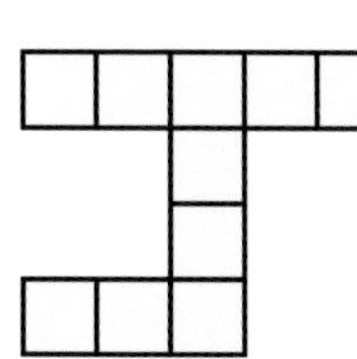

Shape 2 10 squares

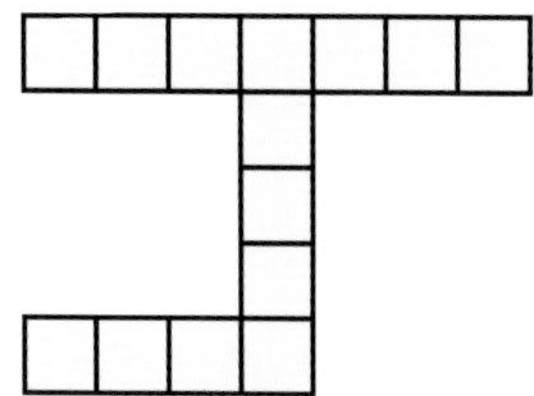

Shape 3 14 squares

13 Carry out an investigation on this pattern similar to the Matchsticks and Counters investigations.
Describe both the term-to-term rule and the position-to-term rule.

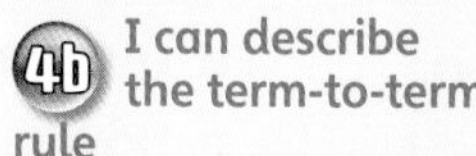

4b I can describe the term-to-term rule

5c I can describe the position-to-term rule

Now try this!

A Shape sequences 1

Use matchsticks or counters to make patterns of shapes.
Ask your partner to continue the pattern and to complete a table of values for the first 5 terms.

B Shape sequences 2

Use matchsticks or counters to make patterns of shapes.
Ask your partner to continue the pattern and to complete a table of values for the first 5 terms.
Now, ask your partner to work out how many matchsticks or counters will be in the tenth shape.
Check whether they are correct by making the tenth shape.

rule **sequence** **term-to-term rule**

Handshakes investigation

Arun, Billy, Charlie and David won the annual four-a-side football tournament.

1 After the game Arun and Billy shook hands once.

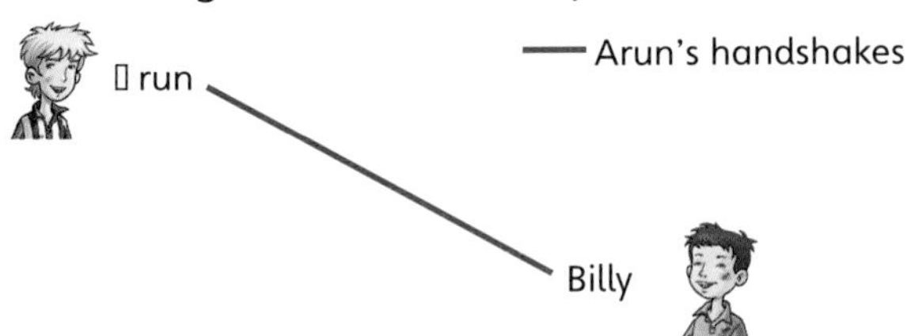

How many handshakes are there? **Level 3**

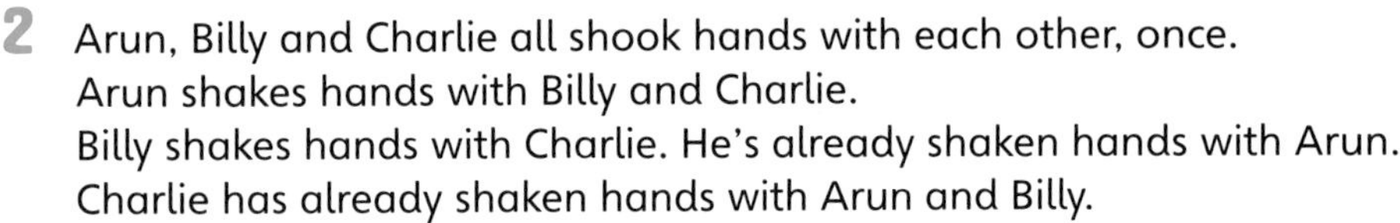

2 Arun, Billy and Charlie all shook hands with each other, once.
Arun shakes hands with Billy and Charlie.
Billy shakes hands with Charlie. He's already shaken hands with Arun.
Charlie has already shaken hands with Arun and Billy.

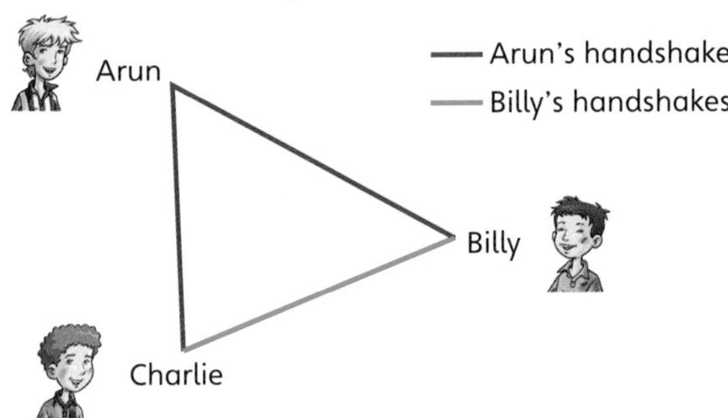

How many handshakes are there between the three of them? **Level 3**

3 Arun, Billy, Charlie and David all shake hands with each other, once.

a Draw a diagram like the ones above to show how many times they shake hands.

b How many handshakes are there between the four of them? **Level 3**

4 How many handshakes can there be between

a 5 people b 6 people c 7 people? **Level 3**

5 Copy and complete this table.

Number of people	2	3	4	5	6	7
Number of handshakes						

a What is the pattern in the number of handshakes?

b What is the term-to-term rule? **Level 4**

6 How many handshakes would there be if the England cricket team all shook hands once with each other? **Level 5**

Hint: You can do this activity by shaking hands with people in your class. There are 11 people in a cricket team.

The BIG ideas

- Each number in a sequence is called a **term**. Level 3
- You can find the missing terms of a sequence by working out the **difference** between the terms. Level 3
- You can describe a sequence using the **first term** and the **term-to-term rule**. Level 4
- You can describe a sequence using the **position-to-term rule**. Level 5
- You can find out the **position** of a term in the sequence using the position-to-term rule. Level 5
- A number multiplied by itself is a **square number** and it makes a square pattern of dots. Level 4
- **Triangle numbers** make a triangular pattern of dots. Level 4
- You can find the **output** from a **function machine** from the **input** and the **rule**. Level 4
- You can find the input to a function machine by using the **inverse operation**. Level 5
- You can find the **rule** of a function machine if you know the input and the output. Level 5
- You can represent a function machine using a mapping and an equation. Level 5
- You can write an **expression** from a word description. Level 5

Find your level

Level 3

Q1 Look at this sequence of numbers going down in steps of 4.
33, 29, 25, 21
Write down the next two numbers in the sequence.

Q2 Look at this sequence of numbers going up in steps of 6.
12, ..., 24, 30, ..., 42
Write down the two missing numbers in the sequence.

Level 4

Q3 a The rule in a number sequence is 'add 7'. Use this rule to write the missing numbers in the sequence.
..., 11, 18, 25, ...

b The rule in a different number sequence is 'double then add 1'. Use this rule to write the missing numbers in the sequence.
..., 9, 19, 39, ...

Q4 a The number sequence below is part of a doubling number sequence.
..., 30, 60, 120, ...
Write down the two missing numbers.

b The number sequence below is part of a halving number sequence.
..., 100, 50, 25, ...
Write down the two missing numbers.

Level 5

Q5 The rule to get the next number in this number sequence is 'multiply by 2 then add 4'.
3, 10, 24, ..., ...
Write down the next two numbers in the sequence.

Q6 a The rule to get the next number in this number sequence is 'multiply by 3 then subtract 5'.
Write down the two missing numbers in the number sequence.
..., 4, 7, 16, ...

b This number sequence has a different rule.
1.8, 3.6, 7.2, 14.4, 28.8
Write what that rule might be.

2 Know your numbers

This unit is about using numbers and getting the decimal point in the right place.

The Afghan Reading Project (ARP) is a charity that helps school children and teachers in Afghanistan. There has been war in Afghanistan for many years. It has been very dangerous for children to attend school, and many schools have been destroyed. The ARP provides books for schools. These books are written and printed in Afghanistan, so this also provides work and income for local people.

So far, the ARP has provided 42 000 books to 60 schools. Nineteen titles have been written already, including story books and a book about drug awareness. A gift of books is a helping hand after years of turmoil and destruction. Being able to read brings hope of a better future for many children and adults.

Activities

A To raise money, the Afghan Reading Project bought baskets and made cards to sell at a town fête. It cost them £18 to buy all the baskets, £34.25 to buy the materials to make the cards and £15 to set up the stall.

- What was the total cost of running the stall?
- On the day the stall took £222.63. How much profit did the charity make?

B The Afghan Reading Project was started by three friends. Get together with a group of friends and plan a charity fund-raising event. Make it as fun as possible.

- How much would your event cost to run?
- Estimate how much money you could raise.
- What would your profit be?
- What could your charity provide for that money?

Before you start this unit...

1 For each of these numbers, write down the digit in the tens position.

a 46 **b** 73 **c** 281

Level Up Maths 1-2 page 8

2 Write down the largest number in each set.

a 16, 160, 16.3

b 2.1, 2.01, 2.11

c 10.09, 9.01, 10.9

Level Up Maths 1-2 page 8

3 Do the calculations and use the code to write three words.

Level Up Maths 1-2 page 9

A	N	R	D	I	U	B	M	E
6	3	1	8	7	2	9	5	4

a 9 − 8 = ☐ 10 − 6 = ☐ 4 + 4 = ☐

b 12 − 3 = ☐ 16 − 15 = ☐ 2 + 4 = ☐

15 − 8 = ☐ 19 − 16 = ☐

c 21 − 18 = ☐ 14 − 12 = ☐ 17 − 12 = ☐

24 − 15 = ☐ 26 − 22 = ☐ 28 − 27 = ☐

Charities like the Afghan Reading Project deal with numbers all the time. They have to be careful to make sure whether they are dealing with millions, thousands, hundreds, tens, or just single units.

Plus digital resources

2.1 Place value

- Read and write whole numbers in figures and words
- Know what each digit represents in numbers with up to two decimal places
- Understand and use decimal notation and place value
- Multiply and divide whole numbers and decimals by 10, 100 and 1000

Why learn this?

On a cheque, you need to write the amount in words and in figures.

What's the BIG idea?

→ The value of a **digit** depends on its position – its **place value**. Level 3

4 7 2 8
- 8 units
- 2 tens
- 7 hundreds
- 4 thousands

→ The **decimal point** separates the whole number part (on the left) from the fractional part (on the right). The place value headings are H T U . t h th Level 3 & Level 4

→ To **multiply** whole numbers and decimals:
- by 10, move the digits one place to the left
- by 100, move the digits two places to the left
- by 1000, move the digits three places to the left. Level 4 & Level 5

→ To **divide** whole numbers and decimals:
- by 10, move the digits one place to the right
- by 100, move the digits two places to the right
- by 1000, move the digits three places to the right. Level 4 & Level 5

Watch out!

Be careful where you place the decimal point – it makes a big difference!

Did you know?

π (pi) is an infinite decimal, it goes on and on and on 3.1415926535… The current world record for reciting π belongs to Chao Lu, who rattled off 67 890 digits over 24 hours in 2005.

Practice, practice, practice!

Level 3

3a I can write numbers in figures

1 Write these numbers in figures.

five hundred and seventy-two

Write under place value headings

H T U
5 7 2

a six hundred and four
b one hundred and thirty-nine
c seven thousand three hundred and eighty-six

3a I can read and write whole numbers and decimal numbers in words and figures

2 To fill in a cheque, you write the amount of money in words and in figures. Complete the amounts in these cheques.

a
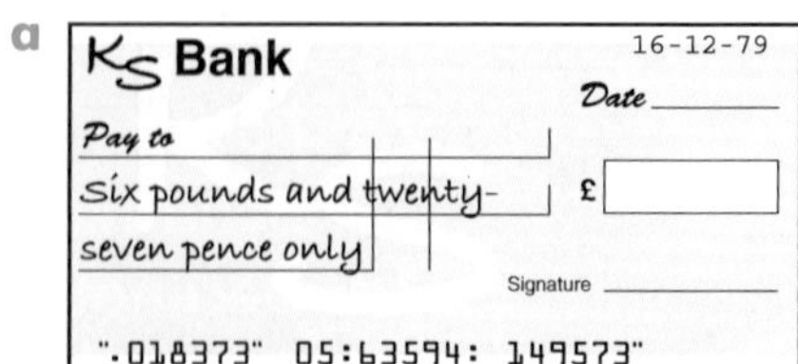
KS Bank 16-12-79
Date
Pay to
Six pounds and twenty-seven pence only £
Signature
".018373" 05:63594: 149573"

b
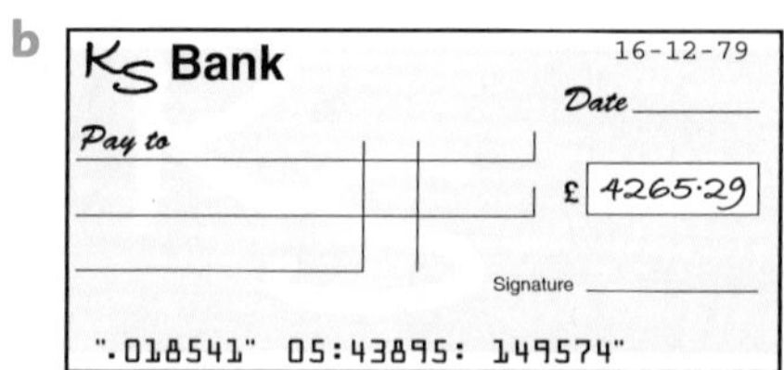
KS Bank 16-12-79
Date
Pay to
£ 4265·29
Signature
".018541" 05:43895: 149574"

c
KS Bank 16-12-79
Date
Pay to
Five thousand and thirty-six pounds only £
Signature
".018371" 05:63986: 149575"

d
KS Bank 16-12-79
Date
Pay to
£ 7934·06
Signature
".018378" 05:93477: 149576"

decimal number | decimal place | decimal point | digit | divide

3 Write down the value of the 5 in each of these numbers.

a 6549 b 87 245 c 72.5 d 392.75

4 Write down these amounts in figures.

a fifteen point three two seven

b two hundred and three point zero two

5 Jasmine has these cards: 4 7 0 9 •

Make the **largest** and the **smallest** number you can using the cards.

6 Work out:

a 87 × 100 b 67 ÷ 10 c 163 ÷ 100 d 253 × 1000

7 Copy and complete these calculations. Fill in the missing digits in.

a _ _ _ × 10 = 2320 b 890_ ÷ 10 = _90 c 45_0 ÷ 10 = _ _6

8 Work out

a 7.2 × 1000 b 0.75 × 100 c 36.4 × 10

d 27.2 ÷ 1000 e 15.1 ÷ 100 f 8.7 ÷ 10

9 Copy and complete these calculations.

a ___ × 0.5 = 5 b 84 ÷ ___ = 0.084 c 103 ÷ ___ = 1.03

10 Use these facts: 1 kg = 1000 g 100 cm = 1 m 1000 m*l* = 1 *l*

Work out

a 750 g = ___ kg b 384 cm = ___ m c 2105 m*l* = ___ *l*

d 5.62 *l* = ___ m*l* e 0.27 kg = ___ g f 6.63 m = ___ cm

3a I know what each digit represents in numbers with up to two decimal places

Level 4

4c I know what each digit represents in numbers with up to three decimal places

4b I can use place value to solve a problem

4a I can multiply and divide integers by 10, 100 and 1000

Level 5

5c I can multiply and divide decimals by 10, 100 and 1000

Now try this!

A Place value challenge

A game for two players. You will need a dice and a game board like this:

	Hundreds	Tens	Units	.	tenths	hundredths	thousandths
Player 1							
Player 2							

Take turns to roll the dice and write your number in a cell on the game board, in your row. The winner is the player with the highest number when all the boxes have been filled.

B How many numbers?

You have four cards: 2 3 7 •

Which numbers can you make between 0 and 50?

hundredth multiply place value tenth thousandth value

2.2 Addition and subtraction

- Add and subtract mentally
- Recall addition and subtraction facts and positive integer complements
- Know how to add and subtract whole numbers and decimals, using a written method

Why learn this?

Mental arithmetic skills are important for many different jobs.

What's the BIG idea?

→ You can use **partitioning** to **add** and **subtract** mentally. **Level 3**

57 + 65 = 50 + 60 + 7 + 5
= 110 + 12
= 122

→ You can use **compensation**, by adding or subtracting too much and then compensating.

57 + 65 = 57 + 70 − 5 = 122 **Level 3**

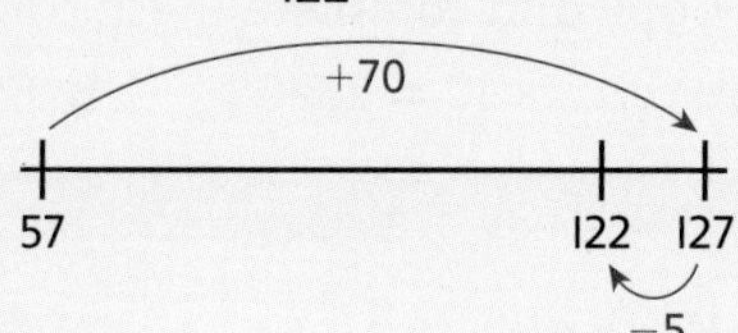

→ You can find a **difference** by **counting on** from the smaller number to the larger number.

95 − 36 = 4 + 50 + 5 = 59 **Level 3**

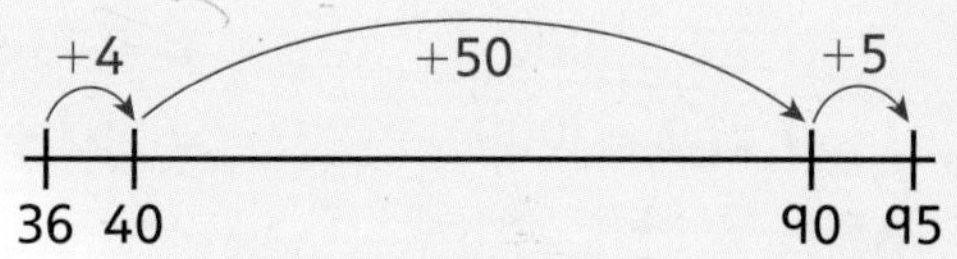

→ **Integer complements** are useful when adding and subtracting mentally.

20 + 80 = 100 6 + 4 = 10 **Level 4**

→ You can use standard column procedures to add and subtract whole numbers and decimals. **Level 4**

Practice, practice, practice!

Level 3

3b I can mentally add pairs of two-digit numbers

1 Mentally add these pairs of numbers. Show your method in writing or with a diagram.

a 27 + 43 **b** 86 + 24 **c** 51 + 46
d 15 + 25 **e** 62 + 30 **f** 98 + 97

3a I can mentally subtract pairs of two-digit numbers

2 Do these subtractions. Show your method in writing or with a diagram.

a 94 − 77 **b** 62 − 41 **c** 89 − 72
d 22 − 20 **e** 75 − 47 **f** 50 − 11

3b 3a I can mentally add and subtract pairs of two-digit numbers

3 On each side of a triangle, the numbers in the two circles add together to give the number in the square between them. Complete these.

a

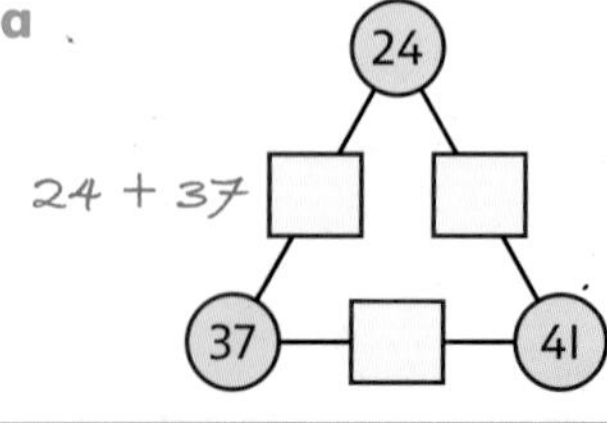

b

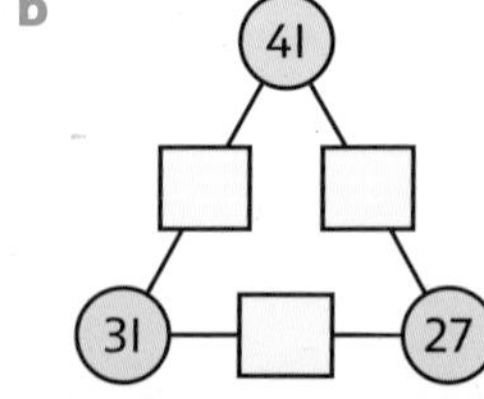

c

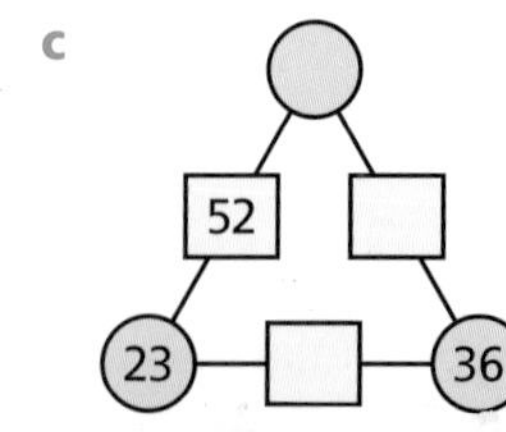

add calculation compensation complements counting on

4 Copy and complete these calculations using complements to 100.

a 17 + ___ = 100 **b** 64 + ___ = 100 **c** 55 + ___ = 100
d 81 + ___ = 100 **e** 28 + ___ = 100 **f** 77 + ___ = 100

5 Work out the change from £1 for these items.

a chewing gum 42p **b** stamp 36p
c bus ticket 75p **d** sweets 68p

6 Work out these additions.

a	b	c	d
272	328	273	779
496 +	897 +	569 +	283 +
___	___	___	___

7 Work out these subtractions.

a	b	c	d
296	371	695	382
142 −	120 −	418 −	195 −
___	___	___	___

8 Work out

a	b	c	d
28.2	243.6	28.3	126.29
13.6 +	17.87 +	1.4 −	37.41 −
___	___	___	___

9 Solve these problems.

a Find the sum of 62.8 and 47.9.
b Find the difference between 87.65 and 49.27.
c Rebecca has £7.27. She is given £4.39 more. How much does Rebecca now have?
d Edward has £19.38. He spends £5.96. How much does he have left?

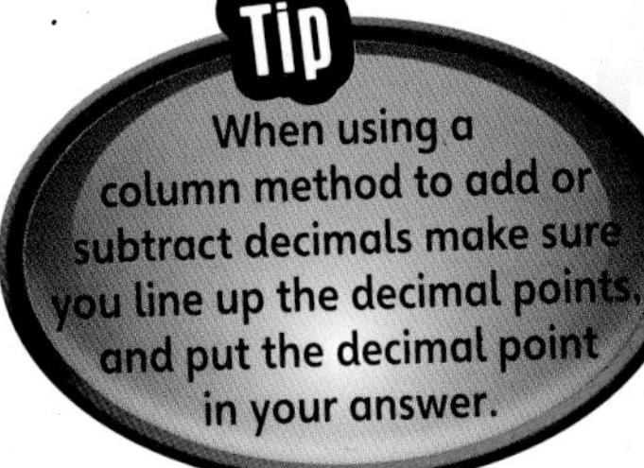

10 Nia cut a length of 0.78 m from a three metre length of wood. Work out the length of wood left over.

11 In these number pyramids, the value in each brick is the sum of the two bricks below it. Copy and complete the pyramids.

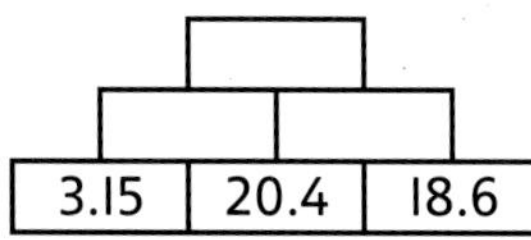

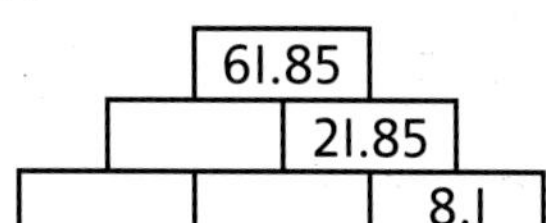

Level 4

4c I can recall the positive integer complements to 100

4c I can use a column method to add together whole numbers

4c I can use a column method to subtract whole numbers

4b I can use a column procedure to add and subtract decimals

Now try this!

This is a magic square. Whichever way you add, you get the same answer.
This magic square adds up to 33.

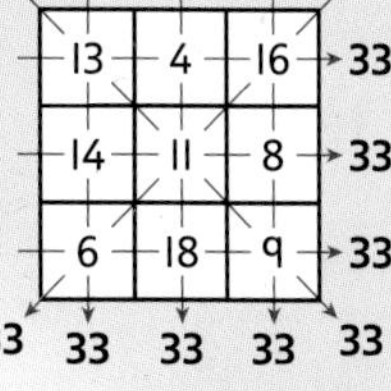

A Magic square 1

This magic square must add up to 18. Find some ways to fill it in.

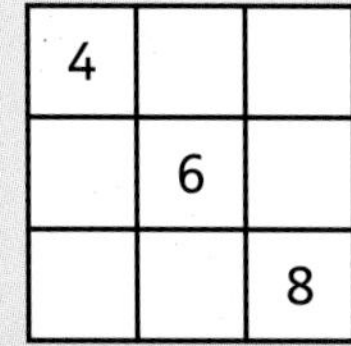

B Magic square 2

This magic square must add up to 37.2. Find some ways to fill it in.

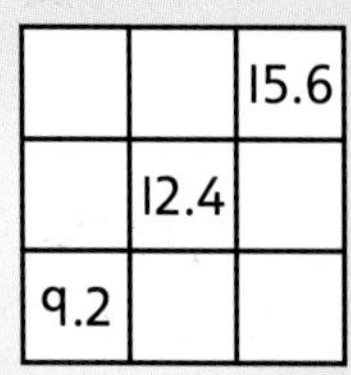

difference integer partition subtract

What's in a number?

The first known use of numbers dates back about 32 000 years – but things have changed a lot since then!

Number pattern

Here is the start of a number pattern:

$$1^2 = 1 \times 1 = 1$$
$$11^2 = 11 \times 11 = 121$$
$$111^2 = 111 \times 111 = 12321$$
$$1111^2 = 1111 \times 1111 = 1234321$$

- What will the next line of the pattern be?
- Will the pattern go on forever?
- Can you explain why the pattern works?

Digit dilemma

- In each of the calculations below, the digits have been replaced by letters.
  What might the original calculations have been?

O N E	M A T H S	N U M B E R
O N E +	S U M S +	N U M B E R +
T W O	S M A R T	D O U B L E

Hint The letters can be worth different amounts in each calculation.

Chinese jigsaw

- How would you fit these jigsaw pieces together to make a number square of the first twenty-five numbers in Chinese? You can use Resource sheet A2 to help you.
- How would you write the number 26 in Chinese characters? What about 43?

2.3 Positive and negative numbers

- Know how to calculate a temperature rise across 0°C
- Know how to calculate a temperature fall across 0°C
- Order positive and negative integers
- Know how to add and subtract positive and negative integers

Why learn this?

You need negative numbers to write very low temperatures.

What's the BIG idea?

- A thermometer shows how high or low a temperature is. Level 3
- Numbers **above zero** are **positive** numbers. Numbers **below zero** are **negative** numbers. Negative numbers are written with a minus sign in front of the number. Level 3
- Positive and negative numbers can be represented on a number line. Level 4

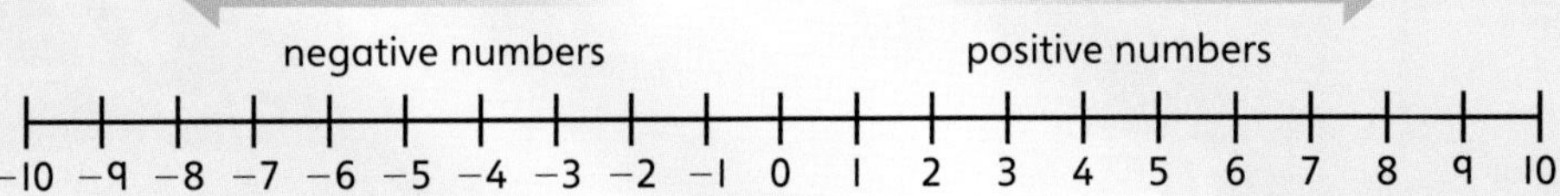

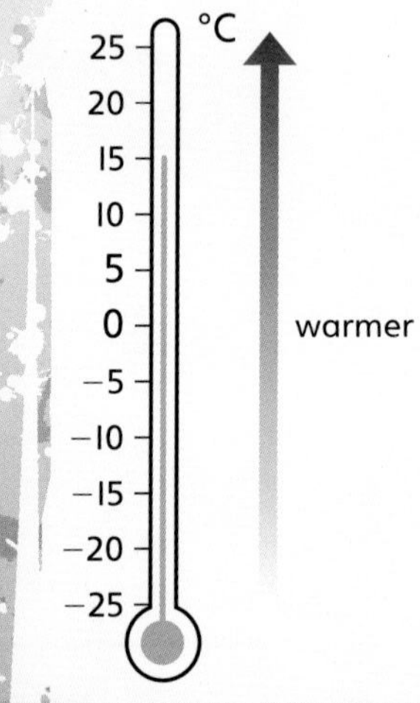

- An **integer** is a positive or negative whole number, or zero. Level 4
- If you **add** a positive number the result is bigger. If you **subtract** a positive number the result is smaller. Level 4
- If you add a negative number the result is smaller. If you subtract a negative number the result is bigger. Level 5

Did you know?

The lowest temperature ever recorded in the UK is −27.2°C at Braemar in the Grampians on 10 January 1982 and at Altnaharra, Highland, on 30 December 1995.

Practice, practice, practice!

Level 3

3b I can calculate a temperature rise across 0°C

1 Calculate the new temperature if the temperature now is

5°C and it rises by 10°C $5°C + 10°C = 15°C$

a 12°C and it warms up by 4°C

b −4°C and it rises by 12°C

c −11°C and it warms up by 6°C.

Hint Use the thermometer or number line to help you.

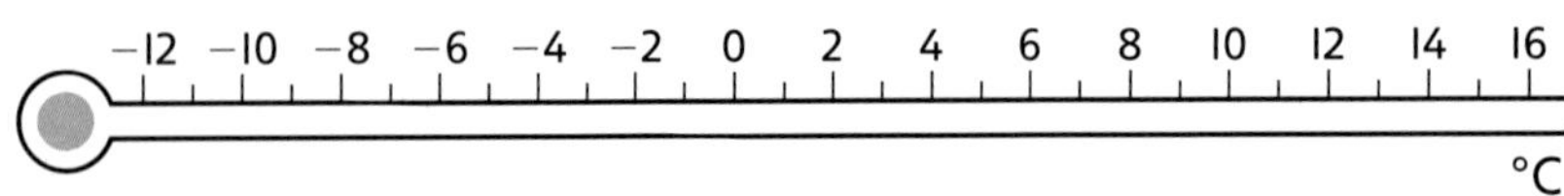

3a I can calculate a temperature fall across 0°C

2 Calculate the new temperature if the temperature now is

a 10°C and it cools down by 9°C

b 5°C and it falls by 7°C

c −5°C and it cools down by 5°C

d −2°C and it cools down by 11°C.

add integer negative

3 These cards show some temperatures.

−1°C	5°C	−9°C	9°C	7°C	−2°C	−8°C	0°C

Draw a number line to help you put the temperatures in order.

Level 4

4b I can show the positions of positive and negative integers on a number line

4 Write each set of temperatures in order, lowest (coldest) first.

−6°C, 12°C, 0°C, −3°C *Use a number line:*

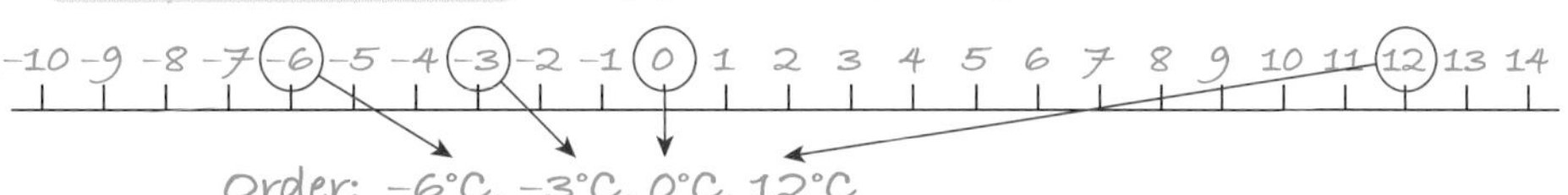

Order: −6°C, −3°C, 0°C, 12°C

a 0°C, −10°C, 4°C, −3°C **b** −8°C, −12°C, −6°C, −7°C
c 4°C, −5°C, 8°C, −10°C **d** −3°C, 3°C, 9°C, −12°C

4b I can order positive and negative integers in context

5 Write these changes to bank accounts as number sentences.
Calculate the final bank balance.

Current balance £25, withdrawal £30. *£25 − £30 = −£5*

a Current balance £12, withdrawal £20.
b Current balance −£9, deposit £15.
c Current balance −£15, deposit £12.
d What does it mean if your bank balance is −£50?

Hint: Withdrawal means taking money out; deposit means putting money in.

4a I can add and subtract positive and negative integers in context

6 Write these temperature changes as number sentences.
Calculate the end temperature.

a −6°C rises by 4°C **b** 3°C falls by 7°C **c** 9°C falls by 13°C

Level 5

5a I can add and subtract positive and negative numbers

7 Copy this number pyramid.
Find each missing number by adding the numbers in the two bricks below it.

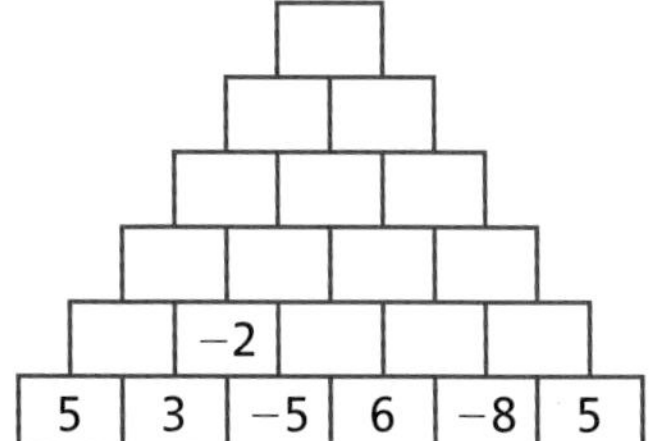

8 Work out the answers to these.

a −3 − 6 **b** 5 − −7
c −4 − −3 **d** −4 + −6

Learn this

Subtracting a positive is the same as adding a negative.
Subtracting a negative is the same as adding a positive.

Now try this!

A Temperature difference

Work with a partner. Make cards showing temperatures from 10°C to −10°C. Shuffle the cards and spread them out face down. Pick two cards each and work out the temperature difference. The person with the highest difference scores 1 point. Repeat five times to find the overall winner.

B Highest wins

Work with a partner. You will need 1–10 number cards. Shuffle the cards and deal them.
Each player uses their cards and + or − signs to make a calculation. The answer closest to zero scores 1 point. Repeat five times to find the overall winner.

order positive subtract

2.4 Decimals

➩ Understand and use decimal notation and place value
➩ Know how to compare and order decimals

Why learn this?

The difference between 0.01 m and 0.1 m is important when it comes to world records!

What's the BIG idea?

→ To **order** decimals, first **compare** the whole numbers, next compare the tenths, then compare the hundredths, and so on. Level 4

→ To compare decimal measures, all the measures must be in the **same units**. Level 4

Did you know?

Stephen Taylor, from the UK, holds the record for the longest tongue. His tongue measures 9.5 cm from the tip to the centre of his closed top lip.

Practice, practice, practice!

Level 4

4b I can compare and order decimals in different contexts

1 The table shows the temperatures at midday in some cities.

 a Which city had the highest midday temperature?

 b Arrange the temperatures in order, starting with the lowest.

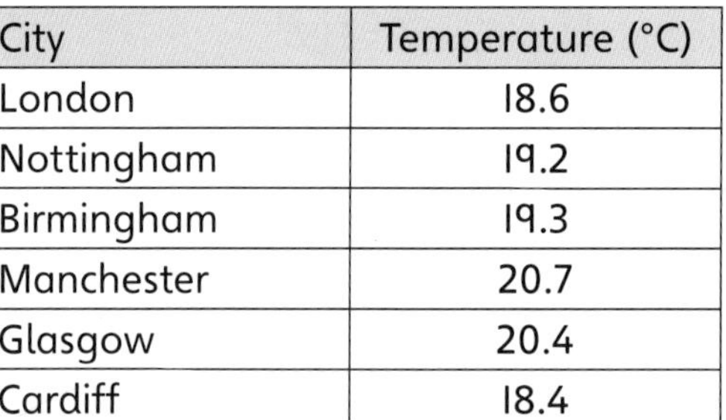

City	Temperature (°C)
London	18.6
Nottingham	19.2
Birmingham	19.3
Manchester	20.7
Glasgow	20.4
Cardiff	18.4

2 Some fruit and vegetables are weighed on digital weighing scales.

Place the weights in order, starting with the lightest.

6.2 KG

6.15 KG

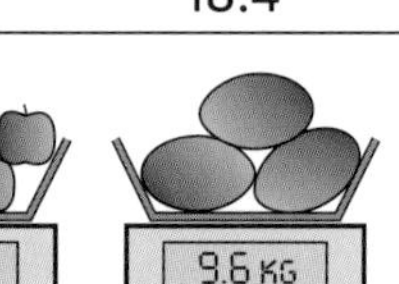

3 The table shows the times taken to solve a sudoku puzzle.

 a Who took the longest to solve the problem?

 b Write the times taken to solve the puzzle, quickest time first.

Student	Time (in minutes)
Ben	3.26
Tom	4.62
Mohammed	4.81
Lily	4.83
Amy	4.65

4 Write the correct sign, > or <, between each pair.

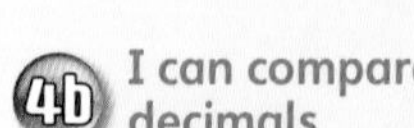

3.4 ☐ 3.5 *3.4 is smaller than 3.5 so use <*
3.4 < 3.5

a 1.32 ☐ 1.4 **b** 12.45 ☐ 12.54 **c** 2.38 ☐ 2.83
d 14.813 ☐ 14.183 **e** 8p ☐ £0.12 **f** −6.7°C ☐ −6.3°C

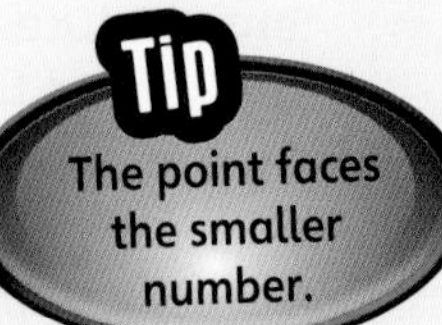

compare decimal number greater than (>) hundredth

5 Rearrange these decimal numbers in order of size, starting with the smallest.

a 6.3, 4.8, 6.02, 6.17, 4.56 b 0.45, 0.09, 0.48, 0.3, 0.5

c 2.05, 1.9, 2.1, 2.23, 1.99 d 7.7, 0.76, 6.7, 7.67, 0.67

Level 4

4b I can order decimals

6 These prices are displayed in a shop window.
Rearrange the prices, starting with the smallest.

4a I can compare measures by changing them to the same units

7 Order each set of measurements, starting with the smallest.

a 8 kg, 800 g, 0.88 kg b 1.46 m, 46 cm, 0.64 m

c 84p, £8.47, £0.48 d 3.5 hours, 4 hours 20 minutes, 65 minutes

e 28 mm, 3.2 cm, 2.4 cm f 1.03 *l*, 993 m*l*, 0.99 *l*

8 The table shows the circuit lengths for the F1 race circuits of different countries.

Country	Circuit length
Belgium	7.00 km
Brazil	4310 m
UK	5140 m
France	4.41 km
Malaysia	5.54 km
Australia	5300 m
Canada	4.36 km

a Which country has the shortest race circuit? **Hint:** 1 km = 1000 m

b Arrange the countries in order of circuit length, starting with the longest.

c Rearrange your list to include
- Bahrain circuit length 5.412 km
- USA circuit length 4192 m
- Hungary circuit length 4.381 km.

Watch out!
Don't forget that to compare measurements they must be in the same units.

Now try this!

A Highest mountains

Find out the heights of some different mountains in the world.
Arrange the heights in order of size, tallest to shortest, to create your own tallest mountain list.

B Decimal ladders

A game for two people. You will need two dice.
Draw a ladder game board with 7 rungs.

Roll both dice to create a decimal number. For example, if you roll a 2 and a 4, the number could be 2.4 or 4.2. You have to decide which position to place your number so that larger numbers are above smaller numbers. You lose when you cannot write a number in the correct space on the ladder.

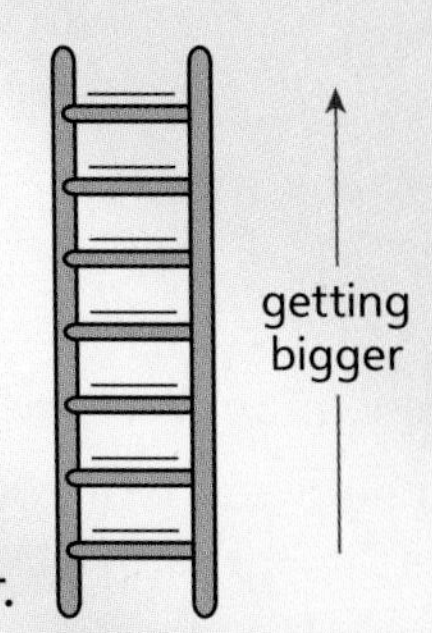

less than (<) order tenth thousandth

2.5 Square numbers and multiplication

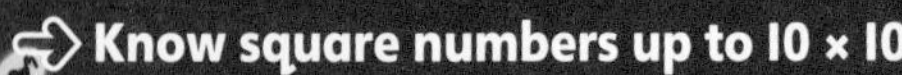

- Know square numbers up to 10 × 10
- Work out square numbers beyond 10 × 10
- Remember multiplication facts up to 10 × 10
- Know how to work out division facts

Why learn this?

Knowing your times tables can help you work out the best buy.

What's the BIG idea?

- Multiplication tables are useful in learning **multiplication** facts. Level 4
- If you know a multiplication fact you can work out a **division** fact. Level 4
- **Square numbers** are numbers that can be represented by the correct number of dots laid out in rows and columns to make a square. Level 4 & Level 5
- To **square a number**, you **multiply** it by itself. Level 4 & Level 5

  2 × 2 = 4 4 × 4 = 16
- You can write 4 × 4 as 4^2. Level 4 & Level 5
- You say 4^2 as '4 to the power of 2' or, more commonly, as '4 **squared**'. Level 4 & Level 5
- Decimals can be written as **fractions**, for example $0.6 = \frac{6}{10}$ and $0.41 = \frac{41}{100}$. Level 5

You need to know your times tables since they are used all the time in mathematics.

Practice, practice, practice!

Level 4

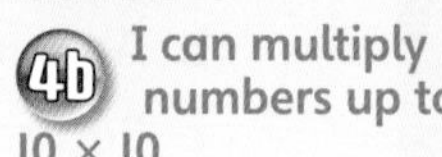

I can multiply numbers up to 10 × 10

1 Work out

a 2 × 6 b 7 × 9 c 10 × 4

d 7 × 3 e 5 × 3 f 8 × 6

2 Copy and complete these multiplication grids.

a

×	2	7	5
4		28	20
3		21	
2	4		10
6	12	42	

b

×	6	3	10
2			
5			
6			
8			

c

×	4	8	9
5			
6			
8			
3			

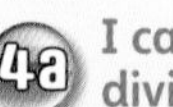

I can work out division facts

3 Work out each multiplication. Then write down all the related division facts.

6 × 7 *6 × 7 = 42 42 ÷ 7 = 6 42 ÷ 6 = 7*

a 8 × 9 b 4 × 8 c 8 × 8 d 7 × 8

e 2 × 5 f 7 × 3 g 6 × 9 h 5 × 4

4a I can multiply integers by 10, 100 and 1000 and work out division facts.

4 Work out the multiplication 9 × 3 = ____

Use your answer to help you work out these divisions.

a ____ ÷ 9 = 30 b 2700 ÷ 300 = ____

decimal number divide division fraction

5 On each side the numbers in the circles are multiplied together to give the numbers in the squares between them. Use division to work out the missing values.

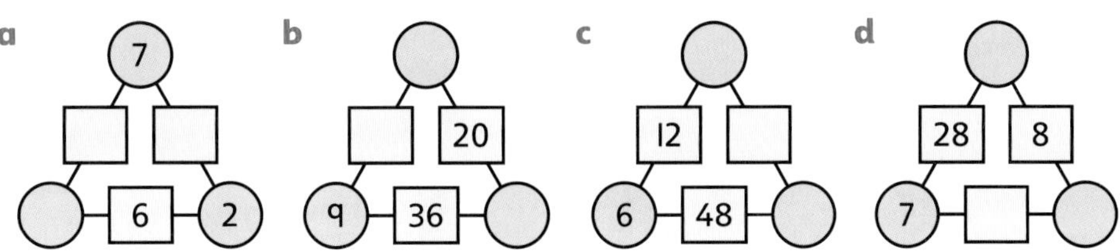

6 Find and write down all the square numbers from this grid.

12	25	26	35	4
21	3	9	42	71
36	5	14	64	76
1	26	72	68	80
27	19	49	19	90

7 Write these using ^{2}.

5 × 5 $= 5^2$

a 6 × 6 b 1 × 1 c 7 × 7 d 9 × 9
e 3 × 3 f 8 × 8 g 10 × 10 h 4 × 4

Level 4

4a I can work out division facts

4a I can recognise square numbers up to 12 × 12

8 Work out
a 12^2 b 15^2 c 20^2 d 22^2
e 14^2 f 25^2 g 17^2 h 19^2

Watch out!
Don't forget that 3^2 means 3 × 3 not 3 × 2!

9 Work out

3.6 × 20 3.6 × 10 = 36
36 × 2 = 72

a 4.2 × 30 b 7.1 × 40 c 5.6 × 20 d 1.24 × 200

10 Work out

1.24 × 50 1.24 × 100 = 124
124 ÷ 2 = 62

a 2.13 × 50 b 1.46 ×50 c 2.68 × 50 d 4.57 × 50

Level 5

5c I know square numbers beyond 10 × 10

5c I can use multiplication facts in more complex calculations.

Now try this!

A Challenge design

Design a multiplication and division quiz for other pupils using multiplication facts up to 10 × 10.

B Design a mathematical crossword

Design a crossword puzzle with multiplication and division problems as the clues.

multiplication multiply squared square number

2.6 Using a calculator

- Enter numbers on a calculator in different contexts
- Correctly interpret the display on a calculator
- Make estimates and approximations of calculations

Why learn this?

Knowing how to use a calculator properly saves time and avoids mistakes.

What's the BIG idea?

- Use the [•] key on your **calculator** to **enter** decimals.
  To work out 25.9 + 16.8 press [2] [5] [•] [9] [+] [1] [6] [•] [8] [=] [42.7] **Level 3**
- Use the [±] key to enter negative numbers. To enter −12 press [±] [1] [2]. **Level 4**
- Be careful reading the display. If you are working with money in pounds, [4.5] means £4.50.
  If you are working with lengths in metres, [4.5] means 4.5 m (or 4 m 50 cm). **Level 4**
- If you enter an amount in pounds, the answer will be in pounds.
  If you enter an amount in pence, the answer will be in pence. **Level 4**
- You can check to see if a calculator answer is correct by making an **estimate**. **Level 4**

Did you know?

When the first pocket calculator was launched in the UK in 1972, it cost £79 plus tax, an amount close to the average monthly wage!

Tip

Your calculator may not have a [±] key. Ask your teacher to check how your calculator works.

Practice, practice, practice!

1 Use your calculator to work these out.

12.7 + 29.8

Press [1] [2] [•] [7] [+] [2] [9] [•] [8] [=] [42.5]

a 25.4 − 16.9 **b** 14.5 × 8.2 **c** 46.8 ÷ 6.5
d 33.6 + 13.2 **e** 12.9 × 8.3 **f** 54.6 ÷ 5.2

Level 3

3c I can use all the operation keys and the decimal point on a calculator

2 Use your calculator to work these out. 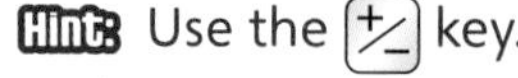

a −17 − 4 **b** 24 + −7 **c** −8 + −12 **d** 100 − −19
e −35 − 17 **f** 8 − −3 **g** 22 + −28 **h** −15 − −39

3 Estimate the answers to these calculations.

799 + 416 *799 + 416 is roughly 800 + 400 = 1200*

a 862 − 324 **b** 9503 − 299 **c** 1911 + 939
d 5635 − 2412 **e** 643 − 379 **f** 1111 − 456

4 Use approximation to see which of these might be correct.

a 998 − 502 = 694 **b** 407 + 398 = 508 **c** 872 − 246 = 626
d 2011 + 974 = 985 **e** 19 × 41 = 79 **f** 9.8 × 6.4 = 62.72

Level 4

4c I can input negative numbers on a calculator

4b I can make estimates and approximations of calculations

approximate calculation calculator

Tip
Always estimate the answer before using your calculator.

Level 4

5 Nicola buys a pair of trainers for £47.19, a pair of jeans for £32.58 and a t-shirt for £8.49.

a Use your calculator to work out the total cost.

b Nicola paid with five £20 notes. How much change did she receive?

(4b I can enter numbers on a calculator in different contexts)

6 Peter is going to the cinema with seven friends. They spend £7.76 on sweets and share the cost between them. How much do they each have to pay? Give your answer in pence.

(4a I can interpret the display on the calculator)

7 Nathan worked out £5.67 plus 54p on a calculator. The display showed 59.67. What did Nathan do wrong?

(4a I can use a calculator correctly)

8 Georgina has £5 to buy 32p stamps for Christmas cards.

a How many stamps can she buy?

b What is the total cost?

c How much change would she have?

(4a I can use a calculator to solve problems)

9 A hedge is 3 km 983 m long. It is to be trimmed by seven farmers. They all trim equal sections. What length does each farmer trim? Give your answer in **a** km and **b** m.

(4a I can use a calculator correctly)

10 Here is Brandon's till receipt. He paid with a £10 note and was given £4.80 change. Brandon thinks his change is wrong.

.67
.85
.36
2.03
.50
.99

a Without using your calculator, explain whether you think he is likely to be right or wrong.

b Use your calculator to check the amount of change he should have.

(4a I can solve different problems using a calculator)

Now try this!

A Target 25

Play 'Target 25' with a partner.

Player 1: Key 1, 2, 3, 4 or 5 into a calculator then hand it to your partner.

Player 2: Add 1, 2, 3, 4 or 5 to the number in the calculator then hand it back.
Keep taking turns. The player who reaches 25 wins the round.
Play several rounds, with a different player going first each time, to find the overall 'Champion 25'.

B Birthday trick

Do this activity with a partner. Use the instructions to find each other's birthdays.

Player 1: Use a calculator to follow these instructions. Only show Player 2 your final answer.

1 Multiply the day of the month you were born in by 5.
2 Add 14 to the answer.
3 Multiply the answer by 4.
4 Subtract 31 from the answer.
5 Multiply the answer by 5.
6 Add the number of the month you were born in.
7 Tell your partner the answer.

Player 2:

1 Subtract 125 from the answer.
2 Read out the day and month of your partner's birthday.
(For example, 205 is 2 May, 1110 is 11 October.) Magic!

display enter estimate

School fête

1 Baker Street School holds a fête to raise money for charity.

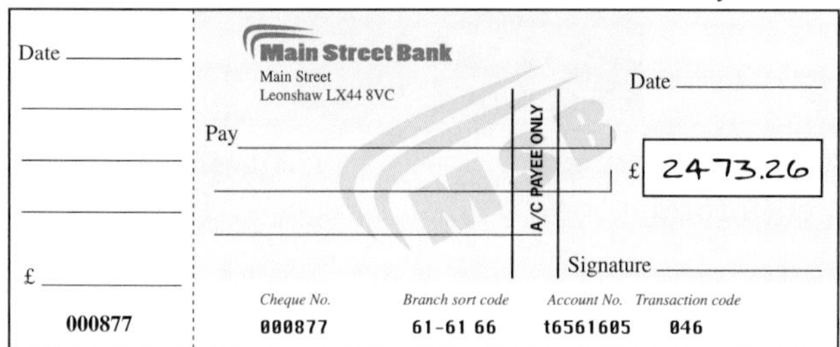

Fête success!

Four hundred and eighty-six people came to our school fête.

Write this number in figures. Level 3

2 The school fête raised £2473.26 in total.
Write this amount in words for the cheque.

Date ______

£ ______

000877

Main Street Bank
Main Street
Leonshaw LX44 8VC

Date ______

Pay ______

A/C PAYEE ONLY

£ 2473.26

Signature ______

Cheque No.	Branch sort code	Account No.	Transaction code
000877	61-61 66	t6561605	046

Level 3

3 Work out how much these three stalls took in total. Level 4

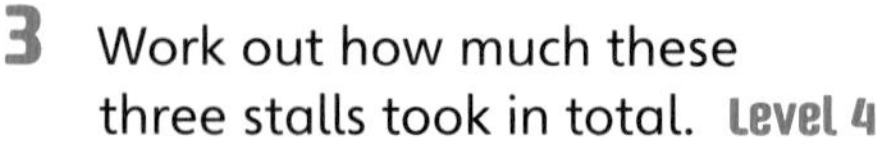

Cake stall	£82.14
Smack the rat!	£41.50
Raffle	£126.71

MAKE MATHS FUNCTIONAL!

4 Class 7 ran the ice cream stall. They had to keep the ice cream in a cool box below 0°C. At the start the cool box temperature was −5°C.

a After 1 hour it was 3°C warmer. What was the new temperature?

b They added more ice and the temperature fell by 6°C.
What was the new temperature? Level 4

5 Use a calculator to find the total cost of these items on the white elephant stall.

Level 4

6 The DVD stall sold 100 DVDs at £0.75 each.
How much money did they make? **Level 5**

The BIG ideas

- Numbers **above zero** are **positive numbers**. Numbers **below zero** are **negative numbers**. They are written with a minus sign in front of the number. Level 3
- Use the [•] key on your calculator to enter decimals. Level 3
- If you enter an amount in pounds, the answer will be in pounds. If you enter an amount in pence, the answer will be in pence. Level 4
- You can use **standard column procedures** to add and subtract whole numbers and decimals. Level 4
- If you add a positive number the result is bigger. If you subtract a positive number the result is smaller. Level 4
- To multiply whole numbers and decimals:
  - by 10, move the digits one place to the left
  - by 100, move the digits two places to the left
  - by 1000, move the digits three places to the left. Level 4 & Level 5
- To divide whole numbers and decimals:
  - by 10, move the digits one place to the right
  - by 100, move the digits two places to the right
  - by 1000, move the digits three places to the right. Level 4 & Level 5
- If you add a negative number the result is smaller. If you subtract a negative number the result is bigger. Level 4 & Level 5

Find your level

Level 3

Q1 a Amy has these coins.

Write the amount in figures.

b Josh has these coins.

Write the amount in words.

Q2 Work out

a 63 + 49 = ____

b 63 − 49 = ____

Q3 Write down these numbers in figures.

a one hundred and sixty-eight

b five hundred and eight

c two thousand four hundred and three

Level 4

Q4 Put these amounts in size order, smallest first.

a 2.369, 269.3, 236.9, 29.63, 293.6, 2396.0

b £34.70, £3.74, £37.04, £4.37, £34.07, £307.40

Q5 Copy and complete this magic square so that all rows and columns, and both diagonals, have the same total.

		1.2
	1.0	1.4
		0.4

Q6 a Elaine has £5.24. She is given £2.36 more. How much does Elaine have now?

b Samia has £16.31. She spends £7.48. How much does Samia have now?

Level 5

Q7 Complete each number sentence using the number 2 or the number −2.

a −4 + ____ = −2

b 2 − ____ = 4

c ____ + 4 = 2

d ____ − 2 = −4

Q8 Copy and complete these calculations.

a ____ × 10 = 12.4

b 725 ÷ ____ = 7.25

c ____ × 100 = 311

d 429 ÷ 10 = ____

3 Sizing up

This unit is about 2-D and 3-D shapes, and the importance of being able to make accurate estimates and measurements.

The Angel of the North is a massive steel sculpture in Tyneside. It was designed by the sculptor Antony Gormley, but it took many people to produce detailed designs, to manufacture it and to put it up. It took many calculations to estimate the amounts of materials needed and to make sure it could withstand winds of over 100 mph.

Whether you're decorating a room, building a stadium or a 20 m sculpture, you need to be able to make estimates of lengths and areas.

Below the Angel of the North, concrete piles 20 m deep anchor it to the rock beneath.

The body of the Angel is attached to the base with bolts 3 m long.

The 3153 pieces of steel needed 10 km of welding.

To make the body of the Angel, Antony Gormley made a cast of his own body. It was then enlarged many times!

Would you have guessed that the average area of skin covering a human body is about 18 000 cm^2? Did you know that the longest fingernails grown by a woman measured 7 m 51 cm 3 mm?

Activities

A Use websites or an encyclopaedia to find ten amazing facts about lengths and areas of the human body, animals or food.

B You are going to design a presentation box for a souvenir bowl of the Angel of the North.

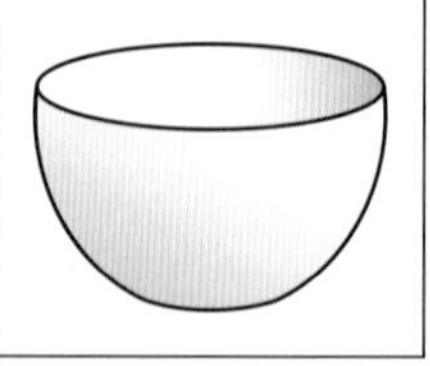

- Cut out five squares of card, each measuring 10 cm by 10 cm.
- How many ways it is possible to arrange these squares to form the net of an open-top box? Sketch each solution so that you can be sure that each one is unique.

Before you start this unit...

1 How many metric units for measuring length can you name?

2 What is the size of the smallest division on a ruler?

3 Which of these shapes is a rectangle?

Level Up Maths 1-2 page 16

How do you know?

4 What is the distance around the edge of a shape called?

Level Up Maths 1-2 page 15

5 What is the name of a flat shape that can fold up to make a 3-D solid?

Level Up Maths 1-2 page 58

The 54 m wingspan of the Angel of the North is wider than a Boeing 757 or 767 jet. It is 20 m high – the height of a five storey building or four double-decker buses.

Plus digital resources

World's Greatest Maths! 3.1

Mission to Mars

Year: 2047
Mission classification: Phoenix 7
Destination: Mars
Objective: design and build a base for interstellar exploration

You are the lead architect on the Phoenix 7 Mars mission. The Phoenix Mars base will be the first manned planetary space base, and the European Space Agency are hoping to use it to launch an interstellar exploration mission.

Can you use your 3-D design skills to build living pods, an antimatter drive and a zero-gee training facility in time for the interstellar mission to blast off?

Design a living pod

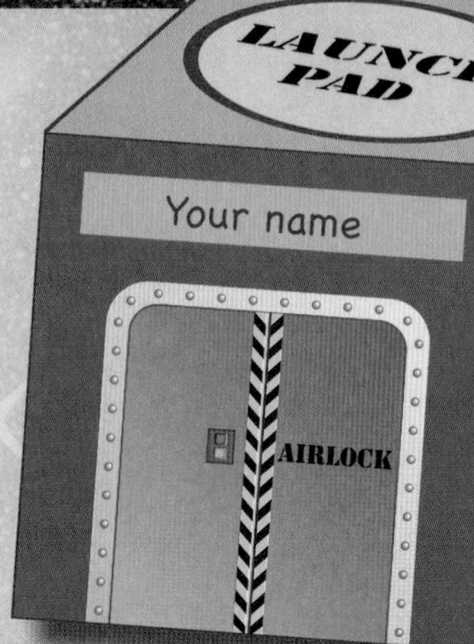

The living pods are the simplest buildings on the Mars base. Each one is in the shape of an upside-down open cube.

- Design your own living pod. You need at least one airlock and one window. There must be a sign with your name on it and a launch pad on the roof.
- Draw your design on the net of an open cube on Resource sheet 3.1. The launch pad has already been drawn for you. Cut out the net and fold it up to make your living pod.
- Draw three different nets of an open cube on plain paper. On each net, mark where your living pod's airlock and launch pad would go.

Shuttle hangars

Shuttle hangars come in three different shapes.

- Name the 3-D shape used to make each type of shuttle hangar.
- How many faces, edges and vertices does each type of hangar have?
- A new building is created by placing a class B shuttle hangar on top of a living pod. It fits exactly.
  How many faces, edges and vertices does this new building have?

Class A

Class B

Class C

Zero-gee training facility

Here are the instructions for building a zero-gee training facility:

- Construct a model of the training facility using multilink cubes.
- Make a drawing of your model on isometric paper.

Join three cubes horizontally in a straight line. Place one cube next to the middle cube. Place one cube on top of each of the end cubes.

Antimatter drive

Here is the design for the revolutionary antimatter propulsion drive for the interstellar mission. It has been shown from three different angles.

Octodrive blueprints

- Use the net on Resource sheet 3.1 to make a 3-D model of this drive.
- Colour the faces correctly and enter the number of faces, edges and vertices on the control panel.

If you haven't got coloured pens or pencils, label the faces with the correct colours.

Laboratory

The research laboratory is a crucial part of the Mars base. It is constructed from four cubes joined together, face to face. Here are two different possible designs for the laboratory.

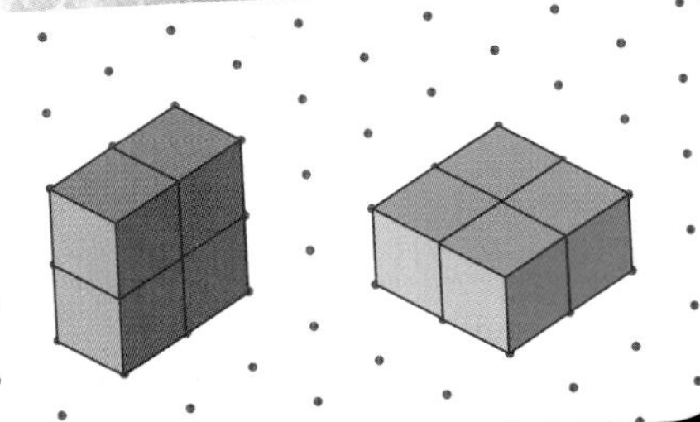

- How many possible designs are there for the laboratory?
- Record your different designs using isometric paper.

Your laboratory must not have any overhanging cubes. So this design would not be allowed:

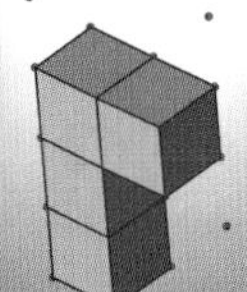

Mars quake!

Falling rocks from a Mars quake have cut a slice through a living pod!

- What is the shape of the new face created after the Mars quake?
- How many faces, edges and vertices does the living pod now have?
- Describe the 3-D shape that has been cut off the living pod.
- What other 2-D shapes could be created by cutting through a cube?
- What 2-D shapes could be created by cutting through a square-based pyramid?

3.2 Measurement

- Read measurements from different scales
- Make sensible estimates of lengths
- Choose which units to use when estimating lengths and areas
- Convert between metric units
- Solve problems involving length

What's the BIG idea?

- Make sure you know what one division on a **scale** represents. Level 3
- How accurately you **estimate** depends on what you are estimating and the scale you use. Level 3
- Units used for **length** are **millimetres (mm)**, **centimetres (cm)**, **metres (m)** and **kilometres (km)**. Level 4
- Units used for area are **square millimetres (mm²)**, **square centimetres (cm²)**, **square metres (m²)** and **square kilometres (km²)**. Level 4
- 10 mm = 1 cm, 100 cm = 1 m, 1000 mm = 1 m, 1000 m = 1 km. **Level 5**
- When you solve problems involving lengths, think about the units and make rough estimates to see if your answers look reasonable. **Level 5**

Why learn this?

A poorly estimated length or height could have disastrous consequences.

Practice, practice, practice!

Level 3

3b I can read scales accurately

1 On each scale, how much does one division represent?
Write down the number the arrow is pointing to.

a 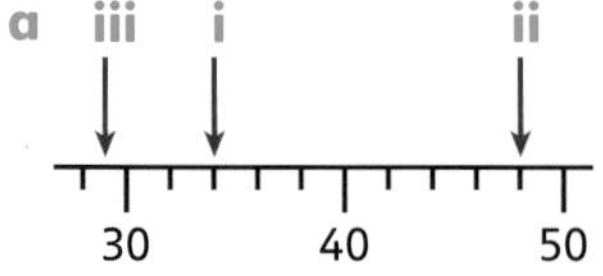

b 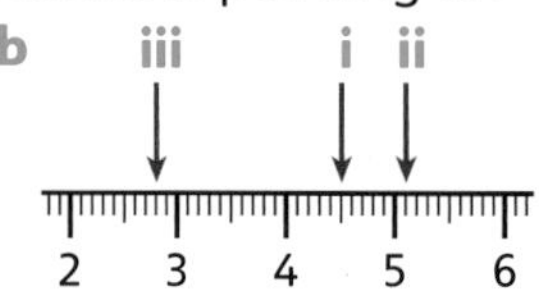

c 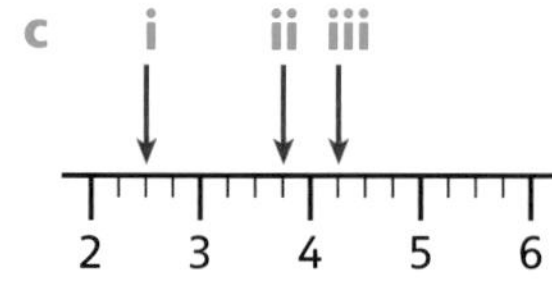

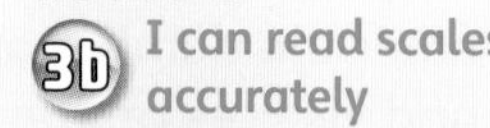

Always work out what one interval stands for before reading a scale.

3a I can estimate readings from scales

2 Estimate where these needles are pointing to.

a 

b 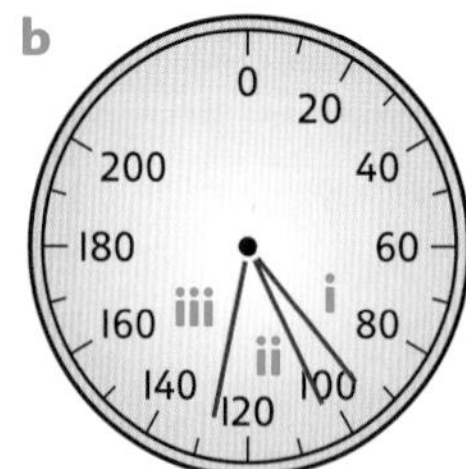

c 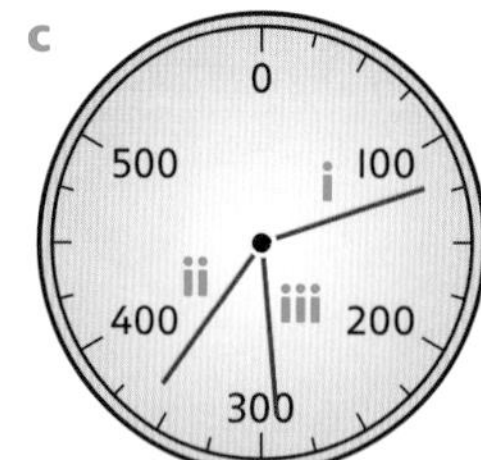

Level 4

4b I can choose a suitable unit for estimates of length

3 Which of these statements is unlikely to be true?
Suggest a more likely unit for the one you think is untrue.
A I went on a 16 km hike this weekend.
B My dog measures 63 m from his nose to his tail.
C The classroom is 6470 mm wide.
D Our classroom door is 195 cm high.
E Our exercise books are 174 mm wide.

area centimetre (cm) estimate kilometre (km) length metre (m) millimetre (mm)

4 a Choose the answer you think is closest to the real value for each of these statements.

i The area of a credit card is... 46 mm² 46 cm² 46 m²

ii The area of the top of a CD case is... 168 mm² 168 cm² 168 m²

iii The area of a desk top is... 0.66 mm² 0.66 cm² 0.66 m²

b Estimate the area of the front cover of your exercise book. Remember to include the correct unit. **Hint:** Use your answers to part **a** to help you.

Level 4

4b I can choose a suitable unit for estimates of length and area

5 a Convert these measurements, where necessary, so that they are all in centimetres.

i 340 mm	**ii** 43 cm	**iii** 0.33 m
iv 3430 cm	**v** 4.3 m	**vi** 3.444 mm

b Put the lengths in order of size, from the smallest to the largest.

6 For a technology project you need to cut ten lengths of wood measuring 350 mm each. There are three lengths of wood in the store cupboard which measure 1.5 m, 1.6 m and 0.65 m. Will you be able to cut enough lengths from these pieces of wood? Explain your answer.

7 A tutor group is planning to raise money for charity by building a line of coins. They hope to raise at least £50. The line will go across the playground, which is 20 m wide. There are three options for coins to collect.

50p = 30 mm wide   20p = 21.4 mm wide   10p = 24.5 mm wide

a What is the total width of **i** two 50p coins **ii** five 20p coins **iii** ten 10p coins?

b What would a 20 m line of **i** 50p coins **ii** 20p coins **iii** 10p coins be worth?

c Which type of coin would raise the amount closest to £50?

8 An internet route finder gives this route from Birmingham to Manchester. It takes 1 hour 27 minutes.

Birmingham to motorway:	4.7 km
A38(M), then M6:	106.5 km
A556:	19.2 km
M56:	7.9 km
Motorway to Manchester:	2 km

Another route avoids motorways. It is 130 km, and takes 2 hours 29 minutes.

a How many kilometres shorter is the slower route?

b Which route would you advise taking? Why?

Level 5

5c I can convert one metric unit for length into another

5c I can solve problems involving lengths

Learn this

'kilo' means a thousand, 'milli' means a thousandth, 'centi' means a hundredth.

Now try this!

A Straight liners

Work with a partner. One of you chooses a length between 0 cm and 5 cm.
Both draw a line that length – without a ruler.
Now measure your line. Score 1 point if you are within 1 cm.
Repeat for lengths between 5 cm and 10 cm, then between 10 cm and 15 cm, 15 cm and 20 cm, and so on.
The highest score after five lines wins.

B Dotters

Work with a partner. Draw ten dots, spread out on A4 paper. Label them A to J. Take turns to choose two dots. Both estimate the distance between them. Then measure the distance to the nearest millimetre.
The difference, in millimetres, between your estimate and the actual distance is the number of points you win. The winner has the *lowest* score after five turns.

scale **square centimetre (cm²)** **square kilometre (km²)** **square metre (m²)** **square millimetre (mm²)**

3.3 Perimeter

- Measure lines to within one millimetre
- Draw lines to within one millimetre
- Calculate the perimeter of a rectangle
- Find the perimeter of other shapes
- Solve problems involving perimeter

What's the BIG idea?

- When you measure a line you must be within one millimetre of the correct length. **Level 3**
- You find the **perimeter** of a shape by adding together the lengths of all its sides. **Level 4**
- A quicker way to calculate the perimeter for a **rectangle** is to add the **length** and **width** together, then double the answer. **Level 4**
- Sometimes you can use what you are told about the lengths of sides to work out the lengths of other sides. **Level 4**
- If you know the perimeter of a rectangle and the length of one side you can work out the length of the other sides. **Level 4**
- Remember to use the correct units (mm, cm, m or km) when you solve problems about lengths. **Level 5**

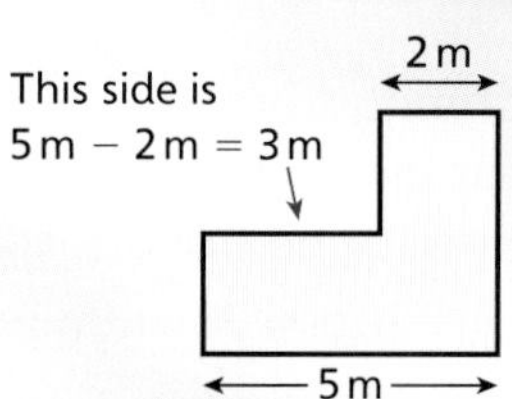

Why learn this?

Fencing in or fencing out? Either way you need to be able to work out how much fencing you need.

Practice, practice, practice!

1 Which of these shapes look as if they have the same perimeter?
Measure the sides of each shape and complete the table to see if you are right.

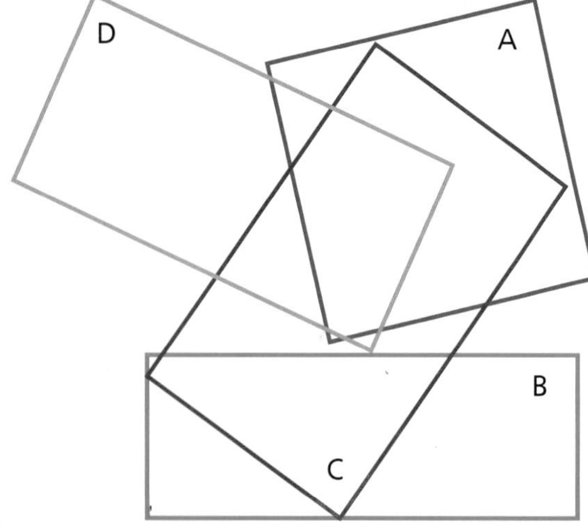

	A	B	C	D
Side 1				
+ Side 2				
+ Side 3				
+ Side 4 (cm)				
= Perimeter (cm)				

Level 3

3b I can measure perimeters accurately

Did you know?

The perimeter fence around Heathrow Airport is over 13 miles long.

2 **a** Draw four rectangles on squared paper with a perimeter of 24 cm.
An example has been started for you.

b Is it possible to draw any other rectangle with a perimeter of 24 cm?

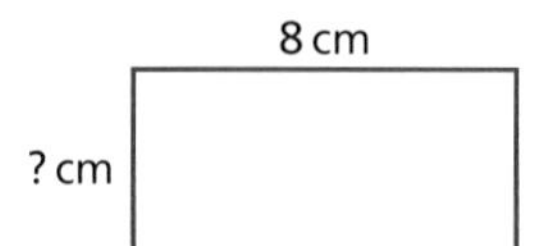

Level 4

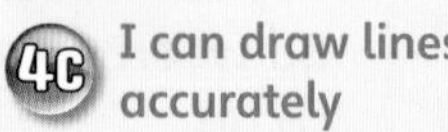

4c I can draw lines accurately

depth distance height high length

3 **a** Calculate **i** $7 + 5 + 7 + 5$
ii $(2 \times 7) + (2 \times 5)$
iii $(7 + 5) \times 2$

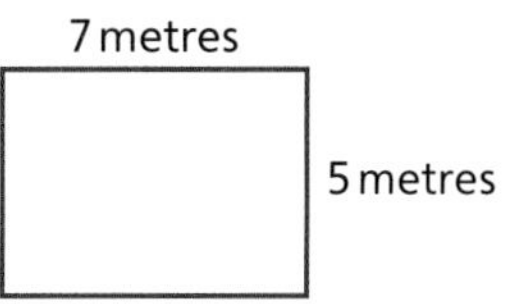

b The calculations in **a** are all ways of working out the perimeter of the rectangle. Which way do you find the easiest?

c Use your chosen way to calculate the perimeter of these rectangles.

i length = 6 cm, width = 9 cm
ii length = 13 cm, width = 7 cm
iii length = 320 cm, width = 30 cm
iv length = $2\frac{1}{2}$ cm, width = $7\frac{1}{2}$ cm
v length = 124 cm, width = 38 cm
vi length = 55 cm, width = 82 cm

4 These letters are drawn on centimetre squared paper. Work out the perimeters of each letter.

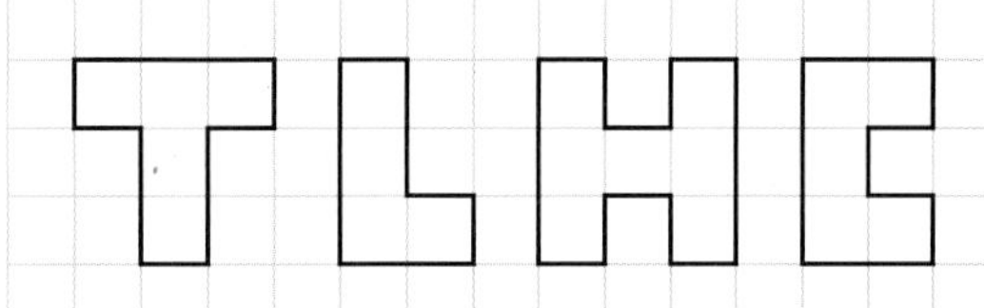

5 Kirsty walks her dog every evening. She goes around the block of flats ten times. She thinks she walks more than 1 kilometre. Is she right?

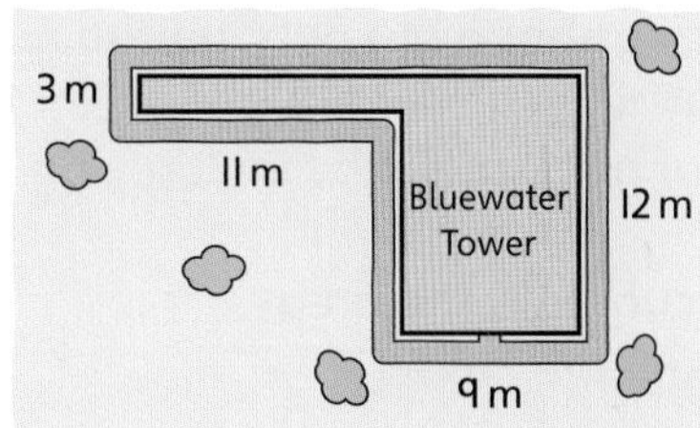

6 Five rectangles each have a perimeter of 60 cm. The lengths of the rectangles are

a 19 cm **b** 16 cm **c** 18.5 cm **d** $20\frac{1}{4}$ cm

What are the widths of the rectangles?

Level 4

4c I can calculate the perimeter of a rectangle

Tip

PAD: To find the Perimeter of a rectangle, Add the length and width, then Double your answer.

4c I can calculate the perimeters of shapes made from rectangles

4a I can calculate the length of a side of a rectangle if I know the perimeter and the length of the other side

7 A robot has to cut all the edges of this lawn.

a How far is it from

i *A* to *B*
ii *C* to *D*
iii *D* to *E*?

b What is the total length of edges that the robot must cut?

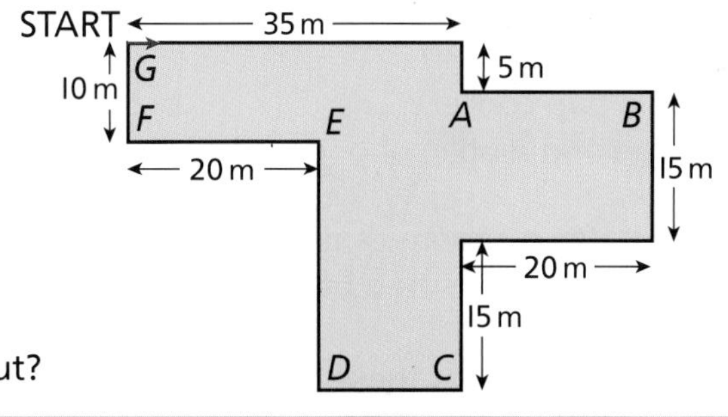

Level 5

5c I can solve problems involving perimeters of rectangles

Now try this!

A Hexominoes

Cut out six squares.
Join them so that they touch side to side to make a hexomino.
Find its perimeter.

They must join like this, *not* like this.

Try other arrangements. Are the perimeters all the same?
Can you find other arrangements with a larger or smaller perimeter?
How many different perimeters are there?

B Robot programs

Look back at Q7. You could write a program to instruct the robot that would start:
Forward 35, RIGHT 90°, Forward 5, LEFT 90°, Forward …
Complete the program to take the robot back to its start position.
How many right turns did it make? How many left turns? What do you notice?
Write a program for a more complicated course. Then check it works by drawing.

perimeter rectangle regular polygon width

3.4 Area of rectangles

- Find the area of a shape by counting the number of square centimetres inside it
- Know the correct units to use when recording areas
- Find the area of a rectangle using the formula $A = l \times w$
- Find the area of shapes made from rectangles
- Calculate the surface area of a cube or cuboid

Why learn this?

When painting a wall, working out the area you are covering helps you work out how much paint to buy.

What's the BIG idea?

→ **Area** is often measured in **square centimetres (cm^2)**. **Level 3**
→ You can also measure area in **square millimetres (mm^2)**, **square metres (m^2)** or **square kilometres (km^2)**. **Level 4**
→ You can find the area of a shape by counting the number of square centimetres inside it. **Level 4**
→ You can find the area of a rectangle by multiplying its **length** by its **width** ($A = l \times w$). **Level 5**
→ The **surface area** of a **cuboid** is the area of all its **faces** added together. **Level 5**

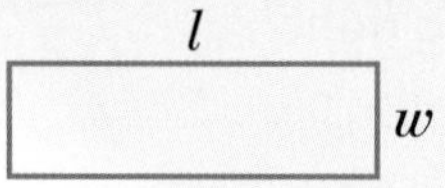

Did you know?

The area of Greater London is 1579 km^2. The area of Jersey is just 116 km^2.

Practice, practice, practice!

Level 4

4b I can choose a suitable unit to measure area

1 Which of these units would you use to measure the area of these shapes?

mm^2 cm^2 m^2 km^2

a tennis court — *You would measure the length and width of a tennis court in metres, so m^2 is the best unit to choose*

a a video screen at a pop concert
b a mobile phone camera lens
c the signal coverage of a mobile phone mast
d a satnav screen

4a I can find areas by counting square centimetres within a shape

2 **a** Each square represents a square centimetre. Count the squares to find the area of each letter.

b Draw a letter covering each of these areas.
i 12 cm^2 **ii** 7 cm^2 **iii** 11 cm^2

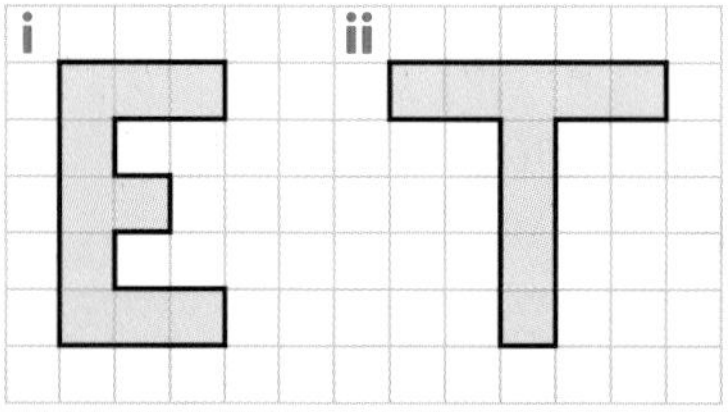

Level 5

5c I can calculate the area of a rectangle using a formula

3 **a** Use the formula $A = l \times w$ to calculate the areas of these rectangles.

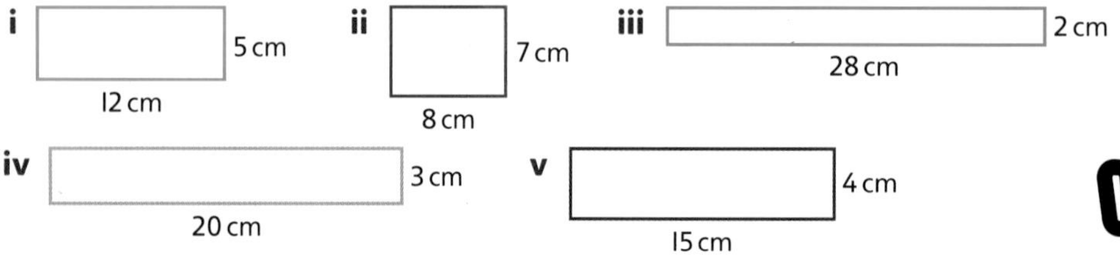

b Which rectangles have an area equal to 60 cm^2?

c Find other pairs of whole number lengths and widths that give a rectangle with area 60 cm^2.

Watch out!

If you double the length and width of a rectangle its area is quadrupled.

area cuboid face length square centimetre (cm^2) square kilometre (km^2)

4 A council has decided to use anti-graffiti paint on the wall by the children's play area in the park. The wall is 2.5 m high and 17 m long. A litre of paint covers 10 m^2. It comes in 5 l and 20 l cans. Which cans do they need?

5 A bottle of lawn food feeds 100 m^2 of lawn. Jim has half a bottle left. He estimates his lawn is roughly 9 m long and 8 m wide. Is there enough lawn food?

6 The area of each of the blue rectangles is 36 m^2.
What is the total area of each shape?

a

b

4 m
4 m
4 m
4 m

7 Calculate the area of each purple shape.

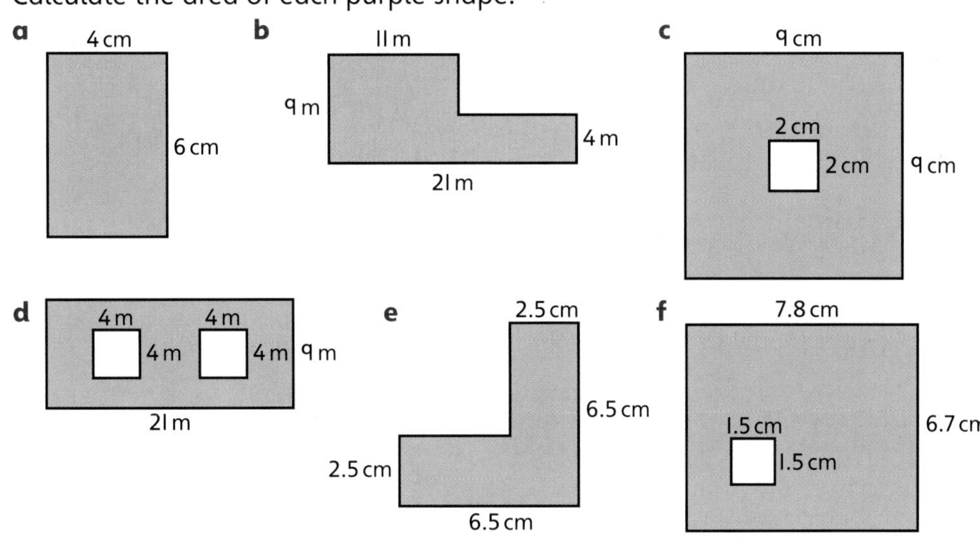

8 **a** Calculate the area of one face of this cube.
b How many faces does the cube have?
c What is the surface area of this cube?

Hint: The surface area is the total area of all the faces.

Level 5

5c I can solve problems involving areas

5b I can calculate the area of shapes made from rectangles

5a I can calculate the surface area of a cube from information about its dimensions

Now try this!

A Picture this

You will need a newspaper.
Ask your teacher to tell you an area in square centimetres. Cut out a picture that you estimate has that area. You can trim the picture if you need to.
Repeat for other areas.

B Rectangle wrestling

A game for two players. Write down the numbers 21 to 30.
The first player chooses a number and crosses it off.
The second player scores a point for every rectangle they sketch with this area.
For example if 20 were in the list, rectangles of 10 cm × 2 cm, 1 cm × 20 cm and 4 cm × 5 cm would score 1 point each.
Swap roles and repeat.
The winner has the highest score once all the numbers have been crossed off.

square metre (m^2) **square millimetre (mm^2)** **surface area** **width**

Design a mobile classroom

In the Indian state of Uttar Pradesh over 1000 computers were distributed to primary schools in villages where there were no power lines. The computers had to run on solar power. Today there are solar-powered computers in schools in rural communities all over the world.

Design a solar-powered computer classroom.

- The classroom will be made of square wall panels so they can be easily transported.
- Each wall panel will be 3 m long and 3 m high.
- There are five computers.
- Each workstation and its chair needs an area of 90 cm × 90 cm.

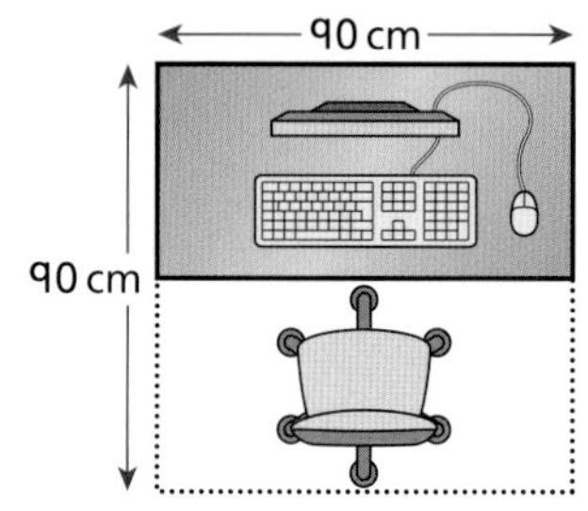

1 Make a model of the classroom by making an open-topped cube measuring 10 cm × 10 cm × 10 cm **Level 3**

2 You need to decide the best place for the workstations and classroom doors.

Cut out five 3 cm × 3 cm squares to represent the workstations.

Position the squares in your model to decide the best place for the workstations.

The classroom needs a door. On your model the door will be 2 cm wide and 7 cm high. Decide the best place for the classroom door. Make a flap in your model to show where it will go. **Level 3**

3 Cabling for the computers will go around the tops of the walls. Calculate the perimeter of the classroom. **Level 4**

4 The classroom will have two solar panels. One will be 1.8 m × 1.2 m and the other will be 1.6 m × 1.2 m. How many square metres is this in total? **Level 5**

5 The inside of the classroom will be painted after it has been put up. Estimate the surface area of the walls. There will be oone window measuring 1 m × 1.2 m. One tin of paint covers 10 m^2. How many tins will you need. **Level 5**

The BIG ideas

- → You can find the perimeter of a shape by adding together the lengths of all its sides. **Level 3**
- → Units used for length are millimetres (mm), centimetres (cm), metres (m) and kilometers. **Level 4**
- → Units used for area are square millimetres (mm^2), square centimetres (cm^2), square metres (m^2) and square kilometers (km^2). **Level 4**
- → You can find the area of a rectangle by multiplying its length by its width ($A = l \times w$). **Level 5**
- → The surface area of a cuboid is the area of all its faces added together. **Level 5**

Find your level

Level 3

Q1 **a** I measure the length of a pencil.

Then I measure the length of the pencil and a rubber.

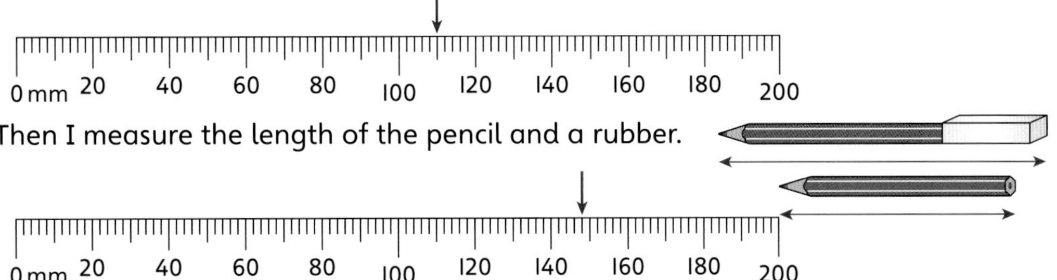

How many millimetres long is the pencil? How many millimetres long is the rubber?

b How many millimetres are there in one metre?

Level 4

Q2 Here is a list of six different units of measure.

millimetres   square metres   kilometres   square centimetres   centimetres   metres

a Which of the units would be the best to use if you wanted to measure
  i the length of an ant
  ii the area of a floor?

b Choose one of the units from the list that you did not use in part a.
Write down the units, then give an example of what it could measure.

Level 5

Q3 Calculate the area of the blue shape.

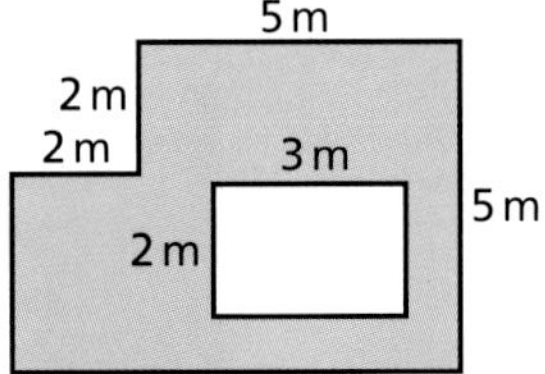

Q4 The square and the rectangle below have the same area.

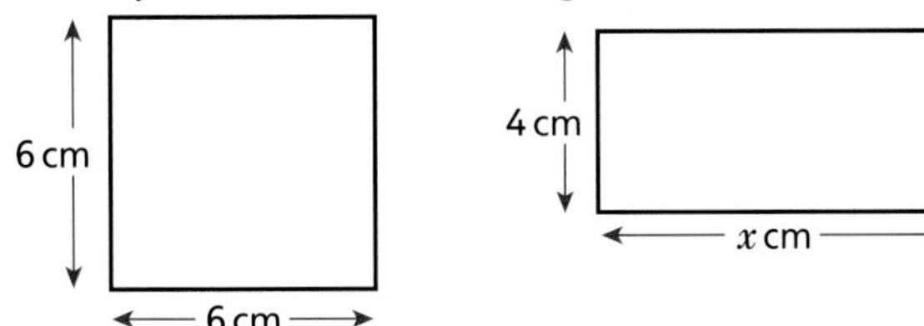

Work out the value of x.

4 Part and parcel

This unit is about fractions and percentages.

Musicians have to think about fractions all the time when they read music. Music is written in 'bars'. Different notes are worth different fractions of a whole bar. It's the combination of the different note values that gives music its rhythm.

Ann Miller is a musician. Her job is to take a composer's handwritten music and get it neatly typed into a score for musicians to play. Most of her work is for films. She needs to make sure that the piece of music lasts the exact time of a particular scene and that all the notes add up to a whole for each bar.

Ann says, 'Occasionally I get scores that are so complicated that I need to work out the note lengths with a calculator! I recently finished a score that had 3 notes, 5 notes, 6 notes, 7 notes and 9 notes all in one beat at the same time. So it worked out the note fractions were $\frac{1}{3}$, $\frac{1}{5}$, $\frac{1}{6}$, $\frac{1}{7}$ and $\frac{1}{9}$.'

Activities

A Here are the note values:

♩ 1 beat 𝅗𝅥 2 beats 𝅝 4 beats ♪ $\frac{1}{2}$ beat

- How many ♪ are there in a ♩ ? What fraction of ♩ is ♪?

B
- Look for a 𝅗𝅥 in the piece of music on the right. What fraction of the bar is this?
- Look for a ♪ What fraction of the bar is this?
- This is a rest 𝄽 It means the musicians keep quiet. What fraction of the bar is it?
- A dot beside a note means 'add half as much again'.
  The ♩ is 1 beat long. So ♩. is $1 + \frac{1}{2} = 1\frac{1}{2}$ beats.
  How many beats is 𝅗𝅥.?

Before you start this unit...

1 Decide whether each of these shapes is divided into halves, quarters, or neither.

Level Up Maths 1-2 page 17

a 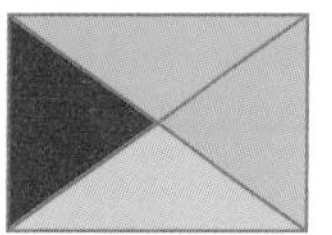

b 

c 

d 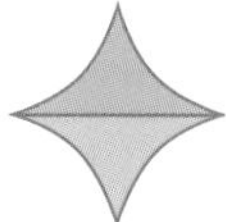

2 Find $\frac{1}{2}$ of these numbers.

Level Up Maths 1-2 page 19

a 60 b 22

c 38 d 52

3 Find $\frac{1}{4}$ of these numbers.

Level Up Maths 1-2 page 19

a 16 b 36

c 88 d 28

This music is called 'The British Grenadiers'. It was a marching song for the British Military from the 17th century to the 19th century.

Plus digital resources

4.1 Fractions

- Recognise when two fractions are the same by using a diagram
- Know how to use fraction notation to describe parts of a shape
- Change an improper fraction to a mixed number
- Know how to add and subtract simple fractions

Why learn this?

Everyday items can be shared by dividing into equal (or not so equal!) fractions.

What's the BIG idea?

- A **fraction** is part of a whole. **Level 3**
- Fractions are **equivalent** when they have the same value. **Level 3**

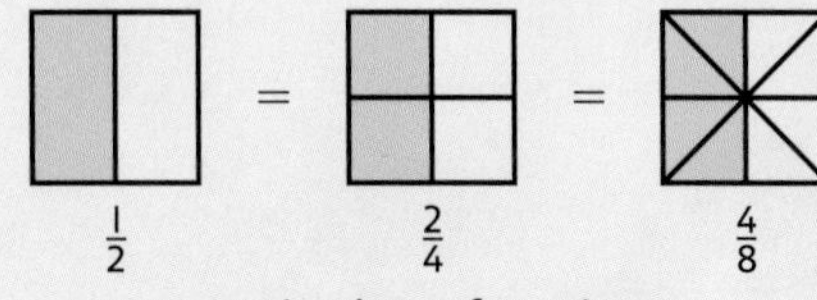

- The top number is called the **numerator**. The bottom number is called the **denominator**. $\frac{6}{8}$ **Level 4**
- $\frac{2}{7}$, $\frac{3}{5}$ and $\frac{7}{9}$ are called **proper fractions** because the numerator is less than the denominator. **Level 4**
- $\frac{7}{5}$, $\frac{3}{2}$ and $\frac{9}{8}$ are called **improper fractions** because the numerator is bigger than the denominator. **Level 4**
- $1\frac{1}{8}$ is called a **mixed number** because it has a whole number part and a fraction part. **Level 4**
- Fractions can be added or subtracted easily if they have the same denominator. **Level 5**

$\frac{4}{6} + \frac{1}{6} = \frac{5}{6}$

Practice, practice, practice!

1 For each pair of diagrams decide whether the shaded fractions are equivalent.

Equivalent. Both shaded parts are $\frac{1}{3}$.

a

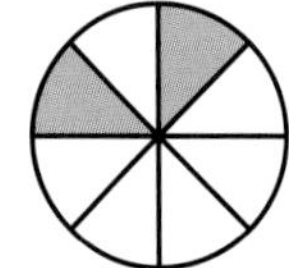

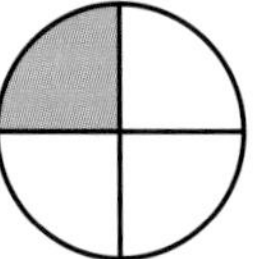

b

c

Level 3

3b I can recognise when two fractions are equivalent

Watch out!

The denominator tells you the number of parts in one whole number.

2 What fraction of each shape is
 i shaded
 ii unshaded?

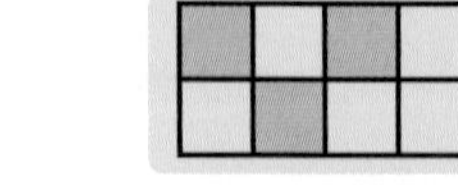

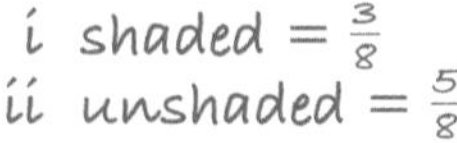

a

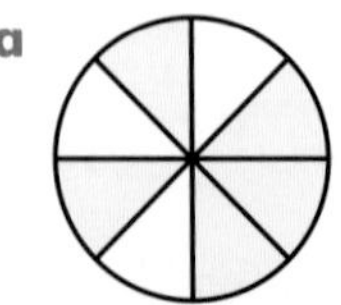

b

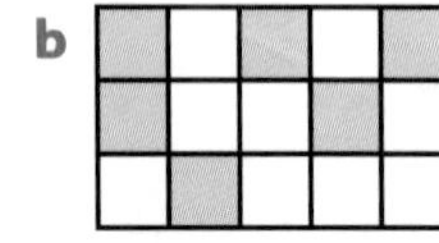

c

d

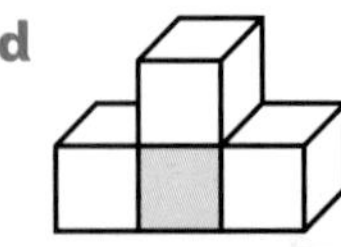

Level 4

4b I can use fraction notation to describe parts of shapes

denominator equivalent fraction improper fraction

3 Copy each diagram and shade the fraction shown.

a $\frac{3}{6}$

b $\frac{2}{5}$

c 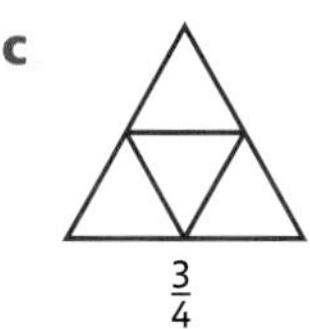 $\frac{3}{4}$

d $\frac{1}{8}$

4 For each of the diagrams below, write what value they show as a mixed number and an improper fraction.

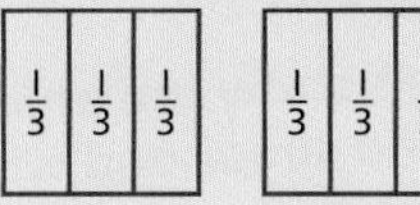

a 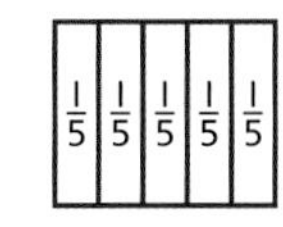 

b 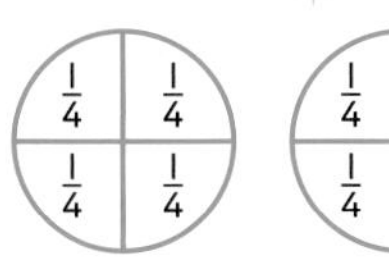

c 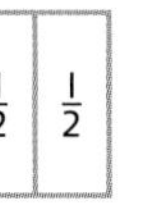 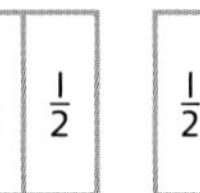

5 Change each improper fraction to a mixed number.

a $\frac{11}{4}$ b $\frac{6}{5}$ c $\frac{12}{7}$ d $\frac{9}{5}$

6 Five pizzas are ordered and then cut into quarters.

a How many slices are there?

b Six slices are eaten. What fraction of the pizzas is left? Write this as a mixed number.

Level 4

4b I can use fraction notation to describe parts of shapes

4a I can change an improper fraction to a mixed number

7 Add these fractions. If necessary, write your answer as a mixed number.

a $\frac{9}{13} + \frac{2}{13}$ b $\frac{12}{17} + \frac{3}{17}$ c $\frac{6}{7} + \frac{3}{7}$

d $\frac{7}{11} + \frac{4}{11}$ e $\frac{1}{7} + \frac{2}{7} + \frac{3}{7}$ f $\frac{1}{5} + \frac{2}{5} + \frac{3}{5}$

8 Subtract these fractions.

a $\frac{5}{7} - \frac{1}{7}$ b $\frac{3}{9} - \frac{1}{9}$ c $\frac{6}{11} - \frac{4}{11}$ d $\frac{12}{21} - \frac{4}{21}$

9 Sukvinder had some sweets. She gave $\frac{3}{7}$ to her friend Amy and $\frac{1}{7}$ to her gran. What fraction did Sukvinder have left?

Level 5

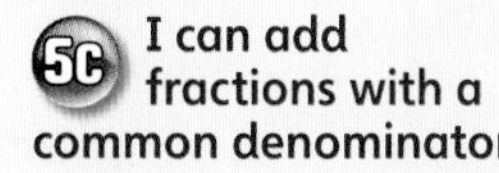

5c I can add fractions with a common denominator

5c I can subtract fractions with a common denominator

Now try this!

A Quarters

This is one way of dividing a 4 × 4 square into quarters using straight lines. Find as many ways as you can to split a 4 × 4 square into quarters. Draw each one and colour in the quarters using different colours.

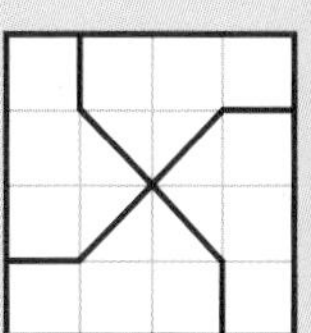

B Rectangle division

This is a 4 × 3 rectangle. Divide the rectangle into four parts. They must be $\frac{1}{2}$, $\frac{1}{4}$, $\frac{1}{6}$ and $\frac{1}{12}$ of the rectangle, and must not overlap.

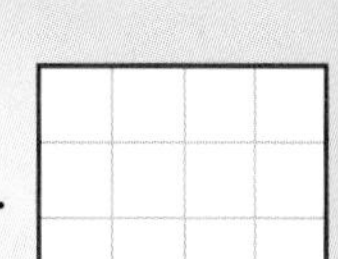

Did you know?

The word fraction comes from the Latin *fractio* – I break.

mixed number **numerator** **proper fraction**

4.2 Equivalent fractions and simplifying

- Identify equivalent fractions
- Use a diagram to compare two or more fractions
- Simplify fractions
- Convert terminating decimals to fractions

Why learn this?

Food labels show the amounts of fat and sugar and what fractions these are of the recommended daily allowance.

What's the BIG idea?

- **Equivalent fractions** are fractions that have equal value but different numerators and denominators. **Level 4** $\frac{1}{2} = \frac{2}{4} = \frac{4}{8} = \frac{8}{16}$
- You can find equivalent fractions by multiplying or dividing the numerator and denominator by the same number. **Level 4** $\frac{5}{7} = \frac{10}{14}$ (×2) $\quad \frac{20}{50} = \frac{2}{5}$ (÷10)
- You can **simplify** fractions by **cancelling**. Divide the numerator and denominator by a common factor. **Level 5** $\frac{12}{15} = \frac{4}{5}$ (÷3) or $\frac{\cancel{12}^4}{\cancel{15}_5} = \frac{4}{5}$
- A fraction is in its **lowest terms** when it has been cancelled down to its **simplest form**. **Level 5**
- A **terminating decimal** is a decimal that ends after a definite number of digits. **Level 5** 0.5 0.123 0.67
- Terminating decimals can be **converted** into fractions. **Level 5** $0.1 = \frac{1}{10}$ $0.89 = \frac{89}{100}$

Practice, practice, practice!

Level 4

4a I can identify equivalent fractions

1 Match each card to a fraction.

$\frac{200}{500}$ $\frac{15}{55}$ $\frac{1}{2}$ $\frac{20}{80}$ $\frac{21}{36}$ $\frac{5}{15}$ $\frac{7}{14}$

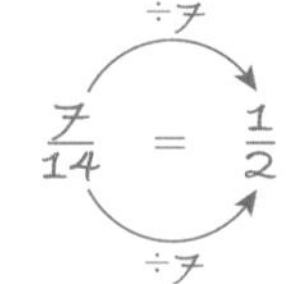

a $\frac{1}{3}$ **b** $\frac{2}{8}$ **c** $\frac{7}{12}$ **d** $\frac{3}{11}$ **e** $\frac{1}{4}$

4a I can calculate equivalent fractions

2 Complete the equivalent fractions in these spider diagrams.

a Centre $\frac{3}{4}$: $\frac{15}{}$, $\frac{24}{}$, $\frac{300}{400}$, $\frac{}{80}$, $\frac{}{16}$, $\frac{}{40}$

b Centre $\frac{2}{5}$: $\frac{30}{}$, $\frac{18}{}$, $\frac{10}{25}$, $\frac{}{105}$, $\frac{22}{}$, $\frac{}{45}$

cancel convert equivalent fraction lowest terms

3 Use a 12 × 12 grid like this. Colour part of each row to represent the fraction given at the side of the row.

Whole											
$\frac{1}{2}$											
$\frac{1}{3}$											
$\frac{2}{3}$											
$\frac{1}{4}$											
$\frac{3}{4}$											
$\frac{1}{6}$											
$\frac{5}{6}$											
$\frac{1}{12}$											
$\frac{5}{12}$											
$\frac{7}{12}$											
$\frac{11}{12}$											

Use your grid to help you answer these questions.

a Put the correct symbol <, > or = between each pair of fractions.

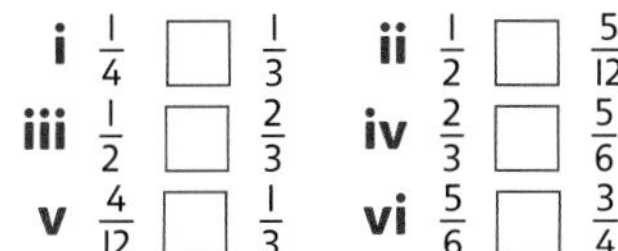

i $\frac{1}{4}$ ☐ $\frac{1}{3}$ **ii** $\frac{1}{2}$ ☐ $\frac{5}{12}$

iii $\frac{1}{2}$ ☐ $\frac{2}{3}$ **iv** $\frac{2}{3}$ ☐ $\frac{5}{6}$

v $\frac{4}{12}$ ☐ $\frac{1}{3}$ **vi** $\frac{5}{6}$ ☐ $\frac{3}{4}$

b Order these fractions, from smallest to biggest.

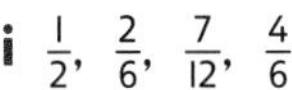

i $\frac{1}{2}, \frac{2}{6}, \frac{7}{12}, \frac{4}{6}$

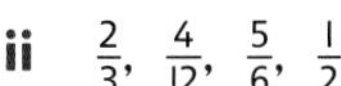

ii $\frac{2}{3}, \frac{4}{12}, \frac{5}{6}, \frac{1}{2}$

iii $\frac{10}{12}, \frac{2}{6}, \frac{2}{3}, \frac{3}{4}$

Level 5

5c I can use a diagram to compare two or more fractions

Tip
The point of the arrow faces the smaller number
2 < 4

4 Use rectangles like this to show which is the biggest fraction, $\frac{1}{3}$, $\frac{1}{2}$ or $\frac{1}{5}$.

5 Simplify these fractions by cancelling.

a $\frac{12}{15} = \frac{\square}{5}$ **b** $\frac{14}{21} = \frac{\square}{3}$ **c** $\frac{6}{30} = \frac{1}{\square}$

d $\frac{24}{36} = \frac{\square}{3}$ **e** $\frac{10}{48} = \frac{5}{\square}$ **f** $\frac{33}{55} = \frac{3}{\square}$

5b I can simplify fractions

6 Put these fractions into their lowest terms.

a $\frac{4}{20}$ **b** $\frac{10}{18}$ **c** $\frac{15}{40}$ **d** $\frac{16}{48}$ **e** $\frac{14}{42}$

7 Convert these terminating decimals into fractions.
Give the fractions in their lowest terms.

a 0.4 **b** 0.72 **c** 0.06 **d** 0.25 **e** 0.5
f 0.75 **g** 0.37 **h** 0.275 **i** 0.027

5a I can convert terminating decimals to fractions

Tip
Always check the decimal place value. 0.25 is 25 hundredths which is $\frac{25}{100}$.

Now try this!

A Fraction pair

Play this game with a partner. Make some fraction cards showing these fractions:

$\frac{1}{4}$ $\frac{2}{8}$ $\frac{3}{12}$ $\frac{4}{16}$ $\frac{8}{32}$ $\frac{5}{15}$ $\frac{1}{3}$ $\frac{3}{9}$ $\frac{9}{21}$ $\frac{12}{20}$ $\frac{6}{10}$ $\frac{3}{5}$ $\frac{5}{14}$ $\frac{10}{28}$ $\frac{10}{16}$ $\frac{5}{8}$

Shuffle the cards and spread them out face down. Take turns to pick two cards.
Keep the pair if they are equivalent fractions. If not, put them back.
The winner is the player who has most cards when they have all been picked.

B Decimal investigation

Here are some fraction and decimal equivalents:

$\frac{2}{10} = 0.4$ $\frac{24}{100} = 0.24$ $0.723 = \frac{723}{1000}$

Using a calculator, investigate how to convert fractions to decimals.
What happens with $\frac{1}{9}$ and $\frac{25}{99}$?
Can you identify other fractions that behave in the same way?

Did you know?
About $\frac{3}{4}$ of the salt we eat is already in the processed foods we buy.

simplest form simplify terminating decimal

4.3 Fractions of amounts

- Understand that fractions relate to division
- Find simple fractions of quantities and measurements

Why learn this?

'One third more free texts when you swap packages.' Are you getting the best deal?

What's the BIG idea?

- Finding one half $\left(\frac{1}{2}\right)$ of something is the same as **dividing** by 2. Level 3
- To find one tenth of an **amount** you divide by 10.
  $\frac{1}{10}$ of £70 = £70 ÷ 10 = £7 Level 3
- You can check your answers by working backwards.
  $\frac{1}{5}$ of 20 = 20 ÷ 5 = 4
  Check by working backwards: 4 × 5 = 20 Level 4
- To find the **fraction** of a quantity, divide the quantity by the **denominator** and then multiply by the **numerator**. Level 5
  $\frac{1}{4}$ of 16: 16 ÷ 4 = 4, 1 × 4 = 4
  $\frac{2}{7}$ of 21 m: 21 ÷ 7 = 3, 2 × 3 = 6 m

Learn this

When finding a fraction of a quantity, **d**ivide by the **d**enominator and multiply by the numerator.

Practice, practice, practice!

Level 3

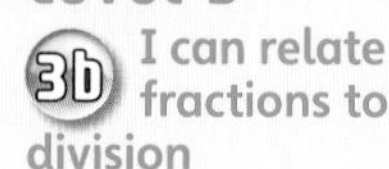
3b I can relate fractions to division

3a I can find simple fractions

1 a Finding one third of an amount is the same as dividing by ☐.
b Finding one fifth of an amount is the same as ☐.
c $\frac{20}{3}$ is another way of writing 20 ☐ 3.

2 a $\frac{1}{2}$ hour = ☐ minutes
b $\frac{1}{4}$ hour = ☐ minutes
c $\frac{1}{3}$ hour = ☐ minutes
d $\frac{1}{2}$ day = ☐ hours
e $\frac{1}{4}$ day = ☐ hours
f $\frac{1}{3}$ day = ☐ hours

3 What is
a one tenth of 240
b one fifth of 35
c half of 62
d one hundredth of 800
e one quarter of 36
f one third of 24

Level 4

4a I can check a result by working the problem backwards

4 A coat was £57.90. Now it is half price, how much will it cost? Use a calculator then check your answer by working it backwards.

Level 5

5b I can calculate fractions of numbers, quantities and measurements

5 Work out
$\frac{1}{2}$ of 16 cm = 16 ÷ 2 = 8 cm
a $\frac{1}{8}$ of 24 kg
b $\frac{1}{4}$ of 20 ml
c $\frac{1}{5}$ of £100
d $\frac{1}{3}$ of 9 km

fraction denominator

Level 5

5b I can calculate fractions of numbers quantities and measurements

6 John is redesigning his garden.
It is a rectangle 12 m long and 8 m wide.
He decides to dig a vegetable plot which is a quarter of the width and length of the garden.

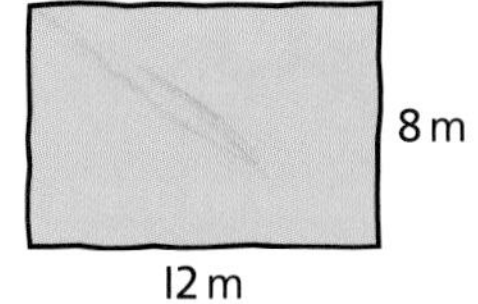

a What is the width of the vegetable plot?

b What is the length of the vegetable plot?

7 Find **a** $\frac{2}{3}$ of 18 **b** $\frac{3}{5}$ of 20 **c** $\frac{7}{12}$ of 48 **d** $\frac{5}{12}$ of 60

8 At the end of the summer, garden furniture is sold in a sale. The price of each piece of furniture is reduced by two thirds.
Work out the amount you save on each item.

9 At a football match, $\frac{3}{8}$ of the crowd support Manchester United. The rest support Chelsea. There are 60 000 people at the match. How many support

a Manchester United **b** Chelsea?

c Explain two ways that you can work out the answer to **b**.

Now try this!

A Fraction investigation

You need some 4 by 3 rectangles for this activity.

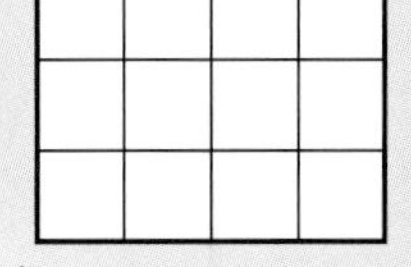

a Find as many ways as possible of splitting the rectangle in half. Draw each different way and colour in each half.

b Find as many ways as possible of splitting the rectangle into thirds. Draw each different way and colour in each third.

c Find as many ways as possible of splitting the rectangle into quarters. Draw each different way and colour in each quarter.

B Dice double

A game for two players. Take turns to roll two dice.
If you throw a double, you score 60.
If you roll two different numbers, use them to make a proper fraction (the numerator is smaller than the denominator). Work out this fraction of 60 to find your score.
The first player to reach 150 wins.

You would score $\frac{1}{4}$ of 60 = 15 for these dice.

numerator

4.4 Percentages

- Know that percentage is the number of parts per 100
- Recognise equivalent percentages, fractions and decimals

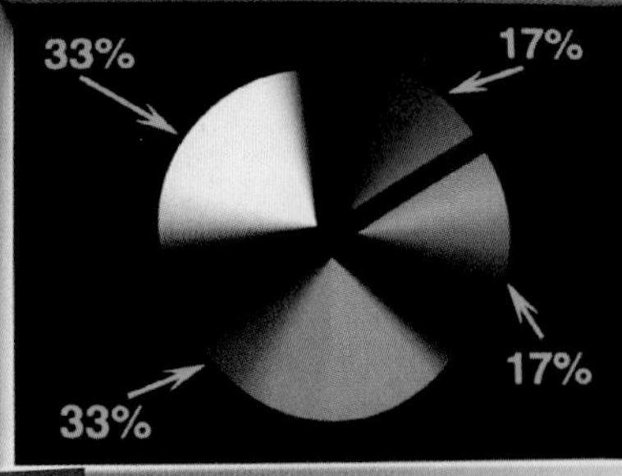

Why learn this?

Survey results are often given as percentages.

What's the BIG idea?

- 'Per cent' means 'out of 100'. So a **percentage** is the number of parts in every 100. For example, 10% means $\frac{10}{100}$. **Level 4**
- You can use % as the shorthand way of writing 'per cent'. **Level 4**
- You can write any percentage as a **fraction** with a **denominator** of 100. **Level 4** $9\% = \frac{9}{100}$ $27\% = \frac{27}{100}$
- You can change a percentage to a **decimal** by dividing by 100. **Level 4** $9\% = \frac{9}{100} = 9 \div 100 = 0.09$ $27\% = \frac{27}{100} = 27 \div 100 = 0.27$
- **Equivalent** fractions, decimals and percentages have the same value. **Level 4**
- Decimals can be written as fractions, for example $0.6 = \frac{6}{10}$ and $0.41 = \frac{41}{100}$. **Level 5**

Learn this

$10\% = 0.1 = \frac{1}{10}$ $25\% = 0.25 = \frac{1}{4}$

$50\% = 0.5 = \frac{1}{2}$ $75\% = 0.75 = \frac{3}{4}$

Practice, practice, practice!

Level 4

4c I can identify percentages

1 What percentage of each block is shaded?

a 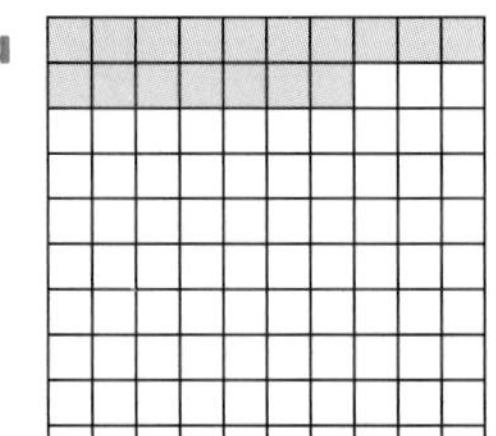

b 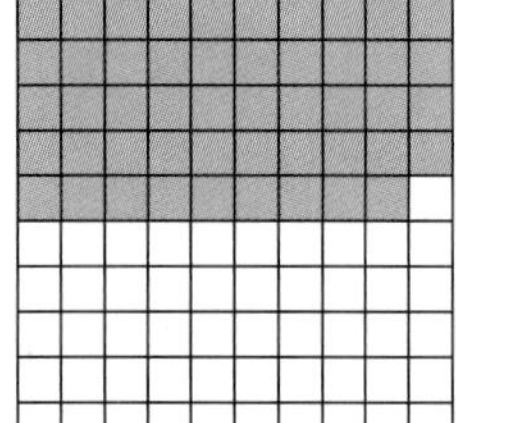

c 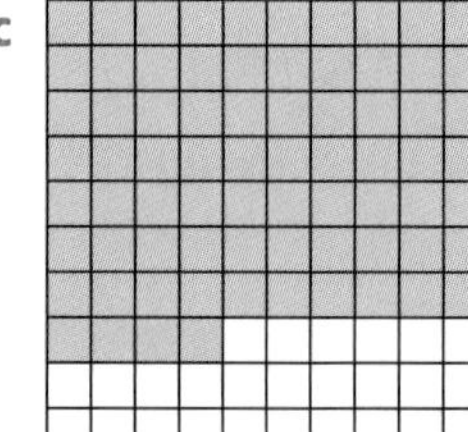

2 Use a 10 × 10 grid like this.

Using different colours, shade the correct number of squares to show

a 12% b 29% c 33%

d What percentage is left unshaded at the end?

4c I can write percentages as a fraction with denominator 100

3 Write each percentage as a fraction.

61% $= \frac{61}{100}$

a 41% b 31% c 97% d 7% e 39%

4c I can understand percentages as the number of parts per 100

4 48% of the pupils in a class are boys.

a What percentage of the class are girls?

b What fraction of the class are girls? Give your answer in its lowest terms.

4b I can work out an equivalent fraction

5 Write each percentage as a fraction in its lowest terms.

70% $= \frac{70}{100} = \frac{7}{10}$

a 10% b 12% c 20% d 95% e 75%

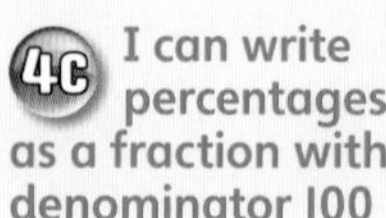

decimal denominator equivalent

6 Copy and complete this number line.

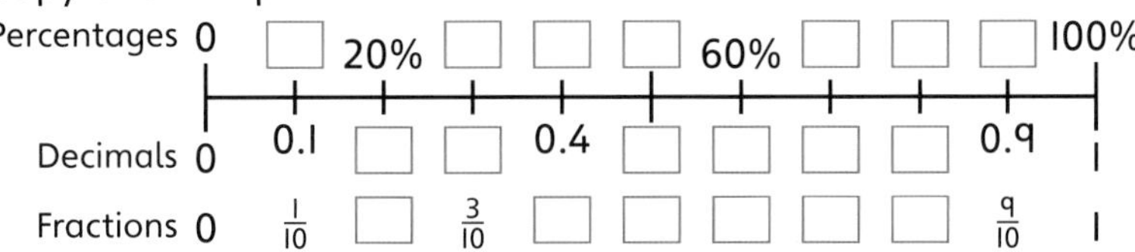

Which decimal is equivalent to

a 50% **b** 90% **c** 45% **d** 18%?

e $\frac{9}{10}$ **f** $\frac{3}{10}$ **g** $\frac{1}{5}$ **h** $\frac{4}{5}$ **i** $\frac{2}{5}$?

7 Copy and complete the table.

	Decimal	Fraction	Percentage
a		$\frac{48}{100}$	48%
b	0.3		30%
c		$\frac{3}{5}$	
d	0.01		
e		$\frac{1}{4}$	
f			8%

8 Group the cards into sets of fractions, decimals and percentages that have the same value.

40% | 0.52 | 81% | $\frac{2}{5}$ | 52% | 0.81 | $\frac{13}{25}$ | 0.4 | $\frac{81}{100}$

9 The bubbles show some fractions and their equivalent decimals.

Match the fractions with the equivalent decimals.

Level 4

4b I can recognise equivalent decimals and percentages

4b I can recognise equivalent fractions, decimals and percentages

Level 5

5a I can recall known facts, including fraction to decimal conversions

Now try this!

A Pick a pair

Work with a partner. Make cards with these fractions and percentages:

25% | 75% | 50% | $\frac{1}{4}$ | $\frac{3}{4}$ | $\frac{1}{2}$ | 99% | $\frac{99}{100}$ | $\frac{33}{100}$ | 33% | 20% | $\frac{2}{10}$

Shuffle the cards and spread them out face down. Take turns to pick two cards. Keep the pair if they are equivalent. If not, put them back. The overall winner is the player with most cards when they have all been picked.

B World statistics

Research facts and statistics on poverty. Pick out three or four facts and produce a poster to illustrate them. Give your statistics as equivalent fractions, decimals and percentages. For example: 50% or $\frac{1}{2}$ or 0.5 of the world's population live on less than \$2 a day.

Did you know?

In the UK roughly 19% of the population are under 16 and 16% are over 65.

fraction percentage (%)

Famous Daft Pirates

Pieces of eight

Jack, Joan and Wavy need to sort out their pieces of eight. Each 8-galleon coin has been cut up for change.

- Can you give the pieces below to the three pirates so that they each get the same total? You can use Resource sheet A4 to help you.

0.5

25%

70%

$\frac{3}{10}$

0.8

$\frac{1}{2}$

0.6

$\frac{1}{10}$

$\frac{3}{4}$

- How many galleons does each pirate end up with in total?

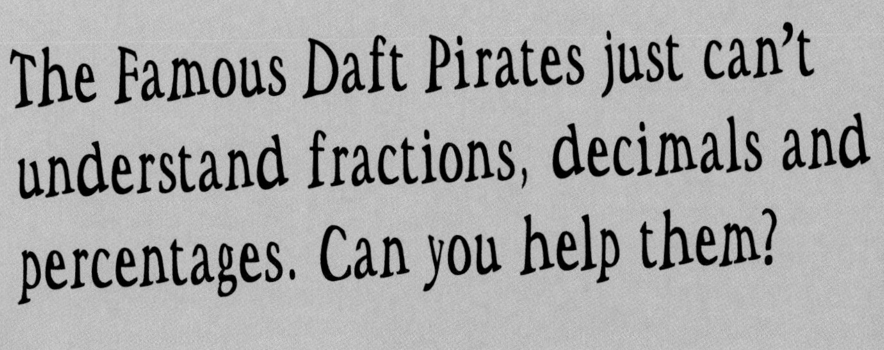

Black Beard's journey

Who let Black Beard take the wheel?
The Famous Daft Pirates have to sail 200 miles to reach land. On the first day Black Beard sails 100 miles, but each day after that he gets lazy, and they sail half as far as they did the day before.

- **How far will they sail on day 2?**
- **How far will they sail on day 3?**
- **How many days will it take them to get to land?**

The piraflute

Captain Jack is playing his piraflute. In music

- **every crotchet ♩ is a quarter of a semibreve 𝅝**
- **every quaver ♪ is a half of a crotchet**
- **half of a quaver is called a semiquaver 𝅘𝅥𝅯**

How many semiquavers can Jack fit into a semibreve?

Wavy Jones

4.5 Finding a percentage of an amount

- Remember percentage/fraction equivalents
- Know how to find a percentage of an amount

Why learn this?

'10% off', 'Reduced by 15%' – how much are you actually saving?

What's the BIG idea?

→ **Percentages** and **fractions** that are **equivalent** have the same value. **Level 4**

→ To find a percentage of an amount change the percentage to a fraction and multiply the fraction by the amount. **Level 4**
50% of £20 → $\frac{1}{2} \times £20 = £20 \div 2 = £10$

→ To find 10% of an amount you divide by 10. **Level 4**
10% of 60 → $\frac{1}{10} \times 60 = 60 \div 10 = 6$

Learn this

$1\% = \frac{1}{100}$
$10\% = \frac{1}{10}$
$20\% = \frac{1}{5}$
$25\% = \frac{1}{4}$
$50\% = \frac{1}{2}$
$75\% = \frac{3}{4}$

Practice, practice, practice!

Level 4

4a I can find 10%

1 Find 10% of
a 40 **b** 90 cm **c** £20 **d** 120 kg

2 In a sale all the marked prices are reduced by 10%.
Find 10% of each of these prices.

$\frac{1}{10} \times £65 = £65 \div 10 = £6.50$

a

b

I can find multiples of 10%

3 Work out
20% of £140 10% is £140 ÷ 10 = £14 20% is £14 × 2 = £28
a 80% of £90 **b** 40% of £400 **c** 70% of 80 cm

4 20% of the pupils in Year 7 won a prize for good attendance.
There are 150 pupils in the year. How many pupils won a prize?

5 In a quiz, Shelly got 50% of the general knowledge questions correct and 60% of the music questions correct.
a There were 40 general knowledge questions. How many did she get correct?
b There were 50 music questions. How many did she get correct in this category?

equivalent fraction

6 Work out:

a 25% of 80 b 25% of £120 c 25% of 16 l

d 75% of 40 mm e 75% of 28 km f 75% of 36 g

Level 4

4a I can find simple percentages

7 There are 64 people on a train and 25% of those got on at the last station. How many people got on at the last station? Use two different methods to work it out.

8 Work out

4a I can find 5%

5% of 60 *10% is 60 ÷ 10 = 6 5% is 6 ÷ 2 = 3*

a 5% of £70 b 5% of £110 c 5% of £200

9 A computer shop is offering a 15% discount on a new laptop computer.
The original price is £480.
How much do you save with the discount?

4a I can find 15%

Watch out!

10% is $\frac{1}{10}$ but 5% is not $\frac{1}{5}$.

Hint: You can work out 10%, and you can work out 5%.

10 Rose is offered a job that pays 20% more than her current job.
She currently earns £6 per hour.
How much extra per hour will Rose earn in her new job?

4a I can find 20%

Now try this!

A True or false?

10% of £50 is less than 15% of £60

30% of 40 m is more than 25% of 50 m

Make up some true-or-false questions like this for a partner. Make sure you know the correct answer!

B Percentage dice

Work with a partner. You will need a dice and a game board each.

Percentage	Amount (£)	Subtotal

Roll the dice eight times. The number on the dice can go in any of the boxes in the first two columns, but once it is placed it cannot be moved. If, for example, you roll a 3 you would either write 30 in the percentage column or 3 in the amount column. Once all the eight boxes have been filled, work out the percentage of each amount and write it in the Subtotal column. Add your four answers together. The winner is the person who gets closest to £5.

Did you know?

An F1 car is made up of 80 000 components. If it were assembled 99.9% correctly, it would still start the race with 80 things wrong!

percentage

4.6 Mental calculation

- Find a difference by counting up
- Carry out mental calculations involving fractions, decimals and percentages
- Know how to check a result

Why learn this?

It is vital to have good mental maths skills and to check all calculations when calculating medicine doses. A mistake could prove fatal!

What's the BIG idea?

- Doubling tricks: e.g. double 36 = double 30 + double 6 = 60 + 12 = 72. **Level 3**
- Halving tricks: e.g. half of 72 = half of 70 + half of 2 = 35 + 1 = 36. **Level 3**
- You can find a **difference** by **counting on** from the smaller to the larger number. **Level 3**

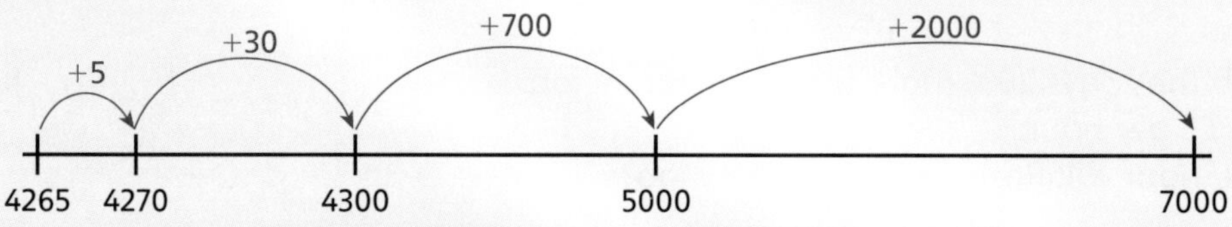

7000 − 4265 = 5 + 30 + 700 + 2000 = 2735

- To find $\frac{1}{4}$ of something, find $\frac{1}{2}$ then **halve** the answer. **Level 4**
- Finding 50% is the same as halving. Halve again to find 25%. Then you can find 75% by adding 50% and 25%. **Level 4**

Did you know?

In some countries people write decimals with a comma instead of a dot. So they write 3,75 instead of 3.75

Learn this

Multiplication undoes division. Addition undoes subtraction.

Practice, practice, practice!

1 Work out the change from £10 for these shopping bills.

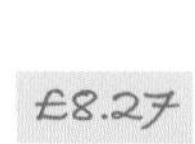

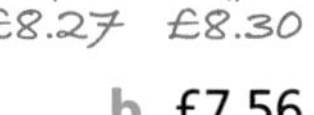

a £8.19 b £7.56 c £2.36 d £4.78 e £1.84

2 Use counting up to work out how long these kings and queens ruled.

a Edward I ruled from 1272–1307
b Henry VII ruled from 1485–1509
c Elizabeth I ruled 1558–1603
d Victoria ruled 1837–1901

3 Find the difference by counting up from the smaller to the larger number.

a 6000 − 1487 b 9007 − 5802 c 7026 − 2915

4 Copy and complete.

a double 34 = ____ b double 1.6 = ____
c double 310 = ____ d double ____ = 48
e double ____ = 1400 f double ____ = 0.86

Level 3

3b I can find a difference by counting up through the next multiple of 100

3a I can find a difference by counting up through the next multiple of 1000

3a I can use the fact that halving is the reverse of doubling

approximately decimal difference double estimate fractio

5 Add these near doubles. **Hint:** Use near doubles.

7.5 + 7.8 *7.5 + 7.8 = double 7.5 + 0.3 = 15 + 0.3 = 15.3*

a 2.5 + 2.7 b 8.5 + 8.2 c 3.9 + 4.3

6 Work out

3.4 × 50 *3.4 × 50 = 1.7 × 100 = 170*

a 2.8 × 50 b 6.2 × 5 c 4.8 × 5 d 8 × 3.5

Hint: Double one number, and halve the other.

7 Work out

a $\frac{1}{2}$ of 36 b $\frac{1}{4}$ of 36 c $\frac{3}{4}$ of 36

d $\frac{1}{4}$ of £72 e $\frac{1}{4}$ of 60 m f $\frac{3}{4}$ of 48 kg

8 Find the missing numbers. **Hint:** Work out $\frac{1}{3}$ first.

a one fifth of 20 = ☐ b two thirds of 18 = ☐

c a quarter of ☐ = 15 d one third of ☐ = 9

9 A storage tank contains 200 litres of water when full.
How much water is in it when it is

30% full $\frac{30}{100} \times 200 = \frac{3 \times 200}{10} = 60$ *litres*

a 50% empty b 25% full c 75% full

d 10% full e 5% full?

10 a What is 50% of £120?

b What is 40% of 90p?

c 25% of a number is 6. What is the number?

d A coat cost £60. The price went up by 10%. What is the new price?

e An MP3 player cost £80. It is 25% off in a sale. What is the sale price?

Level 4

4b I can carry out mental calculations involving decimals

4b I can carry out mental calculations involving fractions

4a I can carry out mental calculations involving percentages

Now try this!

A Dice darts

A game for two players. You need two dice. Each player starts with a score of 301.
Take turns to roll two dice. Make the biggest two-digit number you can.
Use a mental method to subtract this from your score.
The first player to go below 100 wins.

B Percentages

A game for two players.

22	70 cm	34p	£4.50	23 kg	£3.60

Player 1: Pick one of the numbers from the boxes and work out 10%. Say '10% is …'.
Player 2: Work out 20%. Say '20% is …'.
Keep taking turns to work out new percentages. You lose if you get the answer wrong, repeat an answer or cannot think of one.
Player 2 goes first for the second round.

halve **inverse** **multiple** **operation** **percentage**

Putting on a musical

Next year's musical sensation – Mathemagical – is being developed. In the TV competition *Make me magical*, people are competing for the two lead roles – Fred Fraction and Perdita Percentage. Meanwhile, the choreographers and dancers are working hard on the dance routines, the chorus and orchestra are practising their parts, the costumes and set are being designed and the theatre manager is trying to sort out the seating and ticket prices.

1 The theatre manager has drawn these diagrams to show the ticket prices for different seats in the stalls.

Plan 1

Plan 2

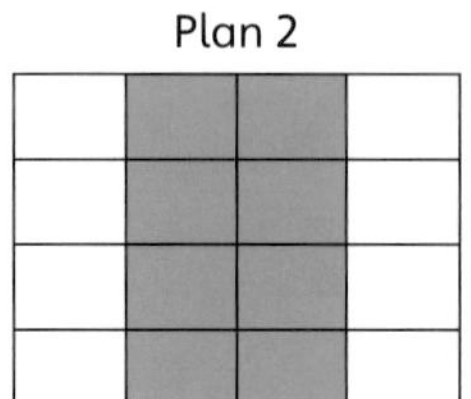

Plan 3

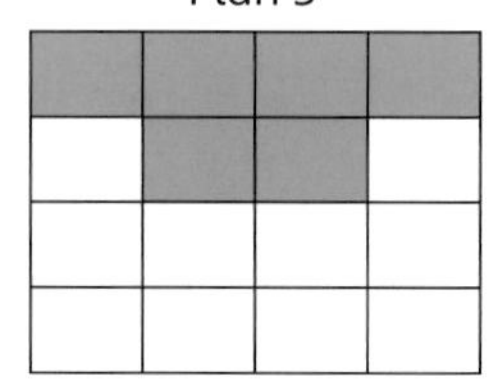

Key:
£30 seats (shaded)
£25 seats (white)

Which plans show the same fraction of £30 seats? **Level 3**

2 The theatre manager and her assistant have both suggested which fraction of the seating should be at the top three prices.
The two of them have used different systems. Are any of their fractions equivalent?

Theatre manager	*Assistant theatre manager*
$\frac{1}{4}$ of seating at £30	$\frac{7}{28}$ of seating at £30
$\frac{1}{8}$ of seating at £25	$\frac{4}{28}$ of seating at £25
$\frac{1}{6}$ of seating at £20	$\frac{3}{18}$ of seating at £20 **Level 4**

3 In *Make me magical*, the studio audience votes for their favourite competitor for each role.

a For the Fred Fraction role, 100 people in the audience voted like this:

Dave	Jas	Charlton	Mitchell
21	33	27	19

Write these votes as percentages.

b For the Perdita Percentage role, the votes are given as fractions:

Shiree	Alix	Ellie	Jade
$\frac{3}{10}$	$\frac{1}{5}$	$\frac{1}{10}$	$\frac{2}{5}$

Write these votes as percentages.

c Which performer got the highest percentage of the votes overall?

d Who wins each role? **Level 4**

4 **a** At the first audition there are 180 dancers. 75% of these are rejected. How many are rejected?

b At the beginning of rehearsals there are 40 musicians in the orchestra.
5% of them arrive late because of the traffic.
How many musicians arrive late? **Level 4**

5 The stage is 16 metres wide. The set designer wants

a a forest scene $\frac{1}{4}$ of this width

b a pair of French windows $\frac{1}{10}$ this width

c an interior scene $\frac{3}{4}$ this width

d a beach scene $\frac{7}{8}$ this width.

Work out the width of each set, in metres. **Level 5**

The BIG ideas

- **Fractions** are **equivalent** when they mean the same thing. Level 3
- Equivalent fractions are fractions that have equal value but different **numerators** and **denominators**. Level 4
- You can find equivalent fractions by multiplying or dividing the numerator and denominator by the same number. Level 4
- '**Per cent**' means 'out of 100'. So a **percentage** is the number of parts in every 100. Level 4
- You can use % as the shorthand way of writing 'per cent'. Level 4
- You can write any percentage as a fraction with a denominator of 100. Level 4
- To find a **percentage of an amount** change the percentage to a fraction and multiply the fraction by the amount. Level 4
- To find a **fraction of a quantity** divide the number by the denominator and then multiply by the numerator. Level 5

Find your level

Level 3

Q1 Calculate
- a half of 18
- b one quarter of 60
- c one third of 24
- d one eighth of 72
- e one hundredth of 160

Level 4

Q2 Here are six number cards.

2	4	6	8	10	12

- a Choose two of the six cards to make a fraction equivalent to $\frac{2}{3}$.
- b Choose two of the six cards to make a fraction that is greater than 0 but less than $\frac{1}{2}$.

$\frac{\square}{\square}$

Q3 a Write the missing numbers.
50% of 60 = ____
5% of 60 = ____
1% of 60 = ____

b Work out 56% of 60.
You can use part **a** to help you.

Q4 Asif scores 30 out of 60 in a test.
Lisa scores 30% in the same test.
Whose score is higher?
How do you know?

Level 5

Q5 What are the missing numbers?
- **a** $\frac{1}{2}$ of 10 = $\frac{1}{4}$ of ____
- **b** $\frac{3}{4}$ of 40 = $\frac{1}{2}$ of ____
- **c** $\frac{1}{3}$ of 90 = $\frac{2}{3}$ of ____

Q6 In a school, $\frac{2}{5}$ of the pupils are in the Infants and the rest are in the Juniors. There are 120 pupils in the school.
- **a** How many pupils are there in the Infants?
- **b** How many pupils are there in the Juniors?

Q7 Here are four fractions.

$\frac{2}{3}$ $\frac{1}{4}$ $\frac{2}{5}$ $\frac{7}{8}$

Look at the number line below.
Match each fraction to an arrow on the number line.

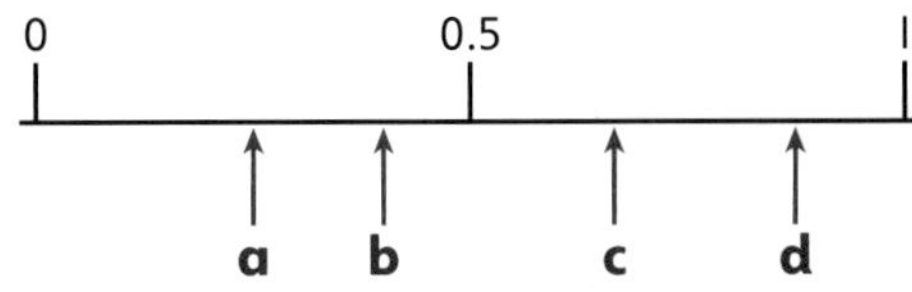

5 More than the average

Marie is a footwear buyer for a supermarket chain. Her job is about buying the right product from manufacturers, getting them to the right stores and at the right time. 'It's all about analysing what's selling,' says Marie. 'Then we can predict what is likely to sell in the future and what to re-order for each store.

'I have to rank the footwear in order of what is going to sell best, predicting the highest and lowest ranked footwear by average rate of sale per store.

'Sometimes my work involves a simple average – the mean. For example, in our range for older girls, one style of ballerina shoe sold 995 pairs last week in 200 stores. So the average rate of sale per store for last week is:

$$995 \div 200 = 4.9 \text{ pairs of ballerina shoes.}$$

'Sometimes the mean isn't very useful. For example, the most popular older girls' size is a 4. But if I work out the mean size of a style, it comes to 3.7. That's not much good when it comes to re-ordering, as no-one makes a size 3.7!'

Activities

A The table below shows the older girls' shoes sold in the supermarket chain throughout the country in one particular week.

Size	1	2	3	4	5	6	7
Unit sales – ballerina	77	111	205	222	111	77	51
Unit sales – court	101	141	253	242	122	91	61
Unit sales – high heel	65	91	156	169	78	58	33
Total unit sales	243	343	614	633	311	226	145

- For each style, which is the modal size?
- Work out the total number of each style sold.
  Which is the most popular style?
- If there are 200 stores, what is the mean number of size 4 ballerina shoes sold in each store?

B Imagine a new store is opening near your school.
Using the data in the table above, suggest how many of each style and size of the shoes should be ordered.

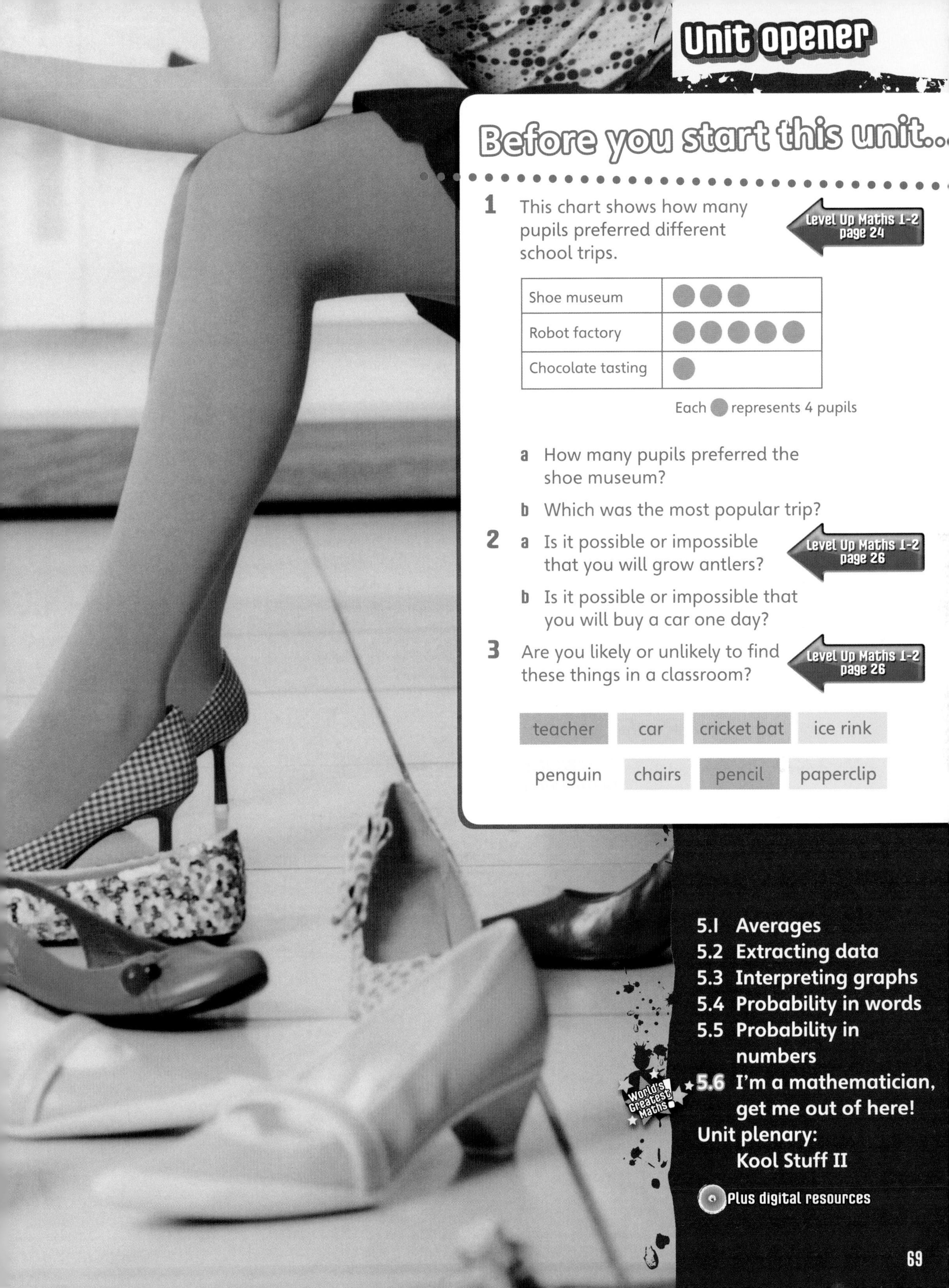

Before you start this unit...

1 This chart shows how many pupils preferred different school trips.

Level Up Maths 1-2 page 24

Shoe museum	● ● ●
Robot factory	● ● ● ● ●
Chocolate tasting	●

Each ● represents 4 pupils

a How many pupils preferred the shoe museum?

b Which was the most popular trip?

2 a Is it possible or impossible that you will grow antlers?

Level Up Maths 1-2 page 26

b Is it possible or impossible that you will buy a car one day?

3 Are you likely or unlikely to find these things in a classroom?

Level Up Maths 1-2 page 26

teacher car cricket bat ice rink

penguin chairs pencil paperclip

World's Greatest Maths

Plus digital resources

5.1 Averages

- Find the mode and range of a small set of discrete data
- Find the modal class for a small set of grouped discrete data
- Calculate the mean and median for a small set of discrete data
- Calculate the mean from a simple frequency table

Why learn this?

If you know your usual average speed you can plan the times for any journey.

What's the BIG idea?

- The **mode** is the data item that occurs most often. Level 3
- The **modal class** is the class with the greatest frequency. Level 4
- The **range** is the difference between the highest and lowest data items. Use it to find out how spread out the data is. Level 4
- The **mean** is calculated by adding up the data items and dividing by the number of data items. **Level 5**
- The **median** is the middle data item when all data items are put in order. Level 4 (up to 10 items) **Level 5** (more than 10 items)

Super fact!

On average, humans shed about 600 000 particles of skin every hour. This is about 675 g a year. By 70 years of age, an average person will have lost over 47 kg of skin!

Practice, practice, practice!

Level 3

3b I can find the most common item for up to 10 data items

1 Terri sorts out her DVDs. She has 10 comedies, 20 music videos, 10 cartoons, 8 adventure films, 7 TV series and 12 romances.
Which type of DVD does she have the most of?

2 A teacher confiscated these items from a class one lesson:
3 mobile phones, 2 packs of chewing gum, 1 bar of chocolate, 1 half-eaten apple and 2 badges.
Which was the most common item confiscated?

Level 4

4b I can find the mode for up to 10 data items

3 Rashmi carried out a survey of seven of his friends to find their favourite crisp flavours. Here are his results.

Chicken Salt 'n' Vinegar Chicken Chicken
Beef Cheese and Onion Plain

Which crisp flavour is the mode?

4b I can find the mode and the range for up to 10 data items

4 Brian was playing darts with Bob. With their first three darts

Brian scored	40	16	20
Bob scored	16	5	19

a Work the range of all their scores.
b Work out the modal score.

average frequency table mean median

5 Paul's football team scored these numbers of goals goals in their last 10 games.

4 2 0 0 1 6 3 4 4 2

a Work out the range of the number of goals.

b Work out the mode of the number of goals.

6 A conservationist collected data on the number of fish in ponds.
Here are her results.

Number in class	15–19	20–24	25–29	30–34
Frequency	0	2	6	2

Which is the modal class?

Level 4

4b I can find the mode and the range for up to 10 data items

4a I can find the modal class for up to 10 data items

7 Gabby scored these marks in her last five maths homeworks.

5 8 5 7 10

Work out

a the mean **b** the median

c the mode **d** the range.

Tip
'Median' has the same number of letters as 'middle'; the median is the middle value

8 Giorgio scored these numbers of points in his last 10 basketball matches.

15 8 15 17 10 12 16 22 20 15

Work out

a the mean **b** the median **c** the mode **d** the range.

9 José rolled a dice 20 times. Here are his results.

Work out

a the mean **b** the mode **c** the range.

Hint: List all the scores e.g. 1, 1, 1, 2, …

Score	Frequency
1	3
2	3
3	4
4	5
5	2
6	3

10 The range of a set of data is 10. The lowest data item is 15.
What is the value of the highest data item?

11 Write five numbers that have a mean of 10 and a range of 2.

Level 5

5c I can find the mean and median for up to 20 data items

5b I can find the mean from a frequency table for up to 20 data items

5a I can solve problems using knowledge of range and mean

Now try this!

A Roll a dice
Roll a dice 20 times and record your results.
What is the mode? What is the mean score?

B Premiership football
Collect data on the number of spectators at each of the Premiership football matches one Saturday. Work out the mean and median numbers of spectators.

modal class **mode** **range** **survey**

Olympic Medal Chart				
Country	Gold	Silver	Bronze	Total
USA	44	32	25	**101**
Germany	20	18	27	**65**
Russia	26	21	16	**63**
C...na	16	22	12	**50**
...tralia	9	9	22	**40**
...ce	15	7	15	**37**
	13	10	12	**35**
...th Ko...			5	**27**
...uba			8	**25**
Ukraine				

5.2 Extracting data

➩ **Extract information such as frequencies, mode and total frequency from bar charts, grouped bar charts, dual bar charts and compound bar charts**

Why learn this?

Information in a league table shows who is in the lead and who might be able to beat them.

What's the BIG idea?

- Data can be shown in many ways; graphs, **frequency tables** and databases all contain **data**. **Level 3**
- A **bar chart** displays data pictorially and shows the frequency of different items. **Level 3**
- A frequency table is a way of recording data from a **survey**. **Level 4**
- You can use bar charts to find the mode. **Level 4**
- You can use **dual** and **compound bar charts** to present more than one set of data. **Level 5**

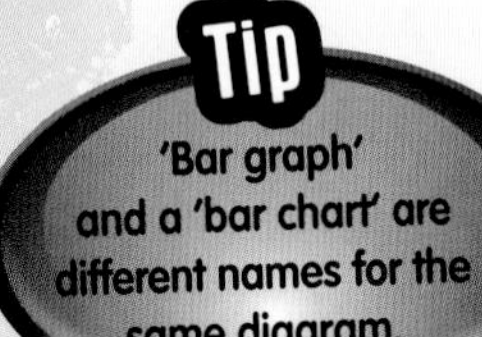

Practice, practice, practice!

Level 3

3a I can read a bar chart to obtain information

1 Jonti asked his friends: 'Which is the best networking site?'
He drew a bar chart of his results.

- **a** What is Jonti's friends' favourite networking site?
- **b** How many people said that Headbook was their favouritenetworking site?
- **c** How many people took part in Jonti's survey?

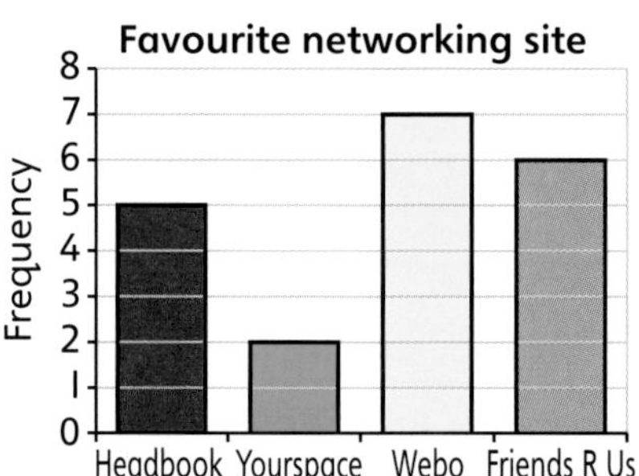

Level 4

4b I can find information from a frequency table

2 Here is a frequency table of the results when Tomas spun a 1–4 spinner.

- **a** What is the modal score?
- **b** How many times did Tomas spin his spinner?

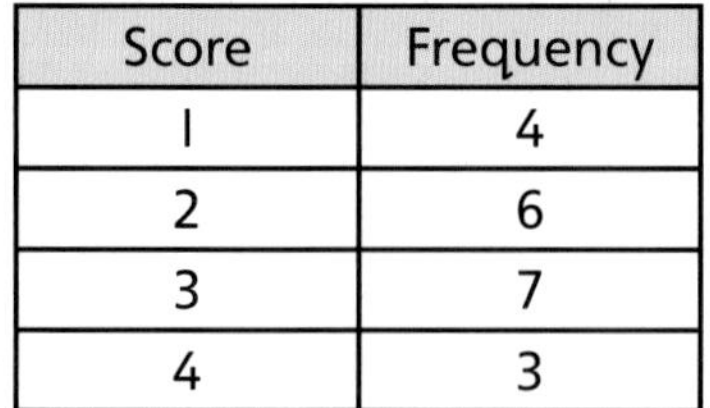

Score	Frequency
1	4
2	6
3	7
4	3

4b I can find the mode from a bar graph

3 Sophie asked some friends which extreme sport they'd most like to try.
She drew a bar chart of her results.

- **a** What is the mode of the sports?
- **b** How many people took part in Sophie's survey?
- **c** How many people chose the least favourite sport?

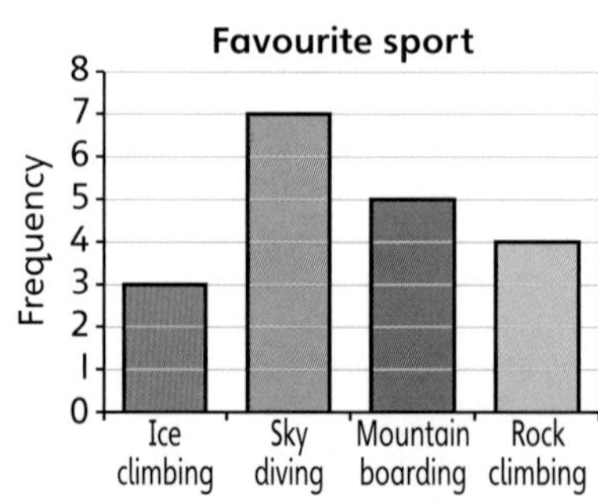

bar chart compound bar chart dual bar chart

4 Dalraj was practising for a darts match. Here is a bar chart that shows the total scores that he obtained from throws of three darts.

a What is the modal group of scores?

b How many times did Dalraj throw three darts?

c Which group of scores did Dalraj score twice?

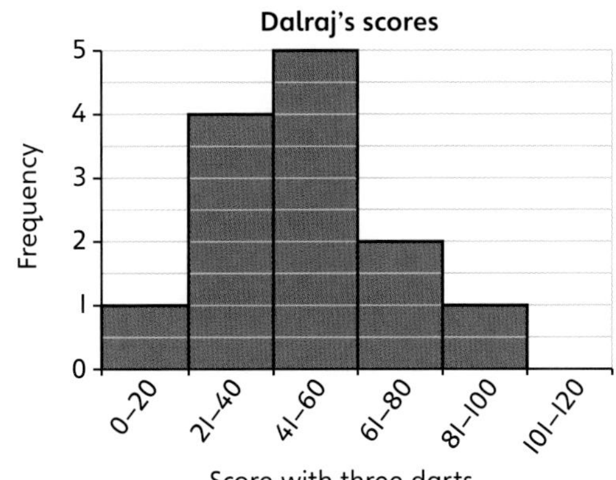

Level 4

4b I can find the modal group from a grouped bar graph

5 This dual bar chart shows the number of hours Helen and Robin worked out in the gym in the last three weeks.

a Which week did Robin work out longest?

b Which week did Helen work out longest?

c Over the three weeks, how many more hours did Robin spend working out than Helen?

Hours in the gym

Week	Helen (hours)	Robin (hours)
Week 1	2	4
Week 2	7	3
Week 3	4	8

Level 5

5b I can find information from a dual bar graph

6 Farmer Boyce runs a campsite. The compound bar chart shows the number of people camping from April to October last year.

a What was the modal month for camping?

b What was the modal month for camping in a caravan?

c What was the modal month for camping in a tent?

d How many people camped in a tent from April to October?

e How many people camped in a caravan from April to October?

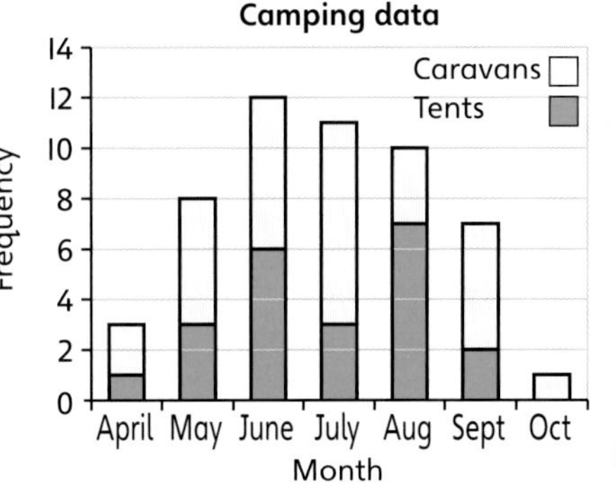

5a I can find information from a compound bar graph

Watch out!

The frequency scale on a bar chart does not always go up in 1s. It might go up in 2s, 5s, 10s, or any other number!

Now try this!

A Get taxed!

Collect information on the month in which the road tax expires on the cars in the car park. Draw a bar chart and find the modal month.

B In a spin

Make a spinner with six sides. Colour each section a different colour. Spin it 20 times and record your results in a frequency table. Remember to put headings in your table. Find the mode.

data frequency table survey

5.3 Interpreting graphs

➩ Extract information such as frequencies and trends from bar charts, line graphs and pie charts

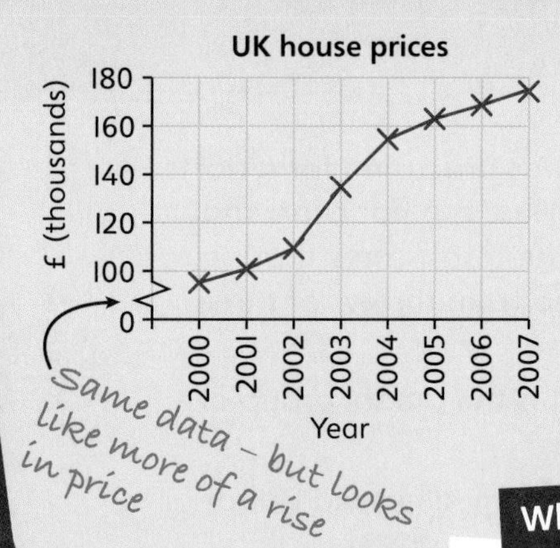

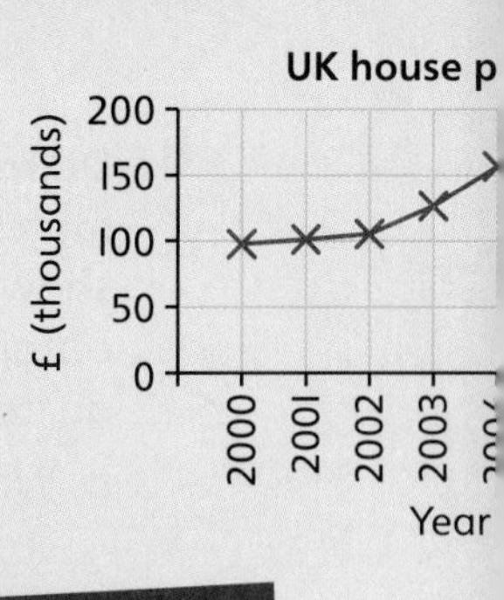

Why learn this?

Graphs and charts can be misleading – keep your wits about you!

What's the BIG idea?

- → Graphs have two labelled **axes** and a **heading** to tell you what data the graph shows. Level 3
- → A **line graph** shows a continuous relationship between two things. Level 4
- → To draw conclusions from a graph you need to relate the shape of the graph to the type of data it displays. Level 4
- → If the items of data are affected, the graph will also change. Level 5

Super fact!

William Playfair, a Scottish engineer and economist who was born in 1759, is credited with inventing bar, line and pie charts.

Practice, practice, practice!

Level 3

3b I can read a graph and interpret information

1 Sam sells ice cream. The graph shows the number of ice creams he sold during one year.

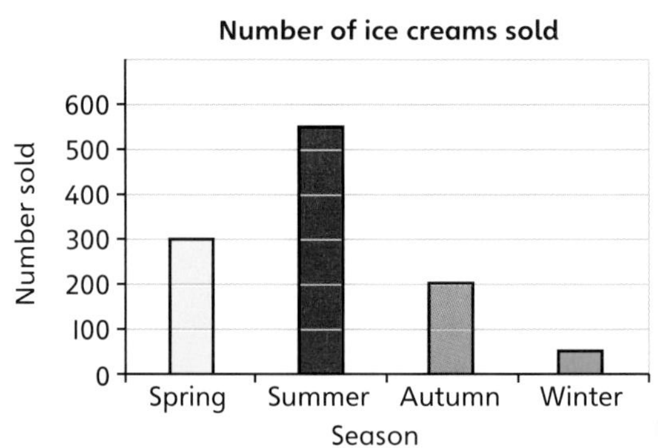

- **a** How many ice creams did Sam sell in the spring?
- **b** In which season did Sam sell 200 ice creams?
- **c** What can you say about the number of ice creams Sam sold?

Level 4

4b I can extract data from a line graph and interpret it

2 Dev had to stay in hospital. Here is a graph of his temperature during one morning.

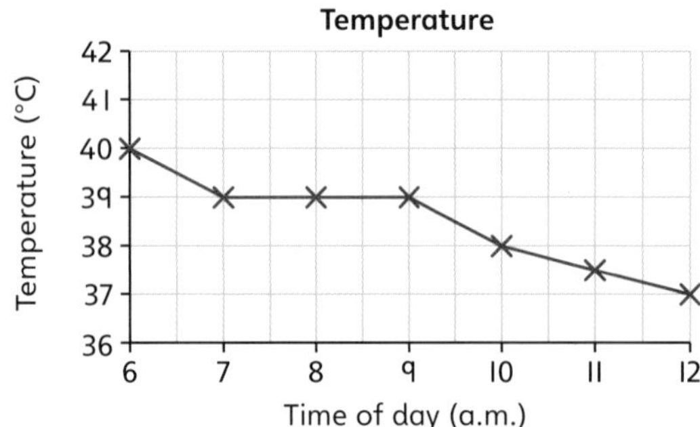

- **a** Between what times was Dev's temperature 39°C?
- **b** What was Dev's highest temperature?
- **c** What can you say about Dev's temperature that morning?

Super fact!

The average normal body temperature is 37 °C.

axes bar chart database frequency

3 Enrico carried out a survey of his friends' favourite takeaways. He drew a bar chart of his results.

a Which was the most popular takeaway?
b How many people did Enrico ask?
c Which takeaway was least popular?

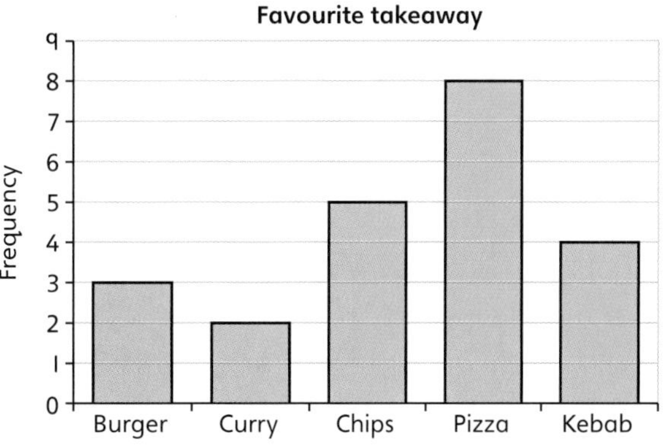

Level 4

4b I can interpret information from a bar graph

4 This graph shows the average monthly temperatures in London and Malaga.

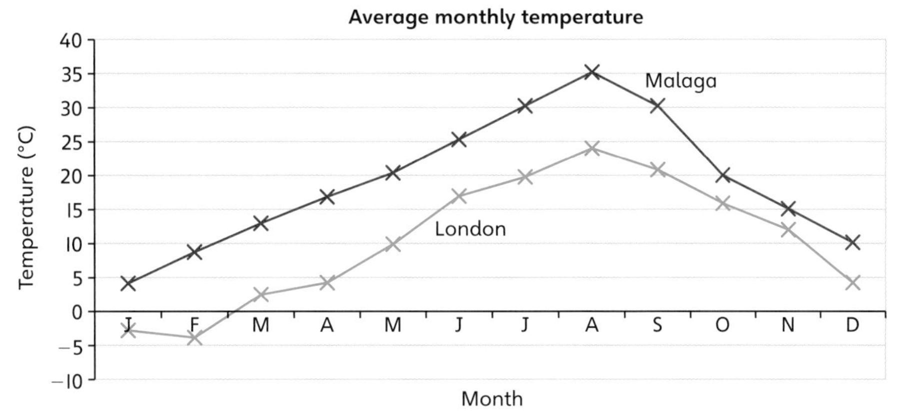

a What is the difference in temperature between London and Malaga in May?
b In which month is there the greatest difference in temperature?
c What can you say about the temperature in the two cities?

4a I can draw conclusions from the shape of line graphs

Level 5

5 Look at the graph in question 4.

a How much hotter is it in London in July than in May?
b What can you say about the weather in London in January?

5c I can draw conclusions from line graphs

6 Here is a pie chart for the number of animals on Mr MacDonald's farm.

a Which animal does Mr MacDonald have most of?
b Which animal does he have least of?

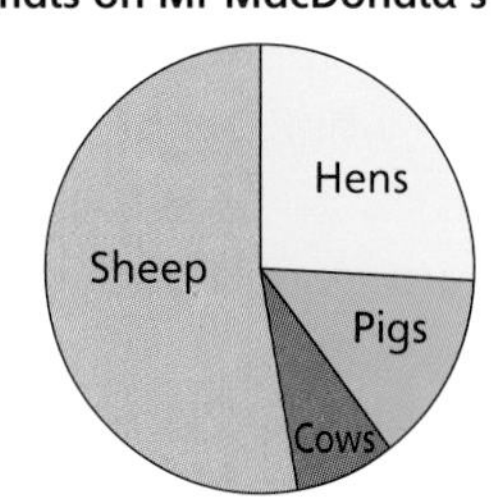

5c I can draw conclusions from pie charts

Now try this!

A Come to Florida!

Find out some information about the weather in Florida. Which months are the hottest? Which months have the greatest rainfall? When is the hurricane season? In your opinion, when is the best time to visit Florida?

B Real-world graphs and charts

Look for graphs and charts in newspapers and magazines. Explain what these diagrams show.

interpret | line graph | pie chart | table

5.4 Probability in words

- Use the vocabulary of probability
- Use a probability scale with words

What's the BIG idea?

- **Probability** is the **chance** that something (an **event**) will happen. **Level 3**
- You can describe the probability of the **outcome** of an event in words. It can be **impossible**, **possible**, **certain**, **even** chance, **likely** or **unlikely**. **Level 4**
- You can use a probability scale to show the outcome of an event in words. **Level 5**

Impossible — Unlikely — Even — Likely — Certain

Why learn this?

Probability helps you work out how likely something is to happen – what is the chance that tomorrow will be sunny?

Practice, practice, practice!

Level 3
3a I can use simple words for probability

1 Write whether these outcomes are certain, possible or impossible.

a You will get younger.

b It will be sunny tomorrow.

c You will get a 1, 2, 3, 4, 5 or 6 when you roll a normal dice.

Level 4
4b I can use the correct words for outcomes in probability

2 For each outcome write whether the outcome is likely or unlikely.

a When you take a card from a pack it will be a King.

b It will rain in Manchester in January.

c When you roll a dice you will get a number greater than 1.

d Someone in your class will break their arm next week.

Tip
Some words for probability aren't exact. They simply give an idea of how likely an event is to occur.

3 Write an outcome which has an even chance of happening. Explain your answer.

4 Here are two spinners.

a Which spinner has an even chance of landing on blue?

b Which colour is Keith's spinner least likely to land on?

Mary's spinner

Keith's spinner

certain chance even event impossible

5 Choose the word that best matches the outcome of each event.

impossible | unlikely | even chance | likely | certain

a Throwing an even number on a dice.
b The number on a dice showing 0.
c Getting an Ace on the top of a pack of cards.
d The sun not rising tomorrow.

Level 4

4b I can use the correct words for outcomes in probability

6 Draw a probability scale. Mark each of these outcomes on the scale.

a A pet dog will live forever.
b You will be dealt a red card from a pack of cards.
c The number on the top face of a dice will be 1.
d The sun will shine in London in June.

Hint: Copy the scale from the Big idea box.

Level 5

5c I can use a probability scale

7 Draw a probability scale.
Mark each of these outcomes on the scale.

a A tree will grow 2 km tall.
b When you spin a coin you will get a tail.
c Your family will go on holiday next year.
d You will land on blue or green when you spin the spinner.
e It will snow on June 18th.
f It will snow at some point in January.

8 Make up a statement that is true for each of these words.

impossible | certain | unlikely | likely | even

Super fact!

Around 500,000 5–14 year olds are injured each year while playing. Around 125,000 of the same age group are injured each year at school. You are probably safer at school!

Now try this!

A Rolling two dice

Roll two dice. Add the two scores and record your results in a frequency table.

Do this at least 50 times. Use your frequency table to help you predict the most likely and least likely scores.

Total score	Tally	Frequency
2		
3		
⋮		

B Spinner design

Design a spinner with four colours so each colour has the same chance of landing.

Design another spinner with three colours. It should have the same chance of landing on red as on yellow, and should be more likely to land on blue than on either red or yellow.

likely | outcome | possible | probability | unlikely

5.5 Probability in numbers

- Understand and use the probability scale 0 to 1
- Find the probabilities of equally likely outcomes
- List all the outcomes when one or two events happen
- Know that if the probability of an event is p, then the probability that it will not happen is $1 - p$

Why learn this?

How do you know if it is fair to use a coin to decide which team kicks off at a football match?

What's the BIG idea?

- All **probabilities** have a value from 0 to 1. **Level 5**
- You can mark the probability of an **event** happening on a probability scale. **Level 5**

Impossible	Unlikely	Even	Likely	Certain
0	$\frac{1}{4}$	$\frac{1}{2}$	$\frac{3}{4}$	1

- The probability of something happening $= \frac{\text{total number of successful outcomes}}{\text{total number of possible outcomes}}$ **Level 5**
- The probability of an event not happening = 1 − the probability of the event happening. **Level 5**

Tip

A probability may be written as a fraction $\left(\frac{1}{2}\right)$, a decimal (0.5) or a percentage (50%).

Practice, practice, practice!

Level 5

5c I can use a probability scale from 0 to 1

1 Draw a probability scale 0 to 1. A dice is rolled.
Mark each of the following outcomes on the probability scale.

- **a** A 6 is rolled.
- **b** An even number is rolled.
- **c** A number greater than 2 is rolled.
- **d** A 7 is rolled.
- **e** A number less than or equal to 6 is rolled.

Hint: You do not need to work out the exact value of each outcome – an estimate will do.

5c I can find the probability of simple outcomes of a single event

2 A coin is spun. Work out the probability of getting

a a head   **b** a tail.

3 An ordinary dice is rolled. Work out the probability of getting

a a 3   **b** an odd number
c a 7   **d** a number greater than 2
e an even number   **f** zero.

certain chance even event impossible

4 Melanie has a bag of 10 coins.
In the bag are three 5p coins, two 10p coins, four 50p coins and one £1 coin.
Melanie chooses one coin at random from the bag.
What is the probability that the coin will be

a 5p **b** 10p **c** 50p **d** £1 **e** worth less than £1?

5 List all the possible outcomes of spinning a coin.

6 List all the possible outcomes of rolling a dice.

7 List all the possible outcomes for spinning two coins.

Hint: For two heads you could write HH.

8 List all the possible outcomes for spinning a coin and rolling a dice.

9 **a** The probability of rain tomorrow is $\frac{1}{4}$.
What is the probability that it will not rain?

b The probability of sun on Wednesday is 70%.
What is the probability that it will not be sunny?

c The probability of fog on Saturday is 0.6.
What is the probability that it will not be foggy?

d The probability of snow next week is 0.05.
What is the probability that it will not snow?

10 A bag contains red and blue counters only. The probability of picking a red counter is $\frac{1}{4}$. What is the probability of picking a blue counter?

Hint: Picking a blue counter is the same as not picking a red one.

Level 5

5c I can find the probability of simple outcomes of a single event

5b I can list all the outcomes of a single event

5b I can list all the outcomes of two events

5a I can work out the probability of an event not happening if I know the probability of it happening

Now try this!

A Pick a ball

Work out how many blue, green and red balls to put in a bag. If you pick a ball the probability of getting each colour should be as follows.

Blue = $\frac{1}{2}$ Green = $\frac{1}{3}$ Red = $\frac{1}{6}$

B Menu choice

Work with a partner.

Each write a café menu, to include five items of food you like.

Swap menus.

You can choose two items from the menu.

List all the possible choices.

What are the possible ways of choosing *three* items?

Learn this

The probability of something happening and the probability of the same thing not happening must add up to 1 (or 100%).

likely outcome possible probability

World's Greatest Maths!

5.6 I'm a mathematician, get me out of here!

Uh oh! Your chief video game designer has just quit! He's taken the answers to some of the trickiest puzzles in your new video game – Escape From Deadly Dungeon – with him!

Can you solve the puzzles in time to get the game programming finished?

Escape from Deadly Dungeon begins with you trapped in a prison cell. There's a control panel next to your cell door, but to escape you need to crack the door code.

```
YT TUJS YMJ ITTW DTZ
SJJI YT UWJXX YMJ
GZYYTSX NS YMJ TWIJW
GQZJ TWFSLJ LWJJS WJI.
```

Each letter in the code represents a different letter in the message. You can decode this message using a **code wheel**.

- Cut out the small circle on Resource sheet 5.6a and place it inside the large circle to make a code wheel.
- Which letter of the alphabet is the most common in an ordinary piece of text? Shade this letter on the outside of the code wheel.
- Complete the frequency table on Resource sheet 5.6a to find the letter which appears most often in the door code.
  Shade this letter on the inside of the code wheel.
- Rotate the code wheel to match up the shaded letters.
- With the code wheel in this position you can decode the message. Write the decoded message under the door code on Resource sheet 5.6a.

Top Tip

If you're not sure, tally the letters in some different sentences. For example, which letter appears most frequently in this tip?

Well done!

You've made it through the cell door, but you've still got to find a way through the final gateway ... and this one has a much more fiendish code to crack!

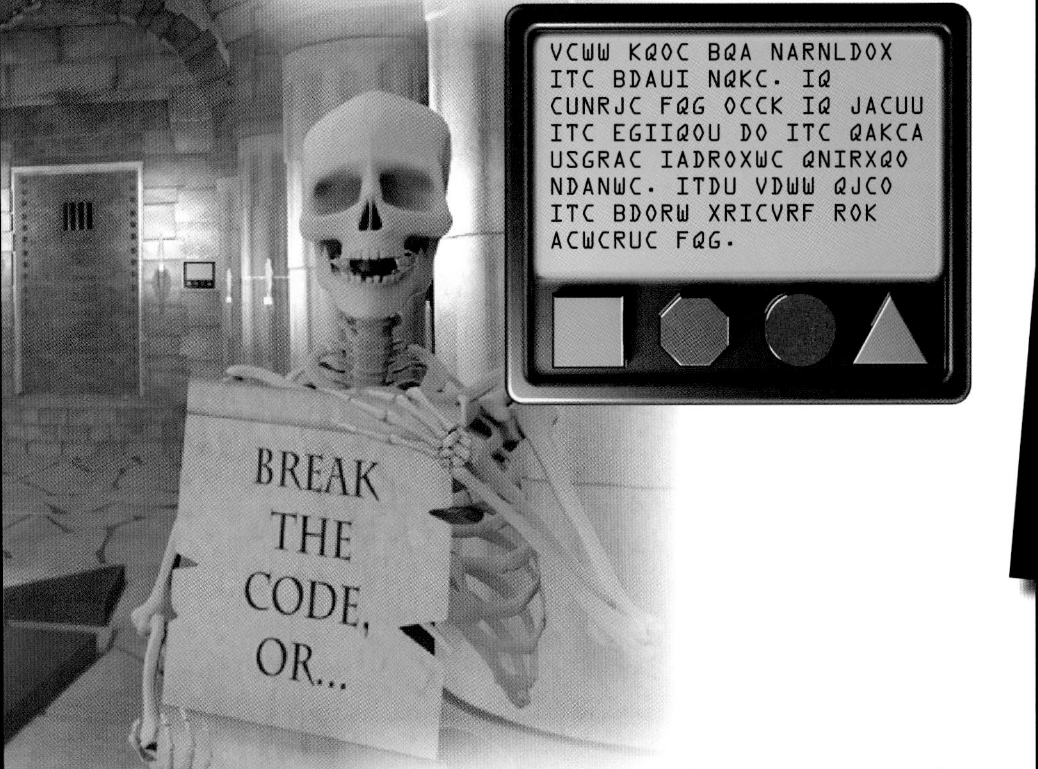

```
VCWW KQOC BQA NARNLDOX
ITC BDAUI NQKC. IQ
CUNRJC FQG OCCK IQ JACUU
ITC EGIIQOU DO ITC QAKCA
USGRAC IADROXWC QNIRXQO
NDANWC. ITDU VDWW QJCO
ITC BDORW XRICVRF ROK
ACWCRUC FQG.
```

BREAK THE CODE, OR...

Look at the bar chart at the top of Resource sheet 5.6b. It shows the frequencies of letters in an ordinary piece of English text. To crack the gateway code you will need to find the frequencies of letters in the coded message and compare them with this bar chart.

- Use the frequency table at the bottom of Resource sheet 5.6b to make a tally of the letters in the gateway code.
- Draw a bar chart of your results. Label it 'Letter frequencies in gateway coded message'.
- Use the two bar charts to decode the message. Start by matching the most common letters. Write your answers on Resource sheet 5.6c.

Top Tip

You might need to use trial and error to find some of the letters.

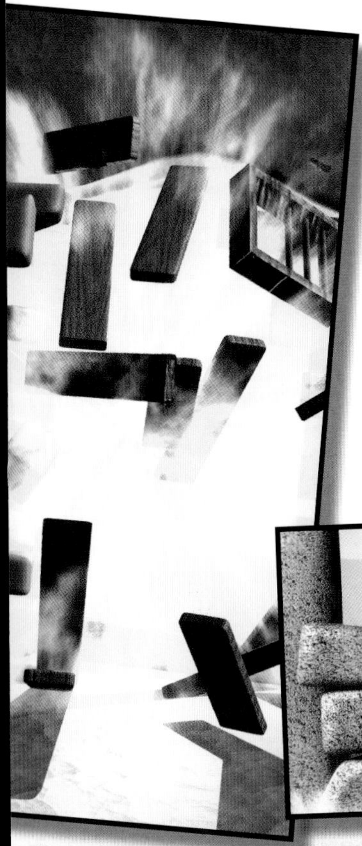

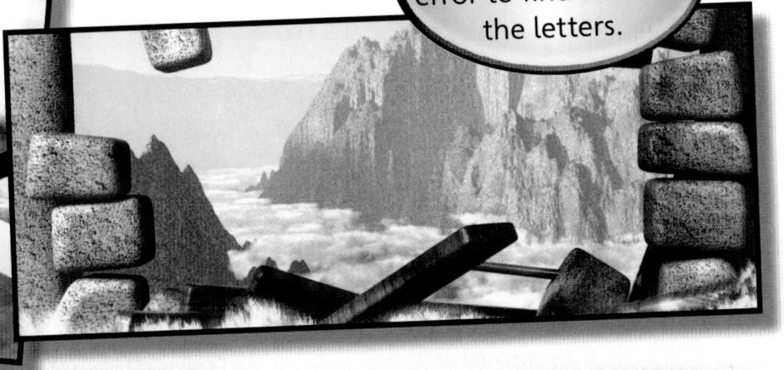

Good news! Mike's on the phone...

He'll come back if you can prove you're as smart as he is. You'll need to use your bar charts and frequency tables from the final gateway.

1. What is the most common letter in an ordinary piece of text?
2. Which six letters appeared most frequently in the coded message?
3. What is the probability of A occurring in an ordinary piece of text?
4. What is the probability of X occurring in an ordinary piece of text?
5. A letter is chosen at random from all the letters on this page. Estimate the probability that it is a vowel.

Kool Stuff II

Kool Stuff II is a new clothes shop in Ayton.
Jay Kool, the owner, has another clothes shop, Kool Stuff I, in Beeton. He is using data from the Beeton shop to plan the stock he needs for the new shop.

1 Last week Kool Stuff I sold these T shirts:
5 red 8 pink 15 blue 6 green 4 striped
Which colour T-shirt sold the most? **Level 3**

2 Last week Kool Stuff I sold these boys' jeans:

Jeans size	Frequency
26″ waist	2
28″ waist	2
30″ waist	5
32″ waist	3
34″ waist	1

a What is the modal size?

b How many pairs of boys' jeans were sold altogether? **Level 4**

3 The graph shows the numbers of hats sold in different seasons last year.

a How many hats were sold in the autumn? **Level 3**

b What can you say about the sales of hats over the year? **Level 4**

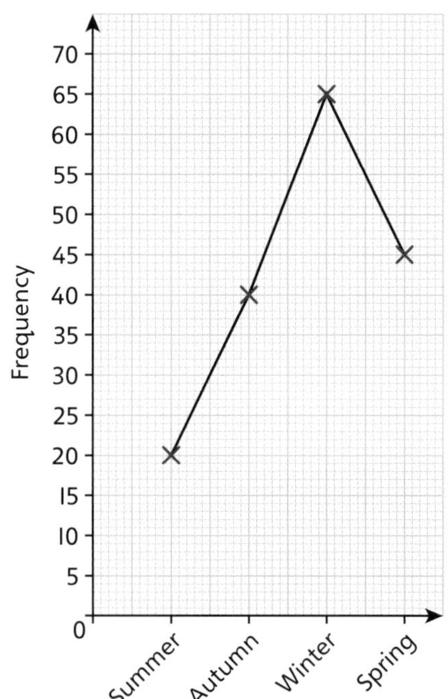

4 The grand opening is in April. Jeff plans to have a stall outside the shop giving away free ice cream.

a Jeff says, 'The sun will shine at the opening.'
Is this outcome certain, possible or impossible? **Level 3**

b In Ayton last April it rained on 15 days.
What is the probability of rain on a day in April?
Choose from likely, unlikely and evens. **Level 4**

c The weather forecast says the probability of rain on the opening day is $\frac{2}{5}$.
What is the probability that it will not rain? **Level 5**

d Do you think Jeff should put his ice cream stall inside or outside? Explain your reasons. **Level 5**

5 Last week Kool Stuff I sold these girls' jeans:

Jeans size	Frequency
6	1
8	3
10	2
12	2
14	1
16	1

a What is the modal size?

b Calculate the mean size.

c Which is the most useful average when planning what stock to buy? Why? **Level 5**

The BIG ideas

- → The **mode** is the data item that occurs most often. **Level 3**
- → **Graphs** have two labelled axes and a heading to tell you what data the graph shows. **Level 3**
- → A **line graph** shows a continuous relationship between two things. **Level 4**
- → You can describe the **probability** of the **outcome** of an **event** in words – it can be impossible, possible, certain, even chance, likely or unlikely. **Level 4**
- → The mean is calculated by adding up the data items and dividing by the number of data items. **Level 4** (up to 10 items) **Level 5** (more than 10 items)
- → You can use **dual** and **compound bar charts** to present more than one set of data. **Level 5**
- → The **probability of an event not happening** = 1 – the probability of an event happening. **Level 5**

Find your level

Level 3

Q1 The table shows some information about drinks sold in a shop.

Name of drink	Number sold
Lemonade	12
Cola	8
Juice	18

The bar chart shows the same information. Write each piece of missing information.

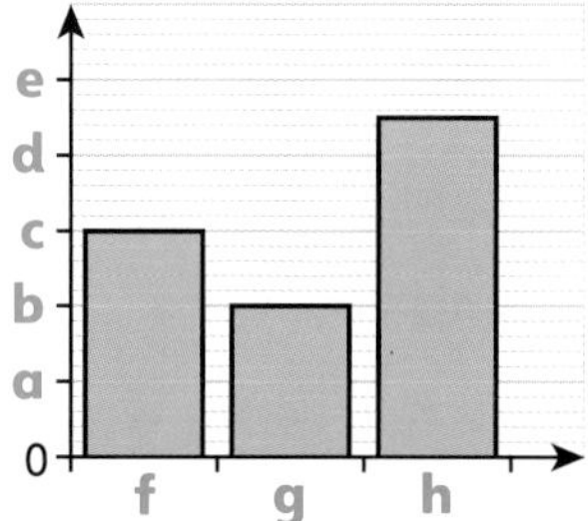

Level 4

Q2 Look at these three numbers.

a Show that the mean of the three numbers is 5.

b Explain why the median of the three numbers is 5.

c Four numbers have a mean of 5 and a median of 5, but none of the numbers is 5.
What could the four numbers be? Give an example.

Level 5

Q3 Jake has a bag of sweets.

Contents
2 red sweets
3 green sweets
8 yellow sweets
1 purple sweet
6 black sweets

He is going to take a sweet from the bag at random.

a What is the probability that Fred will get a green sweet?

b What is the missing colour in this sentence?
The probability that Jake will get a _____ sweet is $\frac{1}{10}$.

Q4 The graph shows the takings for boys' and girls' clothes on 6 days last week.

a Which day had the highest boys' sales?

b Which day had the lowest girls' sales?

c Which day were the takings for boys' clothes higher than the takings for girls' clothes?

d Over the week, which sales were higher – boys' or girls'? **Level 5**

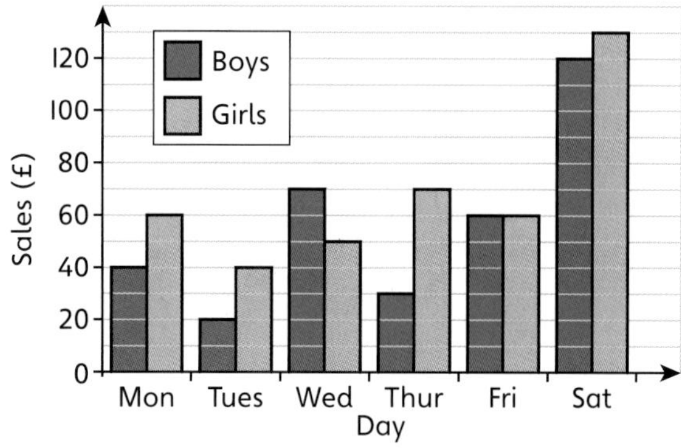

6 Formula one

This unit is about using algebra.

During World War II, instructions were often sent in code. Both the sender and the person receiving the message knew how to read it in order to understand the instructions.

Algebra is a bit like code – you need to know how to read it in order to understand the instructions. You can use algebra to write instructions for a calculation. This is called a formula.

For example, to make tea, the formula is 'one teabag per person plus one for the pot'. In algebra, you could write:
$N = p + 1$
(N stands for the number of teabags and p stands for the number of people)
You can use this formula to work out how many teabags you need for different numbers of people.

A formula can show the relationship between quantities:
Number of toes = 5 × number of feet or $T = 5 \times f$
(T represents the number of toes and f represents the number of feet)

Activities

A Here are instructions for coding and decoding a message.

To put into code ⟶ Use the next letter but one.
To decode ⟶ Go back 2 letters each time.

Y	Z	A	B	C	D	...
↓	↓	↓	↓	↓	↓	
A	B	C	D	E	F	...

- Make up a coding instruction. Use it to write a message. Give it to a partner, with the decoding instructions.

B **a** Make up formulae to describe the relationship between:
- the number of angles and the number of triangles
- the number of weeks and the number of days.

b What could this formula represent?

number of ________ = 6 × number of ________

Make up some more for a friend to solve.

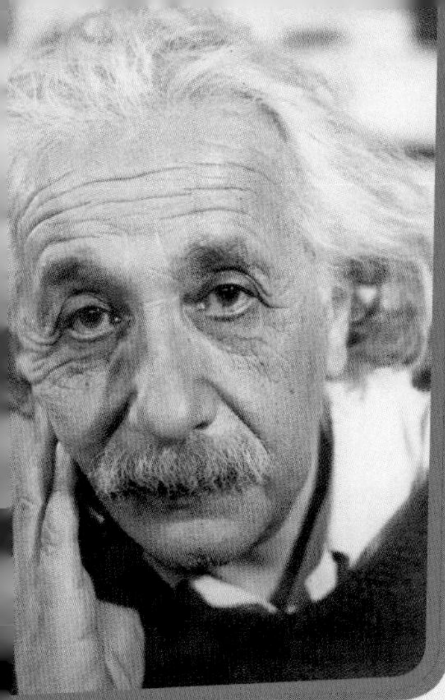

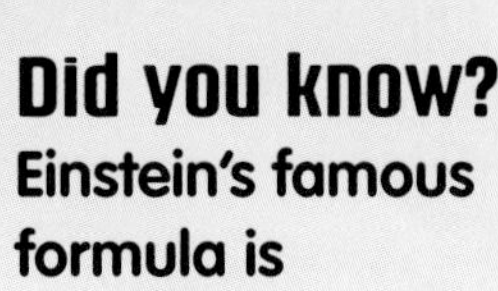

Did you know?
Einstein's famous formula is

$E = mc^2$

It shows the relationship between the energy, E, of an object and its mass, m, and the speed of light, c.

Before you start this unit...

1 Which of these expressions have the same value? Level Up Maths 1-2 page 28

5 × 3 | 3 + 5 | 5 + 5 | 3 × 5 | 5 + 5 + 5

2 What is the value of 4 × 5 − 7? Level Up Maths 1-2 page 29

3 How many days are there in 11 weeks and 3 days? Level Up Maths 1-2 page 29

4 What is 0.5 × 8? Level Up Maths 1-2 page 31

5 What is 48 ÷ 6? Level Up Maths 1-2 page 31

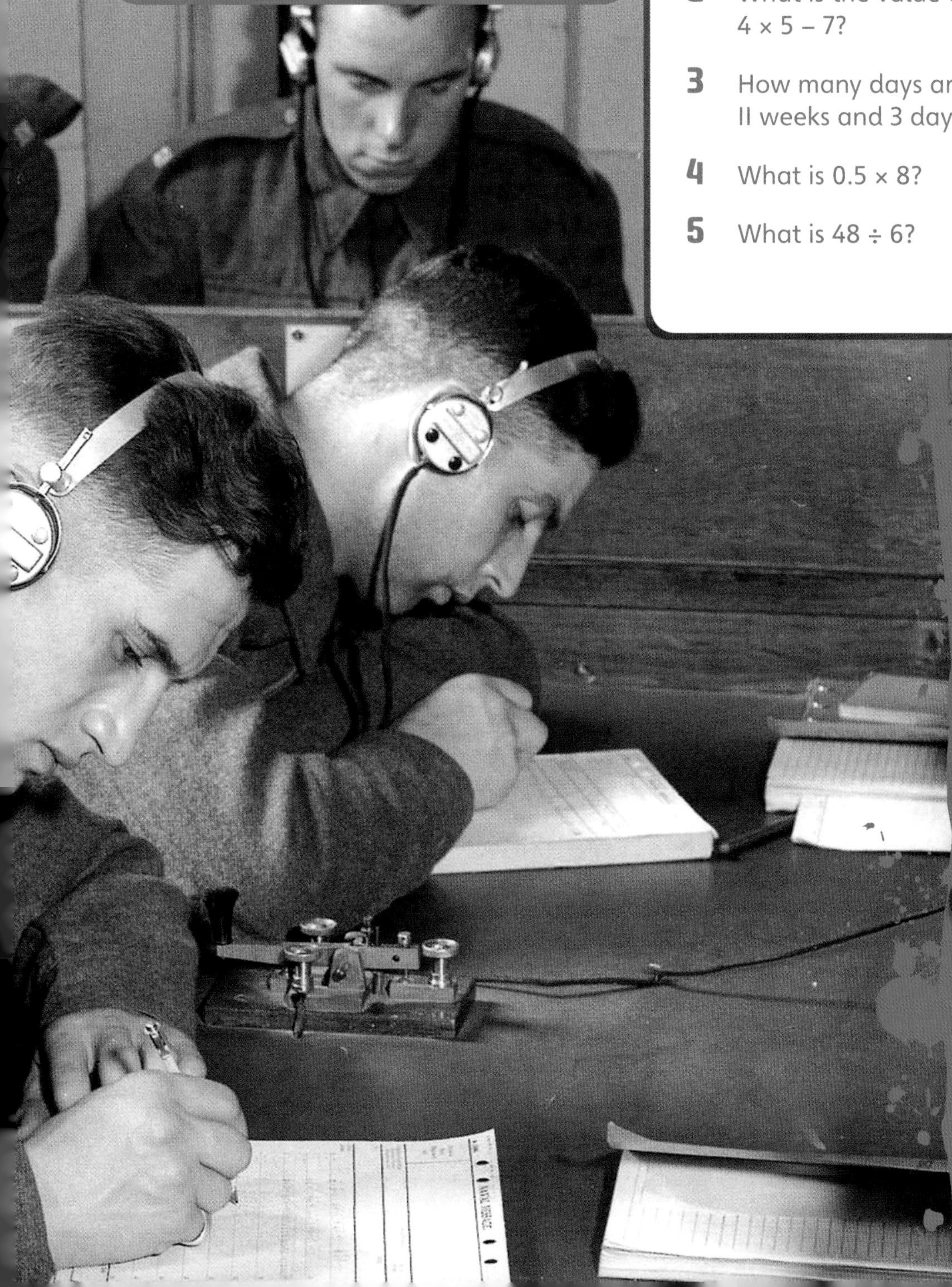

Plus digital resources

6.1 Writing expressions

➩ Write algebraic expressions from descriptions

Why learn this?

We can use words and writing to communicate with each other. To tell someone how to work something out we can use algebra.

What's the BIG idea?

- → You can use **algebra** to write an **expression** that describes how one amount compares with another amount. **Level 5**
- → You can use letters to stand for numbers. **Level 5**
- → If a mystery number is called m, you can write 2 more than this as $m + 2$. **Level 5**
- → m is called a **variable** because its value can change or vary. **Level 5**
- → You can write 3 times the mystery number as $3 \times m$ or $3m$. **Level 5**

Super fact!

In ancient Egypt, they used the word 'heap' instead of a letter to stand for a mystery number in algebra.

Practice, practice, practice!

Level 5

5C I can construct simple expressions

1 Connie has a green envelope containing g counters.
Write an expression for the number of counters she has when

she puts 2 more counters into the envelope.

g counters in the envelope plus 2 more. She has $g + 2$ counters.

a she takes 3 out **b** she has 6 more
c she has 7 less **d** she adds 5 more.

2 Sarbjoht's hair is x cm long. Write expressions for the length of hair that is

a 10 cm longer **b** 2 cm shorter
c 0.5 cm longer **d** the same length.

3 Some friends are comparing their heights. Angela is h cm tall.
Write an expression for each person's height.

a Avnee is 1 cm taller than Angela. **b** Jess is 10 cm taller than Angela.
c Tish is 5 cm shorter than Angela. **d** Adam is 3 cm shorter than Angela.
e Abida is 2.5 cm taller than Angela. **f** Aisha is 3.5 cm shorter than Angela.

4 Kadeem thinks of a mystery number.
Write an expression for the number that is

a 4 more than his number
b 13 less than his number
c the answer after his number has been taken away from 50
d his number then add 8 and take away 6.

algebra expression

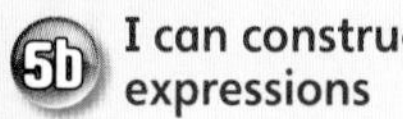

5 Devlin has some red bags each containing r counters and some yellow bags each containing y counters.
Write an expression for how many counters he will have if

a he has one red bag and five more counters
b he has three yellow bags
c he has two red bags and takes five counters out
d he puts together all the counters in parts **b** and **c**.

Watch out!
Some people confuse $b + 3$ and $3b$. $b + 3$ means three more than b and $3b$ means three lots of b.

5b I can construct expressions

6 Asma has a pencil that is y cm long and a pen that is x cm long.
Write an expression for the length that is

a 3 cm longer than the pencil **b** 5 cm shorter than the pen
c twice as long as the pen **d** ten times as long as the pencil
e the length of the pen and the pencil put together.

5b I can construct expressions

7 Tickets for a play cost £p each. Write an expression for the cost of

a two tickets **b** two tickets plus a £5 booking fee.

Student tickets cost £t each. Write an expression for the cost of

c five student tickets **d** one full-price ticket and one student ticket
e four student and three full-price tickets
f two full-price tickets and one student ticket

5b I can construct expressions

8 The mystery number is n. Write expressions for these amounts.

a three times as much as the number
b 20 less than the number in part **a**
c 30 divided by the number
d the square of the result after the number is subtracted from 50
e four times the number and then squared

Watch out!
Some people confuse $2n$ and n^2. The first means two lots of n and the second means $n \times n$.

5a I can construct more complex expressions

Now try this!

A Expression challenge

Work in pairs. Make up five expressions similar to those in the questions you have been doing and write number clues for them. For example, $n + 2$ could have the clue 'two more than a number'. Swap clues with another pair and write the expression.

B The same expression

$b + 5$	$2 \div b$	$b - 3$	$1b$	$3 - b$
$b \div 2$	$\frac{1}{2}b$	b	$b \times b$	b^2
$b + b$	$5 + b$	$2b$	$2 + b$	$b + 2$

Some pairs of these expressions are always the same. Some pairs are only the same for certain numbers. For example, $2b$ is not the same as $b + 2$ unless you choose the value $b = 2$.

Which pairs of expressions are always the same?
Which are the same for certain values? What values are they the same for?

variable

6.2 Order of operations

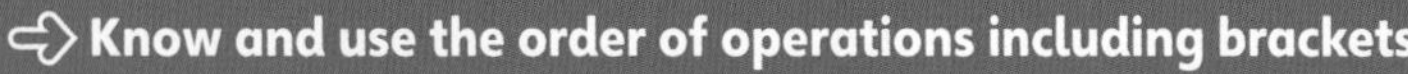

- Know and use the order of operations including brackets
- Multiply a single term over a bracket

Why learn this?

We read English from left to right, but sometimes Chinese writing is read from top to bottom. In maths, we have rules to tell us which way to read a calculation.

What's the BIG idea?

→ $2 \times (5 + 6) = 2 \times 5 + 2 \times 6$
This is called the distributive law. **Level 4**

→ The order of operations is
Brackets – you need to calculate whatever is in brackets first
Indices – powers like ^{2}
Division and **M**ultiplication
Addition and **S**ubtraction
We call this **BIDMAS** to help us remember. **Level 4 & Level 5**

→ A horizontal line acts as a bracket.
$(3 + 4) \div 2$ can also be written as $\frac{3 + 4}{2}$ **Level 5**

Watch out!

When you enter $3 + 4 \times 5$ in a calculator, some give the answer 23, but others give the answer 35. What answer does your calculator give you? Is it correct? If not, you will need to put brackets in the calculation.

Practice, practice, practice!

Level 3

3b I know that numbers can be added or multiplied in any order

1 Match up the pairs of calculations that give the same answer.

2×10 $2 \div 10$ $10 - 3$ $10 - 2$ $2 + 10$
10×2 $2 - 10$ $10 \div 3$ $10 + 2$ $10 \div 2$ $3 \div 10$
$3 + 10$ 3×10 10×3 $3 - 10$ $10 + 3$

Level 4

4c I can use brackets

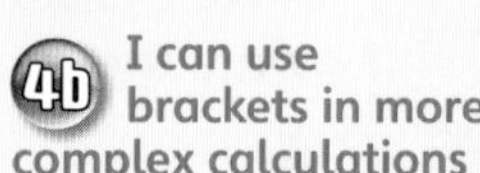

4b I can use brackets in more complex calculations

2 Calculate
a $(6 + 2) \times 5$ **b** $(5 \times 3) + 6$ **c** $4 \times (6 - 3)$
d $(10 - 7) \times 2$ **e** $(6 + 3) \div 10$ **f** $(15 + 3) \div 6$

3 Calculate
a $(17 \times 2) - (6 \times 4)$ **b** $(2 \times 26) - (8 \times 3)$ **c** $7 + (48 \div 3) + 5$
d $\frac{7 + 9}{2 + 10}$ **e** $120 - 5 \times (3 + 5)$ **f** $(120 - 90) \times (3 + 5)$

4 Use these numbers, +, −, ×, ÷ and brackets to make number sentences that give the target answers.
a 5, 5, 2 target = 35 **b** 10, 8, 6 target = 140
c 20, 3, 4 target = 8 **d** 16, 2, 5 target = 13
e 5, 5, 2, 4 target = 39 **f** 4, 4, 3, 2 target = 26

Brackets Indices Division Multiplication

5 Calculate

$5 \times (80 - 2) = 5 \times 80 - 5 \times 2$
$= 400 - 10$
$= 390$

a $5 \times (20 - 1)$ b $4 \times (30 + 3)$ c $4 \times (60 + 5)$ d $8 \times (20 + 7)$

6 Show how brackets and the distributive law can be used to work out these products.

a 3×42 b 5×69 c 18×5 d 7×16 e 3×998

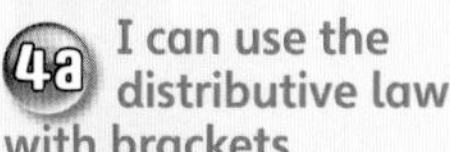

4a I can use the distributive law with brackets

Expanding brackets like this uses the distributive law

7 Calculate

a $4 \times 5 + 3$ b $10 + 2 \times 7$ c $20 - 3 \times 5$
d $10 \times 6 - 7$ e $0.5 \times 8 - 1.5$ f $4.5 + 3 \times 1.5$

8 Calculate

a $6 \times 3 - 7 \times 2$ b $8 + 6 \times 3 - 2$ c $8 \times 10 + 3 + 2$
d $10 + 5 \times 2 \times 3$ e $18 + 36 + 7 \times 9$ f $2 \times 9 - 3 \times 6$

9 Use these numbers and the operations +, −, × and ÷ to make number sentences that give the target answers.

a 4, 5, 3 target = 7 b 18, 2, 6 target = 30
c 18, 2, 6 target = 6 d 3, 7, 9 target = 34

10 Calculate

a $2^2 \times 5 \times 6$ b $(10 \times 6) + 3$
c $5^2 + 3$ d $(6 - 2)^2 + 3$
e $(6 + 3^2) \div 5$ f $4^2 \times (6 - 1) + 5$

Watch out!
Don't confuse squaring and multiplying by 2

11 Put brackets into these calculations to make them correct.

a $4 + 2^2 \times 1 = 8$ b $2 + 3^2 = 25$ c $4 \times 3^2 + 6 = 60$
d $6^2 + 2^2 \times 4 = 160$ e $10^2 - 7 - 2 = 95$

Level 5

5c I can use the order of operations

5b I can use the order of operations in more complex calculations

Now try this!

A Target numbers
Work in pairs. One person picks five numbers under 10, and then the other chooses a target number between 50 and 100. The first person to write a mathematical sentence that gives the target answer using some or all of the five numbers wins 1 point.

Take it in turns to pick the target number. The first person to 3 points wins.

B Number sentences
Make five number sentences that give an answer of 17 – the more complicated the better!

Did you know?
The order of operations can be important in daily life. Which operation should come first – 'leave the house' or 'get dressed'?

Addition Subtraction BIDMAS

6.3 Simplifying expressions

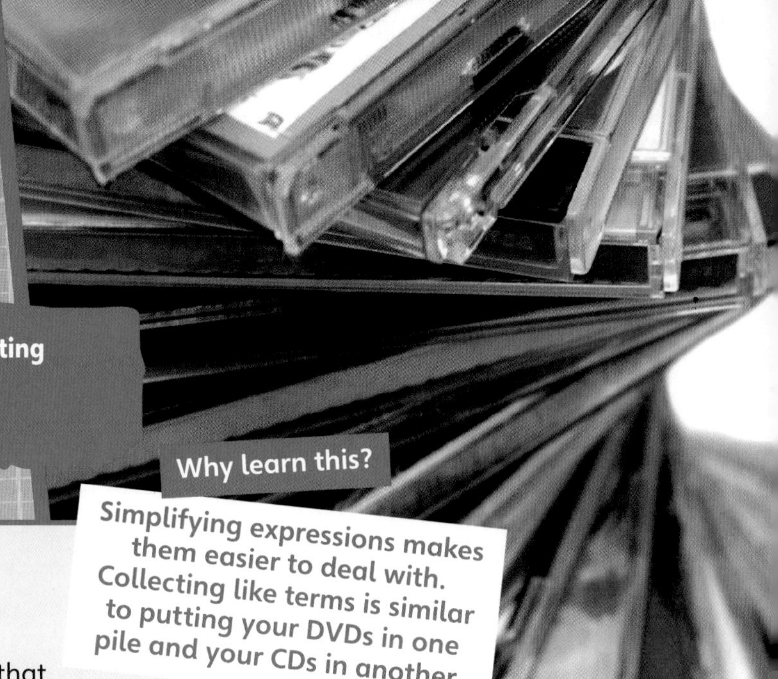

- Know how to simplify algebraic expressions by collecting like terms
- Multiply a single term over a bracket

Why learn this?

Simplifying expressions makes them easier to deal with. Collecting like terms is similar to putting your DVDs in one pile and your CDs in another.

What's the BIG idea?

- An algebraic **expression** is made up of **terms**. For example $a + b + 2$ has three terms. **Level 4**
- You can **simplify** an expression by adding terms that are alike. **Like terms** have the same letter. **Level 4 & Level 5**
- You can also multiply or expand expressions with **brackets**. For example $4(x + 3)$ means four lots of $x + 3$ or $4 \times x + 4 \times 3 = 4x + 12$. **Level 5**

Practice, practice, practice!

Level 4

4a I can collect like terms

1 Simplify these expressions by collecting like terms.

a $f + f + f + f$ **b** $2h + h + 3h - h$ **c** $5 + n + 10$

d $g + 6 + g - 8$ **e** $2a - 8 + 5a - 6a + 7$

2 Copy and complete these addition pyramids.
The expression in any brick is the sum of the expressions in the two bricks below.

a

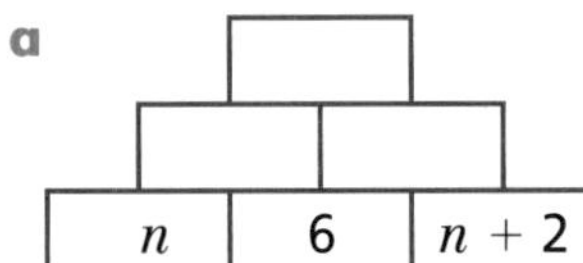

b

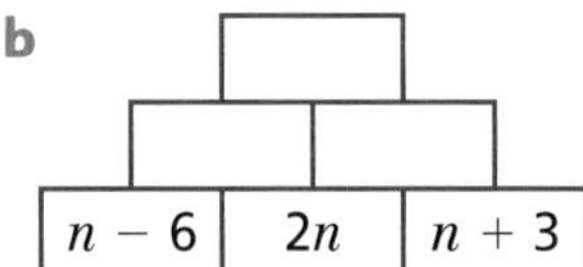

c

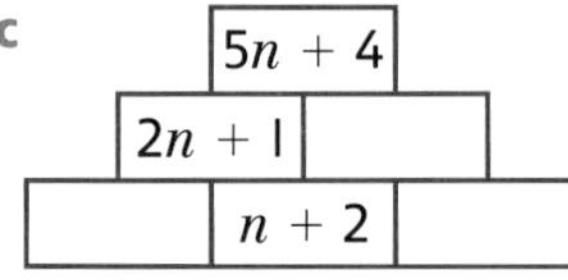

Watch out!

You will have to subtract to find the expression in some bricks.

3 Fill in the missing term and operation to make each statement correct.

$a + a + a + a + 7$ ☐☐ $= 2a + 7$

$a + a + a + a + 7$ makes $4a + 7$
Missing term is $-2a$
then $4a + 7 - 2a = 4a - 2a + 7$
$= 2a + 7$

a $4y + 7 + 2y$ ☐☐ $= 6y + 10$ **b** $y + 6 + 2y$ ☐☐ $= y + 6$

c $3n + 5n - 7 + 2$ ☐☐ $= 8n - 6$ **d** $10n + 8 - 12n + 7$ ☐☐ $= 15$

Level 5

5c I can simplify expressions by collecting like terms

4 Simplify these expressions.

a $g + g + g + h + h + h$ **b** $t + p + t + p + t - p + t$

c $3x + 2y + 2x - y$ **d** $4p + 3r + 7 - p + 2r - 6$

e $3m - 4n + m + 2 - 5 - 3n$ **f** $3a - 7b + 4 + 3b - 6 + 4b$

bracket expression like terms

5 Complete these addition pyramids.

a

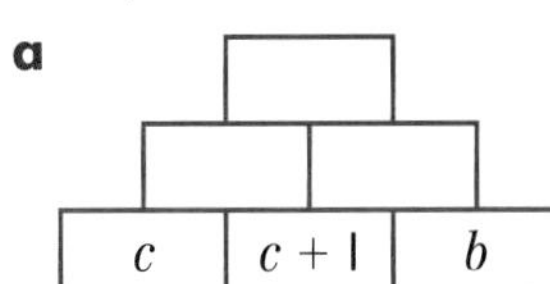

b

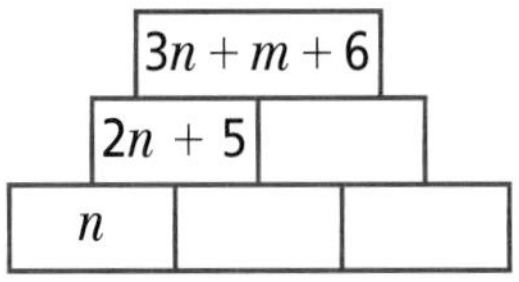

$3n + m + 6$

$2n + 5$

n

c

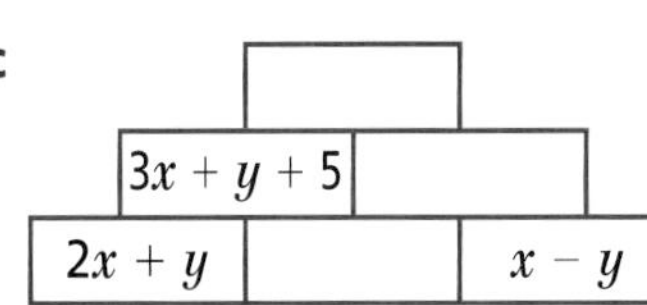

6 Fill in the gaps.

a $2(x + 3) = 2 \times x + 2 \times \square = 2x + \square$ **b** $4(x + 2) = 4x + \square$

c $5(a - 3) = \square - 15$ **d** $6(y - 2) = 6y - \square$

e $3(2a + 5) = \square + 15$ **f** $4(3x - 4y + 1) = 12x \square + 4$

7 Expand the brackets.

a $7(n + 4)$ **b** $4(3x - 10)$ **c** $3(11 + f)$ **d** $2(9 - 6p)$

e $8(x + 2y - 3)$ **f** $7(3p - 5)$ **g** $5(11p - 4 - 6q)$ **h** $\frac{1}{2}(6y + 18)$

8 Match the expressions.

$2(x + 3)$	$8x + 4$
$4(2x + 1)$	$6y + 2x$
$2(x + 3y)$	$6y + 12x$
$2(2x - 3)$	$4x + 4$
$2x + 2(x + 2)$	$6x - 9$
$6(y + 2x)$	$2x + 6$

Hint: There are two that don't match.

Level 4

5c I can simplify expressions by collecting like terms

5b I can expand brackets in simple expressions

Now try this!

A Algebra pyramids

Work in pairs. Each draw a blank pyramid like the ones in Q2.
Write some algebraic terms in the bottom cells. Work out what would be in the top cell. Give your partner the bottom row only. Do they get the same expression in the top cell as you?

B Algebra costs

Chips: c	Chilli: $b - 20$
Burger: b	Family chicken pie: $2b$
Baked beans: $c + 10$	Ice cream sundae: $2b + 40$
Salad: $c + 5$	Fish: $2c$
Jacket potato: $2c + 10$	Veggie hotpot: $2c + 5$

Work in pairs. Secretly, each work out the total cost of several different items. Then ask your partner to guess what you bought. Start with only one type, e.g. five salads, and then combinations if you want to be really challenging.

Hint: There may be more than one combination which gives the same algebraic total.

Super fact!

Algebra was first used by the Babylonians in 1800 BC. It was only introduced in Europe around 1200 BC.

simplify term

maths!

Fior v Tartaglia

In the sixteenth century, to show how talented they were, mathematicians often challenged each other to public contests.
One of the most famous was between Antonio Maria Fior and Niccolò Fontana Tartaglia in 1535.

FIOR FOREVE

$$a + 2a + 3a$$

$$3 \times 7a$$

$$4a + 5c - 2a$$

$$a + 6a^2 - 3a + a^2$$

$$3(a + 6) - 2$$

Fior and Tartaglia each set 30 algebraic questions for the other to solve. The winner would be the person who solved the most correctly in 50 days.

As the deadline approached, Tartaglia had a breakthrough and managed to solve all of Fior's questions in just two hours. Fior was unable to solve any of Tartaglia's questions.

Tartaglia was the winner!

TARTAGLIA ROCKS

$$b + 4b + 2b$$

$$4 \times 6b$$

$$3b + 7d - b$$

$$b + 5b^2 - 4b + b^2$$

$$2(b + 8) - 3$$

Tartaglia became well known as a talented mathematician and went on to further contests and great success.

Fior was exposed as a weaker mathematician who had relied only on being able to solve one type of algebraic question.

- Simplify all the expressions shown.
- Invent five or ten questions of your own and have a contest with a friend.
  Make sure that you can simplify the questions yourself first!

6.4 Substituting into formulae

- Substitute integers into expressions and formulae that are written in words
- Substitute integers into expressions and formulae that are written using algebra

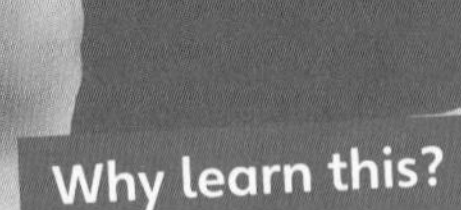

Why learn this?

The amount of medicine a patient needs may be given by a formula. The formula may depend on the age or weight of the patient. The doctor uses the formula to work out the correct dose.

What's the BIG idea?

→ **Formulae** can be written in words or in symbols (using algebra). **Level 4 & Level 5**

→ **Substituting** values into a formula or an expression allows you to work out its value. For example, if $a = 5$ and $b = 4$, the value of the expression $a + b$ is $5 + 4 = 9$. **Level 4 & Level 5**

Practice, practice, practice!

Level 4

4a I can substitute integers into simple word formulae

1 Sandeep runs a limousine service.
He works out how to charge his customers using this word formula:

cost, in pounds = miles × 4 + 80

How much will he charge for these journeys?

a 20 miles **b** 17 miles **c** 36 miles
d 22.5 miles **e** 80 miles **f** 12.25 miles

2 The Han family uses this formula to work out each child's pocket money:

pocket money, in pence = age × 10 + 50

Work out how much each child gets.

a Tony, 12 years old **b** Suzi, 9 years old
c Lily, 8 years old **d** Ho Yin, 4 years old

3 The instructions to cook a chicken say '20 minutes per 500 g + 20 minutes'.
How long will it take to cook a chicken that has a mass of

a 2 kg **b** 1.5 kg **c** 3.5 kg?

Level 5

5c I can substitute integers into simple symbol expressions

4 $a = 4$, $b = 6$, $c = 3$ and $d = 2$. Find the value of

a $2c$ **b** $a + b$ **c** ac **d** $a - 3$
e $10 - c$ **f** $\frac{1}{2}b$ **g** b^2 **Hint:** $b^2 = b \times b$

formula substitute

5 $a = 7$, $b = 6$ and $c = 9$. Find the value of

a $3c$ **b** $37 - a$ **c** $5b$

d ab **e** $a + b - c$ **f** abc

6 The cost of a bunch of flowers at a school fair is $5f$ pence, where f stands for the number of flowers in the bunch.
How much do these bunches cost?

a 12 flowers **b** 7 flowers **c** 15 flowers **d** 11 flowers?

7 $a = 4$, $b = 6$, $c = 3$ and $d = 2$. Find the value of

a $2b + 1$ **b** $a + 3b$ **c** $ac - b$ **d** $5a - 3$

e b^2 **f** $10b - 2c$ **g** $\frac{3}{4}a$ **h** $c^2 + 2a$

8 $x = 7$, $y = 6$ and $z = 9$. Find the value of

a $70 - 3z$ **b** $37 - 5x$ **c** $5y - 2xz$

d $xy - z$ **e** $x^2 - 5z$

9 The formula for converting temperature F in degrees Fahrenheit (°F) to temperature C in degrees Celsius (°C) is

$$C = 5(F - 32) \div 9$$

Work out these temperatures in degrees Celsius (°C).

a 122°F **b** 167°F **c** 50°F

Level 5

5c I can substitute integers into simple symbol expressions

5b I can substitute integers into symbol expressions

Tip
Remember the order of operations when working out values.

Now try this!

A Substitution challenge 1

Work in pairs and take turns. Player 1 picks a value for n between 1 and 10. Player 2 picks one of the expressions below and works out the value.

$3n$	$n - 3$	$20 - n$	$2n$	$12 \div n$	$n \times n$

Work out the total of the three amounts. Swap roles and repeat. Whoever has the highest total wins.

B Substitution challenge 2

Using the expressions in the grid below and the values $x = 6$ and $y = 2$, try to find expressions for all the integers from 1 to 20.

One of the numbers from 1 to 20 is not here – which one?

Hint: There are some expressions which are no use to you at all.

$2x$	$20 - \frac{1}{2}y$	$\frac{1}{2}x$	$2y$	$2x - y$
$20 - y$	$x - y$	$3x - 1$	$2y + 5$	$x + 13$
$2x - \frac{1}{2}y$	$5y$	$10 - y + x + x$	$20y$	$7y$
$y - 4$	$3y - 1$	$10 - y$	$20 - 2y$	$3x$
$10 - 2y$	$2y - 1$	$6x - 4$	$x + y - 1$	$x + y + 1$
$\frac{1}{2}x - 2$	$4y + 3$	$x + x + 3$	$x - y - 1$	$3x - 8y$

Tip
In a team game substituting a player means replacing one player with another. The substitute sits on the subs bench.

variable

6.5 Deriving formulae

➩ **Know how to derive a formula expressed in letter symbols**

What's the BIG idea?

→ A **variable** is a quantity in a formula that can take different values, for example the number of people in a room, or the number of minutes a call lasts. **Level 5**

→ You can use a **formula** to describe how to work out an amount that depends on a variable. **Level 5**

For example, the monthly rental of a phone is £20 and calls cost £2 for 10 minutes. The formula for working out the monthly bill is

cost = $2 \times f + 20$

where f is the number of blocks of 10 minutes used.

Why learn this?

Mobile phone bills are worked out using formulae. The cost of a call usually depends on how long it lasts. You can use the formula to work out a bill for the calls.

Practice, practice, practice!

Level 5

5c I can derive simple formulae using algebra

1 **a** The number of workers in a factory is 20 more than the number of machines. How many workers are there if there are
i 25 machines **ii** 40 machines **iii** 30 machines?
b Write a formula for the number of workers if the number of machines is m.

Hint: Remember to start your formula: 'number of workers ='

2 **a** Avnee is 2 years younger than Rob. How old was Avnee when Rob was
i 14 **ii** 22 **iii** 57?
b Write a formula for Avnee's age when Rob is x years old.

3 **a** Tony has 50 merits at the start of the month. He loses a merit each time he is late. How many merits will he have left if he is late
i 4 times **ii** 12 times **iii** 21 times?
b Write a formula for the number of merits left if Tony is late L times.

5b I can derive formulae using algebra

4 **a** In Binley wildlife park the number of lions is twice the number of keepers. How many lions are there if there are
i 10 keepers **ii** 8 keepers **iii** 15 keepers?
b Write a formula for the number of lions if there are k keepers.

5 **a** Shreena is finding out about sizes of families in her class. Work out how many children there are in a family with
i 3 boys and 2 girls **ii** 3 girls and 1 boy
iii 2 girls and b boys **iv** g girls and 4 boys.
b Write a formula for the number of children in a family if there are g girls and b boys.

algebra expression

6 Draw 4-, 5-, 6- and 7-sided polygons like these. From one corner draw as many diagonals as you can on each shape.

a Copy and complete this table.

Number of sides	Number of diagonals
4	
5	
6	
7	

b How many diagonals will a 10-sided polygon have?

c Write a formula for the number of diagonals if the number of sides on the polygon is n.

7 **a** In Binley wildlife park the age of the animals is given in months. How old will an animal be in years if it is
i 120 months old **ii** 24 months old **iii** 36 months old?

b Write a formula for the age in years if an animal is a months old.

8 **a** In Jamane's school every time you are late you lose 2 merits. At the start of the month he has 40 merits. How many merits will be left if he is late
i 6 times **ii** 12 times **iii** 0 times?

b Write a formula for the number of merits left if Jamane is late L times.

9 The cost of a journey in Glamcabs is £3.50 and then £2 for each mile.

a Work out the cost of a journey that is 10 miles.

b Write a formula for a journey that is m miles.

Level 5

5b I can derive formulae using algebra

Tip

If you're not sure how to derive a formula, put in some numbers. Look carefully at what you are doing to each number. Copy this using a letter instead.

5a I can derive more complex formulae using algebra

Now try this!

A Perimeters

Look at these equilateral triangles.

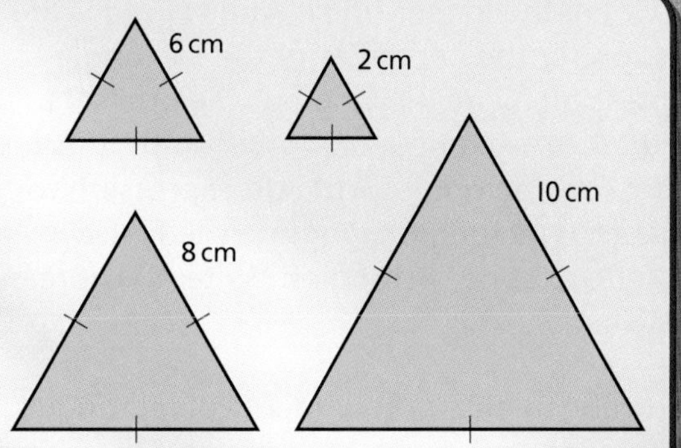

a Write instructions for working out the perimeter of each triangle.

b How would you work out the perimeter if the length of a side is x cm?

c Now try this with other regular polygons such as squares and pentagons.

B Circles and dots

Draw two circles. Label them circle 1 and circle 2. Draw two dots in circle 1 and three dots in circle 2.

a How many lines can you draw joining a dot in circle 1 to a dot in circle 2?

Hint: More than 1 line can come from a dot.

b Try different numbers of dots.

c Choose different letters to represent the number of dots in each circle and write a formula for the number of lines you can draw between the dots.

Super fact!

Coca-Cola was invented by John Pemberton in 1886. His formula has been a closely guarded secret ever since.

formula variable

Perimeters

Farmers and other people who keep animals need to calculate perimeters so that they buy the right amount of fencing to keep their animals safely in fields.

1 This square has sides that are $(b + 3)$ units long.
Its perimeter is $(4b + 12)$ units.

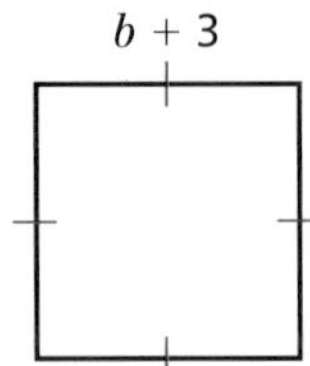

The side length changes to $(a + 7)$ units.
Write an expression for the perimeter of the square. **Level 5**

2 A triangle has a perimeter of $12b$.
Sketch a triangle that could have this perimeter. **Level 5**

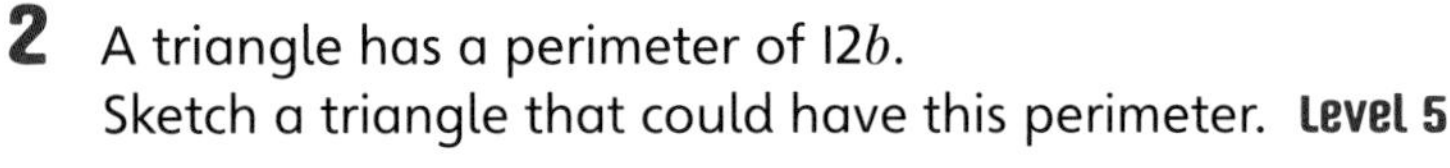

MAKE MATHS FUNCTIONAL!

3 Sketch the following shapes which each have a perimeter of $12b$.
Label each of the sides with its length.

a square
b rectangle
c irregular quadrilateral **Level 5**

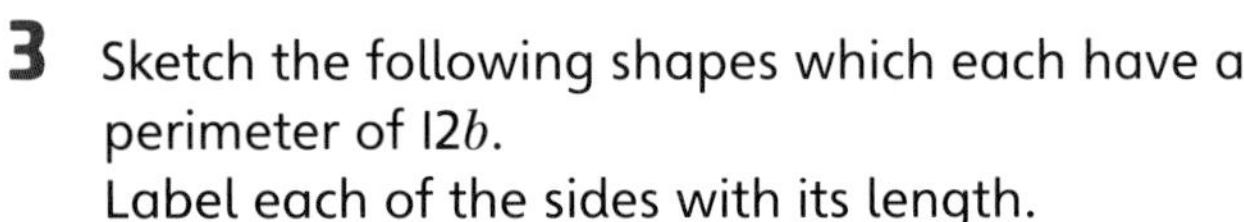

4 Now draw some shapes which have a perimeter of $6x + 12$. **Level 5**

5 Draw a rectangle where the longer side is 4 units longer than the shorter side.

a Write an expression for the perimeter of the rectangle using brackets.
b Simplify the expression by multiplying out the brackets.
c Draw another identical rectangle alongside so that its long side touches a long side of the first rectangle. Write an expression for the perimeter.
d Draw a third identical rectangle alongside the first two, with one side touching one of the existing rectangles. Write an expression for the perimeter. **Level 5**

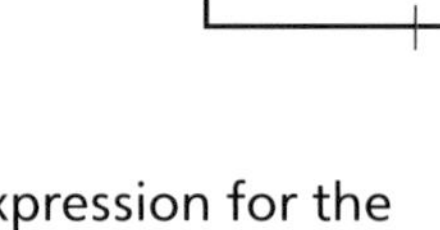

6 Explore different arrangements of four identical rectangles. Write an expression for the perimeter of each arrangement with brackets and then simplify the expression. **Level 5**

7 Let the length of the shorter side of the rectangle be 3 units.
For each of your expressions in **Q5** and **Q6**, work out the perimeter. **Level 5**

The BIG ideas

- → When you work with **algebra**, use the same rules as you use with arithmetic, e.g. $n + 5$ has the same value as $5 + n$. **Level 5**
- → The **order of operations** can be remembered by **BIDMAS**. **Level 4 & Level 5**
  Brackets **I**ndices **D**ivision **M**ultiplication **A**ddition **S**ubtraction
- → You can **simplify** an expression by adding **like terms**. **Level 4**
- → You can multiply expressions which have **brackets**, e.g. $3(b - 2)$ means three lots of $b - 2$ or $3b - 6$. **Level 5**
- → You can use algebra to describe how much or how many an amount is compared with another amount. **Level 5**
- → You can write **formulae** and **expressions** in words or in symbols. **Level 4 & Level 5**

Find your level

Level 3

Q1 Write down the pairs of expressions that have the same value.

5 × 3	3 × 2
2 + 2 + 2	7 − 1 − 1
10 − 2	3 × 5
1 − 7 − 1	2 − 10

Level 4

Q2 Rearrange these numbers and operations into a number sentence that equals the target number.

a 5, 2, 3, +, ×; target  17

b 10, 7, 4, −, ×; target  18

Level 5

Q3 a Ellen has a box of batteries. You cannot see how many batteries are inside the box. Call the number 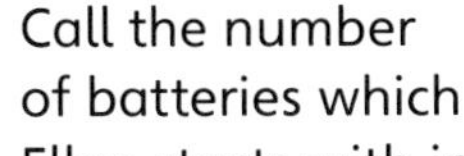 of batteries which Ellen starts with in her box b. 
Ellen puts four more batteries into her box.
Write an expression to show the total number of batteries in Ellen's box now.

b Jamal has another box of batteries. Call the number of batteries which Jamal starts with in his box t. Jamal takes five batteries out of his box.
Write an expression to show the total number of batteries in Jamal's box now.

c Harry has four boxes of batteries. Each box has a batteries inside. Harry takes some batteries out. Now the total number of batteries in Harry's boxes is $4a - 8$.
Which of these statements could be true?

A Harry took one battery out of each of the boxes.
B Harry took two batteries out of one of the boxes and none out of any others.
C Harry took two batteries out of each of the boxes.
D Harry took eight batteries out of one of the boxes and none out of the others.
E Harry took a total of eight out of two of the boxes and none out of the others.
F Harry took four batteries out of one of the boxes and none out of the others.

Q4 Simplify these expressions.

a $7e + 6 + 2e$

b $3 + e + e + 5$

7 Between the lines

This unit is about angles, shapes and coordinates.

Coordinates and angles are used to describe the positions of stars.

Angles of longitude and latitude are used as coordinates to describe positions on the Earth's surface.

Before latitude and longitude were developed maps were often wrong. The 15th century explorer Columbus thought he could reach Asia by travelling west from Europe. Unfortunately he thought Asia was over 6000 miles closer than it actually is. He arrived in the Americas instead!

Activities

A Road atlases use a coordinate system. The maps are drawn on a square grid. The squares are usually labelled with letters in one direction and numbers in the other.

Look up a town in a road atlas index. Use the grid reference given to find the town on the map. What is the grid reference for the place where you live or go to school?

B Cut the corners off a sheet of A4 paper. Then cut what is left into two triangles. You now have six triangles.

Do this again, but this time see if you can make any of your triangles have two equal sides. By changing the rectangle you start with, can you make all of your triangles have two equal sides?

Now cut a sheet of paper into triangles, any way you like, but still using all the paper.

Discuss with a partner how you might group your triangles.

Give your triangles to a partner. Can they put them together to get back the A4 rectangle you started with?

Star fact

If you track a star against a landmark, it takes about 360 days to reappear in the same position.

Before you start this unit...

1 How many right angles make
a a full turn
b half a turn
c a quarter of a turn?

Level Up Maths 1-2 page 33

2 a Name as many of the coloured shapes in this diagram as you can.

Level Up Maths 1-2 page 34

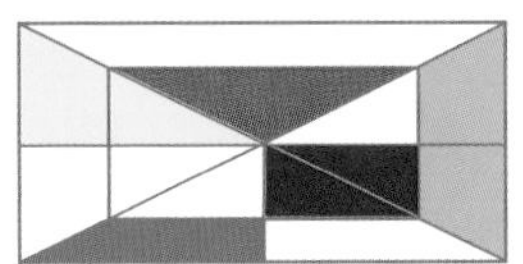

b Now copy the diagram but colour it in differently. Name as many of the coloured shapes as you can.

3 Cut a square into two identical triangles. Describe these triangles.

Level Up Maths 1-2 page 34

4 Cut a square into four identical triangles. Describe these triangles.

Level Up Maths 1-2 page 34

Civilisation began in Mesopotamia, the land between the Tigris and the Euphrates rivers in the Middle East. Over 4000 years ago the Mesopotamians developed a counting system based on the number 60. We still use it today for measuring time and angles. Angles are measured in degrees.

Plus digital resources

7.1 Angles and lines

- Identify right angles, perpendicular lines and parallel lines
- Correctly describe lines, points and angles
- Calculate missing angles in a triangle, on a straight line and round a point
- Recognise vertically opposite angles

Why learn this?

You have to get the angles right when planning and putting up structures – whether they are buildings or sculptures.

→ Two lines that are at 90° to each other are at **right angles**. Level 3

a right angle

→ **Parallel** lines never meet. You can show parallel lines with arrows. Level 4

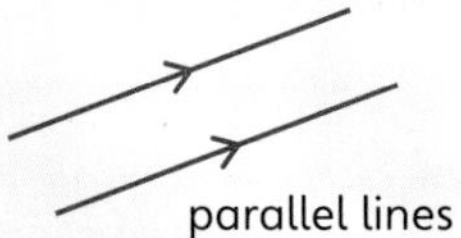

→ **Perpendicular** lines are at right angles to one another. Level 4

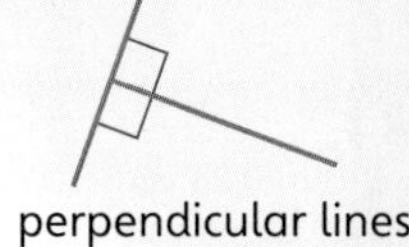

→ The angle at point B enclosed by the lines AB and BC is written $\angle ABC$, $\angle B$ or $\widehat{ABC}$. Level 4

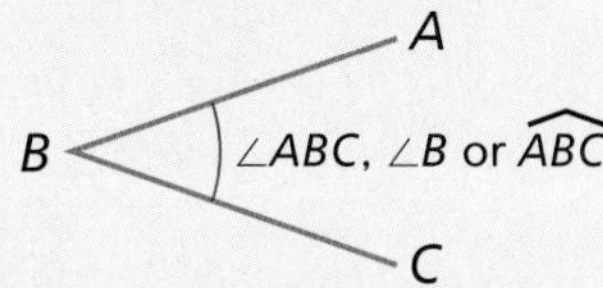

→ A full turn is 360°. The angles around a **point** add up to 360°. Level 5

These angles sum to 360°

→ Half a turn is 180°. The angles on a **straight line** add up to 180°. Level 5

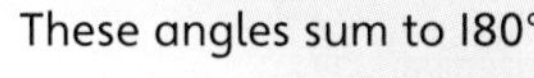

These angles sum to 180°

→ **Vertically opposite** angles are equal. Level 5

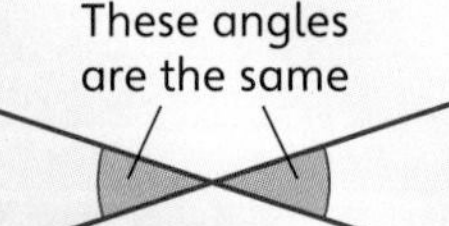

→ The sum of the angles in a **triangle** is 180°. Level 5

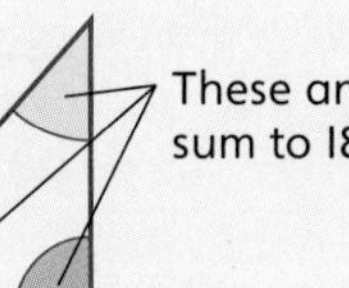

Practice, practice, practice!

Level 3 & Level 4

3c 4c I can identify right angles and parallel lines

1 In the diagram, $\angle DEA$ is a right angle.

a On your diagram mark all the right angles with ⌐

b Which line is parallel to the line BJ?

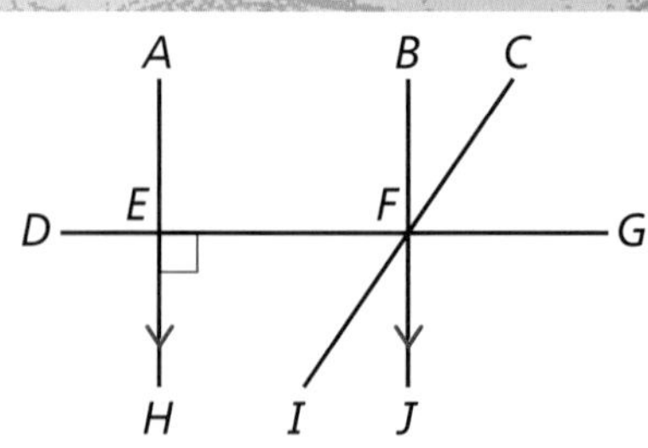

I can identify parallel and perpendicular lines and use the correct labelling

2 a Which line is parallel to AF?

b Which line is perpendicular to AF?

c Write down a right angle.

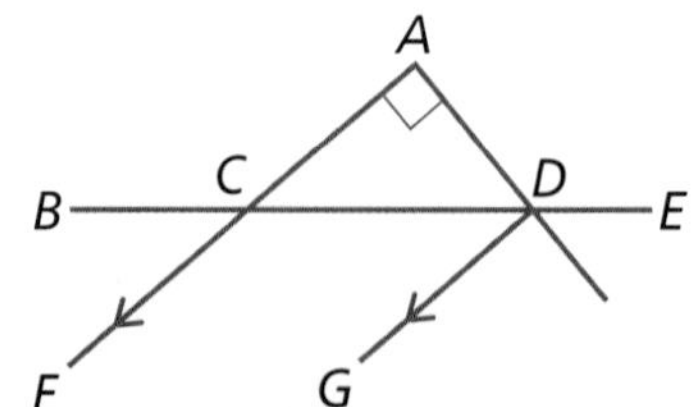

parallel perpendicular point right angle

3 Match the labels to the angles. 35° 325° 90° 125° 55°

a b c d e

f Which label is used twice? Which label doesn't match?

Level 4

4a I am beginning to estimate the size of angles

4 **a** What is $\angle DBE$?

b Copy the diagram. $\angle EBC = 43°$. Show this angle on your diagram.

c Work out $\angle ABD$.

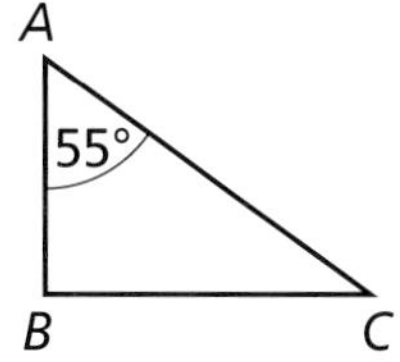

Hint: Your drawing for part **b** doesn't need to be exact.

5 **a** AB and BC are perpendicular. What is $\angle ABC$?

b $\angle BAC = 55°$. Find the size of $\angle ACB$.

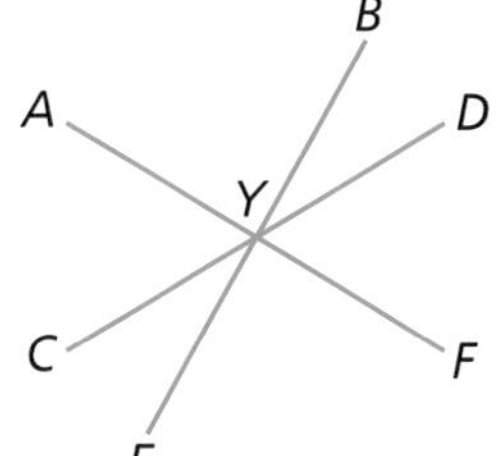

6 **a** Draw a triangle and label its vertices A, B and C.

b $\angle CAB = 50°$ and $\angle ACB = 80°$. Mark these angles on your diagram.

c Work out the size of $\angle ABC$.

7 The lines AF and BE are perpendicular.

a $\angle BYD = 30°$. What is the size of $\angle CYE$?

b Work out the size of $\angle DYF$.

c Which angle is the same as $\angle DYF$? Explain why.

B A D Y C F E

Level 5

5c I can use correct labelling and can find a missing angle on a straight line

5c I can find a missing angle in a triangle

5c I can label a triangle correctly and find a missing angle in a triangle

5b I can recognise and use vertically opposite angles

Now try this!

A The point of a triangle

Draw a triangle. Colour in the tips of the angles.
Cut out your triangle and tear off its corners. Arrange them on a straight line so the tips of the angles meet.
Compare with other pupils' triangles.
What does this show you?

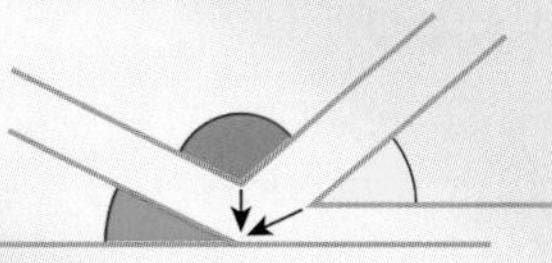

B Make your own 360° protractor

You need a 360° protractor and tracing paper.

1 Draw a large dot in the centre of your paper.
2 Now draw a straight line from your dot.
3 Put the centre of your protractor on the dot and the 0° line on your line. Draw around the protractor.
4 Mark the angles 10°, 20°, 30° and so on.
5 Remove the protractor.
6 Join up your marks with the centre of the circle. Label them (inside the perimeter of the circle) with the angles. Use colour to make it easy to find 90°, 180°, 270° and 0° (360°).

Super fact!

In about 2400 BC the Babylonians divided a circle into 360 degrees and a year into 360 days.

straight line triangle vertically opposite

7.2 Properties of triangles and quadrilaterals

- Recognise and name triangles as equilateral, isosceles or scalene
- Recognise and name angles as acute, right, obtuse or reflex
- Recognise and name quadrilaterals and begin to understand their properties

Why learn this?

When designing patterns or buildings it helps to know how sides and angles are linked. For example, if two sides of a triangle are equal then two of the angles are equal.

What's the BIG idea?

→ A **triangle** can be **scalene, isosceles, equilateral** or **right-angled**. Level 3 & Level 4

Matching angle marks show equal angles.

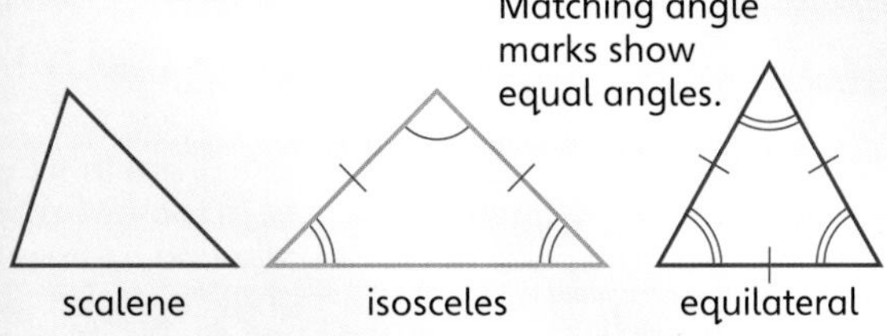

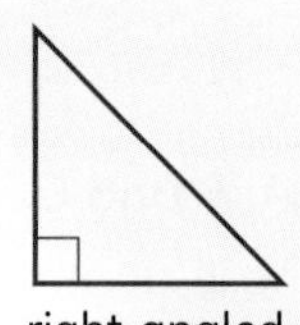

scalene isosceles equilateral right-angled

→ A **square** has four equal sides and four angles of 90°. A **rectangle** has two pairs of equal sides and four angles of 90°. Level 4

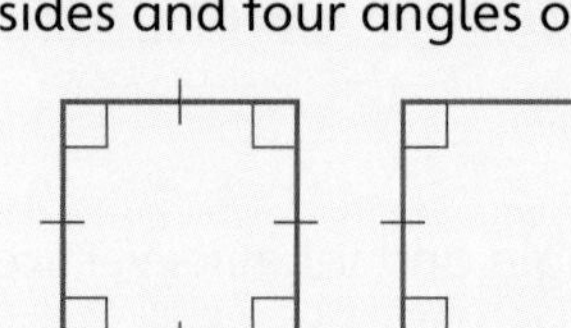

square rectangle

Lines of equal length are marked with dashes.

→ Types of angle: Level 4 & Level 5

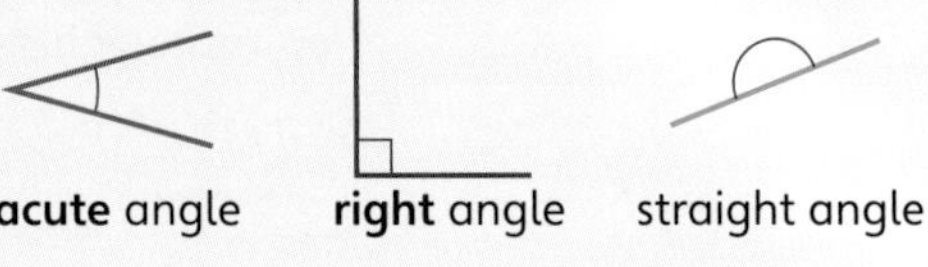

acute angle **right** angle straight angle

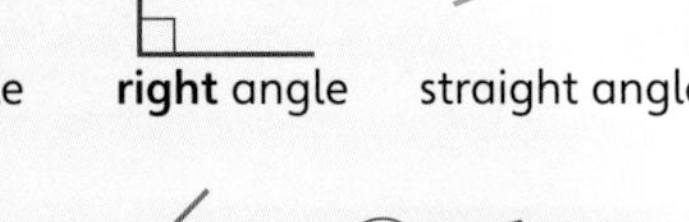

obtuse angle **reflex** angle

→ A **quadrilateral** is named according to its properties, which are based on which angles are equal and which sides are equal. Level 5

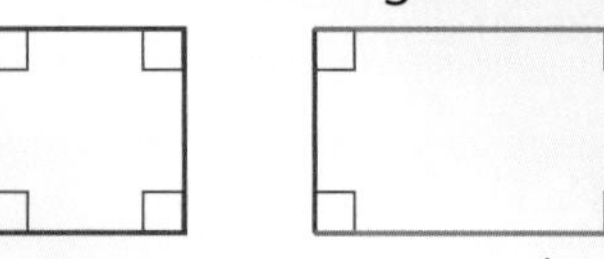

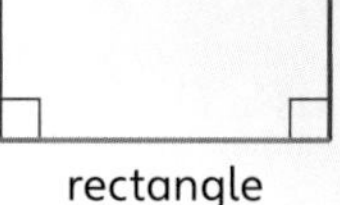

square rectangle

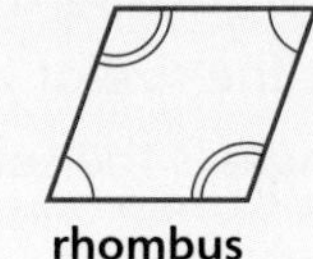

rhombus

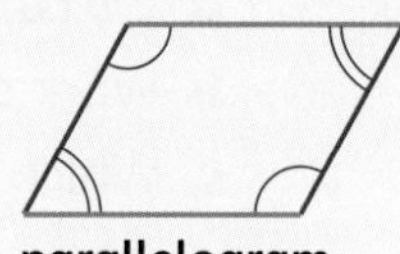

parallelogram

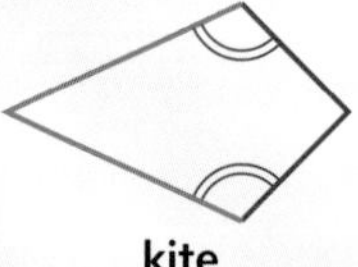

kite

arrowhead

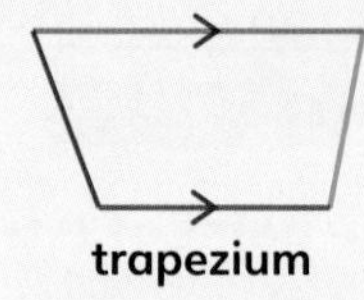

trapezium

Practice, practice, practice!

Level 3

3C I can identify triangles as isosceles, equilateral and scalene triangles

1 Decide whether each triangle is scalene (no sides equal), isosceles (two sides equal) or equilateral (all sides equal).

Hint: Use a ruler to check the lengths of sides.

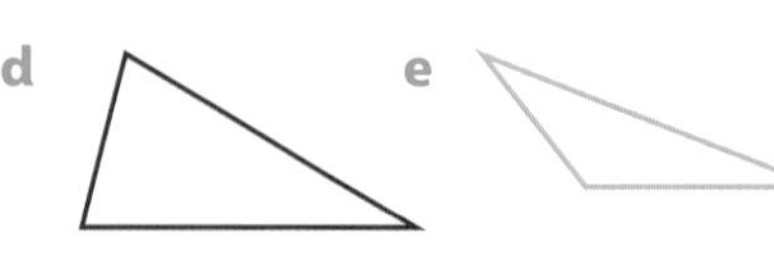

Level 4

4C I can identify triangles, squares and rectangles from their descriptions

2 Name each shape from its description.

Hint: A shape may appear more than once.

a I have three equal sides.
b I have four equal sides and four angles of 90°.
c I have three sides and two equal angles.
d I have four equal angles and two pairs of equal sides.

acute arrowhead equilateral isosceles kite obtuse parallelogram quadrilateral

3 Write the angles of these triangles in the correct place in the table.

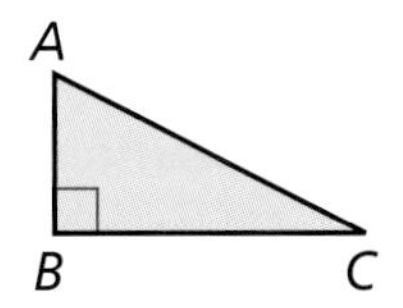

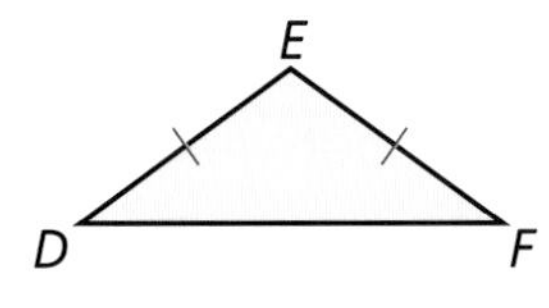

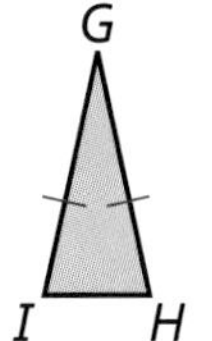

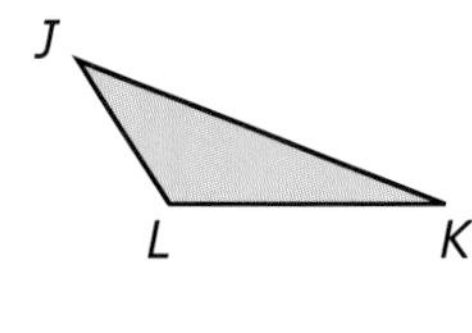

Acute	Obtuse	Right angle
A		*B*

4 **a** Draw an arrowhead and mark the reflex angle.
b Draw the line of symmetry.
c Look at the triangles in part **b**. Is the largest angle in each of them acute, obtuse or reflex?

Hint: It should split your arrowhead into two identical triangles.

5 Pair up each triangle below with a set of angles from the list.
Say whether each triangle is equilateral, isosceles or scalene.

a

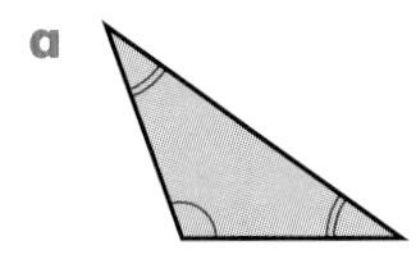

b

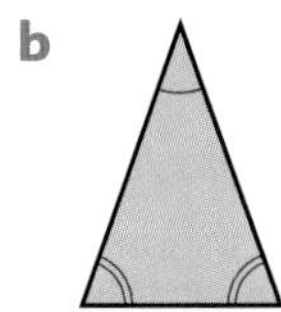

c

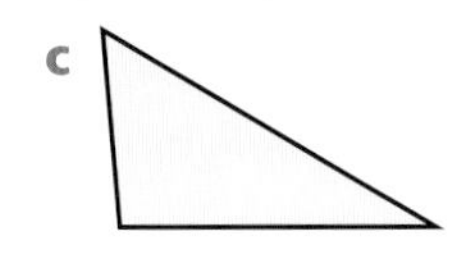

Level 4

4c I can distinguish between acute and obtuse angles

4b I can distinguish between acute, obtuse and reflex angles

4a I can group and identify triangles using simple properties

6 Some of these statements are possible, others are impossible. For each one that is possible, draw a sketch. For each one that is impossible, explain why.
a a triangle with two right angles
b an equilateral triangle with three acute angles
c an isosceles triangle with three acute angles
d an isosceles triangle with one obtuse angle
e a scalene triangle with one obtuse angle
f a scalene triangle with no obtuse angles

Level 5

5c I can group and identify triangles using properties

Now try this!

A Don't be a square!

Start with a square piece of paper. Make as many different shapes as you can by folding one or more corners into the centre. Sketch each shape and name it.

B Name that quadrilateral

A game for two players. Player 1 draws a quadrilateral. Don't show Player 2!

Player 2 asks questions to identify the quadrilateral, for example 'Does it have two parallel sides?'. Player 1 can only answer yes or no.

Keep a record of the number of questions. Player 2 scores 1 point for every question, minus 5 if they guess correctly. Swap roles and repeat. The winner is the player with the lowest score after five rounds.

rectangle reflex rhombus right angle scalene square trapezium triangle

maths!

Angles in sport

In sport, getting the angle just right can make all the difference between success and failure.

Javelin

- What would be the best angle for throwing a javelin?
- What would happen if you threw it at an angle that was too big or too small?
- In events such as the long jump and triple jump, would the angle of take-off be the same as the ideal angle for throwing a javelin?

- In which other sports do you think angles play an important part?

Water-ski jumping

Ramps for water-ski jumps always make an angle of 14° with the water. This allows for the longest jumps.

- Try to explain why.
- Why is a steeper slope not used? Surely a steeper slope would mean you would go higher and further?

Snooker

Angles are used a lot in games like snooker. The angle at which a ball hits the cushion is called the **angle of incidence** and the angle at which it rebounds is called the **angle of reflection**.
These two angles are equal.

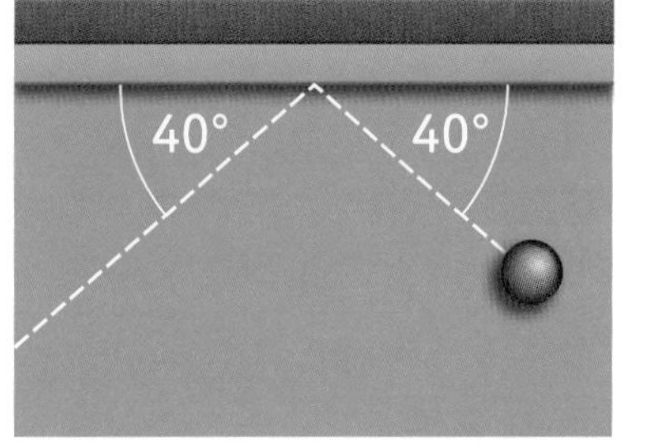

Work out the angles of incidence needed to pot these balls:

- The **red** ball bouncing off cushion 1 into pocket **a**.
- The **yellow** ball bouncing off cushion 2 into pocket **b**.
- The **blue** ball bouncing off cushion 2 into pocket **c**.
- The **pink** ball bouncing off cushion 3 into pocket **d**.

Use Resource sheet A7 to help you.

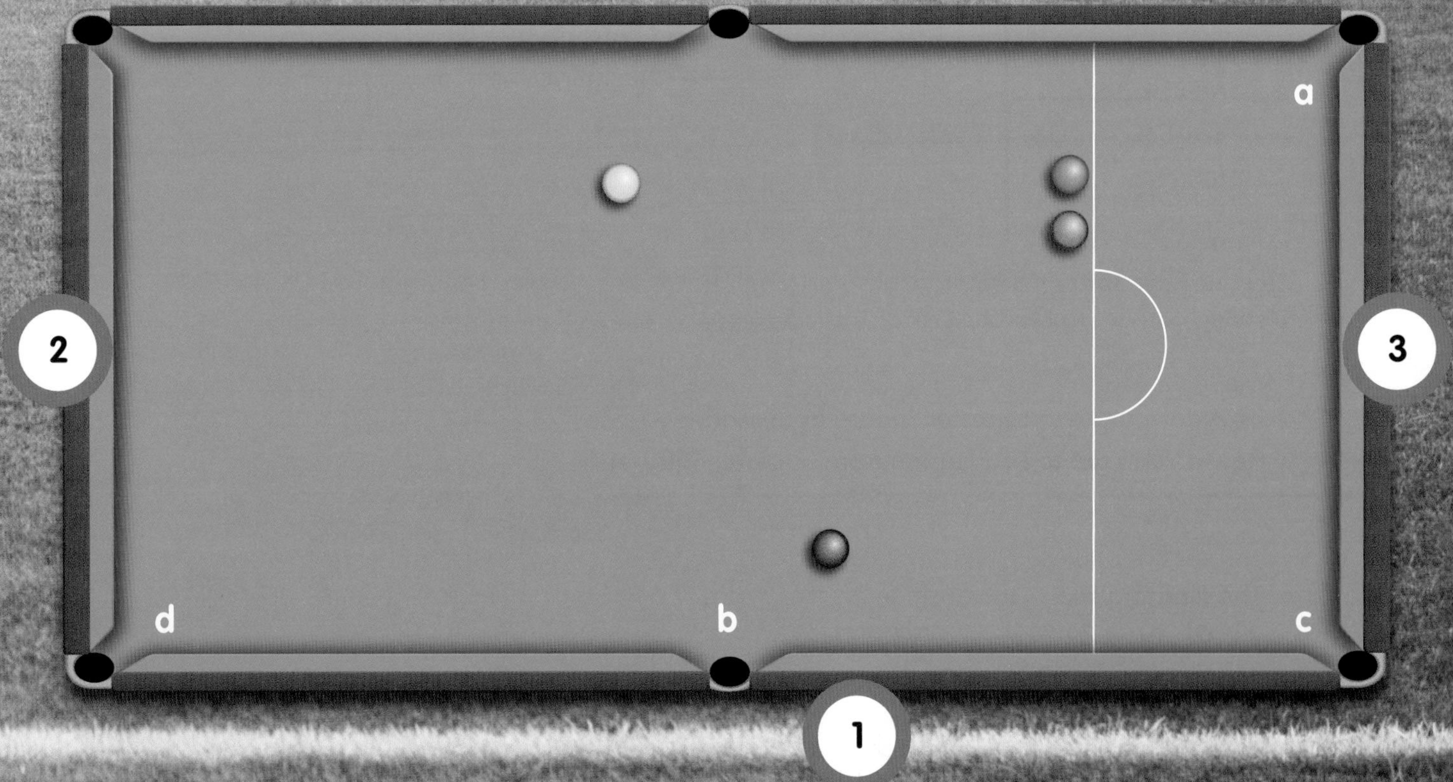

7.3 Using coordinates

- Find a point on a grid
- Read and plot coordinates
- Solve a problem to work out a missing coordinate

Why learn this?

The coordinate grid on a map allows you to find and describe places on the map.

What's the BIG idea?

- You can use **coordinates** to describe a point or to give **directions** to move around a grid. **Level 3**
- You can describe a point by its coordinates (x, y) relative to the **origin** O. **Level 4 & Level 5**
- You can find a missing coordinate of a shape using the coordinates of the other **vertices** and properties of the shape. **Level 5**

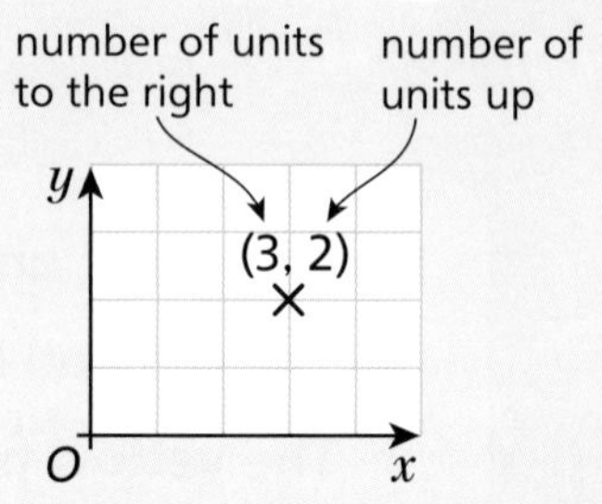

Practice, practice, practice!

Level 3

3a I can recognise positions and directions

1 The diagram shows part of the London Underground.

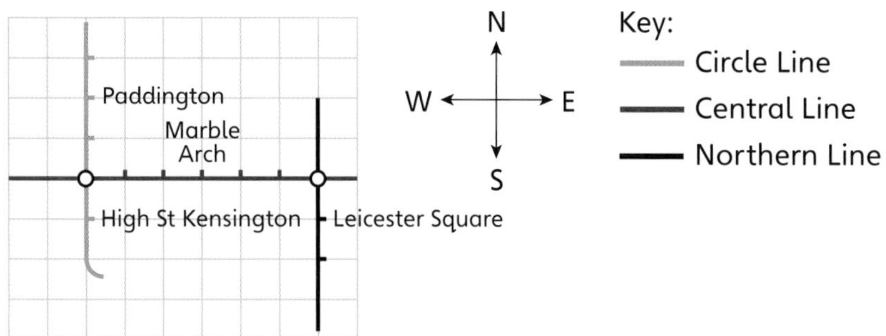

Start at High Street Kensington. How do you get to Marble Arch?

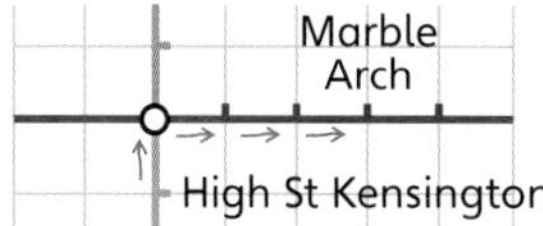

1 stop North, Circle Line
3 stops East, Central Line

a How do you get to Leicester Square from Marble Arch?

b How do you get to Paddington from Leicester Square?

Level 4

4a I can read and plot positive coordinates

2 **a** The diagram shows the position of a boat. Write down the coordinates marked with crosses.

b The boat moves. The new coordinates are (2, 3), (2, 6), (3, 8), (4, 6), (4, 3). Plot these coordinates on a copy of the grid to show the boat's new position.

c Each square on the grid is two metres long. How far has the boat moved and in what direction?

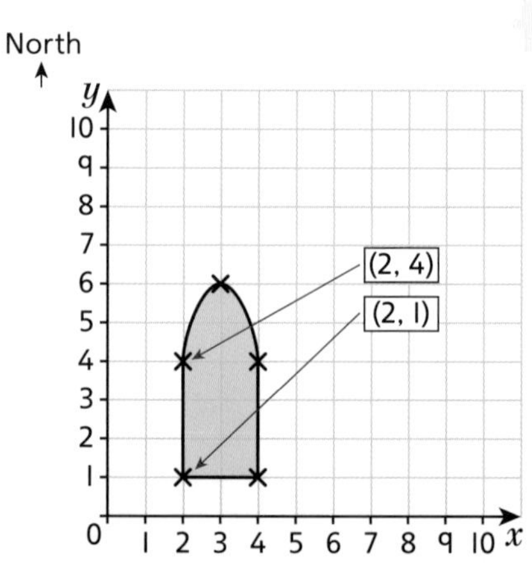

co-ordinate direction origin vertex

3 **a** The points A and B have coordinates (1, −5) and (4, −5). ∠ABC is a right angle. Write down possible coordinates for point C.

b The points D and F have coordinates (−3, −4) and (−1, −2). ∠DEF is a right angle. Write down possible coordinates for point E.

Level 5

5a I can solve simple problems to find coordinates

4 **a** Draw a grid with x- and y-axes from −6 to 6. Plot the points A(−5, 4), B(6, 4) and C(1, −3). Join points A and B with a straight line.

b Lines AB and CD are parallel. Plot and write down possible coordinates for point D. Join the points C and D to form a straight line.

c Lines AB and CE are perpendicular. Plot and write down possible coordinates for point E. Join the points C and E to form a straight line.

Super fact!

The coordinate system with x- and y-axes we use today is called Cartesian. It was developed by Descartes in 1637.

5 Write down the coordinates of the point halfway between

a (3, 2) and (9, 2) **b** (−3, −5) and (7, −5).

6 The line BD is a diagonal of the square $ABCD$.

a Draw a grid with x- and y-axes from −6 to 6. Plot and join the points B(−3, 2) and D(5, 2).

b Find the mid-point of the line BD.

c Use this to help you draw in the other diagonal of the square.

d Write down the coordinates of A and C.

7 The line $x = 3$ is a line of symmetry of a kite. The kite is 6 units high. Two of its vertices are at (2, 4) and (3, −1).

a Draw a diagram of the kite.

b Work out the coordinates of the other two vertices.

Now try this!

A Start plotting

Work in pairs. Secretly plot a quadrilateral on a coordinate grid. Tell your partner the name of your quadrilateral and the coordinates of **three** vertices. They need to work out the missing coordinates. Swap roles and repeat.

B Square up

Draw a square on a coordinate grid, with the origin inside it. The vertices of the square should be at whole-number coordinates.
Now draw a tilted square inside it. Its vertices should touch the sides of the outer square.
How far is each vertex of the tilted square from the nearest vertex of the upright square?
Write down the coordinates of the eight vertices and mix them up.
Swap coordinates with a partner and draw each other's squares. Do your drawings match the originals? If not, why not?

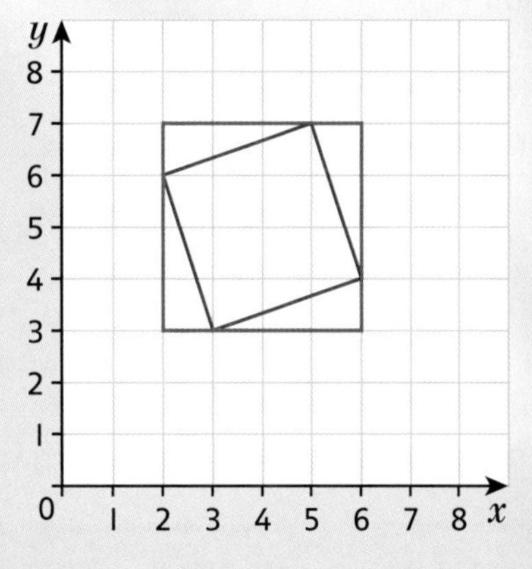

vertices x-axis y-axis

Go cross-country

You are going to use a coordinate grid to plan a cross-country course.

1 Copy this cooordinate grid showing the trees A and B, the start and the patch of nettles.

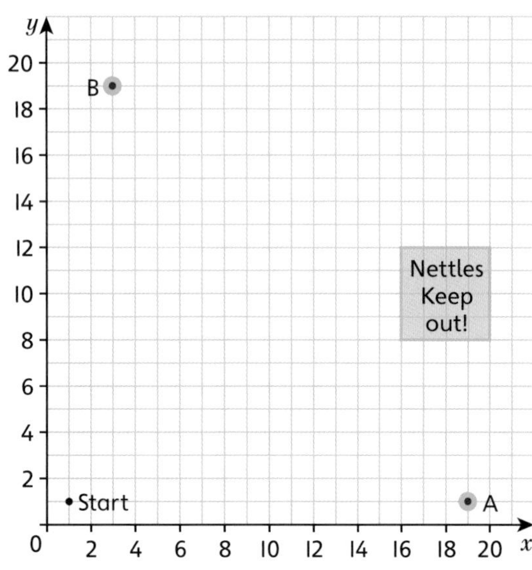

Add trees at the following points:
tree C at (10, 18)
tree D at (4, 8)
tree E at (13, 7)
tree F at (18, 14). **Level 4**

2 The route

start → tree A → tree C → start

makes an isosceles triangle.
What kind of triangle does this route make?

start → tree D → tree E → start **Level 4**

3 There is a rectangular lake.
Three of its vertices are at (11, 8), (14, 10) and (10, 16).
Add these points to your diagram.
Where is the other vertex? Colour the lake blue. **Level 4**

4 The finish is at (18, 18). Mark this on your grid. **Level 4**

5 Work out a route from the start to the finish so the competitors touch each tree once.
They have to run in straight lines.
They can only change direction when they reach a tree. **Level 5**

The BIG ideas

- The different types of triangle are
  scalene – sides all different
  isosceles – two equal sides, two equal angles
  equilateral – sides all equal, angles all 60°. Level 3
- A **rectangle** has two pairs of equal sides and four angles of 90°. Level 3
- You can describe the position of a point with its **coordinates**. Level 3 & Level 4

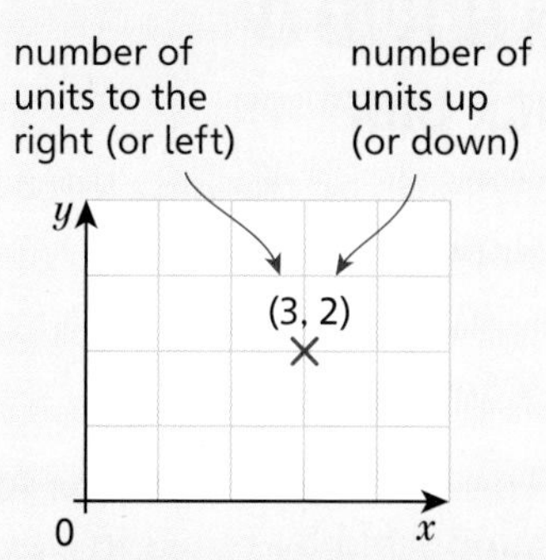

Find your level

Level 3

Q1

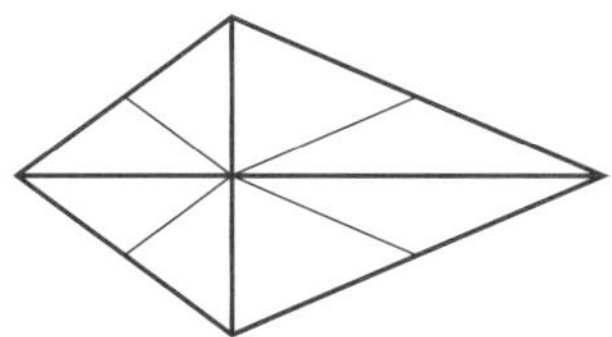

Copy the diagram. Colour in exactly one right-angled triangle.

Level 4

Q2 A is the point (6, 5).
The line AB is 3 units long.
Write down the coordinates of four possible positions for B.

Level 5

Q3

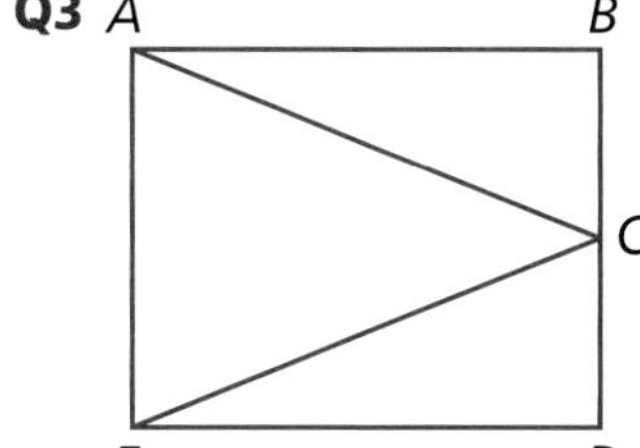

$ABDE$ is a rectangle.
$AC = CE$
$CED = 25°$

a Calculate the size of $\angle AEC$.
b Calculate $\angle ACE$.

Q4 The shaded shape is an isosceles triangle.

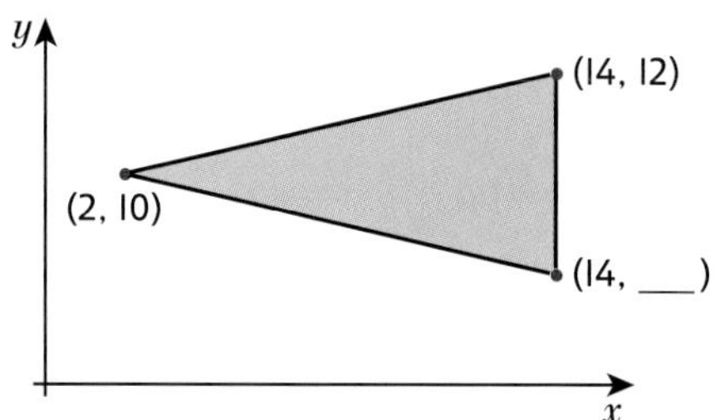

What is the missing coordinate?

Q5 These three shapes fit together at point B.

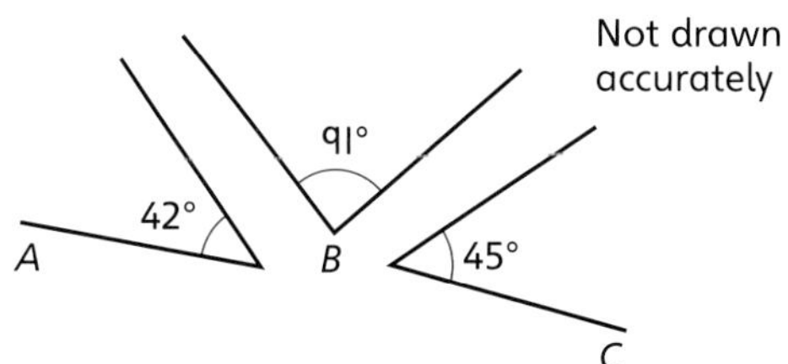

Will ABC make a straight line? Explain your answer.

Revision 1

Quick Quiz

Q1 Write down the next three terms in this sequence.

10, 7, 4, __, __, __

→ *See 1.3*

Q2 This bar chart shows the football teams supported by pupils in David's class.

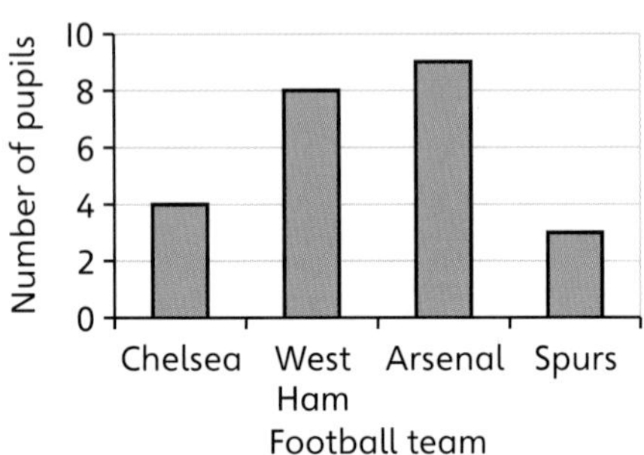

How many pupils support Arsenal?

→ *See 5.2*

Q3 Write down the coordinates of A and B.

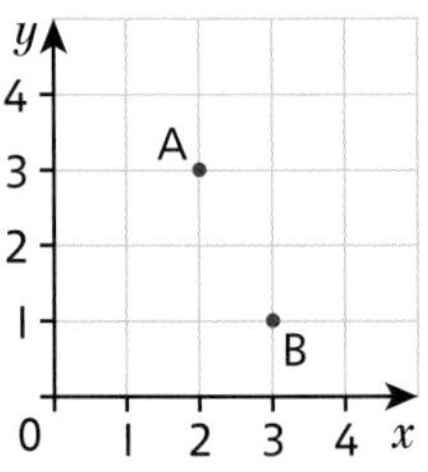

→ *See 7.3*

Q4 Megan cycles to work and back 5 days a week.
The distance from her home to work is 6 miles.
She works 45 weeks a year.
How far does she cycle to work and back in one year?

→ *See 2.6*

Q5 Work out

a $4^2 + 3 \times 2$ **b** $25 \div (9 - 4)$

→ *See 6.2*

Q6 Work out

a 10% of £48 **b** 5% of £48

c 15% of £48

→ *See 4.5*

Q7 A rectangle has an area of 18 cm^2.
The length of the rectangle is 6 cm.
What is the width of the rectangle?

→ *See 3.4*

Q8 Write these fractions in order from smallest to biggest.

$\frac{3}{4}, \frac{1}{8}, \frac{1}{2}, \frac{3}{8}$

→ *See 4.2*

Q9 An ordinary dice is rolled.
Work out the probability of rolling

a a number greater than 4 **b** not a 6

→ *See 5.5*

Activity

You are planning a winter weekend break to a city in Europe.

Q1 On an airplane the maximum length of hand luggage is 56 cm.

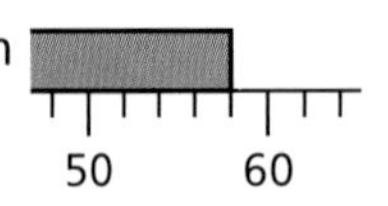

a What is the length shown on this tape measure?

b Would a bag this length be allowed on the airplane as hand luggage?

Q2 The bar chart opposite shows how people rate Barcelona as a weekend break destination.
How many people thought Barcelona was good?

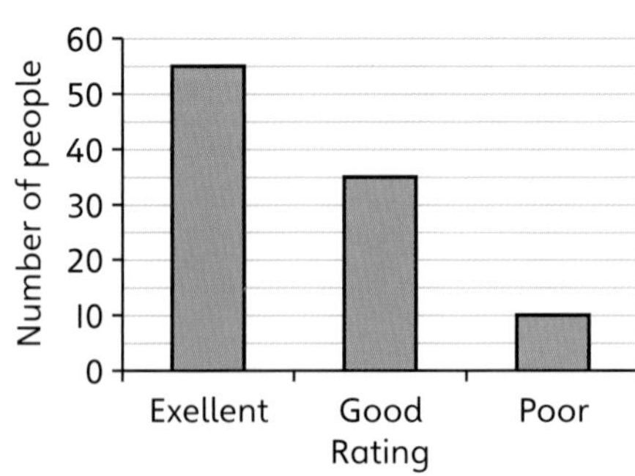

Q3 This table shows the night time temperatures, in January, of five cities.

Barcelona	Prague	Berlin	Rome	Bucharest
4°C	−4°C	−3°C	3°C	−5°C

Write the temperatures in order starting with the coldest.

Q4 The formula to roughly convert pounds (£) into euros (€) is

number of euros = number of pounds × 1.5

Work out how many euros you get for £120.

Q5 This is an advert for holiday insurance.

Insurance
single trip £18
multi-trip £65
buy online and save 10%

a How much will you save if you buy the single trip insurance online?

b How much will the insurance cost?

Q6 This 5-day weather forecast shows the maximum daytime temperature in Barcelona.

Thurs	Fri	Sat	Sun	Mon
12°C	11°C	15°C	14°C	13°C

Work out the mean temperature for the 5 days.

Q7 The price shown for Barcelona is £276. How much does the holiday cost if you book now?

Book Now!
SAVE
$\frac{1}{3}$
on all prices shown

Find your level

Level 3

Q1 A sequence of numbers decreases by 2 each time.
Write the missing numbers in the sequence below.

5 → 3 → □ → □ → □

You can use the number line to help you.

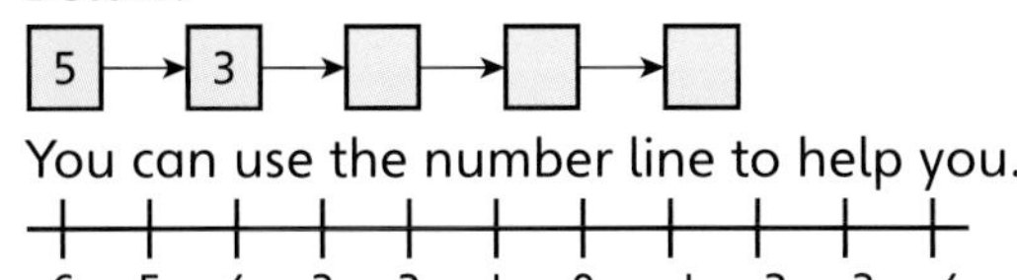

Q2 Look at the graph.

a Write down the coordinates of the points A and B.

b Point D can be plotted so that ABCD is a square.
Copy the graph and plot point D on the graph.

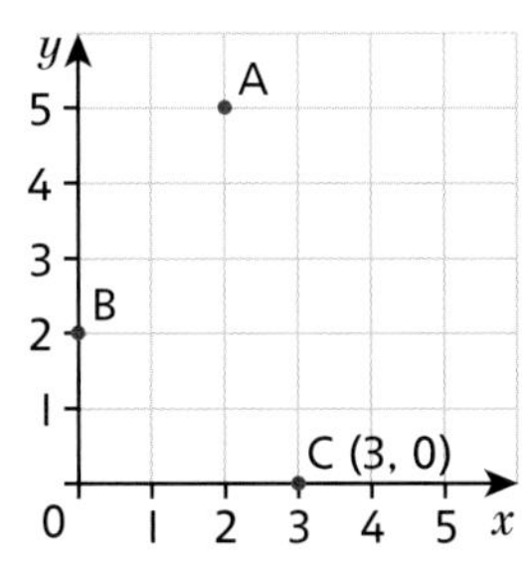

Level 4

Q3 Here is some information about Peter's job.

Peter gets paid £6 per hour.
Peter works 12 hours per day.
Peter works 4 days per week.

Use the information to match each question with the correct calculation.

How much does Peter earn per day?	12 × 6 × 4
	12 + 6
How many hours does Peter work per week?	12 × 6
	12 + 6 + 4
How much does Peter earn per week?	12 × 4

Q4 Write down the missing numbers in the boxes.

a 3 × □ + 5 = 50 **b** 3 × 5 + □ = 50

c □ × 5 − 10 = 50

Level 5

Q5 Here are four fractions.

$\frac{1}{3}$ $\frac{5}{6}$ $\frac{3}{4}$ $\frac{5}{12}$

Copy the number line below.
Write each fraction in the correct box.

Q6 A rectangle has an area of 36 cm^2.
How long could the sides of the rectangle be?
Give three different examples.

____ cm by ____ cm
____ cm by ____ cm
____ cm by ____ cm

8 Get the facts

This unit is about collecting data and displaying it in graphs and charts.

RSPB stands for the Royal Society for the Protection of Birds. It is the largest conservation organisation in Europe, with over 200 nature reserves in the UK. Mark Eaton is a scientist who works for the RSPB:

'We get very useful data from the thousands of people who take part in projects like Big Garden Birdwatch and Big Schools' Birdwatch. These are always done at the same time of year, to make the results reliable. January is best – that's when our gardens and schools can be a vital source of food for hungry birds.

'Everyone is asked to count in the same way: for one hour only and counting the most of each type of bird seen at any one time during that hour.

'As well as counting, we also measure birds. We weigh them and measure the size of certain body parts, like the bill, wing and leg lengths. Before we let them go, we put rings round the birds' legs so we can recognise them if we catch the same birds again.'

Activities

A Bhavna is a keen birdwatcher. Every year she counts the birds in her garden in one hour on February 1st. Here are her results since 1985, for blue tits and sparrows.

Year	Blue tit	House sparrow	Year	Blue tit	House sparrow
1985	2	11	1997	5	4
1986	4	12	1998	2	3
1987	1	8	1999	4	5
1988	didn't count	didn't count	2000	5	4
1989	3	7	2001	3	4
1990	2	8	2002	3	4
1991	3	6	2003	5	2
1992	5	5	2004	4	5
1993	2	4	2005	6	2
1994	2	3	2006	7	4
1995	4	4	2007	5	1
1996	3	5			

What do these figures suggest about the numbers of blue tits and sparrows in the area over the years? Which bird is doing well, and which might need help?

B Count the numbers of birds you can see from the window of your classroom over a period of ten minutes. Record your results clearly.

Before you start this unit...

A group of people were asked which of four countries they preferred as a holiday destination.

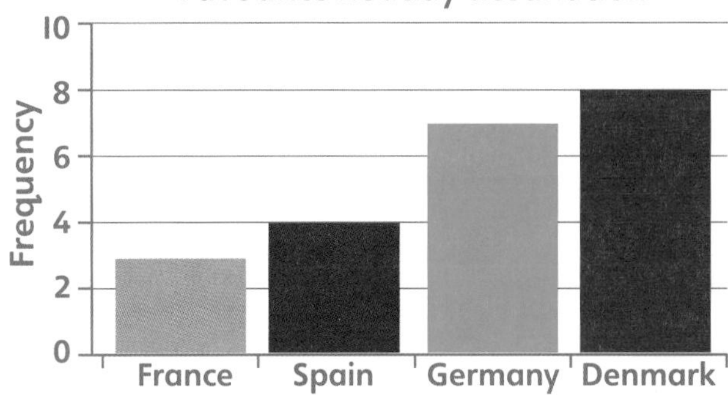

1 Which is the favourite holiday destination?

page 72

2 How many people said that Germany was their favourite holiday destination?

page 72

3 How many people took part in the survey?

page 72

Did you know?
Birds are more active in the morning, so they are more noticeable then and it is easier to count them. Surveys aim to count as many birds as possible to get the best data.

Plus digital resources

8.1 Planning data collection

- Decide what data would be relevant to an enquiry and possible sources
- Plan how to collect and organise small sets of data
- Select a suitable level of accuracy of data
- Select the sample size to use when collecting data
- Design a question for a questionnaire

Why learn this?

Planning to collect data properly will help to provide the information you want.

What's the BIG idea?

- **Data** is collected from different **sources** to answer questions or solve problems. **Level 4**
- To answer a question or solve a problem you need to decide what data is needed. **Level 5**
- It is important to identify which groups of people need to be included in a **survey**. **Level 5**
- Sample sizes need to be large enough to be **representative** but small enough to make it **practical** to collect the data. **Level 5**

Super fact!

A population census has been carried out in the UK every 10 years since 1801 apart from in 1941 (because of the Second World War).

Practice, practice, practice!

Level 4

4a I can identify sources of data

1 Where would you get data to help answer these questions?

a Which country has the largest population?

b What is the largest number of people to fit into a Mini?

c Who uses the local supermarket?

d How many cars use the road outside the school?

Level 5

5c I can select the correct units when planning an experiment or survey

2 Select the most appropriate units to use when collecting this data.

the time it takes to get to school — *minutes*

a the handspan of Year 9 pupils

b the weight of six-month-old babies

c the distance teachers live from school

5c I can decide what data is needed and where to get it

3 Peter wants to find which drinks teachers in his school prefer. He only asks maths teachers. Will his survey provide fair information?

Hint: Think about the sample size and the sample.

data database experiment frequency

4 How could you collect this data?

the favourite colour of your class — *A survey of classmates to ask their favourite colour.*

a the number of times a 6 shows when you roll a dice 60 times
b the number of runs scored by England last season in Test matches
c the number of times tails shows when you flip a coin five times
d the favourite sport of people in a town

Level 5

5b I can plan how to collect data

5 A teacher is organising a Year 9 outdoor activity day.
She wants to estimate which outdoor activity is the most popular.
If there are 150 pupils in the year group, how many pupils should she ask?

A 5 B 25 C 70 D 200

5b I can identify the most sensible sample size when given choices

6 In a survey, which units would you use to measure
a the length of time you can hold your breath underwater
b the length of time you sleep at night
c the time you spend travelling to school
d your absences from school in one year
e your age

seconds years hours days months minutes

5b I can select a suitable level of accuracy when given choices

7 **a** How many times should you carry out an experiment to test whether a dice is fair or not?
b How many pupils should you ask in a survey to find the modal shoe size of pupils in your school?

5a I can identify a suitable sample size

8 Write suitable questions for a survey to find out this information and choose the accuracy with which the answers are required.

the length of time pupils spend on homework each week

How much time do you spend on your homework each week? — *To the nearest half an hour.*

a the time teachers arrive at school each day
b how much water pupils drink each day
c the time people get up in the morning

5a I can plan a question and select a suitable level of accuracy

Now try this!

A Planning an experiment

Carry out an experiment to find out how many times you get a picture card when you cut a pack of cards 100 times.

B Planning a survey

Think of a problem you would like to solve or a question you would like to ask.
Write
- what you are going to ask
- who you are going to ask
- the sample size (how many times you will do the experiment or activity)
- what equipment, if any, you will need.

Watch out!

Don't just ask your friends when you carry out a survey, ask other people as well.

questionnaire source survey

8.2 Collecting data

- Design a data collection sheet
- Construct frequency tables for discrete data
- Construct a grouped frequency table for discrete data
- Construct a simple frequency table for continuous data

Why learn this?

If you know how much the bike you want costs in different places, you can decide where to buy it.

What's the BIG idea?

- → A **data collection sheet** is a good way to organise data as you collect it. **Level 4**
- → A **tally chart** can be used to collect and organise data.
  It is a way of showing **frequency** – 𝍸 means 5. **Level 4**
- → When there is a lot of data you can use grouped **intervals**.
  The intervals must all be the same size.
  How many portions of fruit or vegetables do you eat each day?
  0–1 2–3 4–5 6–7 8–9
  How many days was your last holiday?
  1–3 4–6 7–9 10–12 13–15 **Level 5**
- → Data you can count is called **discrete** data, for example the number of people in a car. **Level 5**
- → Data you measure is called **continuous** data, for example the height of pupils. **Level 5**

Super fact!

Chinese, Korean and Japanese tally marks use the five strokes of 正, which is the character meaning 'correct', 'proper' and 'honesty'.

Practice, practice, practice!

Level 4

4a I can record data in a tally chart

1 Copy and complete the tally chart.

Favourite colour	Tally	Frequency
Red		19
Blue		12
Green	𝍸	
Yellow	𝍸 𝍸 ||	
Black		7
White		3

2 A school netball team played 20 matches last year. Here are the results.

3–0 0–0 4–1 2–3 3–2 0–1 3–2 3–1 3–2 2–0
5–2 7–0 2–1 4–0 4–5 4–2 0–1 6–1 3–1 2–2

Copy and complete the tally chart.

Home team goals	Tally	Frequency
0		
1		
2		
3	𝍸 |	6
4		
5		
6		
7		

continuous data collection sheet discrete

3 This list shows 25 pupils' favourite fruit.
Record the data in a frequency table.

apple	apple	orange	peach	melon
orange	grape	apple	pear	apple
plum	apple	orange	apple	pear
melon	orange	apple	apple	apple
pear	orange	peach	peach	apple

4 Roll a dice and record the number on the top face.
Repeat 60 times. Record the results in a frequency table.

Level 4

4a I can construct a frequency table for discrete data

5 Construct a grouped frequency table to show from a survey how many different vegetables and fruit people eat in a week.

Hint: Make sure your groups have no gaps or overlaps. Start with 0–2.

6 Construct grouped frequency tables for these data.

a number of cars passing the school in different lessons of the day

b the age in years of members of your family

c the length of words in a newspaper

Watch out!

When preparing to collect data in grouped intervals ensure that each interval is the same size.

7 Measure the height of 50 pupils. Record the results in a grouped frequency table with equal class intervals.

8 Use either 'discrete' or 'continuous' to describe these types of data.

a the length of a plank of wood

b the number of people who live in a house

c the number of spectators at a football match

d the weight of a bag of potatoes

e the number of slices of bread in a loaf of bread

f the time taken to walk to the local shop

Level 5

5c I can group discrete data in equal class intervals

5a I can construct a frequency table for continuous data

5a I can identify discrete and continuous data

Now try this!

A Travel to school data

Collect data on how pupils in your year travel to school.
Use a tally chart like this:

Method of travel	Tally	Frequency
Car		
Bus		
Walk		
Cycle		
Other		

B Designing a data collection sheet

Design a data collection sheet to discover pupils' favourite television programmes. Survey pupils in your year and in a different year. Compare and comment on the two surveys.

frequency interval tally chart

8.3 Displaying data

- Construct and interpret pictograms
- Draw conclusions from pictograms and bar charts
- Construct and interpret bar charts for discrete data

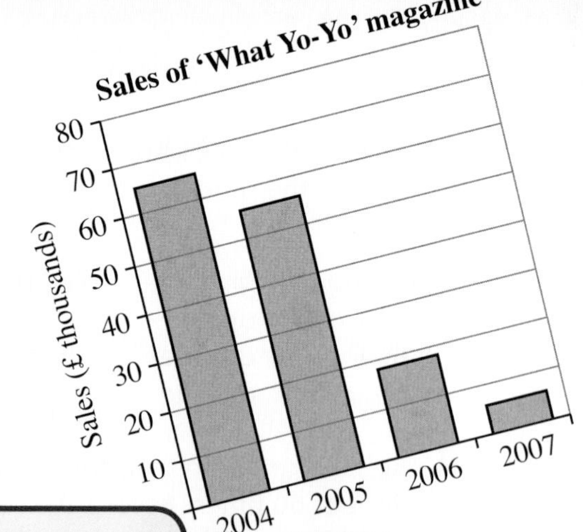

→ A **pictogram** uses pictures to represent data. When large amounts of data need to be represented, one symbol is used to represent more than one item of data. Level 3 & Level 4

→ A **bar chart** uses bars or blocks to show data. Level 3 & Level 4

Why learn this?

Diagrams make it easier to understand and draw conclusions from data.

Practice, practice, practice!

Level 3

3a I can extract and interpret information from pictograms

1 The pictogram shows how many DVDs were sold in a shop in one week.

a How many DVDs were sold on Monday?

b How many DVDs were sold on Wednesday?

c How many DVDs were sold on Saturday?

d On which day did the shop sell the most DVDs?

e On which day did the shop sell the least DVDs?

f How many DVDs were sold in total that week?

Day	DVDs sold
Monday	
Tuesday	
Wednesday	
Thursday	
Friday	
Saturday	
Sunday	

Key: (DVD symbol) represents four DVDs.

3a I can read and interpret information from a bar chart

2 The bar chart shows the number of emails Angus received one week.

a How many emails did he receive on Tuesday?

b On which day did he receive the most emails?

c How many emails did he receive in total that week?

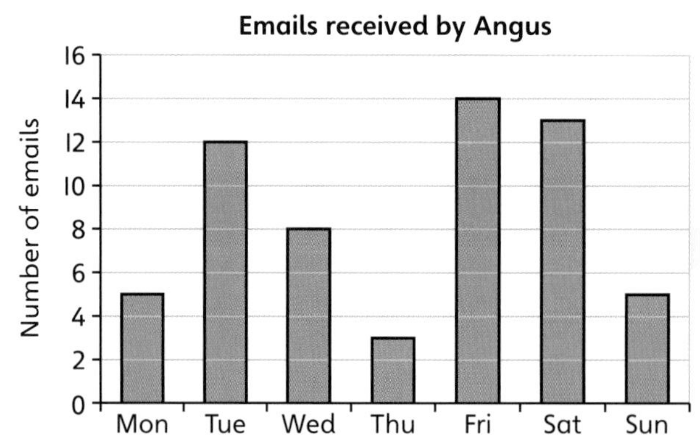

3a 4c I can draw a bar chart

3 This table shows the number of fruit trees in an orchard. Draw a bar chart to show this data.

Fruit tree	Apple	Pear	Cherry	Plum	Crab apple
Number	10	8	6	5	2

4 This table shows how many pupils had school meals one week. Draw a bar chart to show this data. Choose a suitable scale for the vertical axis.

Day	Mon	Tue	Wed	Thur	Fri
Number	25	15	40	35	30

bar chart interpret

5 Mrs Vits sells horses. The pictogram shows how many she sold from 2003 to 2006.

Year	Horses sold
2003	U U
2004	U U (
2005	U U U (
2006	U U U U
2007	

Key: U represents two horses.

a How many horses did she sell in 2003?

b She sold five horses in 2004.
What does (represent?

c How many horses did she sell in 2005?

d She sold 11 horses in 2007.
Copy and complete the pictogram.

e What can you say about the number of horses she sold between 2003 and 2007?

Level 4

4b I can draw conclusions and interpret pictograms

6 People were asked how many holidays they had been on in the last year.

Holidays	0	1	2	3	4
Frequency	2	8	9	4	2

a How many people answered the question in total?

b How many people had three holidays in the last year?

c How many people had one or two holidays in the last year?

4b I can read and interpret information from a frequency table

7 **a** Choose five bands or solo artists. Ask 20 of your classmates which of them they like the most. **Hint:** You will need some way of recording this data!

b Draw a bar chart to show the results of your survey.

c Comment on your results.

4b I can display results in a bar chart and draw conclusions

8 Justin rolled two dice 60 times and found the total each time. His results were:

8	7	6	6	7	9	11	4	9	6
7	7	5	9	12	7	8	6	3	7
7	12	8	8	7	3	6	10	2	8
6	2	10	5	4	3	10	11	4	5
11	6	5	9	7	7	9	10	5	8
8	7	7	10	8	6	11	8	7	5

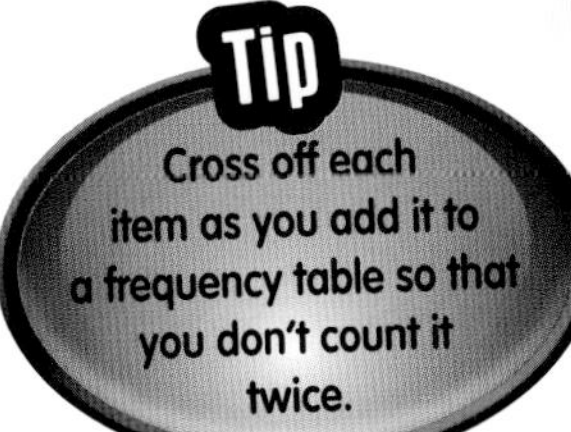

Record the data in a frequency table.

4a I can record data in a frequency table

Now try this!

A Text messages

Ask 5 people how many text messages they sent yesterday.
Draw a pictogram to show the results.
Use ✉ to represent 2 messages

B Dice rolling

Roll two dice 60 times. Record the total each time in a frequency table. Draw a bar chart to show the results. Compare your results with Justin's in Q8.

Watch out!
When you draw a bar chart showing discrete data there should be a gap between each of the bars.

interval pictogram

8.4 Bar charts

- Construct and interpret bar-line graphs
- Construct and interpret compound bar charts
- Construct and interpret dual bar charts

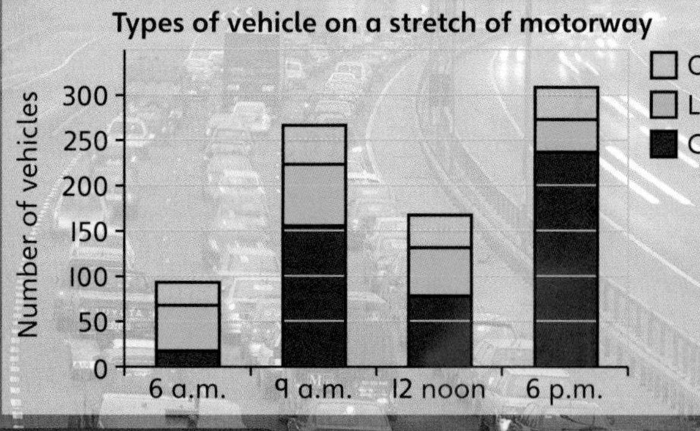

- A **bar-line graph** is similar to a bar chart, but lines are used instead of bars. **Level 4**
- A **compound bar chart** combines different sets of data in one bar. **Level 5**
- A **dual bar chart** is used to compare two sets of data. **Level 5**

Why learn this?

Choosing the right kind of data display can make information available at a glance.

Practice, practice, practice!

Level 4

4b I can interpret bar-line graphs

1 This bar-line graph shows the results of a survey about favourite British cities.

a How many people said Exeter was their favourite city?

b How many more people said Edinburgh was their favourite city than London?

c How many people were included in the survey?

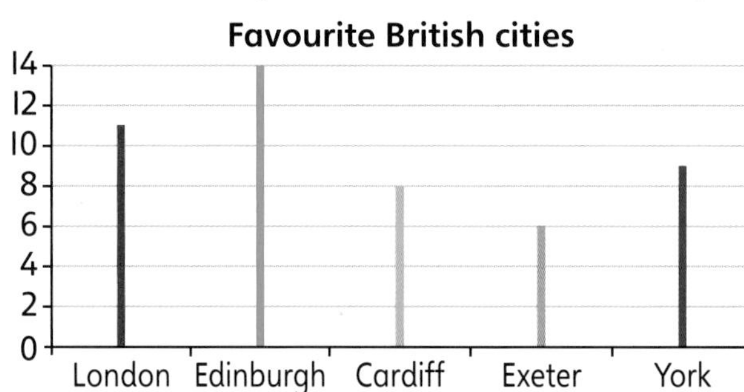

4b I can draw and interpret bar-line graphs

2 The table shows the numbers of goals scored in hockey matches one Sunday.

Number of goals	0	1	2	3	4	5	6	7
Number of matches	5	9	14	11	8	4	3	1

a Draw a bar-line graph to display this data.

b What is the most common number of goals scored? **Hint:** This is the mode.

c In how many matches were three or more goals scored?

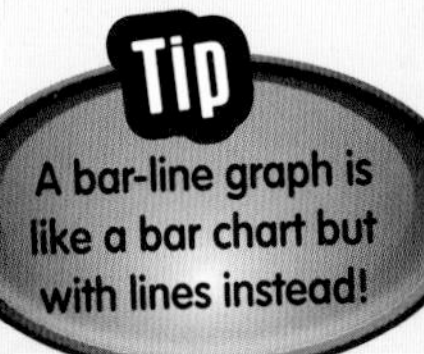

Level 5

5b I can draw and interpret compound bar charts

3 The table shows medals won by five countries at an Olympic Games.

	UK	USA	China	Germany	Russia
Gold	3	15	12	6	8
Silver	2	23	10	0	17
Bronze	6	14	0	5	18

a Draw a compound bar chart to show the different medals won by each country.

b Which country won the most medals?

c Which country won the fewest medals?

d How many gold medals were won?

e How many bronze medals were won?

bar-line graph compound bar chart

4 This dual bar graph shows the sales of five different books online and in a bookshop during a week.

a Which book sold more copies in the bookshop than online?

b How many copies of Book 2 were sold in total?

c How many more copies of Book 1 were sold online than in the bookshop?

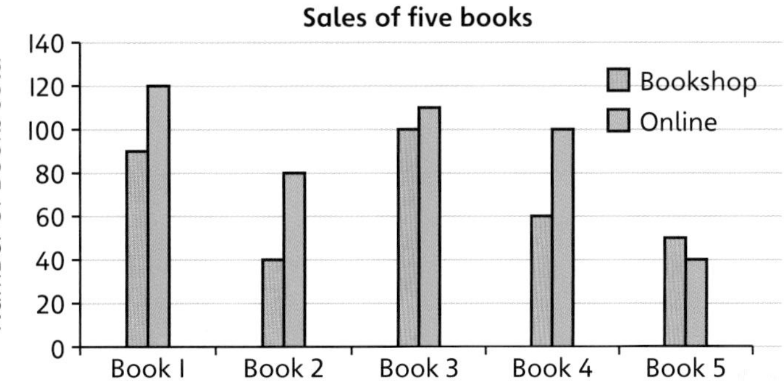

Level 5

5b I can interpret dual bar charts

Watch out!

When interpreting dual and compound bar charts use the key to make sure you look at the correct bar(s).

5 The table shows the absences in two classes during a one-week period.

Day	Mon	Tue	Wed	Thu	Fri
Class 7A	5	6	10	12	15
Class 7B	2	3	5	8	13

a Draw a dual bar chart to show the data.

b On which day were there the most absences for Class 7A and for Class 7B?

c How many absences were there for each class that week?

d Use the table and dual bar chart to write two sentences comparing the absences of the two classes.

e What do you notice about the absences of Class 7A and Class 7B?

f What do you think may have caused the pattern of absences?

5b I can draw and interpret dual bar charts

6 The table shows the average maximum and minimum temperatures in London.

	Jan	Feb	Mar	Apr	May	Jun	Jul	Aug	Sep	Oct	Nov	Dec
Max	6	7	10	13	17	20	22	21	19	14	10	7
Min	2	2	3	6	8	12	14	13	11	8	5	4

a Draw a dual bar chart to show this data.

b In which month was there the greatest difference between the maximum and minimum temperatures?

c Write two things you notice when you compare the two sets of data.

Now try this!

A Constructing charts

Use an ICT package to construct the charts in Q2–7.

B Freetime chart

Ask 10 boys and 10 girls how many hours they spend on these activities at the weekend.
Draw a dual bar chart to show the result.

watching TV

shopping

sport

computer games

sleep

dual bar chart

8.5 Pie charts

- Interpret pie charts
- Construct pie charts using ICT

What's the BIG idea?

- A **pie chart** is a way of displaying data to show how something is shared or divided. Level 4 & Level 5
- Pie charts are circles divided into **sectors**. Level 5
- The size of the angle in each sector represents the **frequency**. Level 5
- The largest sector shows the category with the highest frequency and the smallest sector shows the category with the lowest frequency. Level 5

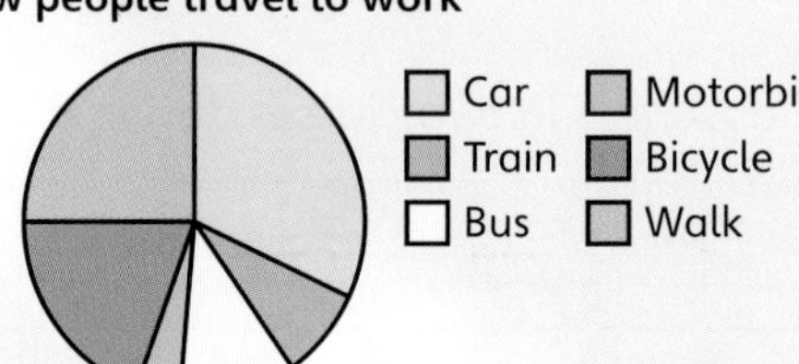

Why learn this?

Pie charts are a good way to show the proportions of different categories of data

Super fact!

Pie charts were invented by Florence Nightingale during the Crimean War. She used them to support her argument that more soldiers were dying from disease than in the battle itself.

Practice, practice, practice!

Level 4

4a I can interpret a simple pie chart

1 The pie chart shows the favourite colours of 40 pupils.

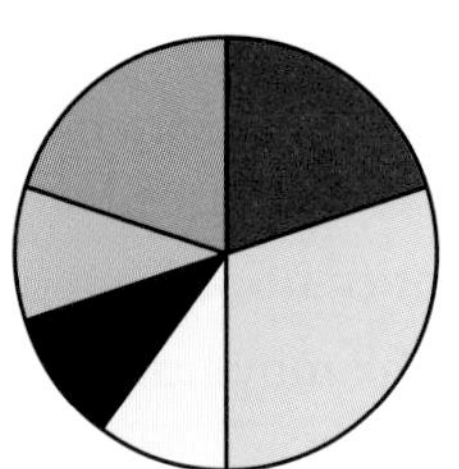

a What is the most popular colour?

b What percentage chose black?

c What percentage chose red?

d How many people chose blue?

Level 5

5c I can interpret pie charts

2 Jasmine surveyed each of her classmates to find out which is their favourite lesson. She drew a pie chart of her results.

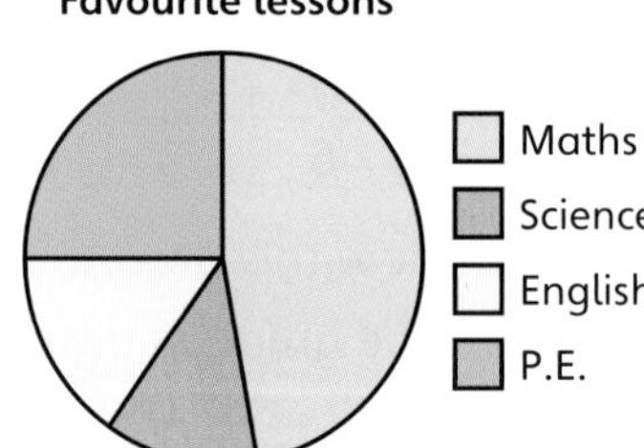

a What is their most popular lesson?

b What is their least favourite lesson?

3 The pie chart shows the number of emails Pritam received last week.

a On Friday Pritam received three emails. Measure the angles using a protractor. Use this information to copy and complete the table.

Day	Angle	Number of emails
Monday		
Tuesday		
Wednesday		
Thursday		
Friday		

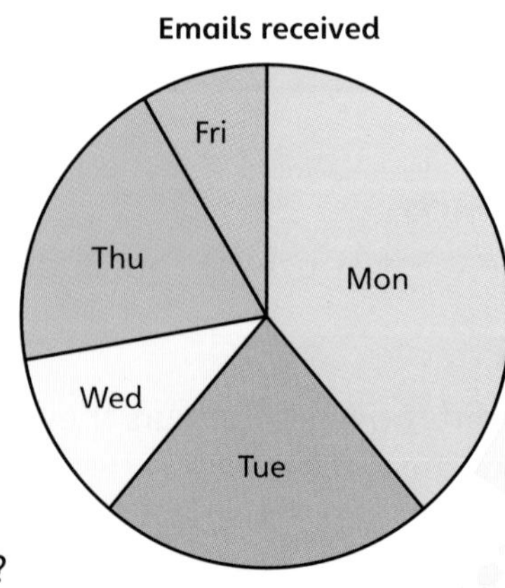

b What is the total number of emails he received?

frequency interpret pie chart

4 These two pie charts show how Alice and Amy spend their money each week.

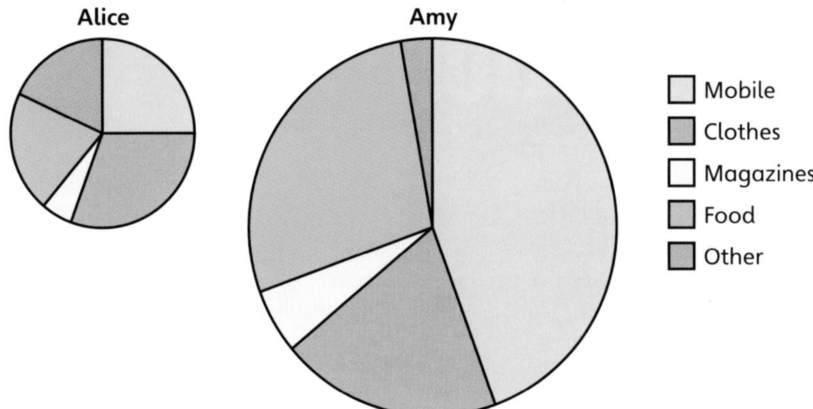

a Who spends the largest fraction of their income on their mobile? Explain your answer.

b Amy says, 'I have more money to spend than Alice each week'. Explain why Amy may be wrong.

c Describe their spending on magazines, food and clothes. Explain each answer.

Level 5

5c I can compare and contrast pie charts

5 The table shows the number of different types of cars in a car park. Use ICT to draw a pie chart for this data.

5a I can use ICT to construct pie charts

Car make	Number
Ford	18
Vauxhall	12
Nissan	10
Toyota	5
BMW	3
Other	12

6 This table shows the numbers of books bought by 180 people in a month. Use ICT to draw a pie chart for this data.

Number of books	0	1	2	3	4	5	6 or more
Frequency	30	51	16	24	36	10	13

Now try this!

A Favourite subject

Ask 30 people 'What is your favourite subject at school'.
Put the information you've collected into a table.
Draw a percentage pie chart to show your results.

B Constructing charts

Do a survey of your friends' favourite bands. Include at least 30 people.
Use ICT to draw a pie chart.
Compare your pie chart with a classmate's and explain any differences.

sector survey

maths!

Insect inspection

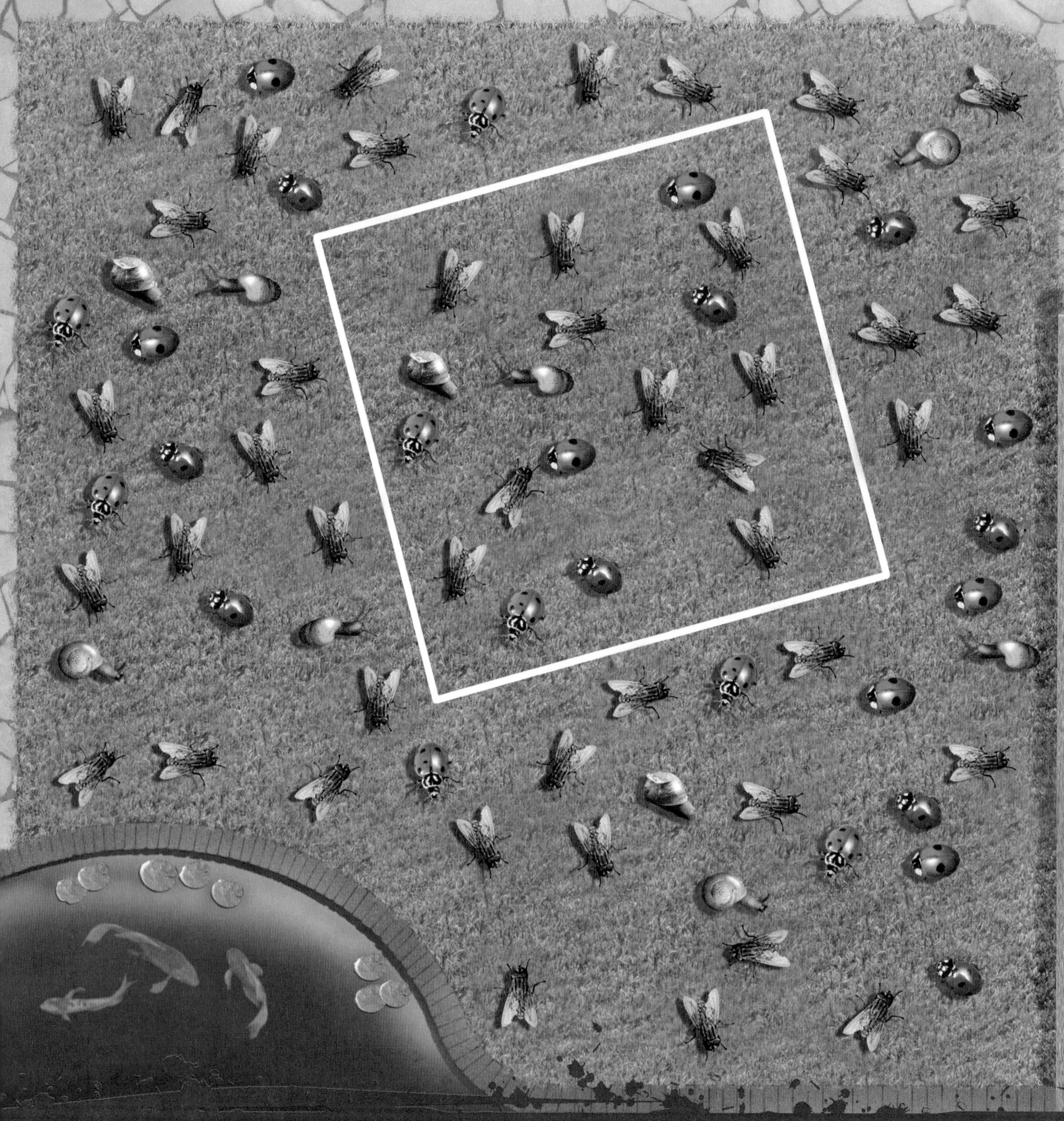

There are creatures all over Mrs Henstridge's lawn!

To work out which species is most common, you can use a quadrat. A quadrat is a square frame which is placed on the ground to surround a sample of the whole population. You simply count the creatures inside it.

- Copy and complete this table.

Species	Fly	Ladybird	Snail
Frequency			

- Use ICT to draw a pie chart of your findings.

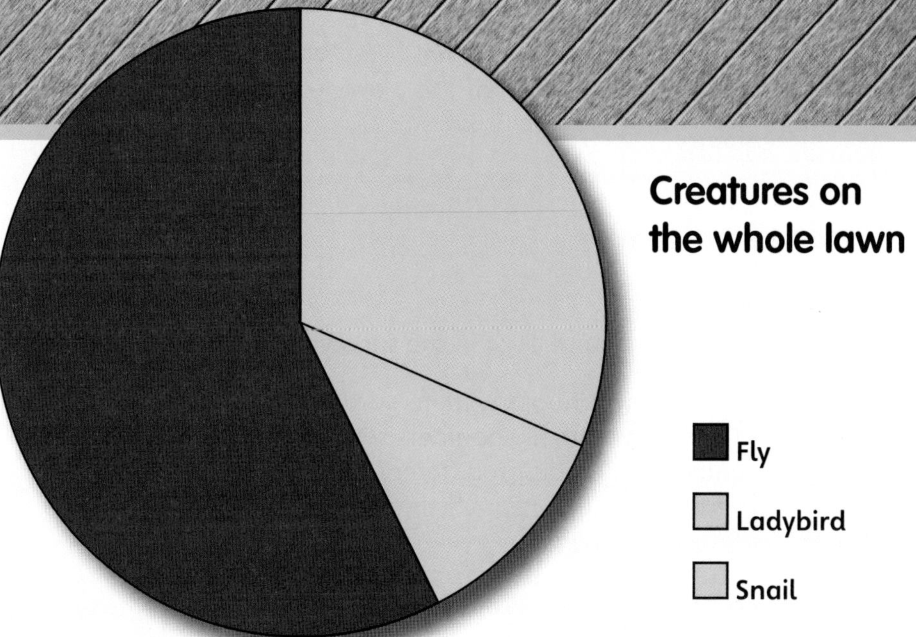

Compare your pie chart with the pie chart for creatures on the whole lawn.

- Did you find similar proportions of creatures?
- Do you think this is a good method of exploring the numbers of creatures?
- Why shouldn't you use this method to estimate the number of fish in the pond?

School wildlife count

At the end of the summer term, pupils at Green School collected information on wildlife around the school.

1 Ruhi and Crystal counted numbers of birds. They counted from 9am to 10am one morning. The pictogram shows some of their results.

Seagulls	⌒⌒ ⌒⌒ ⌒
Pigeons	⌒⌒ ⌒⌒
Crows	⌒⌒
Sparrows	⌒⌒ ⌒⌒
Woodpeckers	⌒

⌒⌒ 2 birds
⌒ 1 birds

a How many woodpeckers did they see? **Level 3**
b Which bird did they see most of? **Level 3**
c How many birds did they see in total? **Level 3**
d They also counted 6 blue tits and 2 blackbirds. Draw two rows for the pictogram to show this data. **Level 4**

MAKE MATHS FUNCTIONAL!

2 Tristan and Michelle recorded the birds they saw at lunchtime. Back in the classroom they designed a frequency chart for this data.

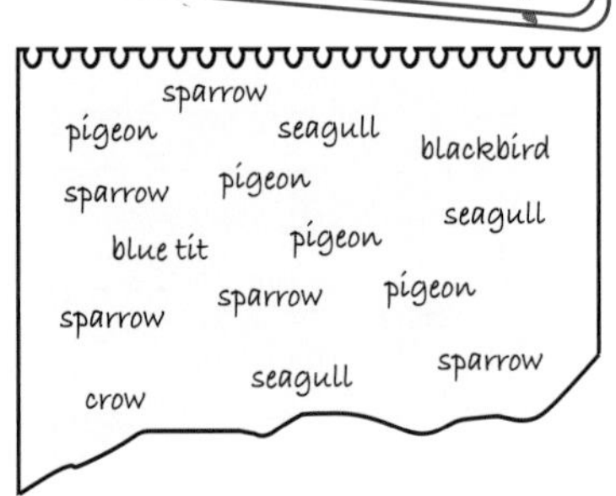

Bird	Tally	Frequency

a Copy and complete the chart for their data.
b Which bird did they see most of?
c Which did they see least of?
d Are these the same birds there were most and least of in the survey in **Q1**? **Level 4**

3 Ashok and Layla investigated the plants in the school's wildlife garden. They each used a square measuring 1 metre by 1 metre. They threw it over their shoulders so it landed randomly in the middle of the rough patch. They counted the number of different plants in the squares.

Ashok's results

Plant	Frequency
daisy	15
dandelion	8
nettle	7
plantain	4
dock	0

Layla's results

Plant	Frequency
daisy	12
dandelion	5
nettle	8
plantain	0
dock	2

a Draw a dual bar chart to show these results.
b Which plant were there most of in total?
c Whose square-metre area had the most plants? **Level 5**

4 The pie chart shows the different butterflies counted during one hour in the wildlife garden.

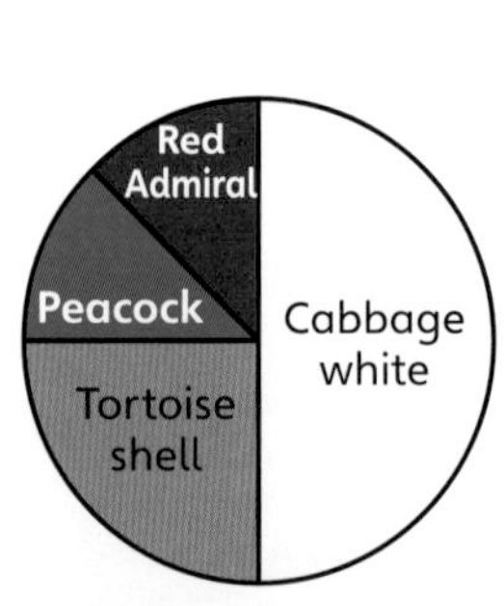

a Which was the most common type of butterfly?
b What fraction of the total were tortoiseshell butterflies?
c 24 butterflies were counted in total. Create a frequency table to show the number of each type. **Level 5**

The BIG ideas

- → A **pictogram** uses pictures to represent data. When large amounts of data need to be represented, one symbol is used to represent more than one item of data. Level 3
- → A **data collection sheet** is a good way to organise data as you collect it. Level 4
- → A **bar chart** uses bars or blocks to show data. Level 4
- → A **dual bar chart** is used to compare two sets of data. Level 5
- → In a **pie chart**, the number of degrees in each sector represents the **frequency**. Level 5
- → The largest sector shows the category with the highest frequency and the smallest sector shows the category with the lowest frequency. Level 5

Find your level

Level 3

Q1 Raj asked 40 pupils if they walk to school.

30 said yes.

10 said no.

He started to draw a pictogram using • to represent 5 pupils.

Copy and complete Raj's pictogram.

Yes	••••••
No	

Level 4

Q2 The bar chart shows the numbers of pets owned by pupils in Mrs Hatton's class.

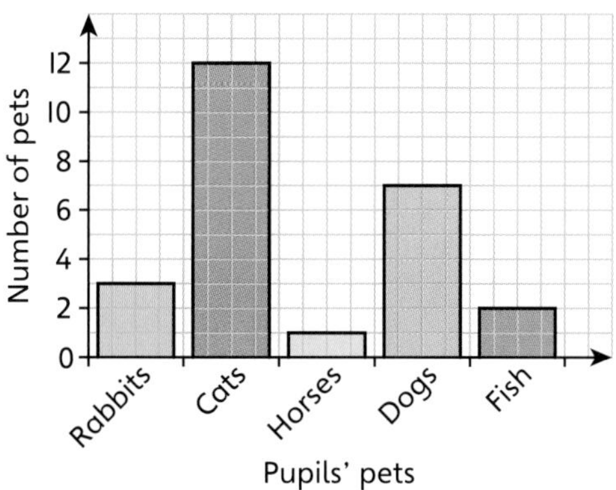

a How many horses are owned by pupils in the class?

b How many more dogs are there than rabbits?

c How many pets are owned by the class in total?

Q3 There are 26 pupils in Mr Payne's class. The bar-line graph shows how many pupils were present in the class on each day for one week.

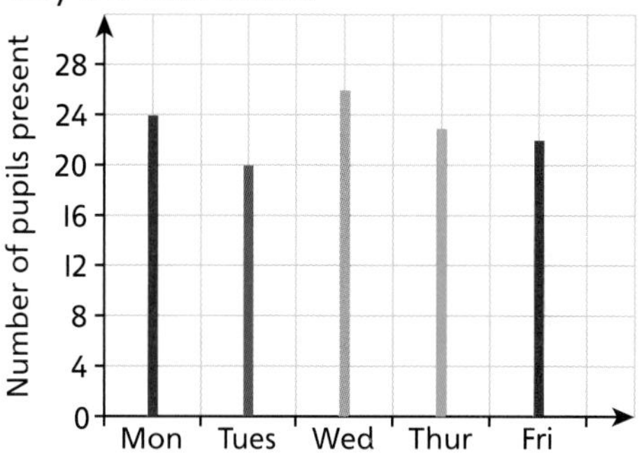

a How many pupils were present on Friday?

b How many pupils were present on Thursday?

c How many pupils were absent on Tuesday?

d How many absences were there in total during the week?

Level 5

Q4 The pie chart shows the distribution of the United Kingdom's population.

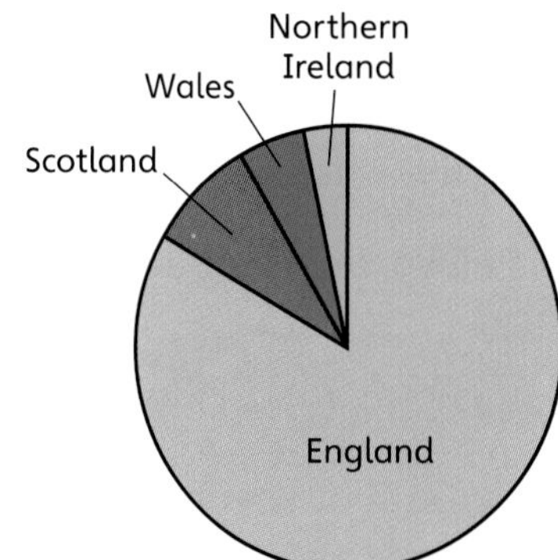

The total population of the United Kingdom is 60 million people.
Estimate the population of Scotland.
Show your method clearly.

9 Work it out

Different countries have different units of currency, for example in the UK we have pounds and pence, and in many EU countries they have euros and cents. These are both decimal systems of money.

Before 1971, the UK used a non-decimal system of money. There used to be 240 old pence in £1. There was a 12 pence coin called a shilling.

In the non-decimal system, you needed to know multiplication facts up to 12 × 12 to be able to do money calculations. With the decimal system you only need to know multiplication facts up to 10 × 10.

This unit explores different mental and written methods of calculation used on a day-to-day basis.

Activities

A Think of a country you would like to visit. Find out about its currency.

- What are the values of their coins and notes?
- What is £1 worth in your chosen country's currency?

B Investigate UK coins used before 1971.

- If there were 12 old pence in a shilling, how many shillings made £1? (Remember: there were 240 old pence in £1.)
- What other coins were there? How could these be used to make £1?

Did you know?
On the island of Yap in the western Pacific ocean, they once used coins made from stone. The value of a coin was determined by its size, and some coins were 4 m in diameter! The Yapese displayed the coins as status symbols. What are the advantages and disadvantages of such large coins?

Before you start this unit...

1 Give an example of something you might measure in

Level Up Maths 1-2 page 44

- **a** centimetres
- **b** grams
- **c** litres.

2 Double these numbers.

Level Up Maths 1-2 page 45

a 8 **b** 34 **c** 2.1

3 What is the value of the 4 in each of these numbers?

Level Up Maths 1-2 page 45

a 142 **b** 4672
c 9.45 **d** 304.5

Plus digital resources

9.1 Measures

- Recognise and use metric units of measure
- Read and interpret scales of measuring instruments
- Know how to convert between metric units
- Recognise imperial units of measure and know how to convert to metric units

Why learn this?

A space mission to Mars once failed because scientists mixed up metric and imperial units in their calculations.

What's the BIG idea?

- You can measure lengths using a ruler, tape measure or trundle wheel. The metric units of **length** are the **millimetre (mm)**, **centimetre (cm)**, **metre (m)** and **kilometre (km)**. **Level 4**
- You can use scales to weigh objects. The metric units of **mass** are the **gram (g)** and **kilogram (kg)**. **Level 4**
- **Capacity** is the amount of liquid a container will hold. You can use a measuring jug to find the capacity in **millilitres (m*l*)**, **centilitres (c*l*)** or **litres (*l*)**. **Level 4**
- Changing to a larger unit means fewer of them, so divide. **Level 5**
- Changing to a smaller unit means more of them, so multiply. **Level 5**
- The imperial units you need to recognise are:
  length: inch, foot, yard, **mile**
  mass: **ounce**, **pound**
  capacity: **pint**, **gallon** **Level 5**

Super fact!

The Anglo Saxons defined an inch as the length of three corns of barley.

Practice, practice, practice!

Level 4

1. Which metric units would you use to measure each of these?
   - **a** the height of a tree
   - **b** the capacity of a kettle
   - **c** the mass of a marble
   - **d** the length of an ant
   - **e** the mass of a bike
   - **f** the capacity of a teaspoon

4b I can choose suitable metric units

2. What equipment would you use to measure each of these?
   - **a** the length of your thumb
   - **b** the mass of an orange
   - **c** the height of a door
   - **d** the capacity of a vase

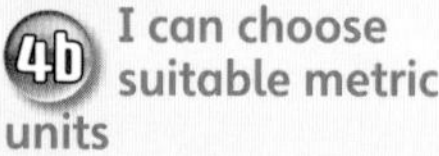

4b I can choose suitable measuring equipment

3. Rearrange the masses of these birds in order, smallest first.
   - A Haast's Eagle 10 kg
   - B Palm Cockatoo 900 g
   - C Tres Marias Amazon $\frac{1}{2}$ kg
   - D Blue and Gold Macaw 1 kg
   - E Barn Owl 300 g

4b I can order metric measures

capacity millilitre (m*l*) centilitre (c*l*) litre (*l*) pint gallon
length millimetre (mm) centimetre (cm)

Level 4

4a I can read and interpret scales

4 Write down the value shown on each of the scales.

a

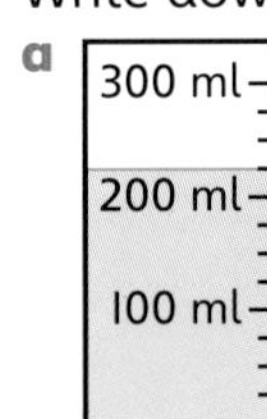

b

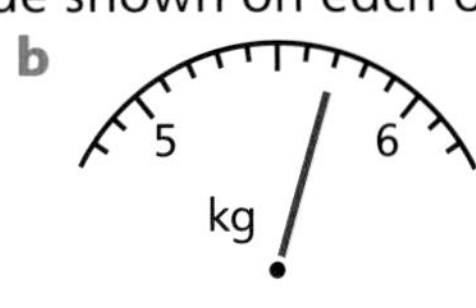

c

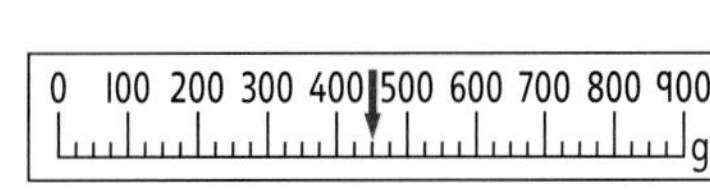

5 The diagram shows a car's speedometer.

a Write down the value shown on the scale.

Hint: Speed is given in miles per hour (mph).

b Copy the speedometer and draw arrows on it to show these speeds.

32 mph 40 mph 66 mph 69 mph

Level 5

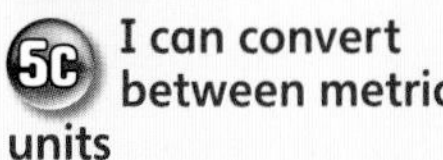

I can convert between metric units

6 Convert into grams.

8 kg

Each kilogram is 1000 g, so multiply by 1000: 8 × 1000 g = 8000 g

a 3 kg **b** $\frac{1}{2}$ kg **c** 2.1 kg **d** 0.9 kg

7 Convert into kilograms.

a 2000 g **b** 600 g **c** 230 g **d** 5476 g

8 Convert into the units shown.

a 5 m = ____ cm **b** 250 g = ____ kg **c** 3.2 km = ____ m

d 4.6 cl = ____ m*l* **e** 1.5 cm = ____ mm **f** 350 m*l* = ____ c*l*

5b I can convert times to decimals

9 Convert these times to decimals.

1 h 15 min $= 1\frac{15}{60}$ h $= 1.25$ h

Hint: You may use a calculator.

a 2 h 30 min **b** 3 h 45 min

c 4 h 25 min **d** 1 h 55 min

5a I can use metric equivalents of imperial measures

10 a 1 gallon ≈ 4.5 litres

A litre of petrol costs 95.5p. Approximately, how much would 1 gallon cost?

b 1 mile ≈ 1.6 km

Asha is doing a sponsored walk. She is sponsored 50p per kilometre. Approximately, how much is she sponsored per mile?

Now try this!

A Unit value

Work in pairs. Each letter of the alphabet is given a value: A = 1, B = 2, C = 3, and so on. You can use these to work out the value of different words. For example, METRE is worth 13 + 5 + 20 + 18 + 5 = 61. Choose a unit name each and work out its value. The person with the highest value scores 1 point. Repeat for four different units each. Who is the winner?

B Can you estimate?

Work in pairs. Choose an item to measure, for example a book or a pencil. First estimate the length and then measure accurately. The person whose estimate is closest to the actual measure scores 1 point. Repeat for four different items to find the overall winner.

mass gram (g) kilogram (kg) ounce pound metre (m) kilometre (km) mile

9.2 Mental methods

- Be able to add, double and halve, and multiply mentally
- Remember multiplication facts up to 10 x 10
- Carry out mental calculations with decimals and percentages

Why learn this?

Mental maths helps you work out scores quickly.

What's the BIG idea?

- When adding numbers in your head, look for **multiples of 10** or **pairs totalling 10**. Level 3
- You can check a calculation by working it backwards. Level 4
  Check 5.8 × 17 = 98.6 98.6 ÷ 17 = 5.8 ✓
- When working backwards you use the inverse (opposite operation). Division is the inverse of multiplication. Subtraction is the inverse of addition. Level 4
- If you know the **multiplication** facts up to 10 × 10 you can work out other multiplications: e.g. 'I know that 8 × 7 = 56, so 80 × 7 = 560'. Level 4
- **Partitioning** turns one difficult multiplication into two easier ones: e.g. 23 × 7 is the same as (20 × 7) + (3 × 7) = 140 + 21 = 161. Level 4

Super fact!

In darts, you have to finish on a double. So, if you have 9 left and one dart, you cannot finish.

Practice, practice, practice!

Level 3

3c I can add multiples of 10

1 Work out these in your head. Write down the answers.

a 40 + 20 + 30
b 80 + 30 + 10
c 90 + 50 + 10 + 40
d 60 + 100 + 70 + 20

3b I can add small numbers mentally

2 Find pairs totalling 10 to help you add these sets of numbers.

a 3 + 8 + 7 + 2
b 1 + 4 + 6 + 9 + 3
c 5 + 7 + 7 + 5 + 3
d 2 + 4 + 8 + 6 + 2 + 8

3a I can add numbers mentally

3 Add these darts scores to find each total score.

a 13, 17, 5
b 24, 1, 16
c 6, 21, 19
d 36, 12, 4
e 15, 8, 25
f 19, 6, 11

Level 4

4c I can use multiplication facts up to 10 × 10

4 Copy and complete the multiplication grids.

a

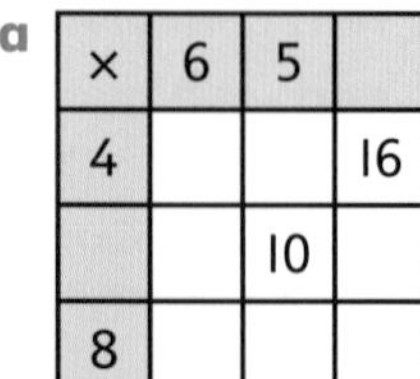

×	6	5	
4			16
		10	
8			

b

×	7		6
10		90	
	35		
8			

c

×		8	
6			18
	25	40	
9			

add inverse multiplication multiply

5 Use partitioning to multiply these.

37 × 8 $\quad 30 \times 8 = 240$
$+ \; 7 \times 8 = 56$
$37 \times 8 = 296$

a 12 × 5 b 15 × 6 c 24 × 7
d 52 × 5 e 11 × 9 f 43 × 8

6 Use a whole-number calculation to help you with these.

5.4 + 3.8 $\quad 54 + 38 = 50 + 30 + 12 = 92$, so $5.4 + 3.8 = 9.2$ (dividing by 10)

a 2.7 + 3.9 b 9.8 − 5.2 c 4.5 + 6.6
d 5.1 − 2.8 e 0.19 + 0.23 f 0.35 − 0.18

7 Use the multiplication facts you know to help you with these.

6 × 0.4 $\quad 6 \times 4 = 24$, so $6 \times 0.4 = 2.4$ (dividing by 10)

a 4 × 0.7 b 5 × 0.2 c 0.3 × 9
d 7 × 0.05 e 0.6 × 8 f 0.02 × 8

8 Use approximation to see which of these answers might be correct.

532 + 309 = 741 $\quad$ 532 + 309 is about 500 + 300 = 800. The answer is wrong.

1.4 × 23 = 32.2 $\quad$ The answer must be between 1 × 23 = 23 and 2 × 23 = 46. The answer might be right.

a 3201 − 1945 = 256 b 430 ÷ 11 = 175
c 9% of 50 = 4.5 d 6.2 + 6.9 = 8.1

9 Use a calculator to work these out. Check your answers by working backwards.

$\frac{1}{5}$ of 300 $\quad \frac{1}{5}$ of 300 = 300 ÷ 5 = 60

Check: 60 × 5 = 300 ✓

a 2.8 ÷ 5 b 1215 ÷ 45 c 4.09 − 2.63 d half of 6.7

Level 4

4c I can use partition to multiply mentally

4b I can add and subtract decimals

4b I can multiply whole numbers and decimals

4b I can check a result by approximation

4a I can check a result by working backwards

Now try this!

A Odd golf

A game for two players. Roll two dice and multiply the numbers.
If the answer is odd, this is your score for the hole. If the answer is even, keep halving until you get an odd number. This is your score. Play nine holes each. The player with the lowest total score wins.

B Penalty shootout

A game for two players. Roll a dice twice to make a two-digit number. Roll it again to make a single-digit number. Multiply the two numbers together. If the answer is even, keep halving until you get an odd number. If the odd number is less than 30, you score a goal. Otherwise you miss. See who has the most goals after five attempts each.

Tip
Make jottings when you do mental calculations.

partition product sum total

World's Greatest Maths!

9.3 Endangered Isle

The marine life around Endangered Isle is being destroyed by pollution. The warden needs to complete her survey to find out how bad the damage is. Can you help her with her calculations?

Jellyfish count

Large numbers of jellyfish can be a sign of overfishing.

- Write the number of jellyfish in each group as an addition
- Write this as a single multiplication
- How many jellyfish are there in each group?

Copy and complete the answers for questions 1 and 2. Write your answers for questions 3 and 4 in the same way.

1

Number of jellyfish = 4 + 4 + 4 = □ × 4 = □

2

Number of jellyfish = □ + 6 + 6 + □ + 6 = □ × □ = □

3

4

Leatherback turtles

Each of these turtles needs to find a mate.

- Use each multiplication or division fact on the left to help you solve a calculation on the right.

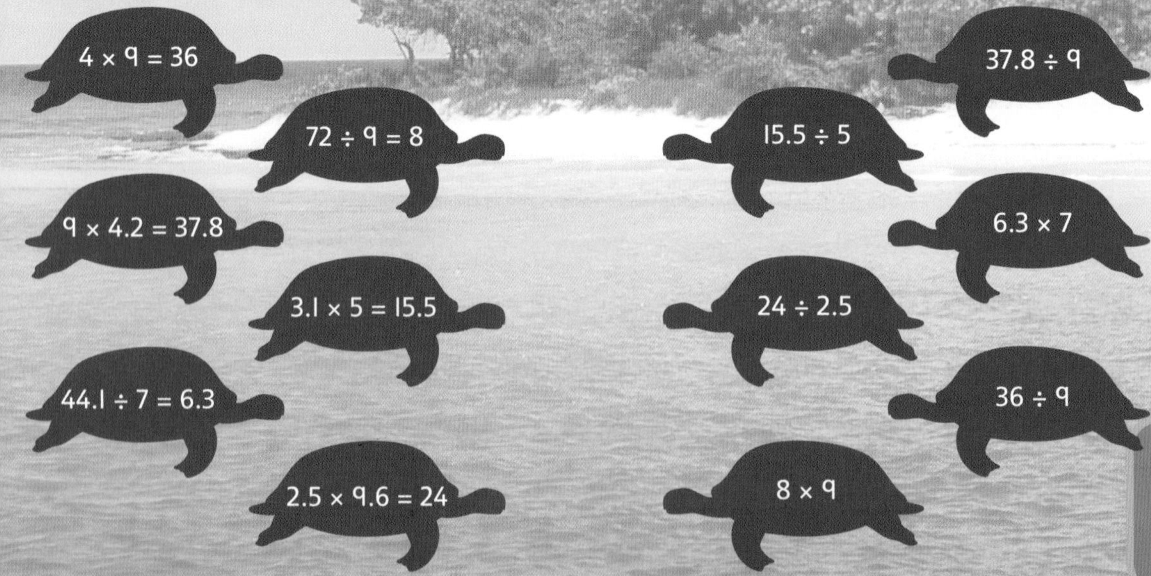

Complete each calculation and write the fact you used.

Shoals of fish

You need Resource sheet 9.3 for this activity.

Sponsored swim (a game for two players)

Aim of the game: To be the first player to collect £1000 for charity

Rules: You are collecting money for a conservation charity. You will swim around the island, collecting sponsorship for each lap you complete.

Player 1 secretly writes down a number between 1 and 9. This is the number of laps you complete. Player 2 secretly writes down a number between 10 and 100. This is the amount of sponsorship money you collect per lap. Both players reveal their numbers at the same time. The player who correctly calculates the total amount of money collected first keeps that amount of money. Keep playing until one player has £1000 or more.

- Play Sponsored swim with a partner.
- Record your game in a table like this one. In this game Lydia wins.

Aaron	Lydia	Amount collected	Strategy	Aaron's total	Lydia's total
6	73	£438	6 × 70 + 6 × 3	£438	£0
4	99	£396	400 – 4	£438	£396
5	80	£400	(5 × 8) × 10	£838	£396
9	78	£702	9 × 80 – 9 × 2	£838	£1098

When one player gives an answer you should check it using a calculator. If it is wrong, the other player collects all the money for that round.

Make sure you jot down the mental strategy you used to work out each calculation.

Warden's notebook

The warden got too close to the water when she was doing her survey! Some of her calculations have been ruined by splashes. ✽
Copy each calculation and fill in the missing values.

1 These calculations all use the **commutative law**. You can do multiplication in any order.

a 12 × 3 × 2 = 3 × 2 × 12 = ✽ × 12 = ✽

b 4 × 9 × 5 = 4 × 5 × ✽ = 20 × ✽ = ✽

c 5 × 7.3 × 2 = ✽ × ✽ × 7.3 = ✽ × 7.3 = ✽

d $\frac{1}{2}$ × 19 × 4 = $\frac{1}{2}$ × ✽ × 19 = ✽ × 19 = ✽

e 2 × 32.7 × 5 = ✽

f 8 × $\frac{1}{3}$ × 9 = ✽

2 These calculations all use the **associative law**. You can break down a number into factors to help with multiplication.

a 15 × 20 = 15 × 2 × 10 = ✽ × 10 = ✽

b 2.1 × 30 = 2.1 × 10 × 3 = ✽ × 3 = ✽

c 18 × 33 = 6 × ✽ × 33 = 6 × ✽ = ✽

d 7 × 24 = 7 × 8 × 3 = ✽ × 3 = ✽

e 11.6 × 20 = ✽

f 15 × 22 = ✽

3 These calculations all use the **distributive law**. You can turn one number into an addition or subtraction and multiply out the brackets.

a 8 × 74 = 8 × (70 + 4)
= 8 × 70 + 8 × 4
= 560 + ✽
= ✽

b 8.1 × 99 = 8.1 × (100 – 1)
= 8.1 × ✽ – 8.1 × 1
= ✽ – 8.1
= ✽

c 12 × 47 = 12 × (50 – 3)
= 12 × ✽ – ✽ × 3
= ✽ – ✽
= ✽

d 3 × 42 = ✽

e 6 × 19 = ✽

f 5 × 212 = ✽

9.4 Rounding

- Round positive whole numbers to the nearest 10, 100 or 1000
- Round decimals to the nearest whole number or one decimal place
- Know how to make estimates and approximations of calculations
- Round positive whole numbers to any given power of 10

Why learn this?

Mount Everest is the highest mountain in the world. It is 8848 m high. You can round this to 9000 m, which is easier to say.

What's the BIG idea?

- → If the **digit** is less than 5, **round** down. If the digit is 5 or more, round up. Level 4
- → To round to the **nearest** 10, look at the digit in the units column. 3827 is **3830** to the nearest 10. Level 4
- → To round to the nearest 100, look at the digit in the tens column. 3827 is **3800** to the nearest 100. Level 4
- → To round to the nearest 1000, look at the digit in the hundreds column. 3827 is **4000** to the nearest 1000. Level 4
- → To round a decimal to the nearest whole number, look at the digit in the first **decimal place**. 8.16 is **8** to the nearest whole number. Level 4
- → To round decimals to one decimal place, look at the digit in the second decimal place. 8.16 is 8.2 to one decimal place. Level 4
- → You can use rounding to **estimate** the answer to a calculation. Level 4
- → Big numbers can also be rounded to the nearest 10 000, 100 000, and so on. **Level 5**

Learn this

Rounding to one decimal place is the same as rounding to the nearest tenth.

Practice, practice, practice!

1 Round these numbers to the nearest 10.

a 92 **b** 314 **c** 502 **d** 3829

2 Round these numbers to the nearest 100.

a 476 **b** 209 **c** 350 **d** 85 **e** 6327

3 These are the lengths of some of the longest rivers in the world.

River	Length (kilometres)
Nile	6690
Amazon	6387
Congo	4371
Danube	2850
Rhine	1320

Round the lengths to the nearest 1000 km.

Level 4

4C I can round whole numbers to the nearest 10

4C I can round whole numbers to the nearest 100

4C I can round whole numbers to the nearest 1000

approximate between compare decimal place

4 Round these numbers to the nearest whole number.

a 1.8 b 3.6 c 4.5 d 51.2 e 0.73

5 Use rounding to estimate the answer to these calculations.
Find the exact answer using a calculator and compare your results.

a $15.4 + 12.7$ b $49.2 - 9.8$ c 3.1×1.6 d $3.99 \div 2.1$

6 This table shows the time taken by the planets to orbit the Sun once.

Round the times to one decimal place.

Planet	Time (years)
Jupiter	11.86
Uranus	84.01
Neptune	164.79
Saturn	29.46

7 This table shows the yearly percentage population growth of five countries.

Round the figures to one decimal place.

Country	Percentage growth (%)
USA	0.89
Bangladesh	2.06
UK	0.28
Uganda	3.57
Sri Lanka	0.98

Level 4

4b I can round decimals to the nearest whole number

4b I can use rounding to estimate an answer

4a I can round decimal numbers to one decimal place

8 292 150 people live in Cardiff. What is this to the nearest 100 000?

9 The highest populated country in the world is China, with 1 321 281 283 people in June 2007. The UK is the 22nd most populated, with 60 764 333 people.

a What is the population of the UK to the nearest million?

b One billion is 1 000 000 000. What is the population of China to the nearest billion?

c Approximately, how many more people live in China than in the UK?

Level 5

5a I can round whole numbers to any given power of 10

Did you know?

China and the USA are approximately the same size (10 million square kilometres) but China has approximately 1 billion more people.

Now try this!

A Highest total wins

A game for two players. Take turns to follow these instructions.

1 Roll a 0–9 dice. This is your tens digit.
2 Roll the dice again. This is your units digit.
3 Round your two-digit number to the nearest 10. This is your score.
4 After five rounds each, the player with the highest total wins.

B Lowest total wins

A game for two players. Take turns to follow these instructions.

1 Randomly enter a four-digit number into your calculator, for example 5978.
2 Divide your number by 20.
3 Round the answer to the nearest whole number.
4 You score the units digit.
5 After five rounds each, the player with the lowest total wins.

digit estimate nearest round

9.5 Written multiplication

➩ Know how to multiply using different written methods

Why learn this?

Engineers multiply the amount of fuel burned per hour by the journey time to find out how much fuel is needed. If they get the calculation wrong, the plane will not reach its destination.

What's the BIG idea?

→ You can use **estimation** to check the answer to a **calculation**. Level 4

→ You can use the grid method or the standard method for **multiplication**. Use the one you like the best. Level 4 & Level 5

Super fact!

The Ancient Greeks used pebbles to help them do multiplications. The Latin word for pebble is 'calculus', from which we get the word 'calculate'.

Practice, practice, practice!

Level 4

4c I can multiply by a single digit

1 Use the grid method to do these multiplications. Estimate the answer first.

436 × 8

Estimate: 436 × 8 is roughly 400 × 10 = 4000

×	400	30	6
8	3200	240	48

3200 + 240 + 48 = 3488 Check: 3488 is close to 4000 ✓

a 219 × 6 **b** 583 × 4 **c** 172 × 9 **d** 351 × 7

2 Use the standard method to do these multiplications. Estimate the answer first.

175 × 6

Estimate: 175 × 6 is roughly 200 × 5 = 1000

```
   175
×    6
  1050
   4 3
```

Check: 1050 is close to 1000 ✓

a 428 × 3 **b** 615 × 4 **c** 287 × 9 **d** 324 × 6

3 On a building project, a window costs £219. The building needs eight windows. How much will the windows cost in total?

Level 5

5c I can multiply by a two-digit number

4 Use the grid method to do these multiplications. Estimate the answer first.

24 × 19

Estimate: 24 × 19 is roughly 20 × 20 = 400

×	20	4
10	200	40
9	180	36

```
  240
+ 216
  456
```

Check: 456 is close to 400 ✓

a 36 × 21 **b** 65 × 42 **c** 29 × 54 **d** 73 × 46

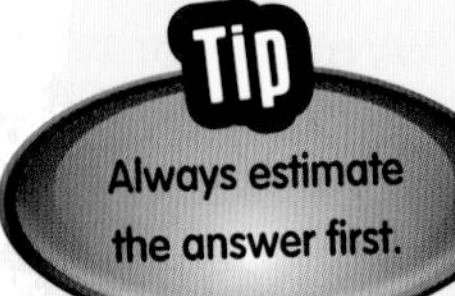

calculate calculation estimate

5 Use the standard method to do these multiplications. Estimate the answer first.

59 × 27

Estimate: 59 × 27 is roughly 60 × 30 = 1800

```
    59
×   27
  1180    (59 × 20)
+  413    (59 × 7)
  1593    Check: 1593 is close to 1800 ✓
```

a 45 × 13 **b** 53 × 32 **c** 36 × 18 **d** 82 × 25

Level 5

5C I can multiply by a two-digit number

6 A rectangular building plot is 34 metres by 21 metres. What is the area of the plot?

7 The lower level of a theatre has 21 rows of 16 seats, and the upper level has 15 rows of 14 seats. How many seats are there in the theatre in total?

8 Use the written method of your choice to do these multiplications. Estimate the answer first.

a 247 × 38 **b** 514 × 32 **c** 629 × 24

9 One strip of laminate flooring is 128 cm by 19 cm. What is the area of the strip?

10 A warehouse contains flatpack furniture stacked in 28 aisles, each containing 314 boxes. How many boxes of flatpack furniture does the warehouse contain?

11 A ream of paper should contain 500 sheets, but there is a problem at the factory. Each ream now has two sheets fewer than it should.

a How many sheets of paper should there be in 16 reams?

b As a result of the problem, how many sheets of paper are there in 16 reams?

Now try this!

A Multiplication puzzle

□□ × □ = ?

Replace each □ with 4, 6 or 7 to make the largest product.

Replace each □ with 4, 6 or 7 to make the smallest product.

B Next door neighbours

Two consecutive numbers multiply together to make 342. What are the two numbers?

Make up some more puzzles like this and swap them with a partner.

What methods do you find most helpful for discovering the answers?

multiplication multiply product

9.6 Multiplying decimals

➩ Know how to multiply decimal numbers by whole numbers
➩ Use an approximate calculation to check answers

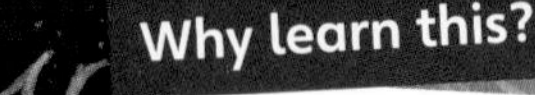

Why learn this?

Being able to work out the total cost of, for example, a restaurant bill is a useful skill.

What's the BIG idea?

→ You can use **estimation** to check the answer to a calculation. **Level 4**
5.2 × 9.8 is about 5 × 10 = 50

→ You can use the grid method to multiply a **decimal number** by a whole number. **Level 5**

→ To **multiply** a decimal number by a whole number using the standard method, ignore the decimal point and multiply the whole numbers. Then work out where to put the decimal point. **Level 5**

Learn this

When you multiply a decimal number by a whole number, the answer has the same number of digits after the decimal point as the original decimal number.

Practice, practice, practice!

Level 5

5b I can multiply decimals by a single digit

1 Copy the grid and use it to multiply the numbers. Estimate the answer first.

6.2 × 8   *Estimate: 6 × 8 = 48*

×	6	0.2
8	48	1.6

48 + 1.6 = 49.6   *Check: 49.6 is close to 48 ✓*

a 3.2 × 7

×	3	0.2
7		

b 1.9 × 4

×	1	0.9
4		

c 6.7 × 9

×	6	0.7
9		

2 Use the grid method to do these multiplications. Estimate the answer first.

a 3.5 × 9   **b** 6.7 × 4   **c** 4.2 × 8

3 A catering size tin of tomatoes weighs 2.6 kg.
How much do six of these tins weigh?

5b I can multiply decimals to two places by a single digit

4 Copy the grid and use it to multiply the numbers.

a 4.15 × 3

×	4	0.1	0.05
3			

b 9.38 × 2

×	9	0.3	0.08
2			

c 2.54 × 8

×	2	0.5	0.04
8			

d 7.62 × 5

×	7	0.6	0.02
5			

decimal number   decimal place   equivalent   estimate

5 Use the grid method to do these multiplications. Estimate the answer first.

a 1.79 × 6 **b** 8.23 × 4 **c** 5.46 × 9

6 At a restaurant, soup costs £3.95. What is the cost of five soups? Use the grid method to work it out.

7 Use the standard method to do these multiplications. Estimate the answer first.

4.9 × 6 *Estimate 5 × 6 = 30*

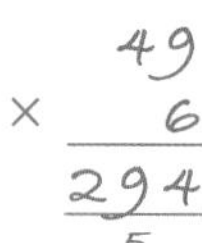

49 × 6 = 294, so 4.9 × 6 = 294 ÷ 10 = 29.4
Check: 29.4 is close to 30 ✓

a 9.2 × 3 **b** 7.6 × 8 **c** 21.3 × 5 **d** 19.3 × 7

8 Use the standard method to do these multiplications. Estimate the answer first.

7.26 × 4 *Estimate 7 × 4 = 28*

726
× 4
2904
1 2

726 × 4 = 2904, so 7.26 × 4 = 2904 ÷ 100 = 29.04
Check: 29.04 is close to 28 ✓

a 1.84 × 9 **b** 4.37 × 6 **c** 0.91 × 8 **d** 6.72 × 3

Hint: 1.84 × 9 is equivalent to 184 × 9 ÷ 100.

9 At a restaurant, roast beef costs £7.49. Four people sitting together all order roast beef. Use the standard method to work out their bill.

10 A length of string is cut into eight equal pieces. Each piece measures 25.25 cm. What was the original length of the string?

Tip
You can use a calculator to check your answers.

Level 5

5b I can multiply decimals to two places by a single digit

5a I can correctly position the decimal point after multiplying

Now try this!

A Target 100

A game for two players. Each roll a dice three times. Use the numbers to make a TU × U multiplication. The player whose answer is closest to 100 wins 1 point. The first player to get 3 points wins.

B Decimal investigation

Arrange the cards to make a multiplication, e.g. 1.2 × 34 or 1.23 × 4.
Which arrangement gives the smallest answer? Which gives the largest answer?

Repeat with the digits 5 6 7 8

Discuss with a partner how you make the largest/smallest answer.
Write down a rule for making the smallest answer.

Super fact!
In computing, 3*4 means 3 × 4.

multiplication multiply product

9.7 Written division

- Know how to divide whole numbers
- Know how to divide decimal numbers
- Use division in practical examples involving amounts of money
- Use an approximate calculation to check answers

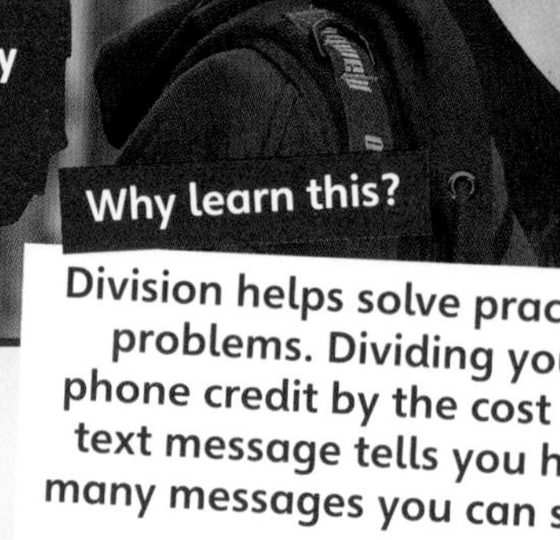

Why learn this?

Division helps solve practical problems. Dividing your phone credit by the cost of a text message tells you how many messages you can send.

What's the BIG idea?

→ You can use **estimation** to check the answer to a calculation. Level 4

→ The number you **divide** by is called the **divisor**. Keep subtracting **multiples** of the divisor until you cannot subtract any more. Then see how many lots of the divisor you subtracted altogether. Level 4 & Level 5

→ Sometimes you will not be able to get to zero by subtracting multiples of the divisor. The number you have left is called the **remainder**. Level 4 & Level 5

→ When you divide a decimal number by a whole number, line up the decimal point in the answer and divide as normal. Level 5

Practice, practice, practice!

Level 4

4b I can divide by a single digit

1 Work out these exact divisions. Estimate the answer first.

234 ÷ 6

Estimate: 240 ÷ 6 = 40

```
6)234
 - 180   (30 × 6)
    54
 -  54   (9 × 6)
     0
```

234 ÷ 6 = 30 + 9 = 39

Check: 39 is close to 40 ✓

a 124 ÷ 4
b 182 ÷ 7
c 351 ÷ 9
d 564 ÷ 6
e 296 ÷ 8
f 340 ÷ 5

Tip

When estimating the answer, look for numbers that are easy to divide.

2 Work out these divisions. They all have remainders.

375 ÷ 7

Estimate: 350 ÷ 7 = 50

```
7)375
 - 350   (50 × 7)
    25
 -  21   (3 × 7)
     4
```

375 ÷ 7 = 53 remainder 4

Check: 53 is close to 50 ✓

a 361 ÷ 8
b 239 ÷ 5
c 487 ÷ 6
d 665 ÷ 9
e 541 ÷ 7
f 333 ÷ 4

divide division divisor estimate exact

3 Antoine has 218p credit on his mobile phone.
It costs 7p to send a text message.
How many text messages can he send?

4 A delivery driver loads her van with packages each weighing 8 kg.
The maximum weight the van will hold is 812 kg.
What is the largest number of packages that the van can hold?

Level 4

4b I can divide by a single digit

5 Work out these divisions.
Some of them have remainders.
Estimate the answer first.

a 378 ÷ 14 **b** 918 ÷ 17 **c** 475 ÷ 11 **d** 859 ÷ 25

6 Sarah is on holiday in Spain.
She has 462p credit on her mobile phone.
It costs 35p to send a text message from Spain.
How many text messages can she send?

7 Work out these exact divisions.
Estimate the answer first.

a 127.8 ÷ 9 **b** 130.4 ÷ 4 **c** 277.2 ÷ 7
d 62.35 ÷ 5 **e** 146.28 ÷ 6 **f** 108.32 ÷ 8

Watch out!
Be careful when dividing decimals. If you don't line up the decimal points, you'll get the wrong answer.

8 Marco works in a gym. He earns £66.80 in one day, working 8 hours.
How much does he earn per hour

9 Seven friends go to a restaurant.
The bill is £123.48.
They share the bill equally. How much do they each have to pay?

10 Mr Parker shares £48.75 between his 15 grandchildren.
How much do they each receive?

11 Bicycle insurance for 12 months costs £50.52.
How much is that per month?

Level 5

5b I can divide by a two-digit number

5a I can divide decimals by a single digit

5a I can divide amounts of money in £s and p

Now try this!

A No remainder challenge 1

A game for two players. You need digit cards 2–9. Take turns to pick three cards. Use them to make a TU ÷ U calculation. If there is no remainder, score 3 points. If the remainder is an odd number, score 2 points. If the remainder is even, score 1 point. The first player to 10 points wins.

B No remainder challenge 2

Do Activity A but pick five cards and make a HTU ÷ TU calculation.

exactly **multiple** **quotient** **remainder**

9.8 More on order of operations

- Understand and use the order of operations
- Develop calculator skills and use a calculator effectively
- Check a result by working the problem backwards

Why learn this?

Mirror... signal... manoeuvre. The order in which you do things is important.

What's the BIG idea?

- You can check an answer by working it backwards.
  25 × 6 = 150   150 ÷ 6 = 25
  ÷ is the inverse (opposite) of ×.
  + is the inverse of −. **Level 4**
- 5^2 is said '5 squared' and means 5 × 5.
  You can use the [5] [x^2] keys on your **calculator** to work out squares. **Level 4**
- **Calculations** must be done in the right **order**:
  Brackets → **I**ndices (powers) → **D**ivision and **M**ultiplication → **A**ddition and **S**ubtraction **Level 4 & Level 5**
- You can write 6 × 6 as 6^2. **Level 4 & Level 5**
- If there are several multiplications and divisions, or additions and subtractions, do them one at a time from left to right. **Level 5**
- Finding the **square root** is the inverse of squaring.
  Use the [√] key on your calculator. **Level 5**

Learn this

BIDMAS
Brackets
Indices (powers)
Division
Multiplication
Addition
Subtraction

Practice, practice, practice!

1 Do these calculations on your calculator. Work from left to right.
- **a** 7.3 + 5.1 + 9.8
- **b** 57 − 8.6 − 3.9
- **c** 2.4 × 3.5 × 8.7
- **d** 728 ÷ 8 ÷ 7

2 180 students are going on a school trip. Each coach holds 49 people. How many coaches are needed?

3 Carly has £43. A ticket for the cinema costs £7.50. How many tickets can Carly afford to buy?

Level 3

3c I can use all operation keys on a calculator

3a I can round up or down after division, depending on the problem

4 Work these out using the memory keys on your calculator.
- **a** 2.7 × (5.2 + 3.1)
- **b** 4.9 × (9.5 − 6.8)
- **c** 151.38 ÷ (19.7 + 6.4)
- **d** 39.52 ÷ (14.2 − 9)

Hint: Work out the calculation inside the brackets first and put the answer in the calculator memory.

Tip
It's easy to make a mistake on a calculator. Repeat the calculation to check you get the same answer.

Level 4

4a I can use the calculator memory

brackets calculation calculator display enter

5 One minute is 60 seconds. One hour is 60 minutes.
How many seconds are there in 12 hours?
Use a calculator. Check your answer by working the calculation backwards.

6 A biscuit weighs 12 g. There are 15 biscuits in a packet.
There are 24 packets of biscuits in a box.
What is the total weight of the biscuits? e a calculator.
Check your answer by working the calculation backwards.

Level 4

4a I can check a result by working it backwards

7 Work these out without using a calculator.

a $6 + 4 \times 5$ b $3 \times 8 + 100$ c $13 + 40 \div 10$

d $8 \div 2 + 11$ e $50 - 6 \times 7$ f $10 - 16 \div 4$

Hint: Do multiplications and divisions before additions and subtractions.

8 Use the bracket keys on your calculator to work these out.

a $(4.1 + 5.2) \times 6.3$ b $10.1 \times (9.3 + 3.2)$

c $270 \div (1.5 + 7.5)$ d $(6.2 + 13.8) \div 4$

Hint: Work out $50 - 22.1$ first and use the calculator memory.

9 Work these out without using a calculator.

a $2 \times 6 + 3 \times 6$ b $72 \div 8 - 2 \times 4$

c $(3 + 4) \times (6 - 1)$ d $36 \div (10 + 5 - 6)$

10 Use a calculator to work these out.

a $202.53 \div (5.4 + 3.7 + 3.8)$ b $9.6^2 + 3.1 \times 7.4$

c $(3.7 + 4.9)^2 - 27.5$ d $\dfrac{357.12}{50 - 22.1}$

11 Use the [√] button on your calculator to find the square roots of these numbers.

a $\sqrt{289}$ b $\sqrt{625}$ c $\sqrt{529}$

d $\sqrt{60.84}$ e $\sqrt{15.6816}$ f $\sqrt{0.5625}$

Level 5

5c I can use the order of operations

5c I can use brackets on a calculator

5b I can use the order of operations in more complex calculations

5b I can carry out complex calculations on a calculator

5c I can use the square root key on a calculator

Now try this!

A Calculator words

Do each calculation on your calculator. Turn the calculator upside down to find the answers to the riddles.

a 939.5×6 Knees are in the middle of these.

b $877\,617.6 \div 15.2$ Ding dong!

c $216 \times 1460 + 648$ Get down on the dance floor!

Investigate other number words on your calculator.

B The value of brackets

Put brackets in this calculation to make the highest possible answer.

$$24 \div 12 - 8 \times 5 + 3$$

What is the lowest possible answer?

inverse key order of operations power square root

Improve your stock car!

You are the proud owner of a stock car.
At the moment it can do a lap in 130 s.
You want to improve it so that it can go faster.
You need a new engine, tyres and brakes.
Your budget is £1000. Spend it wisely!

Engines
V6 engine £390. Reduce lap time by 4 s.
V8 engine £510. Reduce lap time by 6 s.

Tyres
Soft tyres £290. Reduce lap time by 4 s.
Hard tyres £70. Reduce lap time by 1 s.

Brakes
Ceramic brakes £120. Reduce lap time by 2 s.
Carbon brakes £330. Reduce lap time by 4 s.

1 a Choose the engine, tyres and brakes you want.
b Use a calculator to work out how much you have spent in total. **Level 3**

2 If you have spent more than £1000, you must choose some cheaper components.
Work out your new total. **Level 3**

3 Work out how much lap time you will save using the new parts. **Level 4**

4 How long will it take your stock car to complete a lap now? **Level 4**

5 A short race lasts seven laps.
How long would your improved stock car take to complete a short race?
Use a written method to work out the answer. **Level 4**

6 Round your race time to the nearest
a 10 s
b 100 s. **Level 4**

7 A long race lasts 15 laps.
How long would your improved stock car take to complete a long race?
Use a written method to work out the answer. **Level 4**

8 You race your car at a charity event comprising 12 laps.
When you cross the line you are told your race time is 550 s. Use a written method to work out your lap time. **Level 5**

The BIG ideas

- → When adding numbers in your head look for **multiples of 10** or **pairs totalling 10**. Level 3
- → You can use **estimation** to check the answer to a calculation. Level 4
- → When **rounding**, if the digit is less than 5, round down. If the digit is 5 or more, round up. Level 4
- → To round to the **nearest 10** look at the digit in the units column. To round to the **nearest 100** look at the digit in the tens column. Level 4
- → You can use the **grid method** or the **standard method** to multiply by a single-digit or two-digit whole number. Level 4 & Level 5
- → The number you divide by is called the **divisor**. Keep subtracting multiples of the divisor until you can't subtract any more. Then see how many lots of the divisor you subtracted altogether. Level 4 & Level 5

Find your level

Level 3

Q1 Use a calculator to work out these.

a Add 448 to 567, then subtract 341.

b Multiply 269 by 18, then add 956.

c Subtract 248 from 321, then multiply by 13.

Q2 In each part, choose the alternative which is most likely to be true.

a A cup full of coffee holds 2 *l*, 20 m*l* or 200 m*l*.

b The height of a house is 10 mm, 10 m or 10 cm.

c An apple weighs 100 g, 10 g or 1 g.

Level 4

Q3 Use a calculator for this question.

a A hockey club wants to take 2000 supporters to an away match. The coach company tells them that each coach can carry 52 people.
How many coaches do they need for the journey? Show your working.

b If each coach costs £580, what is the total cost of the coaches?

c How much will each supporter have to pay to cover their share of the total cost of the coaches?

Q4 Do not use a calculator for this question.
Copy and complete the calculations.
If $550 \div 25 = 22$, then

a $550 \div \square = 25$

b $\square \times 25 = 550$

c $\square \times 22 = 550$

Q5 The table shows distances of towns from Manchester.

Town	Distance (miles)
Birmingham	95.3
Cardiff	203
Northampton	81.1
London	208
Edinburgh	219

Round each distance to the nearest 10 miles.

Level 5

Q6 **a** In a French oral exam each pupil will spend 25 minutes talking French.
If there are 31 pupils taking the exam, how long will the examiner spend listening to French? Use a written method to work out the answer.

b Each French oral exam is recorded on cassette. If each cassette can record for 60 minutes, how many cassettes will be needed to record all 31 pupils? Use a written method to work out the answer.

Q7 **a** Use a written method to show that $22 \times 36 = 792$.

b What is 440×36?
You can use part **a** to help you.

10 Algebra up close

This unit is about number patterns and how you can use rules to predict the next numbers in a sequence. Patterns and sequences have intrigued many people down through the ages.

The number sequence 1, 1, 2, 3, 5, 8, 13, 21, 34, ... is called the Fibonacci sequence.

It is named after Leonardo Fibonacci, an Italian, who used it as an example in one of his books around 800 years ago. But the sequence was known in India long before that.

Activities

A Look at this addition pattern:

9 + 9 = 18

99 + 99 = 198

999 + 999 = 1998

9999 + 9999 = 19998

Follow the pattern to predict the answer to 99999 + 99999.
Use a calculator to check.

B Work out how to get the next term in the Fibonacci sequence in the box above.

What are the next four terms after 34?

Before you start this unit...

1 (14) (20) (24) (15) (32) (25)

page 4

a Which of these numbers are multiples of 5?

b Which of these numbers are multiples of 3 or 4?

2 Write down two numbers that divide exactly into 12.

page 4

3 Megan has to get across this grid. She starts at the bottom left corner and finishes at the top right corner. She adds on 3 each time she moves to the next number. She can move horizontally, vertically and diagonally. Write down a sequence of numbers that will get her across the grid.

page 6

20	4	18	21	24
15	15	15	18	21
12	12	10	20	21
9	9	13	18	16
6	9	12	15	9

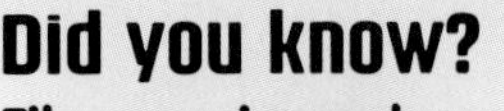

Did you know?
Fibonacci numbers often appear in nature. These flowers have 3, 5, 8 and 13 petals.

Plus digital resources

10.1 Multiples and factors

- Recognise multiples up to 10 × 10
- Know how to apply tests for divisibility by 2, 3, 4, 5, 6, 9, 10 and 25
- Know how to identify factors of numbers with more than four factors
- Recognise and use multiples and factors
- Find common factors including the highest common factor (HCF) of two numbers

Why learn this?

If you know how many seats are in a row, you can use multiples to work out the total number of seats.

What's the BIG idea?

- 3, 6, 9 and 12 are all multiples of 3.
  10, 20, 30 and 40 are all multiples of 10. **Level 3**
- A **factor** is a number which can divide exactly into a given number.
  1, 2, 3, 4, 6 and 12 are factors of 12 because 12 is exactly **divisible** by each of these numbers. **Level 3**
- Numbers exactly divisible by 2 end in a 0, 2, 4, 6 or 8. **Level 3**
- Numbers exactly divisible by 5 end in a 0 or 5. **Level 3**
- Numbers exactly divisible by 10 end in a 0. **Level 3**
- A number is exactly divisible by 3 if the sum of its digits is exactly divisible by 3. **Level 4**
- A number is exactly divisible by 4 if the last two digits are exactly divisible by 4. **Level 4**
- A number is exactly divisible by 6 if it is exactly divisible by 2 and by 3. **Level 4**
- A number is exactly divisible by 9 if the sum of digits is exactly divisible by 9. **Level 4**
- A number is exactly divisible by 25 if the last two digits are 00, 25, 50 or 75. **Level 4**
- A **common factor** is a factor that is common to two given numbers. **Level 4**
- The **highest common factor (HCF)** is the highest factor common to two given numbers. **Level 5**

Practice, practice, practice!

Level 3

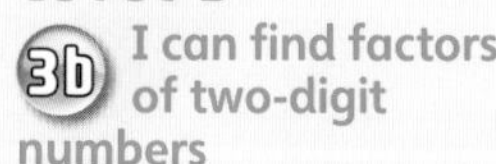

3b I can find factors of two-digit numbers

3a I can find at least four factors of numbers

3a I can use tests for divisibility by 2, 5 and 10

1 Find two factors of

a 18 b 20 c 36 d 28 e 15 f 33

2 Find all the factors of

a 27 b 34 c 45 d 50 e 30 f 42

3 The number 6 has four factors: 1, 2, 3 and 6.
Which other one-digit number has exactly four factors?

4 Copy this grid. Shade each number that is divisible by 2, 5 or 10 to reveal a secret calculation. Work out the answer to this calculation.

1	4	20	16	13	17	25	49	89	55	62	80
3	50	7	35	9	81	60	69	53	29	73	32
101	8	15	40	27	22	32	35	63	39	70	105
11	201	19	100	29	67	44	103	59	73	77	38
87	63	17	30	73	71	50	43	113	45	26	24

common factor divisible factor highest common factor (HCF)

5 Look at these numbers.

27 28 186 140 252 900

Write down the numbers that are divisible by

a 3 b 6 c 4 d 25

6 a Write five multiples of 4.

b Write five multiples of 7.

c Write a number which is a multiple of 5 and a multiple of 9.

d Write a number which is a multiple of 4 and a multiple of 7.

7 a Write a multiple of 15.

b Write a factor of 20.

c Write a number that is a multiple of 8 and a factor of 64.

8 Write all the common factors of

a 8 and 12 b 6 and 10 c 12 and 36.

9 a Which of 70, 60, 180, 72 and 128 are exactly divisible i by 3 ii by 4?

b Which of 54, 145, 108, 162, 234 and 216 are exactly divisible i by 6 ii by 9?

c Which of 125, 100, 200, 325 and 612 are exactly divisible i by 4 ii by 25?

Level 4

4c I can use tests for divisibility by 3, 4, 6 and 25

4c I can find multiples up to 10 × 10

4c I can find and use multiples and factors

4b I can find common factors

4a I can use simple tests of divisibility

10 Write down the highest common factor for each pair of numbers in Q8.

11 Write down the highest common factor of

a 20 and 16 b 30 and 24

c 28 and 42 d 32 and 48.

Tip

First write down all the factors of each number. The HCF is the biggest number that appears in both lists

Level 5

5c I can find the highest common factor of two numbers

Now try this!

A Guess the number 1

I am a factor of 20.
I am a multiple of 5 and a multiple of 2.
The sum of my digits is 1.
What am I?

Make up some statements about a number of your own for your partner to work out. You can include the words 'factor', 'multiple', 'odd' and 'even'.

B Guess the number 2

I am a factor of 24, and a multiple of 3.
What am I?

Make up some statements about a number of your own for your partner to work out. You can include the words 'factor', 'common multiple', 'odd' and 'even'.

Learn this

The word 'multiple' is similar to 'multiplication' – this will help you remember that a multiple is a number in a times table.

multiple prime number

10.2 Generating sequences

➪ Know how to extend sequences, including into negative values
➪ Know how to generate sequences using a term-to-term rule and a position-to-term rule

Why learn this?

You could use a sequence to help you remember the combination of your bicycle lock, or a PIN number.

What's the BIG idea?

→ A **sequence** is a set of numbers that follow a pattern. Level 3
→ Each number in a sequence is called a **term**. Level 3
→ Sequences can be **ascending** (terms getting larger) or **descending** (terms getting smaller). Level 3
→ Sequences can include negative and decimal numbers. Level 3 & Level 4
→ You can **generate** a sequence from the first term and the **term-to-term rule**. Level 4
→ You can use the **position-to-term rule** to find a term in a sequence. Level 5

Practice, practice, practice!

Level 3

3c I can work out number sequences by counting on

1 Write the next three terms of these sequences.

+3 +3 +3 +3 +3 +3 — *Work out the difference between the terms.*
4, 7, 10, 13, 16, 19, 22 — *Carry on adding 3s to find the next term.*

a 4, 9, 14, 19, ..., ..., ...
b 7, 11, 15, 19, ..., ..., ...
c 20, 30, 40, 50, ..., ..., ...
d 45, 48, 51, 54, ..., ..., ...
e 102, 107, 112, 117, ..., ..., ...
f 183, 187, 191, 195, ..., ..., ...

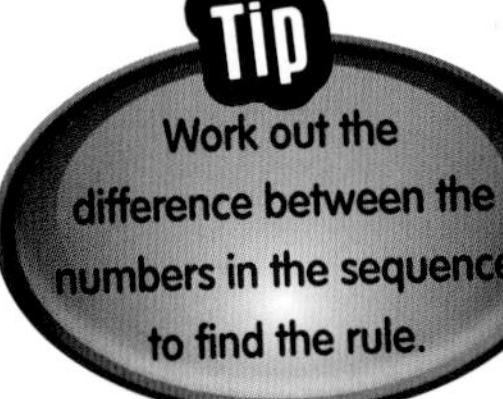

2 Paul plays football every fourth day. He plays on 5th May. Write down the next five dates that he will play football.

3b I can work out number sequences by counting back

3 Write the next three terms of these sequences.

a 27, 24, 21, 18, ..., ..., ...
b 102, 100, 98, 96, ..., ..., ...
c 1000, 900, 800, ..., ..., ...
d 68, 60, 52, 44, ..., ..., ...
e 95, 89, 83, 77, ..., ..., ...
f 217, 213, 209, 205, ..., ..., ...

3a I can work out number sequences extending beyond zero

4 Copy these sequences and write the next three terms.

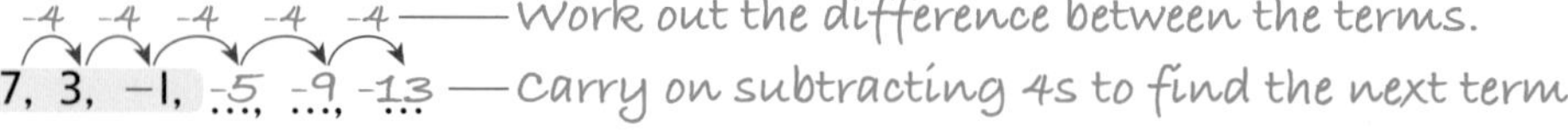

a 3, 2, 1, ..., ..., ...
b 10, 7, 4, ..., ..., ...
c 20, 10, 0, ..., ..., ...
d −1, −3, −5, ..., ..., ...
e 6, 0, −6, ..., ..., ...
f 17, 11, 5, ..., ..., ...

Watch out!
When counting back beyond zero remember that you will need to use negative numbers. You can use a number line to help.

ascending decending generate position

5 Find the missing terms in these sequences.

a 1.6, 2.0, 2.4, …, …, …

b 8.75, 7.25, 5.75, …, …, …

c 3.8, 4.0, 4.2, …, …, …, …, 5.2

d 7.9, 8.3, …, 9.1, …, 9.9, …, …

e …, …, 0.3, 0.1, …, −0.3, …, −0.7

f 0.45, …, …, 0.6, 0.65, …, 0.75, …

6 The first term and the rule of the sequence are given. Write down the first six terms for each sequence.

a first term: 7 rule: add 8

b first term: 1 rule: multiply by 2

c first term: 70 rule: subtract 5

d first term: 6.3 rule: add 0.2

7 Write down the first six terms of each sequence.

a first term: 1 rule: multiply by 2 then add 1

b first term: 4 rule: subtract 1 then multiply by 2

c first term: 6 rule: subtract 2 then multiply by 3

d first term: 800 rule: halve the term

Level 4

4c I can work out sequences with decimals

4b I can work out terms of a simple sequence

4a I can work out terms of a sequence

8 This is part of a calendar for the month of August.

a On what day is 21st August? Explain how you worked it out.

b On what day is 18th August?

c What are the dates of the Saturdays in August?

August						
Mon	Tue	Wed	Thu	Fri	Sat	Sun
1	2	3	4	5	6	7
8	9	10	11			

9 A sequence has position-to-term rule

term number × 3 + 2

a Copy and complete the table.

Term number	1	2	3	4	5	10
Term	5					

b What is the difference between the terms?

10 a Write down the first five terms of the sequence with position-to-term rule

term number × 5 − 2

b What is the difference between the terms?

Level 5

5c I can work out a term of a sequence from its position

Now try this!

A Letter sequences

Look at this sequence: O, T, T, F, F, S, S, E, …

Can you work out what the next letters of the sequence will be?

Make up a letter sequence for your partner.

B Fibonacci sequences

This is a Fibonacci sequence: 3, 3, 6, 9, 15, 24, 39, …

Work out how the next term is formed. Find the next four terms.

Research the Fibonacci sequence on the internet or in books.

sition-to-term rule sequence term term-to-term rule

maths!

Square and triangle numbers

Square numbers

1 = 1 × 1
4 = 2 × 2
9 = 3 × 3
16 = 4 × 4
25 = 5 × 5
36 = 6 × 6
49 = 7 × 7
64 = 8 × 8
81 = 9 × 9
100 = 10 × 10
121 = 11 × 11
144 = 12 × 12
169 = 13 × 13
196 = 14 × 14
225 = 15 × 15
256 = 16 × 16
289 = 17 × 17
324 = 18 × 18
361 = 19 × 19
400 = 20 × 20
441 = 21 × 21
484 = 22 × 22
529 = 23 × 23
576 = 24 × 24
625 = 25 × 25
676 = 26 × 26
729 = 27 × 27
784 = 28 × 28
841 = 29 × 29
900 = 30 × 30
961 = 31 × 31
1024 = 32 × 32
1089 = 33 × 33
1156 = 34 × 34
1225 = 35 × 35
1296 = 36 × 36
1369 = 37 × 37
1444 = 38 × 38
1521 = 39 × 39
1600 = 40 × 40
1681 = 41 × 41
1764 = 42 × 42
1849 = 43 × 43
1936 = 44 × 44
2025 = 45 × 45
2116 = 46 × 46
2209 = 47 × 47
2304 = 48 × 48
2401 = 49 × 49
2500 = 50 × 50

How many toy soldiers are there?

How many squares are there on a chessboard?

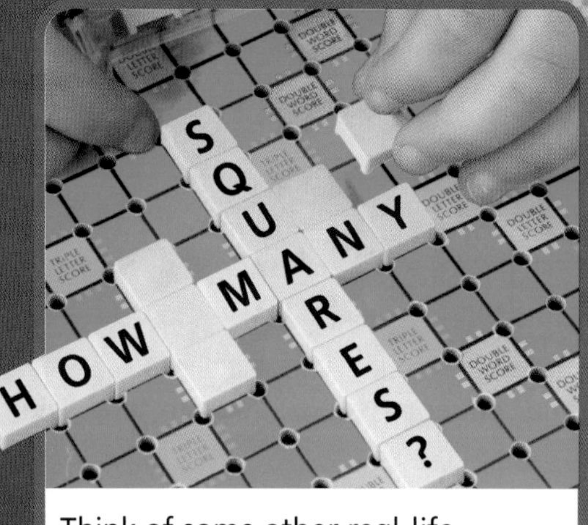

Think of some other real-life examples of square numbers.

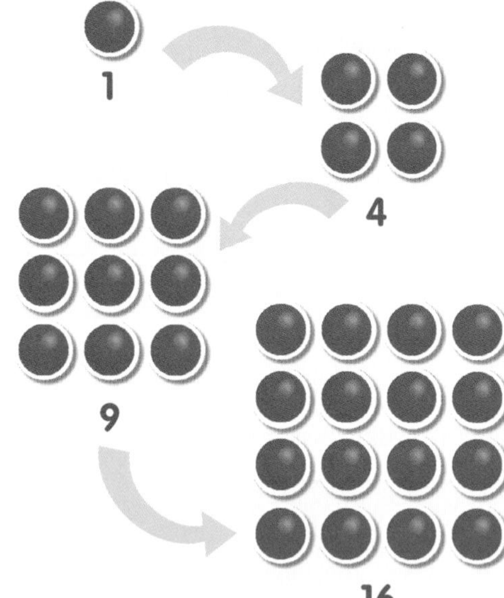

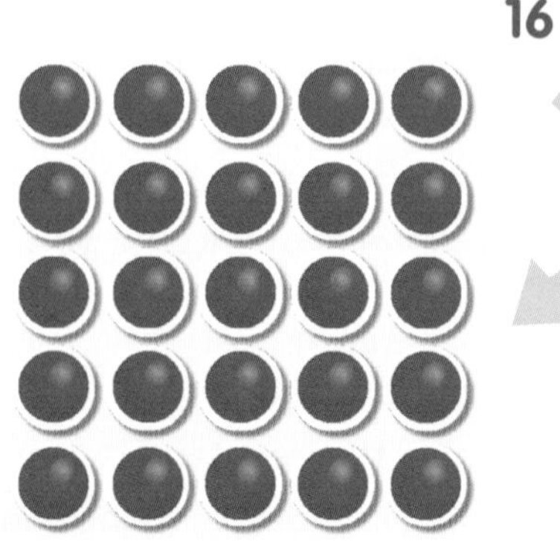

Triangle numbers

1

3

6

10

15

Each row of dots has one more dot, so we can get the triangle numbers by adding up:

1 + 2 = 3
1 + 2 + 3 = 6
1 + 2 + 3 + 4 = 10

1
2
3
4
+ 5
15

So staircases of squares are also triangle numbers.

$12^2 = 144$
12 backwards is 21.
$21^2 = 441$, which is 144 backwards!

The colour values on a snooker table add up to 27, one less than a triangle number. Why is this?

What's the highest number of pins in Wii™ bowling?

Think of some more real-life examples of triangle numbers.

On a calculator, add up

$1 + \frac{1}{3} + \frac{1}{6} + \frac{1}{10} + \frac{1}{15} + \ldots$

where the bottom numbers are triangle numbers. Keep going. What do you notice?

Can you find a number that is both a square and a triangle number?

1	1
2	3
3	6
4	10
5	15
6	21
7	28
8	36
9	45
10	55

11	66
12	78
13	91
14	105
15	120
16	136
17	153
18	171
19	190
20	210
21	231
22	253
23	276
24	300
25	325
26	351
27	378
28	406
29	435
30	465
31	496
32	528
33	561
34	595
35	630
36	666
37	703
38	741
39	780
40	820
41	861
42	903
43	946
44	990
45	1035
46	1081
47	1128
48	1176
49	1225
50	1275

10.3 Generating sequences using rules

- Know how to find terms of a simple sequence by continuing the pattern
- Know how to find a term in a sequence from the position-to-term rule and its position in the sequence
- Know how to use algebra to describe the general rule of a sequence

Why learn this?

Many things around us follow a pattern. Knowing how patterns repeat helps you know what to expect. Can you see how to continue this patterned wallpaper?

What's the BIG idea?

→ To draw the next term in a **sequence** of patterns, work out how the pattern grows. **Level 4**

→ You can **generate** a sequence from the **rule** and the first **term**. **Level 5**

→ You can use the **term-to-term rule** of a sequence to find any term in the sequence. **Level 5**

→ You can write the **position-to-term rule** of a sequence using algebra. **Level 5**

Did you know?

The Italian word for sequence is *sequenza* and the Spanish word is *secuencia*.

Practice, practice, practice!

Level 4

4b I can find terms of a simple practical sequence

1 a Look at this sequence of dot patterns. Draw the next five patterns in sequence.

b Copy and complete the table.

Pattern number	1	2	3	4	5	6	7	8
Number of dots								

Pattern 1 Pattern 2 Pattern 3

2 a Draw the next **two** shapes in this sequence.

b Copy and complete the table.

Shape number	1	2	3	4	5	6	7	8
Number of squares								

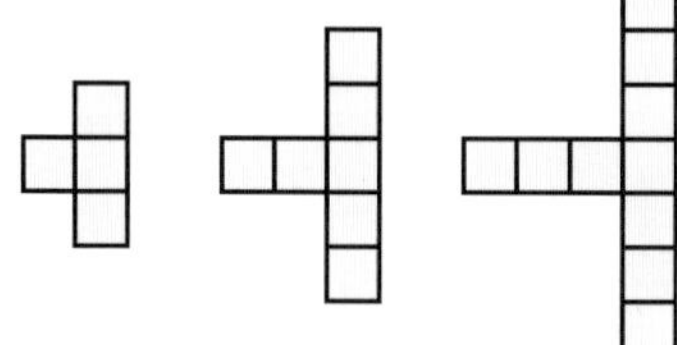

4a I can find terms of a more complex practical sequence

3 In a quadrilateral there is one diagonal from a corner, and this creates two triangles.

a Draw a pentagon. How many diagonals can you draw, starting from one corner?

b How many triangles are there?

c Repeat for a hexagon.

d Copy and complete the table below.
Follow the sequence pattern to complete the number of triangles for 7 sides and 8 sides. Draw diagrams to check you are correct.

1 2

Number of sides of polygon	3	4	5	6	7	8
Number of triangles		2				

generate position position-to-term rule rule

Level 5

5c I can find a term of a sequence from its position

4 Each year Ramesh's gran gives him twice his age in money on his birthday. When he was 6 years old he got £12.

a Copy and complete this table to show how much money Ramesh received from his gran on each birthday.

Age	1	2	3	4	5	6	7	8	9	10
Money (£)						12				

b How much will Ramesh get on his 21st birthday?

c How old will Ramesh be when his gran gives him £50?

5 **a** Copy and complete the table for this sequence of dots.

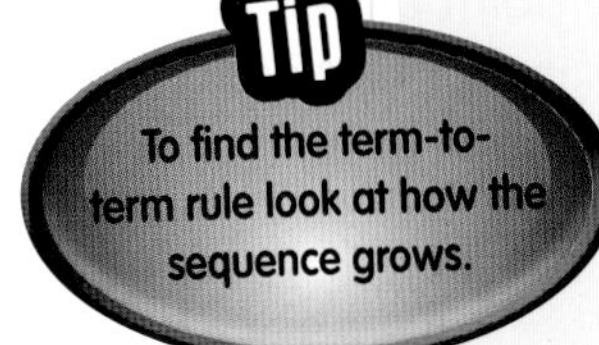

Pattern number	1	2	3	4	5
Number of dots					

b How many dots are there in the 10th pattern? Explain how you worked it out.

c Copy and complete the position-to-term rule for this sequence.
Number of dots = pattern number × ____

6 This sequence is made of sticks.

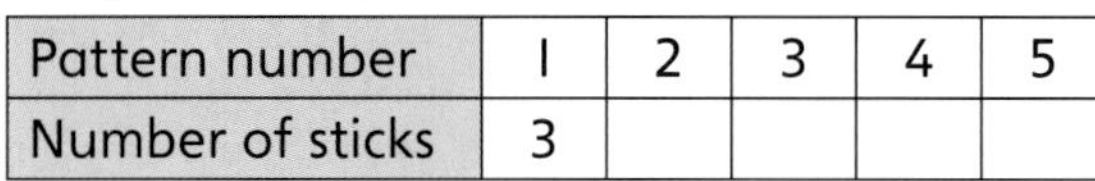

a Copy and complete the table.

Pattern number	1	2	3	4	5
Number of sticks	3				

b How many sticks would you need for the 10th pattern? Explain how you worked it out.

5b I can find terms of a sequence using a term-to-term rule

7 The first term of a sequence is −30. The rule is 'add 5'.

a Write down the first five terms.

b What is the 10th term in this sequence? Don't work out all the terms in between.

5a I can use algebra to describe the rule

8 **a** Write down the position-to-term rule for this sequence.

1st term	2nd term	3rd term	4th term
7	14	21	28

Hint: Use your answers to **a** to help you..

b Write down the position-to-term rules for these sequences.

i 8, 15, 22, 29, … **ii** 5, 12, 19, 26, … **iii** 17, 24, 31, 38, … **iv** 4, 11, 18, 25, …

Now try this!

A Shape patterns 1

Make up a shape pattern.
Draw the first three shapes of your pattern.
Ask your partner to draw the fifth shape. Are they correct?

B Shape patterns 2

Draw the first three dot patterns in a sequence.
Swap sequences with a partner.
Explain how your partner's sequence is growing.
How many dots will there be in the nth pattern?
Using your partner's first pattern, continue the sequence in another way.
How many dots will be in the nth pattern?

sequence term term-to-term rule

10.4 Coordinates

➩ Know how to read and plot coordinates in all four quadrants

Why learn this?

We use coordinates so that we can locate a place or position quickly on a map. Grid references that are used on maps are a form of coordinates.

What's the BIG idea?

- → The point where two axes meet is called the **origin** or (0, 0). **Level 4**
- → Each quarter of the graph is called a quadrant. **Level 4**
- → The first **quadrant** has positive values on the x-**axis** and y-**axis**. Point A is in the first quadrant. **Level 5**
- → When reading **coordinates**, always start at O and read across first and then up or down. The coordinates of A are (2, 3). **Level 4 & Level 5**

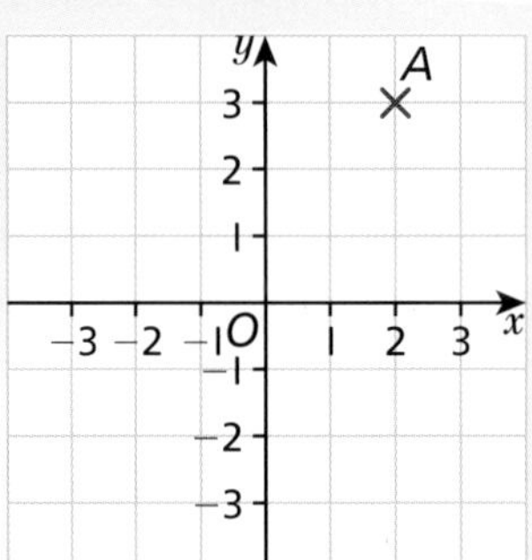

Super fact!

When detectives search a crime scene, they use a coordinate overlay so that they can identify the precise location of each piece of evidence.

Practice, practice, practice!

Level 3

3a I can find a position on a square grid

1 The point C3 is marked by a red dot. Copy the grid and mark these points to reveal a secret calculation

A6, B6, C6, C5, C4, C2, C1, F1, F2, F3, F4, F5, E3, G3, I1, I3, I4, I5, I6, J1, J3, J6, K1, K2, K3, K6.

Work out the answer to this calculation.

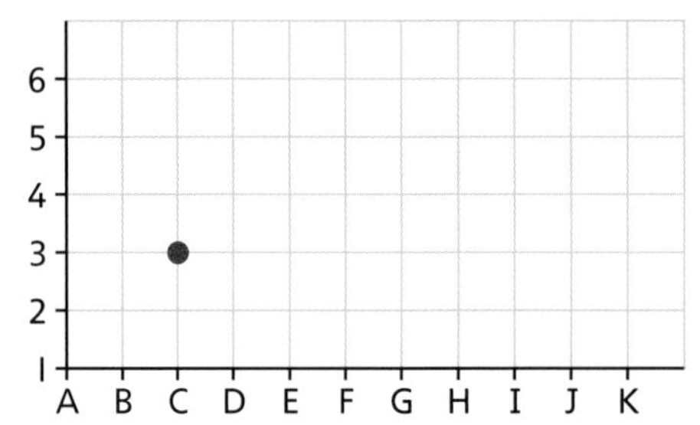

Level 4

4b I can work out the x- and y-coordinates of a point

2 Copy and complete the coordinates of the points with these letters.

 A (5, 2)	B (___, 4)
C (1, ___)	D (___, 1)
E (3, ___)	F (___, ___)
G (___, ___)	H (___, ___)
I (___, ___)	J (___, ___)
K (___, ___)	L (___, ___)

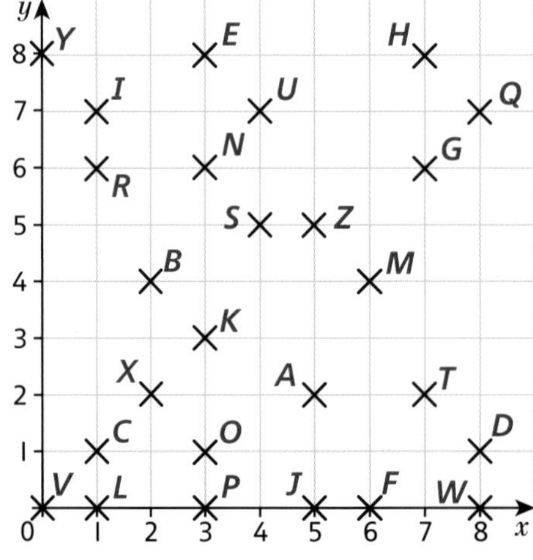

coordinates origin quadrant

3 **a** Draw a grid with x- and y-axes from 0 to 10.

b Plot these coordinates. Join them up with straight lines in the order they are given.

(4, 2) (2, 4) (4, 6) (6, 4) (4, 2)

c Write down the name of this shape.

Watch out!

When plotting coordinates, go along the x-axis first, then up or down the y-axis to find the position.

Level 4

4a I can plot a point in the first quadrant

4 Repeat Q3 for these coordinates, joining the points as you plot them.

(1, 1) (2, 2) (3, 4) (3, 6) (1, 5) (1, 7) (3, 7) (4, 8) (4, 5) (7, 5) (8, 6) (7, 3) (7, 2) (6, 1) (5, 1) (6, 2) (6, 3) (4, 3) (2, 1) (1, 1)

What picture do you get?

Level 5

5c I can work out x- and y-coordinates in all four quadrants

5 Write down the coordinates of each of the holes on the golf course.
For example, hole 1 is at (−2, 3).

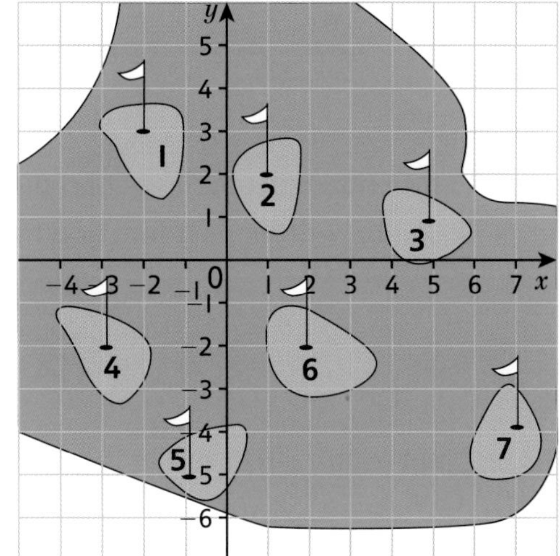

5b I can plot points in all four quadrants

6 Draw a grid with x- and y-axes from −5 to 5.

a Plot these points and join them up in the order they are given.

i (1, 1) (3, 1) (2, 3) (1, 1)

ii (1, 0) (4, 0) (2, −2) (−1, −2) (1, 0)

iii (−3, 0) (−2, 1) (−1, 1) (0, 0) (−1, −1) (−2, −1) (−3, 0)

b Write the name of the polygon you have drawn in each case.

5a I can solve coordinate problems using all four quadrants

7 **a** On a grid with x- and y-axes from −5 to 5 plot these coordinates.
(−3, 4) (3, 4) (3, −2)

b These points are all corners of a square.
Write down the coordinates of the fourth corner.

Now try this!

A Coordinate messages 1

Why was the six scared? Use the letters from the grid in Q2 to work out the answer to this question.

(4, 5) (3, 8) (0, 0) (3, 8) (3, 6)
(3, 8) (1, 7) (7, 6) (7, 8) (7, 2)
(3, 6) (1, 7) (3, 6) (3, 8)

Write a coded message for your partner to work out.

B Coordinate messages 2

Draw your own axes with values of x and y from −4 to 4. Add points and label them *A* to *Z*.

Write a coded message using the coordinates of the letters for your partner to work out.

x-axis y-axis

10.5 Straight line graphs

- Write coordinates in a table
- Find outputs of function machines
- Know the form of equations of straight lines parallel to the x- and y-axes.

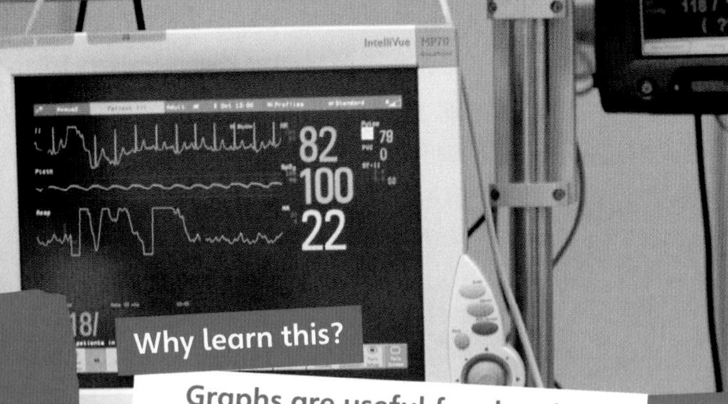

Why learn this?

Graphs are useful for showing a relationship between two variables. You will meet them in many different subjects – Science, Geography, PE. These graphs show heart beat and pulse rate.

What's the BIG idea?

- **Coordinates** can be written in a table. **Level 3**
- You can put numbers in a **function machine** to get an **output** value. **Level 4**
- Functions such as $x \rightarrow 3x$ can be written as a function machine. **Level 5**

  $x \rightarrow$ [×3] $\rightarrow 3x$

- Function machines can help you find pairs of x- and y-values when you have been given a rule. **Level 5**
- Straight line **graphs parallel** to the ***x*-axis** are in the form $y = a$ (where a is a number). **Level 5**
- Straight line graphs parallel to the ***y*-axis** are in the form $x = a$ (where a is a number). **Level 5**

Super fact!

You only need to know the coordinates of three points when plotting a straight line graph. Two show you where to place the ruler and the other is to check you haven't made a mistake.

Learn this

Straight line graphs are also called linear graphs. You can remember this because 'linear' contains the word 'line'.

Practice, practice, practice!

Level 3

3c I can show coordinates in a table

1 Copy and complete the table with the coordinates shown below.

x	1				
y	2				

(1, 2) (4, 5) (6, 7) (7, 8) (8, 9)

3b I can interpret coordinates in a simple table

2 Write the coordinate pairs from this table.

x	3	4	5	6	7
y	2	3	4	5	6

Level 4

4a I can find outputs of simple functions

3 Copy and complete these function machines to find the missing outputs.

a

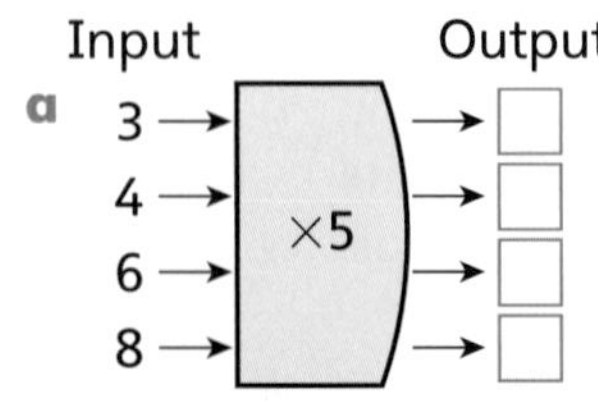

b

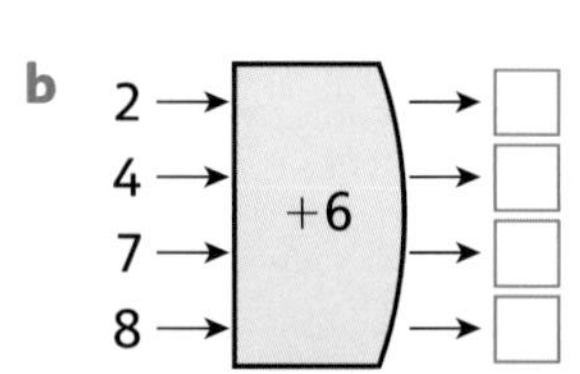

coordinates function machine graph input

4 Copy and complete these function machines to find the missing outputs.

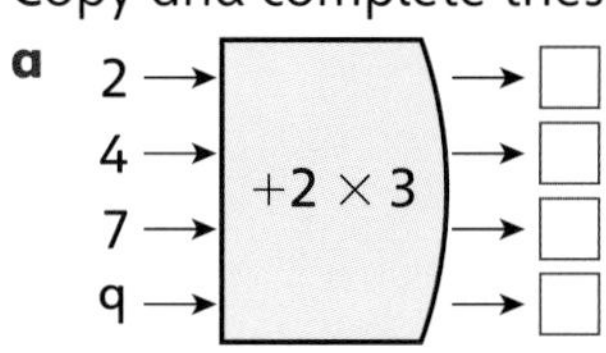

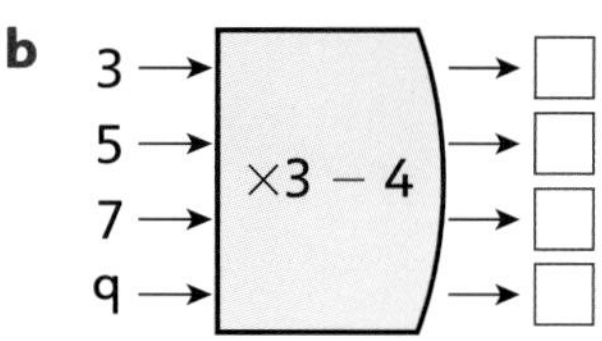

5 The rule $y = x - 1$ can be written as a function machine.
When $x = 3$, $y = 3 - 1 = 2$. The coordinate pair is (3, 2).
Find the coordinate pairs for the rule $y = x - 1$ for these values of x.

$x \rightarrow$ [−1] $\rightarrow y$

a $x = 4$ **b** $x = 7$ **c** $x = 10$ **d** $x = 8$ **e** $x = 15$

6 Copy and complete these tables of values for the rules given.

a $y = 3x$

x	1	2	3	4	5
y	3				

b $y = 6 - x$

x	1	2	3	4	5
y			3		

7 **a** Draw a grid with x- and y-axes from −5 to 5.

b Draw and label the graphs of these functions on your grid.

i $y = 1$ **ii** $x = 4$ **iii** $y = 4$
iv $y = 5$ **v** $x = 2$ **vi** $x = 1$

c What do you notice about these graphs?

8 **a** Draw a grid with the x-axis going from 0 to 5, and the y-axis from 0 to 16.

b Plot the graphs for the functions in Q6.

c Label each graph with the function.

Level 5

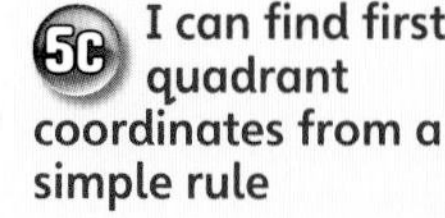

5c I can find outputs of more complex functions

5c I can find first quadrant coordinates from a simple rule

5b I can recognise graphs parallel to the x- or y-axis

5a I can plot a graph of a simple function in the first quadrant

Now try this!

A Coordinates game

A game for two players. Take turns to roll the dice.

1. Each plot eight points on a grid with x- and y-axes from 0 to 6. Do not choose points on the x- or y-axes.
2. Roll a fair six-sided dice two times. The first number you roll is the x-coordinate. The second number is the y-coordinate.
3. If these coordinates match one of your points, circle it on your grid. The winner is the first person to circle all of their points.

B Functions game

A game for two players. Take turns to roll the dice.

1. Each draw a grid with the x-axis from 0 to 6 and the y-axis from 0 to 20. Plot eight points.
2.

$y = x$	$y = 2x$	$y = 3x$	$y = x + 2$	$y = x + 3$
$y = 2x + 1$	$y = 2x + 2$	$y = 2x + 3$	$y = 3x + 1$	$y = 10 - x$
$y = 15 - x$	$y = 7 - x$	$y = 20 - x$	$y = 20 - 2x$	$y = 12 - 2x$

Roll a fair six-sided dice. Choose one of the functions. Put your dice number into the function. If the coordinates you have made match one of your marked points, circle the point on your grid. The winner is the first person to circle five of their points.

output parallel x-axis y-axis

Maps and coordinates

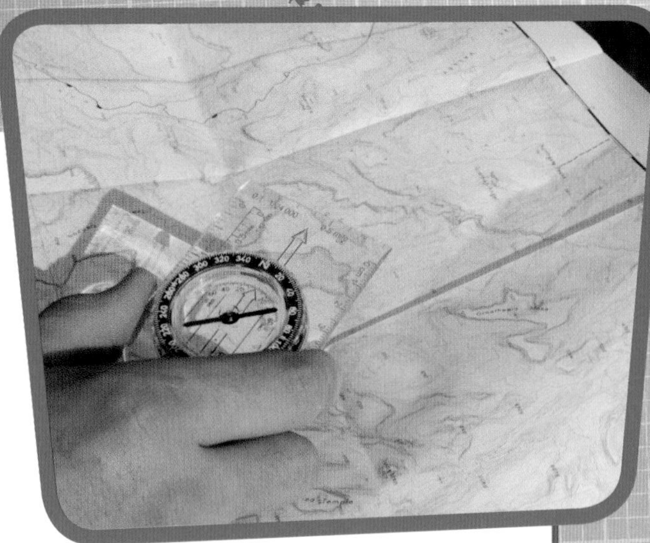

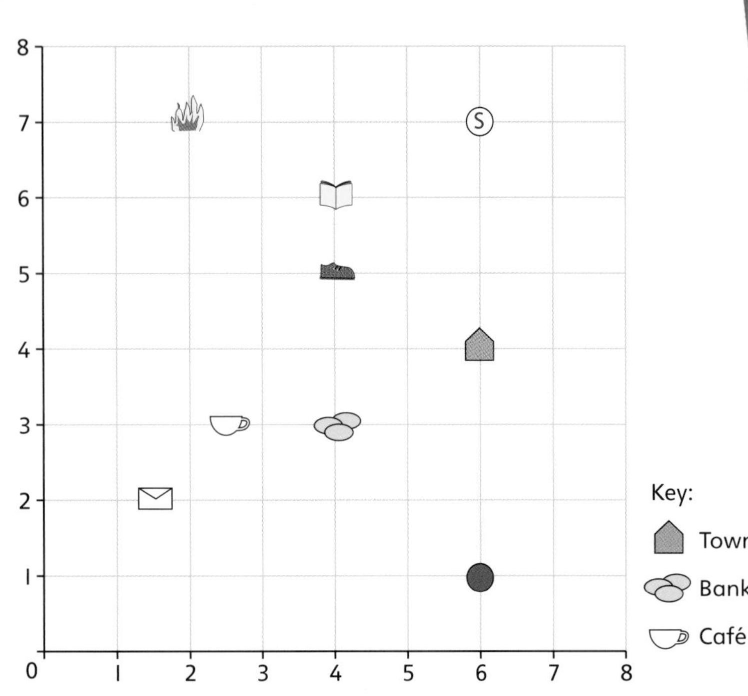

Key:

Town hall	School	Fire station
Bank	Police station	Library
Café	Shoe shop	Post office

1 Coordinates

a Write down the coordinates of the post office and the school.
Put a piece of tracing paper over the map. Mark the two places on the tracing paper and draw a straight line between these two places.
Write down the names of any buildings that the line crosses. **Level 4**

b Mark the position of the police station and the fire station onto the tracing paper.
Draw a straight line between these two places.
Write down the coordinates of any other points on the grid that the line crosses. **Level 4**

c Write down any patterns that you notice in the line that you drew in **b**. **Level 5**

d Write this pattern as a function machine. **Level 5**

e Use this function machine to find the coordinates of other places on the line. **Level 5**

2 Four in a line

A game for two players. Player 1 uses Xs, player 2 uses Os.

- Draw a coordinate grid numbered from 0 to 5 on each axis.
- Player 1 chooses a pair of coordinates, writes them down and marks the point on the grid with an X.
- Player 2 chooses a different pair of coordinates, writes them down and marks the point on the grid with an O.
- Take turns to think of a coordinate for a point.

The game ends when one player gets four points in a line either horizontally, vertically or diagonally. **Level 4**
If the player can describe a pattern that they observe in the numbers they are the winner. **Level 5**
Repeat the game using a coordinate grid numbered from −3 to +3 on each axis. **Level 5**

The BIG ideas

- When reading **coordinates**, always start at 0 and read across first and then up or down. Level 4 & Level 5
- You can generate a **sequence** from the **first term** and the **term-to-term rule**. Level 4
- You can generate a sequence from the **position-to-term** rule. Level 5
- The quarters of a **coordinate grid** are called **quadrants**. Level 5
- The point where two axes meet is called the **origin**. Level 5
- You can use a **function machine** to help you find x- and y-values when you know the rule connecting them. Level 5
- **Straight line graphs** parallel to the x-axis will be of the form $y = a$ (where a is a number). Level 5
- Straight line graphs parallel to the y-axis will be of the form $x = a$ (where a is a number). Level 5

Find your level

Level 4

Q1 Look at the diagram.

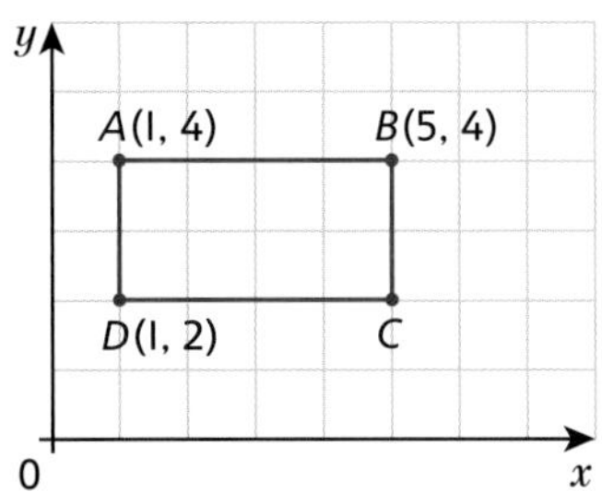

a The point E is halfway between points A and B. What are its coordinates?

b Shape $ABCD$ is a rectangle. What are the coordinates of point C?

Q2 Points A and B are on a line on this grid.

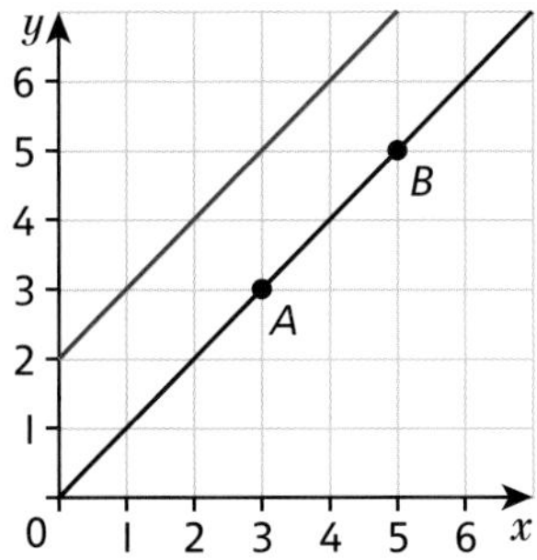

a The coordinates of point A are (3, 3). What are the coordinates of point B?

b Look at the red line on the grid. Write the coordinates of any point on this line.

Level 5

Q3 a Copy and complete the table for this sequence made of sticks.

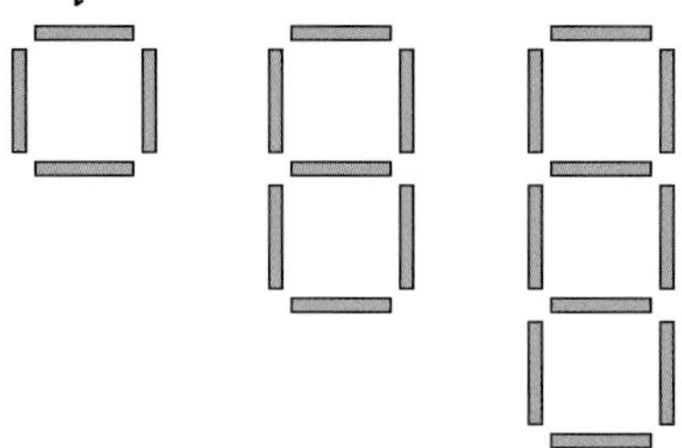

Pattern number	1	2	3	4	5
Number of sticks	4				

b How many sticks are there in the tenth pattern?

Q4 Meia is saving money to buy a bike. She saves £12 per month.

a Copy and complete the table below to show how much Meia saves each month.

Month	1	2	3	4	5
Savings (£)	12				

b Copy and complete this sentence.
amount saved
= number of months × ____

c How much will Meia have saved after 8 months?

d How long will it take Meia to save £180?

11 Taking a different angle

This unit is about reflections and angles.

Watching the path of a snooker ball will help you understand reflection. In snooker, balls bounce off the cushions around the edge of the table. Skilled players can plan where a ball needs to hit a cushion so it will bounce off it and either hit another ball or go into a pocket.

Activities

A Roll a ball, at an angle, towards a wall. What do you notice about the angle it meets the wall and the angle it leaves the wall? With a partner, decide where you will roll the ball from, where it will hit the wall, and where your partner needs to stand to catch the ball.

B A full-size snooker table measures approximately 180 cm by 360 cm.

- Make a scale drawing of a snooker table by drawing a rectangle 9 cm by 18 cm. Mark pockets 0.5 cm wide at each corner, and halfway along the long sides. Draw a white ball and a red ball on the table.
- Draw a path the white ball could take to bounce off a cushion and hit the red ball. Mark what you know about the angles on your diagram.
- Work out another path for the white ball.

Did you know?

The fastest snooker frame on record in a world-ranking tournament lasted just three minutes. The slowest lasted 88 minutes.

Before you start this unit...

1 How many different types of triangle can you name and describe? page 104

2 How many different types of quadrilateral can you name and describe? page 104

3 What other 2-D shapes can you name? page 104

4 Draw a line that is exactly 11.7 cm long. page 132

5 How many degrees are there in a full turn? page 102

In science the angle at which light meets a mirror is called the angle of incidence, and the angle it leaves at is called the angle of reflection.

11.1 Reflection symmetry

- Recognise whether a shape has reflection symmetry
- Know about the symmetry properties of triangles and quadrilaterals

Why learn this?

Symmetry is found in nature. The 'eyespots' on this butterfly help scare off predators.

What's the BIG idea?

- A shape with reflection symmetry has a **line of symmetry**. The line of symmetry divides the shape into two identical halves. **Level 3**
- A shape may have more than one line of symmetry. **Level 3**
- You can check whether a shape has **reflection symmetry** by using a mirror or tracing paper, or by folding it. **Level 3**
- Different types of triangle have different reflection symmetry. **Level 4**
- Different types of quadrilateral have different reflection symmetry. **Level 5**

Super fact!

Security systems that recognise you by your eye work because your iris is not symmetrical.

Practice, practice, practice!

Level 3

3C I can tell whether a shape has reflection symmetry

1 Look at these road signs.

a  b  c  d  e  f  g  h  i  

Copy and complete the table to show their symmetry.

Type of symmetry	a	b	c	d	e	f	g	h	i
Horizontal line of symmetry									
Vertical line of symmetry	✓								
No reflection symmetry									

2 Copy these shapes onto squared paper.

A 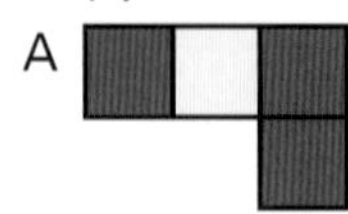 B 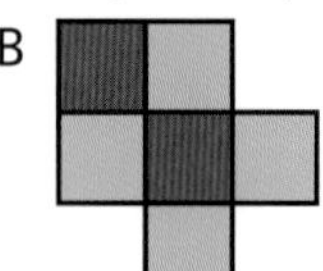 C 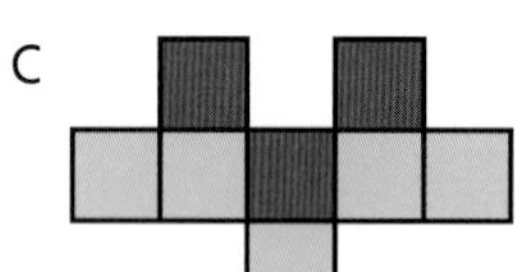 D 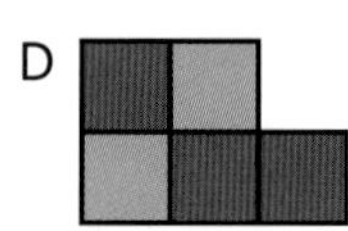

a Add just one black square to each to create a new shape with reflection symmetry.
Use a dotted line to show the line of symmetry.
One possibility for A is shown.

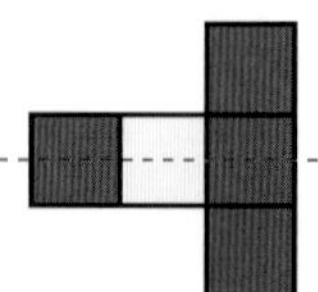

b Say whether the line of symmetry is horizontal, vertical or diagonal.

c Did you find more than one way to do any of these? Draw any extra solutions you found.

diagonal horizontal line of symmetry

3 a Copy and complete the table for triangles A, B, C and D.

	Type of triangle	Number of lines of symmetry
A		
B		
C		
D		

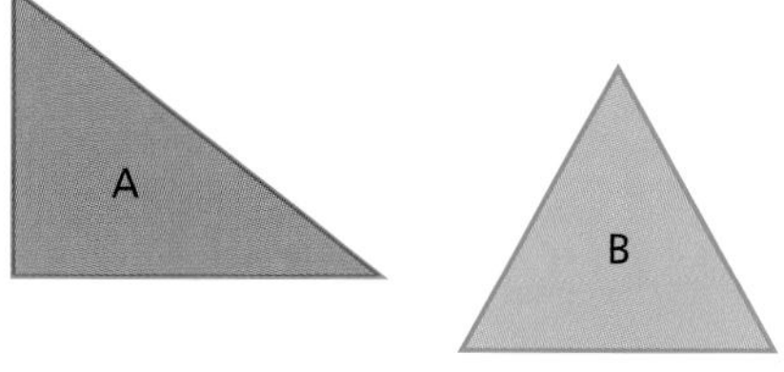

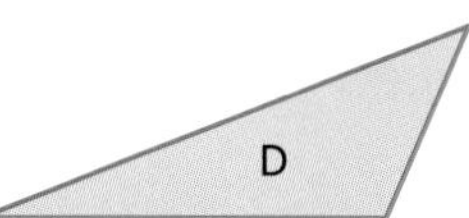

D

b Draw a right-angled triangle which has 1 line of symmetry.

Hint: A right-angled triangle has one right angle.

c How many types of triangle can have three lines of symmetry?

Level 4

4a I can describe the reflection symmetry of any triangle

4 Make three copies of each drawing.

A B

a Add two more straight lines to each drawing to make a quadrilateral that has
 i one line of symmetry
 ii more than one line of symmetry
 iii no lines of symmetry.

b If the quadrilateral you have made has a special name, add this to your drawing. If it does not, write 'An irregular quadrilateral' next to it.

c Show any lines of symmetry on your drawings using a dotted line.

Level 5

5c I can describe the reflection symmetry of any quadrilateral

Now try this!

A Square cut out

Draw a 8 cm square on squared paper. Cut it out and fold it in four to make a smaller square. Now copy this design onto your folded square. Cut out the shaded sections.

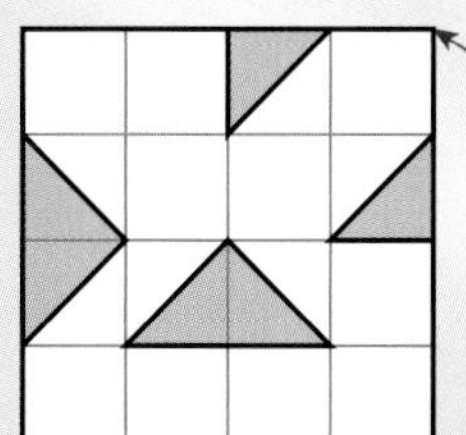

This corner is the centre of your unfolded 8 cm square.

Unfold your shape. Describe its symmetry.
Experiment and design your own shapes.

B Try a tangram

Cut out the tangram pieces from Resource sheet 11.1 and rearrange them to make an arrow, using all seven pieces. There are several ways to do this. How many can you find? What other symmetrical shapes can you make?

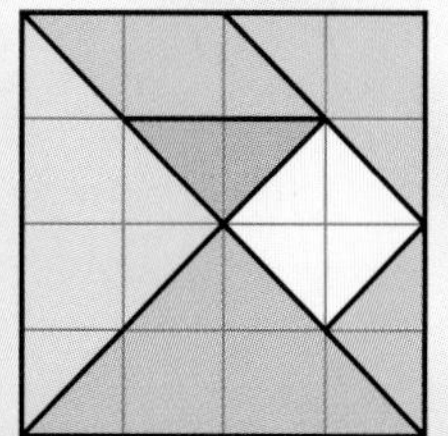

reflection symmetry symmetrical vertical

11.2 Reflection and translation

- Know where a shape will be after it has been reflected
- Know how to translate a shape

Why learn this?
Reflections can be used to create surprising patterns.

What's the BIG idea?

→ When a shape, or **object**, is **reflected** in a **mirror line** you see its **image**. Level 3

→ Lines of symmetry can be **horizontal**, **vertical** or **diagonal** and are usually shown as dotted lines. Level 3

→ You can make patterns with **reflection** symmetry if you reflect in **parallel** or **perpendicular** lines. Level 3

→ You can **translate** a shape by sliding it up, down, to the right or left, or by combining these movements. Level 3

Practice, practice, practice!

Level 3

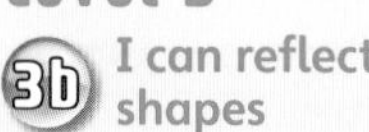

I can reflect shapes

1 Copy these drawings.
Reflect each shape in its mirror line.

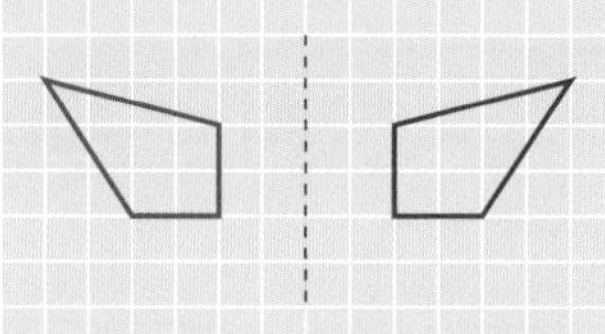

a

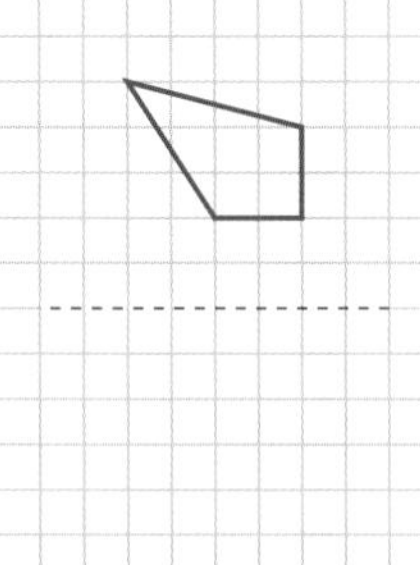

b

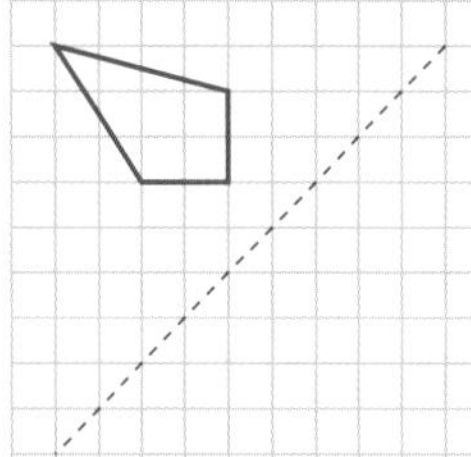

c

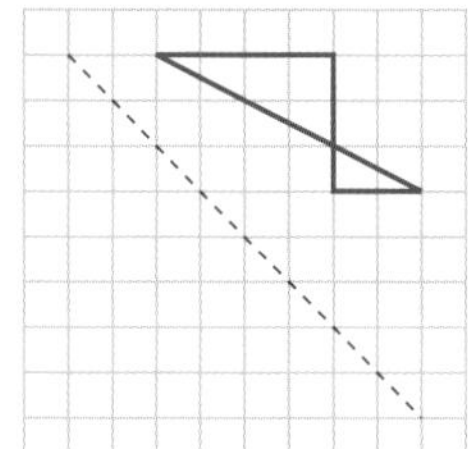

2 **a** Copy this drawing. Reflect shape A in the line Y. Label the new shape B.

b Now reflect both shapes A and B in the line X.

c What shape have you made?

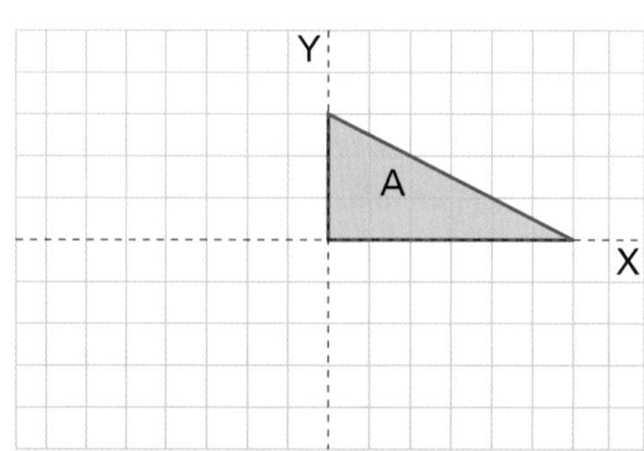

diagonal horizontal image mirror line object

Level 3

3b I can reflect shapes

3 a What's on the menu? Read this without a mirror.

b Add three more choices of your own, written in mirror writing.

pineapple fruit juice
mushroom pizza
chicken korma
strawberry milkshake
cheese and onion crisps

Super fact!

Leonardo da Vinci often used to write his notes using mirror writing.

3a I can translate shapes

4 Copy these drawings and move each shape by the given amount.

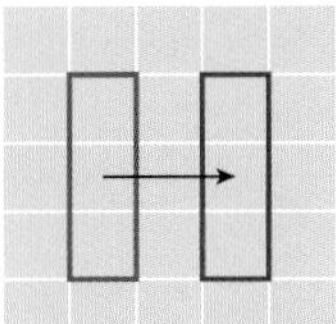

2 squares right

a

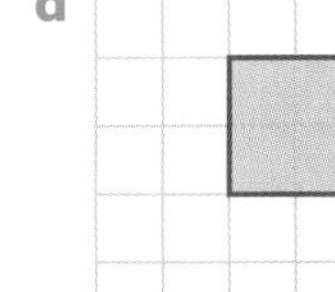

2 squares left

b

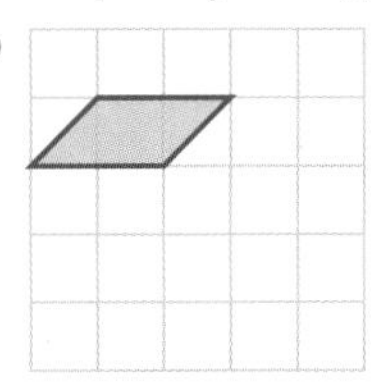

2 squares right
2 squares down

c

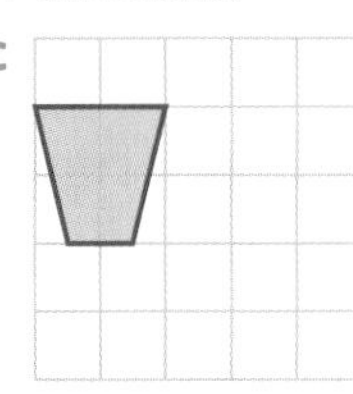

3 squares right
2 squares down

5 Rectangle X has been translated to position A, using the instruction LEFT 2, DOWN 5.

Draw a grid like this. Extend the axes to 10 each way. Mark the new positions of rectangle X when it starts from its original position and moves:

a RIGHT 4, UP 2 (position B)
b LEFT 5, DOWN 6 (position C)
c LEFT 4, UP 1 (position D)
d LEFT 5, UP 0 (position E)
e RIGHT 0, DOWN 7 (position F)
f RIGHT 1, DOWN 3 (position G)

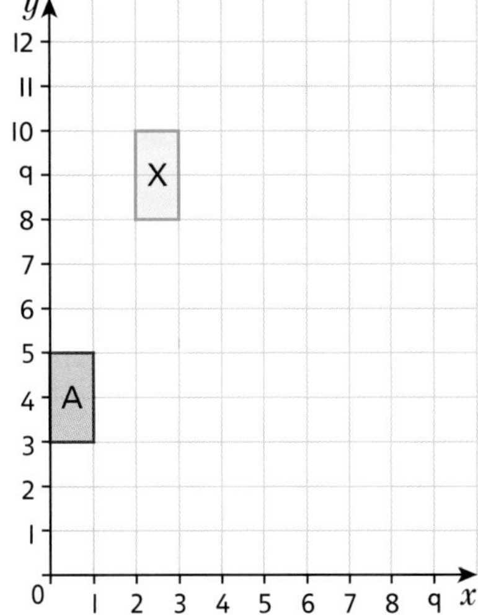

Now try this!

A Make a kaleidoscope

Have you ever thought how a kaleidoscope works? You can make a simple one with two mirrors, sticky tape and a colourful design. You could choose a picture from a magazine or the internet, or design one yourself.

1 Join the two mirrors with a sticky tape 'hinge'.

2 Move the kaleidoscope over your picture and see the patterns it makes.

What do you notice if you increase the angle between the mirrors? What happens if you decrease the angle? Use a protractor to position the mirrors. How many images do you see for angles of 90° and 45°?

Super fact!

If you place an object between two parallel mirrors and look in one of the mirrors you will see several reflections of your object, but they don't all look the same.

B Create wallpaper

Use a simple drawing or part of a letter or number to create some patterned wallpaper. You're allowed to reflect and translate any part of the image you choose.

arallel perpendicular reflect reflection translate vertical

maths!

Rangoli patterns

A rangoli is a colourful design made on the floor near the entrance to a house to welcome guests.

For Diwali, Hindus draw bright rangoli patterns to encourage the goddess Lakshmi to enter their homes.

A rangoli should use a lot of colour. Often these colours reflect the region of the household.

Most rangoli designs are made from geometric patterns formed from dots and lines. They give opportunities for people to show individual artistic skill or to work together. Sometimes many people work as a group for days on a single design.

A common way to draw a rangoli pattern is to use a square with four lines of symmetry.

Only one triangle of the pattern needs to be designed and then it is reflected seven times to complete the square.

Draw a rangoli pattern

- Use these triangles to make rangoli patterns.

You will need Resource sheet A11a and tracing paper.

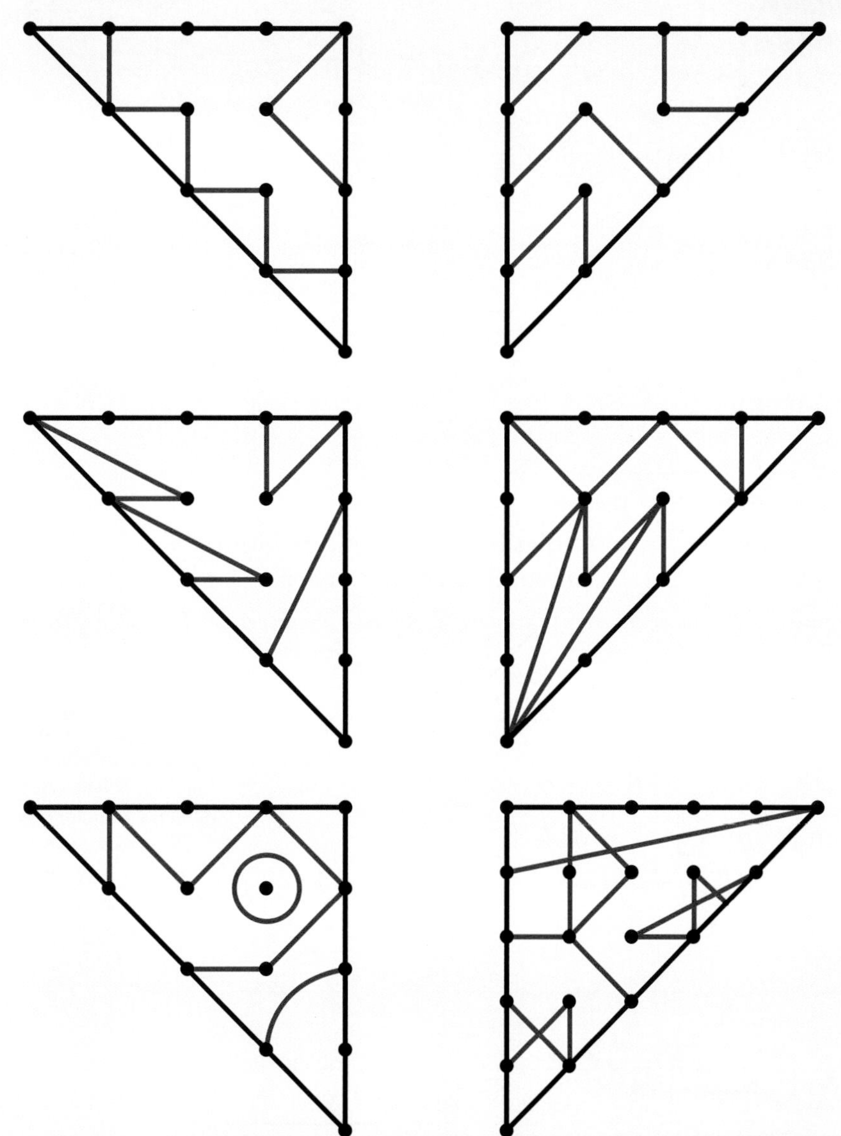

- Use colour to make your patterns even better. Colour them so that they keep four lines of symmetry.

- Use Resource sheet A11b to create your own rangoli patterns.

11.3 Shapes and angle rules

- Be able to name different types of triangles
- Know how to work out missing angles in triangles
- Know the rules about angles that meet on a straight line or around a point

Why learn this?

Architects use angle rules and the properties of shapes when they design structures.

What's the BIG idea?

→ A triangle can be scalene, isosceles or equilateral. **Level 3**

→ A right-angled triangle has one right angle. **Level 4**

right-angled triangle

→ Angles in a triangle add up to 180°. **Level 5**

→ Angles that meet at a **point** add up to 360°. **Level 5**

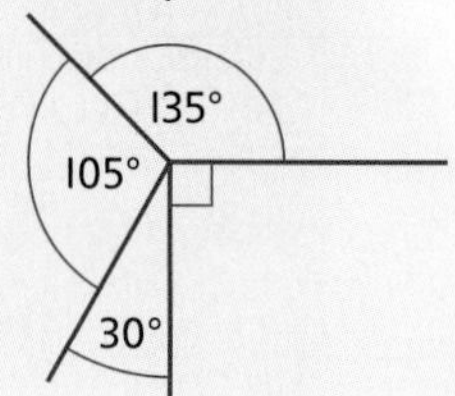

→ Angles that meet on a **straight line** add up to 180°. **Level 5**

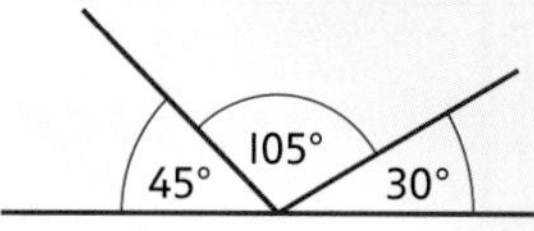

→ Vertically opposite angles are equal. **Level 5**

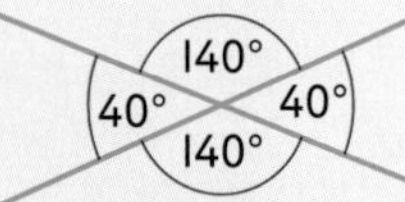

Super fact!

The Bermuda Triangle is a triangular area in the Atlantic Ocean where ships and aircraft are said to have disappeared with no clear explanation.

Practice, practice, practice!

Level 4

4a I can label triangles and identify properties of triangles

1 **a** *EGH* is a triangle. What other triangles can you see in this shape?

b Which triangle is equilateral?

c Which triangle is right-angled?

d List any scalene triangles.

e List any isosceles triangles.

Hint: You'll need to measure the sides of the triangles.

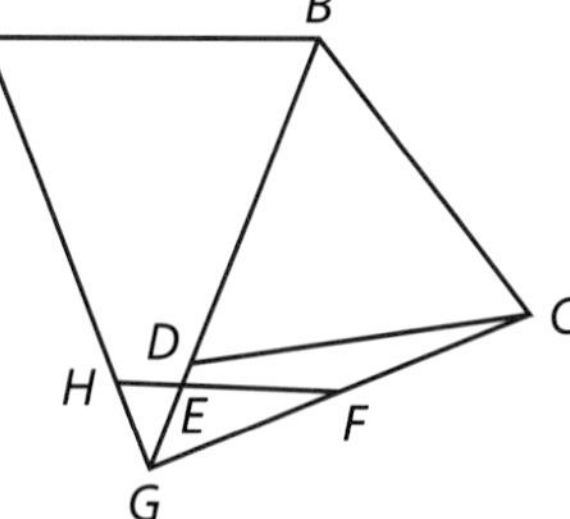

4a I can solve simple problems using the properties of special triangles

2 **a** What types of triangles make this shape?

Hint: Measure the sides to check.

b What size are the angles in each of these triangles?

c What do the angles add up to at the centre of the shape?

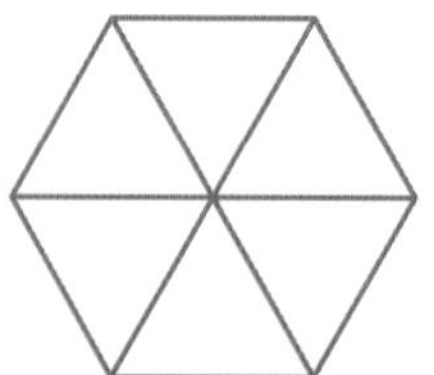

angles at a point | angles on a straight line | degree (°) | equilateral

3 Calculate the missing angle, a, in this shape.

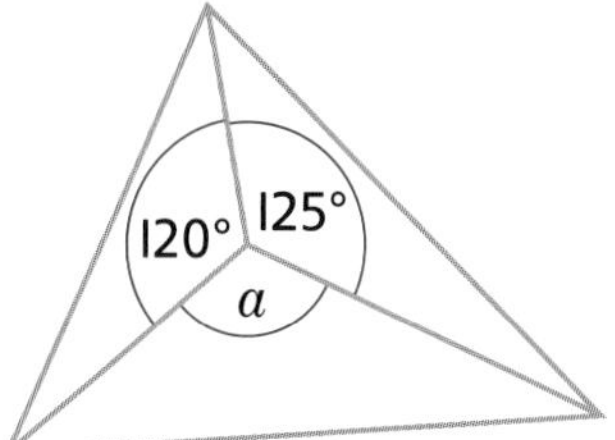

4 Calculate the missing angle in each triangle.

a

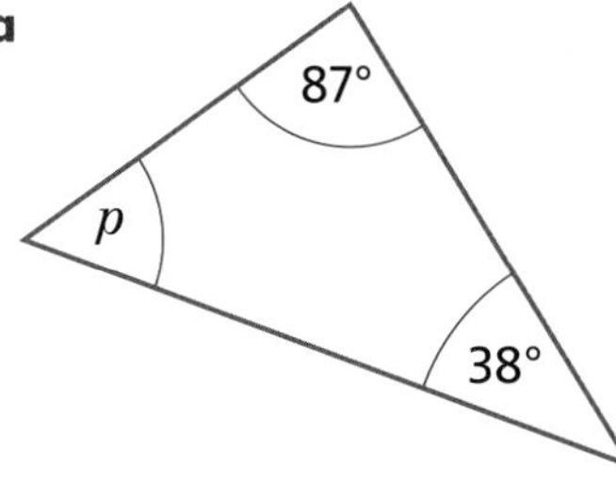

b

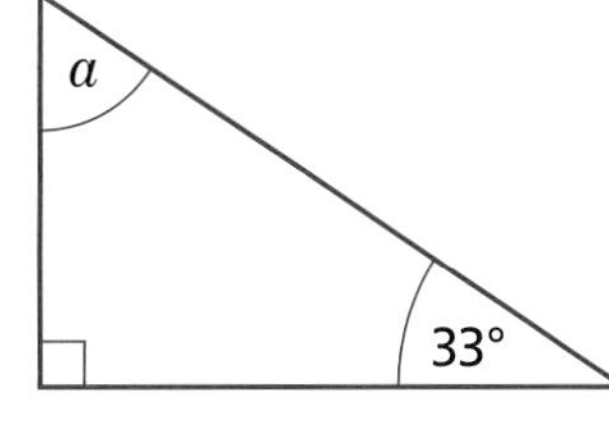

5 Sketch four rectangles and draw in their diagonals.
What do you notice about the angles that meet at the centre of each quadrilateral?

6 An equilateral triangle and a square join to make a straight line.
What is the angle between the two shapes?
Explain how you worked out your answer.

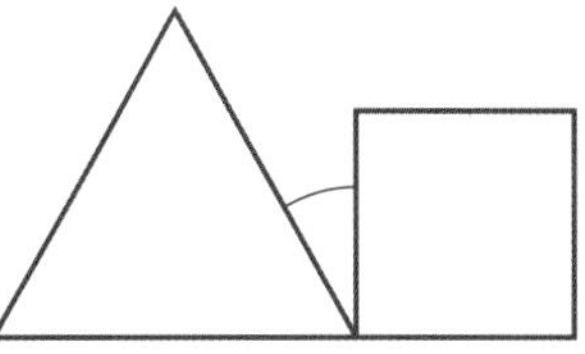

7 **a** Two of the angles in an isosceles triangle are 29°.
Work out the third angle.

b The largest angle of an isosceles triangle is 72°.
Work out the two smaller angles.

c The smallest angle in an isosceles triangle is 20°.
Work out the two larger angles.

Level 5

5c I can calculate missing angles around a point

5b I can calculate angles in a triangle

Tip
If you forget what the angles in a triangle add up to, think of an isosceles right-angled triangle (90° + 45° + 45° = 180°).

5b I can recognise and use vertically opposite angles

5a I can use my knowledge of angle rules to solve problems

Now try this!

A Rectangles and triangles

Draw a rectangle. Cut like this to make three triangles.
Rearrange the triangles to make a different rectangle.
Cut another rectangle like this to make four triangles.
Cut them out then rearrange them to make a different rectangle.
Mix up the seven triangles.
Challenge a partner to make two rectangles out of these pieces.

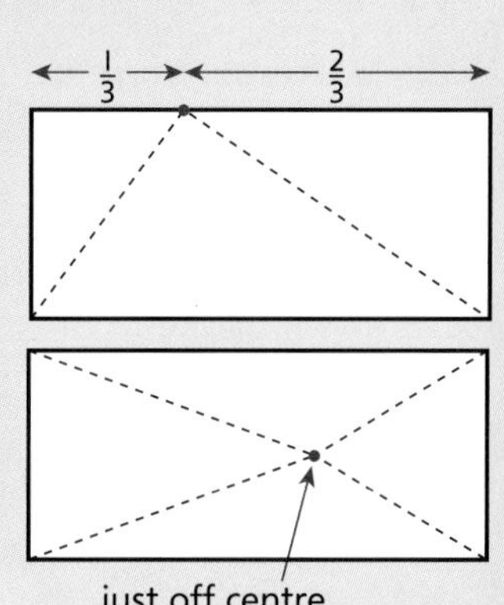

B Constructing polygons

In a regular polygon all sides are the same length and angles are equal.

a Which regular polygons can be made from isosceles triangles with at least one of the angles equal to 45°?

b How can you make a regular hexagon from two identical right-angled triangles and two identical isosceles triangles? How do you know that this is the only regular polygon that can be made?

isosceles right-angled scalene triangle

11.4 Drawing 2-D and 3-D shapes

- Recognise 2-D diagrams and pictures which show views of 3-D solids
- Recognise and describe properties of 3-D solids in isometric drawings
- Measure lines to within one millimetre and angles to within one degree
- Draw lines to within one millimetre and angles to within one degree

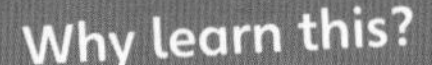

Why learn this?

Artists need to be able to show 3-D objects in 2-D.

What's the BIG idea?

- Lines and angles need to be measured accurately **Level 3 & Level 4**
- You can use isometric paper to create **2-D** representations of **3-D** shapes. **Level 4**
- From simple 2-D representations you can work out the properties of 3-D shapes. **Level 5**

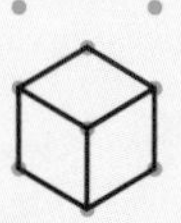

Practice, practice, practice!

Level 3

3a I can measure lines to the nearest millimetre

1 **a** Length A = 1.5 cm. Measure lengths B and C to the nearest millimetre.

b Check you are correct by measuring the height of the giraffe.

c 1 cm on the photo represents 1 m in real life.
How tall is the real giraffe?

Level 4

4c I can draw lines to the nearest millimetre and measure acute angles to within one degree

2 **a** Follow these instructions to draw the three triangles described in the table.
- Draw AB and AC at right angles to each other on squared paper.
- Join B and C with a straight line.

	AB	*AC*
Triangle 1	5.5 cm	6.0 cm
Triangle 2	4.9 cm	6.7 cm
Triangle 3	6.3 cm	4.2 cm

B, x, y, *A*, *C*

b Measure angles x and y in each triangle.

4b I can identify simple 3-D shapes from their 2-D representations

3 **a** What 3-D solid does diagram A represent?

b Do diagrams A and B show the same solid?

A

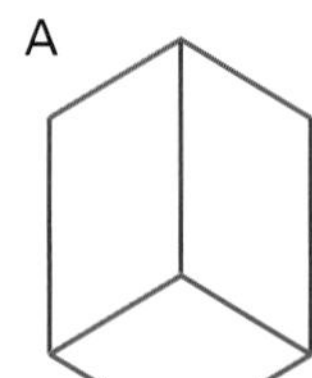

B

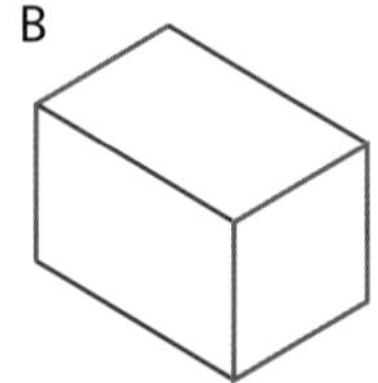

edge face parallel perpendicular protractor

4 How many cubes are needed to make each of these solids?

Hint: There are no hidden cubes.

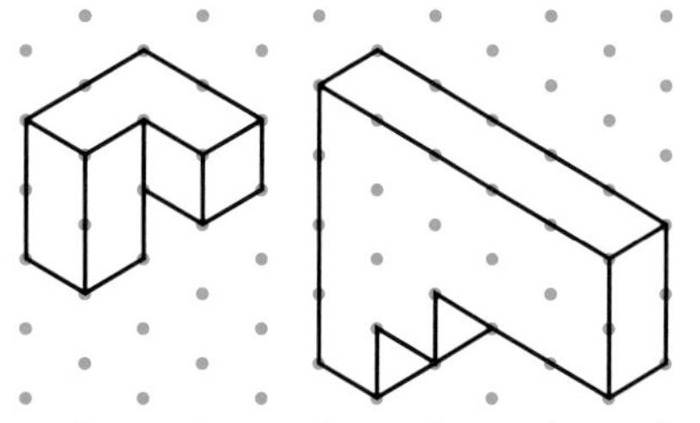

Level 4

4a I can measure obtuse angles to the nearest degree

5 **a** Measure the obtuse angle in each of these triangles.

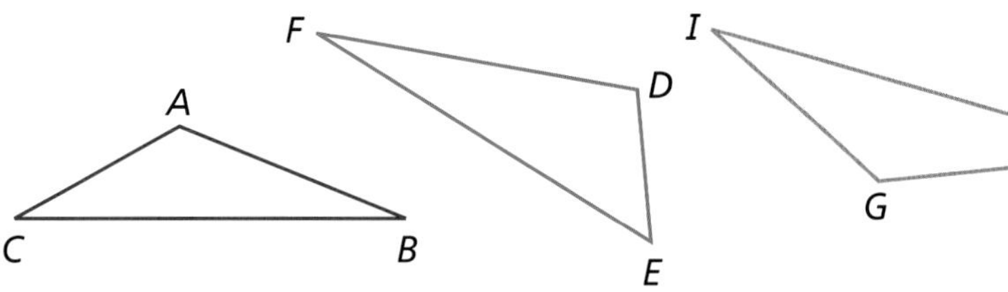

b Work out the reflex angle at the same vertex for each triangle.

c Make accurate drawings of $\angle CAB$, $\angle FDE$ and $\angle IGH$.

Level 5

5c I can use a protractor to draw acute or obtuse angles

Watch out! Make sure you use the correct protractor scale!

6 **a** How many cubes do you need to make this solid?

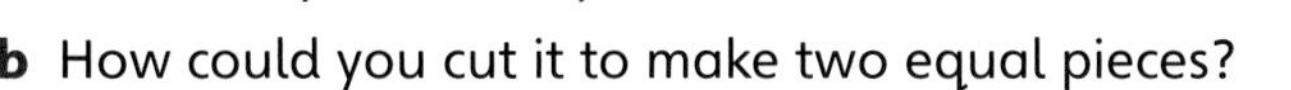

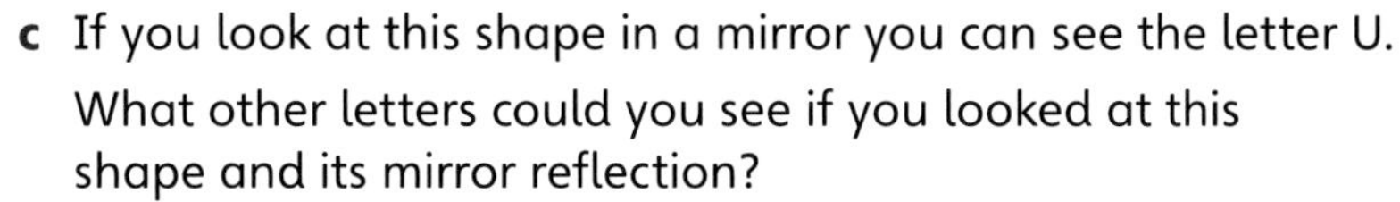

b How could you cut it to make two equal pieces?

c If you look at this shape in a mirror you can see the letter U.

What other letters could you see if you looked at this shape and its mirror reflection?

d How could you rearrange these cubes to make a letter H when looked at in a mirror?

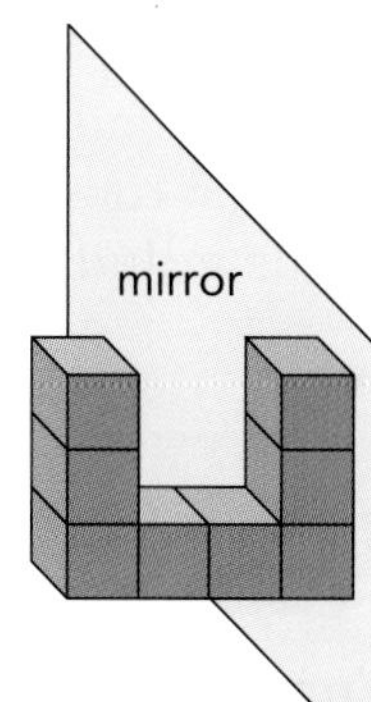

5c I can describe properties of simple 2-D representations of 3-D shapes

Now try this!

A Angle estimation

A game for two to four players. Draw three lines meeting at a point. Each person writes down estimates for the angles. Measure the angles. Score 2 points if you are within 5°, 1 point if you are within 10°. The winner is the person with the most points after five examples.

B Can you clone?

A game for two players. Player 1 (the builder) secretly makes a shape from five cubes. When faces touch they must overlap completely.

Player 2 (the cloner) tries to make exactly the same shape by asking up to 10 questions. The builder can only answer 'yes' or 'no'.

The cloner wins 1 point for a correct shape; otherwise the builder wins 1 point.

Did you know?

Isometric drawing is also used in Technology to draw 3-D objects.

Hint: Use the words vertex/edge/face.

three-dimensional (3-D) **two-dimensional (2-D)** **vertex** **vertices**

11.5 Constructing triangles

- Measure and draw angles, including reflex angles, to within 1° accuracy
- Construct a triangle if you know the lengths of two sides and the angle between them
- Construct a triangle if you know the sizes of two angles and the length of the side between them

Why learn this?

Surveyors use angle and length measurements to create maps and plans.

What's the BIG idea?

- You can **measure reflex angles** to the nearest degree even if you only have a 180° **protractor**. Level 4
- You can use a protractor to draw reflex angles to the nearest degree. Level 5
- If you know the lengths of two sides and the angle between them, you can construct a triangle. This angle is called the **included angle**. Level 5
- If you know two angles and the length of the side between them, you can construct a triangle. This side is called the **included side**. Level 5

Watch out!

Angle questions can start with 'construct', 'calculate', 'estimate', 'draw' or 'measure'. Each is a different type of question.

Practice, practice, practice!

1 Angle $p = 27°$ and angle $q = 47°$.

a Draw these two angles on the same diagram.

b Measure the reflex angle r.

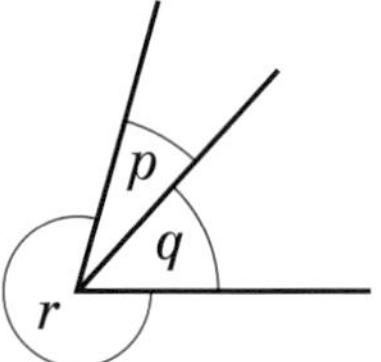

2 **a** Measure the reflex angle between the 3 and the 10 on the clock face.

b Measure the reflex angle between 6 and 4.

c Without using a protractor, explain how you can work out the reflex angle between 5 and 2.

d Measure it to see if you are correct.

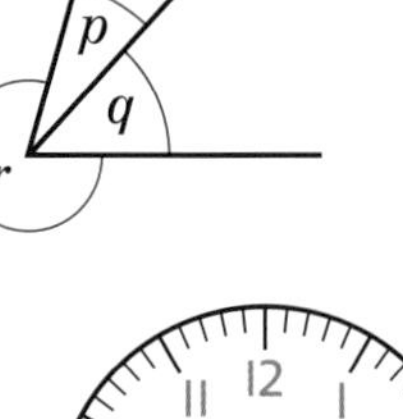

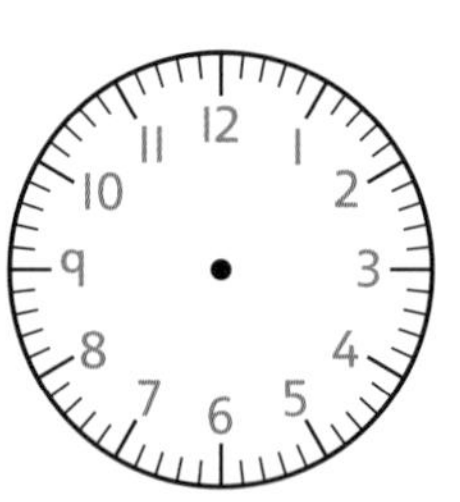

Level 4

4a I can draw acute angles and measure reflex angles to within 1°

4a I can measure reflex angles to within 1°

3 **a** Draw each angle between a pair of 5 cm lines.

i 187° **ii** 200° **iii** 305° **iv** 329°

b Measure the smaller angle between each pair of lines.

c Say whether each angle in **b** is acute or obtuse.

Level 5

5c I can draw reflex angles to within 1°

base construct included angle included side

4 **a** Think of three different numbers that are each between 100 and 150, and add together to make 360.

b Use these numbers to draw three angles that meet at a point.

5 You are going to construct $\triangle ABC$. Choose two sides from the information below.

Sides: $AB = 6$ cm $BC = 10.7$ cm $CA = 7$ cm

Angles: $\angle ABC = 38°$ $\angle BCA = 32°$ $\angle CAB = 110°$

a What is the name of the angle where your two lines meet?

b Construct your triangle using the two lengths and the angle from **a**.

Hint Draw a rough sketch of the triangle and label it with the information first.

c Choose a different pair of sides. Which is the included angle?

d Construct this triangle.

e What do you notice about the two triangles?

6 A mobile phone mast can be seen above the buildings from two schools. Here are some of the measurements pupils have taken.

- Angle above the ground from the primary school: 57°
- Angle above the ground from the secondary school: 28°
- Distance between the schools: 850 m

secondary school   mast   primary school

A primary school pupil says that the distance from her school to the mast is less than half the distance of the mast from the secondary school. Construct a triangle using the information given to see if she is right.

Hint On your diagram let 1 cm represent 100 m.

Level 5

5b I can construct a triangle if I know two lengths and the angle between them

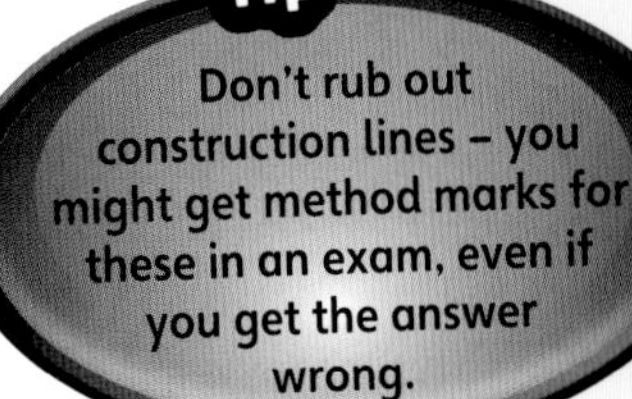

5a I can construct a triangle if I know two angles and the length between them

Now try this!

A Estimate or CRASH

A game for two players.

1 Both players secretly write down a number between 5 and 355 – this is your CRASH number.

2 Take turns to draw two lines that meet at an angle. Your partner estimates the angle between them.

3 Measure the angle. Within 5° score 3 points, within 10° score 1 point.

4 If your partner draws an angle within 10° of your CRASH number call 'CRASH'. Add 10 points to your score and the game ends. The player with the highest score wins.

B Zap it

A game for two players.

1 Draw a line 20 cm long. Write your names at opposite ends.

2 Player 1 draws a cross somewhere above the line.

3 Both estimate the angle from your end of the line to the cross.

4 Measure the correct angles to check.

5 Within 5° score 3 points. Within 10° score 1 point.

6 Player 2 draws a cross at least 5 cm away from any other cross and you play again. The first pupil to score 10 points wins.

measure protractor reflex angle ruler side

Unit 11 plenary

Design a game

A toy manufacturer is developing a new game, Snooball. It is based on snooker and is for children under ten years old.

1 At the start of the game all the balls except the white cue ball are placed in a triangle. There are nine red balls, three black balls and three yellow balls.

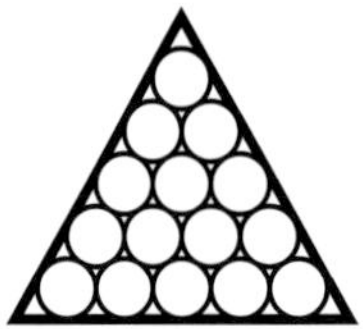

Make two copies of this ball triangle.
Show how you could arrange the balls in the triangle to give

a one line of reflection symmetry

b three lines of reflection symmetry. **Level 3**

2 You need to explain how to make the wooden triangle frame.

a What type of triangle is it? **Level 4**

b What is the angle at each vertex? **Level 4**

c The triangle is 22 cm across the base. Construct a full-size drawing of it to send to the manufacturers. **Level 5**

3 The game will include an instruction booklet. In one section, it will explain what happens when a ball hits the cushion.

Diagram A

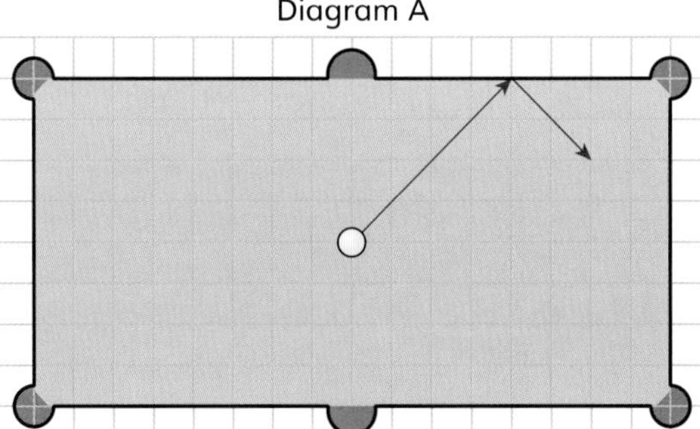

a Copy diagram A onto centimetre squared paper. Show where the ball will go.

b Does the ball go into a pocket? What kind of quadrilateral does its path make?

c Now copy diagram B and show what happens to the ball.

Diagram B

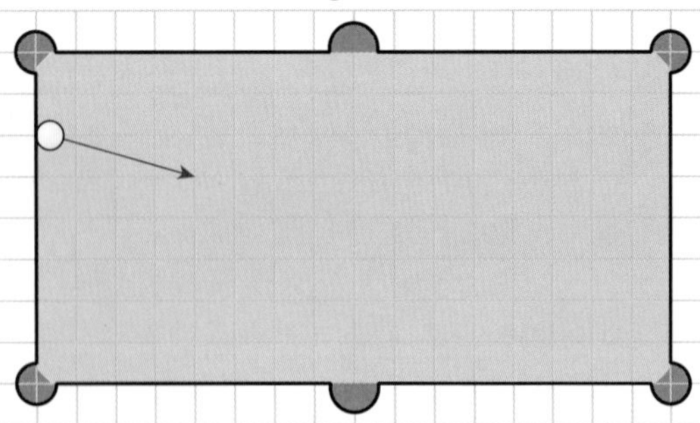

d Measure how far the ball travels in diagram B. **Level 4**

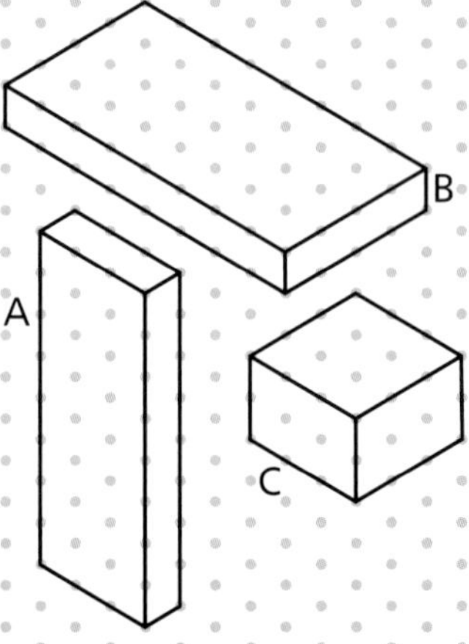

4 The packaging department needs to choose a box to deliver the table in.
Which of these shapes do you think will be best – A, B or C?
Why? **Level 4**

The BIG ideas

- → You can check whether a shape has **reflection symmetry** by using a mirror or tracing paper, or simply by folding a shape. Level 3
- → An **equilateral triangle** has three equal sides, three equal angles of 60° and three lines of symmetry. Level 4
- → A **square** has four equal sides, four equal angles of 90°, four lines of symmetry and opposite sides that are parallel. Level 4
- → Lines need to be drawn and measured to within one millimetre of the correct length. Level 4
- → Angles need to be drawn and measured to within one degree of the correct angle. Level 4
- → You can use **isometric paper** to create 2-D representations of 3-D shapes. Level 4

Find your level

Level 3

Q1 I have a square grid, two triangles and a square. I make a pattern on the grid with the shapes. The first pattern I make has no lines of symmetry.

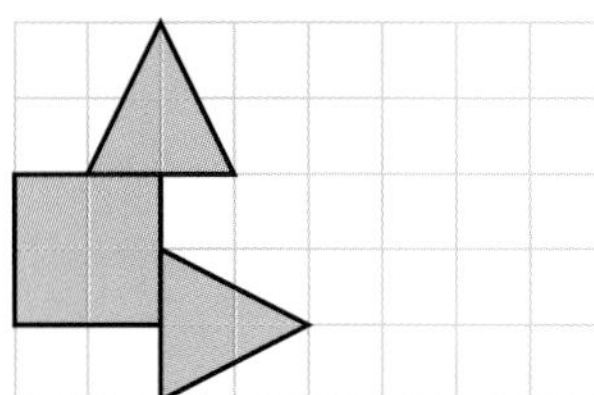

Use squared paper for the grid.

a Draw the square and two triangles on the grid to make a pattern with two lines of symmetry.

b Draw the square and two triangles on the grid to make a pattern with only one line of symmetry.

Level 4

Q2 a Measure the lengths of *AB* and *CD*, correct to the nearest millimetre.

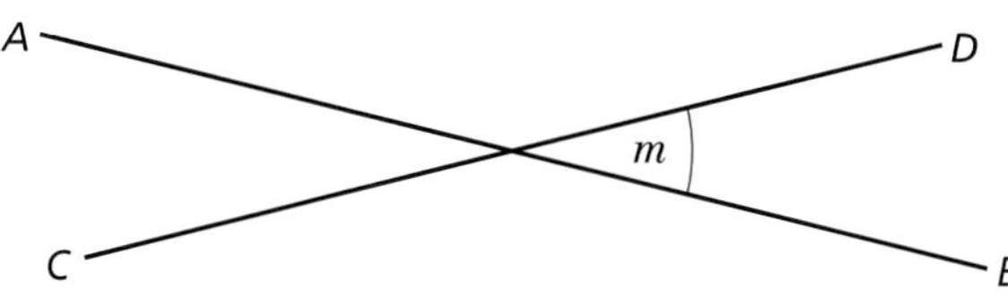

b What are the lengths of *AB* and *CD* in centimetres?

c Measure angle m.

Q3 Triangle *ABD* is the reflection of triangle *ABC* in the line *AB*.

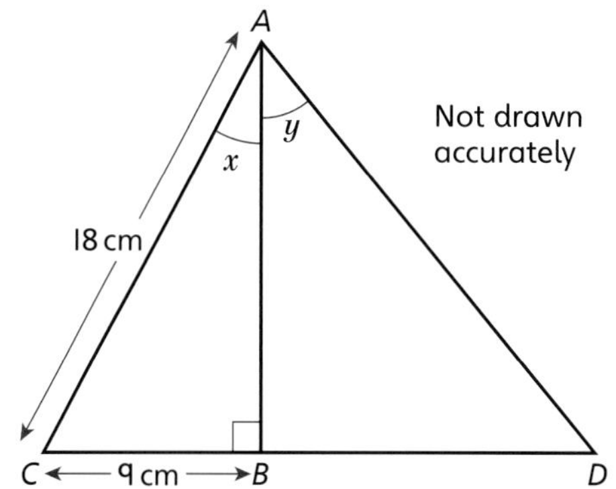

a What is the length of *AD*?
What is the length of *CD*?
How do you know that *ACD* is an equilateral triangle?

b What is the size of angle y?
How do you know?

c What is the size of angle x?
How do you know?

Level 5

Q4 a A pupil measured the angles about a point. She said the angles were 123°, 54°, 29°, and 54°. Was she correct? Explain your answer.

b The diagram shows triangle ABC.
Work out the sizes of angles x, y and z.

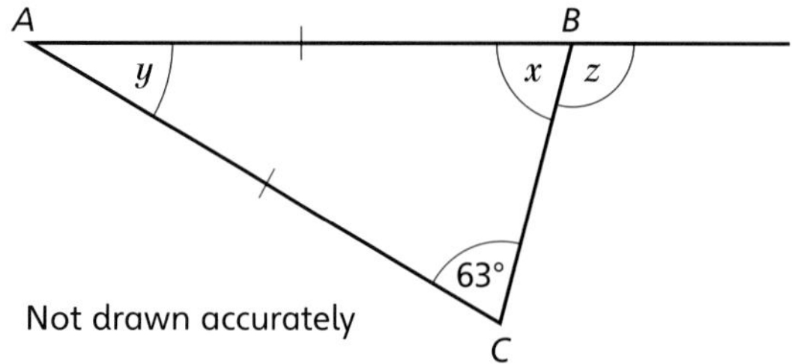

12 More, less or the same?

This unit is about ratio and proportion, and the relationships between quantities.

Good cooks use the correct amounts of ingredients. Add too much salt and your biscuits will taste terrible. Add too much flour and your pastry could be rock hard! Chefs are experts at making sure ingredients are in the right proportions. To help the rest of us, they write down the different quantities of ingredients in recipes.

Recipes are not only used in cookery. Builders have to make sure they use the correct amounts of cement and sand to mix mortar.

Chef Heston Blumenthal uses science to create his food dishes. He uses a science laboratory as well as a kitchen. Some of his popular dishes are snail porridge and bacon-and-egg ice cream!

Activities

A Draw a 6 × 6 grid on squared paper.

Design a pattern using red and white squares, so there is one red square for every three white squares.

What fraction of your pattern is red?

B A recipe for the name Anne Teak is two As, two Es, one K, two Ns and one T.

Write down the recipe for your name.

Who in your class has the most Es in their recipe?

Here are the recipes for the names of three famous chefs. Who are they?

- 2As, 1E, 1H, 2Is, 1L, 1N, 1O, 2Rs, 1S, 2Ts, 1Y
- 2As, 1D, 1G, 1M, 1N, 2Os, 2Rs, 1S, 1Y
- 1A, 2Es, 2Is, 1J, 1L, 1M, 1O, 1R, 1V

1 Write these percentages as fractions of 100. page 58

a 9% **b** 37% **c** 99%

2 Write true or false for each of these. page 54

a $\frac{5}{10} = \frac{1}{2}$ **b** $\frac{6}{9} = \frac{3}{6}$

c $\frac{4}{5} = \frac{1}{2}$ **d** $\frac{8}{10} = \frac{4}{5}$

3 What is page 56

a $\frac{1}{2}$ of 30 cm **b** 50% of £30

c $\frac{1}{10}$ of £80 **d** 10% of 120 g?

4 Copy and complete the table. page 58

Percentage	Fraction	Decimal
25%		0.25
	$\frac{1}{2}$	
		0.75
20%	$\frac{1}{5}$	
10%		
	$\frac{1}{10}$	

Your body has a sort of recipe called DNA. It is found in every cell and controls how each cell develops and behaves.

All the colours in this book are made by combining only four different coloured inks. The inks are cyan, magenta, yellow and black – known as CMYK in the print industry. How would you make green?

Plus digital resources

12.1 Calculating Fractions

- Give a number as a fraction of a larger number
- Calculate fractions of quantities and measurements
- Know how to multiply a fraction by an integer

What's the BIG idea?

→ To find $\frac{3}{4}$ of an amount, divide by the **denominator** and **multiply** by the **numerator**.
$\frac{3}{4}$ of 20 cm = 20 cm ÷ 4 × 3 = 5 cm × 3 = 15 cm **Level 5**

→ You can express part of an amount as a **fraction**.
20p as a fraction of £1 is $\frac{20}{100} = \frac{1}{5}$ **Level 5**

Why learn this?

Fractions can help you to compare things. In 1987 there were about 60 000 orang-utans in the world. In 2001 there were about 30 000, which is half $\left(\frac{1}{2}\right)$ as many.

Practice, practice, practice!

Level 5

5c I can multiply a fraction by an integer

1 Work out

$\frac{2}{7} \times 21$ = (21 ÷ 7) × 2 = 3 × 2 = 6

a $\frac{7}{10} \times 50$ **b** $\frac{4}{7} \times 14$ **c** $\frac{2}{3} \times 12$ **d** $\frac{3}{5} \times 30$

e $\frac{7}{12} \times 48$ **f** $\frac{5}{8} \times 24$ **g** $\frac{1}{6} \times 18$ **h** $\frac{5}{11} \times 55$

2 Copy and complete these calculations.

a $\frac{1}{3} \times 51 = \square$ **b** $\frac{1}{2} \times \square = 18$ **c** $\square \times 28 = 7$

d $\frac{2}{5} \times 40 = \square$ **e** $\frac{4}{9} \times 54 = \square$ **f** $\frac{3}{4} \times \square = 33$

5c I can find fractions of quantities and measurements with fraction answers

3 Find the fraction answers to these.

$\frac{1}{8}$ of 22 m 22 ÷ 8 = 2 remainder 6 = $2\frac{6}{8}$ m

a $\frac{1}{5}$ of 17 **b** $\frac{3}{4}$ of 25 m

c $\frac{2}{3}$ of 140 g **d** $\frac{6}{25}$ of 34

e seven tenths of 32 **f** five eighths of 43

Watch out!

The units in the question will be the units for the answer!

4 Surinder is building a model boat which is $\frac{1}{11}$ of the size of the original boat.

a The original boat is 460 cm long. How long is the model? (Give a fraction answer.)

b The original boat is 120 cm high. How high is the model? (Give a fraction answer.)

5b I can find fractions of quantities and measurements

5 Calculate these fractions of amounts.

$\frac{3}{4}$ of £80 $\frac{1}{4}$ of £80 = £80 ÷ 4 = £20
$\frac{3}{4}$ of £80 = 3 × £20 = £60

a $\frac{2}{5}$ of £300 **b** $\frac{7}{9}$ of 36 g

c $\frac{3}{8}$ of 64 cm **d** $\frac{3}{20}$ of £240

Watch out!

When finding a fraction of an amount, remember to multiply by the numerator if it is greater than 1.

amount denominator divide

6 $\frac{2}{5}$ of the pupils at Bodorgan School have school dinners.

a What fraction of the pupils do not have school dinners?

b There are 900 pupils at the school.
How many school dinners must be prepared?

7 What fraction of £1 is

50p 

50p out of £1
£1 = 100p
$\frac{50}{100} = \frac{1}{2}$

a 20p **b** 25p **c** 98p **d** 45p?

Give your answers in their simplest form.

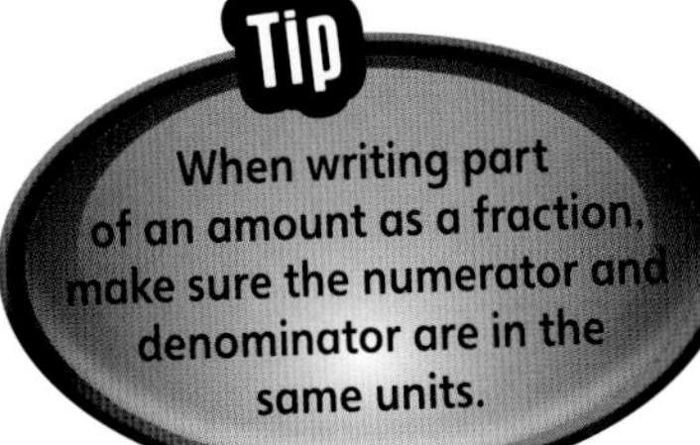

8 What fraction of a metre is

a 15 cm **b** 35 cm **c** 92 cm?

Give your answers in their simplest form.

9 Jarinder is flying from London to Delhi. The total distance is 6800 kilometres. The aeroplane needs to refuel after a distance of 2000 kilometres. What fraction of the journey is left for Jarinder to complete after the refuelling? Give your answer in its simplest form.

Level 5

5b I can find fractions of quantities and measurements

5b I can write part of an amount as a fraction in its simplest form

Now try this!

A Follow me!

Work with a partner. Make a 'follow me' game for the class. You need a card for everybody in the class. Write a fraction calculation on one card and its answer on the next card, with a different calculation below it. The final card, must give the answer to the first calculation. For example:

card 1	card 2	card 3
$\frac{1}{4}$ of 12	I am 3. Work out $\frac{1}{3}$ of 21.	I am 7. Work out $\frac{1}{5}$ of 20.

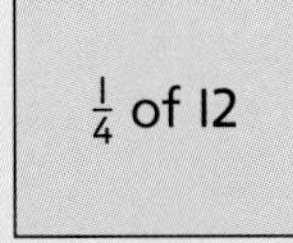

The pupil with the first card reads out the calculation.
Another pupil hold up the card with the answer.
If they are right, they read the next calculation. And so on.

B Fraction dominoes

Work with a partner. Make a set of fraction dominoes.
Divide A4 paper into 16 rectangles.
Each rectangle is a domino.
Write a fraction calculation on one end and write the answer on the next domino:

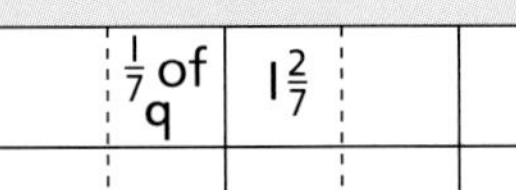

Cut them up. Swap dominoes with another pair and play a game.

fraction multiply numerator simplest form

12.2 Fractions, decimals and percentages

➩ Identify equivalent percentages, fractions and decimals
➩ Check a result by considering whether it is the right size

Why learn this?

You can compare results using fractions, decimals or percentages. A 30% discount is better than $\frac{1}{4}$ off (= 25% discount).

What's the BIG idea?

- → A **percentage** is the number of parts in every 100. **Level 4**
- → To change a percentage to a **decimal**, divide by 100.
  $25\% = \frac{25}{100} = 25 \div 100 = 0.25$ **Level 4**
- → To change a decimal to a percentage, first change the decimal to a **fraction** with **denominator** 100.
  $0.78 = \frac{78}{100} = 78\%$ **Level 4**
- → To change to a percentage, write it as a fraction with denominator 100.
  $\frac{7}{10} = \frac{70}{100} = 70\%$ **Level 4**
- → Equivalent fractions, decimals and percentages have the same value but they are written in a different way. **Level 4**
- → To cancel fractions, divide the numerator and denominator by a common factor. **Level 5**

Learn this

$\frac{1}{2} = 0.5 = 50\%$
$\frac{1}{10} = 0.1 = 10\%$
$\frac{1}{5} = 0.2 = 20\%$
$\frac{1}{4} = 0.25 = 25\%$
$\frac{1}{100} = 0.01 = 1\%$
$\frac{3}{4} = 0.75 = 75\%$

Practice, practice, practice!

Level 4

4c I can write percentages as a fraction with denominator 100

1 Write these percentages as fractions of 100.
a 29% **b** 73% **c** 11% **d** 9%

4b I can find equivalent decimals and percentages

2 Convert these percentages into decimals.
a 85% **b** 12% **c** 99% **d** 6% **e** 150%

3 Convert these decimals into percentages.
a 0.54 **b** 0.38 **c** 0.17 **d** 1.75 **e** 0.09

4b I can find equivalent percentages, fractions and decimals

4 Copy and complete this table.

Percentage	Fraction	Decimal
90%	$\frac{9}{10}$	
	$\frac{7}{10}$	0.7
3%		
	$\frac{1}{2}$	
40%		
		0.65

approximate cancel convert decimal denominator equivale

5 Which shop is giving the bigger discount?

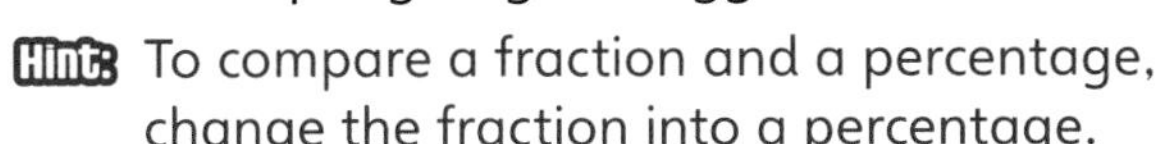

Hint: To compare a fraction and a percentage, change the fraction into a percentage.

Level 4

4b I can recognise the equivalence of percentages and fractions

6 31 out of 95 guests at a party are children. Paul says that 64% of the guests are children. Use approximation to see if Paul is correct.

4b I can use approximation to check a result

7 Copy and complete. Fill in the missing numerator for these equivalent fractions.

$\frac{2}{3} = \frac{10}{15}$ *The numerator and denominator have both been multiplied by 5*

4a I can find equivalent fractions

a $\frac{4}{5} = \frac{\square}{20}$ b $\frac{24}{50} = \frac{\square}{100}$ c $\frac{7}{20} = \frac{\square}{100}$

d $\frac{9}{10} = \frac{\square}{100}$ e $\frac{21}{25} = \frac{\square}{100}$ f $\frac{11}{20} = \frac{\square}{100}$

8 Carlos scored these marks in the summer exams.
Work out the percentage mark in each subject.

4a I can find equivalent fractions and convert to equivalent percentages

History 35 out of 50 *35 out of 50 is the same as $\frac{35}{50}$.*
Using equivalent fractions: $\frac{35}{50} = \frac{70}{100} = 70\%$

a Geography 8 out of 10 b English 13 out of 20 c IT 15 out of 25

d Music 2 out of 5 e Spanish 3 out of 4

9 Convert these percentages into fractions.
Cancel each fraction to its simplest form.

Level 5

5b I can simplify fractions by cancelling

60% *$60\% = \frac{60}{100} = \frac{6}{10} = \frac{3}{5}$*

a 26% b 48% c 35%

d 84% e 95% f 76%

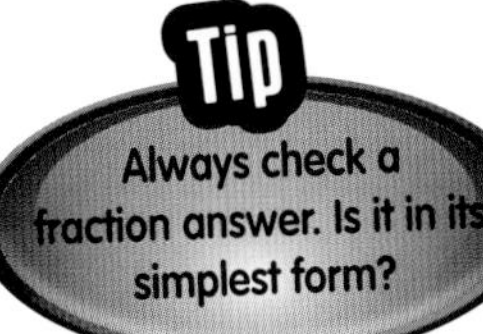

Now try this!

A Shaded fractions

Draw a grid of 10 squares like this.

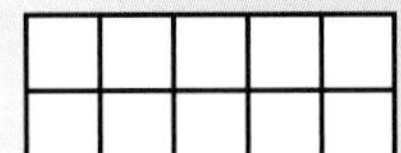

Roll a dice to find how many squares to shade. Write the shaded fraction under the grid. Convert the fraction to a decimal.
Try again with a new grid. If you get the same number, roll the dice again.

B Three of a kind

A game for 2 to 4 players. Make these 12 playing cards.

$\frac{1}{4}$	25%	0.25	$\frac{1}{2}$	50%	0.5	$\frac{3}{4}$	75%	0.75	$\frac{1}{5}$	20%	0.2

Shuffle the cards and deal three cards to each player. See if anyone has an equivalent fraction, decimal and percentage set in their hand, for example $\frac{3}{4}$, 75% and 0.75. This is 'three of a kind'.
The highest value 'three of a kind' wins. If nobody has 'three of a kind', check for 'two of a kind', for example $\frac{1}{2}$ and 50%.
The highest value 'two of a kind' wins. Otherwise call it a draw and play again.

fraction lowest terms numerator percentage (%) simplest form

12.3 Percentages of amounts

- Calculate percentages of quantities
- Know how to use percentages to compare proportions
- Express one quantity as a percentage of another
- Check a result by working it backwards

Why learn this?

Looking after your money means looking for the best deals (20% off) and understanding financial rates (interest rate 5.6%).

What's the BIG idea?

- To find 50% of an amount, divide by 2. **Level 4**
- To find 25% of an amount, divide by 4. **Level 4**
- To find 10% of an amount, you divide by 10. **Level 4**
- You can use 10% to find other **percentages**. For example, 70% is 7 lots of 10%. **Level 4**
- You can use percentages to compare quantities.
  What is 200 g as a percentage of 1 kg?
  To write one quantity as a percentage of another:
  1 Write the quantity as a **fraction** of the other $\frac{200}{1000}$
  2 Find the **equivalent** fraction with denominator 100 $\frac{20}{100}$
  3 Write down the percentage 20% **Level 5**

Practice, practice, practice!

Level 4

4a I can find multiples of 10%

1 Find 50% of
a 30 mm **b** £8 **c** 106 g

2 A loaf of bread weighs 800 g. 10% of the loaf is protein. How many grams of protein are in the loaf?

3 A football team played 12 games. They won 25% and lost the rest. How many games did they lose?

Watch out!
Read the question carefully. It might be asking you to do more than simply work out the percentage.

4a I can calculate percentages

4 Find
a 70% of £110 **b** 15% of 420 g
c 30% of 2 m **d** 40% of 300 m*l*

5 A container holds 480 m*l* of liquid when full. How much liquid is in it when it is
a 10% full **b** 5% full **c** 2.5% full?

4a I can check a result by working the problem backwards

6 Use your calculator to work these out. Check your answers by working backwards.

20% of £495

Pressing [4] [9] [5] [÷] [1] [0] [×] [2] [=] *gives £99*

Check: [9] [9] [÷] [2] [×] [1] [0] [=] *gives 495*

a 40% of 170 **b** 60% of 98 cm **c** 30% of £516

equivalent fraction

7 A Regular drink is 320 m*l*.
A Large drink is 25% more.

a What is 25% of 320 m*l*?

b How many millilitres is a Large drink?

8 The *Feed Me* supermarket is offering 25% extra free on a 260 g bar of chocolate.
The *Superior Food* store is offering 10% extra free on a 300 g bar of chocolate.

a Which offer gives you the most free chocolate?

b If the bars are the same price, which shop is offering the best deal?

9 Put the symbols <, > or = in these to make true statements.

a 75% of £12 ☐ 55% of £18

b 60% of £7.50 ☐ 75% of £6

c 45% of £4.40 ☐ 35% of £5.20

10 Write each of these test marks as a percentage.

23 out of 50 $\frac{23}{50} = \frac{46}{100} = 46\%$

a 34 out of 50 **b** 7 out of 10 **c** 8 out of 25

11 Write

a 550 g as a percentage of 1 kg

b 70 cm as a percentage of 4 m

c 85p as a percentage of £5

d 880 g as a percentage of 4 kg

Tip
When giving one quantity as a percentage of another, check to see that you are using the same units for both.

Level 5

5c I can use percentages to increase and decrease amounts

5c I can use percentages to compare proportions

5a I can express one quantity as a percentage of another

Now try this!

A Follow me 1

Make at least six cards for a 'follow me' game. On each card ask for 10%, 25% or 50% of a number.

Give the answer to each question on the next card.

Example:

card 1	card 2	card 3
Work out 10% of 50	I am 5. Work out 25% of 8	I am 2. Work out 50% of 400

Shuffle the cards. See how quickly you can put them in the correct order.

B Follow me 2

Make a 'follow me' game where the first card gives the answer to the final card.

Use percentages like 40% or 15% in some of your questions.

percentage proportion

12.4 Proportion

- Understand what proportion is
- Use proportion to solve problems

Why learn this?

Recipes make a set amount. To make more or less, you need to keep the ingredients in the same proportions.

What's the BIG idea?

→ A **proportion** can be given as a **fraction**, a **decimal** or a **percentage**.
1 in every 4 squares in this pattern is red.

This means that $\frac{1}{4}$ of the squares are red. Or 0.25 of the squares are red. Or 25% of the squares are red. **Level 4 & Level 5**

→ The more of an item you buy, the more you have to pay. Six items cost twice as much as three items. The cost is in **direct proportion** to the number you buy. **Level 5**

Learn this

'What proportion?' just means 'What fraction?' or 'What percentage?' or 'What decimal?'

Practice, practice, practice!

Level 3

3a I can solve simple problems using proportion

1 One in every three squares in this pattern is red.
This means that $\frac{1}{3}$ of the squares are red.

Make a tile pattern where

a one in every five tiles is red
b two in every four tiles are red
c two in every eight tiles are red
d three in every five tiles are red.

Level 4

4b I can use fractions to describe proportions

2 What proportion of each pattern is shaded? Give your answers as fractions.

a

b

c

3 A bag contains 19 marbles.
12 of the marbles are green.
What proportion of the marbles are green?
Give your answer as a fraction.

decimal direct proportion fraction

4 The pie chart shows the results of a survey into the most popular female singers.

Estimate the

a percentage of those surveyed that liked Girls Aloud best

b proportion that liked Lily Allen best

c percentage that did not choose Beyoncé.

Level 5

5C I can use percentages to describe simple proportions

5 Which shape has the greater percentage shaded? Explain how you know.

Shape A

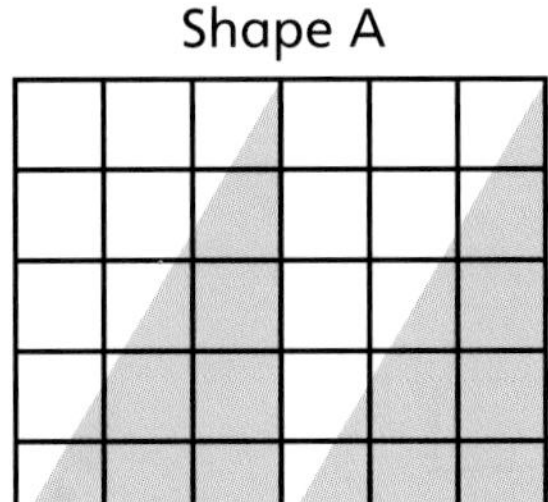

Shape B

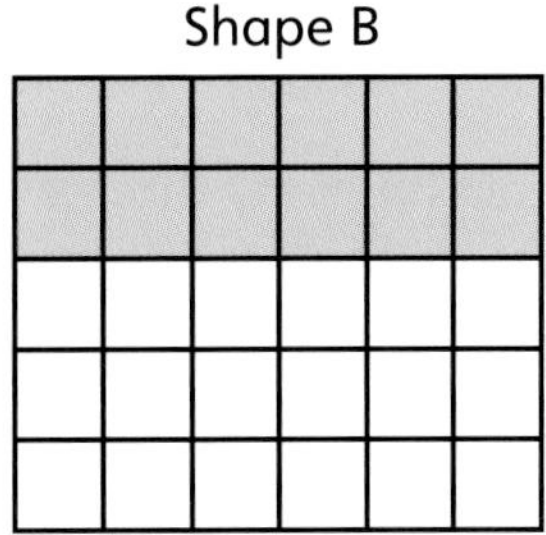

6 One litre of lemonade costs £1.20. How much would

a three litres cost **b** six litres cost?

5C I can use direct proportion in simple contexts

7 A recipe for eight people uses 200 g of flour. How much flour is needed for

a two people **b** 20 people?

8 To make 1 litre of orange squash you need 200 m*l* of orange concentrate.

a How much orange concentrate would you need to make 10 *l* of squash?

b If you have 700 m*l* of orange concentrate, how much orange squash can you make?

9 It costs £1.40 to travel 4 miles on a bus.
How much would it cost to travel 7 miles?

10 Suki and Yasmin go out for a meal on Friday. Suki pays £30 and Yasmin pays £20. Whenever they go out they always pay the bill in the same proportion.

a What proportion does Suki pay?

b On another Friday the meal costs £45 in total. How much does each pay?

Now try this!

A Proportion investigation

Work in pairs. You need 24 cubes. Share the cubes so that Player 1 has

a one cube out of every two cubes

b two cubes out of every four cubes

c three cubes out of every six cubes.

What do you notice?

B 100 square

On a 100 square shade $\frac{1}{2}$ red, $\frac{1}{4}$ black, $\frac{1}{10}$ green and $\frac{1}{20}$ orange.
What proportion is left unshaded? Give your answer as a fraction, a decimal and a percentage.

Super fact!

Although everyone has a different amount of blood, it is always about 8% of their body weight.

percentage **proportion**

12.5 Ratio

- Understand and use ratio notation
- Reduce a ratio to its simplest form
- Divide a quantity into two parts in a given ratio
- Understand the relationship between ratio and proportion

What's the BIG idea?

→ The diagram has one blue part for every three white parts.
For every one blue part there are three white parts.
The ratio of blue to white is 1 to 3. **Level 4**

→ The ratio '1 to 3' can be written as **1 : 3**. **Level 5**

→ You can simplify a ratio if you can divide each side by a **common factor**.

$$15 : 25 \xrightarrow{\div 5} 3 : 5$$

Level 5

→ You can solve ratio and **proportion** problems by reducing one side of the ratio to 1. **Level 5**

Why learn this?

Ratios are used in many situations to describe how two or more quantities are related. Builders mix up concrete using a 1 : 2 ratio of cement to sand.

Practice, practice, practice!

Level 3

3a I can solve simple ratio problems

1 In a junior tennis club, there are five girls for every one boy.
There are five boys in the club.
- **a** How many girls are there in the club?
- **b** How many members are there in total?

Level 4

4a I can divide a quantity into two parts in a given (worded) ratio

2 A decorator mixes blue paint and red paint.
She uses three tins of blue paint for every one tin of red paint.
blue, blue, blue, red
There are eight tins of paint altogether.
Copy and continue the list to see how many tins of blue paint are used.

3 All the front doors on Wellington Avenue are red or blue. There are three red doors for every two blue doors.
There are 20 houses altogether. How many have blue doors?

Level 5

5c I can use ratio notation

4 There are two oranges, three apples and one banana in a fruit bowl.
What is the ratio of
a oranges to apples **b** bananas to oranges?

common factor proportion ratio

5 Write these ratios in their simplest form.

a 20 : 32 **b** 24 : 72 **c** 132 : 88

Tip
When simplifying ratios make sure you divide both sides by the same number.

Level 5

5b I can reduce a ratio to its simplest form

6 Share these amounts in the given ratio.

5b I can divide a quantity into two parts in a given ratio

Marcus and Sue share £50 in the ratio 2 : 3. How much does each receive?

There are 2 + 3 = 5 parts altogether. 1 part = £50 ÷ 5 = £10

£10	£10	£10	£10	£10

= £50

Marcus gets £20 and Sue gets £30.

a Donna and Sarah share £40 in the ratio 1 : 3. How much does each receive?

b A school collected £140 for charity. They decided to divide the money between Children in Need and the RSPCA in the ratio 4 : 3. How much did each charity receive?

7 Find these fractions and percentages.

5a I can understand the relationship between ratio and proportion

Squash is one part orange to four parts water. What fraction of the mixture is orange?

orange	water	water	water	water

There are 1 + 4 = 5 parts altogether, so $\frac{1}{5}$ of the mixture is orange.

a Fizzy orange is one part orange juice to two parts lemonade. What fraction of the drink is lemonade?

b Bird food is one part nuts to three parts seeds. What percentage of the bird food is nuts?

Watch out!
The ratio of orange to water is 1 : 4. The proportion of orange in the squash is $\frac{1}{5}$.

8 **a** To make gingerbread you need fat to flour in the ratio 1 : 3. Jamie has 120 g of flour. How much fat does he need to make the gingerbread?

b A recipe uses 240 g of flour and 600 m*l* of milk for every four eggs used. How much flour and milk are needed if seven eggs are used?

5a I can use the unitary method to solve word problems

Now try this!

A Cube share

Work in pairs. You need 24 cubes. Share the cubes so that

a Player 1 has twice as many cubes as Player 2.

b Player 1 has one cube for every three cubes that Player 2 has.

c Player 1 has two cubes for every four cubes that Player 2 has.

How many cubes does Player 1 get each time?

Super fact!
The ratio of the mass of Jupiter to the mass of the Earth is about 300 : 1.

B Value for money?

In supermarkets you will often find that the price per unit (e.g. per 100 millilitres) is given on the price label on the shelf. You can use this to see which size gives the best value.
Work out the price per 100 m*l* for each size to see which is best value for money.

Volume	Price
200 m*l*	26p
500 m*l*	50p
1500 m*l*	£1.20
3000 m*l*	£2.10

Hint: Work out the price per 1 m*l* first.

ratio notation (e.g. 1 : 3) simplest form simplify

maths!

Human ratios

Ratios aren't just used in maths – in fact, they're all around us!

Vitruvian Man

Some people think that the human body follows set proportions. A Roman architect called Vitruvius wrote down a number of ratios to do with the adult male human body. These were later put in a famous drawing by Leonardo da Vinci.

- The maximum width of a person's shoulders is always a quarter of their height.
- The length of a person's outstretched arms is equal to their height.
- The length of a person's hand is one-tenth of their height.

How would you write these as ratios?

Which of these do you think are true?

Test them on yourself and your friends.

People of the world

- What is the ratio of males to females in your classroom?

The male : female ratio is different all over the world – and it changes as people get older.

The male : female ratio at birth in Germany is roughly 105 : 100. But for older people the ratio of males to females becomes 70 : 100.

- What do these numbers tell you about how the population changes?

Land and water

The ratio of land to water is different for each part of the Earth.

- Copy and complete the table below using the given facts.

	Land : water ratio	Land percentage	Water percentage
Northern hemisphere	2 : 3		
Southern hemisphere		20	

- What might these figures suggest about how big the population is in each hemisphere?

Unit 12 plenary

What's cooking?

You have invited your friends round for a pizza.
Here is the list of ingredients.

1 onion
2 cloves of garlic
2 tablespoons of olive oil
400g tin of chopped tomatoes
half a teaspoon of dried mixed herbs
salt and black pepper
1 ciabatta bread
250g mozzarella cheese
2 tablespoons of grated Parmesan cheese
selection of toppings: ham, pepperoni, peppers, tomatoes

1 You have a 900 g tin of tomatoes. Your gran tells you to use about half for the recipe.
What is half of 900 g?
Is your gran correct? **Level 3**

2 At the supermarket mozzarella cheese is on offer.
Both brands have the same original price.
Which brand should you buy?
Why? **Level 4**

3 With 220 g of ham you get 15% extra free.
How much extra ham is that? **Level 4**

4 Tomatoes come in mixed bags.
For every three red tomatoes there are two yellow ones.
In a bag of 20 tomatoes, how many red ones are there? **Level 4**

5 The pizza recipe is for two people. You have invited seven friends round for the meal.
How much of each ingredient will you need to make enough pizza for everybody?
(Don't forget yourself!) **Level 5**

6 According to the packets, 20 g of Mozza contains 7 g of fat and 5 g of Zarella contains 2 g of fat.
Use percentages to work out which cheese has the smaller proportion of fat. **Level 5**

7 Standard green peppers cost 21p per 100 g.
Organic green peppers cost £1.38 per 375 g.
How much will 250 g of each type of pepper cost? **Level 5**

The BIG ideas

- → Finding one half of something is the same as dividing by 2. **Level 3**
- → To compare a fraction and a percentage, change the fraction into a percentage. **Level 4**
- → To find 10% of an amount, you simply divide by 10.
  You can use 10% to find other percentages. For example, 5% is half of 10%. **Level 4**
- → In a recipe, if you need 200 g of flour for every two eggs, you will need 400 g of flour for four eggs. The ingredients must be kept in the same proportions. **Level 5**
- → To write one number as a percentage of another, write the number as a fraction of the other, find the equivalent fraction with denominator 100, then write down the percentage. **Level 5**

Find your level

Level 3

Q1 **a** Copy the grid and shade $\frac{1}{4}$ of it.

b Make another copy and shade $\frac{1}{8}$ of it.

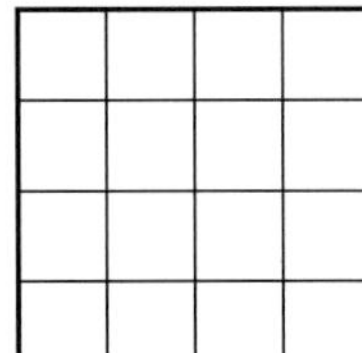

c How much of this grid is shaded – less than half, half or more than half?

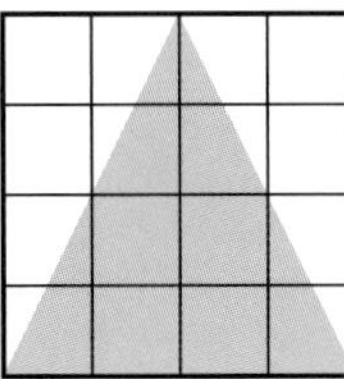

Level 4

Q2 Do not use a calculator for this question.

	£15	£30	£45
5%	75p	£1.50	£2.25
10%	£1.50	£3.00	£4.50

Use this table to help you work out the these:

a 15% of £30 = ______

b 15% of ______ = £2.25

c 20% of £15 = ______

d £9.00 is ______ of £30

e 5% of £60 = ______

f 5% of £90 = ______

Q3 Complete these. Do not use a calculator.

a ______ out of 10 is the same as 70%

b 10 out of 20 is the same as ______%

c 3 out of 4 is the same as ______%

d ______ out of 5 is the same as 20%

Level 5

Q4 An ice cream shop recorded the most popular flavours of ice cream sold on one day.

Flavour	Number sold
Chocolate	120
Vanilla	90
Strawberry	130

a What is the ratio of the number of chocolate ice creams sold to the number of vanilla ice creams sold? Give the ratio in its lowest terms.

b The next day, 160 chocolate ice creams were sold.
If the ratio of chocolate ice creams to vanilla ice creams remained the same, how many vanilla ice creams were sold on that day?

Q5 **a** What percentage of each diagram is shaded?

i

ii

b Cassie says, '$12\frac{1}{2}$% of this diagram is shaded'.
Is she correct? Explain your answer.

c Cassie wants to shade $37\frac{1}{2}$% of this diagram. Copy and complete it for her.

13 Express yourself

This unit is about using algebra to find mystery values.

Magicians often perform 'mystery number' tricks. Sometimes it is easy to explain how these tricks work, using algebra.

Algebra uses logic to work out missing values. Here is a simple example of using logic. This seesaw balances when the weights at either end are equal.

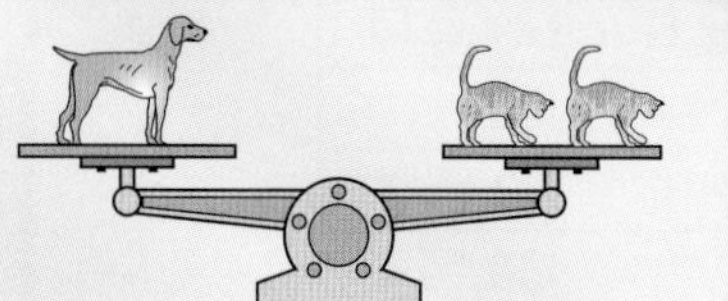

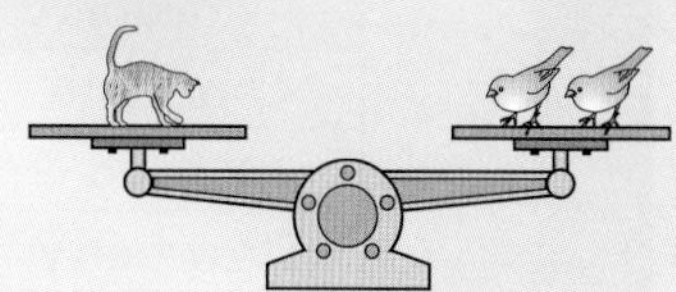

From these two pictures you can work out that:

You use the same sort of skills in some algebra problems.

Activities

A Pick a number.

Add the next (higher) number → Add 9 → Divide by 2 → Subtract your first number

What do you get?
Try this with different starting numbers. What do you notice?

B Work out the price of each type of fruit in this grid.

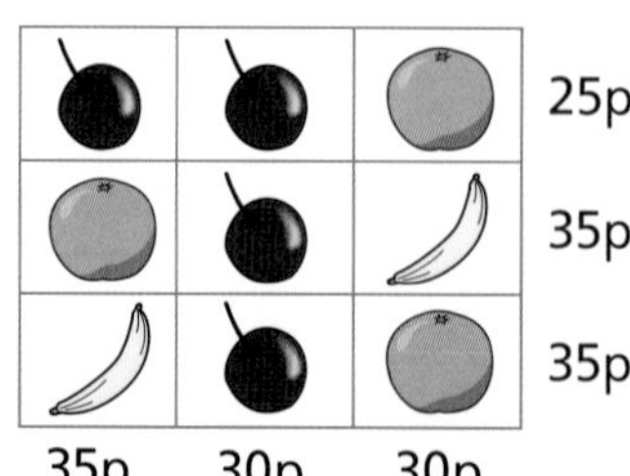

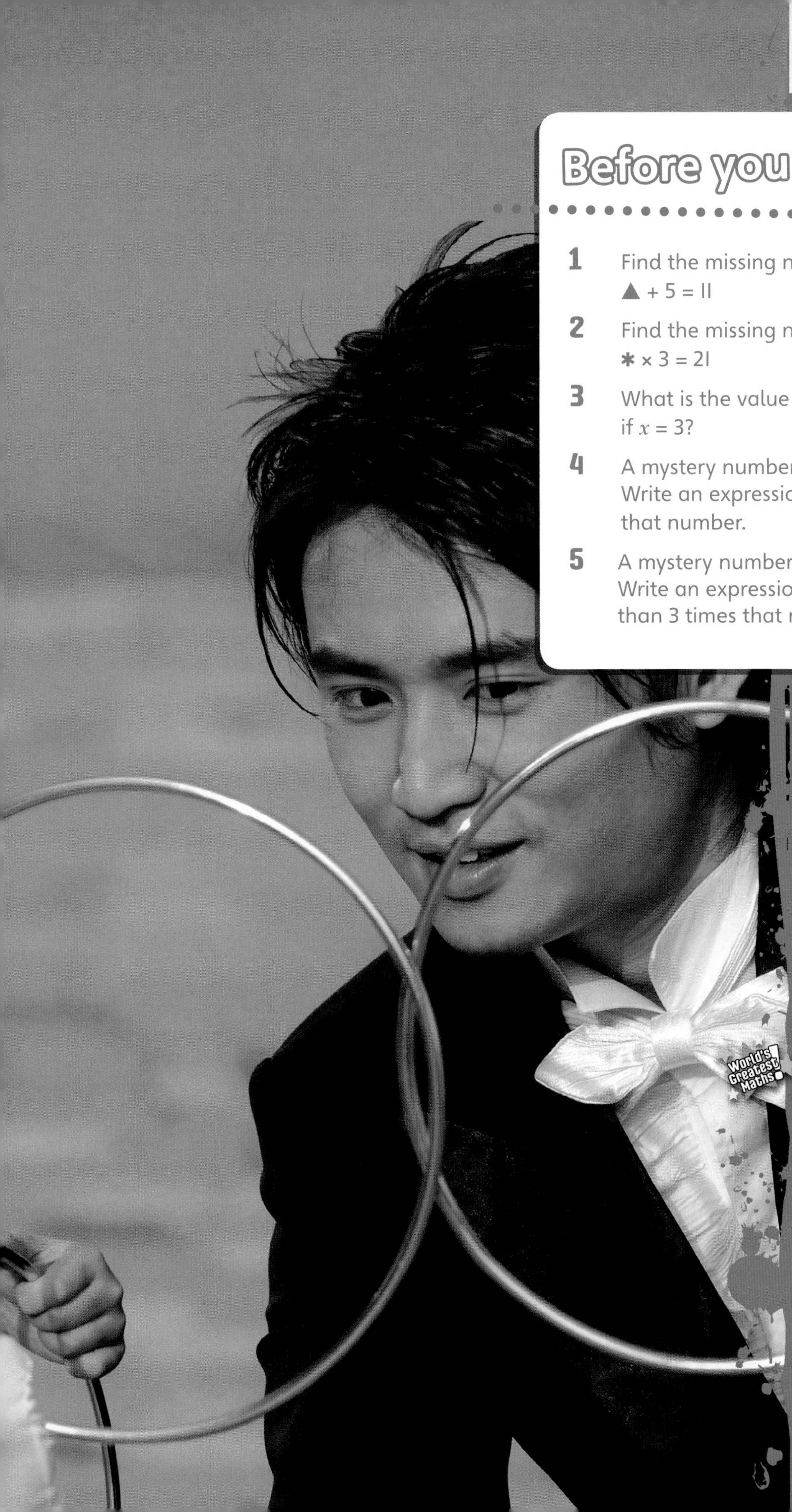

Before you start this unit...

1 Find the missing number: ▲ + 5 = 11 page 14

2 Find the missing number: ✱ × 3 = 21 page 14

3 What is the value of $2x + 4$ if $x = 3$? page 94

4 A mystery number is n. Write an expression for twice that number. page 86

5 A mystery number is y. Write an expression for 4 more than 3 times that number. page 86

Plus digital resources

World's Greatest Maths!

13.1 Brackets blast-off!

Marilyn the Martian has crash-landed in a corn field and you need to help her find her way back to her spaceship.

Unfortunately, Marilyn's crash created a maze through the corn. She also lost 12 important components from her navigation computer and she can't take off without them. The components can be found at the entrance to each chamber in the maze, and they look like this: ❹

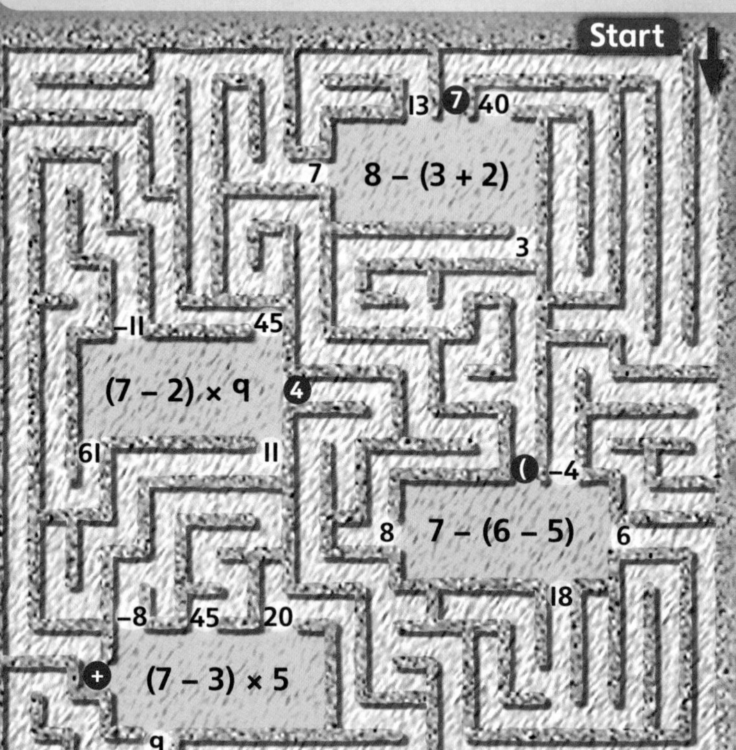

- Find your way through the maze to Marilyn's spaceship.
- Solve the calculation in each chamber to find the correct exit. Write down each calculation and the correct answer.
- Complete each practice session before moving on to the next section of the maze.
- Write down the components you collect – you'll need them to launch the ship!

Use Resource sheets 13.1a and b to help you.

Practice session 1

Work out

1 a 3 + (6 + 4) b (5 + 7) + 2
c 6 – (4 – 3) d (7 + 2) – 4

2 a 8 – (2 – 4) b 5 × (3 + 4)
c (2 + 7) × 3 d 4 × (9 – 5)

3 a 8 – (5 – 3) b (7 – 1) – 3
c 5 × (6 + 2) d (4 + 7) × 5

Practice session 2

1 Work out
a 17 + (25 – 3)
b (74 + 6) – 20
c 2 × (9 + 13)
d (27 – 19) × 8

2 Work out
a 8 ÷ (9 – 7)
b (20 + 10) ÷ 3
c 3 – (14 + 4)
d (39 + 17) ÷ 7

3 Calculate
a $(2 + 1)^2$
b $(12 - 6)^2$
c $4^2 - (3 + 9)$
d $(9 - 2)^2 + 10$

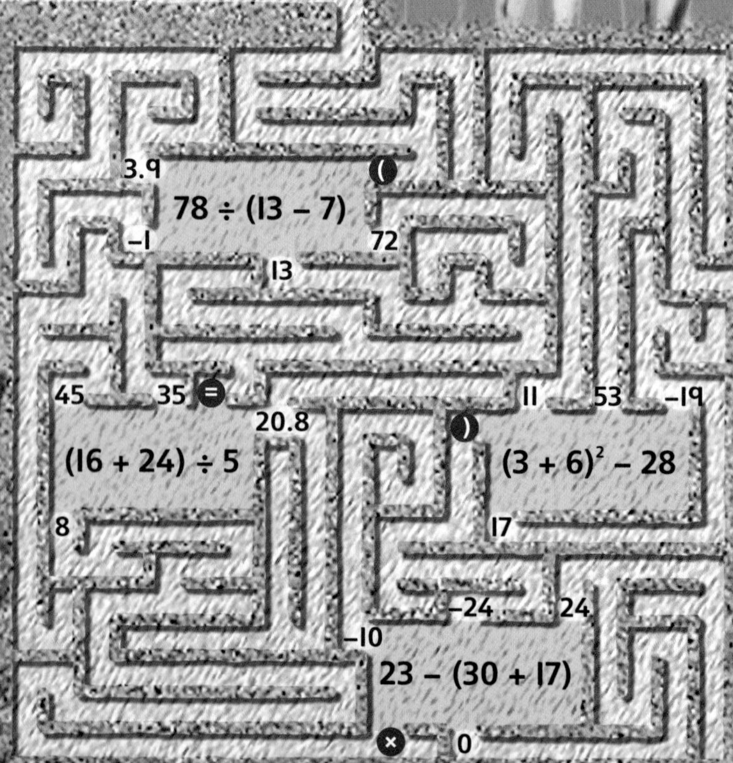

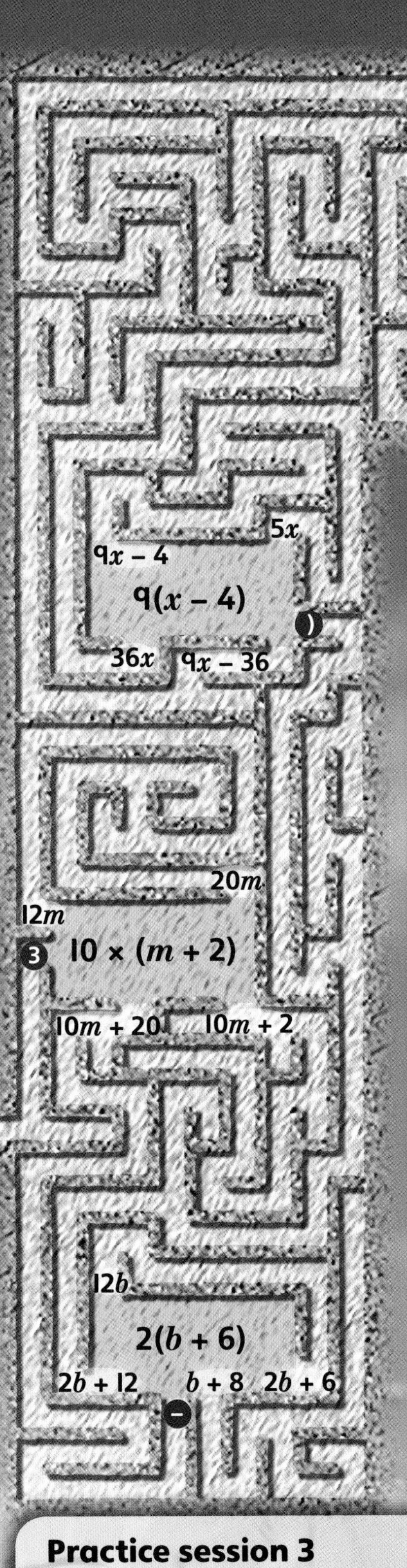

Finish

Congratulations!

You have made it through the maze and helped Marilyn find her spaceship. Have you collected all 12 of the missing components? You need to place the components into the navigation computer in the right order to send Marilyn to the correct galactic sector.

For example, (4 + 6) × 9 = would send the spaceship to sector 90, but 4 + (6 × 9) = would send it to sector 58. Make sure you don't catapult Marilyn to the wrong side of the galaxy!

- The galactic sector of Marilyn's home planet is 52. Find the correct order to place the 12 components into the computer to send Marilyn home.
- Find three other sector numbers that you could program into the navigation computer using these components.
- The higher the sector number, the further away it is. What is the furthest galactic sector you could send Marilyn to with these components?
- What is the nearest galactic sector you could send her to?

Practice session 3

1 Multiply out

a $3 \times (5 + a)$ b $7 \times (3 + b)$ c $2 \times (6 - c)$ d $4 \times (9 - d)$

2 Multiply out

a $5(y - 3)$ b $10(x + 5)$ c $4(c - 7)$ d $8(n + 5)$

3 Remove the brackets

a $9 \times (2a + 4)$ b $3 \times (3f + 7)$ c $8 \times (4 - 2m)$ d $7 \times (2 - 4b)$

13.2 More simplifying expressions

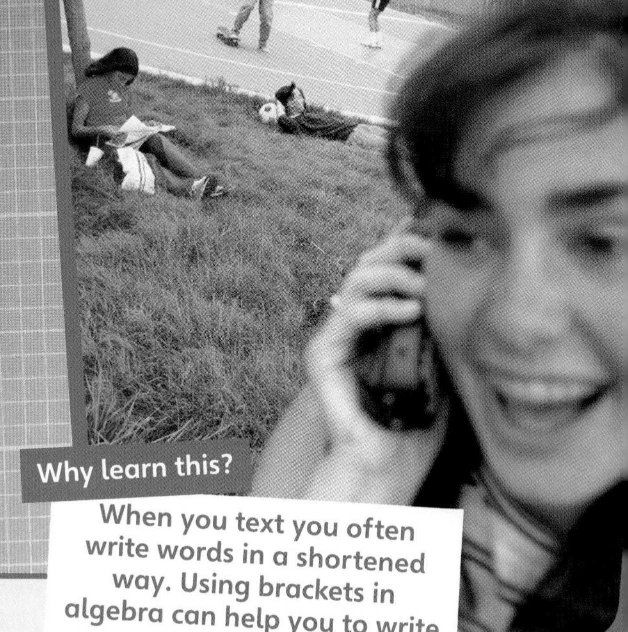

- Use arithmetic operations in algebra
- Simplify algebraic expressions by collecting like terms
- Multiply a single term over a bracket

Why learn this?

When you text you often write words in a shortened way. Using brackets in algebra can help you to write expressions in a short way.

What's the BIG idea?

- An algebraic **expression** is made up of **terms**: the expression $a + a + 2$ has three terms. **Level 4**
- You can **simplify** an expression by adding terms. Like terms have the same letter. **Level 4 & Level 5**
- You can also multiply or expand expressions with **brackets**. $4(x + 3)$ means four lots of $x + 3$, which is $x + 3 + x + 3 + x + 3 + x + 3 = 4x + 12$. **Level 5**

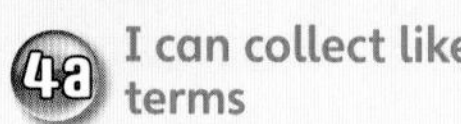

Watch out!

One of the most common student mistakes is writing $3n - n = 3$. The mistake is that $3n$ means 3 lots of n. So $3n - n = (n + n + n) - n = 2n$

Practice, practice, practice!

Level 4

4a I can collect like terms

1 Write these algebraic expressions as simply as possible.

a $c + c + c - c$ **b** $c + c + 2 + c + 2 + c$ **c** $2c + 3 + c$

d $3c + 2 + 2c - 4$ **e** $5c - 8c + 4c$ **f** $3c - 7 + c + 3 - 10$

2 Write an expression for the perimeter of each shape. Simplify the expression.

a

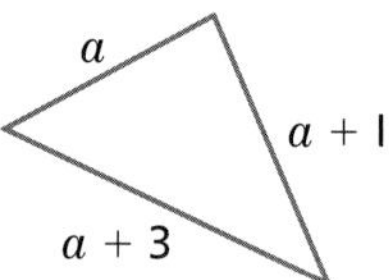

b

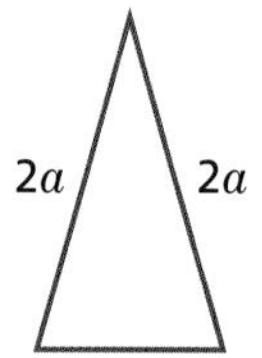

c

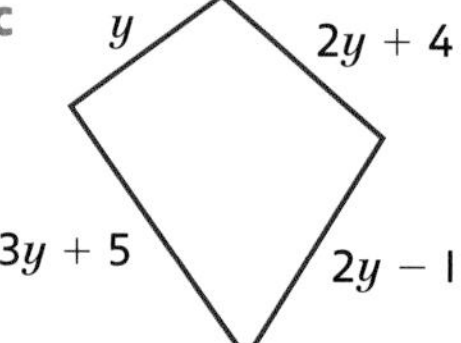

Level 5

5c I can collect more complex like terms

3 Simplify these algebraic expressions.

a $3a + 2a + b + b$ **b** $9a + 4b - 5a$ **c** $4a + b + 5 + 2a + 5b$

d $5a + 3b - 2a + 4b$ **e** $6a - 3b + 7 - 9$ **f** $73a - 50a + 46 - 17$

4 Write an expression for the perimeter of each shape. Collect any like terms.

a

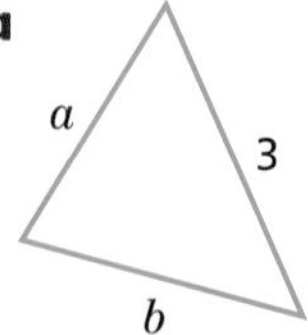

b

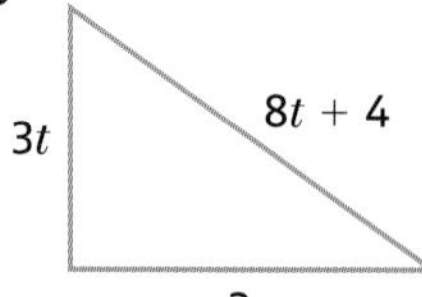

c

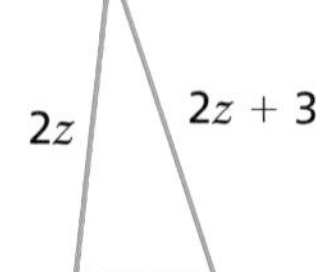

d

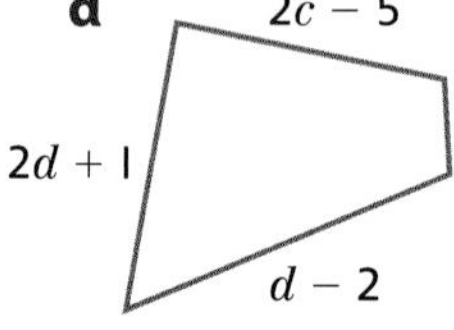

brackets expression

5 Simplify these algebraic expressions.

a $5a \times 2$ **b** $4 \times 2b$ **c** $3 \times 3c$ **d** $10 \times 6d$

e $0.5 \times 8e$ **f** $8f \div 2$ **g** $16g \div 8$ **h** $35h \div 7$

6 Write an expression for the area of each rectangle. Simplify the expression.

a

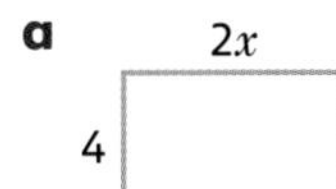

b

c

7 Multiply out these brackets.

a $3(b + 4)$ **b** $11(c - 2)$ **c** $4(6 + x)$ **d** $5(2y + 7)$

e $6(3y - 10)$ **f** $2(6x + 3z + 5)$ **g** $7(4h - 2 + j)$

8 Multiply out the brackets then simplify the expressions.

a $3 + 6a + 4(a + 3)$ **b** $12 + 2(j - 4) + 4$

c $5(y - 3) + 16$ **d** $6(3 + 2b) + 5(2b - 5)$

9 Write an expression for the perimeter of each shape in two ways:
i using brackets and **ii** without using brackets.

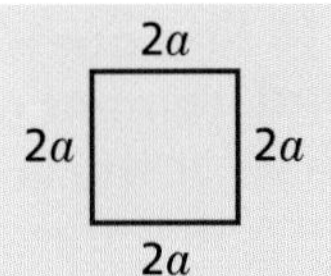

i *perimeter* $= 4(2a)$
ii *perimeter* $= 8a$

a

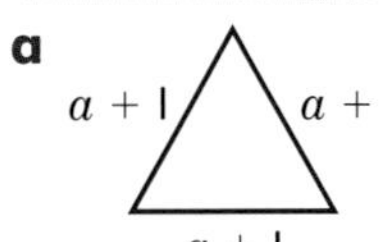

b

c

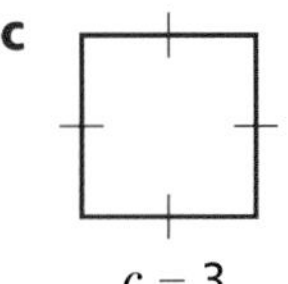

d

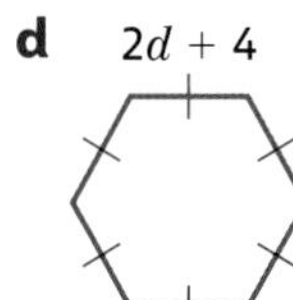

Level 5

5c I can simplify expressions with multiplication and division

5b I can write and simplify expressions involving multiplication

5b I can expand brackets in simple expressions

Now try this!

A Sides and perimeters 1

For each of these shapes write down sets of possible lengths for the sides.
For example, the triangle could have side lengths of d, $3d$ and $4d$.

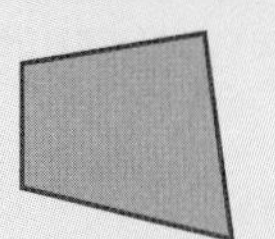

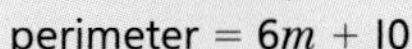

perimeter $= 6m + 10$

perimeter $= 12b + 8$

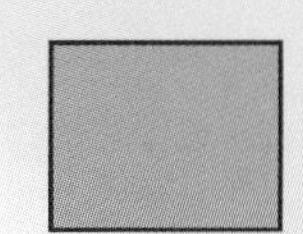

perimeter $= 8f - 4$

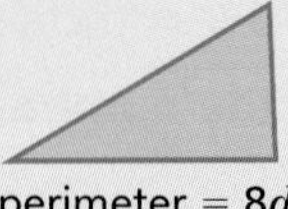

perimeter $= 8d$

B Sides and perimeters 2

For each of these shapes write down sets of possible lengths for the sides.
For example, the first shape could have side lengths of $4z$, $3y$ and $3y$.

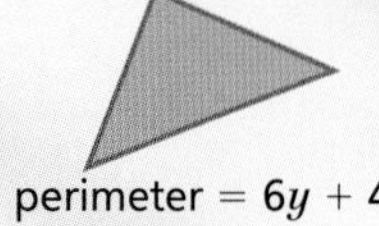

perimeter $= 6y + 4z$

perimeter $= 10y + 16z$

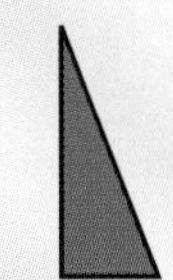

perimeter $= 4a + 4b + 2$

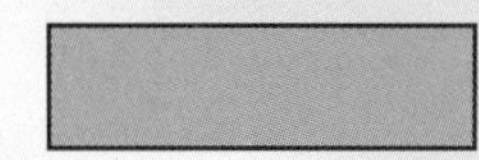

perimeter $= 10w + 6v - 4$

simplify term

13.3 Writing and solving one-step equations

- Write simple equations from worded descriptions
- Solve simple equations

What's the BIG idea?

→ You can use **algebra** to describe an amount by forming an **expression**. For example, a mystery number is n. An expression for 2 more than this number is $n + 2$. **Level 5**

→ You can make an **equation** by putting an expression equal to a number. For example, $n + 2 = 6$. **Level 5**

→ An equation can be solved to find the value of the letter. To **solve** the equation above, subtract 2 from both sides:

$$n + 2 - 2 = 6 - 2$$
$$n = 4$$ **Level 5**

Super fact!
In Egypt archaeologists found old equations written on papyrus. Instead of a mystery letter the ancient Egyptians used the word 'heap'.
heap + 5 = 8

Why learn this?
On building sites, concrete is supplied by volume. Equations are used to find out how much gravel, sand, cement and water are needed for the volume of concrete ordered.

Practice, practice, practice!

Level 3
3a I can solve simple equations using symbols

1 Find the value of each mystery symbol.

a ▲ + 4 = 10 **b** □ − 6 = 3 **c** ◆ × 5 = 25
d 10 + • = 12 **e** 7 + ♣ = 33 **f** ◇ − 1 = 100

Level 5
5c I can construct simple expressions

2 Hannah thinks of a mystery number. She calls her number n. Write an expression that is

a 4 more than the number **b** 10 more than the number
c 7 less than the number **d** double the number
e 5 less than the number **f** 10 times the number
g the number divided by 4

Tip
It's easy to remember the difference between an expression and an equation – an equation has an equals sign (=).

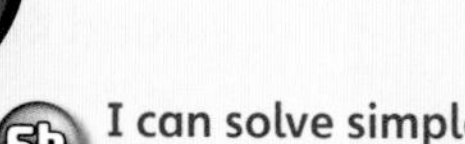
I can solve simple equations

3 Solve these equations to find the value of the letters.

a $a + 4 = 7$ **b** $b + 2 = 10$ **c** $c - 8 = 5$
d $d - 9 = 11$ **e** $e - 16 = 23$ **f** $50 - f = 41$

4 Solve these equations to find the value of the letters.

a $m + 23 = 48$ **b** $n - 17 = 29$ **c** $34 - p = 16$
d $69 = q + 21$ **e** $15 = r - 101$ **f** $23 = 101 - s$

5 Solve these equations to find the value of the letters.

a $2a = 8$ **b** $10b = 50$ **c** $7a = 28$
d $5d = 20$ **e** $\frac{e}{4} = 12$ **f** $\frac{f}{3} = 7$

algebra equation

6 Solve these equations to find the value of the letters.

a $s + 6 = 3$ **b** $t + 12 = 7$ **c** $e - 6 = -17$

d $f - 8 = -4$ **e** $42 = l + 50$ **f** $35 - r = 41$

7 Solve these equations to find the value of the letters.

a $71 = q + 82$ **b** $63 - n = 85$ **c** $3b = -9$

d $7m = -42$ **e** $\frac{d}{3} = -21$ **f** $\frac{t}{6} = -5$

8 I think of a mystery number t and add 5 to it.

a Write an expression for the new amount.

b The answer after I have added 5 is 12.
Write an equation involving t and solve it to find the value of t.

9 I think of a mystery number h and subtract 12 from it.

a Write an expression for the new amount.

b The answer after I have subtracted 12 is 4.
Write an equation involving h and solve it to find the value of h.

10 I think of a mystery number p and multiply it by 3.

a Write an expression for the new amount.

b The answer after I have multiplied by 3 is 15.
Write an equation involving p and solve it to find the value of p.

11 The number of grapes in a bunch of grapes is g. Ben eats 15 grapes.

a Write an expression for the number of grapes that are left.

b The number of grapes left on the bunch is 27.
Write an equation for the number of grapes and solve it to find out how many grapes there were before Ben ate 15 of them.

12 The temperature on the first of July was t °C. The temperature on the first of December was 19 °C less.

a Write an expression for the temperature on the first of December.

b The temperature on the first December was −2 °C.
Write an equation for the temperature and solve it to find the temperature on the first of July.

Level 5

5a I can solve equations

5a I can construct and solve simple equations

Now try this!

A Mystery numbers

Make up five mystery number problems where the mystery number is 6. Write each problem as mystery number expressions as in Q1. Then use algebra to make an equation for each one.
Swap with a partner. Can you work out the mystery numbers?

B Arithmagons

In this arithmagon the numbers in the circles add up to make the number in the square between them.
Write eight different equations from the arithmagon. For example, $p + q = 5$.

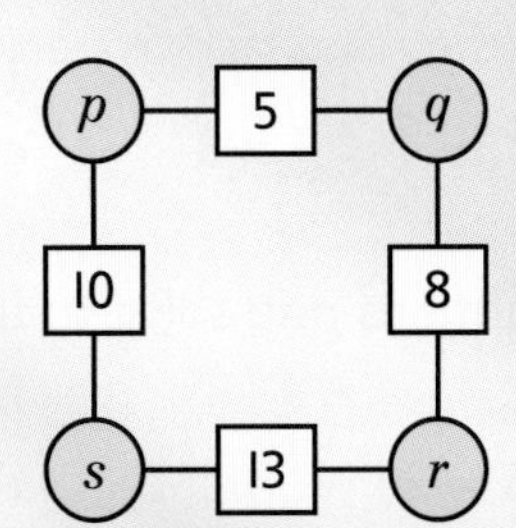

expression solve

13.4 Solving and checking two-step equations

➩ Solve two-step equations and check the answer by substituting the value back into the equation

Why learn this?

We can use equations to describe what happens in a chemical reaction.

What's the BIG idea?

→ You can solve two-step **equations** by making sure that both sides remain balanced.
For example, you can solve the equation $2x + 3 = 7$ like this:
$2x + 3 - 3 = 7 - 3$ subtract 3 from both sides
$2x = 4$
$x = 2$ divide both sides by 2 **Level 5**

→ You can check your answer by substituting it into the original equation $x = 2$ so $(2 \times 2) + 3 = 7$. ✓ **Level 5**

Super fact!

For years mathematicians have tried to find a formula to work out prime numbers. Prime numbers are really useful in writing codes. The larger the prime number, the more secure the code is!

Practice, practice, practice!

Level 5

5a I can use letters to write expressions

1 Ahmed thinks of a mystery number n. Write an expression for a number that is

a double the number
b double the number and then add 5
c 5 times the number less 8
d 3 times the number
e 3 times the number then add 10
f 3 times the number then add 7 and subtract 5.

5a I can solve two-step equations

2 Complete the workings to solve these equations and find the mystery number.

a $2a + 1 = 7$
$2a =$
$a =$

b $3b + 4 = 19$
$3b =$
$b =$

c $5c - 2 = 23$
$5c =$
$c =$

d $\frac{d}{4} + 3 = 13$
$\frac{d}{4} =$
$d =$

3 Solve the equations to find the mystery number.

a $2a + 5 = 13$ **b** $3b - 2 = 13$ **c** $3 + 10c = 43$
d $6d - 2 = 22$ **e** $5e + 13 = 48$ **f** $24 - 4f = 12$

4 Solve the equations to find the mystery number.

a $17 + 4p = 25$ **b** $63 - 3p = 30$ **c** $84 = 6r + 60$
d $2p + 10 = 6$ **e** $17 + 3p = 5$ **f** $2p + 0.4 = 2$

5 Solve the equations to find the mystery number.

a $\frac{x}{6} + 3 = 5$ **b** $\frac{a}{2} - 7 = 3$ **c** $\frac{b}{5} + 17 = 22$ **d** $\frac{y}{5} + 19 = 17$

6 Simplify these equations and solve to find the mystery numbers.

a $2x + 5x + 6 - 3x + 3 = 25$ **b** $3a + a + 5 + 2a = 35$
c $7 + 2y + 6y + 3 = 26$ **d** $p + 45 - 3p - 20 - p = 4$

algebra equation

7 **a** Copy the addition pyramids. The expression at the top is equal to the number value written next to it. Write an equation and solve it to find the mystery number.

i = 52

13 | n | 15

ii

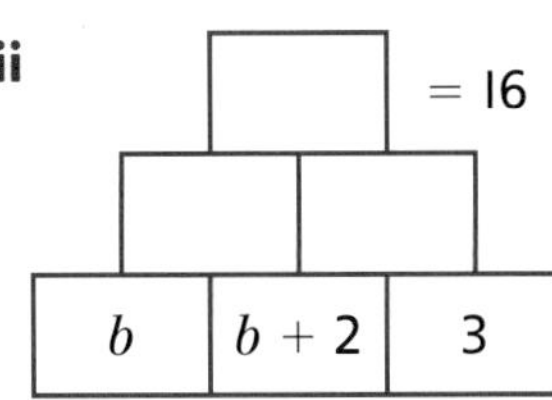

iii

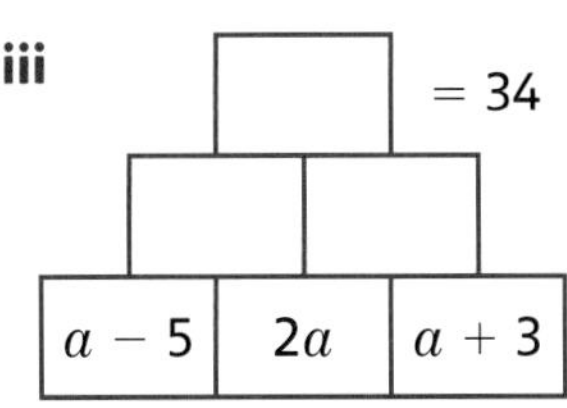

b Check the solution to each part by rewriting the pyramid and substituting your answer for the letters. If you are right you should end up with the correct number in the top brick of the pyramid.

Tip
The expression in any brick is the sum of the expressions in the two bricks below it.

8 $2a + 7 = 35$.
Toni and Chelsea solve this equation. Toni says the answer is 11 and Chelsea says the answer is 14. By putting these answers into the equation decide who has the correct answer.

9 Substitute Toni's and Chelsea's answers into each of these equations. Decide who has the correct answer.

a $4b + 6 = 22$; Toni thinks $b = 4$, Chelsea thinks $b = 5$

b $4t - 3 = 25$; Toni thinks $t = 8$, Chelsea thinks $t = 7$

c $2z + 15 = 39$; Toni thinks $z = 12$, Chelsea thinks $z = 10$

d $16 + 3y = 34$; Toni thinks $y = 8$, Chelsea thinks $y = 6$

10 I have three bags with b counters in each and eight more counters.

a Write an expression for the total number of counters.

b There are 41 counters altogether.
Write an equation and solve it to find the value of b.

11 I think of a mystery number n. I double it and add 5.

a Write an expression for the new number.

b The expression has the value 17.
Write an equation and solve it to find the mystery number.

Now try this!

A Think of a number

I think of a number, multiply it by 5 and add 1. The answer is 21. Solve this problem. Make up four more number puzzles for your partner to solve.

B Equation families

1 Choose a two-step equation and solve it.
For example, $2x + 1 = 7$; the solution is $x = 3$.

2 Now change the end number, e.g. $2x + 1 = 11$, and find the solution again.

3 Do this for three more end numbers. Write down coordinates for each answer: (solution, end number). So for the examples, the coordinates are (3, 7) and (5, 11).

4 Draw axes and plot all five coordinate pairs. What do you notice?

5 Choose another two-step equation and repeat.

Tip
In a two-step equation, two operations are used on the mystery number. For example $2x + 1 = 7$ means
i) multiply x by 2
ii) add 1

expression variable

Number tricks

The Great Stupendo is putting on a magic show.
He specialises in number tricks.
So he gives his instructions as puzzles.
Solve the puzzles to work out what he needs for the show.

1 **a** Use these clues to work out the values of ♦, ♥, ♣ and ♠.

   i $7 + ♦ = 12$

   ii $♥ - 6 = 22$

   iii $♣ + 14 = 21$

   iv $25 - ♠ = 15$

b Now find out how the great Stupendo would like the seats arranged.

> I will need ♥ + ♣ + ♦ + ♠ rows of seats with
> ♥ − ♠ seats in each row.

Level 5

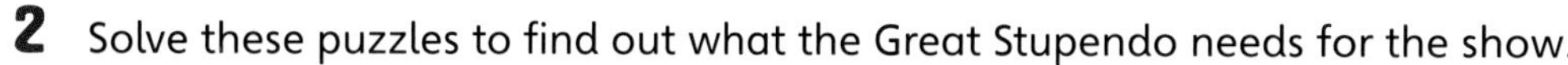

2 Solve these puzzles to find out what the Great Stupendo needs for the show.

a $11 + a = 15$

b $2b = 12$

c $\frac{c}{4} = 2$

d $4d + 5 = 41$

e $25 - 3e = 13$

f $8f - 12 = 4$

g $\frac{g}{2} + 3 = 5$

> I will need:
> a packs of cards
> b white rabbits
> c doves
> d pieces of rope
> e silk scarves
> f assistants
> g litres of coloured water

Level 5

3

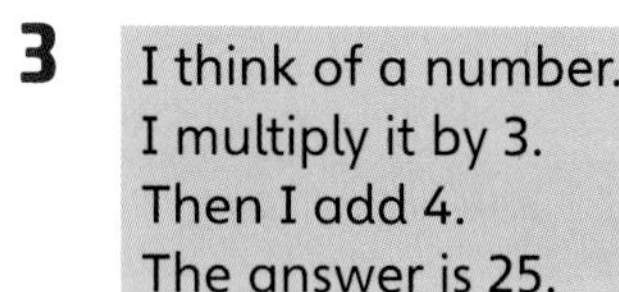

> I think of a number.
> I multiply it by 3.
> Then I add 4.
> The answer is 25.

a Write an equation for this mystery number puzzle.

b Solve your equation to find the start time of the show. **Level 5**

4 The Great Stupendo hasn't decided on the price for the tickets.
Choose a price.
Write a puzzle like the one in Q3, where the mystery number is the price you choose.
Give it to a partner to solve to find the ticket price. **Level 5**

The BIG ideas

→ An **algebraic expression** is made up of **terms**: the expression $a + a + 2$ has three terms. **Level 4**

→ You can use algebra to describe an amount by forming an expression.
For example, a mystery number is n. An expression for 2 more than this number is $n + 2$. **Level 5**

→ You can make an **equation** by putting an expression equal to a number.
For example, $n + 2 = 6$. **Level 5**

→ You can **solve** an equation to find the value of the mystery number.
To solve the equation above, subtract 2 from both sides:
$n + 2 - 2 = 6 - 2$
$n = 4$ **Level 5**

Find your level

Level 4

Q1 Simplify these expressions.
- a $4t + 3 + 2t$
- b $5w + 2 - w + 3 - 2w$
- c $7b - 3b + 5b$

Level 5

Q2 Write an expression for the perimeter of each shape.
Collect any like terms.

a
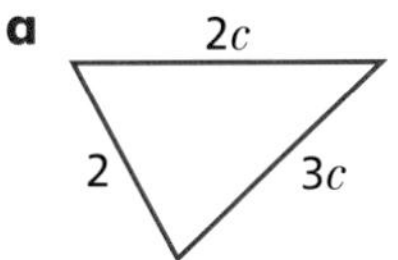

b
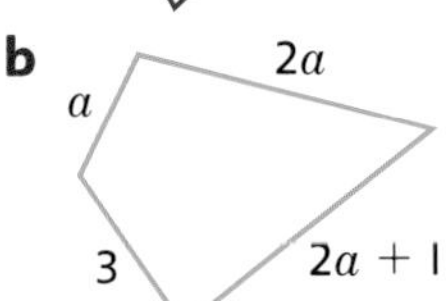

c
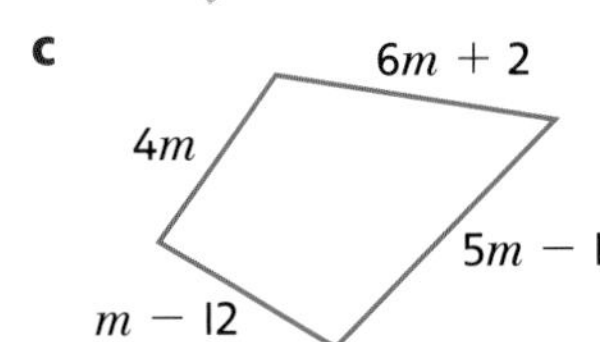

Q3 Write an expression for the area of each shape. Simplify each expression.

a Rectangle with sides $3n$ and 6

b Rectangle with sides 5 and $4x$

c Rectangle with sides $22p$ and 0.5

Q4 Solve these equations.
- a $6e - 4 = 14$
- b $3g + 3 = 18$
- c $11 + 5r = 21$

Q5 Complete these statements.
- a When y is 6, $3y$ is ____.
- b When y is ____, $3y$ is 36.
- c When y is 6, ____ is 36.

Q6 A magic square can be made by substituting numbers into this algebra grid.

$a - b$	$a + c$	$a + b - c$
$a - c$	$a + b$	$a - b + c$
$a + b + c$	$a - b - c$	a

a Copy and complete the magic square using these values.
$a = 6 \quad b = 2 \quad c = 3$

4		
	8	
		6

b The same algebra grid is used but with different values for a, b and c.

7	14	9
6	13	11
17	3	10

What values for a, b and c were used?

Revision 2

Quick Quiz

Q1 This pictogram shows the number of cars washed by 3 people.

John	◯ ◯ ◖
Cerys	◯ ◯ ◯
Shona	◯ ◖

Key: ◯ represents 10 cars

a Who washed the most cars?
b How many cars did Shona wash?

→ *See 8.3*

Q2 Find all the factors of 12.

→ *See 10.1*

Q3 How many lines of symmetry do these shapes have?

a **b**

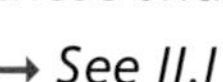

→ *See 11.1*

Q4 Work out 7×0.6

→ *See 9.2*

Q5 Round 2475
a to the nearest 10
b to the nearest 100
c to the nearest 1000

→ *See 9.4*

Q6 Find 15% of 320 kg.

→ *See 12.3*

Q7 Convert these amounts into the units shown.

a 2.3 l = ___ ml **b** 4.2 m = ___ cm
c 3700 g = ___ kg **d** 125 mm = ___ cm

→ *See 9.1*

Q8 Find the highest common factor of 18 and 24.

→ *See 10.1*

Q9 Calculate the missing angle in each of these.

a

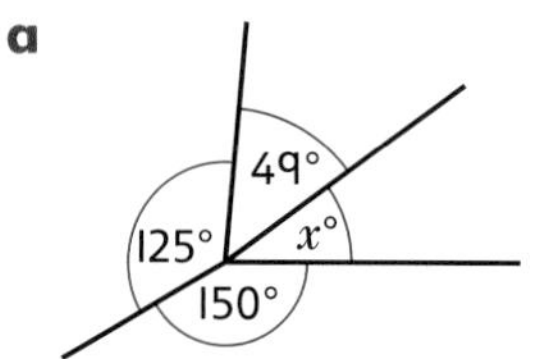

b

55°
y°
62°

→ *See 11.3*

Q10 Work out $\frac{3}{5}$ of £35.

→ *See 12.1*

Q11 Simplify $6p + 2q - 3p + 9q$

→ *See 13.2*

Activity

You are planning to make a cake.
This recipe shows some of the ingredients you need.

300g butter
300g sugar
400g flour
4 eggs

Level 3

Q1 You are going to make a cake using half of all the ingredients in the recipe.
Work out how much of each ingredient you need.

Q2 You also need 150 ml of milk.
What piece of kitchen equipment would you use to measure this amount of milk?

Q3 To prepare the cake tin you need to line the tin with greaseproof paper.
This line shows the accurate height
of the cake tin.
Measure the height of the tin in mm.

height of cake tin

Level 4

Q4 This is a diagram of the cake tin.
What is the name of the shape of the tin?

Q5 Copy these weighing scales. Draw pointers on the scales to show how much flour and how much sugar you need.

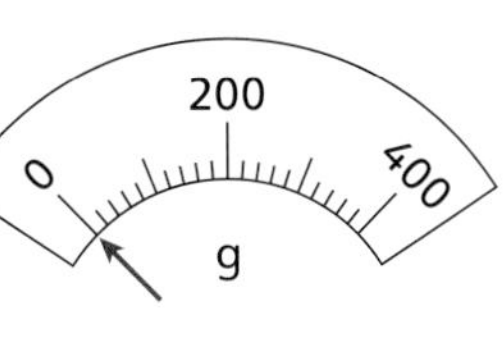

Level 5

Q6 You need 150 ml of milk.
How much is this in litres?

Q7 You can either buy 6 eggs for 96p or 10 eggs for £1.50.
In each case, work out the cost per egg.
Which way gives you best value for money?

Find your level

Level 3

Q1 Amy asked 30 pupils if they walk to school every day.

16 pupils said **yes**

14 pupils said **no**

Amy started to draw a pictogram using the key 🯅 represents 4 people.
Copy and complete the pictogram to show Amy's results.

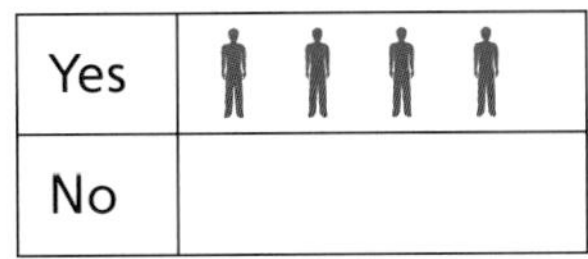

Q2 6 8 12 18 20 24

a Write down all the numbers from the list above that divide by 3 with no remainder.

b Write down all the numbers from the list above that divide by 4 with no remainder.

c Write down all the numbers from the list above that divide by 12 with no remainder.

Level 4

Q3 The members of a youth club had a sponsored walk.
The collected £548.67

a How much is £548.67 to the nearest ten pounds?

b How much is £548.67 to the nearest hundred pounds?

Q4 Here are some number cards.

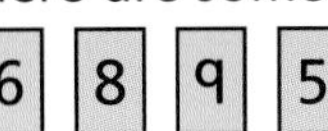

a Choose 2 of these cards to make a fraction that is equivalent to $\frac{1}{4}$ $\frac{?}{?}$

b Choose 2 of these cards to make a fraction that is equivalent to $\frac{2}{3}$ $\frac{?}{?}$

Level 5

Q5 Isobel uses a grid to multiply 34 by 23.

×	30	4
20	600	80
3	90	12

600 + 80 + 90 + 12 = 782

Isobel now multiplies 258 by 79.
Copy and complete the grid.
Write down the answer to the multiplication.

×	200	50	8
70			
9			

Q6 Here is an expression.

$5p + 7 - 2p + 4$

Which expression below shows it written as simply as possible?

$3p + 3$ $7p + 11$

$14p$ $3p + 11$

14 Shape up

This unit is about transformations and problem solving.

We see transformations when we see shapes on the move. For example, a fairground ferris wheel shows turning, or rotation. A car or boat moving in a straight line shows translation.

When you look in the mirror or into still water you see your reflection.

You can make a large design based on a few simple shapes by repeating them in different ways – by translating, rotating or reflecting them. Many wallpaper, rug and fabric designs use transformations to create large patterns.

Activities

A
- Cut out a card pattern of a right-angled scalene triangle like this.
- Now create a star like this by rotating the triangle and tracing round it.
- Colour in each of the triangles in a different colour.

B
- Explain how you would create a border like this, using the triangle in activity A.

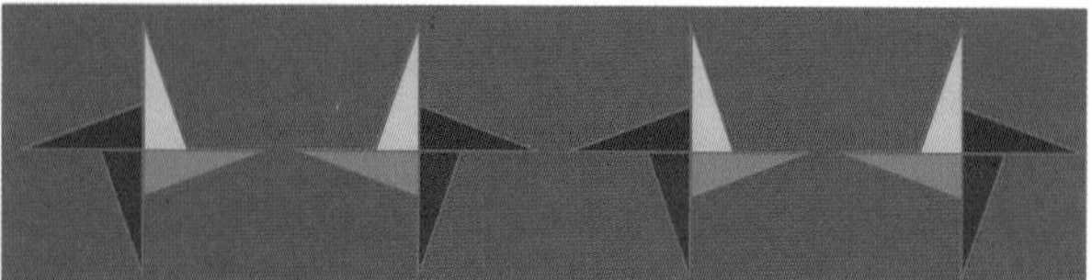

- Describe how the wallpaper design in the main photograph was created.

The London Eye takes 30 minutes to rotate once through 360°. It rotates at a speed of just 26 centimetres per second.

Before you start this unit...

1 Which of the lines A to D are mirror lines for this shape?

page 168

Hint You can use a mirror to help you.

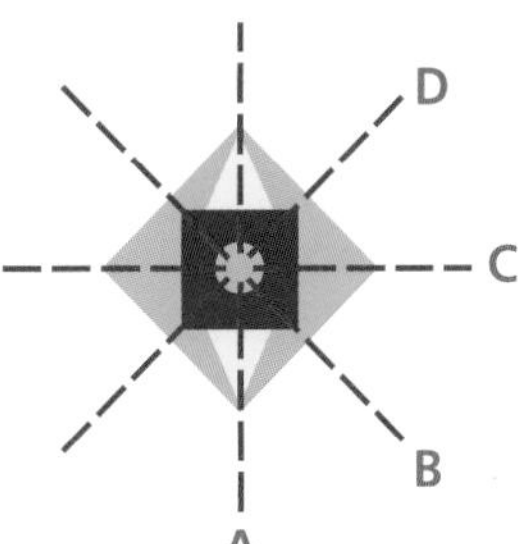

2 a Which of the images A to D are translations of the central G?

page 170

B: G
A: G (rotated) G C: G
D: G (rotated)

b Which image is a reflection?

3 Name and describe as many different types of quadrilateral as you can.

page 104

World's Greatest Maths

Plus digital resources

Did you know?

William Morris (1834–1896) was a writer, designer and socialist. He designed wallpapers and fabrics, inspired by patterns from the Middle East. Many of his designs are still in use today, more than 100 years later.

14.1 Forming shapes with triangles

- Make and name quadrilaterals made from two identical triangles
- Recognise reflections, rotations and symmetry of 2-D shapes

Why learn this?

Using triangles in construction gives stability. All 2-D straight-edged shapes can be created from triangles.

What's the BIG idea?

- A shape with **reflection symmetry** has a line of symmetry. The line of symmetry divides the shape into two identical halves. **Level 3**
- All quadrilaterals can be split into two triangles. All quadrilaterals with two pairs of equal sides can be split into two same-sized triangles. **Level 4 & Level 5**
- The different types of angle are **acute**, **right angle**, straight angle, **obtuse** and **reflex**. **Level 4 & Level 5**

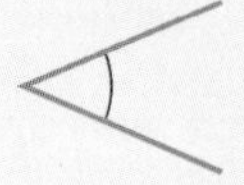
acute angle

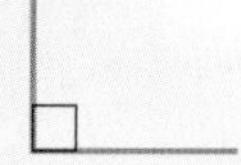
right angle

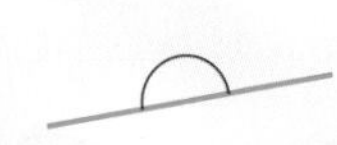
straight angle

obtuse angle

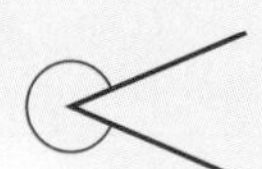
reflex angle

- The order of **rotational symmetry** of a shape is the number of different ways a tracing fits as you rotate it. **Level 5**

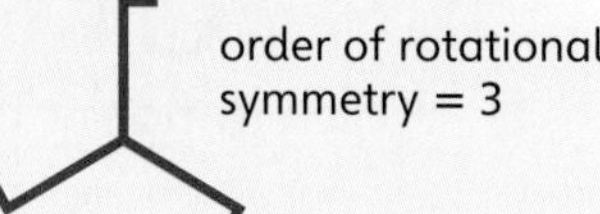

Super fact!

Splitting a quadrilateral along its line of symmetry always gives two identical triangles.

Practice, practice, practice!

Level 3

3a I can identify quadrilaterals

1 **a** Two same-sized right-angled triangles join like this. What shape do they form?

b Make two identical right-angled triangles by cutting a rectangle like this. List the different shapes you can make by joining these triangles.

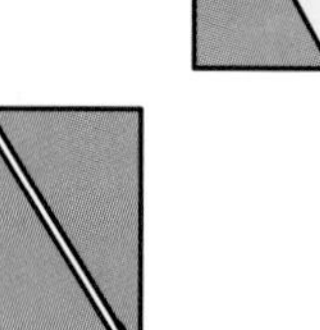

Hint: You should be able to make five different shapes.

Level 4

4a I can identify properties of quadrilaterals

2 Draw a triangle with an obtuse angle. Cut out four copies.

a Use two of the triangles to make an arrowhead.

b Make a different arrowhead with the other two triangles.

arrowhead (delta) isosceles kite parallelogram rectangle reflection symmet

3 **a** Copy these two shapes. Split each into two same-sized triangles.

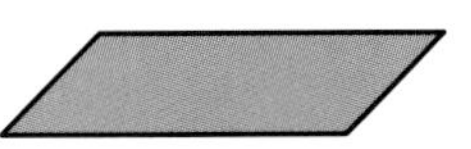

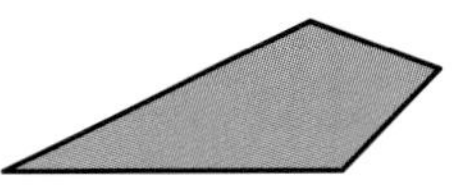

b For each shape, write down whether the triangles are a reflection or a rotation of each other.

4 You can make an isosceles triangle from two identical triangles like this.

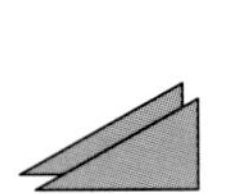

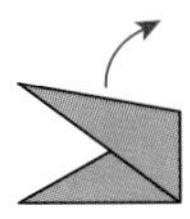

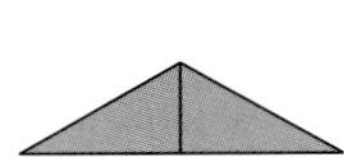

Flip or reflect one triangle.

You can make a parallelogram from two identical triangles like this.

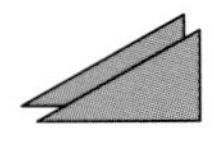

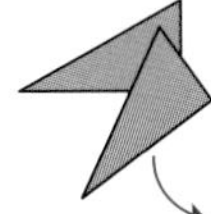

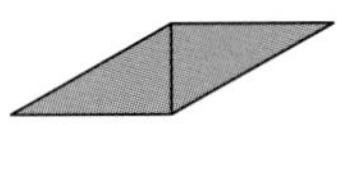

Turn around (or rotate) one triangle.

For each of the shapes, say whether you can make it from two identical triangles. Do you need to use rotation or reflection, or both?

a kite **b** rhombus **c** rectangle **d** square

5 **a** Sketch an equilateral triangle.

i How many lines of symmetry does it have?

ii What is its order of rotational symmetry?

b Split your equilateral triangle into two identical triangles. Work out the angles of one of these triangles.

6 **a** You can make a square using two identical triangles. What type of triangles do you need?

b Work out the angles of the triangle.

Level 5

5c I can recognise reflection or rotation

5c I can recognise and visualise the symmetry of 2-D shapes using line symmetry and rotational symmetry

5b I can identify lines of symmetry and special triangles

Now try this!

A Triangle transformations

1 Draw and cut out two identical triangles.
2 Join the triangles to make a quadrilateral. What type of quadrilateral is it? Make any other quadrilaterals you can.
3 For each quadrilateral you make, work out whether one triangle needs to be reflected or rotated so that it lands on the other one.
4 Repeat using two other identical triangles.

B Transformation perimeters

1 Cut out 12 identical scalene triangles.
2 Make shapes by joining the triangles along a common side. Name each one. Identify whether the triangles are rotated or reflected to make the shape.
3 Find the perimeter of each shape.
4 Which shapes have the same perimeter? Why?

rhombus **rotate (turn)** **rotational symmetry** **scalene** **square**

14.2 Translations

- Identify right angles, perpendicular lines and parallel lines
- Recognise where a 2-D shape will be after a translation
- Correctly describe a translation
- Transform 2-D shapes by simple combinations of translations

Why learn this?

Many patterns used for fabric or decoration are based on repeating patterns. You can form a continuous pattern by translating a basic design.

What's the BIG idea?

- A **translation** is one type of **transformation**. A translation of a 2-D shape is a slide across a flat surface. **Level 3**
- The **object** is the shape you start with before a transformation. The **image** is the shape you end up with. **Level 4**
- To describe a translation, give the movement left or right followed by the movement up or down. For a shape on a grid, a translation of 3 right, 2 down means add 3 to each x**-coordinate** and subtract 2 from each y**-coordinate**. **Level 4**
- You can combine translations by translating a shape, then translating its image. **Level 5**

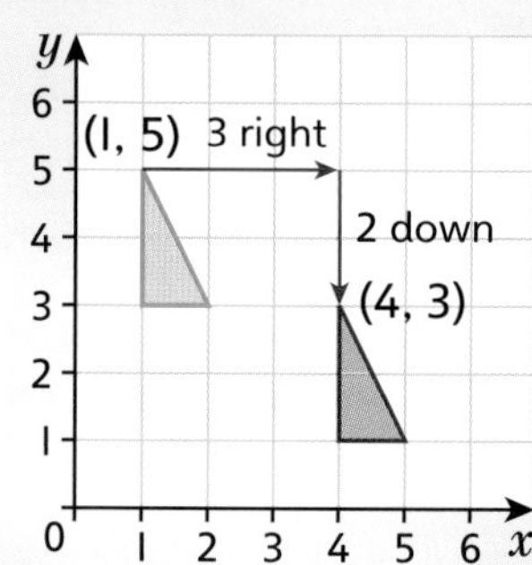

Watch out!

When you are working out a translation, count the movement between corresponding points. Don't count the empty squares between the shapes.

Watch out!

Remember to give the across movement before the up/down movement.

Practice, practice, practice!

Level 3

3a I can recognise where a shape will be after a translation

1 Which is the correct description of the translation of P onto Q?

A Slide P one square to the right.
B Slide P two squares to the right.
C Slide P three squares to the right.

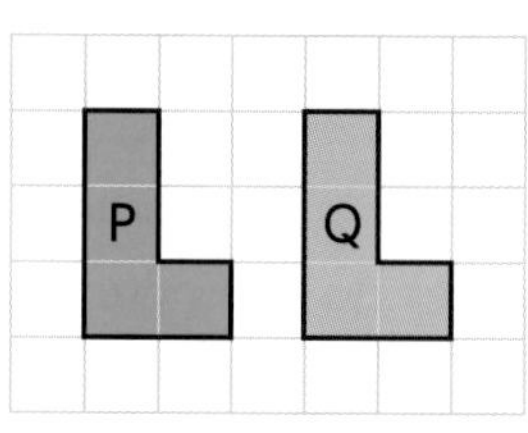
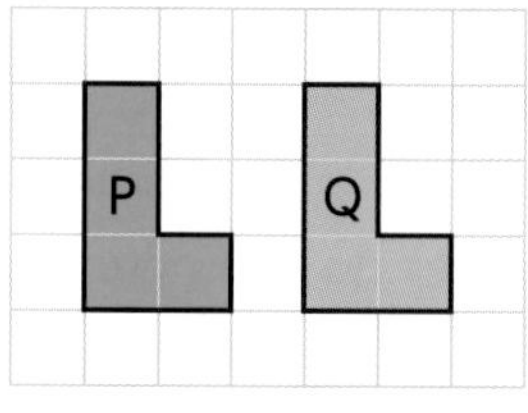

3a I can translate shapes

2 Copy these drawings and move each shape by the given amount.

2 squares left
1 square up

a

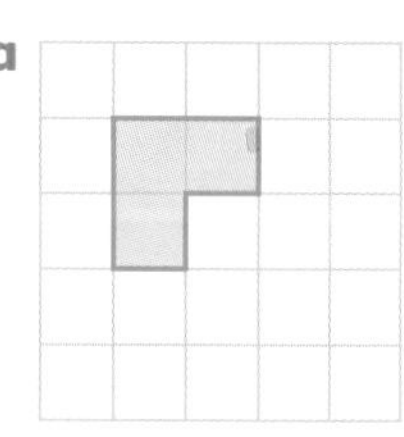

1 square right
1 square down

b

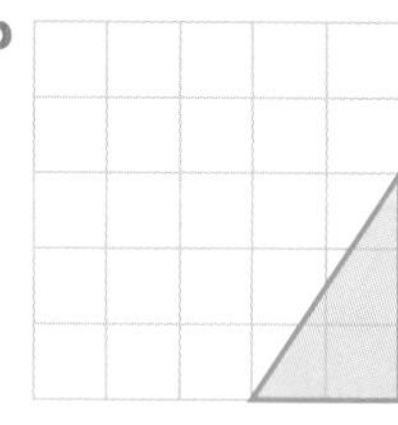

3 squares left
2 squares up

c

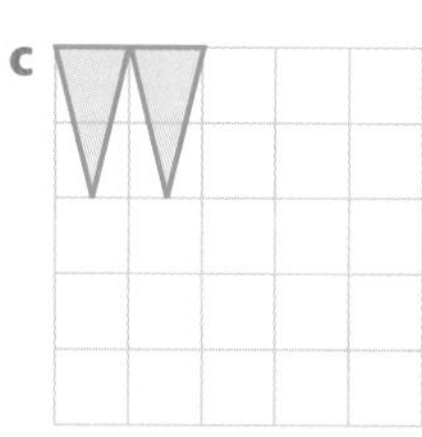

2 squares right
3 squares down

Level 4

4c I can understand and describe translations

3 Describe each translation of P onto Q.

a

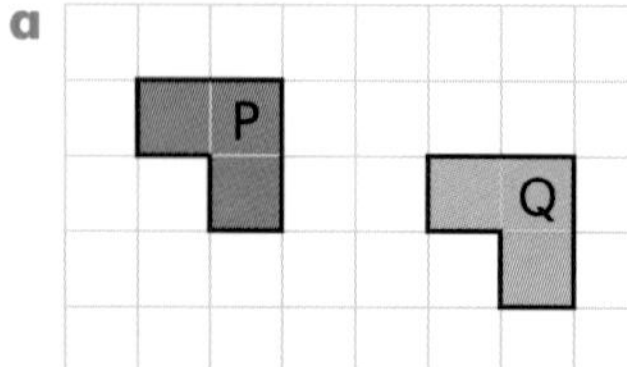

b

Q
P

c

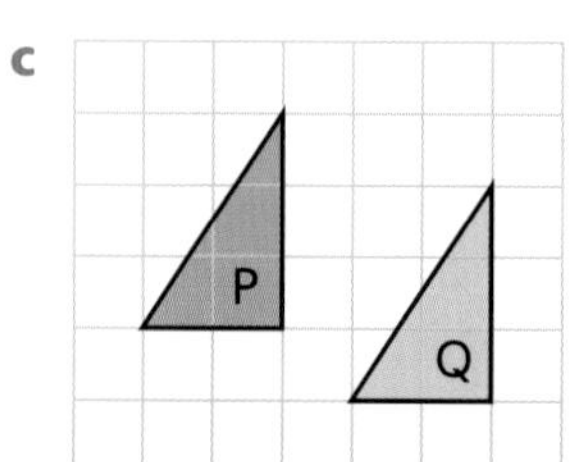

image object transformation

4 **a** Copy and complete the table by filling in the coordinates of the blue triangle.

Point	Yellow (object)	Blue (image)
P	(−5, 1)	
Q	(−5, 3)	
R	(−2, 1)	

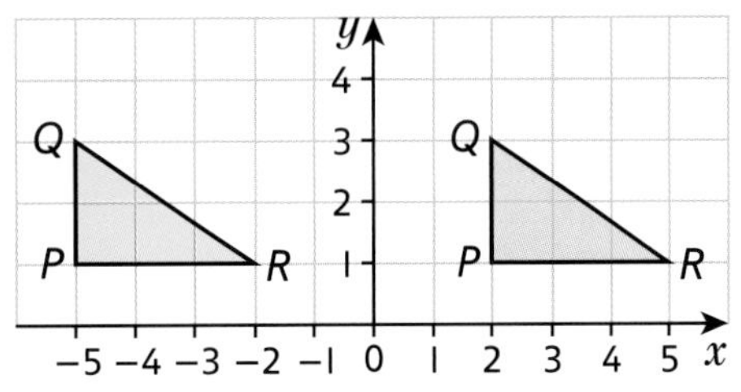

b Describe the translation that takes the yellow triangle onto the blue triangle.

5 Ravi translates a triangle 3 right, 2 up. Copy and complete this table of coordinates.

Point	Object	Image
P	(0, 1)	
Q	(0, 3)	
R	(3, 1)	

6 The translation that takes shape A to shape B is 3 left, 4 up. What translation takes shape B to shape A?

Level 4

4b I can understand and describe translations using coordinates

4a I can work out the position of a 2-D shape after a translation and describe it with positive coordinates

7 Jo translates a quadrilateral 2 right, 10 down.

a Copy and complete its table of coordinates.

b Name the quadrilateral.

Point	Object	Image
A	(5, 4)	
B	(5, 8)	
C		(5, −4)
D		(9, −4)

8 The point *A*(−7, −9) is translated 3 right, 2 down, to point *B*. Point *B* is translated and ends up at point *C*(7, 9). Describe the translation that takes point *B* to point *C*

Level 5

5c I can recognise and visualise the transformation of a 2-D shape after a translation in any quadrant

5a I can transform 2-D shapes by simple combinations of translations

Now try this!

A Another repeat

The length and width of the basic element in a pattern is called the 'pattern repeat'.

Look at the designs on Resource sheet 14.2. Measure the pattern repeat in each direction.

This is the basic pattern

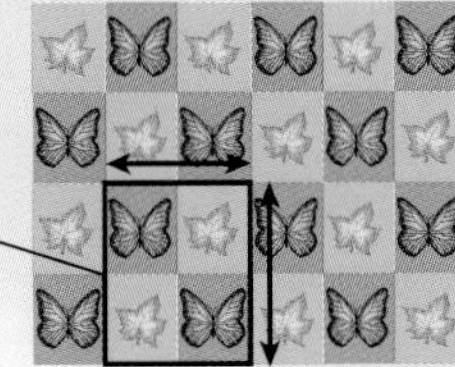

B Wrapping paper design

You can create a design for wrapping paper by repeating a simple pattern.

- Design a simple pattern on a 3 cm by 3 cm grid on squared paper.
  Show your pattern repeated several times.
- Try to make parts of your pattern link up so that it is hard to see where it repeats.
- Design two patterns that you can combine to make a larger repeating pattern.

translation **x-coordinate** **y-coordinate**

14.3 Reflecting shapes

- Recognise reflection symmetry
- Reflect a shape in a mirror line
- Reflect a shape on a coordinate grid

What's the BIG idea?

→ A **reflection** is one type of **transformation**. Level 3

→ You can use a mirror to check the reflection of a shape. Level 3

→ Corresponding points on your original shape (**object**) and reflected shape (**image**) are the same distance from the mirror line, but on opposite sides. Level 4

→ Mirror lines on coordinate grids are described by their equations. For example $x = 4$. Level 5

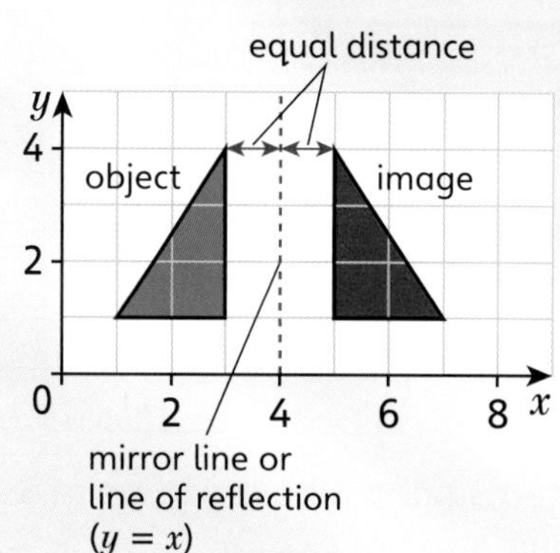

Why learn this?

We often want to make designs symmetrical for practical reasons or visual effect.

Super fact!

The word 'bid' has horizontal or vertical symmetry, depending whether you write it in lower case or capital letters.

BID
BID   bid bid

Practice, practice, practice!

Level 3

3b I can recognise reflection symmetry

1 Which drawings show a correct reflection of the yellow shape?

Hint: Put a mirror on the line if you need to check.

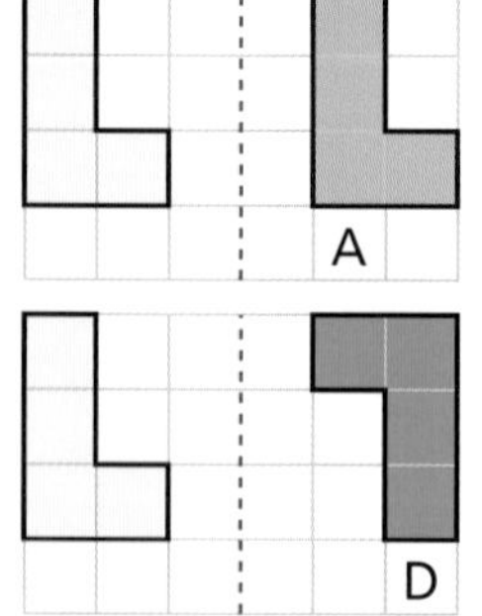

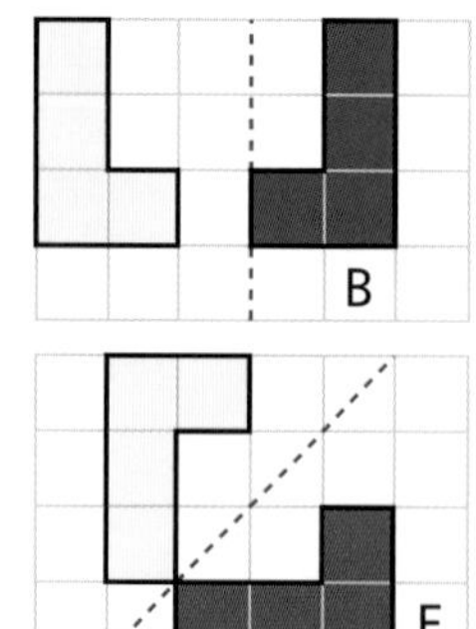

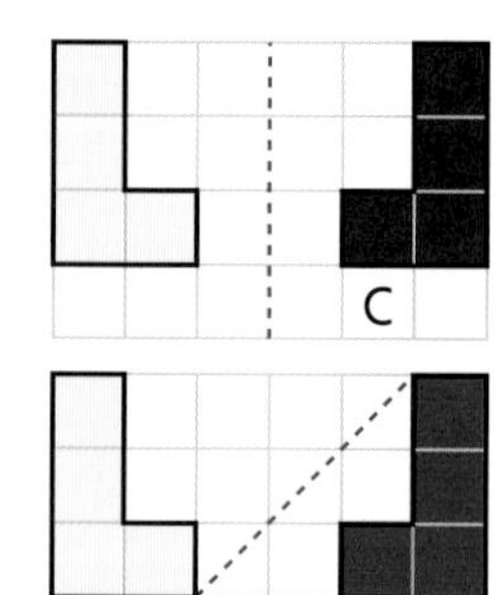

Watch out!

When reflecting in a diagonal line, it often helps to turn the page so that the line of reflection is vertical.

3b I can reflect shapes

2 Copy each diagram and reflect the shape in the red mirror line.

a

b

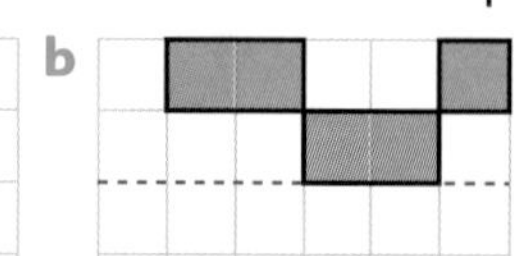

c

d

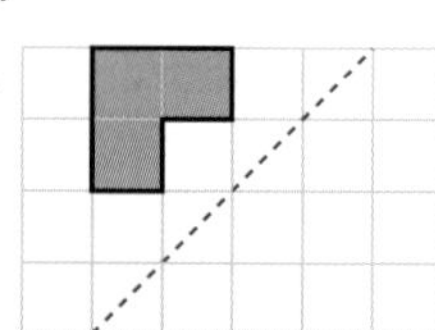

image | line of reflection | mirror line | object | reflection | symmet

3 Copy these diagrams. Add green squares so that the diagrams show a reflection in the red mirror line.

a  b 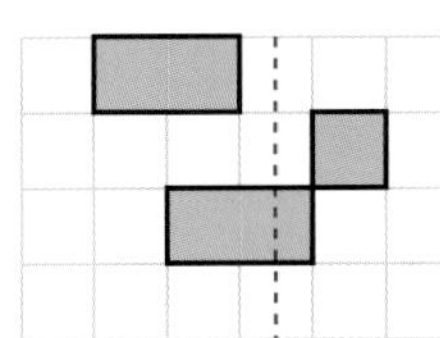 c

4 a Copy this diagram.

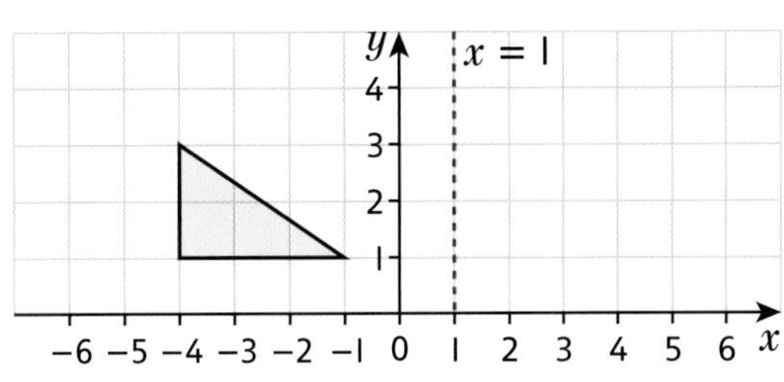

b Reflect the triangle in the line $x = 1$.

c Write down the coordinates of the image (the triangle after reflection).

Level 4

4b I can work out where a shape will be after reflection in a mirror line

5 A triangle is reflected in the y-axis. Without drawing the triangle, copy and complete the table of coordinates.

Object	Image
(−3, 2)	(3, 2)
(−3, 5)	
(−5, 3)	

6 The table shows the coordinates of a triangle before and after a reflection.

a What is the line of reflection?

b How can you tell?

Object	Image
(−3, 2)	(−3, −2)
(−3, 5)	(−3, −5)
(−5, 3)	(−5, −3)

7 a Plot the points $A(-3, 4)$, $B(-3, 2)$, $C(3, 4)$ and $D(3, 2)$. Join them in this order, to form a quadrilateral $ABCD$.

b Name the shape.

c Which of these are lines of symmetry?

the x-axis | the y-axis | $y = 3$ | $x = 3$ | $x = 3.5$ | $y = 2.5$

Level 5

5c I can use coordinates in any quadrant to describe the image of a reflection

5b I can describe mirror lines on a coordinate grid

5a I can recognise a mirror line or line of symmetry on a coordinate grid described by its equation

Now try this!

A Reflection swap

1 Draw a coordinate grid with x- and y-axes from −6 to +6.
2 Draw a triangle on the grid.
3 In pencil, lightly draw a line of reflection parallel to the x-axis or y-axis.
4 Reflect your triangle in the line, then rub out the line of reflection.
5 Swap drawings with a partner.
6 Draw the line of reflection on your partner's grid. Write its equation.

B Coordinate swap

Follow activity A, but instead of swapping drawings give your partner the coordinates before and after the reflection.
Can your partner work out the line of reflection without drawing a graph?

transformation   **x-axis**   **x-coordinate**   **y-axis**   **y-coordinate**

World's Greatest Maths!

14.4 Build a monster trap

Oh no! The school is infested with monsters. They're much too dangerous to catch by hand, and they're too big for a normal mousetrap.

Solve the puzzles to build an ingenious monster trap before it's too late!

Get the ball rolling!

To begin with you need to roll a marble along a platform. Unfortunately, some of the panels have been rotated out of position! The platform is shown in green and the missing panels are shown in red.

- Describe fully the rotation needed to swing each missing panel into place.

To describe a rotation fully, you need to give an angle, a direction of rotation, and the coordinates of the centre of rotation.

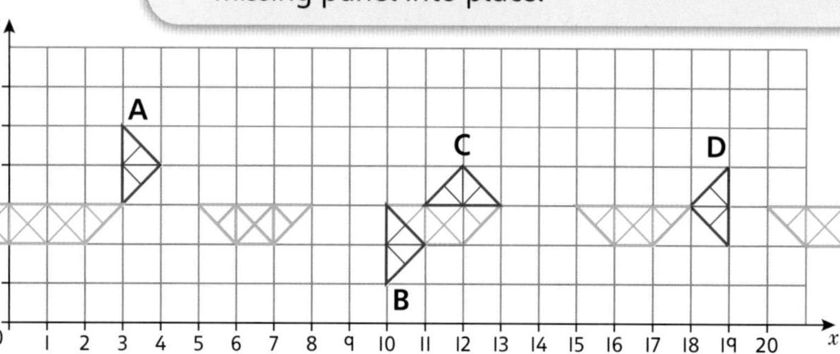

In a spin!

These dials will take your marble to the next stage of the trap. They have to be operated in alphabetical order, and you can only move them one at a time!

- For each dial, choose one angle and one direction from the control box. Each dial has to deliver the marble exactly into the empty slot on the next dial.

Loopy levers

Your marble triggers a series of levers. Each lever is shown in its starting position, and in its finishing position after a rotation.

- Name the shape of each lever.
- Find the coordinates of the centre of rotation for each lever.
- Describe fully the rotation that takes each lever from its starting position to its finishing position.

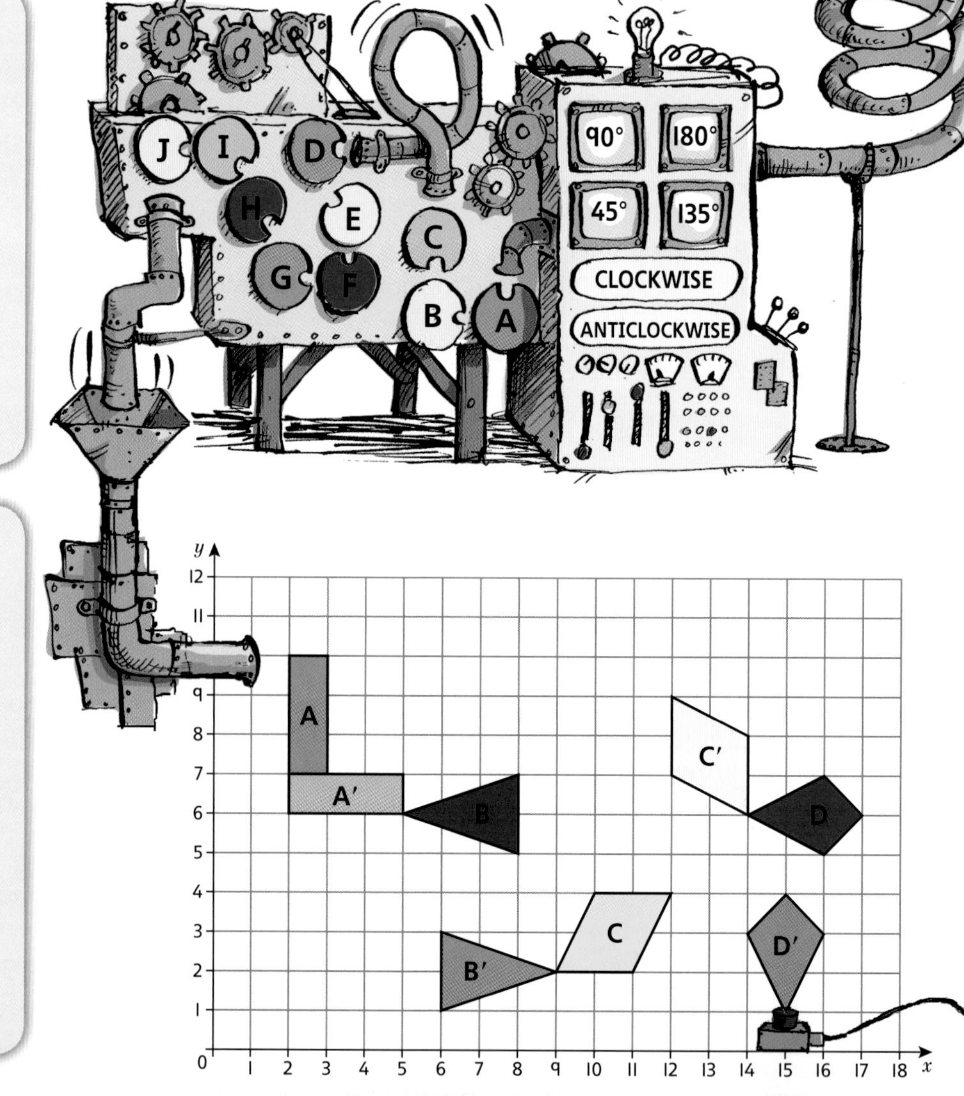

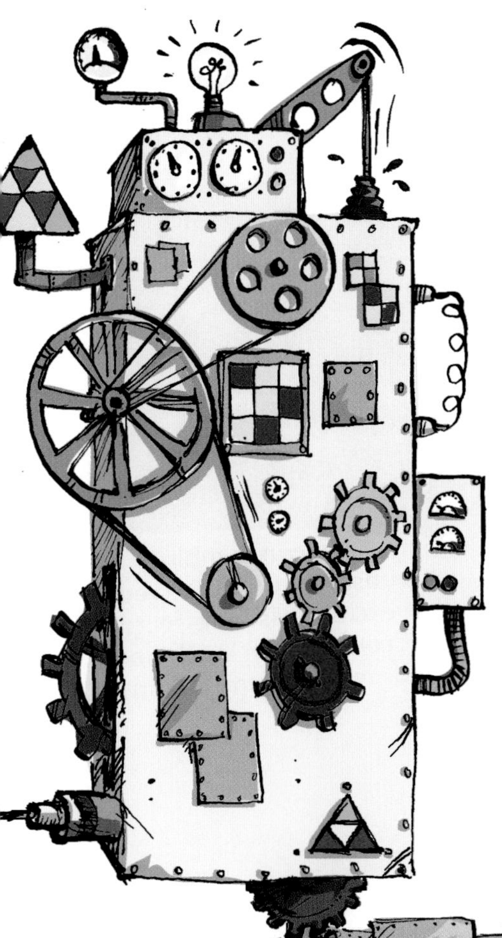

Machinery madness

The final lever has pushed the button which activates the machinery to lower the cage. Unfortunately, some of the components are missing from the machine. Use a copy of Resource sheet 14.4 for this section.

1 Colour each component so that it has the correct order of rotational symmetry.

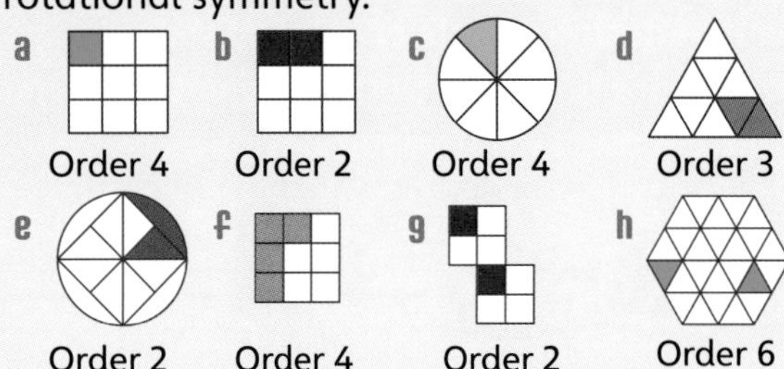

2 Add one square or triangle to each component so that it has the correct order of rotational symmetry.

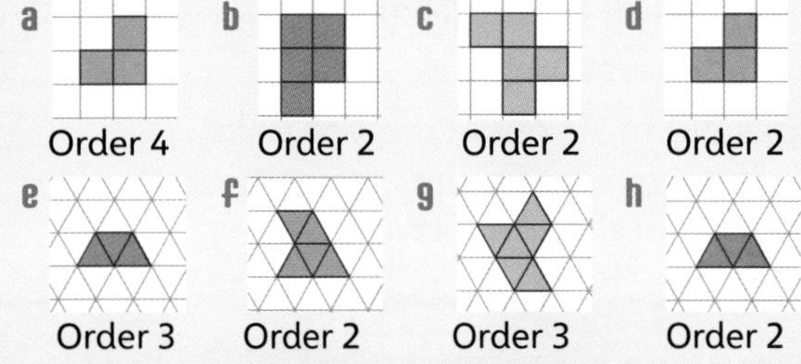

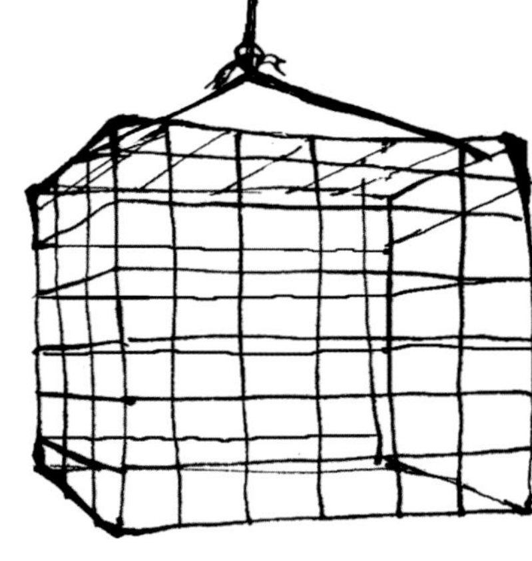

Build a monster cage

To finish the trap you need to build the monster cage. You will need a copy of the coordinate grid from Resource sheet 14.4.

- Draw copies of shapes A and B using the rotations given in these instructions.

Rotate shape A 180° about (4, 4)
Rotate shape B 90° clockwise about (15, 5)
Rotate shape B a quarter turn anticlockwise about (9, 4)
Rotate shape A a quarter turn anticlockwise about (2, 6)
Rotate shape B 90° anticlockwise about (15, 3)
Rotate shape B a half turn about (9, 4)
Rotate shape A 90° clockwise about (11, 1)

- Draw a coordinate grid from 0 to 20 in both directions. Draw your own monster and design a cage to hold it. Choose two different starting shapes and label them A and B. Describe the rotations of A and B that could be used to make your cage.

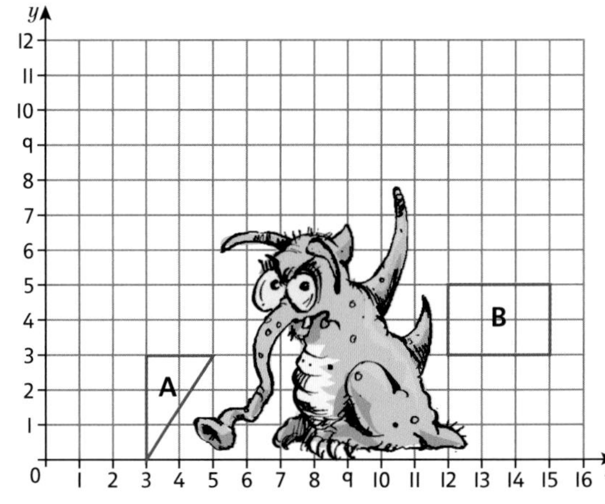

14.5 Combining transformations

- Know how to reflect, translate or rotate a shape
- Follow instructions to make a pattern using transformations
- Design a pattern using transformations

What's the BIG idea?

→ **Translations**, **reflections** and **rotations** are all **transformations**. Level 4

→ In reflection, the mirror line is usually shown as a dotted line. Level 4

→ A translation is a slide. Give the horizontal movement first, then the vertical movement. Level 4

→ Rotations are **turns** about a given point. You need to know the point, the angle and the direction of the turn. Level 5

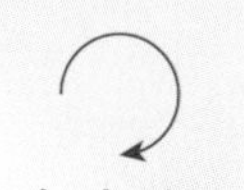
clockwise

anticlockwise

Why learn this?

You can combine transformations to create exciting visual effects. It could be for wallpaper, carpets or flying displays.

Practice, practice, practice!

Level 4

4b I can understand and use the language associated with reflections

1 The blue triangle reflects onto each of the other coloured triangles.

Which triangle is a reflection of the blue triangle in the line

a *DE* **b** *AH* **c** *BG* **d** *CF*?

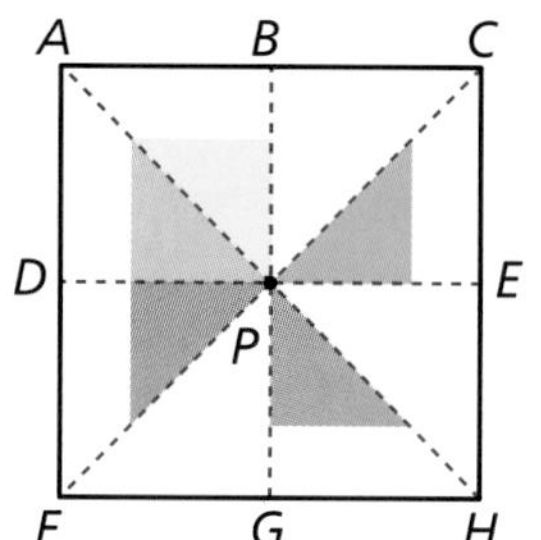

4b I can visualise where a shape will be after a rotation

2 Look at the diagram in Q1. The green triangle rotates about the point *P* onto the yellow triangle. Which colour triangle doesn't it rotate onto?

4a I can understand and describe reflections and rotations

3 Draw a square and its diagonals, like this.

Now copy the pattern carefully. Notice that the green line crosses the mirror line *AC*.

a Reflect the pattern in the line *AC*.

b Reflect both object and image from part **a** in the line *BD*.

c Amy starts with the same pattern. She reflects it in *BD*, then *AC*.

Does she get the same result? Explain your answer.

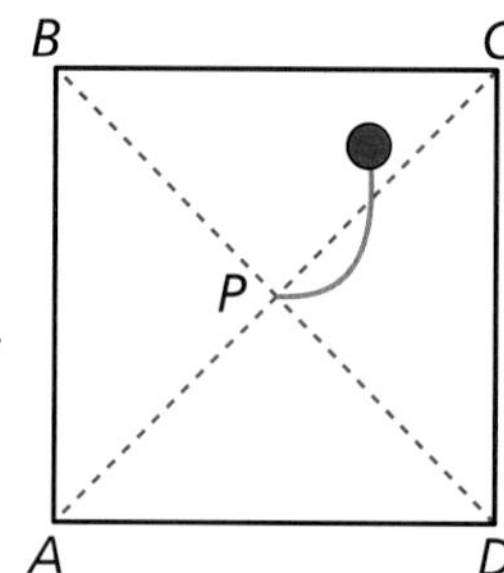

4 Look at the diagram in Q1.

Which colour triangle will the blue triangle land on after

a reflection in the line *AH* and then rotation a quarter-turn clockwise about the point *P*

b rotation a quarter-turn clockwise about *P*, then reflection in the line *AH*

c reflection in the line *DE*, then rotation a quarter-turn anticlockwise about *P*

d reflection in the line *CF*, then rotation a half-turn turn about *P*?

anticlockwise clockwise image object reflection

5 Make another copy of the pattern in Q3.

a Rotate the pattern a quarter-turn anticlockwise about the point P.

b Rotate the result from part **a** a quarter-turn anticlockwise about the point P and repeat until you have four patterns equally spaced.

c What is the order of rotational symmetry of the final design?

6 Copy the diagram.

a Reflect the triangle in the x-axis.

b Reflect the image in the y-axis.

c Is there another way to get the same image using transformations?

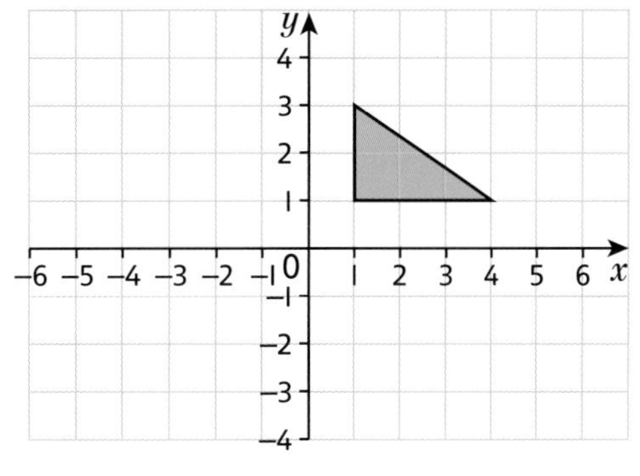

7 Copy the grid and pattern below.

a Rotate the pattern a quarter-turn anticlockwise about the point P.

b Reflect both object and image from part **a** in the line AB.

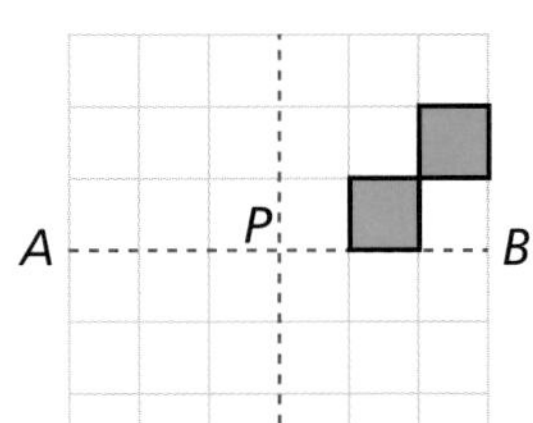

8 Jodie transforms a single triangle in different ways. She makes this beach hut pattern. Draw the triangle on squared paper.

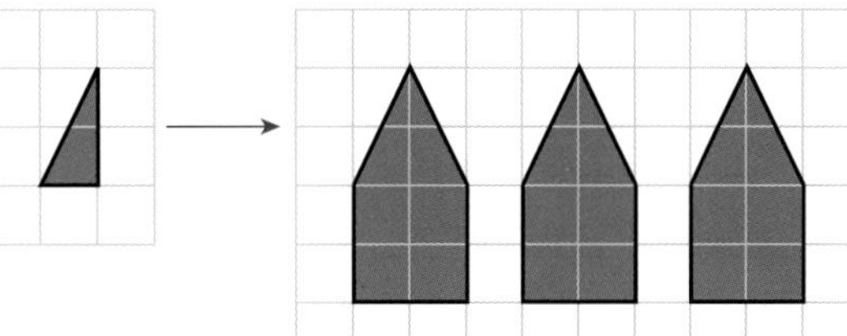

a Work out how to make one beach hut using reflections and translations. Draw in any mirror lines you use.

b Describe the transformation

i to the second beach hut from the first

ii to the third beach hut from the second one.

Level 5

5c I can understand and describe rotations and recognise rotation symmetry

5a I can transform 2-D shapes by simple combinations of rotations and reflections

Did you know?

After a translation the shape still faces the same way.

Now try this!

A Transforming design

Copy this triangle on squared paper.
Create a design on the 6 × 6 grid starting with this triangle.
You can reflect it, translate it, rotate it and change its colour.

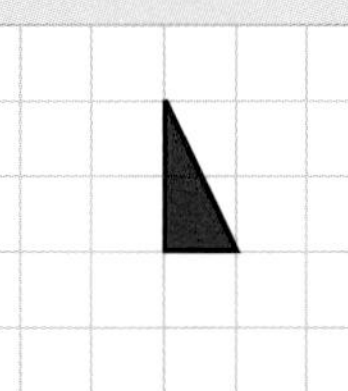

B Transformation swap

1 Draw a triangle on a coordinate grid with x- and y-axes from −6 to 6.
2 Create a design starting with this triangle. You can reflect it, translate it or rotate it. You can do any transformation on all or part of the design.
3 Write instructions for each of your transformations.
4 Swap instructions with a partner. Starting with the original grid, can you re-create each other's designs?

Super fact!

A tessellation is made by rotating, reflecting and/or translating a shape.

rotation transformation translation turn

14.6 Problem solving

- Make and recognise 2-D shapes in different contexts
- Contradict a wrong statement with a counter example
- Choose the maths to use to solve problems

Why learn this?

A farmer needs to know the perimeter of a field to find the length of the hedges that need to be cut, and the area of a field to work out how many crops can be planted in it.

What's the BIG idea?

→ **Perimeter** is the distance around the edge of a shape. **Level 4**

→ **Area** is the number of unit squares inside a shape.
Area of a rectangle $A = l \times w$ (rectangle with sides l and w) **Level 4**

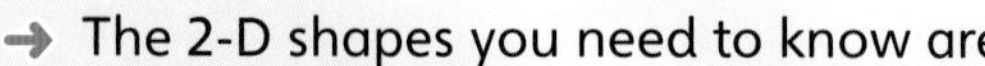

→ The 2-D shapes you need to know are
- triangles: scalene, isosceles and equilateral
- quadrilaterals: square, rhombus, rectangle, parallelogram, kite, arrowhead and trapezium
- others: pentagon, hexagon and octagon. **Level 4**

→ A **counter example** is an example that shows a statement is not true. **Level 5**

Watch out!

Don't muddle area and perimeter. Area is the inside, perimeter is the outside.

Practice, practice, practice!

Level 4

4a I can solve simple problems using perimeter

1 An equilateral triangle has a perimeter of 24 cm.
How long is each side?

2 **a** The line is one side of a rectangle.
Copy the grid onto centimetre squared paper and complete to make a rectangle with a perimeter of 12 cm.

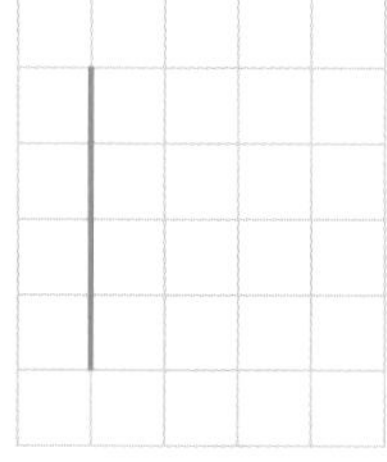

4a I can solve problems using area by counting squares

b The line is one side of a triangle.
Copy the grid onto centimetre squared paper and complete to make a triangle with area 6 cm².

4a I can recognise and visualise 2-D shapes

3 Cut the four corners off a square so that each cut removes just one corner, for example, like this:

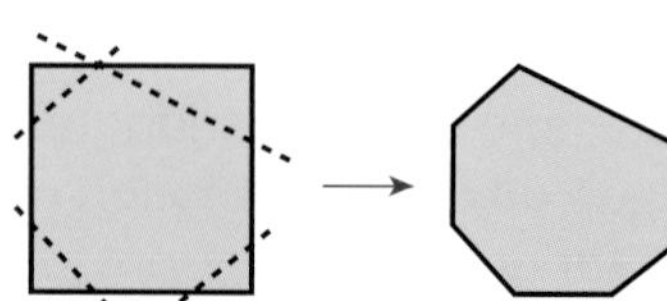

a How many sides can the new shape have?

b Draw three 6 × 6 squares on squared paper.
Draw the cutting lines to make a square, a rectangle and a kite.

area counter example

Level 5

5a I can choose the maths I need to solve problems

4 The area of this square is 81 cm².

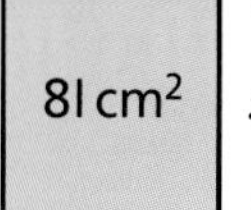

a Find length x.

b Work out the perimeter of the square.

c Ruth says that the perimeter of a square is always a multiple of 4. Give a counter example to show that this is not true.

5 Square *ABCD* has sides of 8 cm. Pete reflects the square in the line *CD*. The combined object and image form a rectangle.

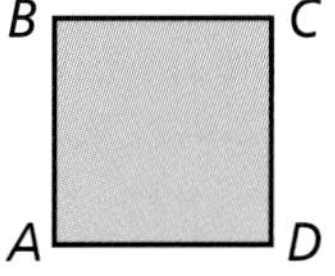

a Work out the area of the square.

b What is the area of the rectangle?

c What is the perimeter of the rectangle?

6 This sequence is made from identical squares. Each square has sides of 5 cm. Here are the first three shapes in the sequence.

a Work out the perimeter of each of the first three shapes in the sequence.

b Work out the perimeter of the 50th shape in the sequence.

c One of the shapes has area 200 cm². Which position is this in the sequence?

7 A regular pentagon and a square have whole number side lengths. They also have the same perimeter.

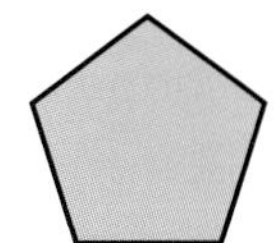

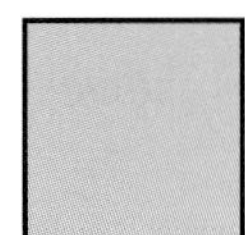

Not drawn accurately

a Caroline says that the perimeter could be any whole number. Give a counter example to show that this is not true.

b One possible perimeter for both shapes is 60 cm. In this case work out

i the side length of the pentagon

ii the side length of the square.

c Write down three other possible perimeters for the pentagon and the square .

Super fact!

'Perimeter' is a Greek word. Its literal translation is 'around measure'. Guess the literal translation of 'periscope'.

Now try this!

A Lemur enclosures

The new lemur enclosure must be rectangular. It needs to have area 12 m². Each side must be a whole number of metres long.

On squared paper, draw all the possible rectangles for the enclosure. Work out the length of fencing for each rectangle.

B Triangle splits

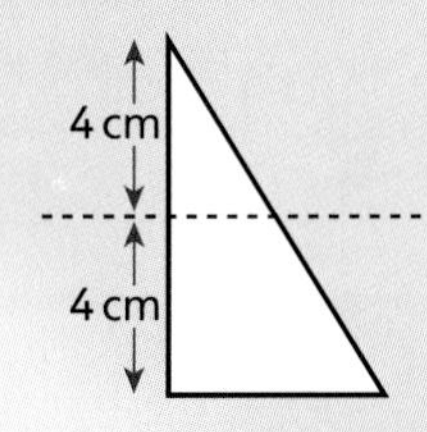

1 Draw a right-angled triangle on squared paper, and cut it out.
2 Cut the triangle in two so that half the height is below the cut and half the height is above the cut.
3 Rearrange the two pieces into a rectangle.
4 Work out the area of your rectangle.
5 Draw another right-angled triangle on squared paper. Write down what you think its area is. Check this by splitting the triangle and rearranging it into a rectangle.

perimeter

Unit 14 plenary

Transformations on the move

The opening ceremonies of events like the Olympics and the Commonwealth Games often have displays where groups of people form moving patterns and symbols.
Adverts also use techniques like these.

A group of people can form themselves into a shape with reflective symmetry.

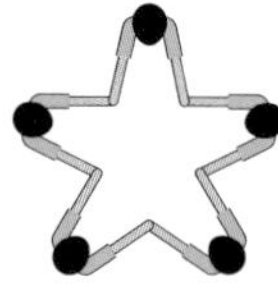

Then they can make their shape rotate and translate.

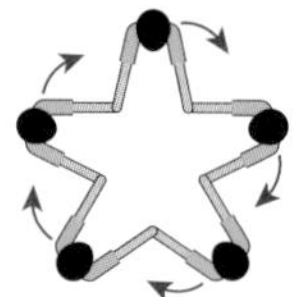

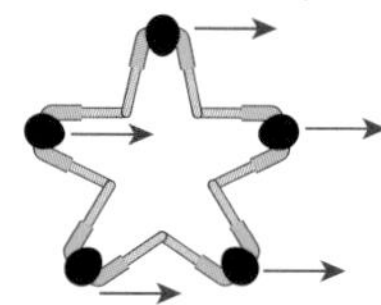

1 In small groups work out at least two shapes your group can form.
Each shape must have at least one mirror line.
Make a drawing of your shapes. **Level 4**

2 Work out how to form your shapes if you all start in a straight line.
The group has to keep at least one mirror line at all times.
Make a drawing to show how each person has to move. **Level 4**

3 With your group practise translations in different directions. **Level 4**

4 Now practise making your shape rotate. Do rotations of 90° and 360°.
Try rotating clockwise and then do the same rotation anticlockwise.
Where do you end up? **Level 5**

5 If you're feeling ambitious try rotating and translating at the same time! **Level 5**

The BIG ideas

- → A **translation** is a slide. The shape stays facing the same way. The **horizontal** movement, x, is given before the **vertical** movement, y. **Level 4**
- → A **reflection** is what you see in a mirror. The **mirror line** is the same distance from the **object** and its **image**. **Level 4**
- → A rotation is a turn about a point. The angle is given as well as the direction of the turn. **Level 5**

Find your level

Level 3

Q1 Copy the shape onto centimetre squared paper. Move the shape 3 to the right and 2 down.

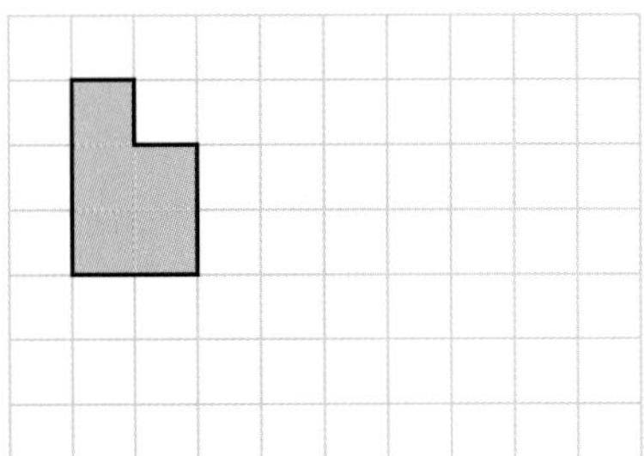

Level 4

Q2 Copy this shape onto centimetre squared paper.

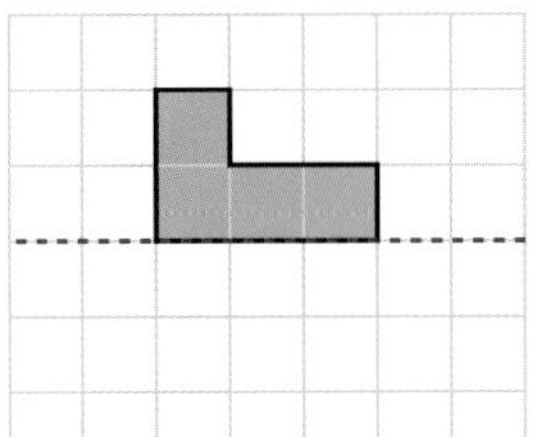

a Reflect the shape in the dotted line.

b Work out the perimeter of the combined object and image.

Level 5

Q3 A square is reflected in the x-axis. Without drawing the square, copy and complete the table of coordinates.

Object	Image
(2, −2)	
(5, −2)	
(5, −5)	
(2, −5)	

Q4 The table shows the coordinates of a triangle before and after a reflection.

Object	Image
(2, 5)	(−2, 5)
(2, 1)	(−2, 1)
(−1, 1)	(1, 1)

What is the line of reflection?

Q5 Copy this diagram.

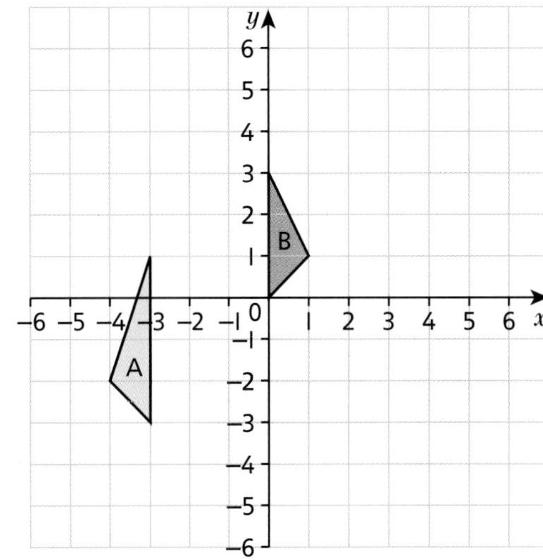

a Write down the coordinates of triangle A.

b Reflect triangle A in the line $x = -3$. Name the quadrilateral formed.

c Reflect triangle B in the line $y = x$. Name the quadrilateral formed.

15 Statistics sorted

Many card games involve chance.

Poker is a popular card game in which players use probability to help them work out whether they have the best cards or not, and place bets accordingly.

Players can also estimate the probability of certain cards being dealt at any point during a hand.

Part of this unit is about probability and the probability of specific outcomes, for example the probability of picking the queen of hearts from a pack of playing cards.

Activities

A
- Investigate card games. Think of and find out about as many different card games as you can. Jot down their rules on paper. Decide how much each card game is based on CHANCE or SKILL.
- Make a scale like this and mark each game on it.

  Chance ——————————————— Skill

- Extend your investigation to include board games. Also think about word and strategy games.

B You have been given an ordinary pack of 52 playing cards with instructions to devise a new card game. The game should involve elements of probability. You do not have to use all 52 cards. Carefully write down the objective(s) and rules of the game. Play the game with a partner. Does it work well? Would you make any changes to the game now that you have tested it?

Did you know?

The playing cards we use today are derived from French designs. Around 1480, the French developed the suits of spades, clubs, diamonds and hearts. The Americans invented the Joker around 1870.

Before you start this unit...

1 Find the mode and range of these sets of numbers.

page 70

a 2, 3, 5, 3, 5, 5, 5, 6, 3, 3

b 2, 3, 8, 7, 5, 8, 8, 7, 2, 2

2 Vikram conducted a survey on bike colours.
His results are as follows.

Red, Yellow, Red, Blue, Blue, Red, Red, Yellow, Red, Blue, Blue, Red

a Show the data on a tally chart.

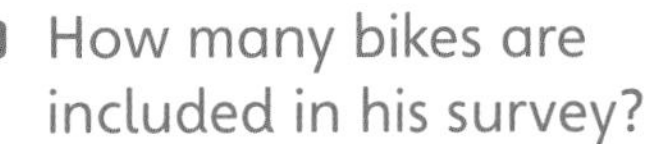

b How many bikes are included in his survey?

page 120

c Draw a bar chart to illustrate the data.

15.1 Probability and outcomes

- Understand and use the probability scale
- Be able to list all the possible outcomes of an event
- Find the probability of equally likely outcomes

Why learn this?

Probability makes it possible to understand everything from batting averages to the weather report, or your chances of being struck by lightning!

What's the BIG idea?

→ You can show the **probability** of something happening on a **probability scale**. **Level 4 & Level 5**

impossible — unlikely — even chance — likely — certain

0 — $\frac{1}{2}$ — 1

→ All probabilities have a value from 0 (**impossible**) to 1 (**certain**). **Level 5**

→ The probability that an event will happen = $\frac{\text{total number of successful outcomes}}{\text{total number of possible outcomes}}$ **Level 5**

→ You can write probability as a fraction, a decimal or a percentage. **Level 5**

Learn this

Picking a card is an event. There are 52 possible outcomes. If the cards have been properly shuffled, each outcome is equally likely.

Practice, practice, practice!

Level 4

4a I can use words to describe probability

1 Choose words to describe the probability of these events.

impossible | unlikely | even chance | likely | certain

a I will pick a red card from a normal pack of cards.
b A human can run at 100 mph.
c I will win the National Lottery.
d The day after Monday will be Tuesday.

Level 5

5c I can use a probability scale from 0 to 1

2 The probabilities of outcomes A, B, C and D are marked on a probability scale. Write a possible event for each.

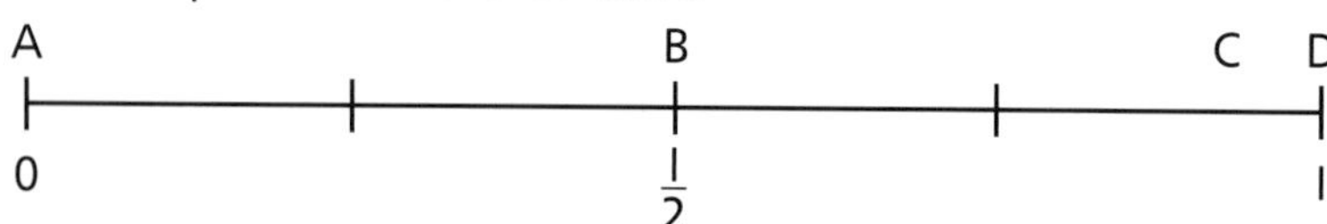

3 Draw a probability scale from 0 to 1.
Each of the probabilities below relates to the spinner in this picture.
Mark each of the probabilities on your scale.

A the probability of getting an even number
B the probability of getting 0
C the probability of getting a number less than 7
D the probability of getting a number greater than 6

5b I can use find the probability of an outcome

certain | even chance | impossible | likely | outcome

Level 5

5b I can list all the possible outcomes of an event

4 What are the possible outcomes when this spinner is spun?

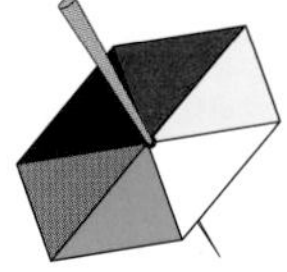

5 What are the possible outcomes when a letter from the word EXTRAPOLATION is picked at random?

6 Nigella is completing her maths homework.
So far she has written:
If this spinner is spun, there are two possible outcomes.

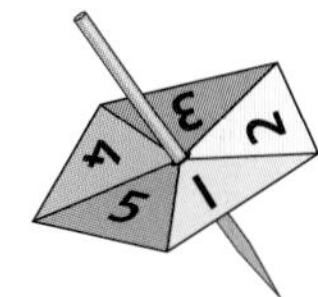

a Is she right?

b List all of the different possible outcomes.

5b I can find the probability of an outcome

7 A normal dice is rolled. What is the probability that it shows

a 1 **b** 6 **c** 7

d an odd number **e** a number less than 6?

8 I have a pack of playing cards (52 cards).
If I pick a card at random, what is the probability that the card is

a a queen **b** an ace **c** a heart

d the king of spades **e** a diamond or a club?

5b I can find the probability of an outcome and mark it on a probability scale

9 A small box of chocolates contains five chocolates with hard centres, six with soft centres and nine with chewy centres.

a Write the probability as a fraction of picking a chocolate with

i a soft centre **ii** a chewy centre

iii a hard or soft centre **iv** a hard or chewy centre

v not a chewy centre?

b Mark your answers on a probability scale from 0 to 1.

c Write the probabilities from **a** as decimals between 0 and 1.

d Write the probabilities from **a** as percentages.

Now try this!

A Probability scale

Draw a probability scale. Mark on it: certain, likely, even chance, unlikely, impossible and 0, $\frac{1}{2}$, 1. Illustrate each with a diagram to explain each term. For example, the even chance illustration could be flipping a coin as there is an equal chance of it landing heads or tails up.

B Spinner design

Design an eight-sided spinner. The segments are equally sized.
Place the numbers 1, 2, 3 and 4 in the segments according to these rules.

- It is more likely to spin a 4 than a 3.
- 3 and 2 have an equally likely chance.
- 4 is three times as likely as 1.
- 3 is twice as likely as 1.

Super fact!

The chance of winning the jackpot on the National Lottery is 1 in 14 million.

possible probability probability scale unlikely

15.2 Sample space diagrams

- Understand the probability of an event not occurring
- Be able to list all the outcomes of combined events
- Record all possible outcomes in a sample space diagram

Why learn this?

Using a table to arrange all the data means you don't forget a vital piece of the information!

What's the BIG idea?

- The **probabilities** of all the possible **outcomes** of an event add up to 1. **Level 5**
- Probability of an event not happening = 1 − probability of the event happening.
  If the probability of picking an 8 from a selection of cards is $\frac{1}{4}$, then the probability of picking a card that is not an 8 is $1 - \frac{1}{4} = \frac{3}{4}$. **Level 5**
- You can use a **sample space diagram** to list all the possible outcomes of a combined event.
  What are the possible outcomes when Spinner 1 (1–3) and Spinner 2 (1–4) are spun?

		Spinner 2			
		1	2	3	4
Spinner 1	1	1, 1	1, 2	1, 3	1, 4
	2	2, 1	2, 2	2, 3	2, 4
	3	3, 1	3, 2	3, 3	3, 4

  Total of 12 possible outcomes. **Level 5**
- The probability of something happening
  $= \frac{\text{total number of successful outcomes}}{\text{total number of possible outcomes}}$ **Level 5**

Super fact!

Two players who shared the jackpot in the Irish Lottery had picked their numbers using the dates of birth, ordination and death of the same priest!

Practice, practice, practice!

1 A normal dice is rolled.

a What is the probability of getting an even number?

b What is the probability of getting an odd number?

c What do you notice about your answers to parts **a** and **b**? Explain.

2 A dice is rolled.

a What is the probability of getting a 3?

b What is the probability of not getting a 3?

Watch out!

It is not harder to roll a 6 than any other number on a dice. If it is a fair dice, all the outcomes are equally likely.

Level 5

5b I can find the probability of an outcome

5a I can find the probability of an outcome not happening

outcome probability

3 An ordinary pack of 52 cards is well shuffled. A card is chosen at random.

a What is the probability that the card is a picture card?

Hint: A picture card is a king, a queen or a jack.

b What is the probability that the card is not a picture card?

Level 5

5a I can find the probability of an outcome not happening

4 The probability that a counter chosen at random from a bag will be red is $\frac{4}{13}$. What is the probability that the counter will not be red?

5 A manufacturer puts its MP3 players through quality testing before they leave the factory.
The probability of failing the quality test is 0.01.
What is the probability of not failing?

6 Nasir spins a coin twice.
List the possible ways that the coin can land in two spins.

5a I can identify all the possible outcomes for a combined event

7 You can choose two pizza toppings from cheese, ham and pepperoni.
What are the possible combinations?

8 **a** Use a sample space diagram to list all the possible outcomes of spinning A and B.

b How many outcomes are there?

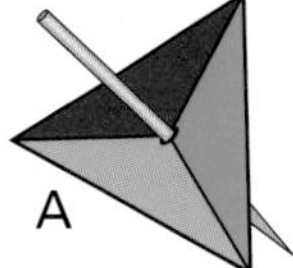

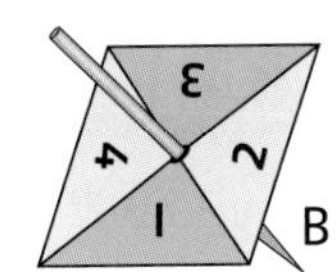

5a I can list all the possible outcomes in a sample space diagram

9 Two normal dice are rolled.

a Use a sample space diagram to list all the possible outcomes of rolling the two dice.

b How many outcomes are there?

Now try this!

A Two-course meal

The local Italian restaurant offers three main course dishes and three desserts.

Mains	*Desserts*
ravioli	*ice cream*
lasagne	*biscotti*
pizza	*torte*

What are all the possible combinations of main course and dessert?

B Two spinners

Design two spinners so that there are 24 different outcomes when they are spun together.

sample space diagram

15.3 Experimental probability

- Collect data from a probability experiment
- Know how to estimate probabilities from experimental data
- Compare experimental and theoretical probabilities

Why learn this?

We cannot always work out the probability of an event. An experiment can help you estimate the probability.

What's the BIG idea?

→ The estimated **probability** of an **outcome** can be worked out after an activity is done several times.

$$\text{Estimated probability} = \frac{\text{number of times the outcome did happen}}{\text{total number of times the activity was done}}$$ **Level 5**

→ The theoretical probability of an equally likely outcome is the predicted value.

$$\text{Theoretical probability} = \frac{\text{number of times the outcome can happen}}{\text{total number of possible outcomes}}$$ **Level 5**

Super fact!

During the 1500s, one of the first people to study probability was Cardano, a well-known gambler!

Practice, practice, practice!

Level 4 & Level 5

4a I can collect and record data

5c I can estimate probability from experimental data

1 In this experiment you will roll a dice 60 times and record which number it lands on.

Outcome	Tally	Frequency
1		
2		
3		
4		
5		
6		

a Write down what you predict the results will be.

b Copy the table.

c Roll the dice 60 times and record your results.
Do your results agree with your predictions?

d What is the estimated probability of each outcome?

Level 5

5c I can estimate probability from experimental data

2 Lucy has put 10 beads in a bag. The beads are red, yellow and blue. Jessica does not know how many of each colour there are. She carries out an experiment to help her guess the number of beads of each colour. She takes a bead from the bag, records its colour then replaces the bead. She does this 30 times.
Her results are shown in this table.

Colour	Tally	Frequency	Estimated probability
Red	卌 ||||		
Yellow	卌 |		
Blue	卌 卌 卌		

a Copy and complete the table.

b Use the estimated probability to calculate the number of red, yellow and blue beads in the bag.

Learn this

Estimated probability is calculated using results from experiments.

experiment experimental probability frequency outcome

Level 5

5c I can compare experimental and theoretical probabilities

3 In this experiment you are going to make a spinner.
Then you will spin it to find the estimated probability of each outcome.

a Make a six-sided spinner in the shape of a regular hexagon.
Number the sections from 1 to 6.

b What is the theoretical probability for each outcome?

c Spin the spinner 60 times and record your results in a table.

d What is the estimated probability of each outcome?
Are these the same as the theoretical probabilities?

e Put a paper clip on one section and repeat the experiment.
What do you notice?
Show the results to a partner. Can they tell where you put the paper clip?

f Design a new spinner where you are more likely to get a 1 or 2 than a 3, 4, 5 or 6. Test this spinner. Show your test results to a partner. Can they tell that 1 or 2 are more likely than 3, 4, 5 or 6?

4 **a** What is the theoretical probability of a coin landing on heads?

b If you spin a coin 50 times, how many times would you expect it to land on heads?

c Spin a coin 50 times and record your results.

d What is the estimated probability for the coin landing on heads?

e Are the estimated and theoretical probabilities the same?

f Repeat the experiment. Spin the coin 100 times and record your results.

g What is the estimated probability for the coin landing on heads?

h Compare the theoretical probability and the estimated probability for 50 and 100 throws. What do you notice?

i Put your class results together for the 50 throws experiment.
What estimated probability did the class get as a whole?

5 **a** Roll a dice 10 times. Record the number of even scores.

b Work out the experimental probability from 10 throws.

c Copy this graph. Plot your experimental probability from **b** for 10 rolls.

Probability
0.10
0.8
0.6
0.4
0.2
0
Theoretical probability
10 20 30 40 50 60 70 80 90 100
Number of rolls

d Repeat for 20, 30, 40 rolls of the dice, up to 100 rolls.

e Compare the theoretical and experimental probabilities. What do you notice?

Now try this!

A New National Lottery game 1

You have been asked by the National Lottery to devise a new game using the numbered balls. A single ball will be drawn, with the winner matching that number. The probability of the winning outcome must be $\frac{1}{4}$. You must decide:

- how many balls will be put in the draw
- which numbers between 1 and 49 will be put in the draw
- how many numbers each entrant picks.

B New National Lottery game 2

You have been given the same task as in Activity A, with the difference that the probability of the winning outcome must be $\frac{1}{10}$.

probability **tally** **theoretical probability**

15.4 More on displaying data

- Construct and use frequency tables
- Draw bar charts for simple and grouped data
- Use ICT to construct pie charts

Why learn this?

Diagrams are a good way to display data because they let you spot patterns or features quickly.

What's the BIG idea?

- A **bar chart (frequency diagram)** uses bars of equal width to show **data**. Level 4
- You can sort data using a **frequency table**. Level 4 & Level 5
- When there is a wide spread of data, you can group the data in equal class **intervals**.
  For example, 0–9, 10–19, 20–29, and so on. Level 4 & Level 5
- A **pie chart** uses a circle to represent data. Each sector of the circle represents a particular category of data. Level 5

Learn this

Discrete data is data which can only take certain definite values.

Practice, practice, practice!

Level 4

1 These are the sales figures for Gameplace, for a Saturday morning in July.

a Draw a bar chart to represent the data.

b How many games consoles were sold in total?

Games console	Frequency
MiMi	8
Playport	5
XY100	11

4b I can draw a bar chart

2 These are the Gameplace sales for a Saturday morning in December.

a Draw a bar-line graph to represent the information.

b How many games consoles were sold in total?

Games console	Frequency
MiMi	14
Playport	20
XY100	16

4b I can draw a bar-line graph

3 The table gives the scores of the first 30 darts thrown in a darts competition. Draw a bar chart to represent this data.

Score	Frequency
0–9	2
10–19	9
20–29	10
30–39	6
40–49	2
50–59	1

4a I can draw a bar chart for grouped data

Watch out!

Bar charts for discrete data need gaps between the bars.

bar chart | bar-line graph | data | frequency diagram

4 The highest scores of a group of professional cricketers are shown in this table.

a Draw a bar chart to represent this data.

b How many cricketers' scores are included?

Score	Frequency
1–10	7
11–20	4
21–30	4
31–40	2
41–50	5
51–60	4
61–70	1
71–80	4

Level 4

4a I can draw a bar chart for grouped data

5 Groups 7X and 7Y recently sat a history test. Their marks out of 40 were

28	19	34	39	21	31	9	32	23	12
22	34	20	5	9	24	27	31	11	18
34	19	15	35	7	22	34	27	24	17
18	22	21	39	21	19	8	26	38	33

a Using class intervals 0–4, 5–9, 10–14 and so on, construct a frequency table for the data.

b Draw a bar chart to represent the data.

Level 5

5c I can group data in equal class intervals

6 Group 7X also sat an English test. Their scores out of 70 were

22	12	15	32	70	45	39	40	60
11	59	27	9	43	48	21	52	28

a Decide on suitable class intervals and construct a frequency table for the data.

b Draw a bar chart to represent the data.

c How many pupils are there in group 7X?

7 Use ICT to construct a pie chart for each set of data given in Q1 and Q2. Remember to give each pie chart a suitable title.

5b I can use ICT to construct pie charts

8 In December, Gameplace sold 1000 games consoles. The table shows how many of each type they sold.

Construct a pie chart to show how many of each game console Gameplace sold. Remember to label each sector of the pie chart and give it a suitable title.

Type	Number
Playport	500
MiMi	125
XY100	250
FFF30	125

5a I can construct pie charts

Now try this!

A Project data

Work with a partner to create a poster about games consoles that you and your classmates have. Include a tally chart and a pictogram or bar chart.

B Charts, charts, charts!

Using data from any of the questions, investigate the types of charts, diagrams and graphs that you can produce using ICT.

frequency table   grouped data   interval   pie chart

15.5 Interpreting charts and graphs

➪ Understand and interpret diagrams, graphs and charts

Why learn this?

Diagrams, graphs and charts are widely used to represent data. But what exactly are they saying?

What's the BIG idea?

→ Graphs need two labelled axes and a heading to tell you what data the graph shows. Level 3

→ A **line graph** shows a continuous relationship between two things. Level 4

→ **Dual** and **compound bar charts** compare different sets of data. Level 5

Practice, practice, practice!

Level 4

4b I can interpret bar charts for grouped data

1 **a** How many songs stayed at Number 1 between 4 and 6 weeks?

b Does this chart show the data clearly? Explain your answer.

Hint: How many songs are included in this survey?

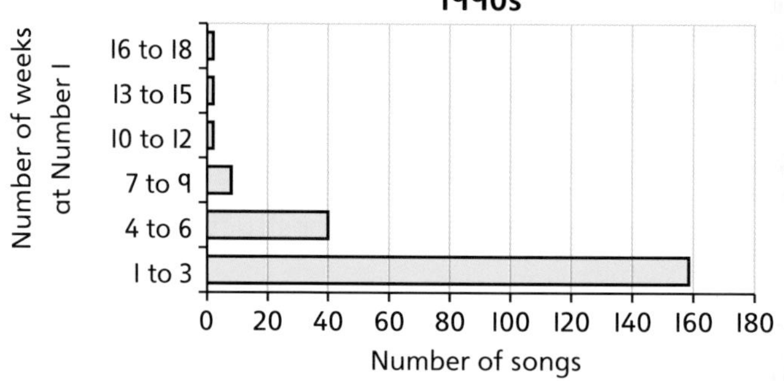

4b I can interpret frequency tables

2 The frequency table shows how long songs stayed at Number 1.

a How many songs stayed at Number 1 for 8 weeks?

b How many songs stayed at Number 1 for 6 weeks or longer?

c What type of chart would you use to display this data? Explain your answer.

Weeks	Frequency
1	47
2	46
3	45
4	22
5	11
6	8
7	5
8	3

4a I can draw conclusions from line graphs

3 **a** When did the sale of CDs reach its peak?

b Which is the only music format for which sales have grown steadily since 1998?

c Write down an explanation for CD sales decreasing after the year 2000.

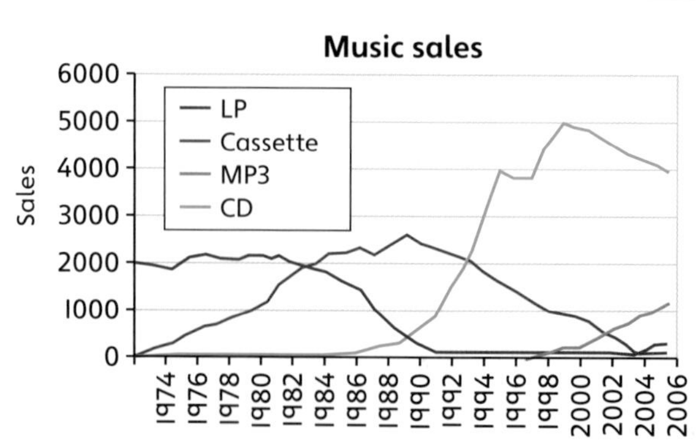

bar chart | bar-line graph | compound bar chart | data

4 The top chart represents music sales in USA.

a Which format sold least?

b Approximately what fraction of the sales were MP3s?

c The total sales in 2008 were 8000 units. Estimate the number of MP3s sold.

d A musical journalist wrote:
"The two pie charts show that fewer LPs are sold in Europe than in the USA."
Explain why the charts do not show this.

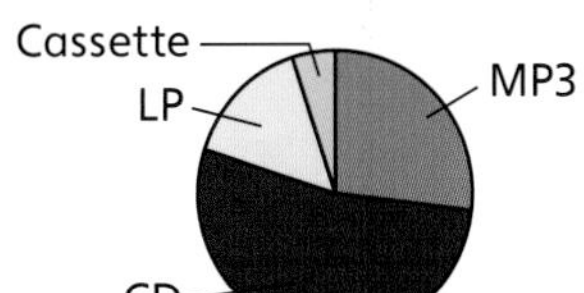

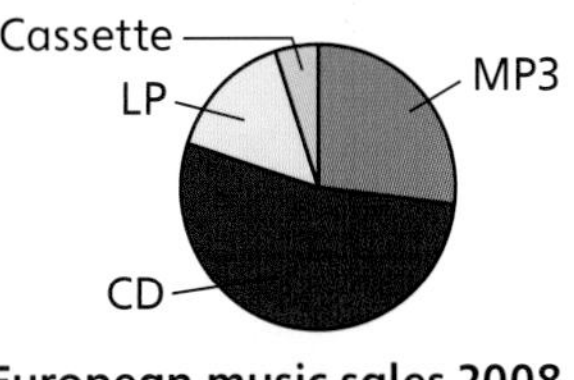

Level 5

5c I can interpret pie charts

Watch out!
You can use pie charts to compare proportions but not actual numbers.

5 The dual bar chart shows what Year 7 and Year 8 pupils chose for lunch.

a How many Year 7 pupils took part in the survey?

b How many more Year 8 pupils had school dinner than went home?

c Describe the trend between the years for **i** bringing sandwiches and **ii** going home for lunch. Suggest reasons for the differences.

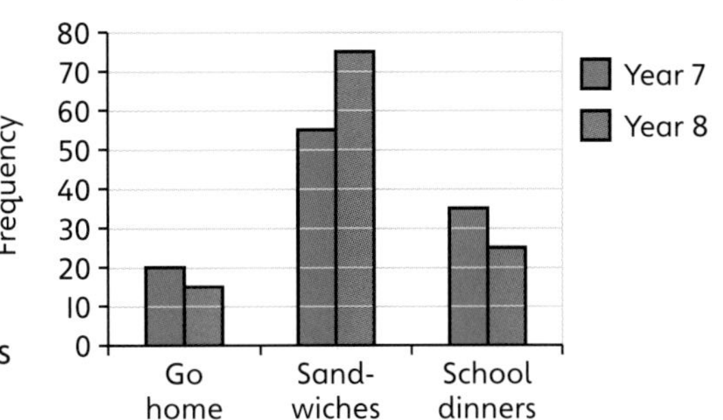

5b I can interpret dual bar charts

5a I can interpret compound bar charts

6 True or False?

a More cassettes were sold in 1975 than in 1980.

b Cassettes were the most popular music format in 1980.

c Fewer LPs were sold in 1990 than in 1975.

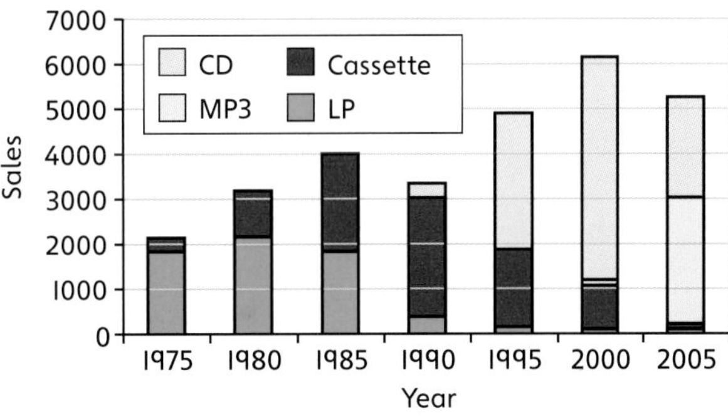

Now try this!

A Poster work
Find as many different types of charts and graphs in newspapers, magazines or on the internet as you can, and turn them into an A3 poster. Give a title to each and explain what each diagram is attempting to show.

B Highest wins
What is wrong with this graph?
Can you find examples of other misleading diagrams?

16
8
4
2
1
0
1 2 3 4

Super fact!
The Sumerians created the earliest known pictograms in around 3200 BC. They were engraved in stone tablets and were used to keep trading records.

dual bar chart | frequency diagram | interpret | pie chart

15.6 Statistics

- Find the mean, mode, median and range
- Use averages to compare distributions

What's the BIG idea?

- The **mode** of a set of data is the value which occurs most often. **Level 3**
- To find the **range** of a set of data subtract the lowest value from the highest value. **Level 4**
- The **modal class** of a set of grouped data is the class which has the greatest frequency. **Level 4**
- The **median** is the middle value when all the data is arranged in order of size. When there is an even number of values, the median is the **average** (mean) of the two middle values. **Level 4** (up to 10 items) **& Level 5** (more than 10 items)
- The **mean** is the sum of all the values divided by the number of values. **Level 5**

Why learn this?

Statistical data is everywhere – the weather, financial markets, and sport.

Practice, practice, practice!

You will need this table to answer Q1–5.

Football Data

Position	Club	Played	Won	Drew	Lost	Goals for	Goals against	Points
1	Manchester United (C)	38	28	5	5	83	27	89
2	Chelsea	38	24	11	3	64	24	83
3	Liverpool	38	20	8	10	57	27	68
4	Arsenal	38	19	11	8	63	35	68
5	Tottenham Hotspur	38	17	9	12	57	54	60
6	Everton	38	15	13	10	52	36	58

Learn this

Mode = most often
Median = middle

Level 4

1 What is the mode of
 a the number of games drawn
 b the number of goals for
 c the total number of points scored?

(4b) I can identify the mode

2 What is the range of
 a the total number of points scored
 b the number of games lost
 c the number of goals for?

(4b) I can calculate the range

3 What is the modal class for this grouped data set?

Points	0–10	11–20	21–30	31–40	41–50	51–60	61–70	71–80	81–90	91+
Frequency	0	0	1	4	5	6	2	0	2	0

(4a) I can identify the modal class

average mean median

4 Look again at the table of football data. What is the median of

the number of games won

15, 17, 19, 20, 24, 28   Median is 19.5

Hint: The numbers must be in size order.

a the number of games lost   **b** the number of games drawn?

5 The points scored by the top six Premiership and Championship teams are:

Premiership 89, 83, 68, 68, 60, 58   Championship 88, 86, 84, 76, 76, 75

a What is the mode and range for each set of data?

b Write two sentences comparing the results using the mode and range.

Level 4

4a I can calculate the median

4a I can compare distributions using the range and mode

6 Look again at the table of football data. Use it to calculate the mean of

a the number of goals for   **b** the number of goals against

c the total number of points scored.

7 **a** Copy and complete this table.

b The mean = $\frac{\text{total number of goals}}{\text{total frequency}}$

What is the mean number of goals?

Number of goals scored	Frequency	Number of goals × frequency
0	1	0 × 1 = 0
1	3	1 × 3 = 3
2	4	
3	1	
4	1	
	Total = 10	Total =

8 Michael and Kevin scored these runs in their last ten cricket matches.

Michael 23, 35, 39, 37, 28, 33, 32, 26, 19, 48

Kevin 18, 54, 21, 20, 39, 32, 27, 26, 28, 35

a Calculate the mean and range for each set of data.

b Who is the better batsman? Give reasons for your answer.

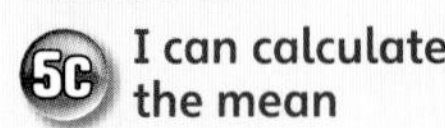

5c I can calculate the mean

5b I can calculate the mean from a frequency table

5b I can compare distributions using the range and mean

Now try this!

A Average pupil?

Carry out an investigation to find out about the school day of an 'average' pupil. By what method do they travel to school? What do they eat for lunch? What activities do they do after school? Use your results to put together a profile of 'an average pupil' at your school. Display the results on a poster.

B Statistical puzzling

What are the missing numbers?

7, 9, 6, ☐ Mean = 6

1, 5, 3, ☐ Mean = 10

11, 19, 18, 13, ☐ Mean = 15

10, 10, 10, 10, ☐, ☐ Mean = 10 and range = 6

Make up puzzles like this for a partner.

Super fact!

One of the first people to study statistics was John Graunt (1620–74). He studied the weekly records of mortality and causes of death in London. He used these to estimate the population of London.

mode   modal class/group   range

maths!

WHODUNNIT?

Scandal at the Tiddlywinks World Cup! ×

Today, 34 competitors took part in the Tiddlywinks World Cup in Franktown.

What started as a civilised tournament ended up in chaos when one of the competitors was revealed to have cheated their way through the tournament!

The identity of the cheat is still unknown.

Your help is needed to catch the culprit.

Look at the crowd of competitors above. What is the probability that the cheat is

- **wearing headgear?**
- **wearing glasses?**
- **female and wearing glasses?**
- **male and wearing glasses and headgear?**

Can probability be used to narrow down the number of suspects?

The police were able to narrow down the suspects to just six people. Here is a picture taken at the police station.

A mathematical clue was left at the scene of the crime.
Use the clue to find the culprit!

THE CHEAT IS THE PERSON

- WHOSE HEIGHT IS CLOSEST TO THE MEAN,
- WHOSE SHOE SIZE IS CLOSEST TO THE MEDIAN,

AND

- WHOSE AGE IS CLOSEST TO THE MEAN.

15.7 Collecting the right data

- Decide which data would be relevant to an enquiry
- Identify possible sources of data
- Identify suitable sample size and type
- Design a data collection sheet and questionnaire

Why learn this?

Surveys are conducted to find out people's views on new theme parks and attractions. Collecting the right kind of data is essential for a successful project.

What's the BIG idea?

→ The most basic **data collection sheet** is a **tally chart**. Level 4

→ **Primary data** is collected from a **survey** or an experiment. **Secondary data** is collected from websites, newspapers and so on. Level 4 & Level 5

→ When choosing a **sample size** for a survey, the bigger the sample the more it will cost to carry out. However, the smaller a sample size the less likely it is to represent the facts. Level 5

→ **Questionnaires** are a good way to collect data. The questions should be simple and clearly worded. Level 5

Super fact!

You can find out how many fish there are in a pond using the capture/recapture method. Catch a sample, mark them and release them. Now catch another sample. You can use the proportion of marked fish in the second sample to work out how many fish there are altogether.

Practice, practice, practice!

Level 4

4a I can decide which data would be important to an enquiry

1 Molten Flowers theme park would like to know how customers travel to the park. Which data would be relevant?

a The method of travel
b The height of the customer
c The distance travelled
d The cost of the journey
e The journey time
f The age of the customer
g The day of travel
h How many people have come together

4a I can design a data collection sheet

2 **a** McRestaurant wants to open a snack bar aimed at children. They plan to sell pizzas, hot dogs, chips, salad, sandwiches and jacket potatoes. Design a data collection sheet to find out what the children might buy.

b Molten Flowers are planning to introduce a new adult ride. Design a data collection sheet that could be used to find out what price adults would be willing to pay for the ride.

Level 5

5c I can decide which data would be relevant to an enquiry

3 What data would you need to investigate these questions?

How do the Molten Flowers employees travel to the theme park?

Data needed for each individual staff member, the method of travel, why that method of travel is used, how long the journey takes, the distance to the theme park.

a How often do customers visit Molten Flowers theme park?

b Why is attendance on Wednesday always lower than on any other day of the week?

data collection sheet primary data questionnaire sample size

4 How should Molten Flowers obtain data to investigate

a opinions on the 'thrill factor' of the water rides

b ticket prices of other theme parks

c the kind of rides available at other parks?

5 Decide on an appropriate sample size for these surveys. Explain your answers.

a Molten Flowers is considering a new staff uniform for their 300 employees. Should they survey 30 employees, 150 employees or all employees?

b Each day Mr Flowers gives a presentation about the animals in the zoo. He wants to find out what people think of his presentation. Should he survey all the people, 15 people or 20 children and 20 adults?

6 The manager of the theme park would like to ask 50% of the people that come to the park every month about their travel arrangements.

a What are the advantages and disadvantages of taking such a large sample?

b What factors are important when choosing sample size?

c What sample size might be better?

7 Give a reason why each of these survey samples is not a good one and suggest a better one.

a *British people like thrilling rides.*
Sample: A random sample of people in the queue for the rollercoaster 'Judgment day'.

b *We need more vegetarian food outlets at the park.*
Sample: People in the queue at MacGreatburger.

c *The entry price to Molten Flowers is too high.*
Sample: A random sample of people at Molten Flowers.

8 Are these quotations suitable for a questionnaire? If not, give a reason and rewrite the question to make it more sensible.

a Age 0–5 ☐ 6–20 ☐ 21–30 ☐ other ☐

b What sports do you play? tennis ☐ football ☐ other ☐

c Are you beautiful? Y ☐ N ☐

d What is your favourite food? chips ☐ salad ☐ other ☐

Level 5

5c I can identify possible data sources

5b I can identify the most sensible sample size given a choice

5a I can identify a sensible sample size

5a I can identify suitable questions for a questionnaire

Now try this!

A Book investigation

The Daily Blurb: **Children don't read books!**

Your school wants to find out if this claim is true. They want to investigate how many books pupils read outside of school and which types of books.

Design a suitable data collection sheet that could be used.

B Healthy food investigation

The Daily Buzz: ***Children don't eat fruit and veg.***

Your school wants to find out if this claim is true. They want to investigate how much fruit and vegetable pupils eat and which types.

Design a questionnaire that could be used.

Tip

Questionnaires should be simple. Try your questions out on a few people first to see if they understand them without you needing to offer an explanation.

secondary data **survey** **tally chart**

15.8 Statistical enquiry

- Prepare a report on a statistical enquiry
- Use appropriate diagrams, graphs and charts to illustrate important facts

Why learn this?

Statistics provides the tools you need to understand information that you hear or see. Then you can decide how to act on that information.

What's the BIG idea?

→ A statistical investigation can be divided into separate stages. **Level 4**

Hypothesis: 'I think girls get more pocket money than boys.'

Collecting the data: Use a **data collection sheet** or a **questionnaire** if you are conducting a **survey**. You need to think carefully about the **sample size**.

Presenting the data: Think about the best way of displaying the results – diagram, graph or chart?

Analysing the data: You may want to find the mode, median or mean.

Conclusions: Discuss whether your results confirm your original hypothesis.

Super fact!

On 14 August 1979, the longest lasting rainbow was recorded on the coast of Gwynedd, North Wales. It lasted for 3 hours.

Practice, practice, practice!

Car colour investigation

'Red is the most popular car colour and white is the least popular'.

To investigate her claim, Greta has conducted an experiment and recorded the colour of the first 40 cars that have passed her house. Here are her results.

B R BL G R R R B B G W S S BL B G W W Y R B BL R B BL G Y S R B R R BL B Y R R B BL BL

Key: B = black, BL = blue, G = green, W = white, R = red, Y = yellow, S = silver

1 Draw up a tally chart of her results.

2 Draw a bar chart to illustrate her data.

3 **a** Which colour appears the least often?

b What is the mode?

c Is Greta's claim correct? Explain your answer.

d How could Greta improve her investigation?

Tip

Always check your diagram, graph or chart has a title and that the axes are labelled.

Level 4

4c I can construct a simple tally chart

4c I can draw a bar chart

4b I can identify the mode

Manufactured goods investigation

'The Raker Design factory manufactures more on average than its competitor, Lakor Design.'

To allow you to investigate this claim, both Raker Design and Lakor Design have supplied you with their manufacturing figures for one week.

Raker Design	26	35	21	13	42	18	9
Lakor Design	37	41	5	11	31	26	21

analysis conclusion data collection sheet hypothesis

4 Draw a dual bar chart for the data given.

5 **a** What is the range of each set of data?
b What does the range tell you about each factory?

Level 4
4b I can draw a dual bar chart
4b I can calculate the range

6 What is the mean of each set of data?

7 Is the claim correct? Explain your answer.

Level 5
5c I can calculate the mean
5b I can compare two distributions using the range and mean

Chocolate bars investigation

'Girls eat as many chocolate bars as boys.'

To investigate this claim, David surveyed 25 girls and 25 boys. He asked them how many chocolate bars they eat in a week.
The results are shown in the table.

Number of bars eaten	Frequency	
	Girls	Boys
0	3	4
1	12	11
2	8	6
3	1	2
4	1	1
5	0	1

8 Draw a dual bar chart to show the data.

9 Find the mode for the boys and for the girls.

10 What is the range for **i** the boys and **ii** the girls?

Level 4
4b I can draw a dual bar chart
4b I can identify the mode
4b I can calculate the range

11 Calculate the mean number of chocolate bars eaten by **i** the girls and **ii** the boys.

12 Compare the mean and the range.
Is David's claim correct? Explain your answer.

13 Use ICT to draw two pie charts for the data, one for girls and one for boys.

Level 5
5b I can use ICT to construct pie charts
5b I can calculate the mean from a frequency table
5b I can compare two distributions using the range and mean

Now try this!

A Questionnaires

Design a questionnaire to find out pupils' shoe sizes and the types of shoes they prefer. Give examples of unsuitable questions and explain why they are unsuitable.

B Stages of enquiry

For each investigation above, prepare a short report stating how you would carry out the enquiry. Consider data collection, sample size, how to present the data and how to analyse the data.

interpret prevention questionnaire sample size survey

The KEO project

The KEO project is an ambitious plan to send a 'time capsule' into space. This time capsule will orbit the Earth on board a satellite and will contain information about our everyday lives at the start of the 21st century. The plan is for it to return to Earth after 50,000 years, when our descendants will face the challenge of accessing the information we have left for them. This is part of an advert for the KEO project:

> KEO would then blast off carrying this unique collection of messages destined for our distant future descendants, 50,000 years from now. A reflection of our way of life, this record would convey both the richness and the diversity of the human experience. Would it give us a glimpse of the answers to the following questions?
>
> Who are we? What are our hopes and expectations? What future do we wish to build together?"
>
> Each one of us has the opportunity to send four pages of information into space.
> What information would you leave to summarise human culture and our species as it is today?

MAKE MATHS FUNCTIONAL!

Information about people today

The first part of your project will be about the kinds of technology that young humans own and use in the early 21st Century. Think of the gadgets that you may use: mobile phone, MP3 player, games machine, etc.

1 Construct a tally chart to collect information on the gadgets that the pupils in your class have. You will need separate charts for the boys and girls. **Level 4**

2 Construct a dual bar chart to illustrate the data. **Level 4**

3 Use ICT to construct a pie chart for each set of data. **Level 5**

The second part of your project will be about the physical characteristics of young humans. **Level 4**

4 Construct a tally chart to collect information on the eye colour and shoe size of the pupils in your class. You will need separate charts for the boys and girls. **Level 4**

5 Draw a bar-line graph for each set of data. **Level 4**

6 Find the median and range of the heights of the pupils in your class. **Level 4**

7 Calculate the mean height of the pupils in your class. **Level 5**

The third part of the project is up to you. Let your imagination take over and let the maths help you!

The BIG ideas

- → A **bar chart** uses bars of equal width to show data.
  A **bar-line graph** is just like a bar chart, but you use thin lines instead of bars. **Level 4**
- → Bar charts can be used to compare different sets of data.
  These are known as **dual bar charts**. **Level 4 & Level 5**
- → You can find the **range** of a set of data by subtracting the lowest value from the highest value. **Level 4**
- → The **median** is the middle value when all the data is arranged in order of size. **Level 4**
- → A **pie chart** uses a circle to represent data.
  Each sector represents a particular category of data. **Level 5**
- → The **mean** is the sum of all the values divided by the number of values. **Level 5**

Find your level

Level 3

Q1 Albert completes a tally chart to find the most popular pet in his class.

Pet	Girls	Boys
Cat	卌 II	III
Rabbit	卌 II	卌
Dog	III	卌 卌
Other	I	II
Total	18	20

a How many girls have a rabbit?
b How many pupils have a dog?
c How many more boys than girls have a dog?
d How many more girls than boys have a cat?
e There are 29 pupils in the class. Why is the total in the tally chart more than 29?

Level 4

Q2 Jared throws a fair coin.
a Jared says, 'The probability of getting a head on each throw is $\frac{1}{2}$.' Is he correct? Explain your answer.
b Jared says, 'If I throw the coin ten times, it is certain that I will get five heads and five tails.' Is he correct? Explain your answer.

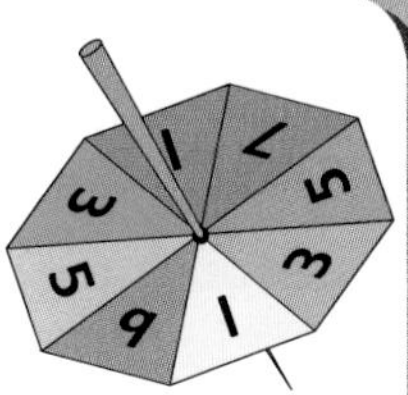

Q3 a What is the probability of spinning a 5?
b What is the probability of spinning an odd number?
c What is the probability of spinning a multiple of 3?

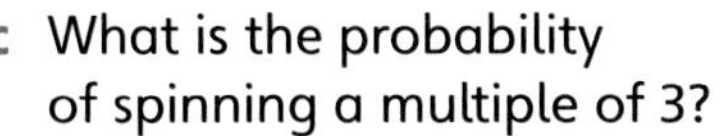

d Copy and complete this spinner so that
  i the probability of spinning an even number is $\frac{2}{3}$
  ii the probability of spinning a 4 is $\frac{1}{3}$
  iii all the numbers on the spinner are less than 10.

Level 5

Q4 Adrian, Luella and Byron are taking part in an archery competition.
a In the first three rounds Adrian scored 7, 8 and 7. In the final round he scored 6. What was his mean score for the four rounds?
b Luella did not qualify for the final two rounds. Her mean score was 6. Her range was 2. What points did she score in rounds 1 and 2?
c Byron completed three rounds. His mean score was 3. His range was 2. What points might Byron have scored in the three rounds?

16 Number crunching

This unit is about doing calculations.

The Ancient Egyptians were doing complex calculations 5000 years ago. The earliest Egyptian number system was called the hieroglyphic system. It used pictures to represent individual numbers. They are known as hieroglyphic numerals.

I stood for 1. **𓍢 stood for 100.** **𓆼 stood for 1000.**

∩ stood for 10.

Activities

A • ∩∩III is 23.

How would you represent: **a** 58 **b** 120 **c** 1580?

- Writing the number 23 uses five hieroglyphic numerals. How many numerals do you need to write these numbers:
  a 5 **b** 11 **c** 48 **d** 321
- Can you see a connection between the number and the number of numerals used?

B Here is a multiplication method that is similar to the one the Ancient Egyptians used.

- To multiply 13 by 15 start by making two columns.
- Keep dividing by 2 (ignoring any halves) down the first column. Stop when you get to 1.
- Keep doubling as you go down the second column.
- Now cross out any rows with an even number in the first column and add the remaining numbers in the second column.

13	15
~~6~~	~~30~~
3	60
1	120

15 + 60 + 120 = 195
so 13 × 15 = 195

Use this Egyptian method for these multiplications.

a 9 × 11 **b** 40 × 25 **c** 33 × 20

Check your answers using a calculator.

Did you know?

Ancient Egyptians loved playing board games. They even buried the board game, *Senet*, with Tutankhamun.

If you go on the internet you can play *Senet* online.

Before you start this unit...

1 Use a mental method to calculate these.

a $40 + 20 + 30$

b $90 + 50 + 10 + 40$

c $2 + 4 + 8 + 6 + 2 + 8$

2 What is the missing number?

a $4 \times 5 =$ ______ b ______ $\times 6 = 42$

c $9 \times$ ______ $= 36$

3 Use a written method to work out these.

a 175×6 b 583×4 c $234 \div 6$

4 Convert each percentage to a fraction in its lowest terms.

a 10% b 25% c 50%

World's Greatest Maths

Plus digital resources

The man representing one million looks as if he has just won the National Lottery!

How would you represent two million?

16.1 More addition and subtraction

- Be able to add and subtract mentally
- Know and use integer complements to 100
- Know how to use the column method to add and subtract whole numbers and decimals
- Be able to make an estimate to check an answer

Why learn this?

Addition and subtraction are used in many sports to work out totals and targets.

What's the BIG idea?

- You can use partitioning, counting up or compensation to help you **add** or **subtract** mentally. Level 3
- To add or subtract whole numbers, line up the units, tens, hundreds and so on, then add or subtract. Level 4
- To add or subtract decimals, line up the decimal points, put the decimal point in the answer, then add or subtract. Level 4
- When you use the column method for decimals, you can replace any empty place values with zeros. Level 4
- To **estimate** an answer to a calculation, round all the numbers and do the calculation with the rounded numbers. Level 4

Watch out!

If you don't line up the decimal points in addition and subtraction calculations, you won't get the right answer.

Practice, practice, practice!

Level 3

3a I can mentally add and subtract pairs of two-digit numbers

1 In these number pyramids, the value in each brick is the sum of the values in the two bricks below.
Copy and complete the number pyramids.

a

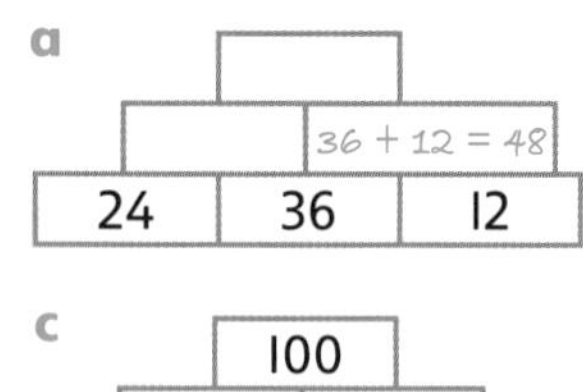

b

Bottom row: 36, 14, 19

c

Top: 100; middle row: ?, 15; bottom row: ?, 9, ?

d

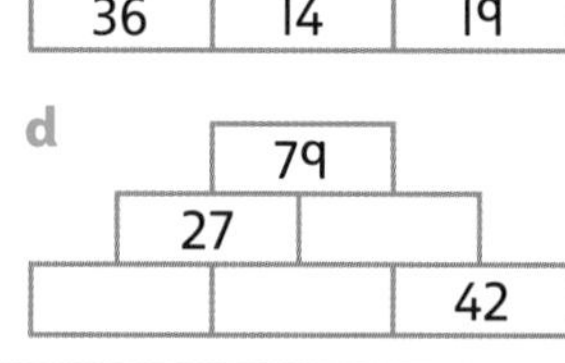

Level 4

4c I can recall whole-number complements in 100

4c I can use the column method to add whole numbers

2 Copy and complete.

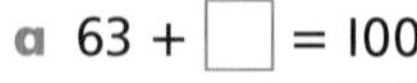

a 63 + ☐ = 100 **b** ☐ + 18 = 100

c 100 = 81 + ☐ **d** £55 + ☐ = £100

3 Use the column method to do these additions.

a 317 + 142 **b** 546 + 58 **c** £467 + £245

add addition complements (in 100) difference estimate

4 Use the column method to do these subtractions.

a 749 − 326 **b** 409 − 72 **c** 531 cm − 248 cm

5 Australia beat Sri Lanka in the Cricket World Cup final in 2007.

a Australia scored 281 runs. India scored 215 runs. By how many runs did Australia win?

b Adam Gilchrist scored 149 of Australia's 281 runs. How many did the rest of the team score?

6 Two of these calculations are wrong. Use approximation to work out which ones. What mistakes have been made?

a
$$\begin{array}{r} 319 \\ +\ 42 \\ \hline 739 \end{array}$$

b
$$\begin{array}{r} 193 \\ +\ 293 \\ \hline 3186 \end{array}$$

c
$$\begin{array}{r} 641 \\ +\ 328 \\ \hline 969 \end{array}$$

7 Use the column method to work these out.

a 39.6 + 14.3 **b** 243.8 + 13.5 **c** 136.2 g + 24.97 g

d 4.72 − 3.51 **e** 218.5 − 54.7 **f** 309.3 km − 68.45 km

8 **a** The London Marathon is 26.22 miles. David passes a water station at 7.9 miles. How much further does he have to run?

b David has raised £380 in sponsorship. So far he has collected £126.49. How much does he have left to collect?

9 The table shows some marathon times in hours, minutes and seconds.

a Who had the fastest time?

b How long after the first person crossed the line did the last person cross it?

Competitor	Time hrs/mins/secs
A	2:27:05
B	2:39:14
C	2:47:16
D	3:02:52

Level 4

4c I can use the column method to subtract whole numbers

4b I can use approximation to check an answer

4b I can use the column method to add and subtract decimals

4a I can choose the maths I need to solve a problem

Now try this!

A Highest total 1

You need a partner and a dice. Both of you copy this: | | | + | | |

Roll the dice. Each write the number in one of your boxes. Repeat until all your boxes are filled. Add your numbers. The player with the higher total wins the round. The first player to win three rounds is the champion.

B Highest total 2

You need a partner and a dice. Both of you copy this:

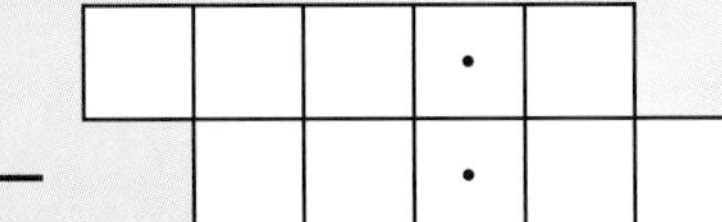

Roll the dice. Each write the number in one of your boxes. Repeat until all your boxes are filled. Subtract your numbers. The player with the higher total wins the round. The first player to win three rounds is the champion.

subtract subtraction sum total

16.2 More multiples and factors

- Recognise and use multiples and factors
- Identify the common factors of two numbers
- Find the highest common factor and lowest common multiple

Why learn this?

If you bottle 30 drinks in a minute, you can use multiples to work out how many bottles are filled in an hour.

What's the BIG idea?

- The **multiples** of a number are the numbers in its times table. Level 3
- The **factors** of a number are the numbers that divide into it exactly. The factors of 6 are 1, 2, 3 and 6. Level 3
- A **common factor** is a factor that is common to two given numbers. Level 4
- The **highest common factor (HCF)** is the highest factor common to two given numbers. Level 5
- To find the HCF, list the factors of each number and pick out the biggest number that is in both lists. Level 5
- The **lowest common multiple (LCM)** of two numbers is the smallest number that is a multiple of them both. Level 5
- To find the LCM, list the multiples of each number and pick out the smallest number that is in both lists. Level 5

Practice, practice, practice!

Level 3

1 What are the factors of these numbers? Find as many as you can.

a 6 b 25 c 8 d 14

3b I can identify at least two factors

2 Use the grid to answer this question.

1	2	3	4	5
6	7	8	9	10
11	12	13	14	15
16	17	18	19	20
21	22	23	24	25

a Write down the first five multiples of
 i 3 ii 5

b What is the biggest multiple of 2 shown in the grid?

c List the multiples of 5 between 9 and 21.

3a I can identify multiples up to 5 × 5

3 Each of these numbers have more than four factors. Find as many as you can.

a 16 b 30 c 28 d 36

Tip
Writing factor pairs helps you find two factors at a time.

3a I can identify at least four factors

common factor factor highest common factor (HCF)

4 Look at these numbers. 42 18 15 27 12 30

Which of the numbers are multiples of

a 2 **b** 3 **c** 6 **d** 9?

5 True or false?

a 27 is a multiple of 3

b 27 is a factor of 3

c 4 is a multiple of 16

d 4 is a factor of 16

e multiples of 6 are all even

f multiples of 7 are all even

6 Find the common factors of these numbers.

6 and 18

The factors of 6 are 1, 2, 3, 6.
The factors of 18 are 1, 2, 3, 6, 9, 18.
The common factors are 1, 2, 3, 6.

a 6 and 8 **b** 15 and 20 **c** 8 and 12 **d** 18 and 27

Level 4

4c I can recognise multiples up to 10 × 10

4c I can recognise multiples and factors

4b I can identify common factors

7 Find the highest common factor (HCF) of these numbers.

12 and 28

Factors of 12: 1, 2, 3, 4, 6, 12
Factors of 28: 1, 2, 4, 7, 14, 28
The HCF of 12 and 28 is 4.

a 8 and 12 **b** 9 and 15 **c** 6 and 30

Watch out!

Always check you have found the highest common factor, not just a common factor.

8 Find the highest common factors of the pairs of numbers in Q6.

9 A group of friends share 15 red sweets and 25 orange sweets. They all get the same number of red and orange sweets. How many friends are there?

10 Find the lowest common multiple (LCM) of these numbers.

6 and 8

Multiples of 6: 6, 12, 18, 24, 30, ...
Multiples of 8: 8, 16, 24, 32, 40, ...
The LCM of 6 and 8 is 24.

a 5 and 10 **b** 4 and 7 **c** 6 and 9

Level 5

5c I can find the HCF

5c I can find the LCM

Now try this!

A Treasure island

You need a 1–100 number square.
Pirate Pete has buried some treasure on a 100-square island.
Cross through the multiples of 6 (/). Cross through the multiples of 9 (\).
In which square is the treasure buried? (X marks the spot!)

B Investigating HCF and LCM

Choose two numbers and find their LCM and their HCF.
Multiply the two numbers together.
Multiply their LCM and their HCF together.
What do you notice?
Try this for other pairs of numbers.

lowest common multiple (LCM) multiple

16.3 Factors, multiples and primes

- Recognise and use multiples and factors
- Recognise prime numbers up to 100
- Find common factors including prime factors
- Find the lowest common multiple (LCM) of two numbers

Why learn this?

When you use a credit card to buy items on the internet, your account is kept safe from hackers thanks to the power of prime numbers. Prime numbers are used to encrypt a secret code.

What's the BIG idea?

- The **factors** of a number are the numbers that divide into it exactly. Level 3
- A **prime** number has exactly two factors, itself and 1. Level 4
- 1 is not a prime number, as it only has one factor. Level 4
- A **prime factor** is a factor that is also a prime number. Level 4
- The **lowest common multiple (LCM)** of two numbers is the smallest number that is a multiple of them both. Level 5

Super fact!

The Electronic Frontier Foundation in America has offered a $150 000 prize to the first person to discover a prime number with at least 100 million digits.

Practice, practice, practice!

Level 4

4C I can apply simple tests of divisibility

1 Copy and complete this table.

Number	Divisible by 4?	... by 6?	... by 25?
34			
96			
126			
148			
240			
412			
650			

4C I can apply simple tests of divisibility

2

56	162	198	64	99
131	108	46	81	83
23	801	127	72	68
54	87	243	257	73
216	189	534	94	491

a Which numbers (between 0 and 10) are all the red numbers exactly divisible by?

b Which numbers are all the blue numbers exactly divisible by?

c Look at the numbers that have not been highlighted.
Write down all of those numbers that are exactly divisible by 6.

divisible divisibility factor

3 None of these numbers are prime numbers. Explain how you can tell.

1245 418 123 316

4 A prime number has exactly two factors.
List the factors of each number and say whether or not it is a prime number.

a 35 **b** 17 **c** 29 **d** 49

5 The prime numbers between 10 and 50 are
11, 13, 17, 19, 23, 29, 31, 37, 41, 43, 47.

a What do these numbers have in common?

b Identify the prime numbers between 50 and 60.
Check the numbers that you have chosen by using factor pairs.

6 **a** Write down all the factors of 50.

b Write down the prime factor of 50.

7 Write down the prime factors of

a 27 **b** 34 **c** 45 **d** 50 **e** 42 **f** 51

8 Which two numbers are the prime factors of 30?

A 1 and 30 B 1 and 3 C 2 and 3 D 1 and 2 E 5 and 6

Level 4

4a I can identify prime numbers

4a I can find prime factors

9 Which is the LCM of 10 and 15?

A 5 B 10 C 150 D 30 E 60

10 Which is the LCM of 12 and 20?

A 6 B 10 C 240 D 120 E 60

Level 5

 I can find the LCM

Now try this!

A Sieve of Eratosthenes

You need a 1–100 number square and a highlighter pen. Use the sieve of Eratosthenes to find the primes to 100:

- Cross out the number 1.
- Circle 2 then cross out all other multiples of 2.
- Circle 3 then cross out all other multiples of 3.
- The next number that is not crossed out is 5. Circle 5 then cross out all other multiples of 5.
- Keep going until all the numbers in your square are either circled or crossed out.
- The circled numbers are the prime numbers less than 100. What are they?

B What number am I?

I am a prime number less than 30. My digit sum is 8. What number am I?
Make up some 'What number am I?' clues of your own. Use the words 'factor', 'prime' and 'divisible' in some of your clues.

Learn this

Memorise the prime numbers up to 30.
They are
2, 3, 5, 7, 11, 13, 17, 19, 23, 29

lowest common multiple prime prime factor

16.4 More multiplication

- Multiply whole numbers and decimals using mental and written methods
- Check answers using approximate calculations
- Understand squares and square roots and use the square and square root keys on a calculator

Why learn this?

Have you got enough money for nine bars of chocolate at £1.20 each? You can use multiplication to help you work this out.

What's the BIG idea?

- If you know the **multiplication** facts up to 10 × 10, you can work out other multiplications by using **partitioning**.
  18 × 7 is the same as (10 × 7) + (8 × 7) = 70 + 56 = 126 **Level 3**
- To estimate an answer to a calculation, round all the numbers and do the calculations with the rounded numbers. **Level 4**
- You can use the grid method or standard method for multiplication. Use the one you like best. **Level 4 & Level 5**
- When you **multiply** a number by itself, you are **squaring** it.
  $8^2 = 8 \times 8 = 64$
  You can use the x^2 key on a calculator to work out squares.
- Finding the **square root** is the inverse (opposite) of squaring.
  $8^2 = 64$, so $\sqrt{64} = 8$.
  You can use the $\sqrt{\ }$ key on your calculator to work out square roots. **Level 5**

Practice, practice, practice!

Level 3

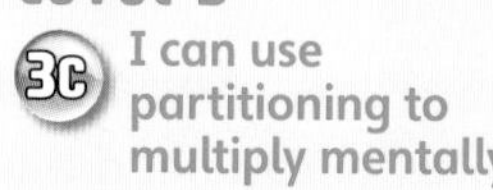

3C I can use partitioning to multiply mentally

1 Use partitioning to work these out mentally.

a There are 31 egg boxes on a supermarket shelf. There are 6 eggs in each box. How many eggs are there altogether?

b There are 24 boxes of fish fingers in the freezer cabinet. There are 6 fish fingers in each box. How many fish fingers are there altogether?

Level 4

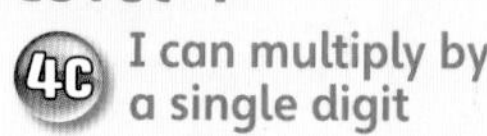

4C I can multiply by a single digit

2 Use the grid method to work these out. Estimate the answer first.

a 3416 × 5 b 9742 × 2 c 7365 × 6

3 Use the standard method to work these out. Estimate the answer first.

a 6418 × 3 b 1576 × 9 c 8143 × 4

4 A school hosts a special charity day. Each pupil donates four objects for sale.

a There are 1839 pupils. How many objects are there in total?

b Each object is sold for £3. How much money is raised for charity?

multiplication multiply partition product

5 Use the grid method to work these out.

a 51×17 b 93×38 c 26×45

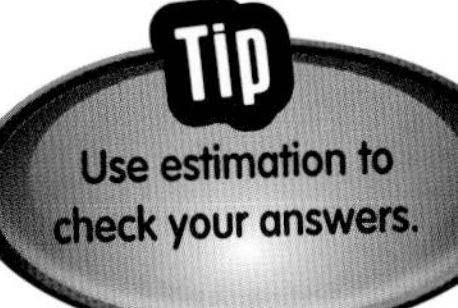

6 Use the standard method to work these out.

a A tin of tomatoes weighs 227 g. How much do 13 tins weigh?

b A tin of sweetcorn weighs 198 g. How much do 24 tins weigh?

7 Use the x^2 key on your calculator to work these out.

a 59×59 b 17×17 c 48×48 d 0.65×0.65

8 Use the $\sqrt{\ }$ key on your calculator to find the missing number.

a $\square^2 = 529$ b $\square^2 = 196$ c $\square^2 = 2500$ d $\square^2 = 12.25$

9 Use the grid method to work these out.

5.7 × 4 *Estimate: 5.7 × 4 is roughly 6 × 4 = 24*

×	5	0.7
4	20	2.8

5.7 × 4 = 20 + 2.8 = 22.8
Check: 22.8 is close to 24 ✓

a 7.3×7 b 8.4×6

c Tom is paid £7.46 per hour. How much is he paid for working 5 hours?

10 Use the standard method to work these out.

A jar or coffee costs £3.64. How much would four jars of coffee cost?

£3.64 × 4 is the same as (£364 × 4) ÷ 100.

```
  3 6 4
×     4
-------
1 4 5 6
  2 1
```

364 × 4 = 1456, so 3.64 × 4 = 14.56
So four jars cost £14.56.

a A box of tea bags costs £2.32. How much do seven boxes of tea bags cost?

b A group of nine children go to the zoo. One child ticket costs £6.25. What is the total cost?

11 Who am I?

a I am a square number. The sum of my digits is 7 and the difference is 5.

b Squaring me is the same as doubling me.

c I am the closest odd square number to 100.

Level 5

5c I can use a written method to calculate TU × TU

5c I can use a written method to calculate HTU × TU

5c I can use the square and square root keys on a calculator

5b I can multiply decimals by single-digit whole numbers

5a I can correctly position the decimal point by considering equivalent calculations

5a I can do mental calculations with squares and square roots

Learn this

You need to know square numbers up to 12 × 12 by heart.

Now try this!

A Magnetic multiplication

David makes this multiplication using fridge magnets.

37 × 5 = 185

Can he use some of these fridge magnets to make another multiplication?

B Multiplication conundrum

In the multiplication 51 × 3 = 153 the same digits are used in the question and the answer. Can you find any other TU × U multiplications where this is also the case?

squared square number square root

16.5 More division

- Understand when to round up or down after division
- Remember multiplication facts up to 10 × 10, and use these to derive division facts
- Divide whole numbers and decimals using written methods
- Check answers using approximate calculations

What's the BIG idea?

- If you know the multiplication facts up to 10 × 10, you also know lots of **division** facts. For example, if you know that 3 × 4 = 12, you also know that 12 ÷ 3 = 4 and 12 ÷ 4 = 3. **Level 4**
- You can use repeated subtraction for division.
  What is 437 ÷ 8?
  Estimate: 437 ÷ 8 is roughly 400 ÷ 8 = 50

$$\begin{array}{rl} 8\overline{)437} & \\ -\ 400 & \rightarrow 50 \times 8 \\ \hline 37 & \\ -\ 32 & \rightarrow 4 \times 8 \\ \hline 5 & \end{array}$$

So $437 \div 8 = 54\frac{5}{8}$. Check: $54\frac{5}{8}$ is close to 50 ✓ **Level 5**

Why learn this?

Friends often divide the cost of a holiday between them. To make sure everyone pays the same amount the division must be done accurately.

Watch out!

Always work out how many lots of the divisor you subtracted altogether. This is the answer you are looking for!

Practice, practice, practice!

Level 3

3a I can round up or down after division

1 Use your calculator for this question.

a A bottle of lemonade holds 1500 ml. A glass holds 350 ml. How many glasses of lemonade can be poured from the bottle?

b 912 pupils are going on a school trip to Buckingham Palace. Each coach can carry 52 passengers. How many coaches will be needed?

Level 4

4b I can use a written method to calculate HTU ÷ U

2 Use a written method to work these out. Write any remainders as fractions.

a 528 ÷ 4   b 497 ÷ 7   c 670 ÷ 9   d 349 ÷ 6

3 Four friends are on holiday. It costs them £276 to hire a car. They share this equally. How much do they each have to pay? Use a written method to work it out.

4a I can use multiplication facts to work out divisions

4 Work these out in your head.

a There are 28 pupils in a class. The teacher asks them to get into groups of four. How many groups are there?

b There are 54 children at a soccer academy. How many six-a-side teams can they make?

divide   division   divisor

5 Use a written method to work these out. Write any remainders as fractions.

a 532 ÷ 14 **b** 713 ÷ 23 **c** 438 ÷ 19 **d** 912 ÷ 31

Level 5

5b I can use a written method to calculate HTU ÷ TU

6 One tin of paint covers 12 m^2. A school needs enough paint to cover 341 m^2. Use a written method to work out the number of tins needed for

a one coat **b** two coats.

7 Use a written method to do these divisions.

5a I can divide decimals by a single-digit whole number

243.6 ÷ 7 Estimate: 243.6 ÷ 7 is roughly 200 ÷ 5 = 40

```
7)2 4 3 . 6
 - 2 1 0 . 0   30 × 7
     3 3 . 6
 -   2 8 . 0    4 × 7
       5 . 6
 -     5 . 6   0.8 × 7
       0 . 0
```

243.6 ÷ 7 = 34.8 Check: 34.8 is close to 40 ✓

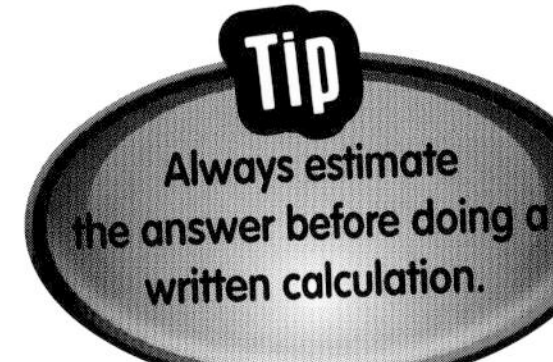

a 98.5 ÷ 5 **b** 117.6 ÷ 4 **c** 64.83 ÷ 3 **d** 107.16 ÷ 6

8 The Olympic torch is passed from person to person in a relay. Seven people run an equal share of 65.8 km.

a Use a written method to work out how far each person runs.

b The first runner is injured after 7.6 km. How far must each of the remaining people now run, if they share the remaining distance equally?

9 A rugby coach bought 15 shirts for the team. The total cost was £91.95. Use a written method to work out the cost of each shirt.

5a I can divide £.p by a two-digit number

10 Katy gets tips at her waitressing job. These were her tips for four Saturdays one month.

£4.72 £5.86 £10.22 £8.12

Work out the mean.

Now try this!

A Divisible by 2 or 3?

A game for two players. You need 1–9 digit cards. Take turns to pick three cards at random. Use these to make a three-digit number.
If your number is divisible by

- 2, you score 1 point
- 3, you score 2 points
- 2 *and* 3, you score 3 points.

The first to 8 points wins.

B Divisible by 2, 3, 5 or 7?

A game for two players. You need 1–9 digit cards. Take turns to pick four cards at random. Use these to make a four-digit number.
If your number is divisible by

- 2, you score 1 point
- 3, you score 2 points
- 7, you score 3 points
- 5, you score 4 points.

The first to 10 points wins.

exactly quotient remainder

16.6 Equivalent fractions, decimals and percentages

- Recognise the equivalence of percentages, fractions and decimals
- Know how to use equivalent fractions to convert fractions to decimals
- Be able to use a calculator to convert fractions to decimals

Why learn this?

If you get 69 tails in 150 spins of a coin, the experimental probability is $\frac{69}{150}$. Converting $\frac{69}{150}$ to 0.46 makes it easier to see that it is about $\frac{1}{2}$ or 0.5.

What's the BIG idea?

- Every **fraction** has an **equivalent decimal** and **percentage**. **Level 4**
- You can simplify a fraction by dividing the **numerator** and **denominator** by a common factor.
  You can write a fraction in its **simplest form** by dividing the numerator and denominator by the highest commmon factor. **Level 5**

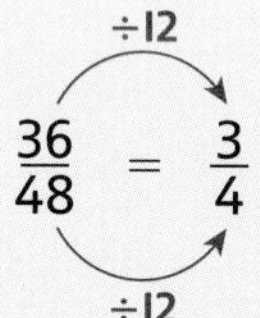

$\frac{36}{48} = \frac{3}{4}$ (÷12)

- You can use equivalent fractions to change a fraction to a decimal. $\frac{21}{50} = \frac{42}{100} = 0.42$ **Level 5**
- You can use a calculator to **convert** a fraction to a decimal. $\frac{21}{50} = 21 \div 50 = 0.42$ **Level 5**

Practice, practice, practice!

Level 4

4b I can recognise the equivalence of percentages, fractions and decimals

1 Are these true or false? Give a reason for each answer.

a Rajiv got 49 out of 100 in his test. He said that he got about half right.

b Seraphina got 72 out of 100. She said that she got about three quarters right.

c Suzie got 76 questions out of 100 wrong. She said that she got about 25% right.

d Bob got 19 out of 100. He said that he got about one fifth of the questions right.

4b I can calculate equivalent fractions

2 Copy and complete these equivalent fractions.

a 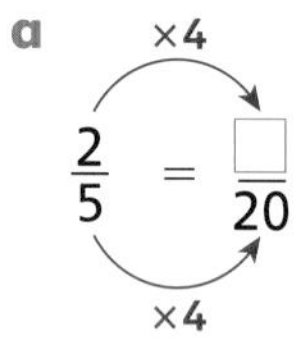

$\frac{2}{5} = \frac{\square}{20}$ (×4)

b 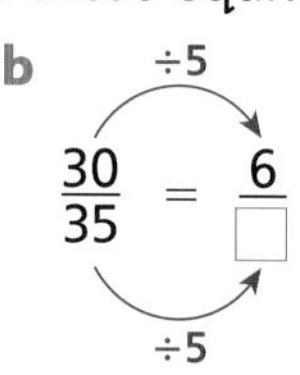

$\frac{30}{35} = \frac{6}{\square}$ (÷5)

c 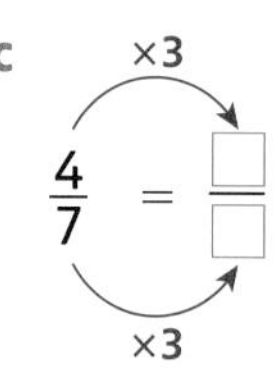

$\frac{4}{7} = \frac{\square}{\square}$ (×3)

3 Write each of these as an equivalent fraction with a denominator of 7.
What do you notice?

a $\frac{20}{28}$ b $\frac{30}{42}$ c $\frac{15}{21}$ d $\frac{35}{49}$

4b I can find equivalent percentages, fractions and decimals

4 Copy and complete this table of equivalent percentages, fractions and decimals.

Percentage	Fraction	Decimal
10%		
		0.02
	$\frac{2}{5}$	
		0.75
	$\frac{8}{10}$	
37%		

cancel convert decimal denominator equivalent

5 Write each of these fractions in its simplest form.

$\frac{18}{24}$ The HCF of 18 and 24 is 6, so $\frac{18}{24} = \frac{3}{4}$ (÷6 numerator and denominator)

a $\frac{14}{28}$ **b** $\frac{12}{30}$ **c** $\frac{30}{36}$

d $\frac{16}{48}$ **e** $\frac{63}{81}$ **f** $\frac{24}{36}$

Level 5

5b I can simplify fractions

6 Use equivalent fractions to convert these fractions to decimals. Use a calculator to check your answers.

a $\frac{9}{20}$ **b** $\frac{3}{25}$

c $\frac{31}{50}$ **d** $\frac{2}{5}$

Tip

When you convert a fraction to a decimal always check your answer. If the fraction was more than $\frac{1}{2}$, the decimal should be more than 0.5.

5a I can convert fractions to decimals and percentages

7 **a** What percentage is $\frac{14}{25}$ equivalent to?

b What is $\frac{14}{25}$ as a decimal?

8 **a** Use your calculator to convert $\frac{1}{3}$ into a decimal. Write down all the numbers on your calculator display.

b Multiply your answer to part **a** by 100 to convert $\frac{1}{3}$ to a percentage. Give your answer to one decimal place.

Hint: One decimal place means you need one digit after the decimal point.

9 **a** What is $\frac{1}{4}$ as a decimal? Use this fact to help you convert $\frac{1}{8}$ to a decimal.

b What is $\frac{1}{5}$ as a decimal? Use this fact to help you convert $\frac{3}{5}$ to a decimal.

c What is $\frac{1}{100}$ as a decimal? Use this fact to help you convert $\frac{1}{200}$ to a decimal.

d What is $\frac{1}{50}$ as a decimal?

10 Convert these decimals to fractions. Write each fraction in its simplest form.

a 0.56 **b** 0.025 **c** 0.84

d 0.375 **e** 0.05 **f** 0.64

Watch out!

$\frac{1}{8}$ is smaller than $\frac{1}{4}$.

$\frac{1}{50}$ is bigger than $\frac{1}{100}$.

5a I can convert terminating decimals to fractions

Now try this!

A Pairs 1

A game for two players. Make 12 cards. Decide on six equivalent fraction and percentage pairs. For example, one pair could be 25% and $\frac{1}{4}$. Write each value on a separate card. Spread out the cards face down. Take turns to turn over two cards. If the cards form an equivalent fraction/percentage pair, keep the cards. If not, turn them face down again. The player with the most cards at the end wins.

B Pairs 2

A game for two players. Make 18 cards. Decide on six equivalent fraction, percentage and decimal sets. For example, one set could be 10%, $\frac{1}{10}$ and 0.1. Write each value on a separate card. Now play 'Pairs' as in **A** above. This time you could have an equivalent fraction/percentage pair or fraction/decimal pair or percentage/decimal pair. There will be six cards left at the end.

fraction | lowest terms | numerator | percentage | simplest form

16.7 Fractions cup final at Wembley

Wembley warm-up

It's the fractions cup final at the new Wembley stadium! Before you play, you've got to do a pre-match warm-up.

1 Half of 52
2 A third of 18
3 $\frac{1}{4}$ of 20
4 $\frac{1}{3}$ of 15
5 $\frac{2}{5}$ of 25
6 $\frac{5}{6}$ of 24
7 $\frac{1}{4}$ of 28 kg
8 $\frac{2}{3}$ of £12
9 $\frac{3}{4}$ of 16 kg
10 $\frac{7}{8}$ of 24 ml
11 $\frac{6}{7}$ of 42 kg
12 $\frac{1}{2} \times 32$
13 $\frac{1}{3} \times 90$
14 $\frac{3}{5} \times 150$
15 $1\frac{1}{2} \times 24$
16 $\frac{1}{3} \times 15$ mm

Wonderful Wembley

1 There are 26 lifts in Wembley stadium. Half of them are in use during a guided tour. How many is this?

2 6000 employees work on a cup final day. A music concert only needs $\frac{1}{3}$ of this number of staff. How many workers is that?

3 Wembley stadium cost £750 million to build. $\frac{2}{15}$ of that was spent buying the land. How much was this?

4 The stadium can seat 90 000 fans. If a tenth of the fans at a game were away supporters, how many fans were supporting the home team?

5 The Wembley arch rises to a height of 135 m. The top of the roof is $\frac{2}{5}$ of this height. Find the height difference between the top of the roof and the top of the arch.

0 m

$\frac{1}{8}$ of 100 m = 12.5 m

GG

Groundsman Gary has chosen $\frac{1}{8}$

Groundsman Gary's game (a game for 2–4 players)

Aim of the game: To get three markers in a row.

How to play: Draw a 10 cm line to represent the pitch. Mark 0 m, 50 m and 100 m.

Dribbling practice

There are lots of different ways of writing the number 8 using fractions:

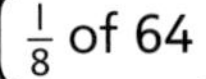

$\frac{1}{8}$ of 64 $\frac{4}{5}$ of 10 Half of 16 $\frac{2}{3}$ of 12

For this challenge you need to find different expressions for the same number using fractions. For each different expression you will dribble around one cone in the slalom. Can you make it all the way to the tenth cone?

- Choose a number from one of the these lists.

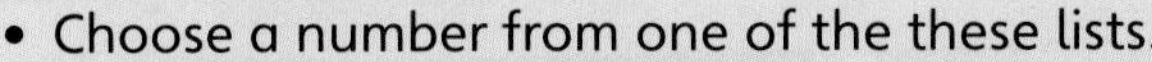

Division 1 (easy) 2, 3, 8, 10

Championship (medium) 7, 18, 24, 27

Premiership (difficult) $3\frac{1}{2}$, 0.75, $\frac{1}{4}$, 2.5

- Write different expressions with your number as the answer.
- Find ten different expressions to beat the challenge and win promotion.

Penalty shoot-out (a game for 2 players)

Aim of the game: To win the penalty shoot-out by finding fractions of 360°.

Rules: The first player to take a penalty chooses a fraction with one of the denominators given below. The second player has 10 seconds to save the penalty by working out that fraction of 360°. Check your answers using a calculator. The player who has scored more goals after five penalties each is the winner. You can play 'sudden death' if both players are level after five penalties.

- Choose whether you are playing in Division 1, the Championship or the Premiership.

Difficulty	Division 1 (easy)	Championship (medium)	Premiership (difficult)
Denominators allowed	2, 3, 4, 6, 10	5, 6, 8, 12, 20	9, 12, 15, 18, 24

- Record your results in a penalty shoot-out table. In this game Chris won in 'sudden death':

Player names	**1**	**2**	**3**	**4**	**5**	**Sudden death...**		
Jade	✓	×	×	✓	✓	×	×	
Chris	×	×	✓	✓	✓	×	✓	

Rules: Take turns to choose a fraction, and use a calculator to work out that fraction of 100 m. Mark the fraction on the pitch and label it with your initials.

The first to get three marks in a row (without someone else's mark in between) is the winner. Play stops after 10 minutes. If no-one has won, the game is a draw.

Hint: Always write down the fraction you choose and the distance in metres. If necessary round your answers to 1 decimal place.

16.8 Calculations with percentages

- Use mental and written methods to calculate percentages of amounts and solve word problems
- Use a calculator to find percentages of amounts
- Understand the calculator display when dealing with money
- Express one number as a percentage of another

Why learn this?

When you save money, it is better to put it in a real bank. The bank will pay you a percentage of the amount saved as interest.

What's the BIG idea?

- To find 10% of an **amount**, you simply divide by 10. **Level 4**
- To find 1% of an amount, you simply divide by 100. **Level 4**
- You can find 11% of an amount by adding 10% and 1%.
  Find 11% of £150.
  10% of £150 = £150 ÷ 10 = £15
  1% of £150 = £150 ÷ 100 = £1.50
  so 11% = £15 + £1.50 = £16.50 **Level 4**
- If you are dealing with money in pounds, 6.8 on the **calculator display** means £6.80. **Level 4**
- You can use a calculator to work out **percentages** of numbers and measures.
  14% of £62 = (14 ÷ 100) × 62
  Pressing [1] [4] [÷] [1] [0] [0] [×] [6] [2] [=] gives £8.68
  12% of 360 = 0.12 × 360
  Pressing [•] [1] [2] [×] [3] [6] [0] [=] gives 43.2 **Level 4 & Level 5**
- To write one number as a percentage of another:
  1 Write one number as a fraction of the other, e.g. $\frac{12}{20}$
  2 Find the equivalent percentage, e.g. $\frac{12}{20} = \frac{60}{100} = 60\%$ **Level 5**

Tip
When using a calculator, using an equivalent decimal to do a percentage calculation uses fewer key presses.

Practice, practice, practice!

Level 4

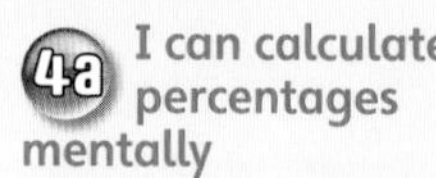

4a I can calculate percentages mentally

4a I can carry out mental calculations involving percentages

4a I can correctly interpret the calculator display

4a I can calculate simple percentages

1 Work these out in your head.
  a 10% of £87 b 50% of 410 g
  c 5% of £9 d 15% of 60 litres

2 A computer cost £800. The price is reduced by 25% in a sale.
  a How much is the computer reduced by?
  b What is the sale price?

3 A caterer charges £325 for a party. 50% of this is the cost of the food. Use your calculator to work out the cost of the food.

4 Without using a calculator, find 11% of each of these.
  a £320 b £260 c £9

amount | calculate | calculator display | clear | decimal number

5 a Half of 50% is 25%. What is half of 25%?

b Use the facts in part a to work out these.

i 25% of £600 ii 12.5% of £200 iii $12\frac{1}{2}$% of £480

6 Sarah has ordered a sofa which costs £1449. She has paid a 50% deposit.

a Use your calculator to work out how much deposit she has paid.

b Check your answer by working the problem backwards.

7 Sue takes out a loan of £482 from the bank. The bank charges 15% interest each year. Use your calculator to work out 15% interest of £482. How much will Sue own the bank after one year?

Level 4

4a I can calculate simple percentages

4a I can check a result by working it backwards

4a I can carry out calculations on a calculator with more than one step

8 There are 520 replica football kits remaining in a sports shop at the end of the season. Five out of ten are Chelsea kits. Five out of 20 are Manchester United kits. 12.5% are Liverpool kits. The remainder are Everton kits.

a Use percentages to work out how many are

i Chelsea kits

ii Manchester United kits.

b i What percentage are Everton kits?

ii How many Everton kits are there?

c List the football teams in order from the smallest to the largest number of kits.

9 Use a calculator to work these out by changing the percentage to an equivalent decimal.

a 12% of 360 b 27% of £46 c 99% of 210 kg d 4% of 570 m

10 Write

a 75 cm as a percentage of 1 m b 45 mm as a percentage of 1 m

c £8 as a percentage of £20 d 220 ml as a percentage of 1 *l*.

Level 5

5c I can use percentages to compare proportions

5a I can use a calculator to find percentages by using decimal equivalents

5a I can express one quantity as a percentage of another

Now try this!

A Anagrams

Unscramble these anagrams.

IDIVED AUNTOM SIDLAPY DOTHEM

Devise some of your own for a partner to unscramble.

B What value am I?

a I am 100% of 10 m. What value am I?

b 50% of me is £36. What value am I?

c $\frac{1}{4}$ of me is £5.50. What is 75% of me?

d 75% of me is 39 g. What value am I?

e If 20% of me is £72, what is 70%?

f 0.35 of me is £70. What is 17.5% of me?

Make up some clues of your own to test out on a partner.

Learn this

50% = $\frac{1}{2}$

25% = $\frac{1}{4}$

10% = $\frac{1}{10}$

1% = $\frac{1}{100}$

display enter fraction key memory percentage

Egyptian mathematics

The Ancient Egyptians used these hieroglyphic pictures to represent individual numbers:

| stood for 1

∩ stood for 10

𓍢 stood for 100

𓆼 stood for 1000

Give your answers to these problems in the decimal system, not the hieroglyphics system.

1 Tutankhamun ruled from 1336 to 1327 BC.
Use a mental method to work out how long he ruled for. **Level 3**

2 Nasir has ||||| camels. Each camel drinks ∩|||||| gallons of water at a time.
Use a mental method to work out the total amount of water Nasir needs for his camels. **Level 3**

3 The Great Pyramid is 𓍢∩∩∩|||||| metres high.
The Statue of Liberty is ∩∩∩∩∩∩∩∩||| metres high.
Use a written method to work out how much higher the Great Pyramid is than the Statue of Liberty. **Level 4**

MAKE MATHS FUNCTIONAL!

4 There is a special offer on at the camel market: all camels are reduced by 25%.
Nasir chooses a young camel with original price LE220 (LE = Egyptian pound).
How much is the camel in the special offer? **Level 4**

5 Nasir gives camel rides to children. Each camel can carry |||| children. In the first group there are ∩∩∩ children.
How many camels does he need for all the children to ride at the same time? **Level 4**

6 The perimeter of the square base of one pyramid is 𓍢𓍢𓍢𓍢𓍢𓍢𓍢𓍢∩∩∩∩∩∩| metres.
Use a written method to work out the length of one side of the pyramid base. **Level 4**

7 The ancient Egyptians divided the year into ∩|| months of ∩∩∩ days each, with ||||| days added on at the end of the year.
Use a written method to work out the number of days in the Egyptian calendar. **Level 5**

8 Ancient Egyptians measured short lengths using parts of a man's arm and hand as standard measurements. 4 digits = 1 palm ≈ 7.5 cm.
Use a written method to work out the length of seven palms. **Level 5**

9 Nasir wins LE 𓆼𓍢𓍢𓍢𓍢.∩∩ on the Egyptian Lottery. He decides to buy new blankets for his hard working camels. Each blanket costs LE∩∩∩|||. Nasir now has ∩||||||| camels.

a Use a written method to work out the total cost of the blankets.

b How much money will Nasir have left from his winnings after buying the blankets? **Level 5**

The BIG ideas

- → You can use **partitioning**, **counting up** or **compensation** to help you add or subtract mentally. Level 3
- → To add or subtract decimals, line up the decimal points, put the decimal point in the answer, then add or subtract. Level 4
- → You can use partitioning for mental multiplication: 18 × 7 is the same as (10 × 7) + (8 × 7) = 70 + 56 = 126 Level 4
- → If you know 3 × 4 = 12, you also know 12 ÷ 3 = 4 and 12 ÷ 4 = 3. Level 4
- → 25% = $\frac{1}{4}$. To find 25% of an amount you divide by 4. Level 4
- → You can use the **grid method** or the **standard method** for multiplication. Level 4 & Level 5
- → You can use **repeated subtraction** for division. Always work out how many lots of the **divisor** you subtracted altogether. This is the answer you are looking for! Level 4 & Level 5

Find your level

Level 3

Q1 Copy and complete these to create three different correct calculations.

a ___ × ___ = 18
b ___ × ___ = 18
c ___ × ___ = 18

Q2 Write down the numbers from this list which are factors of 18.

1, 2, 3, 4, 5, 6, 7, 8, 9, 10, 11, 12, 13, 14, 15, 16, 17, 18

Level 4

Q3 Use a written method to work out these.

a Add together 3.7 and 6.5.
b Subtract 5.7 from 15.2.
c Multiply 254 by 5.
d Divide 342 by 6.

Q4 a For each number given, write a multiple of it between 130 and 180.

Number	Multiple between 130 and 180
40	
35	
27	

b Is 171 divisible by 9? Explain your answer.
c Is 4 a factor of 104? Explain your answer.

Q5 a Which of these numbers are exactly divisible by 8?
60, 228, 24, 96

b Which of these numbers are exactly divisible by 7?
133, 28, 147, 108

c Which of these numbers are exactly divisible by 8?
72, 36, 150, 161, 128, 200, 324, 48, 70

Level 5

Q6 Arc Limited make a range of replica boats. The Model 2 boat weighs 1.58 kg. What is the weight of eight Model 2 boats? Show your working.

Q7 Here is a list of the prime numbers between 29 and 47.

29, 31, 37, 41, 43, 47

a Is 49 a prime number? Explain your answer.
b Use the list above to help you identify the prime numbers between 50 and 60. Prove your answers are correct.
c Look at these numbers.
6, 12, 18, 24, 30, 36, 42, …
Explain how you can tell that there will never be a prime number in this sequence.

17 Algebra rules

This unit is about using rules in sequences, functions, graphs and formulae.

The Ancient Romans realised that they needed rules and regulations to make sure that society ran smoothly. They wrote down their laws, so that every Roman citizen could see them and powerful people couldn't change them to suit themselves. To enforce the law, they introduced courts across the Empire, where people could get a fair trial. In court, each side had a lawyer to argue their case, and a jury voted on whether the accused was innocent or guilty. The judge then decided on the punishment.

This type of court system is still used across the world today.

Activities

A Scale pans balance when the contents in both sides weigh the same.

Work out the weights marked ? in these scales.

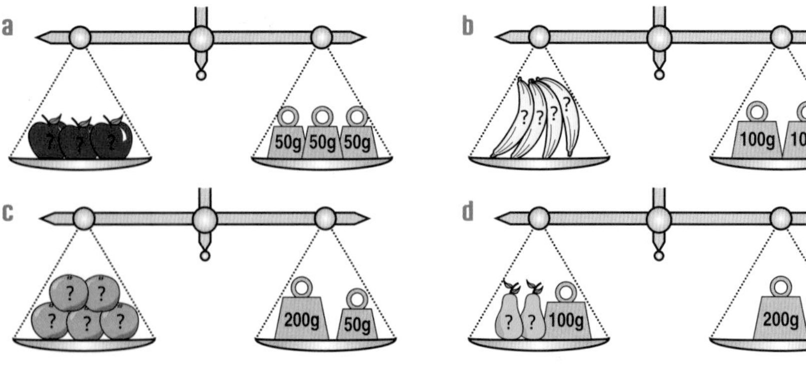

B Here is a list of coordinates: (2, 1) (4, 2) (6, 3) (8, 4).
What is the rule that connects the x- and y-coordinates?
Make up a rule and write four pairs of coordinates for it.
Ask a partner to work out the rule.

Did you know?

The word rule comes from the Latin word 'regula' – which also gives us the word 'regulation'. Justicia, the Roman goddess of justice, holds a pair of scales. She uses these to weigh up the evidence for and against the accused, before she makes a judgement.

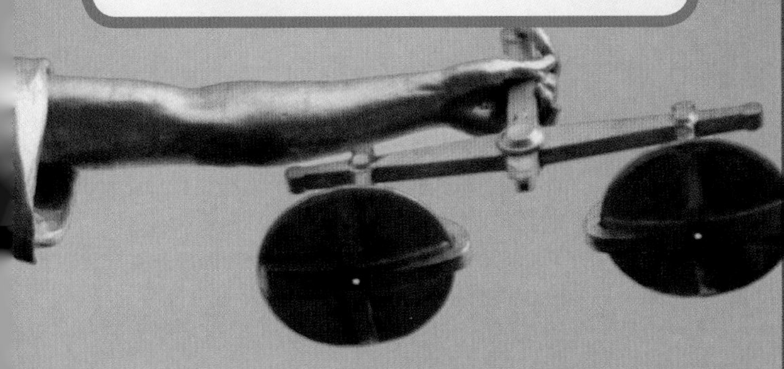

Before you start this unit...

1 Find the missing number:
$4t = 20$

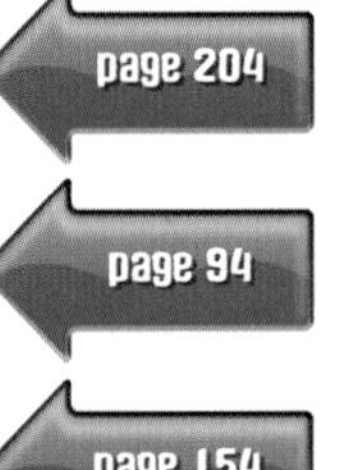
page 204

2 Write down the value of
$3y - 5$ if $y = 7$

page 94

3 Write down the next three terms in this sequence.
2, 9, 16, 23, ...

page 154

4 a Draw a coordinate grid with x- and y-axes from 0–10.

page 163

b Plot these coordinates, joining them up with straight lines in the order they are given.
(5, 4) (8, 4) (6, 7) (3, 7)

c Write down the name of this shape.

Roman punishment

A great event in the bloodthirsty Roman Games was watching criminals fighting to the death. Any survivors could be finished off by gladiators or thrown to wild animals. Thousands of Romans enjoyed watching this 'entertainment'.

Plus digital resources

17.1 Finding terms in a sequence

- Know how to generate terms of a sequence from practical contexts
- Know how to find a term of a practical sequence given its position in the sequence
- Know how to use algebra to describe the rule for the nth term in a sequence

Why learn this?

If a magazine comes out every Wednesday, you can use a sequence to work out which dates the magazine is published on.

What's the BIG idea?

→ You can find the next **term** of a **sequence** by drawing the next **shape** or by finding how much it goes up by each time. **Level 3 & Level 4**

→ You can find a term of a sequence if you know the position of the term in the sequence and the **position-to-term rule**. **Level 5**

Did you know?

The word 'sequence' comes from the Latin word 'sequor' which means 'to follow'. Can you think of other words that include 'sequ...'? What do they mean?

Practice, practice, practice!

Level 4

4b I can find terms of a simple sequence

1 Look at this pattern made from matchsticks.

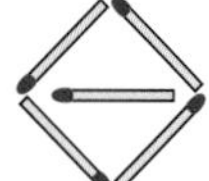

Shape 1

Shape 2

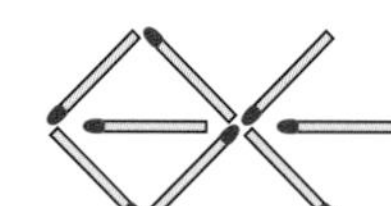
Shape 3

a Copy and complete the 3rd pattern.

b Copy and complete this table of values.

Pattern number	1	2	3	4	5	6
Number of matchsticks						

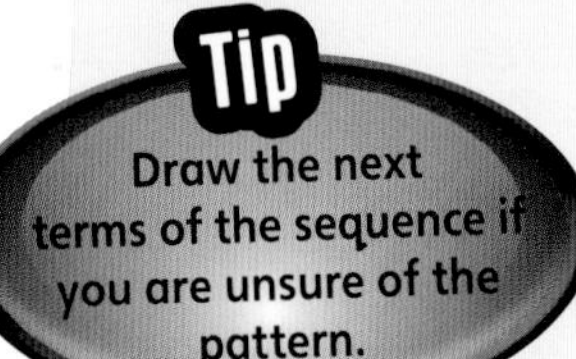

4a I can find terms of a more complex sequence

2 Charlie made a growing pattern of the first letter in his name using counters.

a How many counters are in the 1st, 2nd and 3rd patterns?

How many counters will be in the

b 4th pattern

c 8th pattern?

1st shape 2nd shape 3rd shape

3 Lazarus has £100 in his bank account. He saves £10 per month.

a Copy and complete the table to show how much he has at the start of each month.

Month	1	2	3	4	5	6
Savings	£100	£110				

b How much will he have saved at the end of his first year?

pattern position-to-term rule rule

4 Kelly is raising money for charity. She raises £10 per week.

a How much will she have raised after 5 weeks?

b How much will she have raised after 10 weeks?

c How many weeks will it be before Kelly raises £60?

d Copy and complete this sentence for how much Kelly raises.

money raised = number of weeks × ____

5 Sue goes to a fun park with her family. The price of each ride is £1.50.

a If she goes on 4 rides, how much will she spend?

b If she goes on 6 rides, how much will she spend?

c Sue has £15. How many rides can she afford?

d Copy and complete this sentence for how much money Sue spends.

total spent = ____ × ____

6 These shapes are made with squares.

shape 1
2 squares

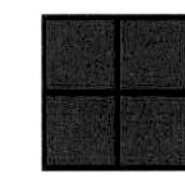

shape 2
4 squares

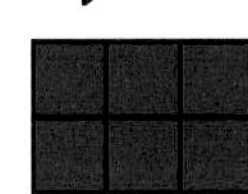

shape 3
6 squares

a How many squares are in

i shape 4 **ii** shape 8 **iii** shape n?

b Copy and complete the position-to-term rule for this sequence.

number of squares = ____ × n = ____

c How many squares will be in shape 10?

7 **a** What is the position-to-term rule rule for this sequence?

1st term	2nd term	3rd term	4th term
4	8	12	16

b Write down the position-to-term rules for these sequences.

i 5, 9, 13, 17, … **ii** 3, 7, 11, 15, … **iii** 7, 11, 15, 19, …

Level 5

5c I can find a term from its position in the sequence

5a I can use algebra to find the nth term

Now try this!

A Term-to-term rules

The term-to-term rule of a sequence is 'add 6'.

1 Write down five sequences that have this rule.
2 Make up a rule for your partner. Ask them to write five sequences for your rule.
3 Check that they are correct.

B Position-to-term rules

The position-to-term rule of a sequence is 'multiply the position number by 3 then subtract 2'.
The first five terms of this sequence are 1, 4, 7, 10, 13.

1 Make up a position-to-term rule for your partner.
Ask them to write the first five terms of the sequence for your rule.
2 Check that they correct.

sequence **term** **term-to-term rule**

17.2 More functions and mappings

- Find outputs of functions in words and symbols
- Find inputs of functions using inverse operations
- Construct functions to describe mappings (completing a function machine)
- Draw a graph of a function

What's the BIG idea?

- You can put numbers into a **function machine** to get an **output** value. **Level 4**
- A function machine can be written as a **function**. For example $y = 4x$. **Level 5**

$x \rightarrow \boxed{\times 4} \rightarrow y$

- Function machines can help you find x- and y-values when you have been given a **rule**. For the function machine above, when $x = 1$, $y = 4$. **Level 5**

Why learn this?

When prices are reduced in a sale, a function machine can be used to calculate the sale prices.

Practice, practice, practice!

Level 4

4a I can find outputs of simple functions

1 This function machine can be used to generate even numbers.

$x \rightarrow \boxed{\times 2} \rightarrow y$

What will the y-value be if the x-value is

a 8 **b** 20 **c** 42 **d** 8.2?

2 Match each table to a function machine and a function.

a

x	10	15	20	25	30
y	2	3	4	5	6

b

x	2	4	6	8	10
y	9	11	13	15	17

c

x	7	8	9	10	11
y	3	4	5	6	7

d

x	3	4	5	6	7
y	9	12	15	18	21

$x \rightarrow \boxed{\text{add } 7} \rightarrow y$ $x \rightarrow \boxed{\times 3} \rightarrow y$ $y = x - 4$ $y = x + 7$

$x \rightarrow \boxed{\div 5} \rightarrow y$ $x \rightarrow \boxed{-4} \rightarrow y$ $y = 3x$ $y = \frac{x}{5}$

Level 5

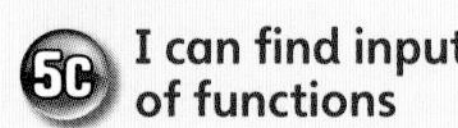

5c I can find inputs of functions

3 Copy these tables and find the missing inputs and outputs to complete them.

a $x \rightarrow \boxed{\times 4} \rightarrow y$

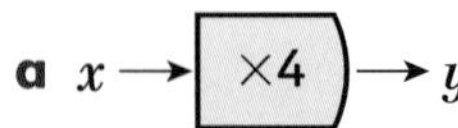

x	1	4			
y			8	12	20

b $x \rightarrow \boxed{\times 2 + 1} \rightarrow y$

x	2	5		8	10
y			13		

function function machine input

4 Claire is playing a game with her friend.
She uses a rule and her friend has to guess the rule used.

$x \rightarrow \square \rightarrow y$

a Find the missing rule for this set of inputs and outputs.

$1 \rightarrow 8 \quad 2 \rightarrow 9 \quad 3 \rightarrow 10$

b What is the output for the input 10?

c What is the input for the output 8.5?

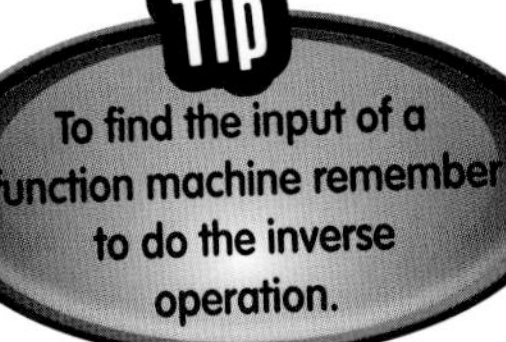

5 Find the missing part of the rule in these function machines.
Write each as a mapping and as a function.

a $x \rightarrow \square \rightarrow \boxed{+5} \rightarrow y$

$2 \rightarrow 9$
$4 \rightarrow 13$
$5 \rightarrow 15$
$7 \rightarrow 19$

mapping: $x \rightarrow$ ____ $+ 5$
function: $y =$ ____$x + 5$

b $x \rightarrow \boxed{-3} \rightarrow \square \rightarrow y$

$6 \rightarrow 12$
$8 \rightarrow 20$
$9 \rightarrow 24$
$10 \rightarrow 28$

mapping: $x \rightarrow$ ____
function: $y =$ ____

Watch out!
Be careful of the order of operations when writing a function from a function machine.

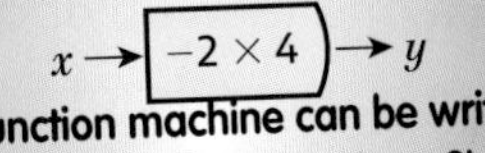

This function machine can be written as the function $y = 4(x - 2)$

6 These three function machines are all equivalent.

$x \rightarrow \boxed{\times 6} \rightarrow y \qquad x \rightarrow \boxed{\times 2} \rightarrow \boxed{\times 3} \rightarrow y \qquad x \rightarrow \boxed{\times 3} \rightarrow \boxed{\times 2} \rightarrow y$

Find another function machine which is equivalent to $x \rightarrow \boxed{\times 8} \rightarrow y$

7 **a** Copy these axes.

b Plot the graph from Q3 **a** on your axes.
Label the graph $y = 4x$

c Plot the graph from Q3 **b** on your axes.
Label the graph.

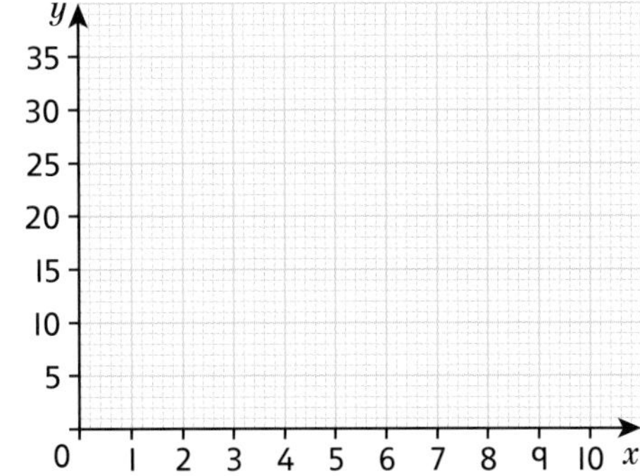

Level 5

5b I can find the rule in a function machine

5a I can draw a graph of a function

Now try this!

A Rule maze

You will need Resource sheet 17.2.
Find your way through the maze using the rule ×3.
You can start at any number in the left-hand column.
You can move up, down, sideways or diagonally.

Hint There is more than one way of getting through.

B Three in a line

A game for two players.
You will need Resource sheet 17.2 and counters in two different colours.
Choose a statement. If you can find a mapping that matches your statement, cover the mapping with your colour counter.
The first person to get three of their counters in a line is the winner.

mapping output rule

17.3 More coordinates

- Plot coordinates in all four quadrants
- Generate coordinates that satisfy a simple rule in the first quadrant
- Plot a graph of a simple linear function in the first quadrant

What's the BIG idea?

- When reading **coordinates**, always start at 0 and read across first and then up or down. **Level 4**
- The first **quadrant** has positive values on the x-**axis** and y-**axis**. **Level 4**

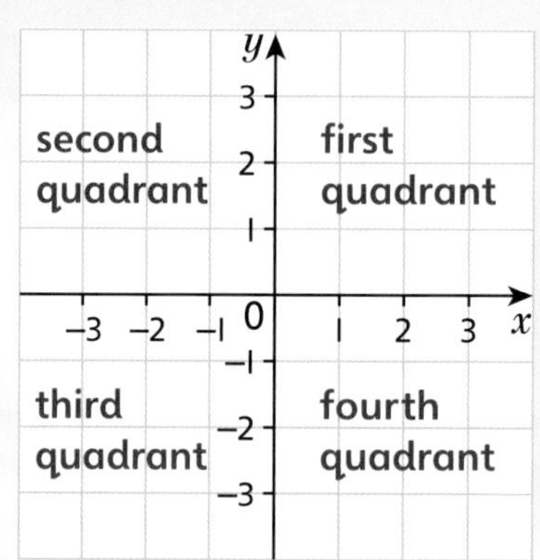

- You can use **linear functions** to generate coordinate pairs. **Level 5**
- You need three coordinate pairs to draw a straight line **graph**. **Level 5**

Why learn this?

Coordinates are used a lot in real life. Every dot of light on a computer screen is described by a coordinate pair.

Practice, practice, practice!

Level 3

3a I can describe and find the position on a grid

1 Look at the metro map.

a Which station is at
  - i E4
  - ii B7
  - iii F2?

b Where on the grid is
  - i Royal Square
  - ii Watford Circus
  - iii Central Station?

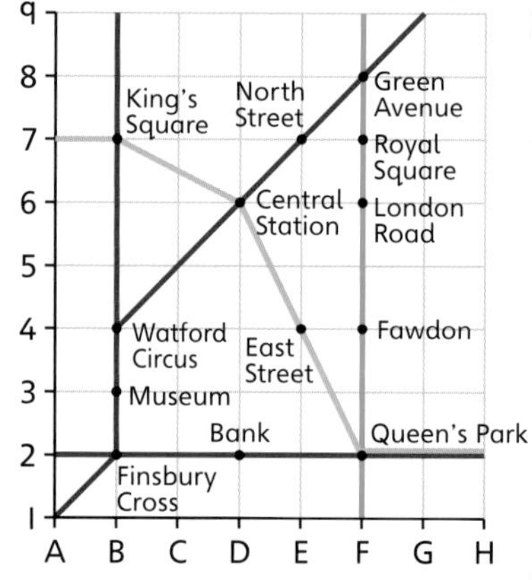

Level 4

4a I can read and plot coordinates in the first quadrant

2 Jason is drawing triangles in a row on a coordinate grid.

a Write down the coordinates of the first four corners marked with a cross.

b Write down one thing you notice about these coordinates.

c Will the point (16, 4) have a cross on it? Explain how you know.

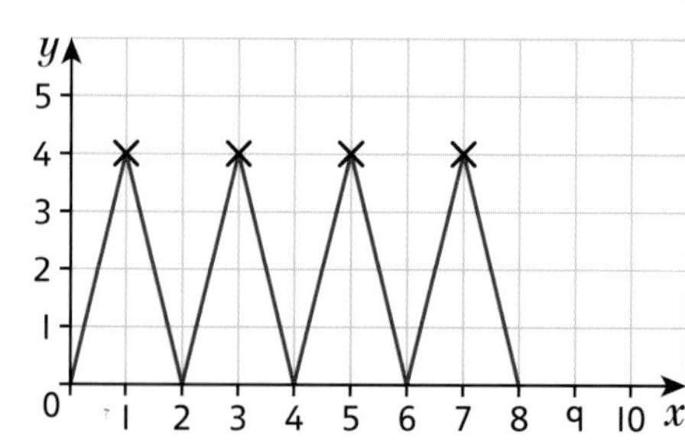

axes axis coordinates function graph

3 Using the rule $y = x + 7$, find the y-value when the x-value is

a 2 **b** 5 **c** 6 **d** 8 **e** 10

4 Copy and complete this table of values for the rule $y = 2x$.

x	1	2	3	4	
y					10

Hint: $2x$ means $2 \times x$.

5 Copy and complete this table of values for the rule $y = 2x + 3$.

x	1	2	3	4	5
y					

6 Copy and complete this table of values for the rule $y = 2x - 2$.

x	1	2	3	4	5
y					

7 Draw a pair of axes from 0 to 5.
Plot the graph for this table of values.

x	4	4	4	4	4
y	0	1	2	3	4

What is the function for this graph?

8 Draw a pair of axes on graph paper. Label the x-axis from −2 to 5 and the y-axis from 0 to 14.

a Plot the graphs of Q4, Q5 and Q6 on the same grid.

b What do you notice about the graphs you have drawn?

Hint: Use a different colour for each line.

9 **a** Draw a pair of axes labelled from −10 to 10. Plot these coordinate pairs and join them up with a straight line.

(−6, −2) (−5, −1) (2, 6)

b Copy this table of values and use your graph to complete it.

x	−3		0	1	
y		2			8

Level 5

5c I can find first quadrant coordinates using a simple rule

5b I can recognise graphs parallel to the x or y-axis

5a I can plot a graph of a line graph in the first quadrant

5a I can plot coordinates in all four quadrants

Watch out!

Remember – if the x-coordinate is negative, read to the left; if the y-coordinate is negative, read down.

Now try this!

A Straight line graphs

1 Plot the graphs of $y = x$, $y = x + 1$ and $y = x + 2$ on the same axes. Is there a pattern?

2 Investigate what happens for $y = x$, $y = 2x$ and $y = 3x$.

B Straight line graphs 2

1 Plot the graphs of $y = 3x + 1$, $y = 3x + 3$ and $y = 3x - 2$ on the same axes. Is there a pattern?

2 Investigate for other straight line graphs.

linear quadrant rule x-axis y-axis

17.4 Plotting real-life graphs

- Complete a table of values
- Plot a graph from a table of values
- Use a real-life graph

Why learn this?

The length of time you use your mobile phone and how much it costs will be a linear relationship. This can be plotted as a straight line graph.

What's the BIG idea?

- The **axes** on a grid should be labelled and the graph should have a title. **Level 4**
- When **plotting** a **real-life graph** you need to decide where the **scale** will start and finish on the x- and y-axes. **Level 5**
- When marking the axes, the same interval between the numbers must be the same distance on the axis. **Level 5**

Learn this

When you draw the straight line between three points, extend it to the edges of the grid.

Practice, practice, practice!

Level 4

4a I can plot a graph from a table of values

1 A shop hires out video cameras.
The price is £10 per hour.
This table shows some costs for hiring a video camera.

Hours	1	3	4
Cost (£)	10	30	40

a Copy the grid. Plot the points from the table.

b Join the points with a straight line.

c Label your axes. Give your graph a title.

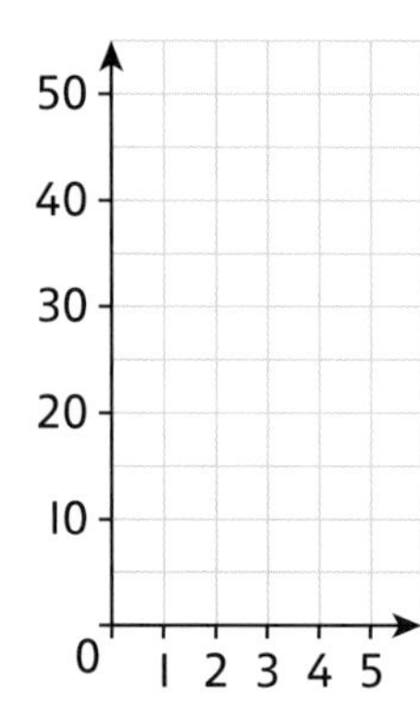

Level 5

5c I can plot a graph from a table of values and use it

2 Mr Morgan wants to convert the marks that pupils got in a maths test to percentages.
The test was out of 25.
This table shows some of the marks and percentages that he calculated.

Mark	5	10	20
Percentage	20	40	80

a Copy and complete the grid, deciding where the scales on the axes should finish.
Plot the points from the table and join them up with a straight line.
Label your axes and give your graph a title.

b Use your graph to find out the percentage for each of these pupils.

i Jamie, 16 marks **ii** Mandeep, 8 marks

iii Anna, 24 marks **iv** Claire, 18 marks

axes plot

3 The price of Carol's mobile phone calls is 20p per minute.

a Copy and complete the table of how much Carol will pay for using her mobile phone.

Number of minutes	10	20	30	100
Cost of call (£)	2		6	

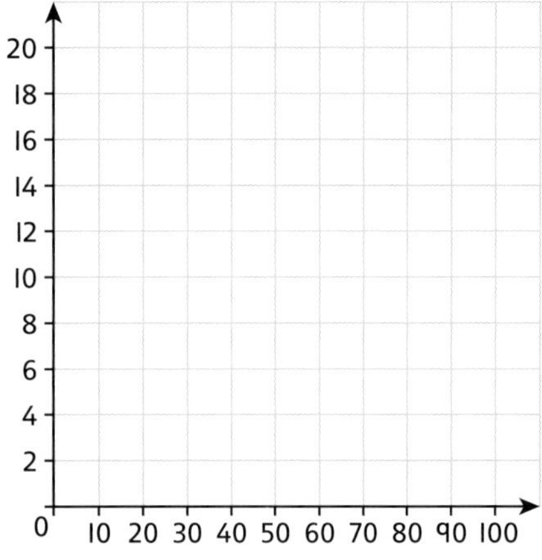

b Copy this grid. Plot the points in your table and join them up with a straight line. Label your axes and give your graph a title.

c Use your graph to find how much Carol will pay if she uses the phone for

i 70 minutes

ii 25 minutes

iii $1\frac{1}{2}$ hours.

d Last month, Carol's bill was £16.
How many minutes did she spend on the phone?

e This month's bill is £13. How many minutes did she spend on the phone?

Level 5

5b I can complete a table of values and plot a real-life graph

4 Mr Juan is booking a coach for a school trip to the Science Museum. The coach company charges £50 for the driver and £25 per hour the coach is used.

a Copy and complete the table.

Hours	0	2	10
Charge (£)	50	100	

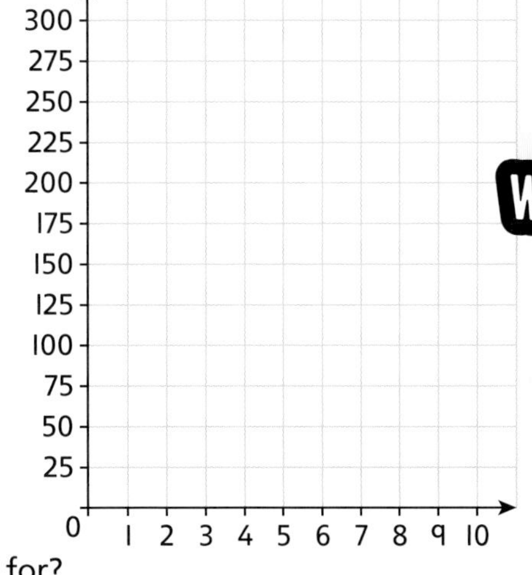

b Copy the grid. Plot the points in your table and join them up with a straight line. Label your axes and give your graph a title.

c How much will it cost if the trip lasts

i 3 hours

ii 8 hours

iii 9 hours?

d The bill for the coach was £200.
How many hours was the coach booked for?

5a I can complete a more complex table of values and plot a graph

Watch out!
Some graphs don't go through the origin.

Now try this!

A Mobile phone charges 1

Investigate pay-as-you-go phone charges for two different mobile phone providers. Compare the costs of using different phones for 60, 100 and 150 minutes each month.

B Mobile phone charges 2

Investigate pay-as-you-go phone charges for two different mobile phone providers. Compare the costs by drawing graphs of their phone charges on the same axes.

real-life graph scale

17.5 Using real-life graphs

➩ Read and plot real-life graphs and interpret information from them

What's the BIG idea?

→ **Graphs** show how one quantity changes in relation to another. **Level 4**
→ You can use **conversion graphs** to **convert** between one value and another. **Level 5**
→ To read the value on a conversion graph, draw a straight horizontal or vertical line to the graph and read the values. **Level 5**

Why learn this?

You can use a conversion graph to convert from euros to pounds. A conversion graph can quickly tell you what prices in euros are in pounds.

Practice, practice, practice!

Level 4

4a I can read information from a real-life graph

1 Look at the graph. Which of these sentences are true?

A The more time spent on the phone the lower the bill.
B The less time spent on the phone the lower the bill.
C The more time spent on the phone the higher the bill.
D As the amount of time spent on the phone increases, the cost of the bill will increase.

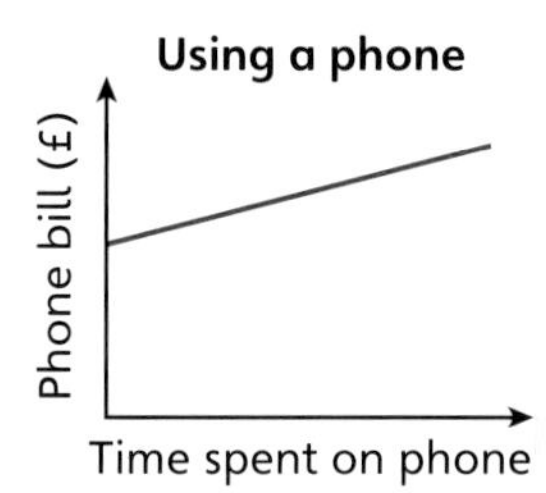

2 Salma measured the temperature in her room one morning in June. The graph shows the temperatures.

a What was the temperature in Salma's room at 10.00?
b At what time was the temperature in the room 24°C?
c What do you think happened between 10.30 and 11.30?

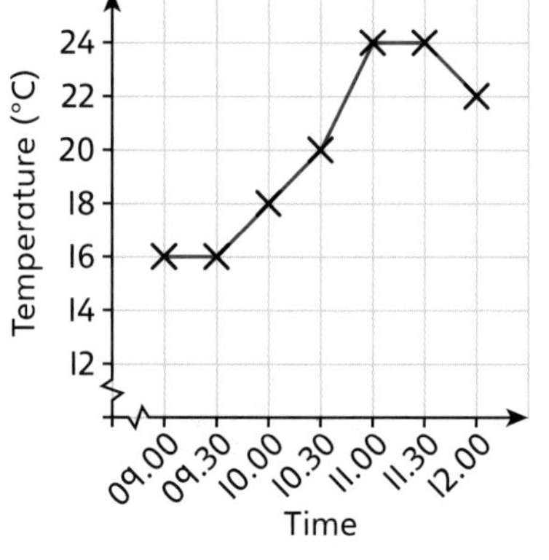

Level 5

5a I can read information from a more complex real-life graph

3 This graph can be used to convert a distance in kilometres to miles.
Use the conversion graph to find the distance in miles from London to these places.

a Luton 40 km
b Colchester 85 km
c Gatwick 65 km
d Oxford 90 km
e Brighton 80 km

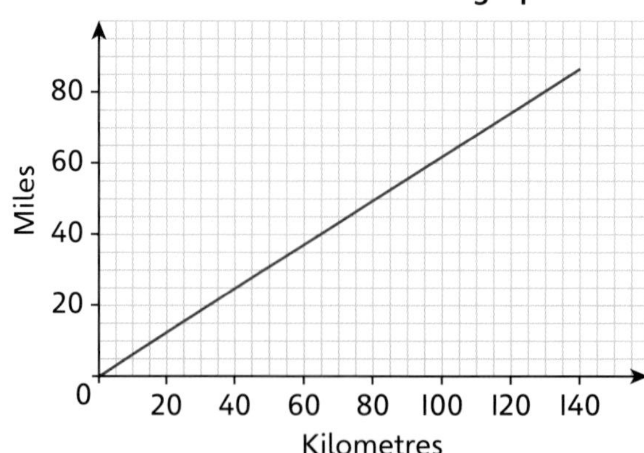

Tip

Use a ruler to follow the line up from the value to the graph. Then follow a line across from the graph to the converted value.

axes conversion graph

4 **a** Jane is going to Spain on holiday and needs to convert some pounds to euros. Approximately how many euros does she get for

i £100 **ii** £150 **iii** £230

b Harry has some euros left over from his holiday. He wants to convert them back to pounds. Approximately how many pounds does he get for

i 30 euro **ii** 90 euro **iii** 300 euro

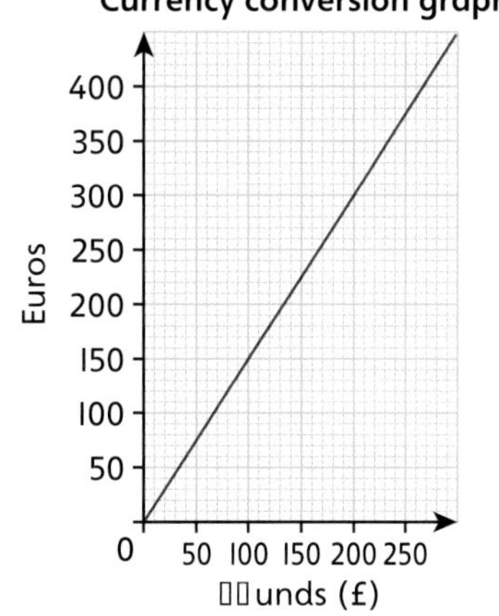

Level 5

5a I can read information from a more complex real-life graph

5 Use the conversion graph in Q3 to convert these distances from miles to kilometres.

a 25 miles **b** 30 miles **c** 10 miles **d** 45 miles

6 The conversion rate from pounds to Australian dollars is approximately £1 = Aus$2.50.

a Copy and complete the table below which shows these conversions.

£	1	2	3	4	5	6	7
Aus$	2.50	5					

b **i** On graph paper, draw a horizontal axis between 1 and 10 and a vertical axis between 1 and 25.

ii Label the horizontal axis 'pounds' and the vertical axis 'Australian dollars'.

iii Plot the conversion graph for pounds and Australian dollars.

c Use your graph to convert

i £5 to Aus$

ii Aus$15 to £

iii £8 to Aus$

iv Aus$25 to £

Watch out!
Be careful when reading the values on the axes.

Now try this!

A Currency conversion rates 1

Research the exchange rates from £ into different currencies.
Find out how much £100 will be converted to in these different currencies.

B Currency conversion rates 2

Research the exchange rates from £ into different currencies.
Choose one of these currencies and draw a conversion graph from £ to your chosen currency.

Tip
You can find currency conversion rates in newspapers, at banks and post offices, and on the internet.

convert graph

maths!

Graphs and graphics

Equations are used for many applications in computing.

When creating a CGI movie, programmers have to explain to the computer what needs to be drawn and where.

They can't just say 'Draw an ant'; they need to program how to draw an ant. Equations can be used for this.

Have a go at this yourself!
How would you explain to a computer how to draw these shapes in the right place?

A square

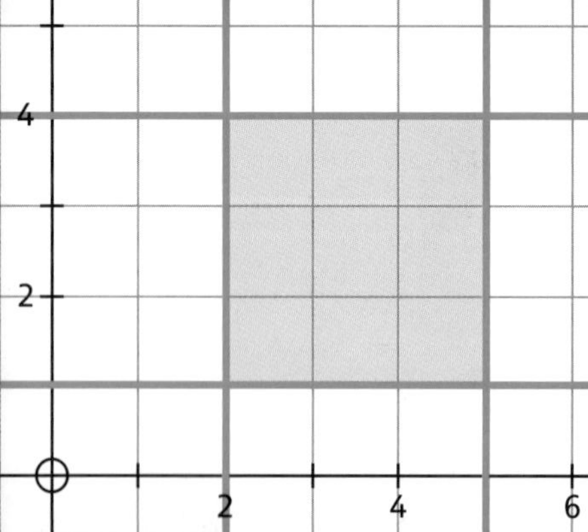

A rectangle

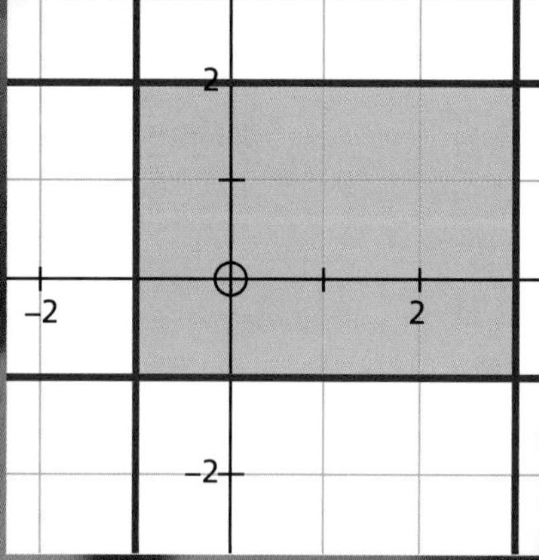

A right-angled triangle

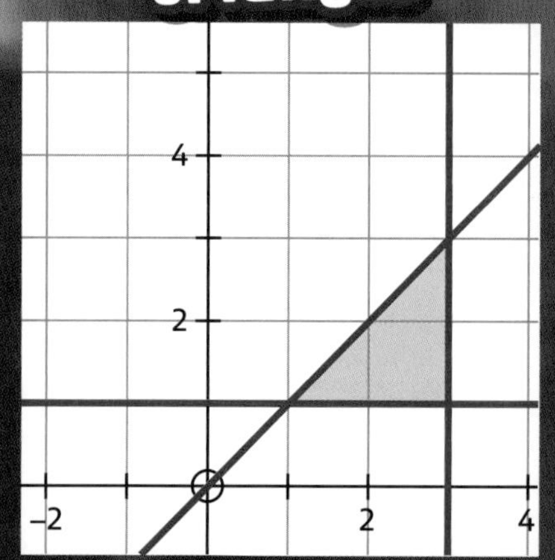

Which four lines are needed for

- the square?
- the rectangle?

- Which three lines are needed for the right-angled triangle?

(Be careful finding the diagonal line. How do the x-coordinates relate to the y-coordinates?)

Mobile costs

The cost of using a mobile phone increases as more minutes of calls are made. Here is a graph showing these costs for both a pay as you go phone and a contract phone.

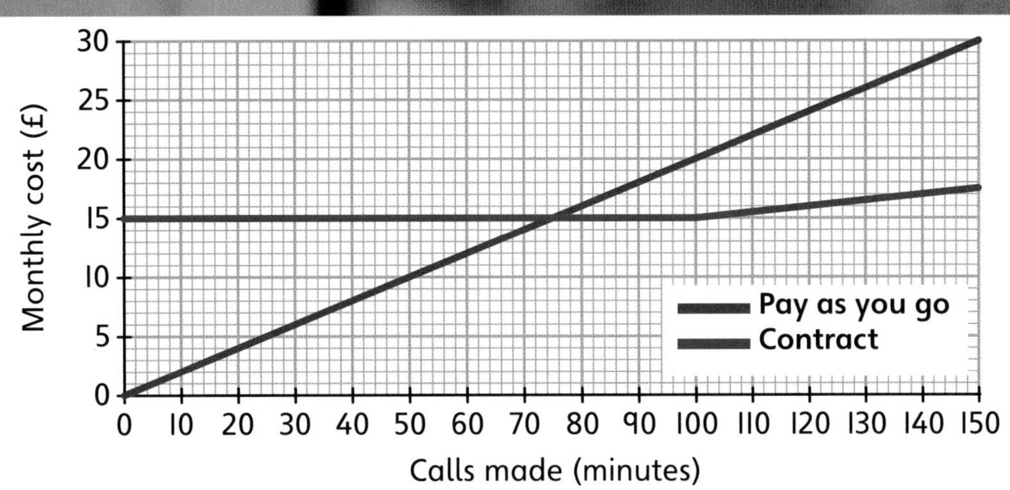

- If you were advising someone who only made one hour's worth of calls each month, which type of phone would you recommend? Why?
- How many minutes of calls would you have to make each month so that the contract phone was better value?

Billy's goat graph

Billy has four goats – Bert, Jeff, Greg and Justin. One day he decides to race them 100 metres across his dad's farm. He marks out a course and regularly notes down their progress. Here is the graph of their race.

- What happens to Justin near the end of the race?
- Why is Bert's graph horizontal between 10 and 18 seconds?
- Imagine you are a commentator watching this race. What would you say?

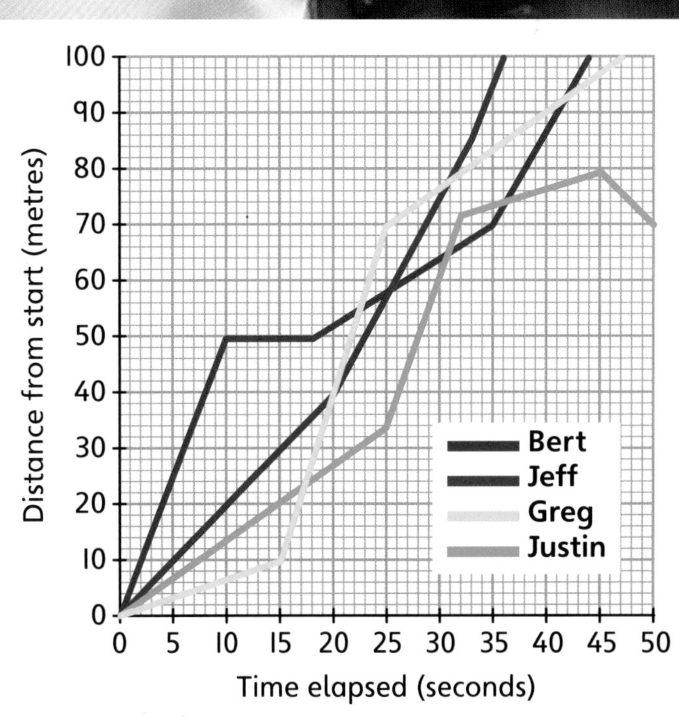

17.6 Using formulae

- Know how to use simple formulae
- Know how to substitute positive integers into formulae

Why learn this?

A recipe tells you how much of each ingredient you need for a certain number of people. You can use a formula to work out how much of each ingredient you need for a different number of people.

What's the BIG idea?

→ A **variable** is a quantity that can change, for example the number of people in a room. **Level 4 & Level 5**

→ A **formula** is a rule for working out an amount that depends on a variable. **Level 4 & Level 5**

→ To **substitute** values into a formula, replace the letters with their values. For example, for the formula $R = 3d$, when $d = 4$, $R = 3 \times 4 = 12$. **Level 5**

Practice, practice, practice!

All about Stan's café

Stan runs a café. The tasks for each day depend on variables. For example, the number of chairs needed depends on the number of tables in the café.
Stan works out how much of each item he needs by using formulae.

Level 4

4a I can substitute integers into word formulae

1 Stan sells sweet snacks at 10p more than he buys them for, so

selling price = buying price + 10p

Work out the selling prices for these buying prices.

a doughnut 25p **b** brownie 40p **c** flapjack 31p **d** giant cookie 54p

2 The money that Stan takes from selling a breakfast depends on price and on how many are sold. The price of a breakfast is £3, so

money from sale of breakfasts = £3 × number sold

What is the total money taken from the sale of

a 100 breakfasts **b** 250 breakfasts **c** 123 breakfasts **d** 89 breakfasts?

3 The money that Stan takes on drinks depends on the price and the number sold.

money from sale of tea = 20p × number of cups sold
money from sale of coffee = 30p × number of cups sold
money from sale of hot chocolate = 45p × number of cups sold

What is the total (in £) taken from the sale of

a 35 cups of tea **b** 26 cups of coffee

c 15 cups of hot chocolate **d** 21 cups of tea and 16 cups of coffee

e 20 cups of tea, 9 cups of coffee and 5 cups of hot chocolate?

formula substitute

4 Stan puts four chairs around each table. This can be written as the formula $c = 4t$, where c is the number of chairs and t is the number of tables.

a Work out the number of chairs needed for
i 12 tables **ii** 15 tables **iii** 9 tables **iv** 27 tables.

b How many tables does Stan need if puts out 64 chairs?

Level 5

5c I can substitute integers into symbol formulae

5 Stan bought too much fruit so he reduced prices using the formula $S = P - 12$, where S is the sale price and P is the old price (all in pence).
Find the sale prices for these old prices.

a banana 45p **b** apple 31p **c** peach 37p
d pineapple 95p **e** kiwi fruit 63p **f** orange 55p

6 The selling price of food is given by the formula $P = 2c + 17$, where P is the selling price and c is the cost of buying the food from the market (all in pence).
Find the selling price P of these items.

a chips $c = 27$p **b** sausage $c = 20$p **c** egg $c = 12$p
d pie $c = 75$p **e** lasagne $c = £1.25$ **f** muesli $c = 35$p

7 Some recipes give cooking temperatures in degrees Celsius (°C) and some in degrees Fahrenheit (°F). Stan converts from one to the other using the approximate rule $F = 2C + 30$, where F is the temperature in degrees Fahrenheit and C is the temperature in degrees Celsius.

a Change these temperatures to degrees Fahrenheit.
i 120°C **ii** 155°C **iii** 140°C

b Change these temperatures to degrees Celsius.
i 190°F **ii** 220°F **iii** 255°F

5b I can substitute integers into equations and solve them

Remember: in algebra, $2a$ means $2 \times a$.

8 Chloe gets paid £5.50 an hour and a bonus of £8 for working on a Sunday. The formula to work out her weekly wages (in £) is $W = 5.5h + 8$, where W is Chloe's wages and h is the number of hours worked.

a Work out Chloe's wages if she works 40 hours a week, including on Sunday.

b Chloe always works on a Sunday. How many hours a week does Chloe need to work to earn
i £63 **ii** £118 **iii** £195 **iv** exactly £100?

Now try this!

A Mrs Osmond's shop

Ben uses this formula to work out the cost, in pence, of things he buys from Mrs Osmond's stationery shop:

cost = 12 × number of pencils + 8 × number of rulers

1 Choose different values to substitute for the number of pencils and the number of rulers.
2 Can you find a way to spend exactly 50p?
3 Can you find a way to spend exactly £1?

B Highest wins

Find recipes that give cooking temperatures both in degrees Fahrenheit and in degrees Celsius. Is the formula that Stan uses in Q7 correct?
Find five examples from recipes to support your argument.

variable

17.7 More deriving formulae

➩ Know how to derive a formula expressed in algebra

What's the BIG idea?

→ You can use a **formula** to describe how to work out an amount that depends on a **variable**.
For example, the post and packing charge is £4 plus £2 for every 1 kg.
The formula for working out post and packing (in £) is

cost = $2 \times n + 4$

where n is the weight in kg. **Level 5**

Why learn this?

Many internet shopping sites use a formula to work out how much you pay for postage and packing, depending on the size of the items, how heavy they are and how many you are buying.

Practice, practice, practice!

Stan's formulae

Stan the café owner is planning to go on holiday and wants to leave instructions for his staff. He needs to make sure that he has written (or derived) formulae for all the jobs in the café.

Level 5

5c I can derive simple formulae using algebra

1 Some formulae depend on the number of customers, C.
Stan has made up these formulae based on estimates.
For each item, find how many are needed for 75 customers and for C customers.

The number of bottles of milk used is 10 less than the number of customers.

Number of bottles for 75 customers = 75 – 10 = 65
Number of bottles for C customers = C – 10

a The number of napkins needed is 21 more than the number of customers.
b The number of teabags used is 9 more than the number of customers.
c The number of spoons is 18 more than the number of customers.

Hint: Remember to start each formula with 'number of … =' or choose a letter!

2 Many formulae for setting up each day depend on the number of tables, T.
For each item, work out the number needed for 10 tables and for T tables.

a The number of water jugs is two less than the number of tables.
b The number of centre plates is five more than the number of tables.
c The number of menus is 10 more than the number of tables.
d Each table needs four chairs.
e Each table needs two sauces.
f Each table needs five mats.

5b I can derive formula using algebra

3 The number of customers is given by C. For each item, work out how many are needed for 80 customers and for C customers.

a The number of pieces of cutlery is 3 times the number of customers.
b The number of cups needed is half the number of customers.
c The number of mugs needed is half the number of customers plus four extra.

algebra derive expression

4 The breakfast special is made up of two eggs, one sausage, three rashers of bacon and 10 mushrooms.

a Work out how many of each are needed for 50 breakfasts.

b Write a formula for the number of each item for b breakfasts.

Hint: Remember to choose a letter for the variable and then write it in the formula, e.g. E is the number of eggs needed.

5 The number of pieces of chicken cooked for an order depends on the number of meals and whether they are for adults or children.
There are three pieces in an adult's meal and two pieces in a child's meal.

a Work out the number of pieces needed for

i four adult's meals **ii** five child's meals.

b Work out a formula for the number of pieces needed for

i a adult's meals **ii** c child's meals

iii a adult meals and two child's meals.

6 The tips are shared out equally among all the staff.

a The tips total £85 and there are five staff. How much does each person get?

b Work out a formula for the tips each person gets for each of these.

i five staff, £X in tips **ii** four staff, £X in tips

iii s staff, £90 in tips **iv** s staff, £112 in tips

v s staff, £X in tips

7 A 'Stan Special' is a cup of tea and a bun.

a The price of a cup of tea is 30p and of a bun is 45p.
What is the price of a 'Stan Special'?

b Write a formula for the price of a 'Stan Special' if the price of a cup of tea is t pence and of a bun is b pence.

c Write a formula for the price of a 'Super Stan Special' – two buns and a cup of tea.

d Write a formula for the change for the 'Stan Special' in **b** from £1.

Hint: Turn £1 into pence.

Level 5

5b I can derive formulae using algebra

5a I can derive more complicated formulae using algebra

Now try this!

A Picnic

Imagine that you are organising a picnic.

1 What will each person eat? How much of each type of food will you need?

2 Write some rules to work out how much of each item to take to the picnic.

B Tables and chairs

Carly wants to introduce a new arrangement for the chairs and tables.

a Copy and complete the table.

Number of tables, T	Number of chairs, C
1	
2	
3	
4	

b Write a formula for the number of chairs when there are T tables.

formula variable

17.8 Using and solving equations

➪ Construct and solve simple linear equations using inverse operations

Why learn this?

You can use and solve an equation to find the average speed of a racing car from the distance travelled round a lap and the time taken to do the lap.

What's the BIG idea?

→ You can use **algebra** to describe an amount by building an **expression**. By setting this equal to a number you can form an **equation**, which can be **solved**. **Level 5**

David pays for a mug of tea and gives the staff a 10p tip. This totals 53p. Use t to stand for the price of a mug of tea.

$t + 10 = 53$
$t + 10 - 10 = 53 - 10$ subtract 10 from both sides
$t = 43$

So the price of a mug of tea is 43p.

Practice, practice, practice!

Simon and Carly's equations

While Stan, the café owner, is away on holiday, his staff have lost the price list. To help them some of the regular customers have remembered how much they used to pay for items.
To work out the price of each item Simon and Carly construct some equations using algebra and solve them to find the prices.

Level 5

5b I can solve simple linear equations

1 Carly has constructed these equations about the prices of the fruit. Solve each equation to find the price of each piece of fruit, where a is the price of an apple, b is the price of a banana, c is the price of a bag of cherries, g is the price of a bunch of grapes, k is the price of a kiwi, m is the price of a piece of melon, n is the price of a nectarine, and p is the price of a peach.

a $a + 12 = 60$ **b** $b - 6 = 22$ **c** $c + 5 = 85$ **d** $100 - g = 20$
e $2m = 64$ **f** $3k = 45$ **g** $6n = 90$ **h** $\frac{1}{2}p = 25$

2 Simon has constructed these equations about the prices of drinks. Solve each to find the price of a drink, where t is the price of a cup of tea, c is the price of a cup of coffee, l is the price of lemonade, o is the price of orange squash, and j is the price of juice.

a $t + 5 = 30$ **b** $c - 8 = 32$ **c** $50 - l = 22$
d $6o = 90$ **e** $3j = £1.20$

5a I can solve simple two-step linear equations

3 Mr Jones says that three cookies (price c pence each) and a 10p chocolate bar cost 85p. Carly writes this as an equation, $3c + 10 = 85$.
Solve this to find the price of a cookie.

algebra equation expression

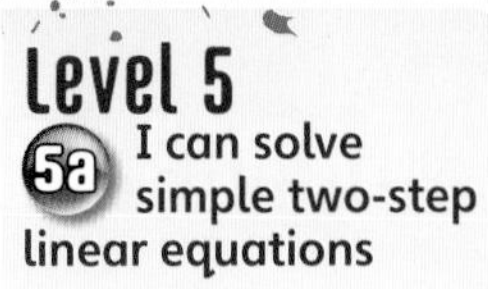

Level 5

5a I can solve simple two-step linear equations

4 Ahmed says that the price of two meat pies (price m pence each) less 25p is 145p. Carly writes the equation $2m - 25 = 145$.
Solve this to find the price of a meat pie.

5 Solve the rest of Carly's equations to find the price of these other items.
b is the price of a rasher of bacon, e is the price of an egg, h is the price of a hash brown, k is the price of a ketchup sachet, s is the price of a sausage, and t is the price of a piece of toast.

a $2b + 7 = 37$ **b** $4s + 25 = 109$ **c** $5e - 12 = 48$

d $8t + 10 = 58$ **e** $3h - 17 = 46$ **f** $12k + 4 = 40$

6 Solve these equations that Simon wrote. c is the price of a chocolate bar, f is the price of a fruit chew, l is the price of a lemon sparkle, m is the price of a mint chew, s is the price of sparkle dust, and t is the price of a toffee stick.

a $6 + 2c = 72$ **b** $5f + 12 = 57$ **c** $18 + 4l = 62$

d $7m - 21 = 42$ **e** $65 - 3s = 14$ **f** $17 + 3t = 35$

7 Solve these equations.

a $5x + 17 = 62$ **b** $17 - 2x = 3$ **c** $8x - 41 = 39$

d $16 + 4x = 26$ **e** $52 = 6x + 16$ **f** $27 = 5x - 3$

5a I can construct and solve a simple equation

8 The price of three iced buns is 63p.

a Construct an equation to find the price of an iced bun, i.

b Solve the equation.

9 12p more than the price of four biscuits is 88p.

a Construct an equation to find the price of a biscuit, b.

b Solve the equation.

10 The price of five fruit slices less 15p is 90p.
Construct and solve an equation to find the price of a fruit slice, f.

11 The price of three orange cookies and a 35p cup of tea is 65p.
Construct and solve an equation to find the price of an orange cookie, o.

Now try this!

A Café word formulae

1 Write down five items that you could find in the café and choose a price for each item. Do not show your partner.
2 Now write clues or word equations for the price of each item.
3 Challenge your partner to solve them.

B Café algebra

1 Write down five items that you could find in the café and choose a price for each item. Do not show your partner.
2 For each item choose a letter to stand for its price.
3 Construct some equations for your partner to solve.

solve variable

Unit 17 plenary

Games and entertainment

Sports clubs need to charge for tickets. They may also raise money in other ways.

1 Minchester United are trying to raise extra money. They sell 'where's the ball' game cards for £2 each. To play, you guess where the ball will be when the whistle blows for half time. The closest one wins a prize.
These are some of the guesses:
Baz A6   Tim F3   Eve C4   Casey D9   Kes H7

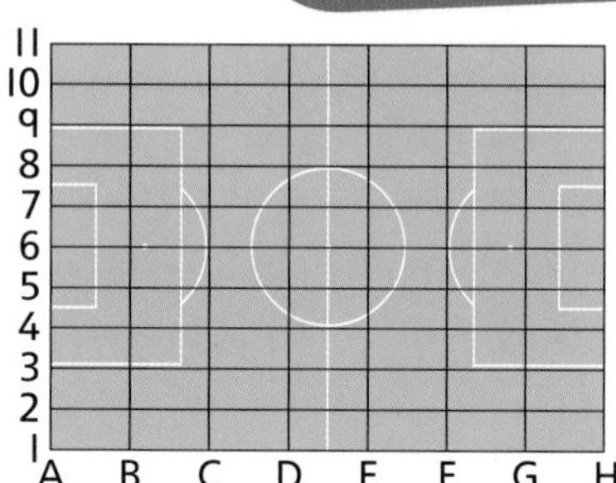

a Copy the grid. Mark the guesses on the grid.

b When the whistle blows the ball is close to E7.
Who wins the prize? **Level 3**

2 Minchester United charge £8 for an adult ticket.
They use this formula to work out the amount they take for adult tickets:
amount taken = number of adults × 8

a Use the formula to complete this table.

Number of tickets	0	10	50	100
Amount taken (£)	0			

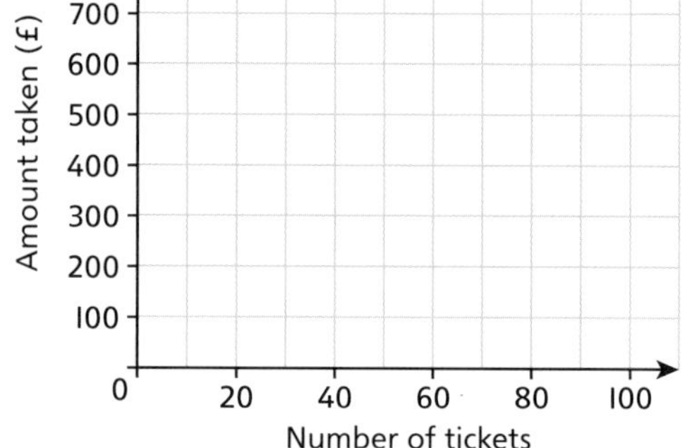

b Copy these axes.
Plot the points from the table of values on the graph. Join them with a straight line.

c One Saturday Minchester United takes £520 from adult ticket sales.
Find how many adult tickets they sold. **Level 4**

3 Minchester United charges £3 for an under-16 ticket.

a Write a formula for the amount they take for child tickets.

b Use your formula to work out the amount taken for
i 10 under-16 tickets
ii 50 under-16 tickets
iii 100 under-16 tickets.

c One Saturday the club takes £240 for under-16 tickets.
Substitute this amount into your formula from part **a** to give an equation.
Solve the equation to find the number of under-16 tickets they sold.

d The ticket office uses this equation for ticket sales:

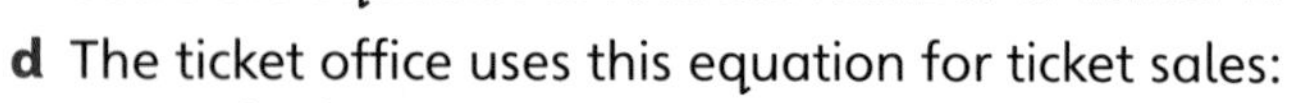

Total taken = $8a + 3u$

where a = number of adult tickets and u = number of under-16 tickets.
One Thursday they take £1170 for tickets. £210 is for under-16 tickets.
Substitute these values into the equation.
Solve the equation to find the number of adult tickets sold. **Level 5**

The BIG ideas

- → When you work with **algebra**, use the same rules as you would use with arithmetic. **Level 4**
- → An **expression** has no equals sign, e.g. $2a + 6$. **Level 4**
- → A **formula** or an **equation** has an equals sign in it, e.g. cost $= 2a + 6$ or $2a + 6 = 14$ **Level 4**
- → You can find the next term of a **sequence** either by drawing the next shape or by finding how much it goes up by each time. **Level 4**
- → When reading **coordinates**, always start at 0 and read across first and then up or down. **Level 4**
- → You can use **conversion graphs** to convert between one unit and another. **Level 5**
- → You can use a **formula** to describe how to work out an amount that depends on a **variable**. **Level 5**
- → You can use algebra to describe an amount by building an expression. By setting this equal to a number you form an equation, which can be solved. **Level 5**
- → You can solve equations using **inverse operations**. For example, to solve $3r = 15$, you use the inverse operation 'divide 15 by 3' to get the answer $r = 5$. **Level 5**

Find your level

Level 3

Q1 This block of lockers has 5 rows.

Row 1	1	6	11
Row 2	2	7	
Row 3	3	8	
Row 4	4	9	
Row 5	5	10	

- **a** In which row is locker number 26?
- **b** In which row is locker number 32?
- **c** In which row is locker number 44?
- **d** Lockers 2 and 7 are in row 2. Write the numbers of three more lockers in row 2.
- **e** Write the numbers of the lockers that will be on the left and right of locker 48.

Level 4

Q2 Ameet puts square tiles on a large grid. The tiles touch at the corners, as shown in the diagram.

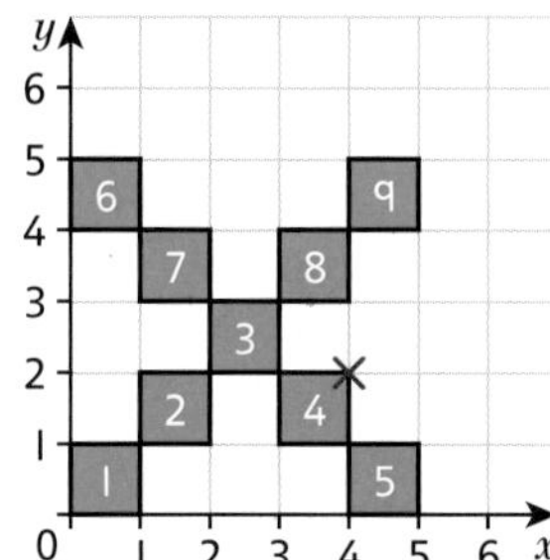

- **a** The top right-hand corner of tile 4 is marked with a cross. Write the coordinates of this point.
- **b** Tile 7 touches two other tiles. Write the coordinates of the points where tile 7 touches two other tiles.

Level 5

Q3 Deeveedee is a company selling DVDs over the internet. The delivery charges are shown on the graph.

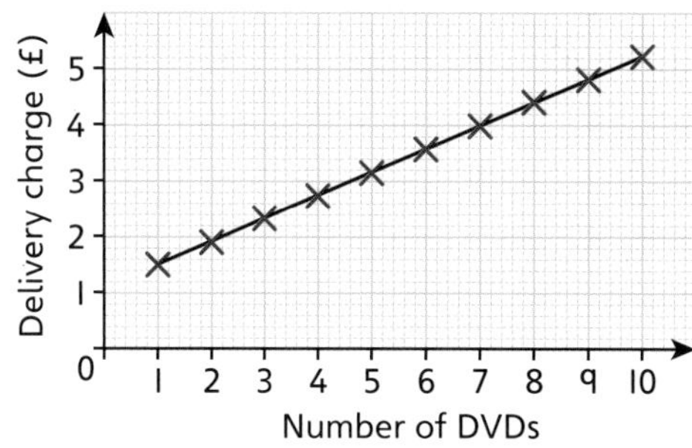

- **a** What is the delivery charge for
  - **i** 7 DVDs
  - **ii** 8 DVDs?
- **b** For every extra DVD you buy, how much more must you pay for delivery?
- **c** Orinoco is another company selling DVDs over the internet. Its delivery charge is £1.00 per DVD. Draw a graph to show this information.
- **d** You buy five DVDs. Which company is cheaper for delivery?

18 Getting into shape

This unit is about constructing shapes and understanding their properties in terms of angles, sides and symmetry.

The Great Pyramid of Giza, in Egypt, is about 4500 years old. It is the oldest built structure on Earth and the only surviving Wonder of the ancient world. It was the tallest structure on Earth for thousands of years until overtaken by Lincoln Cathedral.

It was 147 m high, but it is now 139 m because its top was removed. The faces of the pyramid are at an angle of about 52° to the ground, which is about the same as a natural mountain. Each side of the square base measures 231 m. It was so well constructed that the sides are accurate to within 20 cm.

Activities

A Use Resource sheet 18.0

- Measure each angle and write it on the diagram.
- Cut the net out and make it into a pyramid.

B To protect the Great Pyramid, planes are banned from flying over it. Imagine you could fly over it. What would you see?

Sketch a bird's eye view of the pyramid from above.

The Great Pyramid was originally covered in polished limestone slabs. These were removed and used for other building projects in later centuries.

Unit opener

Did you know?

A more recent pyramid is the main glass pyramid at the Louvre Museum in Paris. It is 21.6 m high, and it is made from 673 glass panes – 603 rhombuses and 70 triangles.

Before you start this unit...

1 Cut out four identical obtuse-angled triangles:

page 214

What two shapes can you form by putting two of the triangles together?

2 Which colour triangles can the blue triangle be

page 222

a reflected onto

b translated onto

c rotated onto?

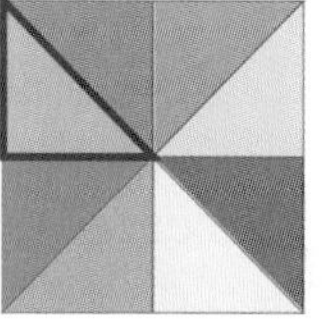

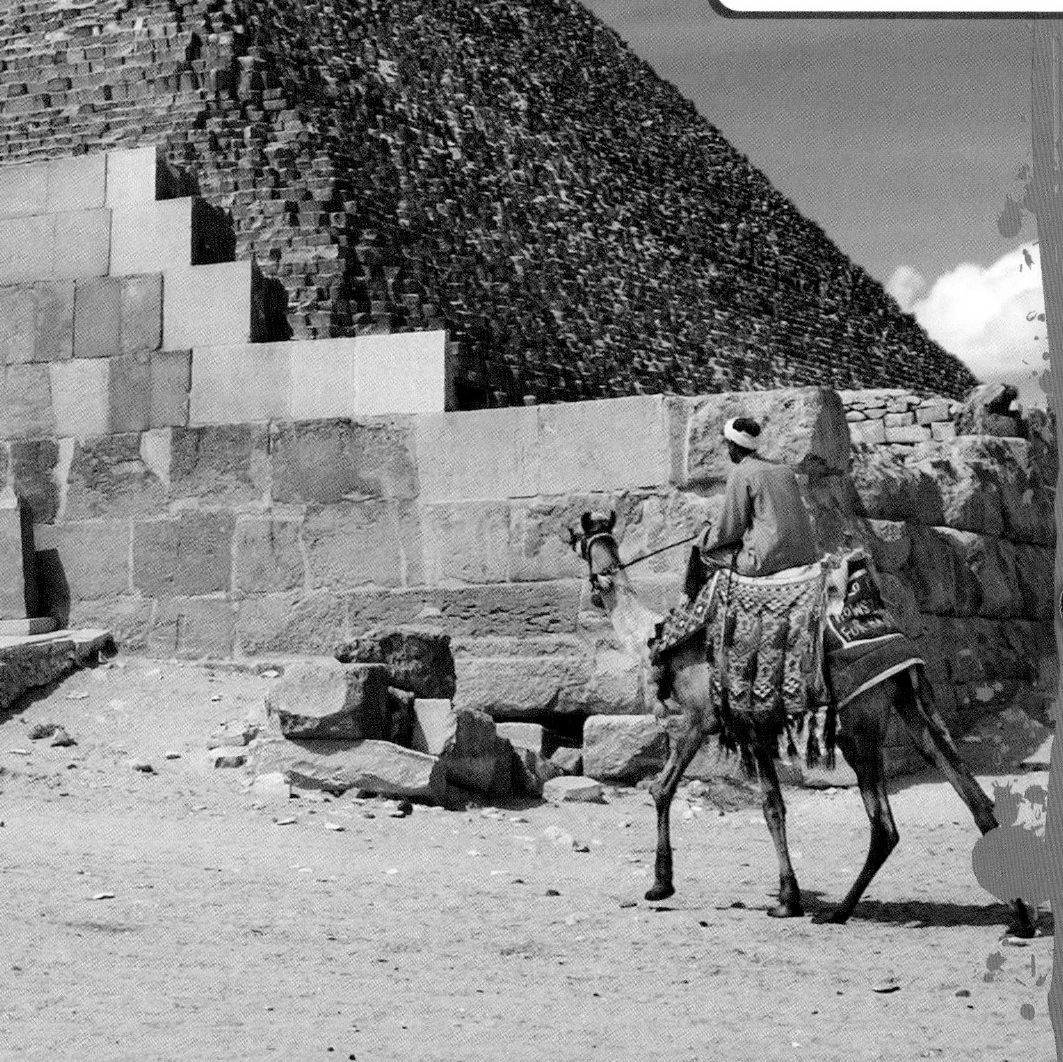

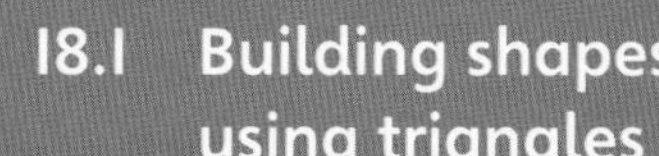

Plus digital resources

18.1 Building shapes using triangles

- Identify types of triangle and quadrilateral and know their basic properties
- Calculate angles around a point
- Calculate angles in a triangle
- Using angle facts to work out the angles of a quadrilateral

What's the BIG idea?

- An isosceles triangle has two equal sides and two equal angles. **Level 4**
- All lines from the **centre** to the **circumference** of a **circle** are equal in length. Each one of these is called a **radius**. **Level 4**
- The angles in a triangle add up to 180°. **Level 5**
- The angles around a **point** add up to 360°. If a circle is divided into eight equal sectors, divide 360° by 8 to find the angle at the centre of each one. **Level 5**
- You can identify **quadrilaterals** (square, rectangle, rhombus, parallelogram, kite, arrowhead (or delta) and trapezium) from their properties. **Level 5**
- If two triangles are joined together to make a quadrilateral, the angles touching each other add together to give two of the angles of the new shape. **Level 5**

Why learn this?

Many designs, like the Palace of Westminster Clock Tower, are based on the symmetry properties of shapes.

Super fact!

The Palace of Westminster Clock Tower is often mistakenly known as Big Ben. Big Ben is actually the name of the main bell housed within the Clock Tower.

Practice, practice, practice!

Level 4

4a I can identify simple angle, side and symmetry properties of triangles

1 Describe the green triangle.

It is an isosceles triangle.

a Describe the red and the blue triangles.

b Describe any equal sides, equal angles or lines of symmetry for each of the three triangles.

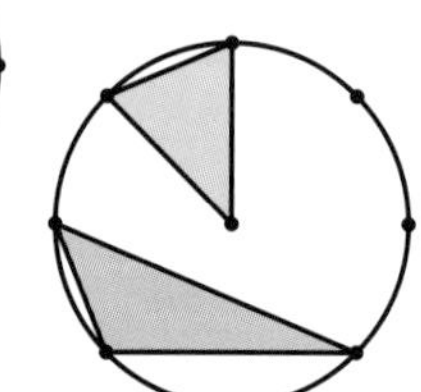

4a I can identify isosceles triangles by looking for equal sides

2 **a** Copy this diagram onto Resource Sheet 18.1.

b Fill the rest of the regular octagon with triangles. Each of your triangles must join three black dots. Write 'I' inside each isosceles triangle.

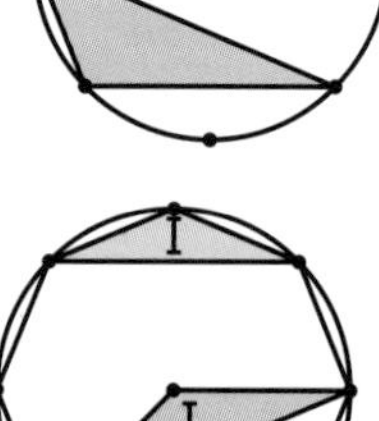

Level 5

5c I can identify quadrilaterals using simple angle, side and symmetry properties

3 **a** Write down the name of the blue shape.

b Using Resource Sheet 18.1, make as many different quadrilaterals as you can by joining four black dots.

c Name each quadrilateral.

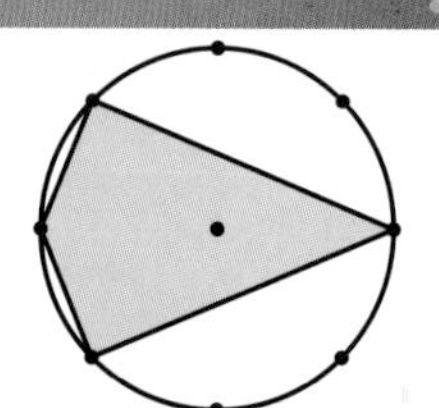

centre | circle | circumference | geometric | isosceles | octagon

4 Work out the angles in the blue triangle.

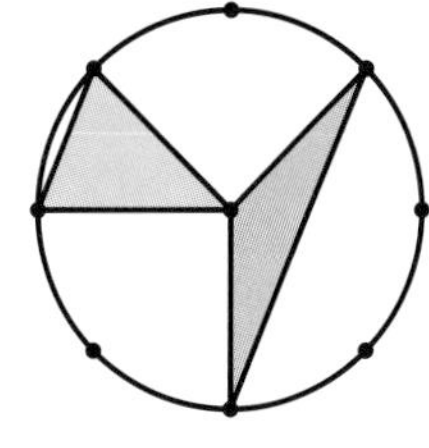

Angle at centre = 360° ÷ 8 = 45°
Sum of remaining angles = 180° – 45° = 135°
(angles in a triangle add up to 180°)
Each remaining angle = 135° ÷ 2 = 67.5°
(triangle is isosceles so remaining two angles are the same)
Angles of the blue triangle are 67.5°, 67.5° and 45°.

Work out the angles in the pink triangle.

5 **a** Name the quadrilateral formed by the two triangles. Explain how you can tell.

b Use the calculation of the angles in the blue triangle in Q4 to help you work out the angles of the quadrilateral.

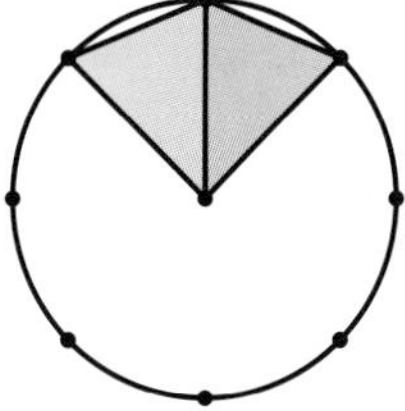

6 **a** Explain how you know that this shape is an arrowhead.

b Work out its angles. Use your calculation of the angles in the pink triangle in Q4 to help you.

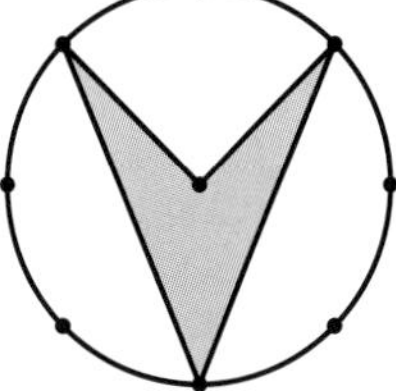

7 **a** Copy this pentagon onto Resource Sheet 18.1.

b Work out the angles in each triangle and write them on your diagram.

c Use your answers to part **b** to help you work out the angles in the pentagon. Write them on your diagram.

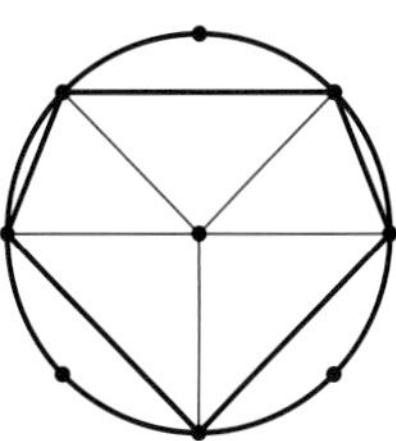

Level 5

5b I can calculate angles around a point and in a triangle

5a I can solve geometric problems using side and angle properties of isosceles triangles

Now try this!

A Octagon divisions

1 Using Resource Sheet 18.1, join the outside black dots to make a regular octagon.
2 Fill this octagon with shapes. Join any of the black dots to form a shape. Your shapes must not overlap.
3 Name each shape. Score 1 point for each different shape. Compare your drawing with a partner's. Who scored the most points? For example, this set of shapes would score 5 points.

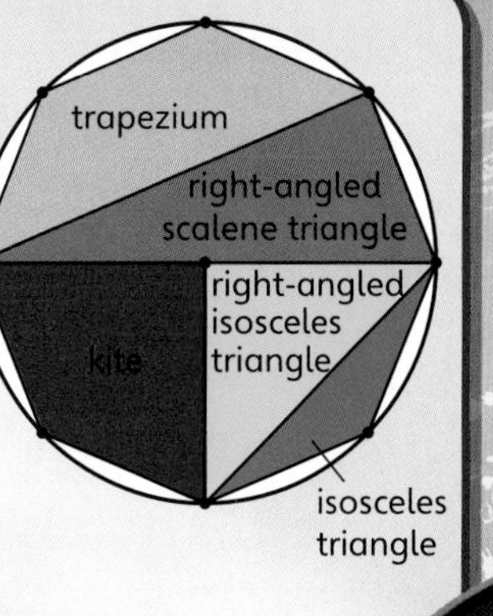

B Angle finds

1 Using Resource Sheet 18.1, draw a quadrilateral by joining four black dots. One dot must be the central one.
2 Split your quadrilateral into two triangles and work out all their angles.
3 Work out the angles of your quadrilateral.

Tip

To work out the properties of a quadrilateral, see if it can be split into two identical triangles. This helps you to see which sides are equal and which angles are equal.

pentagon point quadrilateral radius scalene triangle

18.2 Using ICT to understand reflection

- Use ICT to reflect shapes
- Identify equal sides and equal angles of shapes made by reflection
- Use ICT to position an object or the line of reflection to create a given effect
- Use ICT to create given shapes using reflection

Why learn this?

Dynamic geometry software helps you understand how to construct patterns and allows you to experiment. By predicting 'what would happen if...' you will learn more about reflections.

What's the BIG idea?

- Dynamic geometry software lets you draw and reflect a shape. **Level 4**
- Drag the line of **reflection** towards the object to make the **object** and **image** closer. Drag the line of reflection away from the object to make the object and image further apart. **Level 4**
- You can use one side of a triangle as a mirror line and reflect the triangle to make an isosceles triangle, a square, a kite, a rhombus or an arrowhead. The end shape depends on the type of triangle and the side used. **Level 5**
- You can change the shape formed by a triangle reflected in one of its sides to any of the shapes listed above by dragging a **vertex** of the original triangle. **Level 5**
- You can make patterns by reflecting a shape in a line and then reflecting both the object and the image in at least one other line. **Level 5**

Practice, practice, practice!

Level 4

4b I can use ICT to reflect shapes

1 Use dynamic geometry software to
  a draw a triangle
  b draw a reflection line down the centre of your screen
  c reflect the triangle in the line.

4b I can describe how to drag the line of reflection to have a given effect

2 What do you need to do to the reflection line in QI to make the triangles
  a further apart b closer together c overlap one another?

Level 5

5c I can create shapes by reflecting a triangle

3 How can you can create these shapes by reflecting a triangle?

a square *Reflect a right-angled isosceles triangle like this.*

  a a kite **b** an arrowhead

Hint: Use squared paper to help you.

image object

4 **a** Create a new file.
b Draw a triangle.
c Reflect the triangle in one of its sides.
d Drag one of the vertices of your original triangle to make a new shape.
e Sketch and name each different shape as you make it.
f Mark equal sides on your sketch with dashes.
g Draw in the line of symmetry.
h Use the symmetry to help you colour equal angles the same colour.

5 **a** Construct a triangle in a new file.
b Reflect the triangle in one of its sides.
c Find a triangle which can make a kite by reflecting in one of its sides.
d Find a triangle which can make a kite by reflecting in one of its sides and an arrowhead by reflecting in a different side.
e Sketch each shape, showing the line of symmetry.

6 **a** Construct a triangle and line of reflection like this.

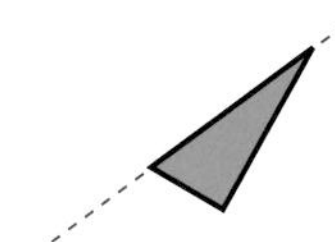

b Use reflection to build up your shape like this.

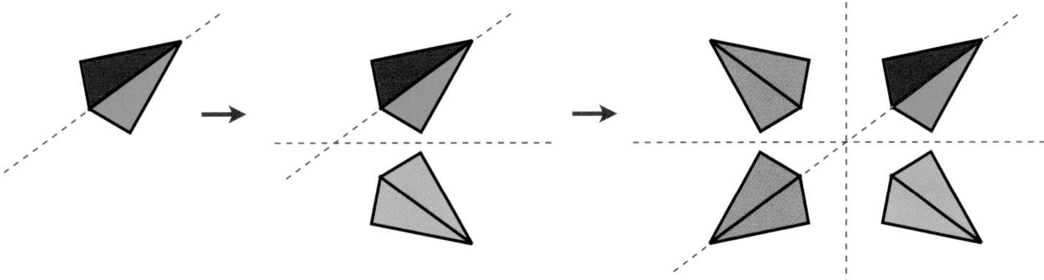

c Predict what will happen if you drag a vertex of the original triangle. Now try it. Were you right?
d Predict what will happen if you drag one of the lines of reflection. Now try it. Were you right?

Level 5

5c I can identify angle, side and symmetry properties of simple quadrilaterals

5b I can use ICT to create given shapes using reflection

Now try this!

A Face up to reflections

Construct half a face using dynamic geometry software. Use reflection to complete the face.

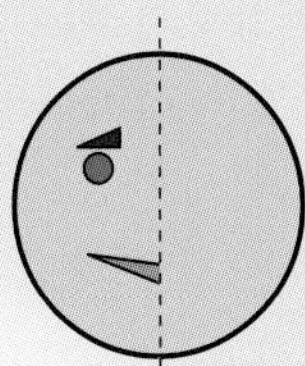

B Card reflections

Using reflection, design a pattern for a greeting card which has rotational symmetry of order 4.

Watch out!

All patterns with rotational symmetry can be made by repeatedly rotating a shape. Some (but not all) of these patterns can also be made by reflection, depending on whether the pattern also has reflection symmetry.

reflection vertex

18.3 Understanding triangles and quadrilaterals

- Recognise different transformations
- Solve problems using properties of triangles
- Make quadrilaterals with two pairs of equal sides from two identical triangles by reflecting or rotating one of the triangles
- Identify equal sides and angles of a quadrilateral by splitting it into triangles and use these to solve problems

Why learn this?

Building shapes using identical triangles helps you to understand how the properties of quadrilaterals can be linked to the transformations of triangles.

What's the BIG idea?

- All **quadrilaterals** with two pairs of equal sides can be made from two identical triangles. **Level 4**
- A square, kite, rhombus or arrowhead can be made by reflecting a triangle in one of its sides. **Level 5**
- A square, rectangle, rhombus or parallelogram can be made from a triangle and a rotation of it. **Level 5**
- An equilateral triangle has three angles of 60°. **Level 5**
- To find the angles of a quadrilateral formed by joining two triangles, add the angles which are joined together – the other angles stay the same. **Level 5**

Super fact!

Kites were invented in China about 1000 BC.

Practice, practice, practice!

Level 4

4a I can identify and use simple angle and side properties of triangles

1 Cut out a 6 cm by 8 cm rectangle
Cut it in half into two triangles.

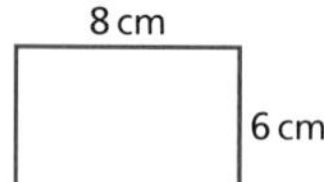

a What is the largest angle in each of your triangles?

b Are these triangles equilateral, isosceles or scalene? Explain your answer.

c Work out the perimeter of one of your triangles.

Hint: You will need to measure the longest side.

4a I can recognise where a shape will be after a translation and I can solve problems using properties of triangles

2 The large triangle has sides of length 6 cm, 8 cm and 10 cm. It is made from four identical triangles.

a What are the side lengths of the small triangles?

b Find the perimeter of one small triangle.

c Which colour triangles can the orange triangle be translated onto?

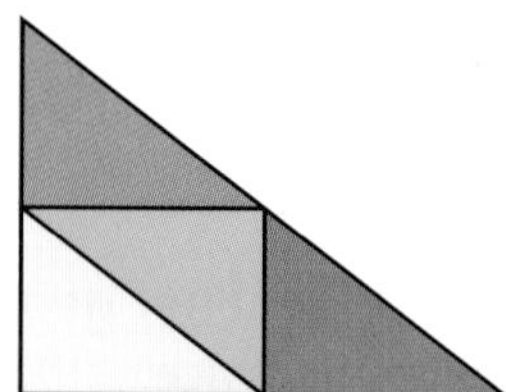

Level 5

5c I can identify angle, side and symmetry properties of quadrilaterals

3 a Copy this right-angled triangle.

b Reflect it in the mirror line.

c What shape is formed by the combined object and image?

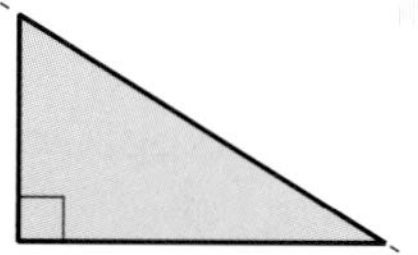

geometrical property quadrilateral

4 This kite is made of two identical triangles.

Calculate the angle

a *CBA*

b *CDB*

c *CDA*

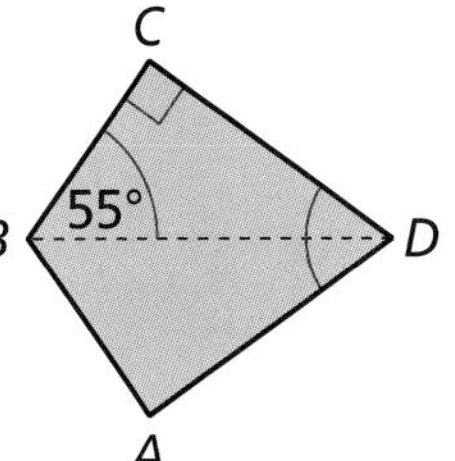

Level 5

5b I can solve simple geometrical problems involving reasoning

5 **a** Work out the top angle in the triangle on the right.

b The quadrilaterals have been made from triangles identical to this one. Sketch each shape. Show where the triangles are joined. Work out the angles of the quadrilateral and mark them on your sketch.

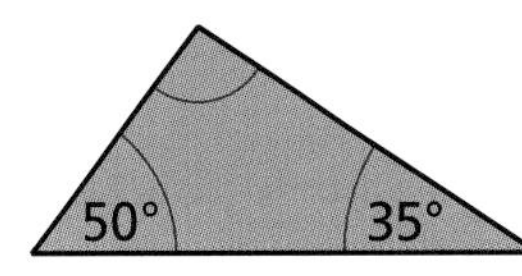

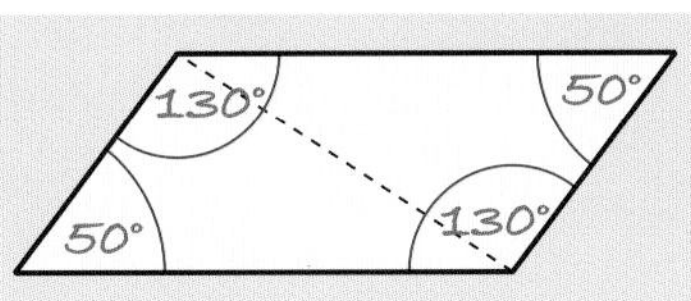

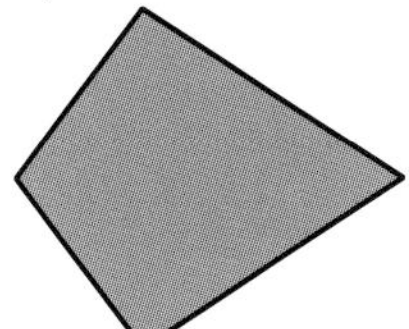

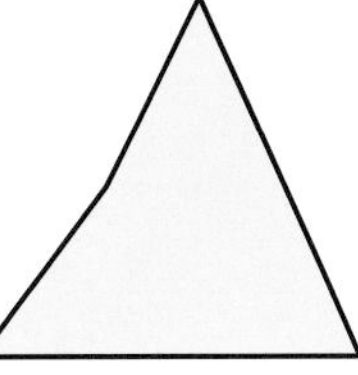

c Which two of these quadrilaterals have the same perimeter? How can you tell?

Tip

Where two angles come together to form a new angle, the new angle is the sum of the other two angles. So if they are the same you only need to double one of them.

6 **a** I join two equilateral triangles. Each triangle has a perimeter of 18 cm. Sketch and name the quadrilateral formed. Work out its angles and write them inside. What is the perimeter of the quadrilateral?

b I join an equilateral triangle with an isosceles right-angled triangle as shown.

Sketch the shape and write in its angles.

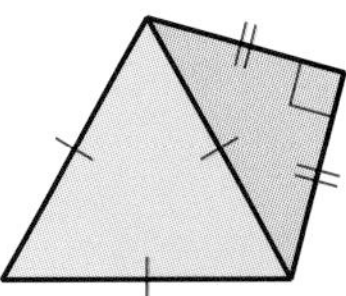

5a I can use side and angle properties of equilateral and isosceles triangles to solve geometrical problems

Now try this!

A Triangle trios

1. Cut out six rectangles 3 cm by 4 cm.
2. Cut each rectangle into two triangles so that you have 12 identical triangles.
3. Make as many different shapes as you can using three triangles for each shape. You may only join sides together that are the same length.
4. Name each of your shapes. This one is done for you.

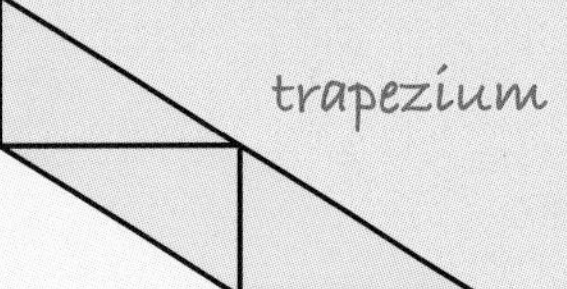

B Split the quadrilateral

1. Cut out two identical triangles.
2. Make a quadrilateral by joining them together, then draw around it.
3. Swap drawings with a partner.
   Divide each other's quadrilaterals into two identical triangles.
4. Estimate the angles in the triangle. (Your estimates must add up to 180°.)
5. Now calculate the estimated angles of the quadrilaterals.
6. Measure the angles to see how good your estimates are.

MATHEMATICAL ORIGAMI

折り紙

Swan shape-spotting

This is an unfolded paper swan.

- How many types of triangles and quadrilaterals can you find in the folds?

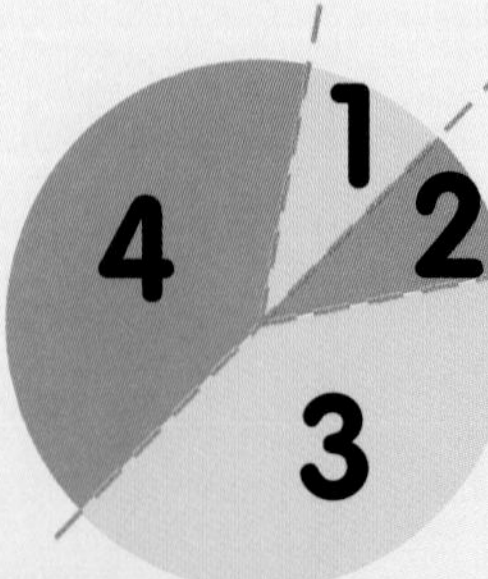

Kawasaki's theorem

Kawasaki's theorem is a rule about angles in origami.

Number the angles about one point on an origami crease pattern. If you add up all the odd-numbered angles about this point, they total 180°.

- Why must the same thing happen if you add up all the even-numbered angles?
- Use a protractor to check the rule on this diagram, or on some unfolded origami of your own.

ORIGAMI – THE ART OF FOLDING PAPER TO MAKE 3-D SHAPES – IS AN ANCIENT PASTIME FROM CHINA AND JAPAN WITH A LOT OF MATHEMATICS BEHIND IT.

The origami cube

With six squares of paper, you can make your own origami cube. Each square makes one of the six faces of the cube.

1 Fold the side edges in to meet at the middle. Unfold.

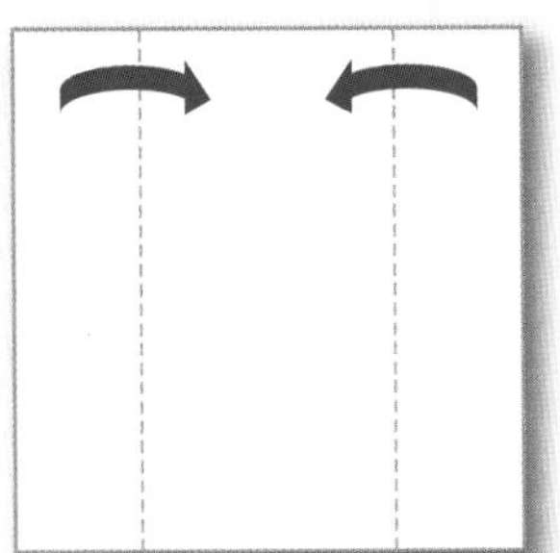

2 Fold the top and bottom edges so that they meet in the middle. Do not unfold.

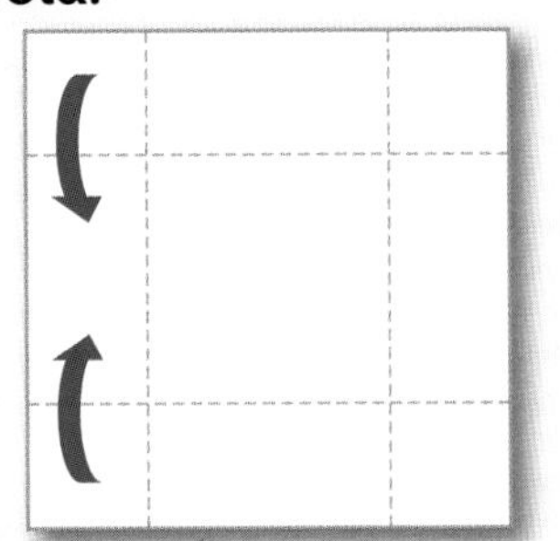

3 Fold along the lines you made in step 1 to make a 'C' shape that stands up on its own.

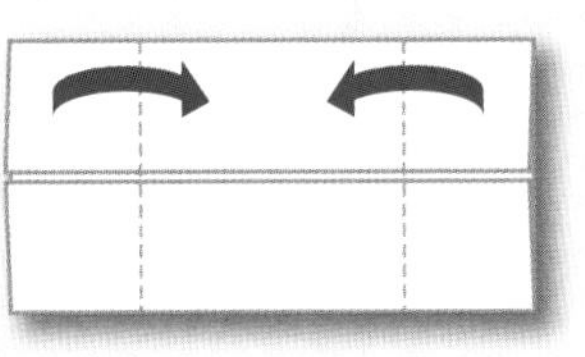

4 Make six of these 'C' shapes. Slot the first two together.

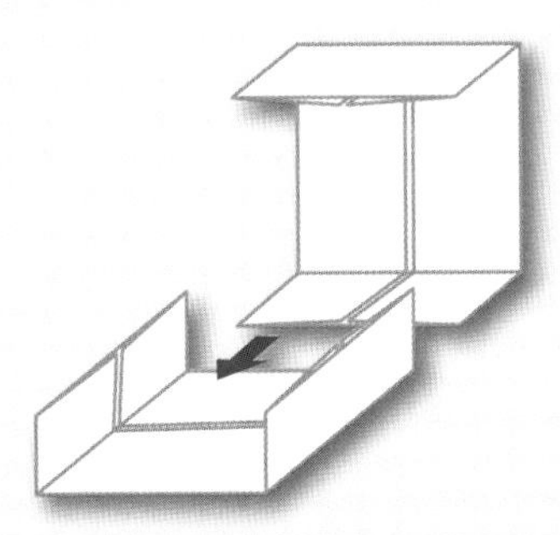

5 Add a third 'C' shape.

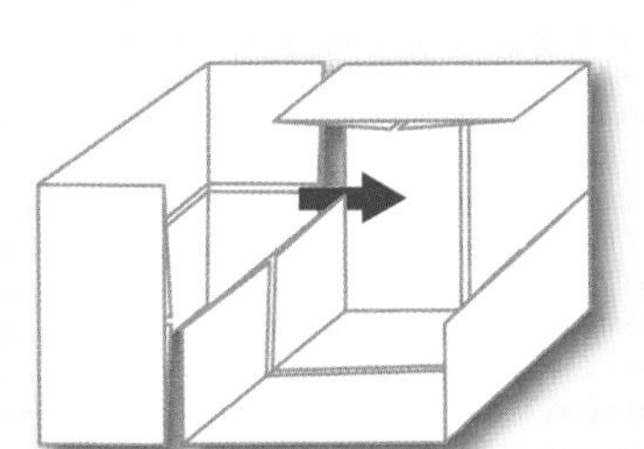

6 In the same way, slot the remaining three 'C' shapes into position to complete the cube.

Origami can create many other mathematical shapes – can you find out how to make any others?

18.4 Cubes and other 3-D shapes

- Describe 3-D shapes, using the correct vocabulary
- Recognise nets that fold up to make a complete cube
- Recognise 3-D shapes from 2-D drawings

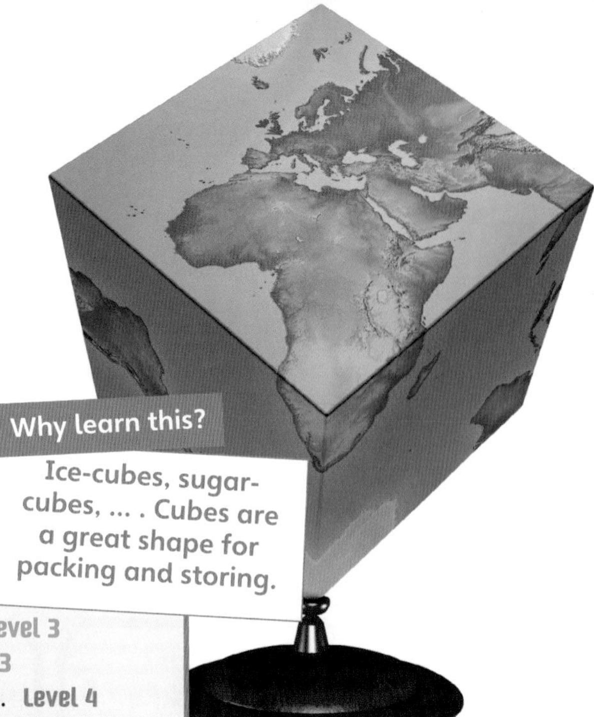

Why learn this?

Ice-cubes, sugar-cubes, ... Cubes are a great shape for packing and storing.

What's the BIG idea?

- Solids are described using the words **face**, **edge** and **vertex**. Level 3
- A **cube** has six square faces, eight vertices and 12 edges. Level 3
- Not every arrangement of six squares folds up to make a cube. Level 4
- A **cuboid** has three pairs of rectangular faces. Level 4
- A **cylinder** has two circular faces and one curved surface. Level 4
- A **sphere** has one curved surface. Level 4
- A **hemisphere** has one circular face and one curved surface. Level 4
- A **pyramid** has a base; all the other faces meet at one vertex. Level 4
- A **tetrahedron** has four triangular faces. Level 4
- A **prism** has two identical faces that are parallel. Level 4

Super fact!

Crystals of sodium chloride (common salt) can be perfect cubes.

Practice, practice, practice!

Level 3

3a I can describe a cube, correctly using the words 'face', 'edge' and 'vertex'

The diagram shows the net of a cube.

C D
A B 2 E F G
1 3 5 6
N M 4 J I H
L K

1 Which faces meet along the edge *BM* in the diagram?

Faces 1 and 3 meet along edge BM.

Which faces meet at *A*?

Faces 1, 2 and 6 meet at vertex A.

a Copy and complete each sentence by identifying the faces that meet along the edge.

i Faces ________ and ________ meet along edge *EF*.

ii Faces ________ and ________ meet along edge *AN*.

iii Faces ________ and ________ meet along edge *LM*.

iv Faces ________ and ________ meet along edge *FG*.

Hint: Make and label your own net to help you answer these questions.

b Which faces meet at i *B* ii *E* iii *F*?

c Letters *A*, *C* and *G* meet at the same vertex. Which two letters meet with *H*?

Level 4

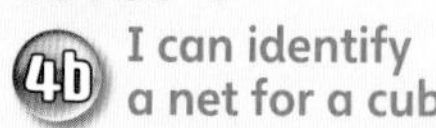

4b I can identify a net for a cube

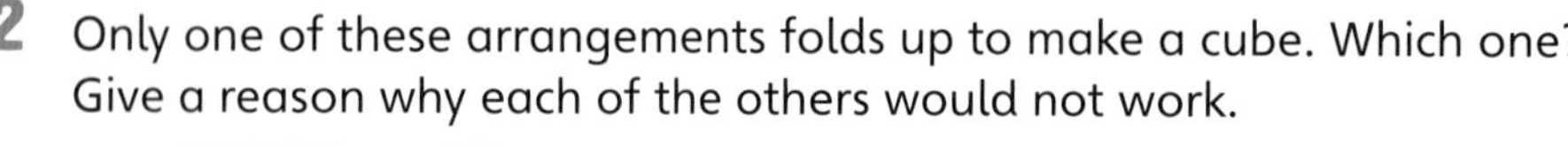

2 Only one of these arrangements folds up to make a cube. Which one? Give a reason why each of the others would not work.

A 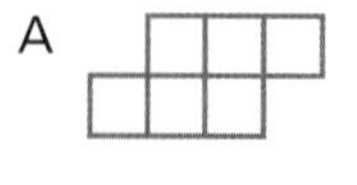 B  C  D 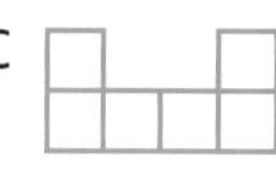 E 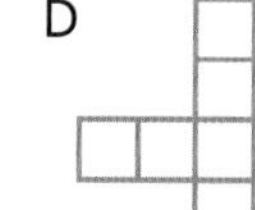 F 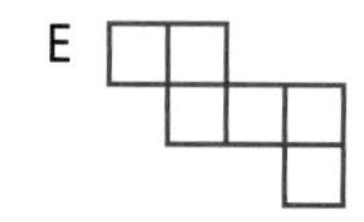

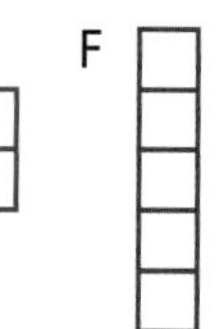

cube cuboid cylinder edge face hemisphere prism

3 Copy and complete the table to describe each of these 3-D shapes.

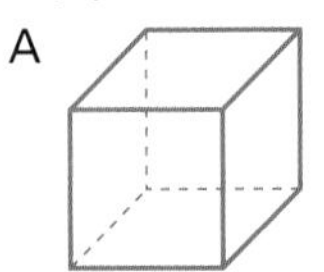
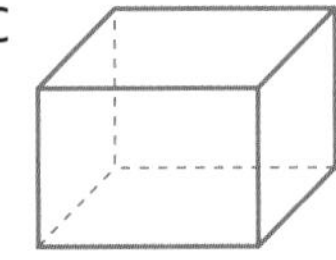
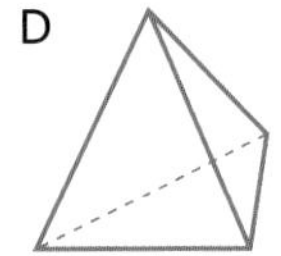
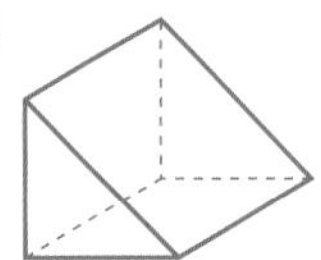

Name of shape	Number of faces	Number of edges	Number of vertices
A			
B			

Level 4

4b I can describe 3-D shapes, correctly using the words 'face', 'edge' and 'vertex'

4 Which of these shapes are prisms?

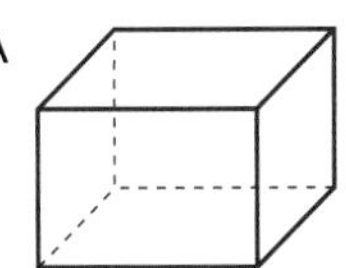
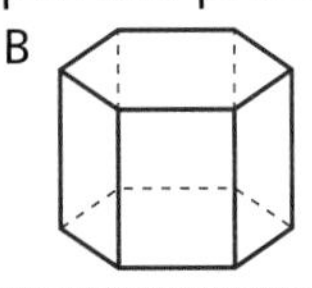
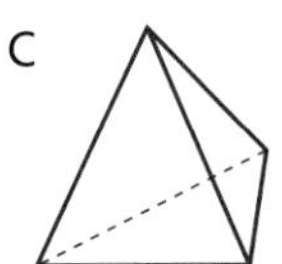
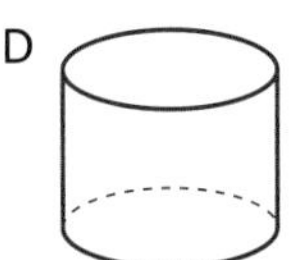

4b I can identify 3-D shapes

5 Sketch the solids in Q3 when seen

a from above **b** from the front.

5c I can identify plan elevations

6 This is a net of a cuboid that is 6 cm wide, 3 cm high and 4 deep.

The area of face A is $6 \times 3 = 18\text{ cm}^2$.

a What is the area of face B?

b What is the area of face C?

c Use these answers to help you calculate the total surface area of the cuboid.

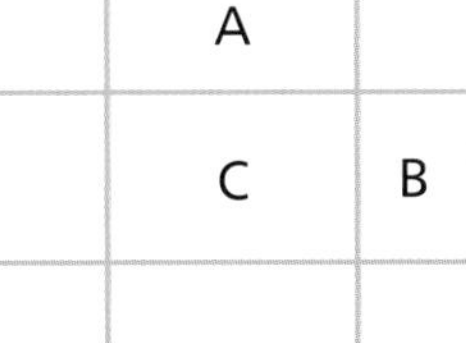

5b I can use nets to help me calculate the surface area of a cuboid

7 Calculate

a the surface area of a 3 cm cube.

b the surface area of a cuboid with height 5 cm, width 4 cm and depth 3 cm.

c the surface area of a cuboid with height 10 cm, width 8 cm and depth 6 cm.

d the height of a cube with a surface area of 150 cm^2.

5a I can calculate the surface area of a cuboid from information about its dimensions

Now try this!

Tip If a word ends in '-hedron' it means it is a 3-D shape. The first part of the name tells you how many faces there are. So a 'hexahedron' is another name for a solid with six faces because 'hex' means 'six'.

A Eight faces

A regular octahedron is made from eight equilateral triangles.

Using isometric paper, draw a net for a regular octahedron. Can you make any other nets for an octahedron?

B Happy families

A game for two players. Each make 12 equal-sized cards like this from a sheet of A4 card.

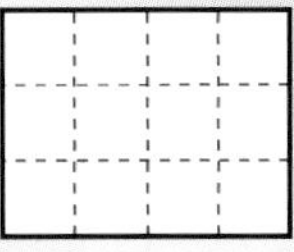

Write these names on your 12 cards: three 'square', four 'equilateral triangle', four 'rectangle' and one 'circle'.

Put the 24 cards together, shuffle and deal four cards each. Put the remaining cards in a pile face down on the table.

Take turns. When it's your go, either swap a card (for example, 'Do you want to swap a square for a triangle?') or take another card from the pack.

When all the cards have been taken from the pack, put down your cards and name the 3-D shapes you can make – you score 1 point for every card in the shape (you can only use each card once).

pyramid sphere square-based pyramid tetrahedron vertex (vertices)

18.5 Constructing 3-D shapes

- Construct triangles, squares and rectangles using a ruler and protractor
- Draw lines to within 1 mm of the correct length
- Draw angles to within 1° of the correct angle
- Construct and combine 2-D shapes to make nets

Why learn this?

Whether it is houses or furniture, knowing how to design and put up 3-D structures from flat packs is big business.

What's the BIG idea?

- A **net** for a **cube** is **constructed** from six squares, where not more than three **faces** meet at a vertex and all the edges meet each other at 90°. **Level 5**
- You can stick a net for a cube together by adding flaps to every other edge. **Level 5**
- A net for a **regular tetrahedron** can be constructed from one large equilateral triangle if the mid-points from each side are joined to divide the large triangle into four smaller triangles. **Level 5**
- A net for a **cuboid** is constructed from three pairs of equal rectangles. (If one pair is square then the other four rectangles will have the same dimensions, with one side equal to the length of the square faces.) **Level 5**
- A **triangular prism** can be constructed from three rectangles and two identical triangles if each side of the triangle equals a side of one of the rectangles. **Level 5**
- A **square-based pyramid** can be constructed from a square and four equilateral, or isosceles, triangles where the base of the triangles is equal to the side length of the square. **Level 5**

Practice, practice, practice!

Level 5

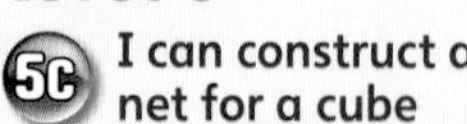

1 A 2.7 m aluminium cube has been launched as the solution to Britain's housing problems.

a Make a scale model of a cube measuring 2.7 m × 2.7 m × 2.7 m. Draw a net with squares of side 5.4 cm.

b Check there are 14 sides round the edge of your net and that the seven flaps each join to a side without a flap.

c Cut out the net and make your cube.

d Make a 4 cm high model to represent a 2 m adult. Do you think the housing idea will catch on?

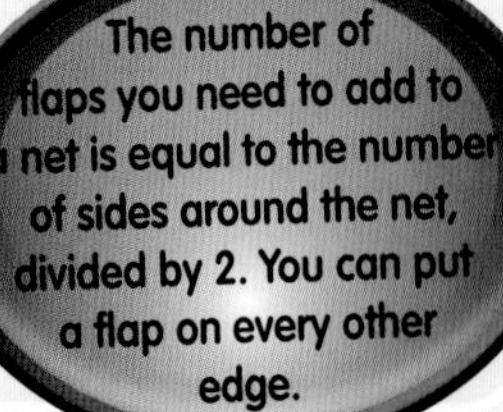

construct cube cuboid face net perimeter

2 Construct a net for this cuboid.
Make the base 6 cm × 4 cm.
Add a flap to every other edge, cut out and stick the net together together.

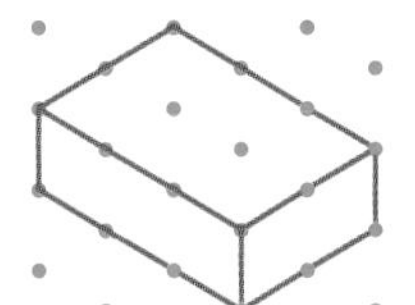

Level 5

5c I can construct a net for a cuboid

3 An article in *My Magazine* in 1918 predicted the world would eventually spin itself into a tetrahedron. Construct a net for a regular tetrahedron:

- Construct an equilateral triangle, with sides 10 cm long.
- Mark the mid-point of each side and join them with straight lines to make four smaller equilateral triangles within your triangle.
- Add a flap to every other edge.
- Sketch Africa, Europe and Asia, North and South America, Australia and Antarctica on your net, cut it out and then fold and glue it together.

5b I can construct a net for a regular tetrahedron

4 Construct a triangular prism to fit exactly on top of the cuboid you made in Q3.

- Construct a base measuring 6 cm × 4 cm.
- Add two triangular faces to the base (along the sides that measure 4 cm) with base angles of 45°.
- Add two rectangular sides on the other two sides of the base, measuring 6 cm × 2.8 cm.
- Add a flap to every other edge. Then cut out and stick the net together.

5b I can construct a triangular prism

5 **a** Construct a net for a square-based pyramid where all sides measure 6 cm.
b Imagine you had constructed two square-based pyramids and stuck the square faces together. What 3-D shape would that make?

5a I can construct a net for a square-based pyramid

Now try this!

A Prime time

A game for two persons. Make two four-sided dice, numbered 1 to 4.
Take turns to roll them.
If the sum of the two hidden numbers equals a prime number, score 1 point. If the sum equals a square number or a cube number, deduct 1 point.
The winner is the first to have at least 10 points and at least 2 more than their opponent.

B Make a simple model of a BoKlok house

1 Make a cuboid, measuring 7 cm × 7 cm × 10 cm.
Draw on the windows and doors before you stick it together.
2 Make a triangular prism with a base measuring 10 cm × 7 cm and triangular ends along the 7 cm sides, with base angles of 31°. Measure the sides of your triangle to work out the width of the two remaining rectangles needed for your net.
3 Stick the prism on top of the cuboid.
4 Cut out a rectangle 13 cm × 11 cm and fold it in half to make a rectangle measuring 6.5 cm × 11 cm. Open the rectangle out and stick it on top of your model to make the roof.

Did you know?

The UK's first BoKlok flat-pack houses were built in 2006. The original design is Swedish. The houses are built indoors and then taken on a lorry to the site where they are assembled. ('BoKlok' means 'live smart' in Swedish.)

regular square-based pyramid tetrahedron triangular prism

18.6 Angles, triangles and pyramids

- Measure and draw angles to within 1° accuracy
- Construct a triangle if you know the lengths of two sides and the angle between them
- Construct a triangle if you know the size of two angles and the length of the side between them

Why learn this?

Pyramids are still used in modern-day designs.

What's the BIG idea?

- You need to **measure** angles to within 1° of the correct answer. **Level 4**
- You need to **draw** angles to within 1° accuracy. **Level 4 & Level 5**
- A triangle can be **constructed** if you know two **sides** and the **included angle** (SAS). **Level 5**
- A triangle can also be constructed if you know two angles and the **included side** (ASA). **Level 5**
- Make a sketch before accurately drawing a triangle. **Level 5**

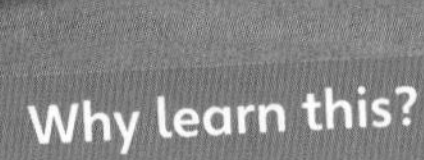

Super fact!

The Great Pyramid was used as a sundial. The Egyptians used the shadows made by the changing angles of the Sun to mark the day of the year and the hour of the day on the pavements around the pyramid.

Practice, practice, practice!

Level 4

1 **a** Measure the angle at the top of the pyramid in the photo.

b Which type of angle is it?

4b I can identify simple angle properties of triangles

2 An obtuse triangle is a triangle where one of the angles is greater than 90°. Which of these triangles are obtuse triangles?

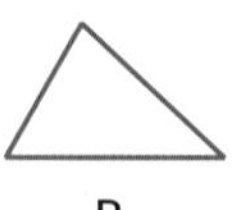
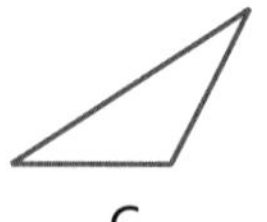
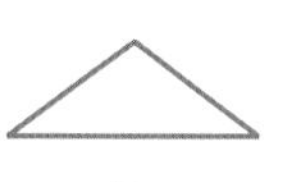
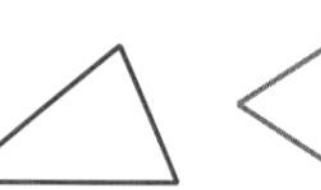

A B C D E F G

4b I can measure obtuse angles accurately

3 Historians think that a stone, weighing two and a half tonnes, could be moved up a 15° ramp by only ten men.

a Draw a line at 15° above a horizontal line. Do you think a block of stone the size of a small elephant could be dragged up a slope like this by ten men?

The passage that descended into the pyramid was 26° below the horizontal.

b Draw a line at 26° below a horizontal line. Could you walk down a slope at this angle carrying something heavy?

4a I can draw acute angles accurately

acute construct draw included angle included side

4 **a** Make an accurate full-size drawing of each diagram.

i A, 5 cm, 102°, 4 cm, B

ii D, C

iii E, F

iv G, H

b Measure the distance between the ends of each pair of lines.

5 The early pyramids had faces with an angle of 60° at each vertex.
Follow these instructions to make a net to see what they looked like.
a Draw a 5 cm square.
b Add a line 5 cm long at an angle of 60° to one of the sides of the square.
c Join the end of the line to complete the triangular face.
d Repeat on the other sides of the square.
e Now cut out and fold up the net.

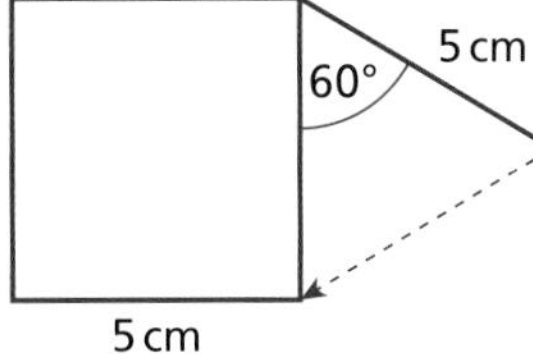

6 Pyramids with an angle of 60° at the top collapsed, so an angle of 70° was tried.
a Calculate the base angles for a pyramid face with an angle of 70° at the top.
b Draw a baseline of 10 cm and construct a triangle using these base angles.
c Measure the angle at the top to check it is 70°. **Hint:** Make a sketch first.

7 Make a net for a pyramid, with a base length of 5 cm and base angles of 55°. Compare it with your net from Q5. Which pyramid would use more stone? Why do you think the 60° pyramids collapsed?

Level 5

5c I can draw obtuse angles accurately

Tip
Use a hard pencil (H or HB) and sharpen it before starting any question using construction.

5b I can construct a triangle if I know two lengths and the angle between them

5a I can construct a triangle if I know two angles and the length between them

Now try this!

A Obtuse triangles and quadrilaterals

Draw two lines of different lengths which meet to form an obtuse angle.

1 What sort of triangle do you make if you join the two ends?
2 Is it possible to make any other sort of triangle starting with your two lines?
3 How many different quadrilaterals you can make if you add two lines to your original lines?
4 If you start off with two lines of equal length, can you make any other types of triangle or quadrilateral?

B Integer peaks

Use dynamic geometry software to investigate obtuse triangles with a base of 10 cm and acute base angles. How many pairs of whole number lengths can you find for the other two sides?

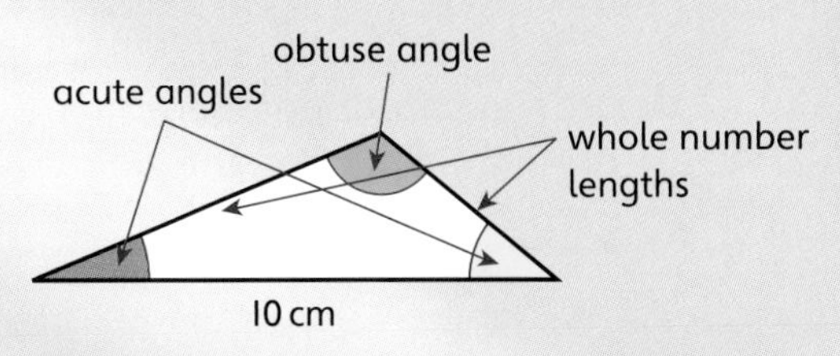

measure obtuse protractor (angle measurer) ruler side

2-D puzzles

Building a pyramid (or any other building) is a bit like a 3-D puzzle. All the blocks need to go in exactly the right places – or the building may collapse!

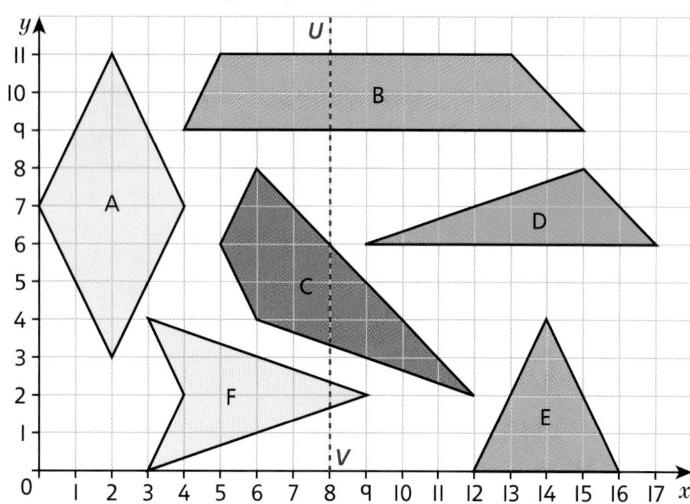

The six pieces on this grid are the six pieces of a mathematical jigsaw puzzle.

1 Describe each shape. Use the names you have learned for special triangles and quadrilaterals. Level 3 & Level 5 **Hint:** One of the shapes is an irregular quadrilateral.

2 Which shapes are symmetrical? Level 3

3 How many lines of reflection symmetry does each shape have? Level 3

4 What are the coordinates of the image of shape C after it has been reflected in the line *UV*? Level 3

5 What are the coordinates of the image of shape D after it has been translated 5 to the left and 2 down? Level 3

6 Measure the obtuse angles in shape B. Level 4

7 Measure the angles in shape E and check your answers add up to the correct total. Level 5

8 Make an exact copy of the shapes on a grid, using centimetre squared paper. Colour and label the shapes. Cut out each shape. Level 3

9 Your challenge is to fit your pieces into a triangle. (Make sure all of your pieces are colour-side up.) Level 5

10 Draw a net for an open-top box that could be used to store a wooden version of your completed puzzle. The wood is 2 cm thick. Level 5

The BIG ideas

- You can check whether a shape has **reflection symmetry** by using a mirror and tracing paper, or by folding it. Level 3
- You can check a **translation**, by choosing the same vertex on the object and image, and checking the movement of this single point. Level 3
- To check a **reflection**, make sure that the distance from the line of symmetry (at right angles to the axis of symmetry) is the same for both an object point and its image. Level 3
- An **obtuse angle** is greater than 90°, but less than 180°. Level 4
- Angles need to be drawn and measured to within 1° of the correct angle. Level 4
- **Angles in a triangle** add up to 180°. Level 5
- You can construct a triangle if you know two sides and the included angle (**SAS**). Level 5
- You can construct a triangle if you know two angles and the included side (**ASA**). Level 5

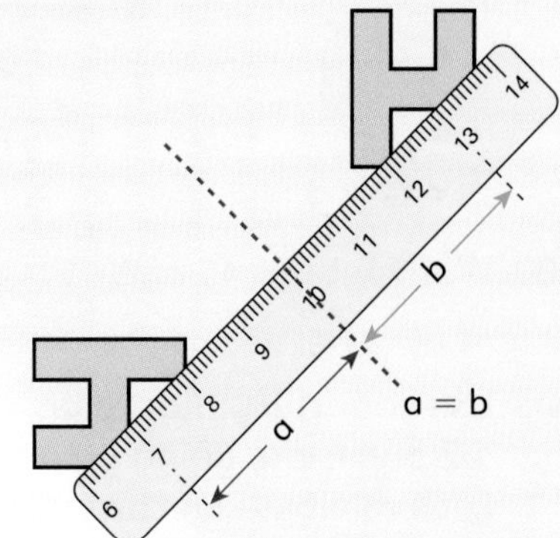

Find your level

Level 3

Q1 a Copy these shapes onto a grid.

Y

Z

b Add the image of the square after it has been translated 1 square to the right and 2 down.

c Add the image of the rectangle after it has been reflected in the line YZ.

d The completed shape could be a net. Add dotted lines to show where you would need to add folds. What would the completed net make if it were folded up to make a 3-D shape?

Level 4

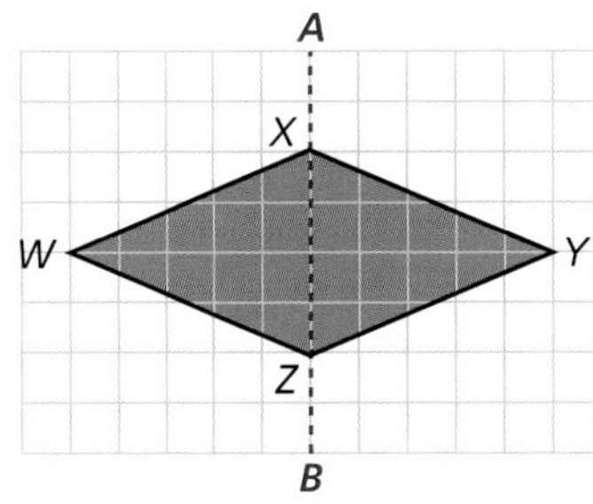

Q2 Look at the diagram. Triangle *XWZ* is the reflection of triangle *XYZ* in the line *AB*.

a i Measure the length of *XY*.
ii Measure the length of *ZY*.
iii Measure the length of *XZ*.

b What sort of a triangle is *XYZ*? Explain your answer.

c What sort of a quadrilateral is *WXYZ*? Explain your answer.

Level 5

Q3 Look at this shape made from seven cubes. Five cubes are white. Two cubes are orange.

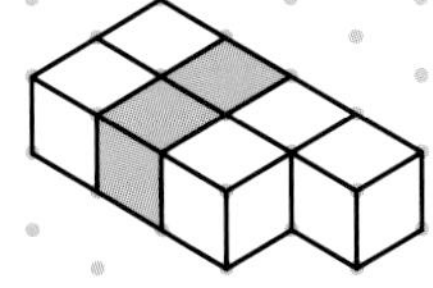

a Part of the shape is rotated through 90° to make this shape.

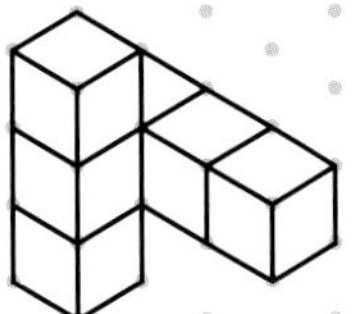

Copy the new shape onto isometric paper and shade the faces that are orange.

b Four of the white cubes are used to make a cuboid. Draw two different shapes for the cuboid on isometric paper.

Revision 3

Quick Quiz

Q1 Copy these shapes. Draw on them the number of lines of symmetry shown.

a

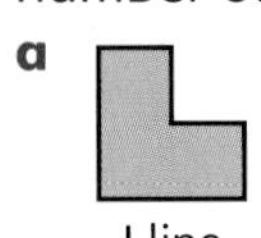

1 line

b

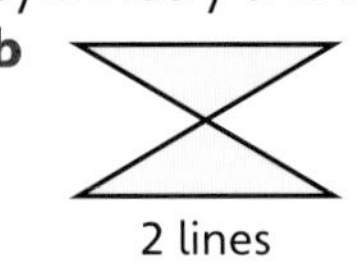

2 lines

→ *See 14.3*

Q2 Work out **a** 45 + 39 **b** 183 − 146

→ *See 16.1*

Q3 Use your calculator to answer this question.
102 pupils are going on a school trip.
Each minibus can carry 15 pupils.
How many minibuses will be needed?

→ *See 16.5*

Q4 These are the weights of five people.

76 kg, 65 kg, 60 kg, 76 kg, 69 kg

a What is the range of the weights?
b What is the mode of the weights?
c What is the median of the weights?

→ *See 15.6*

Q5 The formula to work out the area of a triangle is
Area = $\frac{1}{2}$ × base × height
Work out the area of a triangle with a base of 6 cm and a height of 5 cm.

→ *See 17.6*

Q6 What kind of triangles are these?

a

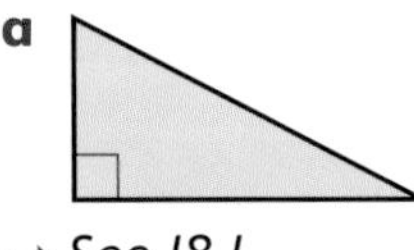

b

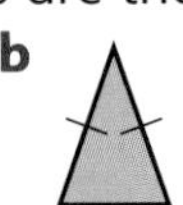

c

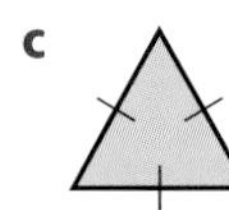

→ *See 18.1*

Q7 Describe the transformation that takes shape A to shape B.

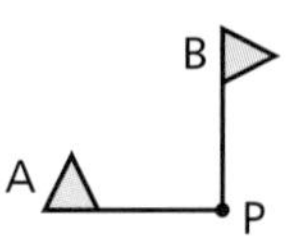

→ *See 14.5*

Q8 The frequency table shows the number of eggs laid by Sally's chickens over a 10 day period.
What is the mean number of eggs laid each day?

Number of eggs laid each day	Number of days
0	1
1	4
2	5

→ *See 15.6*

Q9 Look at this pattern of dots.

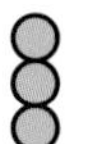 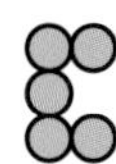 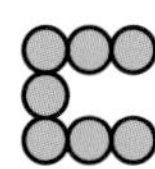

To find the number of dots in pattern n you can use the position-to-term rule number of dots = $2n + 1$
How many dots will be in pattern 15?

→ *See 17.1*

Q10 Find the size of angle ADC in this kite.

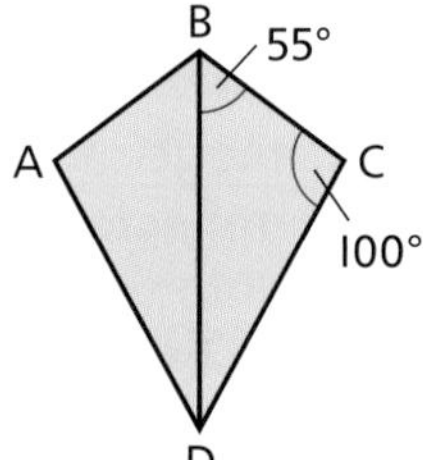

→ *See 18.3*

Activity

You are going to organise designing and ordering new T-shirts for employees in a company.

Level 3

Q1 In the company there are 26 full-time staff and 39 part-time staff.
What is the total number of staff?

Q2 Each employee will be given three T-shirts.
T-shirts come in packs of 10.
How many packs of T-shirts need to be ordered?

Level 4

Q3 On the grid is the old logo for the company.

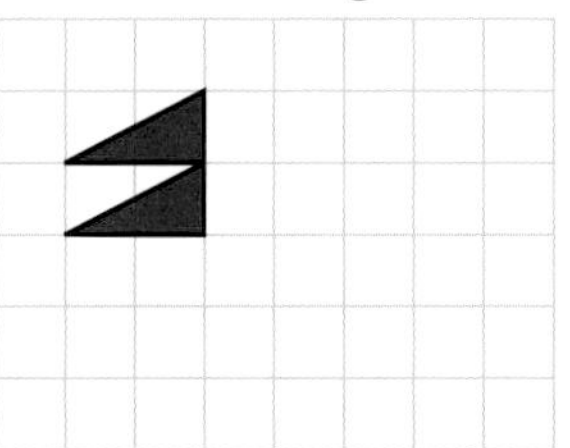

Copy the grid and the old logo.
The new logo is created by adding a translation to the old logo.
Translate the old logo 2 squares right and one square down.

Level 4

Q4 The total cost for the T-shirts can be found using the formula

total cost = cost per shirt × number of shirts

Find the total cost of 220 T-shirts costing £8 each.

Level 5

Q5 The employees are asked what they think of the quality of the T-shirts.
The table below shows the results.

Quality	Fraction of employees	Percentage of employees
Poor	$\frac{1}{5}$	
Good	$\frac{3}{5}$	
Excellent	$\frac{1}{5}$	

Copy and complete the table.

Q6 Draw a pie chart to show the results of the quality survey. Use the table in question 5.

Find your level

Level 3

Q1 These shapes are drawn on square grids.

a

b

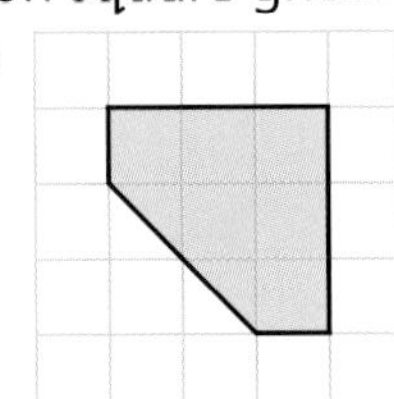

Each shape has one line of symmetry. Copy the shapes and draw the line of symmetry on each shape.

Q2 Copy these diagrams. Fill in the missing numbers in the boxes.

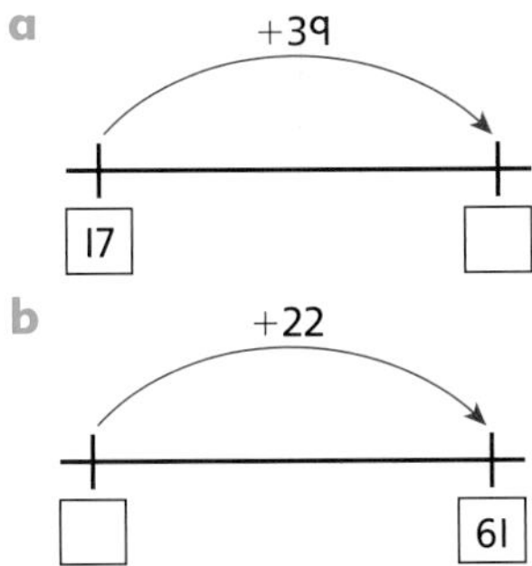

Level 4

Q3 There are five children in the Jones family. Their ages are 6, 6, 9, 12 and 13 years old. Match each question with the correct answer.

Question	Answer
What is the range of their ages?	9 years old
What is the mode of their ages?	7 years old
What is the median of their ages?	6 years old

Q4 This is a kite.
The dotted lines are the diagonals of the kite. To find the area of a kite:

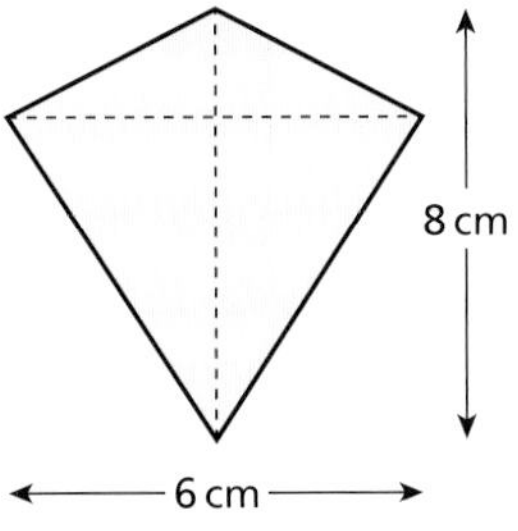

Multiply the length of the diagonals together, then divide the answer by 2

What is the area of this kite?

Level 5

Q5 Look at this sequence of patterns made with counters.

pattern number 1

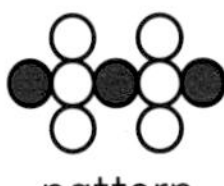
pattern number 2

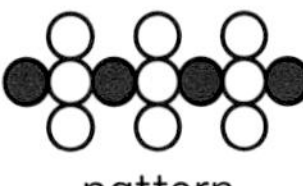
pattern number 3

To find the number of counters in pattern number n you can use these rules:

Number of red counters = $n + 1$
Number of white counters = $3n$

Altogether, what is the total number of counters in pattern number 30?

Q6 This frequency table shows the number of children in 20 families. What is the mean number of children in each family?

Number of children in each family	Number of families
0	4
1	5
2	8
3	1
4	2

Index

q

r

s

t

u

v

w

x

y